Footprint Laos

Jock O'Tailan
4th edition

*It is hard to make these people hate. It is the custom of the
land that a stranger in the village must be well treated.
We were usually met at the river's edge by some elder of
the village with a small silver bowl containing some flowers,
candles and other offerings of welcome to the visitors.*

Dr Tom Dooley's account of a river expedition down the Namtha River
The Edge of Tomorrow, 1958

Laos Highlights

See colour maps at back of book

❶ That Luang
Symbol of Lao nationhood and the country's holiest site

❷ Vang Vieng
Adventure capital en route to Luang Prabang, with caves, rafting and elephant trekking

❸ Kwang Si Falls
Popular get-away from Luang Prabang with prospect of a cooling dip

❹ Luang Prabang
Perfectly formed little city with UNESCO World Heritage status

❺ Pak Ou Caves
4000 images of the Buddha crammed into cliff-side caves with a river view

❻ Phongsali
An upland town surrounded by stunning scenery

❼ Muang Sing
Attractive base for trekking and for visiting minorities

❽ The Mekong
Take a slow boat along the mother river of Southeast Asia

CHINA

MYANMAR
(BURMA)

Phongsali ❻

Muang ❼
Sing

Luang
Namtha

Udom Xai

Xam Neua

Houei Xai

Mekong River

❽

Luang
Prabang ❹

❺

❸

Sayaboury

Plain of Jars ❾

Phonsavanh

Vang Vieng ❷

Nam Ngum
Reservoir

Phonhong

Paksan

VIENTIANE ❶

THAILAND

N

0 km   40

0 miles   40

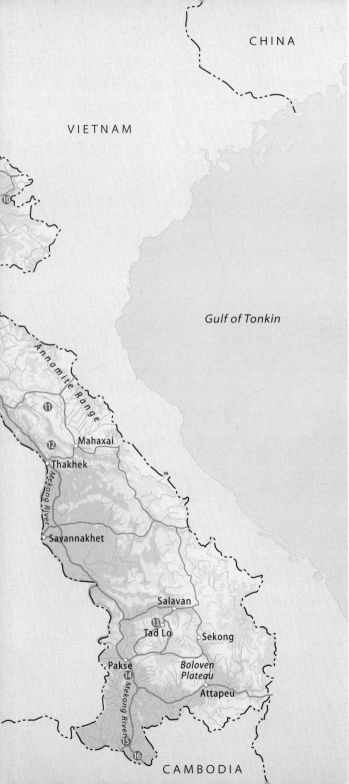

9 Plain of Jars
Perplexing giant stone jars littered over US-bombed grasslands

10 Caves at Vieng Xai
Communist Pathet Lao bolt-hole and command centre

11 Tham Kong Lor
Take a boat through this spectacular river cave

12 Mahaxai
Laos' limestone heartland, peppered with caves

13 Tad Lo
Eco-resort with trekking and minority villages

14 Wat Phou
Stupendous 12th-century Khmer archaeological site

15 Mekong Islands
Land-locked Laos' very own tropical archipelago

16 Li Phi and Khong Phapheng falls
The falls that thwarted French attempts to find a route to China

CHINA

VIETNAM

Gulf of Tonkin

Annamite Range

Mekong River

Mahaxai

Thakhek

Savannakhet

Salavan

Tad Lo

Sekong

Pakse

Boloven Plateau

Attapeu

Mekong River

CAMBODIA

Super stupa
That Luang in Vientiane serves as a symbol of Lao nationhood and is the most revered Buddhist monument in the country.

Contents

Wet and wild
The Laos' landscape is characterized by intricate river systems and spectacular waterfalls. The Kwang Si Falls are among the most famous.

Window dressing
A novice monk watches the world go by from the richly decorated sim at Wat Xieng Thong in Luang Prabang.

A foot in the door

Laos is fast becoming the darling of Southeast Asia, satisfying all the romantic images of perfumed frangipani trees, saffron-robed monks, rusty old bicycles and golden temples, all set amongst a rich tapestry of tropical river islands, ethnic minority villages, cascading waterfalls and vivid, green rice paddies, and bound together by the mighty Mekong River, the country's lifeline. The vernacular architecture that other countries have swept away in a maelstrom of redevelopment survives in Laos. Simple wooden village homes, colonial-era brick-and-stucco shophouses and gently mouldering monasteries mark Laos out as different. Traditional customs are also firmly intact: incense wafts out of streetside wats, monks collect alms at daybreak and the clickety-clack of looms weaving richly coloured silk can be heard in most villages.

As compelling as these sights and sounds are, the lasting impression for most visitors is of the people and their overwhelming friendliness. Many believe the best thing about Laos is the constant chimes of '*sabaidee*' ringing out from schoolchildren, monks and other passers-by, extending an invitation to join their meal. This is a land that endures the terrible legacy of being the most bombed country per capita in the world, yet its people transform bomb casings into flower pots and bomb craters into fish ponds. Regardless of their history and their poverty, people here radiate a sunny, happy disposition.

Life is simple in Laos but the people share with their former French colonists an infectious *joie de vivre* that ensures that good food and great company are the pinnacle of enjoyment. If you're seeking a relaxed lifestyle and a warm welcome, you've come to the right place.

Contemporary Laos

The most frequently used epithet to describe Laos is 'forgotten', owing to its disengagement from the world political scene for two decades. From 1975, when the Pathet Lao government seized power, until the 1990s, the country was isolated from the West and, thus, insulated against many of the negative effects of rapid modernization associated with its near neighbours. Known affectionately by its citizens as 'Laos Please Don't Rush' (PDR), the country continues to exude a timeless, mellow, languorous air and is millennia away from becoming the next up-and-coming Asian giant.

However, a decade since first opening up to visitors, Laos is finally rousing. Incremental changes are noticeable, especially in the country's famously low-key capital, Vientiane: hammer-and-sickle flags adorn computerized ten-pin bowling galleries; cash machines have been installed on street corners – although some have human cashiers to dole out the kip; a couple of traffic lights command the dribble of tuk-tuks and bicycles; women meet for outdoor aerobics sessions, and the local chicken farmer can text the price of eggs to your mobile phone.

Giant jars
These ancient and mysterious jars still dot the landscape of Xieng Khouang Province, despite intensive bombing during the Secret War.

In the countryside, though, home to 80% of the population, life remains relatively unchanged. The odd motorbike, maybe, a Metallica T-shirt, a mobile phone or a television antenna are the only concessions to 21st-century living. The scores of different ethnic groups scattered across the country are still heavily reliant on the land and on traditional ways of farming or hunting. They live in remote villages of wooden or thatched houses, with no proper infrastructure and, therefore, no easy access to markets where they could sell their produce.

For years cynics have warned that it is only a matter of time before Laos becomes a generic Asian country. But, for now, it remains unique because its gradual development has not been at the cost of its culture. The government may have brought in new liberalizing economic policies but, on the ground, bargaining power is still determined by your ability to tell a good joke and friendships are cemented for life by a decent karaoke performance and a bottle of Beer Lao. *Bopenyang*, meaning 'no problem', is one of the country's most commonly used phrases and encapsulates a culture that remains among the most laid-back on earth.

The Akha Way
The Akha are just one of the hill tribes that live around Muang Sing, in northwest Laos. The women wear elaborate headdresses decorated with jewellery and silver coins.

1 *Laos was formerly known as Lane Xang or 'Land of a million elephants'. Visitors today can enjoy elephant trekking around Vang Vieng.* ▶▶ *See page 111.*

2 *The royal city of Luang Prabang is a beautifully preserved highlight of Southeast Asia.* ▶▶ *See page 116.*

3 *Saffron-robed monks collect offerings from residents and pilgrims during the Boun That Luang festival.* ▶▶ *See page 88.*

4 *Wat Xieng Thong in Luang Prabang is arguably the finest monastery in the country. Its side chapels are decorated with intricate mosaics.* ▶▶ *See page 125.*

5 *Women share a joke in Xam Neua, in the far northeast of the country. This area served as a Pathet Lao hideout during the Secret War.* ▶▶ *See page 197.*

6 *The Mekong roars over the Khong Phapheng Falls near the border with Cambodia.* ▶▶ *See page 277.*

7 *Buses may be the most common form of transport but don't miss the chance to travel by boat along one of Laos' many navigable rivers.* ▶▶ *See page 40.*

8 *The Nakai Nam Theun National Protected Area encompasses some of the most pristine wilderness in Southeast Asia.* ▶▶ *See page 219.*

9 *Brightly coloured tuk-tuks are ubiquitous in Laos' towns and are great for visiting outlying attractions.* ▶▶ *See page 43.*

10 *The Nam Ngum river flows into a picturesque reservoir near Vientiane that's dotted with small islands.* ▶▶ *See page 103.*

11 *Wat Phra Maha That is a typical Luang Prabang wat, built in the 1500s and decorated with figures from the Phra Lak Phra Lam.* ▶▶ *See page 128.*

12 *Ban Pak Ou lies in the shadow of limestone cliffs. It's the closest village to the Pak Ou caves, which contain thousands of Buddha images.* ▶▶ *See page 135.*

A lower case capital

In 1827, Siamese King Rama III ransacked Vieng Chan, the capital of Lane Xang, in retaliation for King Chou Anou's failed and foolhardy attempt to defeat the Siamese army. The city lay in ruins until the French took over and the result is that Vientiane is more of a French colonial outpost than an Asian city. It is a low-key place, restrained and understated, with simple shophouses, French villas and a great position on the Mekong. Old and new, East and West meet here. Baguettes and cafés coexist with spicy papaya salad and incense-filled pagodas, all watched over by glistening That Luang, the country's most important Buddhist monument.

A jewel in the crown

Luang Prabang is Laos' single greatest draw: a UNESCO World Heritage site and a former royal capital. Anchored at the confluence of the Mekong and Nam Khan rivers and surrounded by a crown of mountains, its position alone makes it worth the journey. When you add a plethora of gilded temples and French colonial buildings, strung together by ancient cobbled paths, it becomes a place that should be at the top of every traveller's itinerary. Luang Prabang shows the merit of missed opportunities: starved of funds for 40 years from the French withdrawal through to 1990, its eclectic mix of 16th-century monasteries and late 19th- and 20th-century shophouses has survived with scarcely a pimple of redevelopment. UNESCO's recognition of the town's World Heritage status should mean that the core of Luang Prabang, including the incomparable Wat Xieng Thong, is protected for future generations. What's more, Luang Prabang has great little guesthouses, excellent

A monk prays at a shrine in the 12th-century Khmer complex of Wat Phou.

In Vientiane, Pi Mai (Lao New Year) is celebrated with three days of festivities and a water fight.

restaurants and numerous opportunities for rewarding forays into the surrounding countryside, from the 4000 Buddhas of the Pak Ou caves to the waterfalls at Kwang Si.

Head for the hills

Laos has probably the richest forests, the cleanest rivers and the freshest air of all the countries in Southeast Asia. Rafting, trekking, caving and climbing are increasingly popular activities, particularly around Vang Vieng, with its honeycomb of limestone caves and riverside position, but other areas also have enormous potential. Northern Laos is like a Sung Dynasty painting, with jagged mountains, topped by misty cloud formations. Nestled against the border with China are the lofty provinces of Luang Namtha and Phongsali, where brilliant trekking opportunities abound. And, with the opening up of Laos' wild areas has come easier access to the country's minorities. The dominant cultural group in Laos are the Lao: lowland-living, wet-rice cultivating Theravada Buddhists, but more than half the population comprises an array of hill peoples each with their own traditions, beliefs and practices.

Bombed back to the Stone Age

Xieng Khouang in the northeast was unfortunate to lie at the epicentre of one of the war in Indochina's nastier 'sideshows'. It was bombed to bits – something that is still all too evident from the crater-pocked landscape. The war may be over but, day by day, the number of maimed and killed rises, as farmers plough up unexploded bombs and young children play with the detritus of war. Another tragedy was the total destruction of Xieng Khouang town, bombed so thoroughly that not a single building of the original settlement survived. All examples of one of the country's three religious architectural styles were obliterated in the process. However, Xieng Khouang's mysterious giant stone jars did survive – some 300 of them are still littered over the Plain of Jars. Archaeologists argue over their purpose and providence, but the Lao have always known the answer: the jars were left by King Khoon Chuong and his troops after they had used them to brew prodigious quantities of *lao-lao* to lubricate a stupendous victory celebration.

Southern secrets

One of the least explored but arguably most magnificent parts of the country are the central provinces, where imposing, Gothic-style limestone scenery is riddled with elaborate cave systems, including the massive river cave at Kong Lor. Further south, Champasak Province is home to raging waterfalls, coffee plantations and the romantic ruins of ancient, pre-Angkorian Wat Phou.

This fabulous concoction of pavilions, causeways and sanctuaries dates from the 12th century and belongs to another people: the Khmer, whose empire of Angkor extended its power and influence over southern Laos, as well as large areas of central and northeast Thailand. Wat Phou is ample evidence of the economic might and artistic prowess of the Khmer, conveniently left in Laos for another people to exploit.

Finally, right at the southern tip of Laos, the Mekong – the country's defining thread – unravels into a tangle of channels and cascades, surrounding the idyllic, palm-fringed Mekong islands of Siphandon.

Life has changed little over the centuries on Don Khong, the largest of the Mekong Islands.

Essentials

Footprint features

Planning your trip

Where to go

Laos may not be on the travel itineraries of most international tourists or in the brochures of many tour companies, but it is a priceless country with a great deal to offer the discerning traveller. Notwithstanding the country's poverty and lack of development, it is civilized and refined, with elegant towns, sophisticated cuisine, a leisurely pace of life and a population which is probably the most welcoming and relaxed in Asia. Laos has style.

Certainly the former royal capital of Luang Prabang – designated a World Heritage Site by UNESCO – is a fabulous little city. Today's capital Vientiane, as well as the other Mekong towns of Pakse, Savannakhet and Thakhek, is also elegant with its French architectural heritage largely intact. Wat Phou, an outlier of the former Cambodian kingdom of Angkor, is highly satisfying too, and some visitors enjoy the war history and enigmatic stone urns that litter the Plain of Jars. The Mekong islands in the far south are a great place to relax and read at leisure. Laos has also firmly established itself as the region's premier ecotourism destination, with a wide range of ecoactivities ranging from treks to kayaking. But what visitors to this gem of a country tend to remember best of all is the warmth of the people and the pleasure that comes from visiting a country which has so far managed to keep the more lurid and gauche aspects of the modern world at bay.

Timetabling a visit Because travelling in Laos can be a bit of a lottery, it is strongly recommended that you allow some leeway in your schedule. Assuming, for example, that it will be possible to catch a flight from Phonsavanh to Vientiane to connect with another from Vientiane to Bangkok, and from there to the US or Europe, is – to say the least – risky. The same goes for road transport, especially during the wet season. Those on organized tours have some distinct advantages in this regard. They will have the services of a local tour guide to apply pressure and perhaps supply gifts to secure seats on overbooked planes. Local guides are also much more aware of when problems are likely to arise. A lone traveller, with no Lao, will find it hard to strike the same deals and may be left floundering on the tarmac.

Nonetheless, a three- to four-week visit to Laos is sufficient to see much of the country – or at least that fraction of the country that it is possible to see. The main issue, perhaps, is how to couple a visit to the north with a trip to the south where Pakse, Champasak, Wat Phou and the Mekong Islands are to be found. Vientiane to Pakse is a journey of around 750 km and many people (because they have booked a flight into and out of Vientiane) have then to retrace those 750 km to catch their plane out. By air this is bearable; by public bus it may test your patience, although now air-conditioned overnight buses make the journey in about 10 hours. The alternative is to enter and exit at different ends of the country. This used to be impossible because visas stipulated the entry and exit points. But now it is possible to enter at Chiang Khong/Houei Xai in the far north, travel south, and then exit at Pakse/Chongmek. There is also the option of entering or departing from Vietnam, Cambodia and China (see the box on border crossings on page 32).

When to go

Best time to visit The best time to travel is during the relatively cool and dry winter months from November to March. Not only is the weather more pleasant at this time of year but roads are also in better shape. However, temperatures in upland areas like the Plain of Jars, the Boloven Plateau and some towns in the north of the country can drop to below freezing in winter. From April onwards, temperatures can exceed 40°C in many lowland areas, although it remains dry through to May. From June or July, as the wet season wears on, so unsurfaced roads begin to deteriorate and overland transport in some areas becomes slower and more difficult. In the north, the months from March through to the first rains in May or June can be very hazy as smoke from burning off the secondary forest hangs in the air. On the worst days this can cause itchiness of the eyes. What's more, it means that views are restricted and sometimes flights are cancelled. See page 343 for more details on climate. For daily weather reports for Champasak, Pak Lai, Pakbeng, Pakse, Phongsali, Savannakhet, Vientiane, Xam Neua and Xepon, see www.wunderground.com.

Tour operators

UK and Ireland
Audley Travel Ltd, 6 Willows Gate, Stratton Audley, Oxfordshire, OX27 9AU, T01869-276200, www.audleytravel.com.
Coromandel , 29a Main St, Lyddington, Oakham, Rutland LE15 9LR, T01572-821330, www.coromandelabt.com.
Explore Worldwide, 1 Frederick St, Aldershot, Hants GU11 1LQ, T0870-3334001, www.exploreworldwide.com. Arranges small group tours (average 16 people), with many different types of trip offered including

cultural excursions, adventure holidays and natural history tours.
Exodus Travels, 9 Weir Rd, London, SW12 0LT, T0870-2405550, www.exodus.co.uk.
Guerba Expeditions, Wessex House, 40 Station Rd, Westbury, Wiltshire BA13 3JN, T01373-858956, www.guerba.co.uk.
Magic of the Orient, 14 Frederick Place, Clifton, Bristol BS8 1AS, T0117-3116051, www.magic-of-the-orient.com.
Maxwells Travel, D'Olier Chambers, 1 Hawkins St, Dublin 2, Ireland, T01-677

9479, F01-679 3948. An agent for **Explore Worldwide**.
Regent Holidays, 13 John St, Bristol BS1 2HR, T0117-9211711, regent@regent-holidays.co.uk. One of the leading UK tour operators to Cambodia.
Silk Steps, Deep Meadow, Edington, Bridgwater, Somerset TA7 9JH, T01278-722460, www.silksteps.co.uk.
Steppes Travel, 51 Castle St, Cirencester, Gloucestershire GL7 5ET, T01285-880980, www.steppestravel.co.uk.
Symbiosis, Holly House, Whilton, Daventry, Northamptonshire NN11 5NN, T0845-1232844, www.symbiosis-travel.com. A highly reputable company that offers tailor-made tours and expeditions for individuals and groups small and large – especially bicycle tours.
Tennyson Travel, 30-32 Fulham High St, London SW6 3LQ, T020-7736 4347, http://www.visitasia.co.uk.

North America
Adventure Centre, 1311 63rd St, Suite 200, Emeryville, CA 94608, T510-6541879, 1-800-228-8747 (USA toll free) www.adventurecenter.com. A company supporting 'Trees for Life' which aims to re-forest denuded areas. Offers 7 different trips in Southeast Asia for 15-30 days.

Global Spectrum, 3907 Laro Court, Fairfax, VA 22031 USA, T1-800-4194446, www.asianpassages.com.
Journeys, 107 April Drive, Suite 3, Ann Arbor MI 46103, T734-6654407, www.journeys-intl.com.
Hidden Treasures Tours, 162 West Park Av, 2nd Floor, Long Beach, NY 11561, T888-8899906 (USA toll free), www.hiddentreasuretours.com.
Himalayan Travel Inc, 8 Berkshire Place, Danbury, CT 06810, T203-7432349, www.himalayantravelinc.com/.
Nine Dragons Travel & Tours, 2136 Fullerton Drive, Indianapolis, IN 46224-0105, T1-800-9099050, www.nine-dragons.com.

Australia
Adventure World, Level 20, 141 Walker St, North Sydney, NSW 2060, Australia, T028913-0755, info@adventureworld.com.au.
Intrepid Travel Pty Ltd, 11 Spring St, Fitzroy, Victoria, T1300-360 667, www.intrepidtravel.com.au.
Travel Indochina, 403 George St, Sydney. NSW 2000, T+61 02 9244 2133, www.travelindochina.com.

South Africa
Shiralee Travel, 32 Main Rd, PO Box 1420, Hermanus, 7200, South Africa, T027 11 452 6394, www.harveyworld.co.za.

Finding out more

Useful websites
Up-to-date information on Laos is not easy to come by. The best bet is to browse Lao-related or Lao-dedicated websites. The best sites, in our experience, are:
www.travelfish.org
www.visit-laos.com
www.ecotourismlaos.com
www.laohotelgroup.org
www.laopdr.com
www.asean-tourism.com
www.muonglao.com
www.mekongcenter.com
www.visit-mekong.com

Language

Lao is the national language but there are many local dialects, not to mention the ubiquitous languages of the minority groups. French is spoken by government officials and hotel staff, and many educated people over 40. Most government officials and many shopkeepers have some command of English.

Lao is closely related to Thai and, in a sense, is becoming more so as the years pass. Though there are important differences between the languages, they are mutually intelligible – just about. To many Thais, Lao is a rather basic version of their own more sophisticated language – they often describe it as 'primitive'. Of course the Lao vehemently reject, and resent, such a view and it represents, in microcosm the 'big-brother-little brother' relationship that exists between the two countries and peoples. (It is not accidental that the Lao of the poverty-stricken northeast of Thailand are often regarded as country bumpkins in Bangkok.) The Lao language is a lot more egalitarian with less of the class and gender implications of the Thai counterpart. Today, though, many Lao watch Thai TV, their antennae aimed to receive transmissions from the west. As a result Thai expressions are becoming more common and familiarity with Thai is spreading. Even written Thai is more in evidence. As Thailand dominates mainland Southeast Asia in economic terms (they are the largest investor in Laos) this linguistic imperialism is seen by Thailand's critics as just another facet of a wide-ranging Thai cultural colonization of Laos.

Raintree Books, Pang Kham Road, and **Monument Books**, Nokeo Khoummane Road, both in Vientiane, stock a reasonable selection of **dictionaries** and **'teach yourself' books**. Khamphan Mingbuapha and Benjawan Poomsam Becker's *Lao-English/English-Lao Dictionary* (Paiboon Publishing) can be found at bookshops in Thailand and occasionally in Laos. ▸▸ *For a list of other recommended titles, see Books, page 344.*

Lao script computer software can be downloaded from www.travelphrases.info/gallery/Fonts_Lao.html and from www.home.vicnet.net.au/~lao/lswin. It is also available from local computer stores for around US$10. In 2005, several different version of script were present, making it difficult to make worldwide recognized websites in Lao scripts, but the government was working on a standardized Lao computer script.

Specialist travel

Disabled travellers

Laos is not an easy country for the disabled traveller; pavements are often uneven, there are potholes and missing drain covers galore, pedestrian crossings are ignored, ramps are unheard of, lifts are few and far between and escalators are seen only in magazines. On top of this, numerous other hazards abound, amongst the most dangerous of which must number the tuk-tuk drivers, whose philosophy on road safety remains either undeveloped or eccentric. However, while there are scores of hurdles that disabled people will have to negotiate, the Lao themselves are likely to go out of their way to be helpful. After all, one of the legacies of the war in Indochina is a large population of amputees.

Gay and lesbian travellers

Gay and lesbian travellers should have no problems in Laos. But, unlike Thailand, Laos does not have a hot gay scene and the Lao government is intent on avoiding the mushrooming of the gay and straight sex industry. Officially it is illegal for any foreigner to have a sexual relationship with a Lao person they aren't married to. Openly gay behaviour is contrary to local culture and custom and visitors, whether straight or gay, should not flaunt their sexuality. Any show of passion or sexually orientated affection in public is taboo. In Vientiane there aren't any gay bars, per se, although there are some bars and clubs where gays are known to hang out; Luang Prabang has a few more gay-orientated options.

Student travellers

In the past, the Lao government has not been overly eager to attract student travellers. It has not wanted to suffer from the problems that Thailand has encountered, where

Living in *sinh*

A lovely experience is to wear the *sinh*, the Lao traditional banded sarong. It isn't at all necessary to wear one but the Lao love the fact that you are taking an interest in their culture and are likely to shower you with compliments. If you are attending a wedding, funeral or plan to visit a government office, it is a sign of respect to wear one. Depending on the fabric, a *sinh* can be whipped up in most markets in a day and can be bought for around $US10.

hoardes of tourists descend upon 'hotspots', spending little money and generally degrading the place (or that, at least, was the generally accepted view). However, in recent years, this anti-backpacker attitude has moderated and the government has come to realize that backpackers do spend money, that they bring income to places where other forms of development are lacking, and that today's backpackers are tomorrow's big spenders. The result is that many more students are visiting the country, and its reputation as a cracking place to enjoy a cheap, culturally rich and wonderfully relaxing stint during a gap year or summer holiday is growing. That's all to the good. But there are few savings that come from being a student in Laos. In short, don't expect massive discounts on travel, entry fees and such like. But you don't really need student concessions, as everything is ridiculously cheap anyway.

ISIC Anyone in full-time education is entitled to an International Student Identity Card (ISIC, www.isic.org). These are issued by student travel offices and travel agencies across the world and offer special rates on all forms of transport and other concessions and services. They sometimes permit free admission to museums and sights, at other times a substantial discount on the entry fee.

Women travellers

While women travelling alone can generally face more potential problems than men or couples, these are far less pronounced in Laos than in most countries. Women have considerable autonomy in Laos (although this does not apply to all ethnic groups), and while their status is not equal to that of men, the level of bias is comparatively small. Women play a critical role in trade, household and reproductive decision-making, they are prominent in Lao history, and even the Lao language is notable for its lack of gendered pronouns. Some scholars have even argued that men and women are equal. This is difficult to sustain and on the other side of the coin it is notable that the practice of Buddhism accords men a higher status and in national politics, women play a very minor role. But the relative power, autonomy and status of women means that it is rare for women to be harassed. Nonetheless, women should take care to dress modestly, especially in the smaller, more provincial towns. Here in particular, skimpy tops and micro-shorts still arouse in locals the sort of embarrassed shock their urban counterparts have had to get used to. The best piece of advice for female travellers is to spend a while watching how Lao women behave and dress and appropriate where possible.

Though Laos is very safe, women should also take the usual precautions. It is illegal for a foreigner to be in a sexual relationship with a local unless married. You may often get asked if you are married, just a friendly conversation starter.

Affection in public is not looked upon highly, especially in rural areas. What may be considered in the west as friendly affection, such as putting your arm around someone, could be misconstrued as romantic love in Laos, so try not to be too tactile with the men.

Bring ample underwear and swimwear as the local synthetic underwear is uncomfortable (and very, very small) and some might find it hard trying to squeeze into the Madonna-style, conical brassieres. If you are bathing in a waterfall or river, please wear a sarong, as the locals are easily embarrassed or offended by the sight of bare flesh. Tampons and sanitary napkins can be purchased in major towns but are in short supply in other areas, so bring a backup supply from home.

Travelling with children

Many people are daunted by the prospect of taking a child to Laos: travelling is slower and more expensive and there are additional health risks for the child or baby. But it can be a most rewarding experience and, with sufficient care and planning, it can also be safe. Children are excellent passports into a local culture. You will also receive the best service and help from officials and members of the public when in difficulty.

Children in Laos are given 24-hour attention by parents, grandparents and siblings. They are rarely left to cry and are carried for most of the first eight months of their lives. A non-Asian child is still something of a novelty and parents may find their child frequently taken off their hands, even mobbed in more remote areas. This can be a great relief (at mealtimes, for instance) or most alarming. Some children love the attention, others react against it; it is best simply to gauge your own child's reactions. Restaurants are particularly child-friendly; don't be surprised if the staff entertain your child during your meal. Lao children are very friendly and like to meet foreign kids, although at times they can be painfully shy; this shouldn't be misconstrued.

Practicalities

Disposable nappies These can be bought in Vientiane and other larger provincial capitals, but are often expensive. If you are staying any length of time in one place, it may be worth taking terry (cloth) nappies. All you need is a bucket and some double-strength nappy cleanse (simply soak and rinse). Cotton nappies dry quickly in the heat and are generally more comfortable for the baby or child. They also reduce rubbish – Laos is not geared to the disposal of nappies.

Food and drink The advice given in the health section on food and drink (see page 55 and page 58) should be applied even more stringently where young children are concerned. Be aware that even expensive hotels may have squalid cooking conditions; the cheapest street stall is often more hygienic. Where possible, try to watch food being prepared. Stir-fried vegetables and rice or noodles are the best bet; meat and fish may be pre-cooked and then left out before being re-heated. Fruit can be bought cheaply: papaya and banana are excellent sources of nutrition, and can be self-peeled ensuring cleanliness. Powdered milk is available in provincial centres, although most brands have added sugar. If travelling with a baby, breast feeding is strongly recommended. Powdered food can also be bought in some towns – the quality may not be the same as equivalent foods bought in the West, but it is perfectly adequate for short periods. Avoid letting your child drink tap water as it may carry parasites. Bottled water and fizzy drinks are sold widely. If your child is at the 'grab everything and put it in mouth' stage, a damp cloth and some antiseptic liquid (such as Dettol) are useful. Frequent wiping of hands and tabletops can help to minimize the chance of infection. Ensure that older children wash their hands before all meals.

Sleeping At the hottest time of year, air conditioning may be essential for a baby or young child's comfort. This rules out many of the cheaper hotels, but air-conditioned accommodation is available in all larger towns. Check the accommodation sections in this book for information on which hotels provide air-conditioned rooms.

Transport Public transport may be a problem; long bus journeys are restrictive and uncomfortable. There is a reasonable domestic air network. Chartering a car is undoubtedly the most convenient way to travel overland but rear seatbelts are scarce and child seats even rarer.

Health

More preparation is probably necessary for babies and children than for an adult and perhaps a little more care should be taken when travelling to remote areas where health services are primitive. This is because children can become ill more rapidly than adults (on the other hand they often recover more quickly). Diarrhoea and vomiting are the most common problems, so take the usual precautions, but more intensively. The treatment of diarrhoea is the same for adults, except that it should start earlier and be continued with more persistence. Children get dehydrated very quickly in hot countries and can become drowsy and uncooperative unless cajoled to drink water or juice plus salts. Never allow your child to be exposed to the harsh tropical sun without protection. A child can burn in a matter of minutes. Loose cotton clothing, with long sleeves and legs and a sunhat are best. High-factor sun-protection cream is essential. Upper respiratory infections, such as colds, catarrh and middle-ear infections are also common; if your child normally suffers from these take some antibiotics with you in case. Outer-ear infections after swimming are also common and antibiotic eardrops will help. Wet wipes are always useful and can be found in the large cities. Baby powder might help reduce some of the chaffing that comes with the dauntingly hot weather.

Vaccinations Children should already be properly protected against diphtheria, poliomyelitis and pertussis (whooping cough), measles and HIB all of which can be more serious infections in Southeast Asia than at home. Measles, mumps and rubella vaccine is also given to children throughout the world, but those teenage girls who have not had rubella (German measles) should be tested and vaccinated. Hepatitis B vaccination for babies is now routine in some countries.

Emergencies Babies and small children deteriorate very rapidly when ill. A travel insurance policy which has an air ambulance provision is strongly recommended. When planning a route, try to stay within 24 hours' travel of a hospital with good care and facilities (see page 54).

Checklist Baby wipes; child paracetamol; disinfectant; first aid kit; flannel; immersion element for boiling water; decongestant for colds; instant food for under-one-year-olds; mug/bottle/bowl/spoons; nappy cleanse, double-strength; ORS (Oral Rehydration Salts) such as Dioralyte, to alleviate diarrhoea (it is not a cure); portable baby chair to hook onto tables; sarong or backpack for carrying child (and/or light weight collapsible buggy); sterilizing tablets (and container for sterilizing bottles, teats, utensils); cream for nappy rash and other skin complaints such as Sudocrem; sunblock; sunhat; terry towelling (cloth) nappies, liners, pins and plastic pants; thermometer; zip-lock bags.

Suggested reading

Pentes, Tina and Truelove, Adrienne (1984) *Travelling with Children to Indonesia and South-East Asia*, Hale & Iremonger: Sydney.

Working and studying in Laos

Work is not easily available in Laos and is in great demand. Laos has one of the highest retention rates of foreign workers in the region, as once they get there they don't want to leave. There is a vibrant expat community, mostly of aid workers (with

NGOs or bilaterial/multilateral agencies; see www.directoryofngos.org) as well as the usual diplomatic corps. But unlike Thailand there is not great scope for people to teach English for a few months, for example. Jobs are advertised in the *Vientiane Times*. The *Vientiane Guide*, published by the **Women's International Group** and available from bookshops in Vientiane is a useful tool for those proposing to live in the country. It's a bit out of date these days but has handy tips on how to rent a house and so on. Courses available to foreigners tend to be more fun-orientated than career-focused. Details of cooking, weaving, language and meditation courses are given in the relevant area chapter.

Volunteer programmes

Volunteer opportunities exist all over the world, for people of all ages, nationalities, cultures and skills. This can take the shape of long-term professional posts for humanitarian specialists and aid workers or short-, medium- and long-term positions of two weeks up to nine months for those taking sabbaticals and gap years, or young people looking for 'hands-on' practical field experience or the chance to join an expeditionary conservation project. Volunteering abroad and working with local grassroots NGOs brings benefits to everyone involved. Volunteers can spend time working with local populations, exchanging cultures and gaining experience in the field in the non-profit sector, and local grassroots NGOs in turn can receive support and funding from volunteers. All of this can be done on a grassroots level without the involvement of governments and politicians. For this reason many local organizations are developing more and more volunteer programmes. As a general rule, social work and the environment are the main sectors within the programmes of local NGOs.

There are several umbrella groups offering useful information and links to vetted organizations. **WorkingAbroad** (www.workingabroad.com) offers information on local grassroots volunteer and professional work opportunities in over 150 countries worldwide. These include social and community development, environment and conservation, wildlife expeditions, teaching English, organic agricultural projects, human rights observing, working with children and orphans, providing medical care, nursing and lots more. A good one-stop shop is **www.yearoutgroup.org**, a not-for-profit group representing, among others, **SWP, i-to-I, Outreach International, Bunac, Greenforce** and **Raleigh International**. Also worth checking out is **WorldWide Volunteering** (www.wwv.org.uk), which has projects with more than 1000 organizations in over 200 countries. This service costs £10 for three searches in a year, or is free if used in public libraries, universities and schools in the UK.

Other worthwhile organizations include **VSO** (www.vso.org.uk) in the UK; the Youth Ambassador Program (www.ausaid.gov.au/youtham) in Australia; **CUSO**, (www.cuso.org) in Canada and the **United Nations Volunteers** website, www.unv.org.

Before you travel

Getting in

The economic potential of tourism and the hospitable nature of the Lao people has helped wean the government off its historically paranoid view of the outside world and embrace tourism – as long as visitors stick to approved activities. Despite a significant drop in the number of arrivals following the SARS hysteria in 2003, Lao has rebounded and 2004 saw almost 900,000 tourists visit the country, up from under 150,000 a decade earlier. Travelling in Laos is far simpler than it used to be unless you happen to choose one of the rare occasions when the government restricts tourist entries into Vientiane.

Fifteen-day single-entry visas can be obtained for $US30 at Wattay International Airport, Vientiane (see page 64), Luang Prabang International Airport (see page 116), Pakse International Airport (see page 238) and at officially recognized international border crossings (see page 32). 'Overtime fees' are often charged if you enter after 1600 or at a weekend. You will need a passport photo (sometimes two).

30-day visas If you want to stay for longer than two weeks, most Lao embassies and consulates (see below) will issue 30-day visas. Many visitors to Laos arrange these in a neighbouring country, usually Thailand but also Cambodia, China, Myanmar and Vietnam. You generally need to allow three working days, although a one-day express service is sometimes available on payment of a surcharge.

Bangkok is the best place to arrange a 30-day visa in advance. The Laos embassy has moved north to quite an inaccessible spot, so many visitors find it easier to arrange their visa through one of the Thai capital's many travel agents, who usually only slap a ฿300 to ฿500 charge on top of the basic cost. The greatest concentration of tour agents is around Khaosan Road in Banglamphu but agents in other tourist areas will also arrange visas at similar rates. The service can also be provided for a fee by travel agents and tour operators in Chiang Khong, Chiang Mai, Khon Kaen, Mukdahan, Nakhon Phanom, Nong Khai, Ubon Ratchathani and Udon Thani (Thailand), in Phnom Penh (Cambodia) and in Yangon/Rangoon (Myanmar/Burma).

Visa extensions These can be obtained from the **Lao Immigration Office** in the Ministry of the Interior opposite the Morning Market in Vientiane, T021-212529. Visas can be extended for 30 days at the cost of US$3 per day; paid in kip or US$. You will need one passport photo. The Immigration Office staff are pleasant and issue extensions politely and with little fuss – sometimes in as little as a few hours. Numerous tourist shops and travel agencies in Vientiane and other major centres can also handle this service for you (although they are likely to add a service charge). Visitors who overstay are charged US$10 for each day beyond the visa's date of expiry.

❧ It is useful to take several passport photographs with you for visa extensions, etc.

Transit visas

Usually valid for seven to 10 days, transit visas (US$15) can be obtained by tourists with a confirmed onward airline ticket. They are available from Lao embassies in Bangkok, Hanoi, Phnom Penh, Beijing and Yangon (Rangoon) and from Lao consulates in Kunming (China), Ho Chi Minh City (Saigon, Vietnam) and Danang (Vietnam). As with regular tourist visas you can pay extra for an 'express' service. Transit visas cannot be extended. Those who do overstay are fined when they leave the country (see above).

Business visas

Business visas, valid for 30 days, with multiple entries and exits, may be obtained from Laos' embassies and consulates, although the Lao Embassy in Bangkok often operates as an intermediary. Business visas can be indefinitely extended or renewed in Vientiane for repeated 30-day periods. The visa must be approved in Vientiane and requires a formal request from a business, government organization, family or friend in Laos. Approval for issuing the visa is sent to the appropriate embassy from Vientiane.

Lao embassies and consulates

Australia, 1 Dalman Crescent, O' Malley Canberra, ACT 2606, T02-864595, F02-2901910.

Cambodia, 15-17 Mao Tse Toung Boulevard, Phnom Penh, T023-26441, F023-85523.

China, Beijing: 11 Dongsi Jie, Sanlitun, 100600, T65321224, F65326746. **Yunnan**: Room 3226, Camelia Hotel, 154 East Dong Feng Rd 650041, T3176623-24, F3178556.

France, 74 Ave Raymond-Poincaré 75116 Paris, T01-4553 0298, F01-4727 5789. This is the nearest embassy to the UK.
Myanmar (Burma), A1 Diplomatic quarters Fraser Road, Yangon, T01-22482, F01-27446.
Singapore, 101 Thomson Rd, No 05-03A, United Square, Singapore 307591, T2506044, F2506014
Thailand, Bangkok: 502/1 Soi Ramkamhaeng 39, Thanon Pracha Uthit, Wangthonglang, 10310, T02-539 6667, F02-539 6678. Khon Kaen: 19/1-3 Phothisan Rd, Muang District,

40000 T043-221961, F043-223849.
USA, 2222 S St NW, Washington DC, 20008, T1-202 332 6416/17, F1-202 332 4923. Permanent Mission United States, 317 East 51 St, New York, 10022, T1-212 832 2734, F1-212 750 0039.
Vietnam, Hanoi: 22 Tran Binh Trong, T04-254576, F04 228414. Danang City, 12 Tran Quy Cap, T051-21208, F051-22628. Ho Chi Minh City, 181 Hai Ba Trung, T08-299275, F08-299272. Open 0830-1100, 1430-1600.

Onward travel

Visas for Cambodia Cambodia visas are not available at the land border with Laos and must be obtained in advance from the Cambodian embassy in Vientiane (see page 96). Three-day applications cost US$20; 24-hour applications cost US$30. You need a minimum of three valid months on your passport, otherwise you will be rejected.

Visas for China Sixty-day visas must be obtained in advance from the Chinese Embassy in Vientiane (see page 96). They take three days to process, or 24 hours on payment of a surcharge.

Visas for Myanmar The embassy in Vientiane (see page 96) processes visa applications in two days for $US20. Note that foreigners are not permitted to cross by land between Laos and Myanmar (Burma).

Visas for Thailand It is no longer necessary for nationals of most countries (including EU member states, USA, Canada, Australia, New Zealand and South Africa) to obtain a visa for Thailand for tourist stays of up to 30 days. For those that require them, visas are issued at the Friendship Bridge, see page 97. For longer stays, 60-day visas (฿300, payable in baht only) are available from the Thai Embassy in Vientiane (see page 96) and at the Thai Consulate in Savannakhet (see page 234); it takes one to three days to process an application.

Visas for Vietnam Thirty-day visas are not available at land borders and must be arranged in advance. They are available from the embassy in Vientiane (see page 96) and from the consulates in Savannakhet (see page 234) and Pakse (see page 252). They take three days to process and cost US$50 in Vientiane (more from Savannakhet or Pakse).

Customs

Duty free allowance 500 cigarettes, two bottles of wine and a bottle of liquor can be brought into the country duty free. There is a small but well-stocked duty-free shop on the Lao side of the Thai-Lao Friendship Bridge and at Wattay Airport.

Export restrictions Due to ridiculous amounts of looting, Laos has a strictly enforced ban on the export of antiquities and all Buddha images. There are no restrictions on the import or export of foreign currencies.

Vaccinations

No mandatory inoculations are required for Laos except yellow fever and cholera, if coming from an infected area. However, it is advisable to take the whole spectrum of relevant vaccinations, including the seris hepatitis (A and B) shots, rabies, Japanese encephalitis, yellow fever, tetanus, typhoid, measles, polio, cholera, etc. You should visit a doctor before going to Laos and specify exactly where and how you will be travelling. ➤➤ *For further information, see Health page 53.*

What to take

Laos is not noted for its shopping, although it is now possible to buy most toiletries, as well as things like photographic supplies and peanut butter, in Vientiane. Luang Prabang, Savannakhet and Pakse also stock most basic items. Outside these cities little is available beyond such items as soap, washing powder, batteries, shampoo, and the like. Suitcases are not appropriate if you are intending to travel overland by bus. A backpack, or even better a travelpack (where the straps can be zipped out of sight), is recommended. Travelpacks (hybrid backpacks-suitcases) can be carried on the back for easy porterage, but can also be taken into hotels without the owner being labelled a 'hippy'. In terms of clothing, dress in Laos is relatively casual – even at formal functions. Suits are not necessary, although most people dress tidily and modestly. Don't pack too may clothes; laundry services are cheap, and the turnaround is rapid.

Medical checklist antacid tablets for indigestion; antibiotics for travellers diarrhoea (eg Ciproxin/Ciprofloxacin); antiseptic ointment (eg Cetrimide); anti-malarials (see page 56); condoms; contraceptives; diarrhoea treatments; disposable gloves; fungicidal dusting powder for feet; MedicAlert bracelet or pendant; mosquito repellents; motion sickness tablets; pain killers; sterile syringes and needles; sun protection cream and sun block; tampons (expensive in parts of Southeast Asia).

For longer trips involving jungle treks taking a clean needle pack, clean dental pack and water filtration devices are common-sense measures. However, be wary of carrying disposable needles as customs officials may find them suspicious. If you are popular target for insect bites or develop lumps quite soon after being bitten, carry an Aspivenin kit. This syringe suction device is available from many chemists and draws out some of the allergic materials and provides quick relief.

Other items bumbag; cotton sheet sleeping bag; digital camera memory card; earplugs; film; inflatable pillow; international driving licence; money belt; mosquito mats/coils; mosquito net; padlock; passport (valid for at least six months); passport photographs; photocopies of essential documents; soap; student ID card; sun glasses; Swiss Army knife; toilet paper; torch; travel wash; umbrella; wet wipes; zip-lock bags.

Insurance

Always take out comprehensive travel insurance and read the small print carefully. Check which activities are covered; exactly what level of medical cover you will receive (including emergency flights back home); the excess payable on any claim and the payment protocol. Keep details of your policy and the claims telephone number with you at all times; you should also give these details to a reliable person at home.

Money

The kip is the currency unit and has plummeted in value over the last decade. In the mid-1990s there were 1,200 kip to the US dollar. Be prepared for further significant change in the costs of goods and services. There are no coins in circulation. Notes used to start at the diminutive – and useless – one kip; now 10-, 20- and 50-kip notes are also worthless and the lowest commonly used note is the 500 kip. More useful are the 1,000 and 5,000 kip notes, but 10,000 and 20,000 kip notes are now in circulation (even the latter, the highest denomination note available, is worth little more than US$2). As a result pockets tend to bulge with huge wads of kip. It is partly because of the sheer inconvenience of carrying pockets full of Lao notes that people sensibly opt for Thai currency or US dollars, instead. US dollars and Thai baht can be used as cash in most shops, restaurants and hotels. In some northern areas Chinese yuan can be used. A certain amount of cash (in US dollars or Thai baht) can also be useful in an emergency. Keep it separate from your traveller's cheques.

> ⚑ In December 2005, US$1 was worth around 10,800 kip. To check the latest exchange rate see www.oanda.com

Exchange

The Lao kip tends to shadow the Thai baht but with a rather quaint one week delay. It is getting much easier to change currency and traveller's cheques in Laos. Traveller's cheques denominated in US dollars and pounds sterling can be changed in major centres. Euro denominations are also now widely accepted. Banks are generally reluctant to give anything but kip in exchange for hard currency but US dollar traveller's cheques can sometimes be exchanged into US dollars cash or Thai baht at major banks.

There are now a host of foreign banks – mostly Thai – with branches in Vientiane. Other major branches include the **Lao Development Bank** and **Le Banque pour Commerce Exterieur Lao** (BCEL), which change most major international currencies (cash) and traveller's cheques denominated in US dollars and pounds sterling. Many of the BCEL branches offer cash advances on Visa/MasterCard.There is a barely significant difference in the rates of exchange offered by banks and money changers but some banks charge a hefty commission of US$2 per traveller's cheque, so take traveller's cheques in larger denominations. In regional areas facilities to change traveller's cheques can be difficult, so it is better to organize exchange in major towns and cities. In general, it is easier to carry small denominations of US dollars cash or Thai baht, changing them as you go.

More expensive items such as tours, car hire, hotels, etc, tend to be quoted in dollars (or baht) while smaller purchases are quoted in kip. Thai baht are readily accepted in most towns but it is advisable to carry kip in rural areas (buses, for example, will usually only accept kip). It is quite normal to be quoted a price in kip, US dollars and baht. Nor is it unheard of to pay for a meal in three different currencies and certainly to be handed a bill quoting the total in kip, baht and US dollars.

The kip is pretty much non-convertible, so once you leave Laos any remaining notes are useless unless you can pass them onto someone about to enter the country.

ATMs

There are now several ATMs in Vientiane, the most prominent being at the BCEL bank. Many are less than reliable and at least one has a man behind the machine handing out the money. Others will only dispense a maximum of 700,000 kip at a time. A number of local Visa ATMs are appearing, but they aren't always functional. At weekends, the only other options for exchange or obtaining cash are the BCEL booth along the river and the ATM booth (complete with a bank staffer hiding behind it) across from the Lao Plaza, both in Vientiane. It makes sense, if you are arriving from Thailand, to draw a few thousand baht out of an ATM before arriving in Laos.

Credit cards

Now that Laos has reformed its banking laws and welcomed foreign investment, payment by credit card is becoming easier – although beyond the larger hotels and restaurants in Vientiane and Luang Prabang do not expect to be able to get by on plastic. American Express, Visa, MasterCard/Access cards are accepted in a limited number of more upmarket establishments. There is an ATM in Vientiane, which accepts credit cards. Note that a commission is charged by some places on credit card transactions. If they can route the payment through Thailand then a commission is not levied; but if this is not possible, then 3% is usually added.

Many banks will now advance cash on credit cards in major centres including Luang Prabang, Vientiane, Pakse, Phonsavanh, Savannakhet and Vang Vieng (not not all cards are accepted at these banks, so it's better to check in advance).

Cost of living

Budget travellers will find that a little goes a long way in Laos. Numerous guesthouses offer accommodation at around US$4-5 a night (often considerably less if you're sharing) and more and more are beginning to throw in free water and bananas. Food-wise, the seriously strapped can easily manage to survive healthily on US$5-6 per day, so an overall daily budget (not allowing for excursions) of US$10 should be just enough for the really cost-conscious, but requires scrimping. For the less frugally minded, a daily allowance of $12-20 should see you relatively well housed and fed, while at the upper end of the scale, there are usually plenty of accommodation and restaurant opportunities for those looking for Lao-levels of luxury. A mid-range hotel (attached bathroom, hot water and air conditioning) will normally cost around US$20 per night. A good meal at a restaurant, perhaps US$4-5.

Cost of travelling

The cost of travelling around Laos is dependent largely on your chosen method of transport. The variety of available domestic flights means that the bruised bottoms, dust-soaked clothes and stiff limbs that go hand-in-hand with some of the longer bus/boat rides can be avoided by those with thicker wallets and deeper pockets. Air travel costs are standardized, and the same prices are offered by all travel agents, usually lower than from the airlines directly (or should be). Foreigners pay more than locals. Boats traditionally formed the cornerstone of domestic travel requirements. Now, though, as more of the country becomes accessible by land (although beware the rainy season, when some previously adequate roads become at best treacherous and at worst impassible), the popularity of boat travel has diminished while the cost has rocketed. As the roads improve and journey times diminish, buses have emerged above both planes and boats as the preferred (not to mention most reasonably priced) transportation option. Usually buses are also the cargo carriers, so don't be surprised when you are sitting beside a motorbike, a few sacks of rice, some chooks or a goat for that matter. Motion sickness is a common issue on bus transport and Laos people tend to vomit a lot. On any remotely hilly trips it is worth taking some motion sickness medicine in order to avoid participating in the chain reaction, projectile vomiting out of the window.

Getting there

Air

There are international flights to Vientiane from the following countries: **Cambodia** (Phnom Penh and Siem Reap), **China** (Kunming), **Taiwan** (Taipei), **Thailand** (Bangkok and Chiang Mai) and **Vietnam** (Hanoi and Ho Chi Minh City/Saigon). Most people visiting Laos from outside the region, travel via Bangkok. ▸▸ *For details of domestic services, see Getting around, page 40.*

From Thailand

Bangkok (BKK) This is the main gateway to Vientiane. If you want to visit Bangkok as well as Laos, the best way is to include the Bangkok-Vientiane sector on your long-haul ticket. This is a cheaper option than purchasing tickets separately in Bangkok. There are daily flights between Bangkok and Vientiane operated by **THAI** (www.thaiairways.com) and **Lao Airlines** (www.laoairlines.com). The official fares on each airline vary slightly but both can be purchased from travel agents. It's worth checking the schedule on the Lao Airlines website as they are forever curtailing/adding/changing flights. **Bangkok Airways** (www.bangkokair.com) has recently started flying from Bangkok to Luang Prabang.

Chiang Mai (CNX) Lao Airlines (www.laoairlines.com) now runs a thrice-weekly service between Chiang Mai (northern Thailand) and Vientiane; and one flight a week between Chiang Mai and Luang Prabang.

Udon Thani (UTH) While most visitors to Laos fly into Vientiane, the preferred route in and out of Laos for many expats is via Udon Thani in northeast Thailand, about 50 km south of the Friendship Bridge border. This is because the single domestic airfare between Bangkok and Udon is a third of the international fare between Bangkok and Vientiane, while a domestic return costs half the price of the international ticket. Discount airline, **Air Asia** (www.airasia.com) flies this route so there are now around six flights a day between Bangkok and Udon. The service works very efficiently and is fairly hassle-free. From Udon Thani, you can catch a minibus or taxi to the Friendship Bridge or a bus directly to the Talaat Sao bus terminal in Vientiane for only ฿80. (You could also overland it from Udon Thani to Pakse in southern Laos.) All in all, taking the Udon/Friendship Bridge option between Bangkok and Vientiane will probably only add one hour to your journey, since immigration at Wattay Airport tends to be slow.

From other neighbouring countries

Cambodia There are daily flights between Phnom Penh (PNH) and Vientiane with **Vietnam Airlines** (www.vietnamairlines.com) and **Lao Airlines** (www.laoairlines.com). **Lao Airlines** also runs flights between Siem Reap and Vientiane and between Siem Reap and Pakse.

China Lao Airlines (www.laoairlines.com) and **Southern Airlines** (merged with China Yunnan Air; www.cs-air.com/en/) both run flights between Kunming (KMG) and Vientiane.

Taiwan There are two flights a week between Taipei (TPE) and Vientiane with **Eva Air** (www.evaair.com).

Vietnam There are flights between Vientiane and Hanoi and Vientiane and Ho Chi Minh City (Saigon) operated by **Lao Airlines** (www.laoairlines.com) flies three times a week between Hanoi and Vientiane. **Vietnam Airlines** (www.vietnamairlines.com) runs a daily service between Hanoi and Vientiane and also between Ho Chi Minh City and Vientiane.

Road and river

Laos is a land-locked country and hopes to establish itself as a regional transit point, with new international highways dissecting the country at 100 km intervals. For the moment, however, foreign visitors travelling overland between neighbouring

⁚ Official border crossings

Cambodia-Laos
Stung Treng-Voen Kham, page 284.

China-Laos
Mohan-Boten, page 177.

Myanmar (Burma)-Laos
Foreigners are currently not
permitted to either enter or leave
Laos through Myanmar (Burma).

Thailand-Laos
Mittaphab (Friendship) Bridge,
Nong Khai-Vientiane, page 97.
Chiang Khong-Houei Xai, page 178.
Bueng Kan-Paksan, page 213.
Nakhon Phanom-Thakhek, page 224.
Mukdahan-Savannakhet, page 233.
The Thai-Lao Friendship Bridge at
Savannakhet is supposed to open
in 2006 but might well be delayed
until 2007.

Chongmek-Vang Tao (near Pakse),
page 252.
    At the time of publication, the
crossing between Houei Kone,
Thailand, and Muang Ngoen, Laos,
was only open to Lao and Thai
nationals.

Vietnam-Laos
Nam Khan-Nam Khan
(Xieng Khouang), page 190.
Na Maew-Nam Xoi, page 196.
Cau Treo-Nam Phao, page 211.
Lao Bao-Dansavanh, page 232.
This is the most popular crossing.
    At the time of publication, the
crossings between Tay Trang,
Vietnam, and Tai Xang, Laos, and
between Huoi Puoc, Vietnam (near
Dien Bien Phu), and Na Son, Laos,
were only officially open to Lao and
Vietnamese nationals.

countries are restricted to a handful of key crossing points (see Official border crossings, above). For much of its length, the Lao-Thai border is defined by the Mekong, with bridges and ferries to link the two countries. To the east, the Annamite mountain range forms a spine separating Laos from Vietnam, with a few cross-border buses running from Vientiane and Savannakhet. There is only one official border crossing between Laos and Cambodia in the south and between Laos and China in the north. Foreigners are not permitted to cross between Laos and Myanmar (Burma).

Touching down

Airport information → *Flight information: T020-212066 .*

Wattay International Airport is about 6 km from Vientiane. Until a couple of years ago Wattay Airport was a throwback to an earlier age of aviation when pilots were aviators and airports were air fields. There wasn't an escalator or moving walkway in sight. Sadly for those with a nostalgic turn of mind, this is all in the past. A new, Japanese-financed (but Lao designed) terminal has opened, fully air conditioned and painted in soothing – and very 21st century – grey. There's even an escalator as well as a small number of air bridges for the few airplanes that require such advanced technology. Visitors can now complete their visa application forms in air-conditioned comfort while listening to piped international music. (But all is not lost: the old terminal has now become the domestic terminal.) The airport also has a restaurant, hotel booking counter, foreign exchange desk, duty free shop, gift shop, and post office. In other words, most of the things that you could possibly want from an airport.

Visas are issued on arrival (see page 26). Depending on the numbers of incoming vistors, the process usually takes about 30 minutes and is fairly efficient. It is much quicker if you already have passport photos to hand. If you intend returning to Laos, it is handy to take a few extra visa application forms with you so you can fill one in before landing. ⟩⟩ *For information on transport to and from the airport, see Ins and outs page 64.*

Airport tax International airport tax is US$10; domestic airport tax is 5000 kip. This hasn't changed for years and years, so expect a price hike soon.

Tourist information

In the past, the official government-run **National Tourism Authority**, Lao Lane Xang Avenue, Vientiane, T021-212251, F212769, was not renowned for its skills in information dissemination, but it is getting better. Recently, it has teamed up with local tour operators to provide a number of ecotourism opportunities throughout the country (www.ecotourismlaos.com). The provincial offices are usually very obliging and, as long as you are patient, they will usually come through with the information you need. There are particularly good tourism offices in Thakhek, Savannakhet, Xam Neua and Luang Namtha. Before you arrive, another source of up-to-date information are comments and advice from recent travellers, which are documented in scrapbooks in Nong Khai guesthouses (across the river in Thailand). Certain tour agencies in Bangkok also keep bulletin boards of up-to-date records and travellers' tips, although these informal sources are becoming less necessary as travelling in Laos becomes easier and information on the country is more widely available.

Local customs and laws

Bargaining/haggling

While bargaining is common in Laos – in the market or in negotiating a trip on a *saamlor* or tuk-tuk for example – it is not heavy duty haggling. The Lao are extremely laid back and it is rare to be fleeced; don't bargain hard with them, it may force them to lose face and reduce prices well below their profit margin. For most things, you won't even really need to bargain. Having said that, beware the tuk-tuk drivers in Lak Xao, and some of the more transparent petitions for more money 'for medicine' you'll hear in some pockets of the country where opium is abundant. Approach bargaining with a sense of fun; a smile or joke always helps.

Clothing

Informal, lightweight clothing is all that is needed, although a sweater is vital for the highlands in the winter months (November to March). An umbrella is useful during the rainy season (June and July). Sleeveless shirts and singlets, very short shorts and skirts are not ideal. When visiting monasteries (wats) women should keep their shoulders covered and take their shoes off. One of the main reasons for the tight controls on tourism in Laos is because of the perceived corrosive effects that badly dressed tourists were having on Lao culture. The assumption was that scruffy dress was a reflection of character. Today, 'scruffy' travellers are still frowned upon and officials are getting utterly fed up with people wandering around skimpily clad, particularly in Vang Vieng and Siphandon. If you are bathing in public, particularly in rural areas, you should try to bathe with a sarong. It is expected that people will take their shoes off before entering a Lao home.

Touching down

Business hours Government offices: usually Mon-Fri 0800-1200, 1300-1630 (lunch break usually drags on a bit longer). **Banks:** 0830-1600 (some close at 1500, so check in advance). **Business:** usually Mon-Fri 0900-1700; businesses that deal with tourists open a bit later and usually over the weekend. **Bars and nightclubs** Usually close around 2200-2300 depending on how strictly the curfew is being reinforced. In smaller towns, most restaurants and bars will be closed by 2200.

Directory enquiries T16 (national), T170 (international).

Emergencies Ambulance: T195.

Fire brigade: T190. **Police:** T191.

IDD code T+856.

Official language Lao; Thai is understood, as are French and English in the main tourist areas.

Official time Seven hours ahead of GMT.

Voltage 220 volts, 50 cycles in the main towns. 110 volts in the country. Two-pin sockets are common so adaptors are required. Blackouts are common outside Vientiane and many smaller towns are not connected to the national grid and only have power during the evening.

Weights and measures Metric along with local systems of measurement.

Conduct

Particular rules apply when visiting minority villages, for details, see page 38.

Wats Monks are revered, don't touch their robes. If talking to a monk your head should be lower than his. Avoid visiting a wat around 1100 as this is when the monks have their morning meal. It is considerate to ask the abbot's permission to enter the *sim* and shoes should be removed before entry. When sitting down, feet should point away from the altar and main image. Arms and legs should be fully covered when visiting wats. A small donation is often appropriate (kneel when putting it into the box).

Forms of address Lao people are addressed by their first name, not their family name, even when a title is used.

Greeting The *nop* or *wai* – with palms together below your chin and head bowed, as if in prayer – remains the traditional form of greeting. Shaking hands, though, is very widespread – more so than in neighbouring Thailand. This can be put down to the influence of the French during the colonial period (whereas Thailand was never colonized). 'Sabaidee' (hello) is also a good way to greet. Avoid hugging and kissing to greet Lao people, as they tend to get embarrassed.

In private homes Remove your shoes. When seated on the floor you should tuck your feet behind you.

Eating etiquette In Laos, who eats when is important. At a meal, a guest should not begin eating until his host has invited him or her to do so. Nor should the guest continue eating after everyone else has finished. It is also customary for guests to leave a small amount of food on their plate; to do otherwise would imply that the guest was still hungry and that the host had not provided sufficient food for the meal. Sharing is a big thing at meal times, where plates of food are ordered and shared amongst everyone. Lao people often invite tourists to eat with them or share on buses, and it is a nice gesture if this is reciprocated. Though Lao people tend to be shy so don't take any refusal as a rejection, sometimes they also get embarrassed about their clothes, etc. Most Lao are very tolerant of other cultures and don't expect things such as eating etiquette to be strictly adhered to.

General Pointing with the index finger is considered rude. If you want to call someone over, gesture with your palm facing the ground and fingers waving towards you (as opposed to the other direction). In Lao your head is considered 'high' and feet are considered 'low'. So try to keep your feet low, don't point them at people or touch people with your feet. Don't pat children on the head (or touch people's heads in general) , as it is the considered the most sacred part of the body.

Lao people have a passive nature. Yelling or boisterous people tend to completely freak them out and they go into panic mode. If a dispute arises, a smile and a few jokes will do the trick every time. Likewise for bargaining, keep a sense of humour, and the funnier you are, the more likely you are to get your desired price.

The Lao are proud people and begging is just not the done thing, so don't hand out money (or medicine) to local villagers. If you want to give a gift or a donation to someone, it is best to channel it through the village elder.

Drugs

Drug use is illegal in Laos and there are harsh penalties for those that indulge, ranging from fines for possession through to imprisonment or worse. Police have been known to levy heavy fines on people in Vang Vieng for consuming the 'happy' foods that are on sale. What's more, the 'happy' pizzas, shakes and other items on sale in Vang Vieng have been known to make people extremely unwell and should be avoided. Opium has officially been eradicated in Laos but it is still often for sale in northern areas, particularly around the former Golden Triangle. Needless to say, the police will punish anyone found in possession. The nasty drug *yaa baa* is also available, to a lesser extent, and should be avoided at all costs.

Photographs

Sensitivity pays when taking photographs. Be very wary in areas that have (or could have) military importance – such as airports, where all photography is prohibited. Also be careful when photographing official functions and parades without permission. Always ask permission before taking photographs in a monastery. You should always ask people's permission before you take a photograph of them.

Tipping

It is not common practice to tip, even in hotels. However, it is a kind gesture to tip guides and some more expensive restaurants, mostly in Vientiane, appreciate a 10% tip if service charge is not included on the bill.

Responsible tourism

'Tourism is like fire. It can either cook your food or burn your house down'. This sums up the ambivalent attitude that many people have regarding the effects of tourism. It is the world's largest single industry, yet many people in receiving countries would rather tourists went home. Tourism is seen to be the cause of rising prices, loose morals, consumerism and much else besides.

In a survey of the industry in 1991, *The Economist* pointed that "the curse of the tourist industry is that it peddles dreams: dreams of holidays where the sun always shines, the children are always occupied, and where every evening ends in the best sex you have ever had. For most of its modern life, this has been matched by a concomitant dreaminess on the part of its customers. When asked, most tourists tell whopping lies about what they want on holiday..." (*The Economist*, 1991).

Most international tourists come from a handful of wealthy countries. This is why many see tourism as the new 'imperialism', imposing alien cultures and ideals on sensitive and unmodernized peoples. The problem, however, is that discussions of the effects of tourism tend to degenerate into simplifications – culminating in the drawing up of a checklist of 'positive' and 'negative' effects. Although such tables may be useful in highlighting problem areas, they also do a disservice by reducing a complex issue to a simple set of rather one-dimensional 'costs' and 'benefits'. Different destinations will be affected in different ways; these effects are likely to vary over time; and different groups living in a particular destination will feel the effects of tourism in different ways and to varying degrees. At no time or place can tourism (or any other influence) be categorized as uniformly 'good' or 'bad'. Tourism can take a young Australian backpacker on US$10 a day to a guesthouse in a small town in northern Laos, a family to a first-class hotel in Luang Prabang where a room can cost more than US$100 a night, or a businessman or woman to Vientiane.

Some tourists are attracted to Laos because of its exotic 'tribal' ethnic groups. When cultural erosion is identified, the tendency is to blame this on tourism and tourists, who become the 'suntanned destroyers of culture'. The problem with views like this is that they assume that change is bad, and that indigenous cultures are unchanging. It makes local peoples victims of change, rather than masters of their own destinies. It also assumes that tourism is an external influence, when in fact it quickly becomes part of the local landscape. Cultural change is inevitable and ongoing, and 'new' and 'traditional' are only judgements, not absolutes. Thus new cultural forms can quickly become key markers of tradition. Tourists searching for an 'authentic' experience are assuming that tradition is tangible, easily identifiable and unchanging. It is none of these.

Views of tourist art, both material (such as sculpture) and non-material (like dances,) also sharply diverge. The mass of inferior 'airport' art on sale to tourists demonstrates to some the corrosive effects of tourism. It leads craftsmen and women to mass-produce second-rate pieces for a market that appreciates neither their cultural and symbolic worth, nor their aesthetic value. Yet tourism can also give value to craft industries that would otherwise be undermined by cheap industrial goods. So, some people argue that the craft traditions of Laos may be given a new injection of vitality by the demands that tourism is increasingly creating. Indeed, this has already happened: witness the re-birth of top-quality textile production.

The environmental deterioration that is linked to tourism is due to a destination area exceeding its 'carrying capacity' as a result of overcrowding. But carrying capacity, though an attractive concept, is notoriously difficult to pin down. A second dilemma facing those trying to encourage greater environmental consciousness is the so-called 'tragedy of the commons', best explained as follows: when a group of people go to a restaurant with the intention of sharing the bill, each customer will tend to order a more expensive dish than he or she would normally do, based on the logic that everyone will be doing the same and the bill will be split. In tourism terms, it means that hotel owners will always build those few more bungalows or that extra wing to maximize their profits, reassured in the knowledge that the environmental costs will be shared among all hotel owners in the area. So, despite most operators appreciating that over-development may 'kill the goose that lays the golden eggs', they expand their operations anyway. Many areas of Laos have few other development opportunities and those with beautiful landscapes and/or exotic cultures find it difficult to resist the temptation to market them and attract the tourist dollar. And why shouldn't they?

One of the ironies is that the 'traveller' or 'backpacker' finds it difficult to consider him or herself a tourist at all. This, of course, is hubris built upon the notion that the

Wildlife conservation

The opportunity to buy or consume wildlife will probably present itself throughout your travels in Laos . However, while the Government of Lao PDR permits subsistence hunting for local rural villagers, the sale and purchase of any wildlife is illegal in the country, and is damaging to biodiversity and local livelihoods.

You may see live wild animals for sale as meat or pets in rural areas and cities. Some travellers buy these live animals out of pity, and then release them. Please do not be tempted to do this, as the vendors do not know your motivation and the sale simply increases the demand for wildlife. Also, by this stage the animal could be sick, and could infect other wild animals if released.

You may also encounter rat snakes, soft-shelled turtles, mouse deer, sambar deer, squirrel, bamboo rat, muntjac and pangolins as food in markets and on the menus of Lao and Chinese restaurants in Vientiane, Luang Prabang and in the provinces. Some French restaurants in Vientiane and Luang Prabang serve deer – usually this is muntjac, a wild animal from the forest. Many of these species are either endangered themselves or are a prey source for endangered species, such as the Indochinese tiger.

Neither should travellers be tempted to purchase stuffed wild animals, animal products such as bags and wallets or insects in framed boxes (eg butterflies and beetles). Also to be avoided are animal teeth sold as rings and necklaces – sellers often state this is buffalo bone but it may be bear or wild pig bone. Do not buy bottles of alcohol with snakes, birds or insects inside. Though widely sold, all these items are illegal in Laos, and most travellers will find that their purchases are confiscated by customs in their home country (particularly in Australia and America). Only products with a CITES-certified label are legal to buy in Laos and take home.

As a part of many festivals and temple visits in Laos, Buddhists release small birds to gain merit. You are likely to see these tiny birds, frequently native munias and swallows, in small rattan cages outside temples. The Wildlife Conservation Society-Lao PDR Program, is working with the Lao Buddhist Association to discourage this practice. The birds, weakened by being caged, probably perish shortly after release. Please don't participate in buying and releasing birds.

For many species of wildlife in Laos, populations are at critically low levels. The Wildlife Conservation Society-Lao PDR Program is collaborating with the Vientiane Capital City government to monitor and control wildlife trade. Government staff patrol restaurants, markets and households with suspected trade or captured species, and confiscate the wildlife. Live wildlife is released or euthanized; dead wildlife is periodically burnt in ceremonial public fires (for project transparency and to raise awareness). The Wildlife Conservation Society (WCS) appreciates the support of all visitors and residents in Laos to help conserve wildlife. For more information visit www.wcs.org/international/Asia/laos.

Dr Renae Stenhouse, Wildlife Conservation Society.

traveller is an 'independent' explorer who is somehow beyond the bounds of the industry. Anna Borzello in an article entitled 'The myth of the traveller' in the journal *Tourism in Focus* (No 19, 1994) writes that "Independent travellers cannot acknowledge – without shattering their self-image – that to many local people they are simply a good source of income. ...[not] inheritors of Livingstone, [but] bearers of urgently needed money".

The Lao government has really tried to protect the country from adverse effects tourism can have. To this end, they have distributed lots of literature to try and make tourists aware of what is culturally sensitive in the country. Despite their efforts, many tourists still continue to disregard their wishes, particularly when it comes to dressing modestly.

Visiting minority villages It is becoming increasingly popular for travellers to Laos to visit minority villages. This raises a whole series of questions about conduct which cannot be covered in a general discussion because of cultural differences between the many different ethnic peoples. There is certainly a case for advising that visitors, where possible, employ the services of a local guide. Just as was the case in northern Thailand when trekking became popularized there, the actions of a few are tarring the reputation of the many. In more than a few cases, visitors have no idea how to behave with minority people. Many seek to buy drugs, female travellers potter around scantily clad, they have little notion of local customs, where not to go, what not to bring (many bring sweets), and so on. Because the numbers of travellers visiting minority villages has exploded in recent years this has become quite a serious problem.

Safety

Before travelling, check your country's official advice on travel to Laos (**Australia**, www.smartraveller.gov.au; **Canada**, www.voyage.gc.ca; **UK**, www.fco.gov.uk; **USA**, www.travel.state.gov). For information on women travelling alone, see page 22.

Air travel Laos has a pretty terrible reputation for domestic air safety. Lao Airlines has three types of aeroplane: French-built *ATR 72s*, and Chinese-built *Y-7s* and *Y-12s*. The latter two hardly inspire confidence and some foreign embassies in Vientiane request that their staff do not fly on the *Y-7s* and *Y-12s*, viewing them as simply too risky. Safety standards and maintenance of the *ATRs* has improved but it is still advisable to check travel advisories before departing on a **Lao Airlines** flight.

Bombs and mines Xieng Khouang province, the Boloven Plateau, Xam Neua and areas along the Ho Chi Minh Trail are littered with bombies (small anti-personnel mines and bomblets from cluster bomb units). There are also numerous large, unexploded bombs in many villages that have been left lying around. They are very unstable so DO NOT TOUCH. Five to 10 people are still killed or injured every month in Laos by inadvertently stepping on ordnance, or by hitting bomblets with hoes. Only walk on clearly marked or newly trodden paths.

Crime Crime rates are very low but it is advisable to take the usual precautions. There has been a reported increase in motorcycle drive-by thefts in Vientiane, but these and other similar crimes are still at a low level compared with most countries. If riding on a motor-bike or bicycle, carry a backpack rather than a bag with a long strap and don't leave valuables in a bike basket. In the Siphandon and Vang Vieng areas, theft seems more common, so, if a security box is available at your guest-house/hotel, it is advisable to use it.

Hmong insurgency A few years ago foreign embassies were advising tourists in Laos not to travel along certain roads and in certain areas (in particular, route 13

How big is your footprint?

- Learn about the country you're visiting and start enjoying your travels before you leave by tapping into as many sources of information as you can.
- Think about where your money goes – be fair and realistic about how cheaply you travel. Try and put money into local people's hands; drink local beer or fruit juice rather than imported brands and stay in locally-owned accommodation.
- Open your mind to new cultures and traditions. It can transform your holiday experience and you'll earn respect from and be more readily welcomed by local people.
- Think about what happens to your rubbish - take biodegradable products and a water filter bottle.
- Be sensitive to limited resources like water, fuel and electricity.
- Help preserve local wildlife and habitats by respecting rules and regulations, such as sticking to footpaths, not standing on coral and not buying products made from endangered plants or animals.
- Use your guidebook as a starting point, not the only source of information. Talk to local people, then discover your own adventure!
- Don't treat people as part of the landscape, they may not want their picture taken. Put yourself in their shoes, ask first and respect their wishes.

This information is taken from the Tourism Concern website (**www.tourismconcern.org.uk**) which provides further elaboration of the points noted here.

between Vientiane and Luang Prabang, and route 7 between Phonsavanh and route 13) because of the risk of attacks by Hmong rebels. Today these risks have effectively disappeared and most areas of Laos are safe. However, the government will sometimes make areas provisionally off-limits if they think there is a security risk and Saysomboun (see page 102) continues to be off-limits to tourists.

Road travel This is becoming more hazardous as the number of motorized vehicles increases. The US State Department in July 2005 put it like this: "Theoretically, the traffic moves on the right, but most cars, like pedestrians and bicycles, use all parts of the street. Cyclists pay little or no heed to cars on the road, and bicycles are rarely equipped with functioning lights or reflectors. This makes driving particularly dangerous at dusk and at night. Defensive driving is necessary". The hiring of motorbikes by tourists is also becoming more popular and consequently tourist injuries are increasing. The utmost care should be taken. If you do rent a motorbike ensure it has a working horn (imperative) and buy some rear-view mirrors so you can keep an eye on the traffic. Wear a helmet – it may not be cool but neither is a fractured skull.

Waterways Be careful around waterways, as drowning is one of the primary causes of tourist deaths. Be particularly careful during the rainy season (May to September) as rivers have a tendency to flood and can have extremely strong currents. Make sure if you are kayaking, tubing, canoeing, travelling by fast boat, etc, that proper safety gear, such as life-jackets, is provided. 'Fast boat' river travel can be dangerous due to excessive speed and the risk of hitting something in the river and capsizing. Many rivers also carry the schistosomiasis bacteria (see page 57).

Getting around

Air

Lao Airlines (www.laoairlines.com) runs domestic flights between Vientiane and Luang Prabang, Phonsavanh, Houei Xai, Udom Xai, Luang Namtha, Sayaboury, Phongsali and Pakse. For now, all flights must either depart or arrive in Vientiane but this could all change, as flight schedules alter almost on a daily basis. Notwithstanding the safety concerns (see page 38), flying is still the quickest and most convenient form of travel. Fortunately, the most reliable, comfortable and newest machines – the *ATR-72s* – operate on the most popular routes (Vientiane-Bangkok and Vientiane-Luang Prabang). **Lao Airlines**, at least on its minor domestic routes, seems to operate on the rather charming principle of *c'est la vie*. Planes are overbooked, underbooked, leave 30 minutes early, two hours late, or not at all. Even the official **Visit Laos** website used to admit that 'timetables cannot be relied upon' and exhorts visitors to 'please be flexible'. Some passengers have even been ticketed (in Lao) to towns they had no wish or intention of visiting. As a tourist this can be amusing, even enchanting; as a businessman or woman it can be frustrating. However, letters from readers suggest that the airline is becoming more professional and efficient as each year passes.

Tickets can be purchased from the **Lao Airlines** office in Vientiane ① *2 Pang Kham Rd, T021-212054, F021-212065, www.laoairlines.com*. All flights whether domestic or international, have to be paid for in US dollars. Kip is not acceptable. Some offices will also accept Thai baht or other Western currencies but the exchange rate is usually unfavourable. Lao Airlines accept Visa and AmEx on their international routes.

River

It is possible to take river boats up and down the Mekong and its main tributaries. The Mekong is navigable from Houei Xai on the border with Thailand downriver to south of Pakse. The most popular route is between Houei Xai and Luang Prabang (see pages 147 and 179). Other Mekong boat services to Vientiane, Thakhek and Savannakhet, as well as smaller towns and villages, are unscheduled and may be limited during the dry season. Boats leave at the last minute and speaking Lao is definitely an advantage. Boats are basic but cheap; take food and drink and expect somewhat crowded conditions aboard. The most common riverboats are the *hua houa leim*, with no decks, the hold being enclosed by side panels and a flat roof; note that metal boats get very hot. Speedboats also chart some routes, but are dangerous and never enjoyable. Prices vary according to size of boat and length of journey; downriver from Luang Prabang to Vientiane, for example, takes four days, travelling up to 10 hours a day.

While river transport remains important in a country with lots of rivers and few roads, it seems to be in terminal decline. As roads are upgraded and the cost of road transport goes down and speed goes up, so travellers are abandoning the river for the road. This means that scheduled passenger ferries on some routes are a thing of the past; it is still possible to charter a vessel, but the price is relatively high.

Road

Laos is a very poor country and has been ravaged by a terrible war, experiencing, in the process, some of the heaviest bombing the world has ever witnessed. Couple this with the mountainous terrain and a tropical climate of seasonal torrential rains, and it is no wonder that road construction poses a considerable challenge in many areas. The country was also cut off from the West from 1975 until the mid-1980s, when it hesitatingly embraced a programme of economic reform and international integration. All this means that roads in Laos are not exactly 'good' but they are slowly improving. Many have been repaired or upgraded and and new vehicles are gradually being introduced, making journeys infinitely more comfortable, as well as faster.

Practicalities Quite a few bus, truck, tuk-tuk, songthaew and taxi drivers understand the rudimentaries of English, French or Thai, although some of them (especially tuk-tuk drivers) aren't above forgetting the lowest price you thought you'd successfully negotiated before hopping aboard! It is best to take this sort of thing in good humour. Even so, in order to travel to a particular destination, it is a great advantage to have the name written out in Lao. Map reading is out of the question, and many people will not know road names, even if it's the road right outside their front door. However, they will know where all the sights of interest are – for example wats, markets, monuments, waterfalls, etc.

Bus/truck

It is now possible to travel to most areas of the country by bus, truck or *songthaew* (converted pick-up truck) in the dry season, although road travel in the rainy season can be trickier if not downright impossible. The accessibility of the further-flung towns and villages can depend to a certain extent on the time of year, and also, sometimes, on the willingness of passengers to get out and help build the very road the bus is meant to be driving along. There is a variety of public transport on Laos' roads, and also a rather intriguing north-south divide.

In the north, Nissan and Mitsubishi trucks are used as *songthaew* and these are often the fastest form of land-based public transport. For longer journeys, big Langjian (Chinese) trucks are sometimes used. On certain long routes, such as Vientiane/Luang Prabang to Xam Neua/Nam Nouan/Vieng Thong, the trucks have been converted into colourful buses with divided wooden seats and glassless windows. In more remote places (Xam Neua to Vieng Xai, for instance), ancient jeeps are common. In the south of the country, Japanese-donated buses are used, although you may see the occasional shiny Volvo bus.

Journey times are inevitably delayed by toilet stops, loading, unloading and overloading, so vehicles never seem to pick up any speed. One journey may be twice or half as long as another on the same stretch of road, in the same season and with the same type of vehicle. Many roads or parts of road are unsealed and breakdowns, though not frequent, aren't uncommon either. For some connections you may need to wait a day. During the rainy season (June to December) expect journey times to be longer than those quoted; indeed some roads may be closed altogether. Travellers can often negotiate a price if travelling by truck.

Bicycle

Bicycles are available from guesthouses in many towns and are a cheap way to see the sights. Chinese bikes tend to be better than Thai ones. Long-distance touring is not yet overly popular in Laos, so you'll need to bring your own bike and spare parts. However, there is great potential: the roads are not heavily used (but this could all change with the new Chinese-Thai super-highway) and traffic speeds are modest. That said, traffic volumes are increasing and road knowledge is limited (for road safety, see page 38).

Car

Car hire is anything from US$40-80 per day, depending on the vehicle, with first 150 km free, then US$10 every 100 km thereafter. The price includes a driver. For insurance purposes you will probably need an international driver's permit, which can be picked up before you leave for Laos. Insurance is generally included with car hire but it's best to check the fine print. A general rule of thumb: if you are involved in a traffic accident, you, the foreigner, are likely to be expected to bear the costs as you have more money. Metered taxis are common in Vientiane, mostly at markets and the airport. Outside Vientiane taxis are not so common, although you can charter a car (see above).

Hitchhiking

Hitchhiking alone or even in pairs carries risks anywhere in the world. Laos is probably safer than most places in that respect and drivers are more likely to stop here than in, for example, Thailand, but you should exercise caution and avoid hitching in areas that are known for Hmong insurgency. Hitchhiking can be more convenient than Lao public transport and is sometimes the only option in more out-of-the-way spots and at certain border crossings, although there are relatively few private vehicles on some roads. It is a good idea to offer some money for the journey.

Motorbike

Motorbike trips are one of the best ways to see the country, if you are an experienced rider that is! Nearly all roads between provincial capitals are sealed and shouldn't pose too much of a problem but other roads may become dangerous or impassable In the wet season. Some of the most sensational rides are around Pakse and beyond, where you can explore all of Champasak's ruins and waterfalls, and in the north between Phonsavanh and Xam Neua, where you will be rewarded with some of the country's finest scenery. Day trips from Vientiane to Phou Khao Khouay National Park are also worthwhile and one of the best ways to explore this vast area.

Motorbikes are increasingly available from guesthouses and other shops: 110cc bikes go for around US$7 a day, while 250cc Hondas are around US$20 per day. Dirt bikes can be rented from **PVO**, 344 Samsenthai Road, Vientiane, T214 444, and **Fuark**, T2 Road (between the Shell petrol station and northern bus station) Ban Nakham, Vientiane, T261970. In Pakse, the **Lane Kham** hotel has dirt bikes for rent. It is advisable to bring a good helmet with you and you will need an international licence for insurance purposes. Even whistle-stop towns have mechanics (usually thinly disguised as a restaurant or shop – look for the give-away dead tyres) who can change your tyre/oil but it is best to bring a repair kit with you for more complex issues. If you are renting a motorbike in Laos it is a good idea to buy some side-mirrors and check that the milometer is hooked up. A good map, such as the GT-Rider map, is essential as sites aren't necessarily sign-posted. Petrol can be bought from small stalls on the side of the road, and it is usually kept in old soft-drink bottles (regular petrol is red and diesel is yellow). Make sure you always have half a **43** tank of petrol, as in some areas petrol stops are few and far between. Depending on where you are coming from, you will need to organize permits, insurance, etc, at the border. Check your insurance policy, as many don't cover motorcycle accidents. **Golden Triangle Rider**, www.gt-rider.com, is an excellent source of information for those planning on motorcycling around Laos.

Tuk-tuk

The majority of motorized three-wheelers known as 'jumbos' or tuk-tuks (a name derived from the noise they make) are large motorbike taxis with two bench seats in the back. You'll find them in most cities and metropolitan areas; expect to pay around 5000-10,000 kip for a short ride. They can also be hired by the hour or the day to reach destinations out of town.

Maps

The **GT Rider** Lao map found in bookstores and other shops in Vientiane is probably the most accurate map of the country. The National Tourism Authority has also put together pretty good provincial maps of Laos, using the GT Rider Map as a base. These are available at provincial tourism offices. There are also numerous glossy maps of Vientiane and Luang Prabang, including 3D maps, and a series of locally produced town maps which cover the major settlementsof Vientiane, Luang Prabang, Thakhek, Savannakhet and Pakse. The best selection in the UK is available from Stanfords, 12-14 Long Acre, London WC2E 9LP, T020-7836 1321.

Sleeping

Rooms in Laos are rarely luxurious and standards vary enormously. You can end up paying double what you would pay in Bangkok for similar facilities and service. However, the hotel industry is expanding rapidly, many older buildings are under renovation, and new hotels are springing up – some in conjunction with overseas companies. The **Tai-Pan, Settha Palace, Novotel, Lao Plaza** and **Don Chan Palace** in Vientiane, and the **Villa Santi, Phou Vao, Villa Santi Resort, 3 Nagas, Sala Luang Prabang, Apsara, Sala Luang Prabang** and **Maison Souvannaphoum** in Luang Prabang come into the first-class bracket and could be said to approach international standards in terms of the range of facilities on offer. There is a reasonable choice of hotels of different standards and prices in Vientiane, Luang Prabang and Pakse and an expanding number of budget options in many towns on the fast-developing tourist trail.

The majority of guesthouses and hotels have fans and attached bathrooms, although more and more are providing air-conditioning where there is a stable electricity supply, while others are installing their own generators to cater for the needs of the growing tourist trade. Smaller provincial towns, having previously had only a handful of hotels and guesthouses – some of them quaint French colonial villas – are now home to a growing number of rival concerns as tourism takes off. In rural villages, people's homes are enthusiastically transformed into bed and breakfasts on demand. While there is evidence of profound change in the tourism infrastructure, Laos still has a long way to go before it approaches international standards.

Until the mid 1990s, Laos was a relatively expensive place for budget travellers. While mid-range hotels offered reasonable value for money compared with Thailand, guesthouses at the lower end of the market were overpriced. However, as independent tourism has expanded and the number of guesthouses has increased, so the ensuing price wars have kept costs competitively low. In addition, the fall in the value of the kip has meant that, in international terms, Laos has become cheaper. Many towns in the north, such as Vang Vieng, Muang Ngoi, Muang Sing, Pak Beng and Luang Namtha, have a large choice of very cheap, and in some cases very good accommodation. A double in a guesthouse can be found for 40,000 kip (around US$4). In addition, many towns, especially in the north, have rock-bottom dorm rooms that many Lao use for around 20,000 kip per bed (around US$2). In the Siphandon region budget accommodation is ubiquitous and possibly the cheapest in the country, ranging from $US2-3/night.

Camping

Although it is possible to free camp in many places in Laos, camping facilities are quite thin to the ground. At the time of publication the only real option (with tents for hire, etc) was Phou Khao Khouay National Park, near Vientiane (see page 101). Many tour companies offer home-stay in ethnic minority villages and camping as part of a package tour. **Asian Safari** (www.asiasafari-laos.com) offers pricier camping trips. For tents with all the mod-cons, try staying at **Kamu Lodge** in Udom Xai Province (see page 169); the permanent structures are luxuriously fitted out.

Eating

Food

Food in Laos is surprisingly good – for a country so poor. The cuisine is similar to that of Thailand, although the Chinese influence is slightly less noticeable. Lao dishes are distinguished by the use of aromatic herbs and spices such as lemon grass, chillies, ginger and tamarind. Coconut fat is used sparingly. Food takes a long time to prepare and does not keep well, which goes some way to explaining why many restaurants do not offer local dishes, or if they do, they demand advance warning. The best place to try Lao food is often from roadside stalls or in the markets.

The staple Lao foods are *kao niao* (glutinous rice), which is eaten with your hands and fermented fish or *pa dek* (distinguishable by its distinctive smell), often laced with liberal spoons of *nam pa*, or fish sauce (see box).

Being a landlocked country, most of the **fish** is fresh from the Mekong. 'Mutton' (goat) is relatively scarce and 'beef' (water buffalo) is expensive; most of the dishes are variations on two themes: fish and bird. There are also practical and health reasons for this: without refrigerators, anyone slaughtering a cow, goat, pig or water buffalo needs to be sure there are enough buyers to purchase all the meat in one day. Outside big towns there is rarely the demand to warrant such a slaughter – except when there is a festival or other significant events, like a wedding. But the Lao cookbook does not stop at **chicken** and **turkey**. The rule of thumb is that if it has wings and feathers, it's edible. In some areas, such as Luang Prabang, the birds have long since been eaten. In the south, where the forests have not (yet) been denuded, wild foods are more plentiful and it is not unusual to see pangolin, deer and turtle on the menu.

Laap, also meaning 'luck' in Lao, is a traditional ceremonial dish made from (traditionally) raw fish or meat crushed into a paste, marinated in lemon juice and mixed with chopped mint. It is said to be similar to Mexican *ceviche*. It is called *laap sin* if it has a meat base and *laap paa* if it's fish based. Beware of *laap* in cheap street restaurants which is sometimes concocted from raw offal and served cold; this should be consumed with great caution. *Phanaeng kai* is stuffed chicken with pork, peanuts and coconut milk with a dash of cinnamon. *Kai ping* is grilled chicken eaten with sticky

▪ Hotel price codes explained

L US$100+ First class plus: business services, sports facilities, Asian and Western restaurants, bars and discos. Only a handful of hotels in Vientiane and Luang Prabang could be said to meet this level of facilities.

AL US$60-100 First class: business services, sports facilities, Asian and Western restaurants, bars and discos. Only hotels in Vientiane and Luang Prabang will conform to international 'First Class' standards. Other hotels in this category are likely to be smaller and unable to support a wealth of facilities but they should be comfortable and may well make up in terms of personal service and friendliness what they lack in size and grandeur.

A US$30-60 Tourist class: air-conditioning, en suite bathrooms and cable films and/or satellite television. Restaurant, coffee shop/room service and, occasionally, a swimming pool.

B US$15-30 Economy: air-conditioning, en suite bathrooms with hot water. Restaurant and room service.

C US$8-15 Budget: probably air-conditioned with en suite bathroom. Bed linen and towels provided. There may be a restaurant.

D US$4-8 Guesthouse: small, fan-cooled rooms, possibly en suite bathroom facilities. Mixture of bathroom technologies from Asian to Western. Bed linen and towels provided.

E US$2-4 and **F** US$2 Guesthouse: fan-cooled rooms, shared bathroom facilities. Asian toilets. Variable standards of cleanliness.

Unless otherwise stated, the prices and codes in this guide are based on the cost of a double room for one night, not including service charges or meals.

rice. Another popular Lao dish is *tam som* – often called *som tam* – a spicy green shredded papaya salad served with chilli peppers, spices and fish sauce. This dish can be fiery hot at times, so you should stipulate how hot (*phet*) you want it! There are several different types of **soup** – include *keng no mai* (bamboo shoot), *keng khi lek* (vegetable and buffalo skin), *ken chut* (without pimentos) *keng kalami* (cabbage with fish or pork), *kenghet bot* (mushroom), *tom khaa kai* (chicken with coconut milk).

The most common **vegetables** are aubergines, tomatoes, cabbage, corn, cucumbers and lettuce, often cooked together, pureed and eaten with sticky rice. Soups usually accompany meals – they are usually a mixture of fish and meat infused with aromatic herbs.

The Lao are partial to **sweets**: sticky rice with coconut milk and black beans (which can be bought in bamboo tubes in the markets) and grilled bananas are favourites. One would have thought, in a place like Laos, that **fruit** would be on every menu. But, perhaps because familiarity breeds contempt, many restaurants will have no fruit of any kind – even at breakfast and particularly in places not geared to foreigners.

There is a well-ingrained **Vietnamese** culinary tradition and **Chinese** food is never hard to find. *Feu*, Vietnamese noodle soup, is itself an import from China but often masquerades in Laos as a Lao dish. It is usually served with a plate of raw vegetables. Most restaurants outside the main towns do not have menus but will nearly always serve *feu* and *laap* or local specialities. Indeed, their generic name is *raan khai feu* – restaurants that sell *feu*. Vietnamese spring rolls are also very popular – you can either have *yaw jeun* (deep-fried spring rolls) or *yaw dip* (fresh spring rolls) and both are usually served with fresh herbs and rice noodles.

⦂ Nam pa

No meal would be complete without a small dish of *nam pa* to spoon onto almost any savoury dish. Like *nam plaa* in Thailand, *nuoc mam* in Vietnam and *ngan-pyaye* in Myanmar (Burma), *nam pa* is an essential element of Laotian gastronomic life. To make the sauce, freshwater fish is packed into containers and steeped in brine. Elsewhere, it is made mostly from small saltwater fish, but because Laos is landlocked, freshwater fish is used instead. The resulting brown liquid – essentially the by-products of slowly putrifying fish – is drained off and bottled. A variation is *pa dek*, *nam pa* with small chunks of fermented fish added, often with rice husks too. This variation tends to be used in cooking rather than as a condiment and is usually kept in an earthenware pot – often outside as the aroma is so strong!

The French left a legacy of sophisticated cuisine in Laos. **French** food is widely available, with street cafés, serving delectable fresh croissants, baguettes, *pain au chocolat* and a selection of sticky pastries, which can be washed down with a powerful cup of Lao coffee. Bread or *khao jii* is baked daily and often served with vegetables, pâté, fried eggs or an omelette. The Lao however have a habit of eating baguette sandwiches with fish sauce sprinkled on top (these are available in Vientiane, Savannakhet and Pakse). Menus in many of Vientiane's restaurants still have a distinctly French flavour to them. Vintage Bordeaux and Burgundies occasionally emerge from the cellars of restaurants too – although most of the fine vintages have now been consumed. Hotels in main towns often provide international menus and continental breakfasts. Even in small towns it is easy enough to create a continental breakfast: baguettes are widely available, wild honey can usually be tracked down, and fresh Boloven' coffee is abundant (although, tragically, 'Nescafe' seems to be making insidious inroads). Some people recommend taking a jar of jam or peanut butter to spread on the baguettes. The Lao prefer theirs either with 'pâté' (more like spam) or with thick and sweetened condensed milk. *Surn saap* – enjoy your meal!

Drink

Urban areas have access to safe water, but all water should be boiled or sterilized before drinking. Less than a third of rural areas have safe water. Bottled water is widely available, however, and produced locally, so it is cheap (about 1000 kip for a litre). Soft drinks are expensive (they are imported from Thailand); a can of coke in a stall costs about 5000 kip, a bottle 1500 kip. *Nam saa*, weak Chinese tea, is also served. There is now local fresh milk production, so milk and yoghurt are available.

The local brew is rice wine which is drunk from a clay jug with long straws. The white variety is called *lau-lao* (Lao alcohol) and is made from fermented sticky rice; *fanthong*, or red *lao-lao* is fermented with herbs. Bottled *lao-lao* is also widely available. Imported beers, wines and spirits can be found in hotels, restaurants, bars and nightclubs but are not particularly cheap. *Beer Lao* is available as a light lager (although the alcohol content is 5%) best served ice-cold or as a dark ale. In towns without electricity it is normal to add ice although most places are now on the grid. *Beer Lao* also has the advantage of being reasonably priced (about US$1 for a large bottle, depending on the restaurant or bar). Chinese beer is cheaper still and can be found in the northern provinces. French wines can be purchased (at a price) in some supermarkets and quite a few restaurants.

Restaurant price codes explained

▦▦▦	US$10+	A three-course meal in a restaurant with pleasant decor. Beers, wines and spirits available.
▦▦	US$5-10	A two-course meal in reasonable surroundings.
▦	Under US$5	A single course meal in spartan or makeshift surroundings, such as a street kiosk with simple benches and tables. In many cases a simple meal will cost less than US$1.

Eating out

Restaurant food is, on the whole, hygienically prepared, and as long as street stall snacks have been well cooked, they are usually fine and a good place to sample local specialities. Expect to pay between US$3-10 per head for a meal in main towns and less outside. By eating Lao food in local restaurants it is possible to pay US$1 or less for a meal.

Really classy restaurants are only to be found in Vientiane and Luang Prabang (especially the former). Good French cuisine is available in both cities. Salads, steaks, pizzas and more are all on offer. Expect to pay anywhere over US$5 for a reasonable meal. A better bet in terms of value for money are the Lao restaurants. Indian restaurants are starting to find their way around the country

Far more prevalent are lower-end Lao and Chinese-Lao restaurants which can be found in every town. Food in these places is usually good and excellent value for money. You'll find a cold beer and a good range of vegetarian and meat-based dishes all for between US$3 and US$5. In towns on the tourist trail these local restaurants are complemented by places geared to the vicarious demands of tourists. Here you'll find fruit smoothies, Indian food, burgers and more for anywhere between US$2 and US$5. Finally, right at the bottom end – in terms of price if not necessarily in terms of quality – are stalls that charge a US$1-2 for filled baguettes or simple single-dish meals.

Entertainment

If you are looking for evenings out at cultural events, or are keen to dance the night away, Laos is not the place for you. Until about five years ago the country seemed to shut down from about 2100. Even today, anywhere outside the capital is unlikely to provide much in the way of night-time revelry. Excepting perhaps the odd lock-in in a Luang Prabang pub or at a bar in Vientiane, a quiet evening sipping Lao beer by the Mekong is as good as it gets. Today, even in towns, a 2200 curfew exists; sometimes bars and clubs will push it and stay open to 2300 or 2400, but since the police cracked down in 2004, closing scores of establishments (as punishment), they are more likely to play by the rules.

The pace of life in Laos is slow; certainly nothing is super-developed – you can even count the number of cinemas on one hand, so the nearest you should expect to get to seeing the hottest new Hollywood blockbuster would generally be the nightly videos shown at some guesthouses. All this, of course, is part of the inherent appeal of the country and most visitors wouldn't have it any other way.

Most larger towns have bars and 'discos'. But a Lao disco is usually a place where live rather than recorded music is played. In 1996 the government tried to crack down on what was felt to be Thai cultural imperialism and stipulated that bands had to play at least 70% Lao music (as opposed to Thai or Western). They also banned karaoke bars

: The universal stimulant – the betel nut

Throughout the countryside in Southeast Asia, and in more remote towns, it is common to meet men and women whose teeth are stained black, and gums red, by continuous chewing of the 'betel nut'. This, though, is a misnomer. The betel 'nut' is not chewed at all: the three crucial ingredients that make up a betel 'wad' are the nut of the areca palm (Areca catechu), the leaf or catkin of the betel vine (Piper betel), and lime. When these three ingredients are combined with saliva they act as a mild stimulant. Other ingredients (people have their own recipes) are tobacco, gambier, various spices and the gum of Acacia catechu. The habit, though also common in South Asia and parts of China, seems to have evolved in Southeast Asia and it is mentioned in the very earliest chronicles. The lacquer betel boxes of Myanmar and Thailand, and the brass and silver ones of Indonesia, illustrate the importance of chewing betel in social intercourse. Galvao in his journal of 1544 noted: "They use it so continuously that they never take it from their mouths; therefore these people can be said to go around always ruminating." Among Westernized Southeast Asians the habit is frowned upon: the disfigurement and ageing that it causes, and the stained walls and floors that result from the constant spitting, are regarded as distasteful products of an earlier age. But beyond the elite it is still widely practised.

for the same sort of reason: moral depravity. This latter edict seemed to be weakly enforced in smaller towns and may have been lifted by the time this book is on the shelves. There is a growing number of bars and clubs in Vientiane, and a handful in the other major centres (mostly geared to locals rather than the foreign/expat markets).

Festivals and events

Being of festive inclination, the Lao celebrate New Year four times a year: the international New Year in January, Chinese New Year in January/February, Lao New Year (Pi Mai) in April and Hmong New Year in December. The Lao Buddhist year follows the lunar calendar, so many of the festivals are movable. The first month begins around the full moon in December. There are also many local festivals (see under individual regions). **Note** The list below is not exhaustive, but does include the most important festivals. There are many Chinese, Vietnamese and ethnic minority festivals which are celebrated in Laos and there are many regional variations.

January

New Year's Day (1 Jan) Public holiday celebrated by private *baci* throughout the country.
Pathet Lao Day (6 Jan) Public holiday, parades in main towns.
Army Day (20 Jan) Public holiday.
Boun Pha Vet (movable) To celebrate King Vessanthara's reincarnation as a Buddha. Sermons, processions, dance, theatre. Popular time for ordination.

February

Magha Puja (movable) Celebrates the end of Buddha's time in the monastery and the prediction of his death. It is principally celebrated in Vientiane and at Wat Phou, near Champassak.
Chinese New Year (movable, Jan/Feb) Celebrated by Chinese and Vietnamese communities. Many Chinese and Vietnamese businesses shut down for three days.

☃ Baci

The baci ceremony is a uniquely Lao *boun* (festival) and celebrates any auspicious occasion – marriage, birth, achievement or the end of an arduous journey, for instance. The ceremony dates from pre-Buddhist times and is therefore animist in origin. It is centred around the *phakhouan*, a designer tree made from banana leaves and flowers (or, today, some artificial concoction of plastic) and surrounded by symbolic foods. The most common symbolic foods are eggs and rice – symbolizing fertility and fecundity. The *mophone* hosts the ceremony and recites memorized prayers, usually in Pali, and ties cotton threads (*sai sin*) around the wrists of guests symbolizing good health, prosperity and happiness. For maximum effect, these strings must have three knots in them. It is unlucky to take them off until at least three days have elapsed, and custom dictates that they never be cut. Many people wear them until, frayed and worn, they fall off through sheer decreptitude. All this is accompanied by a *ramvong* (traditional circle dance) which in turn is accompanied by traditional instruments – flutes, clarinets, xylophones with bamboo crosspieces, drums, cymbals and the *kaen*, a hand-held pipe organ that is to Laos what the bagpipes are to Scotland.

March

Women's Day (8 Mar) Public holiday.
People's Party Day (22 Mar) Public holiday.
Boun Khoun Khao (movable) Harvest festival, local celebration centred around the wats.

April

Pi Mai (13-15 Apr) Public holiday to celebrate Lao New Year. The first month of the Lao New Year is actually Dec but festivities are delayed until Apr when days are longer than nights. By Apr it's also hotting up, so having hosepipes levelled at you and buckets of water dumped on you is more pleasurable. The festival also serves to invite the rains. Pi Mai is one of the most important annual festivals, particularly in Luang Prabang (see page 88). Statues of the Buddha (in the 'calling for rain' posture) are ceremonially doused in water, which is poured along an intricately decorated trench (*hang song nam pha*). The small stupas of sand, decorated with streamers, in wat compounds are symbolic requests for health and happiness over the next year. It is celebrated with traditional Lao folksinging (*mor lam*) and the circle dance (*ramwong*). There is usually a 3-day holiday. Similar festivals are celebrated in Thailand, Cambodia and Burma. It's good if you keep your money, cameras, etc, in plastic. 'Sok Dee Pi Mai' – good luck for the New Year – is usually said to one another during this period.

May

Labour Day (1 May) Public holiday with parades in Vientiane.
Visakha Puja (movable) To celebrate the birth, enlightenment and death of the Buddha, celebrated in local wats.
Boun Bang Fai (movable) The rocket festival, is a Buddhist rain-making festival. Large bamboo rockets are built and decorated by monks and carried in procession before being blasted skywards. The higher a rocket goes, the bigger its builder's ego gets. Designers of failed rockets are thrown in the mud. The festival lasts 2 days.

June/July

Children's Day (1 Jun) Public holiday.
Khao Phansa (movable) The start of Buddhist Lent and a time of retreat and fasting for monks. These are the most usual months for ordination and for men to enter

the monkhood for short periods before they marry. The festival starts with the full moon in Jun/Jul and continues until the full moon in Oct. It all ends with the *Kathin* ceremony in Oct when monks receive gifts.

August

Lao Issara (13 Aug) Public holiday, Free Lao Day.
Liberation Day (23 Aug) Public holiday.
Ho Khao Padap Dinh (movable) A celebration of the dead.

September

Boun Ok Phansa (movable) The end of Buddhist Lent when the faithful take offerings to the temple. It is in the '9th month' in Luang Prabang and the '11th month' in Vientiane, and marks the end of the rainy season. Boat races take place on the Mekong River with crews of 50 or more men and women. On the night before the

race small decorated rafts are set afloat on the river.

October

Freedom from the French Day (12 Oct) Public holiday which is only really celebrated in Vientiane.

November

Boun That Luang (movable) Celebrated in all Laos' *thats*, although most enthusiastically and colourfully in Vientiane (see page 88). As well as religious rituals, most celebrations include local fairs, processions, beauty pageants and other festivities.

December

Hmong New Year (movable).
Independence Day (2 Dec) Public holiday, military parades, dancing and music.

Shopping

Popular souvenirs from Laos include handicrafts and textiles, which are sold pretty much everywhere; the local market is usually a good starting point as are some of the minority villages.

As far as 'best buys' go, it's really a matter of taste, although many visitors stock up on **silks**, which are sold in smaller, less touristy towns for about 40,000 kip a length. The best kind of Lao silk to buy is naturally dyed and comes from Hua Phan Province; **OckPopTok** in Luang Prabang specializes in this kind of silk. A wide variety of modern materials are sometimes used to make the *pha sinh*, the Lao sarong, and *pha baeng*, or shawl, worn by Lao women. The bridal *sinh* is a popular buy; it is usually plain with a single motif repeated over most of the material, but with an elaborate border. Gold and silver thread, *tdinjok*, is often woven into the border pattern. Lao weavers have been isolated from external influences and have maintained many of their original patterns and styles (see page 331). Most of the materials are sold in weaving villages or are available from markets in the main towns, which offer a wide selection of patterns and embroidery. Perhaps the best places to go are Talaat Sao or the cheaper Talaat Kudin, in Vientiane, which has a textile section in the covered area, although both were undergoing renovations at the time of publication. If you wish to have something made, most tailors can whip up a simple *sinh* (Lao sarong, see page 22) in a day but you might want to allow a little bit longer for adjustments or other items. Those on a frugal budget will find some tailors who can churn out a decent pair of trousers on Sisavangvong in Luang Prabang and around Nam Phou in Vientiane. If you get the right tailor, they can be much better than those found in Thailand both in terms of price and quality, but you do need to be patient and allow time for multiple fittings/adjustments. It is also a good idea to bring

a pattern/picture of what you want with you and if you are interested in anything in 51
stretch fabrics, lace, etc, you might need to bring fabric with you. Vientiane and Luang
Prabang offer the most sophisticated line in boutiques, where you can get all sorts of
clothes from the utterly exquisite to the frankly bizarre. **Antique textiles** are getting
more expensive and harder to come across. It is hard to find 'antique' textiles in good
condition as old *pha sinh* (sarongs) are worn over new ones for work or bathing and so
wear out quickly. **Carol Cassidy** in Vientiane (see page 91) has revived high-quality
traditional weaving and her weavers are producing work of an exceptionally high
quality. Prices, though, can run into thousands of US dollars for these
museum-quality pieces. Thai-style clothes boutiques can be found everywhere. Beer
Lao t-shirts are ubiquitous and have almost become the backpacker uniform for Laos.

Silverware, usually in the form of jewellery and small pots, is traditional in Laos.
Luang Prabang is reputed to produce the best silverware (see page 145) but this may
just reflect received wisdom rather than reality. Chunky antique ethnic-minority
jewellery, bangles, pendants, belts and earrings, are often sold in markets in the main
towns, or antique shops in Vientiane.

Craftsmen in Laos are still producing **wood carvings** for temples and coffins.
Designs are usually traditional, with a religious theme. Craftsmen produce carved
panels and statues for tourists, which are available in outlets in Vientiane. The
higher-quality handicrafts can usually be found in Luang Prabang and Vientiane,
although prices will be correspondingly high. Some of the best bargains are to be
found when you're not looking for them, amongst the local villages.

Sport and activities

Laos is starting to garner a reputation for itself as one of the prime adventure and
ecotourism destinations in the region. The pleasure of floating lazily down the Nam
Xong, stopping every so often to get out of your inner tube and explore a cave or two,
is indisputable, and people come back for more time and again. Canoeing is also an
option, but gear yourself up for a pleasant, rather tame day out rather than a
foam-flecked white-knuckle ride.

Caving
Laos has some of the most extensive and largest caves in the region. Some of the best
grottoes can be found around Vang Vieng, where caving tourism has been developed.
Other interesting areas are Muang Sui (a day trip from Phonsavanh); around Thakhek;
the Kong Lor river cave (which runs right through a mountain); and the old Pathet Lao
hide-outs at Vieng Xai. It's best to go caving with a local tour operator, such as **Green
Discovery**, www.greendiscoverylaos.com.

Cycling
Organized and independent cycling tours are starting to become popular in Laos.
Organized bike tours can only be arranged in Luang Namtha for now, but expect a few
more places to crop up over the next few years. Most cities and small towns have
guesthouses that rent bicycles (for around $US1 per day), though these bikes,
generally, aren't suitable for riding around the country. If you wish to cycle around
Laos it is best to either bring an appropriate bicycle with you or purchase one in
Thailand. You will also need to bring a proper helmet as they aren't available in Laos.
Traffic is quite light but often speeds along the highways, particularly the southern
roads. Most major roads are sealed now and for the most part traverse quite hilly
areas. **Green Discovery**, www.greendiscoverylaos.com, organizes bicycle tours.

⁞ The best wildlife experiences

- Look for wild elephants while trekking through the stunning wilderness of Phou Khao Khouay National Park, www.trekkingcentrallaos.com, page 102.
- Visit a camp 15 km out of Luang Prabang, set up by Tiger Trails for the rehabilitation of elephants previously employed in the logging trade, www.tigertrail-laos.com, page 129.
- Catch a glimpse of the rare, black-cheeked crested gibbons chortling out soprano tunes from the jungle's canopy, with the Gibbon Experience, T084-212-021, jf@clemastecs.net, page 176.
- See the beautiful, rare freshwater dolphins in Siphandon, page 276.

Kayaking and rafting

Laos is criss-crossed by fantastic rivers, which carve their way through pristine wilderness and stunning mountain scenery. Kayaking/rafting is offered around the country: the Nam Lik, Nam Ngum, near Vientiane is good for die-hard enthusiasts, while the Nam Xong at Vang Vieng hosts a variety of water-borne tours suitable to most travellers' tastes. Water-based activities are also run out of Luang Prabang, Sekong, Pakse and Luang Namtha. There is also fantastic kayaking on the Hin Boun River in Khammouane Province. The National Tourism Authority recommends the four-day trip down the Nam Fa from Vieng Phouka, describing it as the most intense and magnificent rafting trip available in Laos.

Before undertaking a trip ensure that the boats are in good condition and that you are supplied with safety equipment, such as helmets and life-jackets. Most kayaking and rafting trips will need to be organized from a provincial capital or Vientiane. Tour operators specializing in rafting and kayaking in Laos are **Green Discovery Laos**, www.greendiscoverylaos.com, and **Paddle Asia**, www.laosadventure.com.

Rock-climbing

Owing to Laos' stunning karst rock formations, caves and cliffs, it is an ideal destination for rock-climbers. However, rock-climbing is still relatively new to Laos and the only area which has really developed facilities is Vang Vieng. It is expected that over the next few years this adventure sport will be established in other areas around the country. **Green Discovery**, www.greendiscoverlaos.com, runs rock-climbing trips out of Vang Vieng. You can pick up a copy of the *Rock Climbing – Vang Vieng Guide*, by Dr. Volker Schoeffl (2005) for US$5 at all **Green Discovery** offices.

Trekking

Treks are offered in abundance and the most northerly parts of the country are especially geared up for this sort of activity. Luang Namtha, Muang Sing, Vieng Phouka and Phongsali all offer trekking in areas inhabited by a diverse range of ethnicities. When trekking in Laos, it is imperative that visitors abide by local rules and customs in order to support the country's efforts to keep tourism sustainable and as low impact as possible. There are also treks offered out of Udom Xai, Luang Prabang, Vang Vieng, Phou Khao Khouay National Protected Area, in the Phou Hin Poun National Protected Area, in Dong Phou Vieng National Protected Area, in Xe Pian National Protected Area and in Bokeo.

For futher information, refer to the websites www.trekkingcentrallaos.com and www.ecotourismlaos.com/activities/act_trekking

Health

Most visitors return home from Laos having experienced no problems at all beyond an upset stomach. With the following advice and precautions you should keep as healthy as you do at home. It largely depends on how and where you travel. Laos has a mainly tropical climate; nevertheless, the acquisition of a tropical disease by the visitor is probably conditioned as much by the rural nature of the surroundings and standards of hygiene than by the climate. However, if you do get critically ill or have a serious accident, the best advice is to head straight for a hospital in Thailand. ▸▸ *For information on children's health, see page 24.*

The following advice was provided by Prof Larry Goodyer, Head of the Leicester School of Pharmacy and director of **Nomad Medical**.

Before you travel

You should see your GP, practice nurse or travel clinic at least six weeks before your departure for advice on travel risks, malaria and recommended vaccinations. Your local pharmacist can also be a good source of advice. Make sure you have travel insurance, get a dental check (especially if you are going to be away for more than a month), know your own blood group and if you suffer a long-term condition, such as diabetes or epilepsy, make sure you inform your travelling companion or that you have a Medic Alert bracelet/necklace with this information on it. Start taking your anti-malarials.

Vaccination and immunization

The following vaccinations are commonly recommended for Laos. The final decision, however, should be based on a consultation with your GP or travel clinic. Shots should be organized four to six weeks in advance. Smallpox vaccination is no longer required anywhere in the world and cholera vaccination is no longer recognized as necessary for international travel by the World Health Organization.

Diphtheria Yes, if none in last 10 years
Hepatitis A Yes
Hepatitis B Yes
Measles Yes
Polio Yes, if none in last 10 years
Rabies Yes
Tetanus Yes, if none in last 10 years, but five doses is enough for life.
Tuberculosis Consult your doctor for advice on tuberculosis inoculation; the disease is still widespread in Laos.
Typhoid Yes, if none in last three years.
Yellow fever Yellow fever vaccination is not required, although you may be asked for a certificate if you have been in a country affected by yellow fever immediately before travelling to Laos.

Other vaccinations Vaccinations against meningococcal meningitis and Japanese B encephalitis (JVE) might be considered necessary in the case of epidemics; consult a specialist clinic before travelling. There is an extremely small risk of these rather serious diseases; both are seasonal and vary according to region. Meningitis can occur in epidemic form. JVE is a viral disease transmitted from pigs to humans by mosquitoes.

When you arrive

Medicines

There is very little control on the sale of drugs and medicines in Laos. You may be able to buy any and every drug in pharmacies without a prescription. Be wary of this because pharmacists can be poorly trained and might sell you drugs that are unsuitable, counterfeit, dangerous or old. Many drugs and medicines are manufactured under licence from American or European companies in Thailand, so the trade names may be familiar to you. This means you do not have to carry a whole chest of medicines with you, but remember that the shelf life of some items, especially vaccines and antibiotics, is markedly reduced in hot conditions. Buy your supplies at the better outlets where there are refrigerators, even though they are more expensive and check the expiry date of all preparations you buy. Immigration officials occasionally confiscate scheduled drugs if they are not accompanied by a doctor's prescription. Doctors in Thailand are notorious over-prescribers, as they make their money from doling out drugs rather than charging high service fees.

❖ Remember that it is risky to buy medicine, and in particular anti-malarials, in developing countries, as they may be sub-standard or part of a trade in counterfeit drugs.

Medical facilities

Hospitals are few and far between and medical facilities are poor. Expats living in Laos tend to fly to Bangkok or even further afield should they need hospitalization or sophisticated medical care. Medical services are restricted by a lack of trained personnel and facilities and standards are poor, particularly at district and rural level. There is only one doctor to every 4545 people. Emergency treatment is available at the **Mahosot Hospital** and **Clinique Settathirath** in Vientiane (see page 98). The Australian embassy also has a clinic – for Commonwealth citizens– for minor problems (see page 96); $US50 per consultation. Better facilities are available in Thailand and emergency evacuation to Nong Khai or Udon Thani (Thailand) can be arranged at short notice (see below).

It is wise to carry a first-aid pack in case of emergency. Pharmacies in rural areas are usually poorly stocked, but basic drugs are available. The likelihood of finding good medical care diminishes very rapidly as you move away from larger towns. Especially in the rural areas there are systems and traditions of medicine wholly different from the Western model and you will be confronted with less orthodox forms of treatment such as herbal medicines and acupuncture.

Hospitals in Thailand

Aek Udon Hospital, Udon Thani, T+66 42-342555. Quite good facilities. A 2½-hr trip from Vientiane.
Bangkok Nursing Home, 9/1, Convent Road, Silom Bangkok 10500, T+66 2-686 2700, www.bnhhospital.com.

Bumrungrad Hospital, Soi 3 Sukhumvit, Bangkok, T+66 2-667 1000, www.bumrungrad.com. The best option: a world-class hospital with brilliant facilities.
Nong Khai Wattana General Hospital, T+66 42-465201. The closest hospital is a 40-min trip from Vientiane. Open 24 hrs daily, good medical services and dentist.

A-Z of health risks

AIDS/HIV

Aids is increasing its prevalence in Laos and is not confined to high risk sections of the population (homosexual men, intravenous drug abusers, prostitutes and the children of infected mothers). Heterosexual transmission is now the dominant mode of infection and so the main risk to travellers is from casual sex. The same precautions should be taken as when encountering any sexually transmitted disease (see below). The AIDS virus (HIV) can be passed via unsterile needles which have been previously used to inject an HIV positive patient, but the risk of this is very small indeed. It would, however, be sensible to check that needles have been properly sterilized or disposable needles are used. The chance of picking up Hepatitis B in this way is more of a danger. The risk of receiving a blood transfusion with blood infected with the HIV virus is greater than from dirty needles because of the amount of fluid exchanged. Supplies of blood for transfusion are supposed to be screened for HIV in all reputable hospitals so the risk should be small. The only way to be sure if you feel you have been put at risk is to have a blood test for HIV antibodies on your return to a place where there are reliable laboratory facilities. However the test does not become positive for many weeks.

Bites and stings

Insect bites are usually more of a nuisance than a serious hazard and, if you try, you can prevent yourself entirely from being bitten. Some insects, such as mosquitoes are, of course, carriers of potentially serious diseases, such as malaria, dengue fever, leishmaniasis and filariasis, so it is sensible to avoid being bitten as much as possible. If you are popular target for insect bites or develop lumps quite soon after being bitten, carry an Aspivenin kit. This syringe suction device is available from many chemists and draws out some of the allergic materials and provides quick relief.

Insects aside, it is very rare for travellers to be bitten by a venomous creature but if you are unlucky (or careless) enough to be bitten by a snake, spider or scorpion, try to identify the culprit, without putting yourself in further danger (do not try to catch a live snake). Snake bites in particular are very frightening, but in fact rarely poisonous – even venomous snakes bite without injecting venom. Victims should be taken to a hospital or a doctor without delay. It is not advised for travellers to carry snake bite antivenom as it can do more harm than good in inexperienced hands. Reassure and comfort the victim frequently. Immobilize the limb with a bandage or a splint and get the patient to lie still. Do not slash the bite area and try to suck out the poison. This also does more harm than good. You should apply a tourniquet in these circumstances, but only if you know how to. Do not attempt this if you are not experienced.

Dengue fever

This is a viral disease spread by mosquitoes that tend to bite during the day. The symptoms are fever and often intense joint pains, also some people develop a rash. Symptoms last about a week but it can take a few weeks to recover fully. Dengue can be difficult to distinguish from malaria as both diseases tend to occur in the same countries. There are no effective vaccines or antiviral drugs though, fortunately, travellers rarely develop the more severe forms of the disease (these can prove fatal). Rest, plenty of fluids and paracetamol (not aspirin) is the recommended treatment

Diarrhoea and intestinal upset

Diarrhoea can refer either to loose stools or an increased frequency of bowel movement, both of which can be a nuisance. Symptoms should be relatively short-lived but if they persist beyond two weeks specialist medical attention should be sought. Also seek medical help if there is blood in the stools and/or fever.

Adults can use an antidiarrhoeal medication such as loperamide to control the symptoms but only for up to 24 hours. In addition keep well hydrated by drinking plenty of fluids and eat bland foods. Oral rehydration sachets taken after each loose stool are a useful way to keep well hydrated. These should always be used when treating children and the elderly.

Bacterial traveller's diarrhoea is the most common form. Ciproxin (Ciprofloxacin) is a useful antibiotic and can be obtained by private prescription in the UK. You need to take one 500 mg tablet when the diarrhoea starts. If there are so signs of improvement after 24 hours the diarrhoea is likely to be viral and not bacterial. If it is due to other organisms such as those causing giardia or amoebic dysentery, different antibiotics will be required.

The standard advice to prevent problems is to be careful with water and ice for drinking. Ask yourself where the water came from. If you have any doubts then boil it or filter and treat it. There are many filter/treatment devices now available on the market. Food can also transmit disease. Be wary of salads (what were they washed in? who handled them?), re-heated foods or food that has been left out in the sun having been cooked earlier in the day. There is a simple adage that says wash it, peel it, boil it or forget it. Also be wary of unpasteurised dairy products as these can transmit a range of diseases. River water is likely to be contaminated by sewage and so swimming in such dilute effluent can also be a cause of intestinal problems.

Hepatitis

Hepatitis means inflammation of the liver. Viral causes of the disease can be acquired anywhere in the world. The less serious, but more common form is hepatitis A . The most obvious symptom is a yellowing of your skin or the whites of your eyes, pains in the stomach and lack of appetite. However, prior to this, all that you may notice is itching and tiredness. The other, more serious, version is hepatitis B, which is acquired as a sexually transmitted disease or by blood transfusion. It can less commonly be transmitted by injections with unclean needles and possibly by insect bites. The symptoms are the same as for hepatitis A but the incubation period is much longer (up to six months compared with six weeks) and there are more likely to be complications. Pre-travel vaccine is the best prevention. A combined hepatitis A and B vaccine is now available. You should also take care in the preparation of food, avoid contaminated drinking water and pay scrupulous attention to toilet hygiene. Avoid unprotected sexual intercourse and any contact with blood.

Japanese encephalitis B

This is a viral disease of the brain spread by mosquitoes in parts of Asia. It is very rare in travellers but those visiting rural areas during the wet season may be advised to have the vaccine.

Malaria

Malaria is prevalent in Laos and remains a serious disease; about a third of the population contracts malaria at some stage in their lives. You are strongly advised to protect yourself against mosquito bites and to take prophylactic (preventative) drugs. In parts of Laos, there has been an increase in cases of *falciparum malaria* which is resistant to the normally used drugs. Always get up-to-date advice from a travel health specialist. Information regarding country-by-country malaria risk can be obtained from the World Health Organization (WHO) or in Britain from **The Ross Institute**, London School of Hygiene and Tropical Medicine, Keppel Street, London WC1E 7HT.

Malaria can cause death within 24 hours and can start as something just resembling an attack of flu. You may feel tired, lethargic, headachy, feverish; or more seriously, develop fits, followed by coma and then death. Have a low index of suspicion because it is very easy to write off vague symptoms, which may actually be malaria. If you have a temperature, visit a doctor as soon as you can and ask for a malaria test. On your return home, if you suffer any of these symptoms, have a test as soon as possible. Even if a previous test proved negative, this could save your life.

Treatment is with drugs and may be oral or into a vein depending on the seriousness of the infection. Remember ABCD: Awareness (of whether the disease is

To prevent mosquito bites wear clothes that cover arms and legs, use effective insect repellents in areas with known risks of insect-spread disease and use a mosquito net treated with an insecticide. Repellents containing 30-50% DEET (Di-ethyltoluamide) are recommended when visiting malaria endemic areas; lemon eucalyptus (Mosiguard) is a reasonable alternative. The key advice is to guard against contracting malaria by taking the correct anti-malarials and finishing the recommended course. If you are popular target for insect bites or develop lumps quite soon after being bitten use antihistamine tablets and apply a cream such as hydrocortisone.

Rabies

Rabies is endemic throughout Laos so it is advisable to have an anti-rabies jab before travelling. Avoid contact with dogs and bear in mind that other animals also carry the disease. If you are bitten by a domestic or wild animal, always scrub the wound with soap and water and/or disinfectant, try to determine the animal's ownership, and seek medical assistance at once. The course of treatment depends on whether you have already been vaccinated against rabies. If you have (advisable) then some further doses of vaccine are all that is required. If not already vaccinated then anti rabies serum (immunoglobulin) may be required. It is important to finish the course of treatment.

Schistosomiasis (bilharzia)

Schistosomiasis, or bilharzia, is a disease caused by parasitic worms, which are usually carried by snails and are found in the Mekong River in Laos. The parasite penetrates the skin and can cause a local itch soon after, fever after a few weeks and much later diarrhoea, abdominal pain and spleen or liver enlargement. Avoid infected waters, check the CDC, WHO websites and a travel clinic specialist for up-to-date information. A single drug cures this disease.

Sexual health

The range of visible and invisible diseases is awesome. Unprotected sex can spread HIV, Hepatitis B and C, gonorrhea (green discharge), chlamydia (nothing to see but may cause painful urination and later female infertility), painful recurrent herpes, syphilis and warts, just to name a few. You can cut down the risk by using condoms, a femidom, but the best prevention is to avoid sex altogether.

Sun and heat

Always protect yourself against the sun. Overexposure can lead to sunburn and, in the longer term, skin cancers and premature skin aging. The best advice is simply to avoid exposure to the sun by covering exposed skin, wearing a hat and staying out of the sun if possible, particularly between late morning and early afternoon. Apply a high factor sunscreen (greater than SPF15) and also make sure it screens against UVB. Note that high-factor sun screens are often not available in Laos so bring your own.

A further danger in tropical climates is heat exhaustion or more seriously heatstroke. This can be avoided by good hydration, which means drinking water past the point of simply quenching thirst. Also, when first exposed to tropical heat, take time to acclimatize by avoiding strenuous activity in the middle of the day. If you cannot avoid heavy exercise, it is also a good idea to increase salt intake.

Tuberculosis

The disease is still widespread in Laos.

Typhoid

A disease spread by the insanitary preparation of food. People have been known to pick up typhoid in Laos. A number of new vaccines against this condition are now available; the older TAB and monovalent typhoid vaccines are being phased out. The newer, for example Typhim Vi, cause less side effects, but are more expensive. For those who do not like injections, there are now oral vaccines.

Typhus
Can still occur carried by ticks. There is usually a reaction at the site of the bite and a fever. Typhus is quite common in Laos and symptoms can include a nasty rash and high fever. Seek medical advice.

Water
Tap water in Laos is rarely safe, especially in the rainy season, and river water is often contaminated by local communities. However, filtered or bottled water is usually available and safe, although you must make sure that the bottles have not been re-filled from the tap. Ice for drinks is rarely made from boiled water, so stand your glass on the ice cubes, rather than putting them in the drink. If your hotel has a central hot water supply, this water is safe to drink after cooling. The better hotels have water-purifying systems. If you have any doubts about the water then boil it or filter and treat it. Dirty water should first be strained through a filter bag and then boiled or treated. Bring water to a rolling boil for several minutes. There are sterilising methods that can be used and products generally contain chlorine (eg Puritabs) or iodine (eg Pota Aqua) compounds. There are a number of water sterilisers now on the market available in personal and expedition size. Make sure you take the spare parts or spare chemicals with you and do not believe everything the manufacturers say.

Other diseases and risks
The WHO website (www.who.int/en/) gives up-to-date information on current disease outbreaks and pandemics. As of January 2006 there had been no human cases of avian flu in Laos, however, cases (and deaths) had been reported in all neighbouring countries, so check the WHO website for travel advice and precautionary measures. It is also worth checking the current situation regarding a range of insect-borne diseases, such as sleeping sickness, river blindness and leishmaniasis, and water-borne diseases, such as bilharzia and leptospirosis.

When you get home

Remember to take your anti-malarial tablets for six weeks after leaving the malarial area. If you have had attacks of diarrhoea it is worth having a stool specimen tested in case you have picked up amoebas. If you have been living rough, blood tests may be worthwhile to detect worms and other parasites. If you have been exposed to schistosomiasis by swimming in lakes etc check by means of a blood test when you get home, but leave it for six weeks because the test is slow to become positive. Report any untoward symptoms to your doctor and tell the doctor exactly where you have been and, if you know, what the likelihood of disease is to which you were exposed.

Further information

Websites

www.fco.gov.uk Foreign and Commonwealth Office (FCO) (UK)
www.nathnac.org/ The National Travel Health Network and Centre (NaTHNaC)

www.who.int World Health Organization
www.fitfortravel.scot.nhs.uk This Fit for Travel site from Scotland provides a quick A-Z of vaccine and travel health advice requirements for each country.

Books

Dawood R, editor. *Travellers' health*. 3rd Ed. Oxford: Oxford University Press, 2002.

Expedition Medicine (The Royal Geographic Society) Editors David Warrell and Sarah Anderson ISBN 1 86197 040-4.

Keeping in touch

Internet

Internet cafés have been popping up all over Laos over the last few years. The connections are surprisingly good in major centres. Fast, cheap internet is available in Vientiane, Luang Prabang, Vang Vieng and Savannakhet for around 100-200 kip per minute. Less reliable and more expensive internet (due to long-distance calls) can be found in Xam Neua, Phonsavanh, Don Khone, Don Deth, Luang Namtha and Udom Xai. There is often fierce rivalry between neighbouring outlets and the ensuing price wars only benefit the customer. Many internet cafés also offer international phone services. Wireless internet is not available yet but you can buy prepaid internet cards for use with a landline from **PlaNet Internet** and **Phimpone Market**, Vientiane.

Postal services

In general, post offices are open from 0800 to 1700, with a one-hour lunch break at midday. In the provinces the post offices usually close around 1600 or 1630. There is a poste restante at the central post office in Vientiane. In provincial areas, Lao Telecom is usually attached to the post office.

International service The outbound service is inexpensive and, although long-term foreign residents cast aspersions on its reliability, it reaches its destination most of the time. Expect to pay around 3000-5000 kip to send a postcard overseas. Contents of outgoing parcels must be examined by an official before being sealed. EMS (Express Mail Service) is available from main post offices in larger towns. In-coming mail should use the official title, 'Lao PDR'. For long-term visitors post boxes can be arranged, although it's probably better to get your mail delivered to your hotel. A small fee is required when picking up parcels, determined by the weight of the item.

Freight forwarders/couriers Advertisements for freight and packaging companies in Vientiane are published in the *Vientiane Times* every other day.

Telephone services → *Three-digit area codes are given throughout the guide.*

All major towns are now linked by phone. Public phones are available in Vientiane and other major cities. You can also go to **Lao Telecom** offices to call and fax overseas. Most towns in Laos have at least one telephone box with IDD facility. The one drawback is that you must buy a phonecard. Because these are denominated in such small units, even the highest-value card will only get you a handful of minutes talk time with Europe. All post offices, telecommunications offices and many, many shops sell phone cards.

Many places have fax facilities, particularly guesthouses and hotels. A telephone and **fax service** is also available at the Lao Telecom, Settathirath, Vientiane. Mark incoming faxes with the recipient's telephone number and he/she will be informed immediately. However, it's probably more convenient and reliable to get faxes sent straight to your hotel.

⁞ Useful numbers

- Laos country code (for international calls to Laos): +856. If ringing from Thailand, dial 007 before the country code.
- IDD code (for international calls from Laos): 00
- Operator: 16.
- International operator: 170.
- Area code information: 178 (in Vientiane only).
- Emergency services: Ambulance 195; Fire 190; Police 191

Mobile phones

Bringing your mobile phone is a good way to stay in contact, as you can buy **Tango** (www.tangolao.com) or **Laotel** phone cards from most mini-marts or phone shops for about US$10. Laotel gets better coverage in provincial areas but you can send and receive international text messages with Tango and its starter kit includes US$5 extra credit. Mobile telephone coverage is now quite good.

Media

Newspapers and magazines The *Vientiane Times*, established in 1994, is published five days a week and costs 3000 kip. It provides quirky pieces of information and some interesting cultural and tourist-based features. It is available in several outlets around the capital and in many hotels and guesthouses and is also, remarkably, available online at www.vientianetimes.com. *KPL News*, the English output from the government wire, is not as informative and can be a bit bland.

Sayo Magazine is a monthly publication, which features interesting lifestyle and travel articles. *Newsweek* and *The Economist* are available, as is the French-language *Le Renovateur* (3000 kip). The *Bangkok Post* (costing more than its cover price of ₿20) is the most recent addition to newstands. *Asiaweek* (weekly) is a lightweight Far Eastern Economic Review; rather like a regional *Time* magazine in style.

Television The national TV station broadcasts in Lao but there is a distinct preference for Thai soaps and game shows. These can be received in the Mekong basin but not in mountainous areas, including Luang Prabang. Even Vientiane's poorest communities sport forests of aluminium antennae orientated to receive signals from across the Mekong. In Vientiane, **CNN, BBC, ABC** (Australia) and a range of other channels, including some Russian, Thai and Vietnamese television, are available. Thailand's **Channel 5** gives English subtitles to overseas news. Many homes have VCRs imported from Thailand and some upmarket hotels also subscribe to Asia's **Star TV**, which transmits news as well as sports, music, film and general channels). In rural areas there is concern over the effects that a growing penchant for pornographic videos is having among Laos' youth.

Radio The **Lao National Radio** broadcasts news in English. The **BBC** Southeast Asian service can be picked up on shortwave on 3915, 5990, 6195, 7105, 7160, 9410, 9740, 11760, 11955 and 15360 kHz. Its **Dateline East Asia** provides probably the best news and views on Asia. **Voice of America** broadcasts its Southeast Asian service on 1143, 1575, 7120, 9760, 9770, 15185 and 15425 Mhz. Every day in many of the cities and towns loudspeakers blare out broadcasts of the municipal radio station. These days, socialist slogans have been replaced with commercials for soft drinks, washing powder and toothpaste. Also with a strong Asia focus are the broadcasts of the **ABC** (Australian Broadcasting Corporation).

⁂ Footprint features

Introduction

In 1563, King Setthathirat made the riverine city of Vientiane the capital of Laos. Or, to be more historically accurate, Wiang Chan, the 'City of the Moon', became the capital of Lane Xang. In those days it was a small fortified city on the banks of the Mekong with a palace and two wats, That Luang and Wat Phra Kaeo (built to house the Emerald Buddha). The city had grown prosperous from the surrounding fertile plains and taxes levied from trade going upriver.

Today Vientiane is, perhaps, the most charming of all Southeast Asia's capital cities. Cut off from the outside world and foreign investment for much of the modern period, its colonial heritage remains largely intact. While the last few years have brought greater bustle and activity, it is still a quiet city of tree-lined boulevards, where the image of the past is reflected in the present.

Snuggled in a curve of the Mekong, Vientiane is also the region's most modest capital. It is much more than a town, but it doesn't quite cut it as a conventional city. Here, colourless concrete Communist edifices sit alongside chicken farmers; outdoor aerobics fanatics are juxtaposed against locals making merit at the city's wats; and a couple of traffic lights command a dribble of chaotic cars, bikes, tuk-tuks and buses on the city's streets.

Around Vientiane are a number of places of interest, some of which, including Ban Pako and Nam Ngum, make for worthwhile stopovers or weekend retreats. Vang Vieng and Kasi are on the road north to Luang Prabang and the former, particularly, merits more than just a brief visit.

Vientiane Region

★ Don't miss...

1 **That Luang** Visit Laos' most revered Buddhist monument for its annual festival, when monks flock to the city, pages 67 and 88.

2 **National Museums** Check out Wat Phra Kaeo and the former Revolutionary Museum for a highly subjective history lesson, pages 71 and 74.

3 **Floating restaurants** Enjoy a sunset dinner as you cruise along the Mekong, page 82.

4 **Boun Ok Phansa** The end of Buddhist Lent in mid to late October is a highlight of the Laos' calendar, with entertaining boat races (*souang heua*) on the second day, page 88.

5 **Phou Khao Khouay National Park** Explore the mountains, rivers and waterfalls of this protected area, easily accessible from the capital, page 101.

6 **Tubing on the Nam Xong** Vang Vieng is the adventure capital of Laos, with caving, climbing and river sports, page 112.

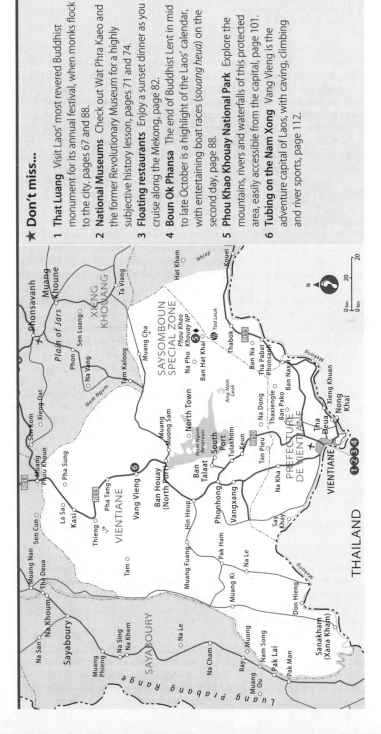

Vientiane

Vientiane's appeal lies in its largely preserved fusion of Southeast Asian and French colonial culture. Baguettes, plunged coffee and Bordeaux wines coexist with spring rolls, pho soup and papaya salad. Colourful tuk-tuks scuttle along tree-lined boulevards, past old Buddhist temples and cosmopolitan cafés. Hammer-and-sickle flags hang at ten-pin bowling discos, locals carry sacks of devalued currency and green and pink chickens wander the streets. But as in the rest of Laos, the best thing about Vientiane, is its people. Take the opportunity to stroll around some of the outlaying bans *(villages) and meet the wonderful characters who make this city what it is.* ▸▸ *For Sleeping, Eating and other listings, see pages 76-98.*

Ins and outs → *Phone code: 021. Colour map 2, B2.*

Getting there

Air Most visitors arrive in Vientiane by air, the great bulk on one of the daily connections from Bangkok, with **Thai Air** or **Lao Airlines** (www.laoairlines.com), which also run international flights to/from Chiang Mai, Hanoi, Ho Chi Minh City, Phnom Penh, Siem Reap and Kunming. **Wattay International Airport** lies 6 km west of the town centre, T021-212066. Vientiane is the hub of Laos's domestic airline system and to travel from the north to the south or vice versa it is necessary to change planes here. The international terminal is the bigger building on the west side. Both terminals have restaurants, telephone box, taxi service and information booth. The desk near the exit handles all outgoing taxis, according to posted rates depending on where you're going in Vientiane. Only taxis are allowed to pick up passengers at the airport (US$5 to the centre of town, 20 mins), although tuk-tuks can drop off here. But tuk-tuks can be taken from the main road and sometimes lurk at the far side of the airport parking area, near the exit (40,000 kip to the centre). The dual carriageway into town is one of only a handful of such stretches of road in the country.

A cheaper alternative from Thailand is to fly from Bangkok to **Udon Thani** on the budget airline **Air Asia** (www.airasia.com). There are several flights a day to and from Bangkok, usually costing between ฿700 and ฿1500. Continue by road to Vientiane via the Friendship Bridge (see Border essentials, page 97), which lies just 25 km downstream from the capital (allow three hours). Shuttle buses from Udon Thani airport usually run to the border after every flight. ▸▸ *For further details, see Essentials, page 31.*

Bus There are three public bus terminals in Vientiane. The **Southern bus station** is 9 km south of the city centre on Route 13. Most international buses bound for Vietnam depart from here as well as buses to southern and eastern Laos. The station has a VIP room, restaurants, a few shops, mini-mart and a guesthouse nearby.

The **Northern bus station** is on Route T2, north of the centre before the airport, T021-260255, and serves destinations in northern Laos. Most tuk-tuks will take you there from the city for 10,000-15,000 kip; ask for "*Bai Thay Song*". There are English-speaking staff at the help desk.

The **Talaat Sao bus station** is across the road from the Morning Market, in front of Talaat Kudin, on the eastern edge of the city centre. This station serves destinations within Vientiane Province, buses to and from the Thai border and international buses to Nong Khai and Udon Thani in Thailand. It is also a good place to pick up a tuk-tuk. Lak Sao, on the border with Vietnam, can be reached by a single 350-km public bus journey from Vientiane. There are also international connections with the private

The charm of Laos lies precisely in the fact that you can't find an espresso at three in the morning or a nightclub meeting your strange desire for techno. There's little point reaching for your Palm organizer and mapping out a day minutely planned to the last moment. But, for what it's worth… Get up at **dawn** and wander out on to the streets to watch the city's monks collecting alms from crouching women and girls (rarely men). After the final victory of the Pathet Lao in 1975 monks were encouraged – none too gently – to work for their living. Depending on your budget either buy a baguette from one of the roadside carts or get a Lao coffee and croissant or baguette from one of the cafés around the Nam Phou Fountain. If it's the dry season and it is still not too late in the day, **hire a bicycle** from one of the shops near here or from your guesthouse. Ride north on Lane Xang Avenue and That Luang Road to **That Luang**, the symbol of Lao nationhood and one of the holiest sites in the country. The ride back into town is slightly downhill, all the better if the day is hotting up. Near the bottom of Lane Xang Avenue are Vientiane's two finest monasteries as well as the **Morning Market** or *Talaat Sao*, which is being developed into a shopping mall. Among the cornucopia of tack from Thailand and China are textiles and silver from Laos. Recharged, head to **Wat Sisaket** and **Wat Phra Kaeo**. If your time (or your interest in Buddhist architecture) is limited, head for the first of these: much more satisfying with its shaded cloisters and elegant, perfectly proportioned *sim*. By now it is time for lunch. Save the big spend for the evening and tuck into some roadside barbecued chicken – and make sure you choose a thin and scrawny Lao bird and not one of the plump, hormone- filled creatures from Thailand. The stalls around the Morning Market are usually a good bet for a meal.

Doing nothing much at all may seem the most enticing prospect during the hot season. But if it's reasonably cool, or you are full of energy, a nice outing is to cycle downstream along the **Mekong**. A track (no cars) follows the river beginning at around Km 5 off the main road. Turn onto one of the many paths and ride for as long as you like. The path, shaded by trees, passes monasteries and attractive riverside houses. There are shops for cold drinks and snacks along the way.

Make sure you get your bike back before the sun has set and make your way to **Quai Fa Ngum** and the Mekong. There are numerous tables right on the banks of the river, where beers and snacks are served to visitors and locals. Have a cold Beer Lao on ice and watch some of the aerobics (6-7pm daily) in the pavilion before getting stuck into the evening's revelries. Use those tens of thousands of kip you saved at lunch and have dinner at **Le Nadao** or **Le Silapa**. To round off the day, **Sticky Fingers** is good for cocktails and coffee.

company **SDT Transport,** T021-740521. All services depart from the Southern bus station. For destinations beyond Vientiane, most people either travel by bus (slow but cheap), tuk-tuk (slower and cheaper) or plane (quick and still cheap by Western standards). ▸▸ *For further details, see Transport, page 93.*

Although Vientiane is the capital of Laos, it is no Bangkok. It is small and manageable and is one of the most laidback capital cities in the world. The local catchphrase 'bopenyang' (no worries) has permeated through every sector of the city, so much so that even the mangy street dogs look completely chilled out, often found asleep in the middle of major intersections. The core of the city is negotiable on foot and even outlying hotels and places of interest are accessible by bicycle. Although traffic has increased substantially over the last five years or so, it is nothing like Bangkok or Saigon, and cycling remains the best and most flexible way to negotiate the city. It can be debilitatingly hot at certain times of the year but there are no great hills to struggle up. If bicycling doesn't appeal, a combination of foot and tuk-tuk or small 110-125cc scooters take the effort out of sightseeing. There is a limited city bus service but it really serves outlying destinations on the Vientiane Plain rather than the city. Larger motorbikes, cars and taxis can also be hired, although these are mainly used for longer journeys and day trips.

Orientation The capital is divided into *bans* or villages, mainly centred around their local wats, and larger *muang* or districts: **Muang Sikhottabong** lies to the west, **Muang Chanthabouli** to the north, **Muang Xaisettha** to the east and **Muang Sisattanak** to the south. Vientiane can be rather confusing for the first-time visitor as there are few street signs and most streets have two names, pre- and post-revolutionary, but, because Vientiane is so small and compact, it doesn't take long to get to grips with the layout. The names of major streets or *thanon* usually correspond to the nearest wat, while traffic lights, wats, monuments and large hotels serve as directional landmarks.

Maps Government-produced tourist/town maps are available from **Venus**, Samsenthai (opposite the Asian Pavilion Hotel). The best tourist map is the one produced by **Golden Triangle Rider**. Although it's geared towards bike riders and will cost you around US$5, it's a great all-round map for Vientiane. You can pick one up at **Phimphone Market**. The most common map of Vientiane in wide circulation is a well-produced 3-D map available for free at the airport and around town. Rather large, and not particularly useful from a tourist viewpoint, it makes a nice souvenir. (It is also sold in some places with the 'free' cunningly blanked out.) The **National Geographic Office** ① *west of the Victory Monument, Mon-Fri 0900-1200 and 1300-1600*, provides plenty of maps at reasonable prices, although they may not be up to date. ▸▸ *For alternatives, see Shopping, page 88.*

Tourist information

Tourist office Lao National Tourism Authority ① *Lane Xang (towards Patuxai), T021-212769, T021-212248 for information, F021-212769,* can provide information regarding ecotourism operators and brilliant trekking opportunities offered in provincial areas. This is a good starting point if you want to organize a trip to Phou Khao Khouay. The Tourist Police are located next door.

History

Vientiane is an ancient city. There was probably a settlement here, on a bend on the left bank of the Mekong, in the tenth century but knowledge of the city before the 16th century is thin and dubious. Scholars do know, from the chronicles, that King Setthathirat decided to relocate his capital here in the early 1560s. It seems that it took him four years to build the city, constructing a defensive wall (hence 'Wiang', meaning a walled or fortified city), along with Wat Phra Kaeo and a much enlarged That Luang.

Vieng Chan, as it was called, remained intact until 1827 when it was ransacked by the Siamese; this is why many of its wats are of recent construction. Francis Garnier in 1860 wrote of "a heap of ruins" and having surveyed the "relics of antiquity" decided that the "absolute silence reigning within the precincts of a city formerly so rich and populous, was ... much more impressive than any of its monuments". A few years later, Louis de Carné wrote of the vegetation that it was like "a veil drawn by nature over the weakness of man and the vanity of his works".

The city was abandoned for decades and erased from the maps of the region. It was only conjured back into existence by the French, who commenced reconstruction at the end of the 19th century. They built rambling colonial villas and wide tree-lined boulevards, befitting their new administrative capital, Vientiane. At the height of American influence in the 1960s, it was renowned for its opium dens and sex shows.

Vientiane today

Today Vientiane is a quiet capital with an urban population of perhaps 205,000 (up from 70,000 in 1960). There are around 500,000 inhabitants (about 10% of the population of Laos) in the Vientiane municipality but this extends far beyond the physical limits of the city. Before 1970 there was only one set of traffic lights in the whole city and, even with the arrival of cars and motorbikes from Thailand in recent years, the streets are a far cry from the congestion of Bangkok. Unlike Phnom Penh and Saigon, there are only scattered traces of French town planning; architecture is a mixture of east and west, with French colonial villas and traditional wooden Lao buildings intermingled with Chinese shophouses and more contemporary buildings. Some locals worry that foreign investment and redevelopment will ruin the city – already some remarkably grotesque buildings are going up – but officials seem to be aware that there is little to be gained from creating Bangkok in microcosm.

For the moment, the city retains its unique innocence: DJs are officially outlawed (although this is not enforced); there is a 2330 curfew; a certain percentage of music played at restaurants and bars every day is supposed to be Lao (overcome by banging out the Lao tune quota at 0800 in the morning) and women are urged to wear the national dress, the *sinh*. However, to describe the Lao government as autocratic is unfairly negative. Vientiane's citizens are proud of their cultural heritage and are usually very supportive of the government's attempts to promote it. The government is trying, by and large, to maintain the national identity and protect its citizens from harmful outside influences, which becomes more understandable when you consider that every country bordering Laos is facing an AIDS epidemic.

If you are out after curfew, a concerned policeman is likely to ask you if you are alright.

Sights

Most of the interesting buildings in Vientiane are of religious significance. All tour companies and many hotels and guesthouses will arrange city tours and excursions to surrounding sights but it is just as easy to arrange a tour independently with a local tuk-tuk driver; the best English speakers (and thus the most expensive tuk-tuks) can be found in the parking lot beside Nam Phou. Those at the Morning Market (Talaat Sao) are cheaper.

That Luang
ⓘ *That Luang Rd, 3.5 km northeast of the city centre. Daily 0800-1200 and 1300-1600 (except 'special' holidays). Admission 2000 kip; a booklet about the wat is on sale at the entrance.*

That Luang is considered Vientiane's most important site and the holiest Buddhist monument in the country. The golden spire looks impressive at the top of the hill, northeast of the city.

According to legend, a stupa was first built here in the third century AD by emissaries of the Moghul Emperor Asoka; it is supposed to have contained the breast bone of the Buddha. Excavations on the site, however, have only located the remains of an 11th- to 13th-century Khmer temple, making the earlier provenance doubtful in the extreme. The present monument, encompassing the previous buildings, was built in 1566 by King Setthathirat, whose statue stands outside. Plundered by the Thais and the Chinese Haw in the 18th century, it was restored by King (Chao) Anou at the beginning of the 19th century. He added the cloister and the Burmese-style pavilion

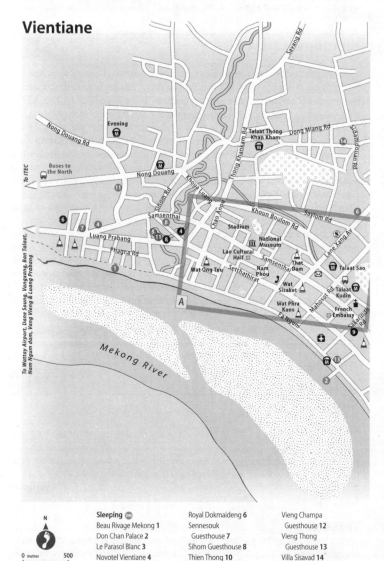

Vientiane

N

0 metres   500
0 yards   500

containing the That Sithamma Hay Sok. The stupa was carefully restored again by l'Ecole Francaise d'Extreme-Orient (whose conservators were also responsible for the restoration of parts of Angkor Wat at the beginning of this century) but was rebuilt in 1930 because many Lao disapproved of the French restoration.

The reliquary is surrounded by a square cloister, with an entrance on each side, the most famous on the east. There is a small collection of statues in the cloisters, including one of the Khmer king Jayavarman VII. The cloisters are used as lodgings by monks who travel to Vientiane for religious reasons and especially for the annual **That Luang festival** (see page 88). The base of the stupa is a mixture of styles, Khmer, Indian and Lao, and each side has a *hor vay* or small offering temple. This lowest level represents the material world, while the second tier is surrounded by a

Related maps
A Vientiane centre, p72
B Around Nam Phou, p80

Wonderland	Le Ranch **3**	Bars & clubs 🍸
Guesthouse **16**	Le Silapa **4**	Abstract **10**
	Nong Vong **5**	Wind West **11**
Eating 🍴	Sakura **6**	
Koto **1**	Tamnak Lao **8**	
Le Nadao **2**	Vegetarian **9**	

lotus wall and 30 smaller stupas, representing the 30 Buddhist perfections. Each of these originally contained smaller golden stupas but they were stolen by Chinese raiders in the 19th century. The 30-m-high spire dominates the skyline and resembles an elongated lotus bud, crowned by a stylized banana flower and parasol. It was designed so that pilgrims could climb up to the stupa via the walkways around each level. There was originally a wat on each side of the stupa but only two remain: **Wat Luang Nua** to the north and **Wat Luang Tai** to the south. The large new wat-like structure is the headquarters of a Buddhist organization. The monument's outer walls often feature art exhibitions.

Although That Luang is the most important historical site in Vientiane, most visitors will feel that it is not the most interesting, impressive or beautiful, largely because it seems to have been constructed out of concrete. Both Wat Sisaket and Wat Phra Kaeo (see opposite) are more memorable. Nonetheless, it is important to appreciate the reverence in which That Luang is held by most Lao, including the many millions who live in neighbouring Thailand. The *that* is the prototype for the distinctive Lao-style angular *chedi*, which can be seen in northeast Thailand, as well as across Laos.

Revolutionary Monument

Also known as the **Unknown Soldier's Memorial**, this hilltop landmark is located just off Phon Kheng Road and is visible from the parade ground (which resembles a disused parking lot) in front of That Luang. Echoing a *that* in design, it is a spectacularly dull monument, built in memory of those who died during the revolution in 1975. The **Pathet Lao Museum**, to the northwest of That Luang, is only open to VIPs and never to the public but there are a few tanks, trucks, guns and aircraft used in the war lying in the grounds, which can be seen from the other side of the fence.

Patuxai (Victory Monument)

ⓘ *Junction of That Luang Rd and Lane Xang Av. Officially Mon-Fri 0800-1100 and 1400-1630, but these hours seem to be posted only for fun. Admission 1000 kip.*

At the end of That Luang is the Oriental answer to Paris's Arc de Triomphe and Vientiane's best-known landmark, the monstrous Victory Monument or Patuxai. It was originally called Anou Savali, officially renamed the Patuxai or Victory Monument, but is affectionately known by locals as 'the vertical runway'. It was built by the former regime in memory of those who died in the wars before the Communist takeover, but the cement ran out before its completion. Refusing to be beaten, the regime diverted hundreds of tonnes of cement, part of a US aid package to help with the construction of runways at Wattay Airport, to finish off the monument in 1969. In 2004 the Chinese funded a big concrete park area surrounding the site, including a musical fountain; it's a pity they didn't stretch the budget to finance the beautification of the park's centrepiece.

A small introductory sign explains that, although Patuxai might look grand from a distance, on closer inspection "it appears like a monster of concrete". The top affords a bird's eye view of the leafy capital, including the distant glittering, golden dome of the old Russian circus, now the rarely used National Circus. The interior of the monument is reminiscent of a multi-storey car park (presumably as a counterpoint to the parade ground next to the Revolutionary Monument), with graffiti sporadically daubed on top of unfinished Buddhist bas-reliefs in reinforced concrete. The frescoes under the arches at the bottom represent mythological stories from the Lao version of the Ramayana, the Phra Lak Pralam. Until 1990 there was a bar on the bottom floor; today Vientiane's youth hang out on the parapet, listening to the 'lambada' in Lao.

① *Junction of Lane Xang Av and Setthathirat Rd. Daily 0800-1200 and 1400-1600. Admission 2000 kip. No photographs in the sim.*

Further down Lane Xang is the **Morning Market** or **Talaat Sao** (see page 90) and beyond, where Setthathirat meets Lane Xang, is one of Vientiane's two national museums, **Wat Sisaket**. Home of the head of the Buddhist community in Laos, Phra Sangka Nagnok, it is one of the most important buildings in the capital and houses over 7,000 Buddha images. Wat Sisaket was built in 1818 during the reign of King Anou. A traditional Lao monastery, it was the only temple that survived the Thai sacking of the town in 1827-28 (perhaps out of deference to its having been completed only 10 years before the invasion), making it the oldest building in Vientiane. Sadly, it is badly in need of restoration.

The main sanctuary, or **sim**, with its sweeping roof shares many stylistic similarities with Wat Phra Kaeo (see page 71): window surrounds, lotus-shaped pillars and carvings of deities held up by giants on the rear door. The *sim* contains 2,052 Buddha statues (mainly terracotta, bronze and wood) in small niches in the top half of the wall. There is little left of the Thai-style *jataka* murals on the lower walls but the depth and colour of the originals can be seen from the few remaining pieces. The ceiling was copied from temples King Anou had seen on a visit to Bangkok. The standing image to the left of the altar is believed to have been cast in the same proportions as King Anou. Around the *sim*, set into the ground, are small *bai sema* or boundary stones. The *sim* is surrounded by a large courtyard, which originally had four entrance gates (three are now blocked). Behind the *sim* is a large trough, in the shape of a *naga*, used for washing the Buddha images during the water festival (see page 88).

The **cloisters** were built during the 1800s and were the first of their kind in Vientiane. They shelter 120 large Buddhas in the attitude of subduing Mara (see page 334), plus a number of other images in assorted *mudras*, and thousands of small figures in niches, although many of the most interesting Buddha figures are now in Wat Phra Kaeo. Most of the statues date from the 16th to 19th centuries but there are some earlier images. Quite a number were taken from local monasteries during the French period and have ended up here.

The whole ensemble of *sim* plus cloisters is washed in a rather attractive shade of caramel and, combined with the terracotta floor tiles and weathered roof, presents a most satisfying sight. An attractive Burmese-style library, or *hau tai*, stands on Lane Xang outside the courtyard. The large casket inside used to contain important Buddhist manuscripts but they have now been moved to protect them against vermin.

Just behind Wat Sisaket is an entire complex of colonial houses in a well-maintained garden.

Wat Phra Kaeo

① *Setthathirat Rd. Daily 0800-1200 and 1300-1600. Closed public holidays. Admission 5000 kip. No photographs in the sim.*

Almost opposite Wat Sisaket is the other national museum, **Wat Phra Kaeo**, also known as **Hor Phra Kaeo**. It was originally built by King Setthathirat in 1565 to house the Emerald Buddha (or Phra Kaeo), now in Bangkok, which he had brought from his royal residence in Chiang Mai. It was never a monastery but was kept instead for royal worship. The Emerald Buddha was removed by the Thais in 1779 and Wat Phra Kaeo was destroyed by them in the sacking of Vientiane in 1827. The whole building was in a bad state of repair after the sackings, the only thing remaining fully intact was the floor. Francis Garnier, the French explorer, who wandered the ruins of Vieng Chan in 1860 describes Wat Phra Kaeo "shin[ing] forth in the midst of the forest, gracefully framed with blooming

❧ *Adjacent to the museum is the old royal palace, where the King from Luang Prabang resided. Today it is the presidential palace and closed to the public.*

lianas, and profusely garlanded with foliage". Louis de Carné in his journal, *Travels in Indochina and the Chinese Empire* (1872), was also enchanted, writing when he came upon the vegetation-choked ruin that it "made one feel something of that awe which filled men of old at the threshold of a sacred wood".

The building was expertly reconstructed in the 1940s and 1950s and is now surrounded by a garden. During renovations, the interior walls of the wat were restored using a plaster made of sugar, sand, buffalo skin and tree oil.

The **sim** stands on three tiers of galleries, the top one surrounded by majestic, lotus-shaped columns. The tiers are joined by several flights of steps and guarded by *nagas*. The main, central (southern) door is an exquisite example of Lao wood sculpture with carved angels surrounded by flowers and birds; it is the only notable remnant of the original wat. (The central door at the northern end, with the larger carved angels supported by ogres, is new.) The *sim* now houses a superb assortment of Lao and Khmer art and some pieces of Burmese and Khmer influence, mostly collected from other wats in Vientiane. Although people regularly come and pray here, the wat's main purpose is as a quasi-museum.

Vientiane centre

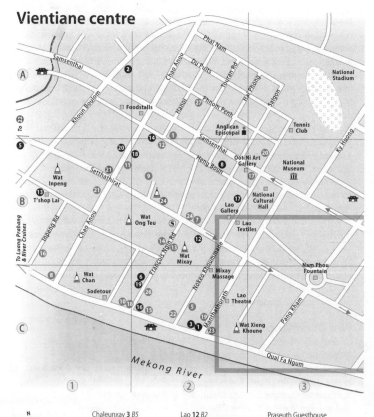

3, 4, 17: Bronze Buddhas in typical Lao style.

294, 295: Buddhas influenced by Sukhothai style (Thailand), where the attitude of the walking Buddha was first created (see page 334).

354: Buddha meditating made of lacquered wood, shows Burmese influence, dates from the 18th century.

372: Wooden, Indian-style door with erotic sculpture, dating back to the 16th century, originally from the Savannakhet region.

388: Copy of the Pra Bang, the revered statue associated with the origins of Buddhism in Laos (see pages 118 and 122).

❧ The garden has a small jar from the Plain of Jars (p185), which was transported to Vientiane by helicopter.

412, 414, 450: Khmer pieces.

415: A hybrid of Vishnu and Buddha.

416: A Khmer deity with four arms.

430, 431: 18th-century copies of the famous Khmer apsaras, the celestial nymphs of Angkor in Cambodia.

Vientiane Region Vientiane

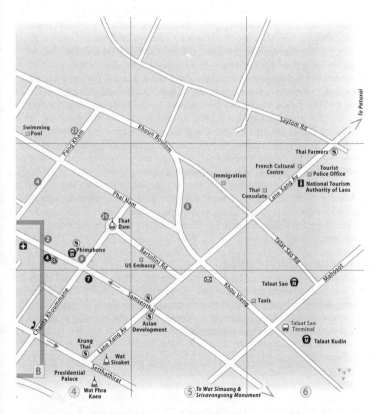

Settha Palace **23** *A4*	Chinese Liao-Ning	Le Croissant d'Or	Tokyo Kitchen **18** *B2*
Soukchaleun	Dumplings **2** *A1*	(French Bakery) **12** *B2*	
Guesthouse **24** *B2*	Côte d'Azur **3** *C2*	Le Vendôme **13** *B1*	**Bars & clubs**
Tai-Pan **26** *C2*	Delight House of	Nam Nuang **14** *A2*	Blue Sky **21** *B1*
Vannasinh	Fruitshakes **4** *B4*	Nazim **16** *C2*	Marina **22** *A1*
Guesthouse **27** *A2*	Fuji Wara **5** *B1*	Sticky Fingers **19** *C2*	Music House **23** *C2*
	Full Moon Café **6** *C2*	Sweet Home	Samlor Pub **24** *B2*
Eating	Happy Garden **8** *B2*	& Bakery **20** *B1*	That Dam Wine
Alexia **1** *C2*	Kua Lao **7** *C4*	Thongphet Cakes **17** *B2*	House **25** *B4*

698: This stone Buddha is the oldest piece of Buddhist art in Laos, dating from the sixth to ninth century.

Also look out for a collection of stelae, inscribed in Lao and Thai script, including one with a treaty delineating a 16th-century agreement between Siam and Lane Xang. And an 'Atom-struck Tile', found on the site of Sairenji Temple, Hiroshima.

That Dam

Travelling north on Chanta Koummane, the distinctive brick That Dam, or **Black Stupa**, can be seen. It is renowned for the legend of the seven-headed *naga*, which is supposed to have helped protect the city from Thai invaders (conveniently forgetting that the city was comprehensively sacked by the Thais in 1827). The *naga* now lies dormant inside, waiting for another chance. The stupa was renovated in 1995 but still has a neglected feel.

National Museum

ⓘ *Samsenthai Rd, in the centre of town, near the stadium. Daily 0800-1200 and 1300-1600 (but these hours are interpreted flexibly). Admission 5000 kip.*

This place was formerly called the Revolutionary Museum but in these post-revolutionary days it has been redesignated a National Museum. To emphasize the change it also moved to new premises, a colonial mansion, in 1985. The museum exhibits a selection of historical artefacts including prehistoric remains, pre-Angkorian sculptures and other displays from the country's history from earliest times, mostly in the form of photographs depicting the 'wicked colonial years and the struggle for freedom'. As in most countries trying to build a sense of national identity after a divisive and destructive civil war, history is carefully patrolled and, if necessary, sanitized. Having said that, there are some fantastic photographs and some lively captions to accompany them, including black-and-white images of victorious elderly women wielding dog machine guns and of "running-dog" Western imperialists. Several displays are only captioned in Lao.

In part, the museum is a shrine to the revolutionary leader Kaysone. Tourists will be understandably flabbergasted by a dazzling array of his personal effects, including his exercise machine, a spoon he once used and the coconut he once had a sip from. There are also some mini jars from the Plain of Jars in the museum's grounds. Recommended.

Lao National Culture Hall

Facing the National Museum on the other side of the road is the **Lao National Culture Hall**. The hideous wedding cake-style building was a gift in kind by the Chinese and sticks out like a sore thumb. It is built in such monumental proportions that you can imagine tumbleweed blowing through the corridors at some of the ill-promoted events. ▶ *For further details, see Entertainment, page 87.*

Wat Ong Teu

Wat Ong Teu (identified by its bright orange monks' quarters) is located on Setthathirat, which runs parallel to Samsenthai. It was constructed by King Setthathirat in the 16th century, was ransacked by the Siamese in 1827 and then rebuilt during the late 19th and 20th centuries. The wat houses one of the biggest Buddhas in Vientiane, weighing several tonnes, which sits at the back of the *sim* and gives the monastery its name: Temple of the Heavy Buddha. The wat is also noted for its magnificent sofa and its ornately carved wooden doors and windows, with motifs from the Phra Lak Pralam (the Ramayana). The monastery runs one of the larger Buddhist schools in Laos and is home to the Deputy Patriarch of the Lao monastic order, Hawng Sangkharat. The wat comes alive every year for the That Luang festival (see page 88).

❊ The story of Quan Am

Quan Am was turned onto the streets by her husband for some unspecified wrong doing and, dressed as a monk, took refuge in a monastery. There, a woman accused her of fathering, and then abandoning, her child. Accepting the blame (why, no one knows), she was again turned out onto the streets, only to return to the monastery much later when she was on the point of death – to confess her true identity. When the Emperor of China heard the tale, he made Quan Am the Guardian Spirit of Mother and Child, and couples without a son now pray to her. Quan Am's husband is sometimes depicted as a parakeet, with the Goddess usually holding her adopted son in one arm and standing on a lotus leaf, the symbol of purity.

Wat Chan

A short walk away, on the banks of the Mekong (junction of Chao Anou and Fa Ngum), is Wat Chan, or **Wat Chanthabuli**. It was wrecked by the marauding Thais in 1827 and now only the base of a single stupa remains in front of the *sim*. The stupa originally had Buddha images in the 'Calling for Rain' attitude on each side (see page 334) but only one remains. Inside the reconstructed *sim* is a remarkable bronze Buddha from the original temple on this site. The wat is also renowned for its panels of sculpted wood on the doors and windows.

Chua Bang-Long

For those who have had their fill of Theravada Buddhist wats, there is a fine Mahayana Buddhist *chua* (pagoda) tucked away down a narrow lane off Khoun Boulom, near Chao Anou. The Chua Bang-Long was established by Vientiane's large and active Vietnamese population, who are said to have outnumbered Lao in the city before the outbreak of the Second World War. A statue of the Chinese goddess Quan Am (see above) stands in front of a Lao-style *that* which, in turn, fronts a large pagoda, almost Cao Dai in style. The pagoda has been extensively renovated and embellished over the last few years. Not far away, at the intersection of Samsenthai and Khoun Boulom is another, much smaller and more intimate pagoda.

Wat Simuàng

ⓘ *Setthathirat Rd, east of town. Daily 0600-2000; during celebrations the temple stays open until 2200.*

Wat Simuang contains the town foundation pillar (*lak muang*), which was erected in 1566 when King Setthathirat established Vientiane as the capital of the kingdom of Lane Xang. It is believed to be an ancient Khmer boundary stone, which marked the edge of the old Lao capital. Although the temple means 'Holy City Monastery' many locals vouch that it's named after pregnant Madame Simuang, who sacrificed herself, her baby and her horse by jumping in the hole dug for the foundation pillar before the consecrated stone was erected. The *sim* was reconstructed in 1915 around the foundation pillar, which forms the centre of the altar. In front of the altar is a stone Buddha, which is thought to have magical powers and is often consulted by worshippers because it survived the temple's razing. It is believed that if you lift the Buddha off the pillow three times and make a wish then you are indebted to return an offering of fruit and flowers. Wat Simuang may not be charming, refined or architecturally significant but for many locals it is the most important monastery in the capital and, certainly, considered the luckiest. Street hawkers selling offerings of fruit, flowers, candles and incense line the surrounding streets, supplying the scores of people who come here hoping for good fortune. In the grounds of the wat are the ruins of what appears to be a Khmer laterite *chedi*.

Statue of King Setthathirat

Just beyond Wat Simaung, where Setthathirat and Samsenthai meet, is the statue of King Setthathirat, the founder of Vientiane. The original statue, carved by a Lao sculptor, apparently made the king look like a dwarf so it was destroyed. The present statue (there's a copy of it in Luang Prabang) was, peculiarly, donated by the Russians and, just as strangely, it survived the revolution.

● Sleeping

Vientiane *p64, maps p68, p72 and p80*
Vientiane has just 5 hotels that could really be considered international grade: the **Don Chan Palace**, **Novotel Vientiane**, **Lao Plaza Hotel**, **Settha Palace** and the boutique **Beau Rivage Mekong**. However, there are a large number of very well run and elegant, converted former colonial villas as well as some good mid-range places. A few years ago there were few budget places to stay but this shortage has eased considerably. Hotels usually insist on payment in US$ or Thai ฿, although most guesthouses will take kip, or a combination of the 3 currencies. As a rule of thumb, hotels priced over US$30 (ie our A category and above) accept major credit cards.

L Don Chan Palace, Ban Piawat (just off Fa Ngum Rd, on the Mekong), T021-244288, F021-244111/2, donchanpalace@laopdr.com. This 14-storey eyesore was built for the 2004 ASEAN summit and is now considered the most prestigious hotel in town (and the most vulgar). It's built so close to the river that locals joke that it's going to sink but its location ensures stunning views of Thailand and the Mekong to the north and panoramic views of Vientiane to the south. The facilities and rooms are also 5-star. Standard rooms have internet access, IDD telephone, cable TV, digital room safes, plus all the usual amenities. The more expensive rooms also have jacuzzis and wide-screen TVs. The hotel also boasts a business centre, well-equipped gym, spa, sauna, pool, sky bar, Chinese restaurant, coffee shop and karaoke. Although the rack rates quoted are between US$130 and US$500 a night, the hotel is having trouble filling rooms, so it is possible to get rooms cheaper.
L Lao Plaza Hotel, 63 Samsenthai Rd, T021-218800/1, www.laoplazahotel.com. Centrally located, this Thai-managed,

140-room hotel is no doubt useful for business visitors but seems rather incongruous in Vientiane. Non-guests may use the hotel's extensive facilities for a set fee. These include 2 restaurants, a fitness centre, pool, conference centre, satellite TV, IDD telephones, karaoke bar and shopping arcade. Most major credit cards accepted.
L Novotel Vientiane, Samsenthai Rd, near the junction with Luang Prabang, T021-213570/1, www.novotel.com. Large international-style hotel (332 rooms), with a good range of facilities including restaurant, pool, gym, tennis court, sauna, Lao massage, nightclub, business centre and games room. A/c throughout. The hotel often holds art exhibitions and concerts but the building itself is completely characterless and suffers from a poor location on the edge of town towards Wattay Airport (free airport transfer). Room rates include breakfast, but tax is extra; most major credit cards accepted.
L Settha Palace, 6 Pang Kham Rd, T021-217581/2, www.setthapalace.com. The only French hotel in town, Settha Palace was built in 1936 and opened as a hotel in 1999. Its French architecture, colonial decor, period furniture and landscaped gardens are really lovely, and sit more easily with the fundamental essence of Vientiane than the glitz and glamour of the other top-level hotels, whilst providing the same level of convenience for both business and leisure guests. The **Belle Epoque** restaurant serves mouthwatering French cuisine. Generally considered the best place in town. Recommended.
AL Tai-Pan, 2-12 François Ngin Rd (off Fa Ngum Rd, near Wat Mixay), T021-216906, -7, -8, -9, www.travelao.com. The service here is hard to fault and facilities are good: restaurant, bar, basic gym, small pool and

free airport pick-up. The lobby is rather more impressive than the 36 rooms, but they are reasonably well equipped with a/c, IDD telephones, satellite TV and flowers and fruit on arrival. Room rates include a good breakfast. Most major credit cards accepted.

A Beau Rivage Mekong, Fa Ngum Rd, T021-243350, www.hbrm.com. One of the first Western-style boutique hotels in Vientiane is beautifully furnished and offers superb Mekong River views. Its location, just out of the centre of town, ensures peace and quiet but it's still only a 5-min walk to the hustle and bustle. Perfect for the executive on the go or people who like to spend a couple of extra dollars on comfort. Recommended.

A Lane Xang Hotel, Fa Ngum Rd, T021-214100/7, F021-214108, CLHotel @yahoo.com. This was the original 'luxury' hotel in Vientiane, built by the French in the 1960s. It has an undefinable charm, despite the fact that some of its retro-hip Soviet fittings and furniture have been ripped out to make way for a more contemporary look. The a/c rooms are now well equipped, with excellent bathrooms, making the hotel the best value in town, with a great central position on the river. Go for a deluxe room, with its own bar and velour bed fittings, to indulge in a 1970s, porn-flick nostalgia trip. The service here is unmatched. The international restaurant has traditional Lao dancing shows every night and a cabaret on Wed, with a bird impressionist and contortionist. Other facilities include a pool, nightclub, bar, putting green, snooker hall, sauna and fitness centre. Major credit cards accepted. Recommended.

A Lani I, 281 Setthathirat Rd (set back from the road next to Wat Hay Sok), T021-214919/ 216103, F021-215639. This auberge was one of the first to open in Vientiane and remains popular with those who have been acquainted with the country since the late 1980s. It is clean, well run and elegant, with a good central position set back from the road in a quiet garden next to a wat. The building is decorated with lovely antiques and handicrafts and has a/c, telex and fax services, bicycles for hire, an outside bar and a restaurant (excellent Chinese, cooked by Lani's father on request). But, it is overpriced, considering the much better choice of

accommodation that is now available. Rooms are often taken by long-term visitors so booking in advance is recommended. The rooms on the ground floor can be dark.

A-B Hotel Day Inn, Pang Kham Rd, T021-214792, F021-222984, dayinn@laotel.com. Run by a friendly Cambodian, this renovated villa is in a good position in a quiet part of town, just to the north of the main concentration of bars and restaurants. Attractive, airy, clean, large rooms, with a/c and excellent bathrooms. Restaurant serves tasty food. Also bike hire. Good value, recommended.

A-B Inter Hotel, 24-25 Fa Ngum Rd/Chou Anou (next to Wat Chan), T021-242842, www.laointerhotel.com. This Thai-owned hotel is one of the oldest in Vientiane, now operating for over 30 years. Recent renovations have made it sparkle: mosaics, relief sculptures and murals adorn the walls, and traditional shutters, silk hangings and furniture feature in every room. The a/c rooms are light and spacious, with slick bathrooms and fantastic balconies overlooking the Mekong. Lovely atrium in the centre of the hotel, a good restaurant (excellent steak) and a great gift shop with beautiful antique costumes. Unbeatable for this price range but the staff are a bit *bopenyang*. Recommended.

A-B Royal Dokmaideng, Lane Xang Av, not far from the Victory Monument, opposite the Morning Market, T021-214455, F021-214454, laoroyal@laotel.com. A refurbished hotel of 80 rooms with a Chinese feel, thanks to its heavy furniture, marble and the high-pressure Karaoke Bar. Other facilities include a/c, restaurant and pool but, at this price, there are several other places which offer more ambience and a better location. Major credit cards accepted.

B Anou, 1-3 Heng Boun Rd, T021-213630/1, F021-213632, anouhotel@laotel.com. Fairly recently renovated with welcoming elevator, the Anou has the same owners as the Phousi Hotel in Luang Prabang (see p138). Rooms are clean and serviceable but impersonal, with satellite TV. Restaurant serves Lao and European cuisine with live traditional music. Credit cards accepted.

B Asian Pavilion, 379 Samsenthai Rd, T021-213430/1, F021-213432, asianlao @loxinfo.co.th. Vientiane's new hotels and guesthouses have left the Asian Pavilion for dust. This hotel offers 44 shabby a/c rooms (rates include breakfast), with views of a bare brick wall. Its only notable attributes are its history and the enthusiasm of the staff. It used to be the **Hotel Constellation** made famous by John Le Carré in *The Honourable Schoolboy*. The original owner was a colonel in the Royal Lao Army, who was sent to a re-education camp after 1975. He wasn't released until 1988, whereupon he reclaimed his hostelry and renamed it the Vieng Vilai. Major credit cards accepted.

B **Douane Deuane**, Nokeo Khoummane Rd, T021-222301/3, www.bookings-asia.com/la/ hotels/douangdeane. From the exterior, this looks like a classic Communist edifice, but the rooms are fantastic: parquet wood floors, art deco furniture, excellent bathrooms, satellite TV and a decent size. Try and get a balcony room for lovely patchwork views of the roofs of the city. Also has restaurant, free airport transfer, DHL service and cars for rent. The room rates have remained competitive and include breakfast. Credit cards accepted. Recommended.

B **Ekkalath Metropole**, Samsenthai Rd (not far from That Dam), T021-213420, F021-222307. Worn and bleak. The rooms in the main block are vast, with ugly metal doors. Some have an attached sitting area ('suite' is too grand a word for these spartan affairs) and a/c. Cheaper rooms are housed in a guesthouse attached to the hotel and are very basic with no hot water but are fairly clean. The scary-looking electrics in some of the bathrooms might jazz up your stay. Professional electricians should either stay away or ask for a job.

B **Hotel Lao**, 53/9 Heng Boun Rd, T021-219281, F021-219282, hotellao@laotel.com. Opened in early 1999, this hotel has 30 enormous a/c rooms, with satellite TV, telephone, mini-bar, even a hairdryer in the en suite bathrooms. Credit card facilities should be available soon. Friendly staff are still enthused with the idea of working in the service sector.

B **Lao Paris**, 100 Samsenthai Rd, opposite Lao Plaza Hotel, T021-213440, F021-216382. Clean but uninspired. Central location. Rooms with a/c and private bathrooms with hot water, some have TV. Cheaper rooms on top floor are drab.

B **Le Parasol Blanc**, behind National Assembly, close to Victory Monument (not very well marked), T021-216091, F021-215444. This is a very attractive leafy haven. Spacious a/c rooms, with wooden floors and sizeable bathrooms. Some look onto the garden, with sitting area in front, the most expensive are alongside the good-sized pool. Charming place, well run, mostly patronized by French visitors. Restaurant (see Eating, below). Recommended.

B **Mali Namphu Guesthouse**, 114 Pang Kham Rd (next door to Phonepaseuth Guesthouse), T021-215093, www.mali.com. Difficult to spot as it looks like a small shopfront but the façade is deceiving, as the foyer opens onto a beautifully manicured courtyard surrounded by quaint, terraced rooms. Clean, bright rooms are traditionally decorated with a modern twist and come with a/c, hot water, cable TV and a fantastic breakfast. Friendly staff. One of the best deals in town. Highly recommended.

B **Vayakone Guesthouse**, Nokeo Khoummane Rd, T021-241911, vayakone@laotel.com. Centrally located and clean, with friendly staff. Wonderful airy rooms, tastefully decorated, with hot water, a/c, satellite and cable TV. Small restaurant serves fruit, coffee and snacks. Highly recommended.

B **Vieng Thong Guesthouse**, Ban Phiawat, opposite Wat Phiavat in a side street, T/F021-212095. Family-style house in a nice garden with a café and big aviary. Large rooms with thick comforting duvets, rattan furniture, TV, china tea-sets and hot water showers. Pleasant but perhaps a little expensive. Car for hire.

B **Villa That Luang**, 307 That Luang Rd, 1.5 km north of town centre, T021-413370, F021-412953, ecolodge@laotel.com. Another converted villa with large and attractively furnished rooms with a/c, TV, fridge, phone and sitting area. Laundry is included in the room rate. Attached restaurant. Well run with friendly staff.

B-C **Vannasinh Guesthouse**, 51 Phnom Penh Rd (off Samsenthai Rd), T/F021-218707. Huge warren-like house, well managed, with friendly staff (good English and French spoken). Clean, large rooms, some with a/c. Bicycles for hire. Well priced and very popular.

C **Chaleunxay Hotel**, Khou Vieng Rd (opposite the Forestry Department) T021-223407/222878, F021-223529. Newly converted into a hotel, Chaleunxay has a laidback, ramshackle, slightly untidy air that persists despite the brace of cleaners whose jobs never seem to be quite done. Temperamental hot water supply. Very friendly staff, and convenient location very close to the Morning Market and bus station. Endearing.

C **Chanta Guesthouse**, Setthathirat Rd (opposite Mixay Temple), T021-243204, guesthouse_chanta_m@yahoo.fr. The shabby foyer doesn't do this place justice. Rooms are homely, with polished floorboards, TV, good bathrooms, wooden furniture and great cotton bedclothes. Cheaper rooms have shared facilities.

C **Orchid Guesthouse**, 33 Fa Ngum Rd, T021-252825, F021-216588. Friendly staff, and jolly nice, spotlessly clean rooms with fan or a/c and breakfast included. Take a table and chairs onto the tiled roof for a lovely view of sunset on the river. Slap bang on the noisy Fa Ngum Rd, so only recommended for deep sleepers.

C **Pangkham Guesthouse**, 72/6 Pang Kham Rd, T/F021-217053. A Chinese-run guesthouse offering basic, clean rooms in a featureless block. More expensive rooms have a/c, all have hot showers, cheaper rooms have no windows. Service is drone-like. Building is currently being extended. Bikes for hire.

C **Phonepaseuth Guesthouse**, 97 Pang Kham Rd, T021-212263/217053, www.phonepaseuth-gh.com. Popular, clean guesthouse with cable TV, hot water and good bathroom. Roof top garden. Good location. Pricey restaurant.

C **Phornthip Guesthouse**, 72 Inpeng Rd (behind Wat Inpeng), T021-217239. A quiet, family-run and very friendly guesthouse. It's almost always full (pre-booking is recommended) and perhaps a trifle overpriced (due, no doubt, to its popularity). Large rooms, with en suite bathrooms, some have a/c. Courtyard at the back, but no garden. Bicycle hire. Recommended.

C **Saysana Guesthouse**, Chao Anou Rd, T021-218636. The Saysana looks smarter than it is but facilities include a/c, restaurant, beauty salon, car rental and ancient

telephones on an antique switchboard. Major credit cards accepted.

C **Saysouly Guesthouse**, 23 Manthathurath Rd, T021-218383/4, F021-223757, saysouly@hotmail.com This is the only guesthouse in town to have cooking facilities. A well-maintained suite of 4 doubles opens out onto a sitting and dining area, with attached kitchen equipped with 2 electric rings. Some rooms have a/c and en suite bathrooms, with hot water. Good value. Motorbike hire at US$10 per day. Very clean. Recommended.

C **Sennesouk Guesthouse**, 100 Luang Prabang Rd, just west of Novotel Hotel on airport side, T021-213375, F021-217449. A guesthouse and restaurant located a little out of town. Rooms are OK and some have en suite bathrooms and a/c, but there is a nightclub next door and it can be noisy when the restaurant is in full swing.

C **Soukchaleun Guesthouse**, 121 Setthathirat Rd (opposite Mixay temple), T021-218723, soukchaleungh@yahoo.com. Simple, clean rooms with fan, a/c, hot water and cable TV. Try and get a balcony room for a beautiful view over the temple.

C **Thien Thong**, Sok Paluang Rd, T021-313782, F021-312125. Has 13 clean rooms, with a/c, fridge and tiled hot water shower room en suite. House is in an attractive and leafy compound about 1500 m from the town centre, so bicycles needed. Good food. Recommended.

C **Thongbay Guesthouse**, off Luang Prabang Rd, turn right before the Novotel, Ban Non Douang, T/F021-242292, thongbay @laotel.com. Lovely traditional Lao house set in a lush tropical garden. Rooms have traditional-style fittings, mosquito nets and fan or a/c. The guesthouse also runs cooking classes on request (US$10), including purchasing ingredients at the local market. The only drawback of this place is its distance from the city centre. Perfect if you wish to relax. Recommended.

C **Villa Sisavad**, 12/117 Sisavad Neua Rd, north of the centre, near the Victory Monument, T/F021-212719. This is situated slightly out of town but has the big selling point of a pool. Otherwise only adequate rooms with en suite hot water showers and a restaurant. Mostly caters to Asian tourists. Major credit cards accepted.

C **Wonderland Guesthouse**, Phonsavan Tai Rd (off Khou Vieng, south of town), T021-312894. Small guesthouse in private villa down a quiet lane some way from the centre of town. Attractive garden, birds, verandahs and restaurant. 10 clean, good-sized rooms with en suite bathrooms and a/c. Consider staying here if you don't mind (or prefer) being out of the town centre. Easily accessible by bicycle along attractive, tree-lined Khou Vieng but no bikes are for hire at this guesthouse.

C-D **KPP Guesthouse**, 123/4 Chao Anou Rd, T021-218601, F021-219559, pholsena @laotel.com. German-owned guesthouse with exceptionally well-appointed rooms for this price range, with fan or a/c. Shared bathrooms have hot water. Recommended.

C-D **Phet Phim Guesthouse** (aka PP Guesthouse), on the corner of Francois Ngin Rd and Fa Ngum Rd, T021-252757, phetphim@yahoo.com. Basic, no-frills backpacker guesthouse offering standard rooms, with fan and shared facilities. Only real positive is its good location on the river-front, with many restaurants and bars nearby. Guests receive a 10% discount at the internet café downstairs. The staff can be a bit iffy and at times absolutely creepy.

C-D **Praseuth Guesthouse**, 312 Samsenthai Rd, T021-217932. This nondescript building contains 10 small a/c rooms, many without windows. Walls and floor are wooden, which enhances the gloomy feel, but facilities are clean. Some rooms have en suite bathrooms. Bikes for hire. Central location, with the popular Xayoh Café next door.

C-D **Samsenthai Guesthouse**, 15 Manthathurath Rd, T021-212116. This hotel is a bit of a mixed bag. Cheaper rooms are grubby and depressing, while the top-end rooms were large and have a/c and en suite bathrooms but don't stretch to great cleanliness, either. The overall impression is not good: a hideous block with a fusty aroma. Restaurant attached. Central location.

Around Nam Phou

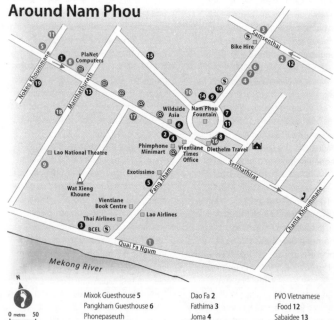

N
0 metres 50
0 yards 50

Sleeping 🛌
Lane Xang 1
Lao Paris 2
Lao Plaza 3
Mali Namphu
  Guesthouse 4

Mixok Guesthouse 5
Pangkham Guesthouse 6
Phonepaseuth
  Guesthouse 7
Sabaidee Guesthouse 8
Saysouly Guesthouse 9
Syri II Guesthouse 10
Vayakone Guesthouse 11

Eating 🍴
Café Indochine 1

Dao Fa 2
Fathima 3
Joma 4
Just for Fun 5
Khop Chai Deu 6
La Cave de Chateau 7
La Terrasse 19
L'Opera 8
Le Provençal 9
Maison du Café 10
Nam Phou 11

PVO Vietnamese
  Food 12
Sabaidee 13
Scandinavian
  Bakery 14
Soukvimarn 15

Bars & clubs 🎵
Déjà Vu 16
Jazzy Brick 17
Muzaik 18

C-D **Santisouk Guesthouse**, 77/79
Nokeo Khoummane Rd (above **Santisouk Restaurant**), T021-215303. 9 a/c rooms,
some with shared facilities, others with en
suite showers. All are clean but the shared
bathroom is pokey and a bit grungy. Those
situated over the popular restaurant can be
noisy too, but are good value at this rate.

C-D **Syri II Guesthouse**, off Namphu Rd,
T021-241345. Riding on the success of
Syri I (its not so great counterpart near the
National Stadium), this handsome 4-storey
house offers a range of rooms and steep
twisting staircases. The more expensive
rooms have a/c and en suite bathrooms and
are gaudily furnished, but the cheaper rooms
with small wall fans and shared bathrooms
are barely larger than the double beds they
hold and gloomy without windows. The
house is cluttered with an interesting array
of bizarre objects. Breakfast is included.

D **Joe Guesthouse**, 112 Fa Ngum Rd, T021-
241936, F021-215848, joe_guesthouse
@yahoo.com. Wonderful family-run
guesthouse on the river-front. Light,
clean, airy. Good coffee shop downstairs.
Fantastic service. Recommended.

D **Laosakonh Guesthouse**, 26 Francois Ngin
Rd, T021-216571, pongfuji@hotmail.com.
Musty, dingy rooms, decorated with Beer
Lao girl posters. A/c, fan and hot water. If
you can ignore the horrendous decor, it's
not too bad for this price range.

D **Mimi Guesthouse**, 9 Francois Ngin Rd,
T021-250773. Dark, hobbit-hole backpacker
guesthouse with shared facilities, hot water
and fan. Nothing to write home about but
cheap enough. Also rents bicycles.

D **Mixok Guesthouse**, 188 Setthathirat Rd
(opposite Mixay Temple), T021-215606,
bucnong@hotmail.com. Spotless double and
twin rooms, soft mattresses, hot water, fan.
Right next to an internet café for those
virtual trips home. Some visitors have
complained that the walls are too thin.

D **RD Guesthouse**, 37/1 Nokeo Khoummane
Rd, T021-262112 (mobile), songkwangsuk
@hotmail.com. Definitely one for
backpackers, the guesthouse offers
exceptionally cheap dorm accommodation.
Shared facilities, basic rooms, very clean.

D **Sihom Guesthouse**, 27 Sihom Rd,
T021-214562. Mixture of rooms, some with
TVs, some with a/c. All with rattan furniture

and huge hot water bathrooms en suite. The
rooms are kept in excellent condition and a
café out front serves snacks and drinks. Good
value for fan rooms. Recommended.

E-F **Vieng Champa**, Tha Deua Rd, south of
town, just up from the Australian Club,
T021-314412. Some of the cheapest rooms
in Vientiane are available here. Stone cells
with old twin beds, all fan cooled, communal
showers and toilets. Grubby and decaying.

F **Sabaidee Guesthouse**, Setthathirat Rd,
the cheap price reflects the facilities.
Turquoise, swimming pool-esque rooms
with fans. Proprietor speaks reasonable
English if cajoled out of his habitual grump.
Communal washrooms, and always a queue.

Serviced apartments

LL **Parkview Executive Suites** , Luang
Prabang Rd (near the Novotel), T021-250888,
Parkview@laotel.com. Serviced residence
complex of 116 units, catering for both long-
and short-term stays. Fitness centre, pool,
sauna, jacuzzi, tennis court, office space and
secretarial support. A bit off the beaten track.

🍴 Eating

Vientiane *p64, maps p68, p72 and p80*
Cafés, cakeshops and juice bars
Pavement cafés are ten a penny in Vientiane.
You need not walk more than half a block
for some hot coffee or a cold fruit shake.
On Chao Anou you'll find **Liang Xiang
Bakery**, **Sweet Home** and **Nai Xiang
Chai** (good juices and shakes).

♥♥♥-♥♥ **Joma** (aka Healthy and Fresh Bakery),
Setthathirat Rd, T021-215265, bakers
@laopdr.com, 0700-2100 Mon-Sat. Hugely
popular. A very crisp, a/c space that's an
ideal retreat from the streets when it's
scorchingly hot. Nicely decorated with
modern furniture and wireless internet
(about 20,000 kip per hr). Good selection
of tasty pastries, bagels, sandwiches, pastas,
salads, pizzas, yoghurts and coffee. The
service is McDonalds-style efficient but the
food is miles ahead. Highly recommended.

♥♥ **Le Croissant d'Or**, top of Nokeo
Khoummane Rd, T021-223740, 0700-1800
daily. French bakery, small selection but
good cheap croissants.

♥♥ **Maison du Café**, 70 Pang Kham Rd
(near Nam Phou), T021-214781, 0700-1930

Tue-Sun. Specialist coffee shop with proper *baristas* and dozens of different types of coffee to choose from. Also pastries, cakes and snacks.

Scandinavian Bakery, 71/1 Pang Kham Rd, Nam Phou Circle, T021-215199, scandinavian@laonet.net, 0700-2000 daily. Delicious pastries, bread, sandwiches and cakes. Friendly *falang* chef/baker, who made the President of Tanzania's daughter's wedding cake – and has the photo to prove it. Great place for a leisurely coffee and pastries. Pricey for Laos but a necessary European fix for many expats. Recommended.

Delight House of Fruit Shakes, Samsenthai Rd opposite the Asian Pavilion Hotel, T021-212200, 0700-2200 daily. The finest fruit shake in town. Also fruit salads.

Thongphet Cakeshop, Nokeo Khoummane Rd, T021-252818, 0700-1500 daily. Surreal cakes and delicious éclairs. No English spoken. Ridiculously cheap.

Chinese

The Chinese quarter is around Chao Anou, Heng Boun and Khoun Boulom and is a lively spot in the evenings. There are a number of noodle shops here, all of which serve a palatable array of vermicelli, *muu daeng* (red pork), duck and chicken.

Chinese Liao-ning Dumpling Restaurant, Chao Anou Rd, T021-240811, 1100-2230 daily. This restaurant is a firm favourite with the expats and it isn't hard to see why: fabulous steamed or fried dumplings and a wide range of vegetarian dishes. The place is spotlessly clean but the birds in the cages outside are a bit off-putting. No one is ever disappointed with the meals here. Highly recommended.

Happy Garden, Hengboun Rd, T021-241381, 0800-2200 daily. Quiet little restaurant that serves up quick food. Doubles as a massage place (1000-2200) for a great post-dining experience.

Floating restaurants

A couple of floating restaurants are docked on the Mekong, off Fa Ngum Road (just past the Inter Hotel). They cruise down the river for an hour or so in the evening. It's a good idea to get there early so you can watch the sunset, as much of the cruise takes place in the dark. The food is as cheap as chips, so the cruises are exceptionally good value. Recommended.

Champadeng, a bit further along from Lane Xang Av, T020-5526911, 1000-2200 daily, cruise at 1930. This is probably the most popular out of the two. Quite a good selection of Lao dishes and some hilarious English translations: 'fish fried flog' and 'fried fish with three taste'. The food here is as good as you will find anywhere else and when you get bored, you can pop down to the lower level and belt out a few tunes on the karaoke – the Lao diners will love it.

Lane Xang, T021-243397, 1000-2230 daily, cruise at 1900. Most meals are around US$2.50.

French and Italian

Cote D'Azur, 63/64 Fa Ngum Rd, T021-217252, jmdazur@laotel.com, 1130-2230 daily. Fine selection of dishes from the south of France, plus excellent wood-fired pizzas and delicious seafood dishes. Recently renovated kitchen and menu. Recommended.

Dao Fa, Setthathirat Rd (across from Kop Chai Deu), T021-215657, www.daofa-bistro.com, 0800-2200 daily. Modern European restaurant offering homemade pasta, crêpes and wood-fired pizza. Great atmosphere with a miscellany of pop-art paintings adorning the white walls.

La Cave de Chateau, Nam Phou Circle, T021-212192, 1100-1400 and 1800-2200 daily. This restaurant around the Nam Phou Fountain is supposed to look like a grotto but is just a little odd. Pretty good set menu, with delicious grilled squid and steaks. Dine on the upstairs balcony.

Le Nadao, Ban Donmieng (on the right-hand side of the Patuxai roundabout), T020-550 4884, 1100-1400 and 1700-2230 daily. This place is difficult to find but definitely worth every second spent searching the back streets of Vientiane in the dark. Sayavouth, who trained in Paris and New York, produces simply delectable French cuisine: soups, venison, lamb, puddings. Fantastic. The US$5 set lunch menu is one of the best lunches you will get in town. Recommended.

Le Provencal, Nam Phou Circle, T021-216248, 1100-1400 and 1800-2200 daily. Long-standing quaint Italian restaurant that generally gets dwarfed by its partners on the other side of the fountain. Serves a good plate of pasta.

Le Ranch (aka Caravan), Phonxay Rd, T021-413700, 1100-1400 and 1800-2200 daily. Looks like a country and western bar but offers distinctly European food. Good family restaurant offering pizzas, barbecue and other French delicacies. Playground for children.

Le Silapa, Sihom Rd, opposite Shell petrol station near traffic lights, T021-219689, 1130-1400 and 1800-2200 daily. Anthony and Fred provide a fantastic menu and atmosphere for fine dining without blowing the budget. Great set lunch menu. Part of the profits are donated to disadvantaged families, usually for expensive but life-saving surgical procedures. Recommended. Closes annually for a month during Jul.

Le Vendôme, Soi Inpeng Rd, T021-216402,1030-1400 and 1800-2230 daily. Run by a Frenchman whose son trains the Lao bicycle squad. A/c inside and an outside terrace, good ambience. Food is quite stodgy and old-fashioned: fish, deer, rabbit, steaks, pizzas, plus soufflés made from anything and everything. Choice of wines. The propietor is renowned for shouting at his staff, who are said to live in perpetual fear.

L'Opera, Nam Phou Circle, T021-215099, 1130-1400 and 1830-2200 daily. A/c Italian restaurant, pompous, cold and overpriced but with delicious ice cream and a wide range of pizza and pasta dishes, also barbecue steaks.

Nam Phou, 20 Nam Phou Circle, T021-216248, 1100-1400 and 1800-2000 daily. Opened 20 years ago. French, upmarket and quietly sophisticated, with staggering French wine list. Includes some unique Lao dishes.

La Terrasse, 55/4 Nokeo Koummane Rd, T021-218550, bpricco@yahoo.fr, 1100-1400 and 1800-2200 Mon-Sat. This is the best European restaurant in town in terms of variety and price. Large fail-safe menu offering French, European, Lao and Mexican

food. Good desserts, especially the rich chocolate mousse and a good selection of French wine. Fantastic service. Reasonable prices with excellent *plat du jour* each day. Highly recommended.

Indian

Taste of India, Lao Hotel , 53/9 Hengboun Rd, T020-525 5403, 1200-1400 and 1700-2230 daily. By far the best Indian in Vientiane. A delicious lunch buffet is available for 40,000 kip. A bit pricier than the other Indian restaurants but worth it.

Fathima, 2/26 Fa Ngum Rd (near Lang Xang Hotel), T021-219097, 0900-2200 daily. Cheapest and fastest Indian in town. North and south Indian cuisine as well as Malaysian food. Scrumptious. Fantastic service.

Nazim, 39 Fa Ngum Rd, T021-223480, 1000-2230 daily. Authentic Indian (north and south) and Halal food, very popular with backpackers. Indoor and outdoor seating. They have another restaurant in Vang Vieng as well as a branch in Luang Prabang.

International

Quite a few places listed here under 'international' also serve good Lao/Thai food and a handful are also experimenting with fusion cuisine.

Sticky Fingers, Francois Ngin Rd (opposite the Tai Pan Hotel), T021-215972, 1000-2300 Tue-Sun. Very popular small restaurant and bar serving Lao and international dishes including fantastic salads, pasta, burgers and such like. Fantastic comfort food and the best breakfast in town. Great cocktails, lively atmosphere, nice setting. The staff, particularly Mr Nam, are as sharp as a tack. Deliveries available. Stickies should be the first pit-stop for every visitor needing to get grounded quickly, as food aside, the expats who frequent the joint are full to the brim with local knowledge. Highly recommended.

Alexia, 7 Fa Ngum Rd, T021-241349, 1100-2300 daily. Popular with tourists, Alexia specializes in Mexican cuisine. The food is a tad overpriced and can be pretty standard. On the up side there is live music after 2000.

Full Moon Café, François Ngin Rd (opposite the Tai Pan Hotel), T021-243373, 1000-2200 daily. Delectable Asian fusion cuisine and Western favourites. Huge pillows, good lighting and great music make this place very relaxing. Fantastic chicken wrap and some pretty good Asian tapas options. Book exchange. Recommended.

Inter, Chao Anou Rd (part of hotel), 1100-1400 and 1800-2200 daily. Locally renowned for its steaks and Western-influenced meals, which can be less than average at times. When they're good, they're great but when they're bad they're terrible. Check that your chips are cooked and that fish is defrosted. Reasonably priced and quite funky since its recent renovations.

Sabaidee, diagonally opposite PlaNet Computers on Setthathirat Rd. Serves a good American breakfast alongside its menu of cheap Lao food in a nice lantern-lit setting. TV often shows BBC news. Open 0800-2200 daily.

Santisouk, 77/79 Nokeo Khoummane Rd, entrance to stadium just off Samsenthai, 0700-1400 and 1800-2200 daily. This place looks like a Communist diner but the food is good for the price. Extensive French menu and reasonably priced sizzling steaks. Also serves good breakfast.

Xayoh, Nokeo Khoummane Rd, T021-262111, www.xayoh.com, 0800-2330 daily. Attractive bar and restaurant next to the hideous Lao National Cultural Hall. The name of this place gives little hint of the cuisine. Salads, pizzas, burgers plus Lao/Thai food. The restaurant's speciality is a Sunday roast of beef and Yorkshire pud etc for homesick Brits. Double-check your order as the staff have a tendency to serve the wrong thing. Deliveries available.

Japanese

Fuji Wara, Luang Prabang Rd, west of Wat Inpeng, T021-222210, 1200-2200 daily. Elegant restaurant with traditional Japanese decor. Great atmosphere that will keep you reaching for extra sake after a delicious meal.

Koto, Phoneexay Rd, T021-412849, 1000-1400 and 1700-2200 Sun-Fri. A good Japanese restaurant but without the reputation of the Sakura; a touch cheaper, too, with traditional floor level tables.

Sakura, Luang Prabang Rd, Km 2/Soi 3 (the Soi runs along the side of the Novotel), T021-212274, 1030-1400 and 1730-2200 Tue-Sun, closed lunch Mon. Regarded as the best Japanese food in town. Expensive for Vientiane but good value by international standards. The restaurant is in a converted private house.

Tokyo Kitchen, 3/127 Chao Anou Rd, T021-214924, kitchen@jumping-lao.com. Great little restaurant and usually quite busy. However, it has a limited menu and doesn't offer a lot of the traditional favourites.

Korean sindat

The Korean-style barbecue, *sindat*, is extremely popular, especially among the younger Lao, as it is a very social event and very cheap. It involves cooking your finely sliced meat on a hot plate in the middle of the table, while forming a broth with your vegetables around the sides of the tray. Reminiscent of a '70s fondue evening.

Seendat, Sihom Rd, T021-213855, 1730-2200 daily. This restaurant has been in existence for well over 20 years and is a favourite amongst the older Lao for its clean food and good atmosphere. About US$1 per person more expensive than most other places but this is reflected in the quality. Recommended

Seendat Somphouthong, Luang Prabang Rd, T021-250540, 1030-2200 daily. Distinguishes itself from many other barbecue restaurants by using a delicious prawn sauce instead of the standard peanut. A bit far from the centre of town but worth the trip.

Lao

The absolutely best place to get Lao food is from the open-air stalls that line the banks of the Mekong along Fa Ngum. The restaurants are ridiculously low on price and high on atmosphere, particularly at night with their flickering candles. From time to time the government kicks all the eateries off the patch but they usually return with a vengeance. The **Dong Palane Night Market**, on Dong Palane, and the night markets near the corner of Chao Anou and Khoun Boulom Rd are also good places to go for Lao stall food. There are various other congregations of stalls and vendors around town, most of which set up shop around 1730 and close down by 2100. Be sure to sample Lao ice cream with coconut sticky rice.

Kua Lao, 111 Samsenthai Rd, T021-215777, F021-215777, 1000-1400 and 1700-2230 daily. A tastefully refurbished colonial house-turned-restaurant provides a sophisticated atmosphere for quality Lao and Thai food. Avoid the set menu. Good Lao music and traditional dancing. Some locals believe that the restaurant has sold its Lao culinary credentials to the tourist dollar but most visitors to Laos will enjoy their meal here. Pricey for Laos.

Lane Xang Hotel Restaurant, Fa Ngum Rd, T021-214100, 1100-2200 daily. Overlooks the river and produces Lao specials such as baked moose, grilled eel, baked turtle. Some international dishes also available. On Wed the restaurant hosts a cabaret show (which includes a contortionist and bird impressionist).

Mekong, Km 4, Tha Deua Rd, near the Australian Club, towards the bridge, T021-312480, 0900-2200 daily. Good food beside the Mekong, drinks on the balcony at sunset, international and Lao cuisine.

Soukvimarn, Bartolomie Rd, Ban Sisaket, near That Dam, T021-214441, 1100-1400 and 1800-2100 daily. Heavily influenced by traditional southern Lao flavours. Well worth the experience as it offers the opportunity to tempt the tastebuds with a wider variety of Lao cuisine than most other eateries offer.

Tamnak Lao Restaurant, That Luang Rd, T021-413562, 1200-2200 daily. It's well worth deviating from the main Nam Phou area for a bite to eat here. This restaurant and its sister branch in Luang Prabang have a reputation for delivering outstanding Lao and Thai food, usually prepared with a modern twist.

Airport Buffet, Wattay International Airport. The buffet is a favourite with senior-ranking Lao government officials and local VIPs who make the long hike out during their lunch hour. It represents unparalleled value: 50,000 kip for as much Lao food (curries, fried dishes etc), Japanese food (sushi), dessert, coffee and tea as you can stomach. Very popular, open for lunch and dinner, highly recommended.

Just for Fun, 57/2 Pang Kham Rd, opposite Lao Airlines. Good Lao food with vegetarian dishes, coffees, soft drinks and the largest selection of teas in Laos, if not Southeast Asia. The atmosphere is relaxed with a/c, newspapers and comfy chairs (also sells textiles and other handicrafts). No smoking. A bit slow but recommended.

Khop Chai Deu, Setthathirat Rd, on the corner of Nam Phou Rd, 0800-2330 daily. This recently renovated bar/restaurant is one of the city's most popular venues with both locals and travellers. Garden seating, good atmosphere at night with soft lantern lighting, and an eclectic menu of Indian, Italian, Korean and international dishes (many of which come from nearby restaurants). The best value are the local Lao dishes though, which are made on site and toned down for the *falang* palate. Also serves draft or bottled beer at a pleasant a/c bar. Excellent lunch buffet.

Vegetarian

Joy Vegetarian in the Talaat Sao food court comes highly recommended for vegetarian meals. Also try to find the unnamed restaurant in the lane behind Talaat Kudin, which serves a spectacular vegetarian buffet for 10,000 kip. Other restaurants which do good vegetarian dishes are **Just for Fun** (see Lao section, above), the **Full Moon Café** (see International, above) and **Nazim** (see Indian, above).

Vietnamese

For cheap Vietnamese food, there's a good selection of stalls on Sisangvong Rd (Ban Sisanvong) near the Japanese Embassy, a couple of km north of the centre. There is also a conglomeration of Vietnamese restaurants around That Luang.

Café Indochine, 199 Setthathirat Rd, T021-216758, 1030-2230 daily. Intimate restaurant with delectable cuisine, including zucchini flower salad and grilled chicken.

Nam Nuang, Heng Boun Rd, 0800-2200 daily. Known for its pork barbecue, spring rolls and the best fish sauce in town. Recommended.

Nong Vong Restaurant, on the road between Sisavong Rd and That Luang, T021-415818. This little, tucked away eatery is an all-time favourite with long-term expats who endearingly refer to it as "Vongs". Impeccable service and a huge selection of superb Lao, Thai and Vietnamese-inspired dishes. You can take 4 people to dinner and still come back with change from US$10. Open for dinner, but lunch really seems to be their forte. Highly recommended.

PVO Vietnamese Food, 344 Samsenthai Rd, T021-215265, 0700-2100/2200 daily (sometimes closes earlier if baguettes run out but never before 2100). A firm favourite. Full menu of freshly prepared Vietnamese food but best known for its baguettes, stuffed with your choice of paté, salad, cheese, coleslaw, vegetables and ham. Fantastic fresh spring rolls. Bikes and motorbikes for rent too. Keep an eye out for the miniature dog wearing the Hannibal Lector style dog-mask – a very popular doggy accessory with those Vientiane citizens paranoid about rabies. Brilliant cheap food and a joyfully raucous atmosphere make this a fantastic choice.

○ Bars and clubs

Vientiane p64, maps p68, p72 and p80
Bars
The bars of the debauched pre-revolutionary days have faded into legend: the **Purple Porpoise**, the **White Rose** and the renowned **Les Rendezvous des Amis**, run by Madame Lulu, which reportedly offered patrons 'warm beer and oral sex', are now only dim and distant memories.

There are a number of bar stalls, which set up in the evening along Quai Fa Ngum (the river road); a good place for a cold beer as the sun sets and the evening breeze picks up. A new promenade has sprung up on the banks of the river, and quite a few restaurants have moved a few metres to exploit the better views offered by this river frontage.

As a general rule most bars will close at 2300 in accordance with the local curfew laws; some places seem to be able to stay open past this time although that varies on a day-to-day basis. Vientiane government officials go through phases of shutting down clubs and bars and restricting curfews.
Abstract, Tha Deua Rd, T020-771138. The original version of the Jazzy Brick (see below) is located away from the city centre so it's not as popular with tourists. As the name suggests, the subdued bar has adopted an artistic theme and has a few paintings and decorations to reflect this. Serves bar snacks. The only problem is that if you stay out drinking past curfew here, it may be hard to get back to the centre as tuk-tuks can be a bit thin on the ground.
Déjà Vu, Nam Phou Circle. Very upmarket, intimate cocktail bar, with a plethora of

drinks available. Set in a small, white minimalist room, it is a bit out of place in Vientiane. The proprietor takes his cocktails very seriously. Recommended.
Jazzy Brick, Setthathirat Rd, near Phimphone Market, brown building on the corner of the lane that leads to Wat Xieng Khoune, T020-7711138. New in 2005. Very sophisticated small modern den, ambient jazz, dim lighting and good wines. This place somehow manages to stay open past curfew most nights due to its low profile. Good spot for quiet or last drinks.
Khop Chai Deu on Setthathirat Rd (near the corner with Nam Phou). Probably the most popular bar for tourists in Vientiane. Casual setting, with beer garden and 2 floors. Also serves food (see Eating: Lao, above). Recommended.
Muzaik, Manthathurath Rd, T020-770 7899. A funky little bar that is a popular haunt with locals as the last stop on Fri and Sat nights. Usually a DJ present but the clientele prefers to drink rather than dance.
Samlor Pub, Setthathirat Rd. Snooker, darts, pizza and the only place in town where you can play table-soccer. Sometimes the clientele can be a bit so-so.
Sticky Fingers, Francois Ngin Rd, opposite the Tai Pan Hotel. The main drinking hole for expats. Small and intimate bar and restaurant run by 2 Australian women. Very atmospheric and a lot of fun. Cheap cocktails 1800-2000 Wed and 1800-1900 Fri. Also serves food (see Eating: International, above). Highly recommended.
Sunset Bar (aka **The End of the World**), end of Fa Ngum Rd. Open wooden house overlooking the Mekong with good atmosphere. Another favourite meeting place for expats to watch the sunset.
That Dam Wine House, next to That Dam, T021-222647. Offers a great selection of international wines in a pleasant and relaxing environment.
Wind West, opposite Russian Cultural Centre by traffic lights, Luang Prabang Rd. Very popular with expats and tourists, as it usually stays open after 2300. Many wild nights happen here.

Clubs
Many of the discos in town, both those in hotels and independent set-ups, sometimes

feature live bands usually playing a mixture of Lao and Thai music and cover versions of Western rock classics. Vientiane lacks good places to dance, since the most popular Western-style clubs were closed down in late 2004. Some Lao places are still running but you are advised to take earplugs as they like to play the music extremely loud.

Marina, Luang Prabang Rd, behind the Marina Bowling Centre. Popular with wealthy young Lao. Drinks of choice are either Beer Lao or Johnny Walker Black. Bring earplugs.

Meena, Km 3, Tha Deua Rd, just before the turn-off for Sok Paluang Rd. You'll hear the music before you see the over-the-top lighting arrangement. Somehow this place continues to operate despite being a noise nuisance to the surrounding residential area. Men should not be startled by the complimentary massage in the urinals – it doesn't go any further than a shoulder rub. The topless dancers are long gone but it's a popular spot among younger Lao people.

● Entertainment

Vientiane *p64, maps p68, p72 and p80*
Circus
The National Circus, known as **Hong Kanyasin**, holds infrequent performances in an old Russian tent, usually in conjunction with the French Cultural Centre. The Performances usually include acrobatics and clowns and are worthwhile if you're in town at the right time.

Fairs and amusements
There's often a ferris wheel and bouncy castle at **That Luang** in the evenings, particularly if it is a public holiday or celebration. A more reliable option is to make the haul out to the **ITEC Centre**, where there is a collection of rides, including a ferris wheel, merry-go-rounds and dodgem cars. Popular at weekends.

Film
Blue Sky Café, on the corner of Setthathirat and Chao Anou rds. DVD movies are generally shown daily at 1200 and 1900 on the 2nd floor.
French Cultural Centre, Lang Xang Rd, T021-215764, 1930 Tue and Thu, 1530 Sat,

US$1. Screens the occasional French film and also hosts the Southeast Asian film festival. The programme is distributed around restaurants in town, like Sticky Fingers, and often promoted in the *Vientiane Times*.
Lao International Trade Exhibition Centre (ITEC), T4 Rd, Ban Phonethane Neua, T021-416374, laoitecc@hotmail.com. A range of international films, screened on quite a random basis.

Karaoke
This could almost be the Lao national sport and there's nothing like bonding with the locals over a heavy-duty karaoke session. Karaoke places are everywhere – just keep your ears out for the off-key bellowing. Good spots include the **Blue Note** in the Lao Plaza Hotel or the more expensive, upmarket **Don Chan Palace** (for both, see Sleeping). **Champadeng Cruise** also has a good karaoke room below deck (see Eating: Floating restaurants). And no one can hear your howling when you're out on the river. Recommended.

Live music
Bands will perform almost every night at **Khop Chai Deu** and **Alexia** (see Eating, above) and at the **Music House**, on Fa Ngum. The **French Cultural Centre**, on Lang Xang, hosts a variety of musical performances, from local bands through to hip-hop ensembles. Look out for **Overdance**, a Thai-influenced pop fusion band, and **The Cells**, who perform everything from death metal to sappy love songs (they also like a costume change or two). At the time of writing there was a very popular Western cover band called **The Reunion** playing regular gigs around town on their self-titled 'Revoke My Visa Tour'.

Occasionally, music concerts and beauty pageants are held at the **Lao National Culture Hall**, opposite the National Museum. No official notice is given of forthcoming events but announcements sometimes appear in the *Vientiane Times* and large banners will flank the building.

Traditional dance
Lane Xang Hotel puts on an excellent traditional dance show every night 1900-2145 in its restaurant, accompanied

by Lao musicians, while you eat. **Kuo Lao Restaurant** also has traditional Lao performances nightly (for both, see Eating). **Lao National Theatre**, Manthatulat Rd, opposite Mixay Guesthouse, T021-242978. Daily shows of traditional Lao dancing, from 2030. Tickets, US$7, available at the theatre.

⊕ Festivals and events

Vientiane *p64, maps p68, p72 and p80*
1st weekend in Apr Pi Mai (Lao New Year) is celebrated with a 3-day festival and a huge water fight. It is advisable to put your wallet into a plastic bag and invest in a turbo water pistol. There are numerous *bacis* (good luck celebrations) and the traditional greeting at this time of year is "*Sok Dee Pi Mai*" (good luck for the new year).
12 Oct Freedom of the French Day is a public holiday.
Oct Boun Ok Phansa is a beautiful event on the night of the full moon at the end of Buddhist Lent. Candles are lit in all the homes and a candle-lit processions take place around the city's wats and through the streets. Then, thousands of banana-leaf boats holding flowers, tapers and candles are floated out onto the river. The boats signify your bad luck floating away. On the second day, boat races (*souang heua*) take place, with 50 or so men in each boat; they power up the river in perfect unison. Usually, a bunch of foolhardy expats also try to compete, much to the amusement of the locals. An exuberant event, with plenty of merrymaking.
Nov (date varies each year) Boun That Luang is celebrated in all of Vientiane's *thats* but most notably at That Luang (the national shrine). Originally a ceremony in which nobles swore allegiance to the king and constitution, it amazingly survived the Communist era. On the festival's most important day, **Thak Baat**, thousands of Lao people pour into the temple at 0600 and again at 1700 to pay homage. Monks travel from across the country to collect offerings and alms from the pilgrims. It is a really beautiful ceremony, with monks chanting and thousands of people praying. Women who attend should invest in a traditional *sinh*. A week-long carnival surrounds the festival with fireworks, music and dancing.

The entertainments range from dodgems to 'freak' shows, a fascinating cavalcade of people and events. Recommended

⊙ Shopping

Vientiane *p64, maps p68, p72 and p80*
Books
A small selection of maps and books on Laos can be found in the **Lane Xang** and **Lani I** hotels and in **Phimphone Market**. The **Full Moon Café** has a book exchange.
Kosila Books, Nokeo Khoummane Rd, T021-241352. A good selection of English, Lao, German and French books, maps and guides. Kosila has also opened another shop near That Dam.
Vientiane Book Centre (previously Raintree Books), 54/1 Pang Kham Rd, T/F021-212031. Raintree was the first English-language bookshop in Laos and still has the best selection in town. Coffee-table books, glossy magazines and maps as well as specialist Lao PDR publications. Book exchange.

Clothing
See also Tailors and Textiles, below.
Cama Craft, Mixay Rd, T021-501271. Handmade clothes in Hmong styles.
Coleur d'Asie, Nam Phou Circle. Modern-style Asian clothing, very well known and a favourite of locals and expats. Pricey but high-quality fusion fashion.
Ekhor Boutique, Pang Kham Rd, T021-517247/668, F021-416677. A small shop boasting a high-quality selection of clothes and handicrafts, with prices to match.
Laha, Francois Ngin Rd. Cotton/silk-blend clothing of a more modern Japanese style.
Mandarina, Samsenthai Rd, T021-223857. Beautiful contemporary fashions in Lao silk, great colours, designed by stylish half-French Isabelle Souvanlasy.
Yani, Mixay Arcade, Setthathirat Rd. French-designed fashion using local fabrics, good quality and good value (by European standards), also a small selection of crafts.

Food
Phimphone Market, Setthathirat Rd, opposite Khop Chai Deu Restaurant. Known for its red chicken logo, this supermarket has everything a foreigner could ask for in terms of imported food,

drink, magazines, translated books, personal hygiene products, household items and much more. Friendly efficient service and Phimphone herself is a source of information on Vientiane and Laos.

Simuang Minimarket, Samsenthai Rd, east end of Wat Simuang. Supermarket with a very good selection of produce, including Western food, wines, cheese and meats.

Udom Pathana, Dong Palane Rd, T021-214256. Has a reasonable range of cheap food imports.

Vinotheque La Cave, 354 Samsenthai Rd, with the big wine barrel out front, T021-217700. French wine shop with a large range of wine, run by Claude Monnier, who serves aperitifs with cheese.

Galleries

Lao Gallery, Nokeo Khoummane Rd. Exhibits by local artists.

Mask Gallery, Nong Bong Rd, before the Japanese embassy, 0800-1600 Mon-Fri.

Oot-Ni Art Gallery, 306 Samsenthai Rd, with another door on Heng Boun Rd, T021-215911, T020-51453. A real Aladdin's cave of handicrafts and artefacts, including cottons and silks. Quite pricey but worth a look. Also a branch in the Morning Market.

T'Shop Lai Gallery, Wat Inpeng Soi. Funky studio exhibiting local sculptures and art. Artists can be seen at work Mon-Sat. Proceeds are donated to Lao Youth projects.

Hair and beauty

There are several hairdressers dotted around the city. Men should be careful not to wind up with a bowl cut.

Barber Jam, just off Khou Vieng Rd (opposite swampland). Cute Lao barbershop (and youth centre) where you can get a haircut for under US$1 while someone plays the guitar to you. Don't ask for anything too complex. Also have a 'ear coning' service.

Cha Ae Beauty Salon, 10 Ban Watchaan (same street as Inter Hotel), T021-241523. Hair cuts and dying, plus facials, manicures, pedicures and waxing. A good range of international beauty products.

Elly Boutique, Setthathirat Rd near the Kodak shop, T021-243675. Women's and men's fashion cuts, dying, facials and waxing, plus reportedly the best manicure and pedicure in Vientiane.

Rd, T021-216542. Soukanh Chantarath, the proprietor, trained at Vidal Sassoon and Tony and Guy in London. Great place to get a reasonably cheap hairdo from an internationally acclaimed hairdresser. Cutting, colouring, straightening, manicures, pedicures, waxing and eyelash tinting.

Handicrafts and antiques

The main shops are along Setthathirat, Samsenthai and Pang Kham. The Morning Market (**Talaat Sao**) is also worth a browse, with artefacts, such as appliquéd panels, decorated hats and sashes, basketwork both old and new, small and large wooden tobacco boxes, sticky-rice lidded baskets, axe pillows, embroidered cushions and a wide range of silver work. The likelihood of finding authentic antiques is pretty low as the Thai dealers scavenged their way through the country many years ago. **Talaat Kudin** offers cheaper artefacts and silks but not as great a selection as Talaat Sao. Across the road from Talaat Sao is a small ethnic handicraft market, which offers a range of cane baskets, trinkets, weaving and silk.

Ekhor Boutique, Pang Kham Rd. Textiles, clothes and handicrafts.

Indochine Handicrafts, Samsenthai Rd next to the big wine barrel, T021-263619, maiphone@hotmail.com. Larger size collectibles, not really suitable for the suitcase shopper.

MaiChan Fine Arts & Handicrafts, Samsenthai Rd, T021-263619, maiphone @hotmail.com. Neat little shop with lots of treasures.

Mixay Boutique, Setthathirat Rd, Ban Mixay. Wooden and textile products.

Namsin Handicrafts, Setthathirat Rd. Wooden objects.

Jewellery and silverware

Many of the stones sold in Vientiane are of dubious quality, but silver and gold are more reliable. Gold is always 24 carat and is good value. Silver is cheap but not necessarily pure silver. Nevertheless, the selection is interesting, with amusing animals, decorated boxes, old coins, earrings and silver belts. There's a particularly wide selection in the Morning Market (**Talaat Sao**). Silver, gold and gem shops on Samsenthai are concentrated

The art of ikat

In the handicraft shops and at the Morning Market in Vientiane, it is possible to buy distinctively patterned cotton and silk *ikat*. *Ikat* is a technique of patterning cloth characteristic of Southeast Asia and is produced from the hills of Burma to the islands of Eastern Indonesia. The word comes from the Malay word '*mengikat*' which means to bind or tie. Very simply, bundles of warp or weft fibres (or, in one Balinese case, both) are tied with material or fibre (or more often plastic string these days), so that they resist the action of the dye. Hence the technique's name – resist dyeing. By dyeing, retying and dyeing again through a number of cycles it is possible to build up complex patterns. This initial pre-weaving process can take anything from two to 10 days, depending on the complexity of the design. *Ikat* is distinguishable by the bleeding of the dye which inevitably occurs no matter how carefully the threads are tied; this gives the finished cloth a blurred finish. The earliest *ikats* date from the 14th-15th centuries.

To prepare the cloth for dyeing, the warp or weft is strung tight on a frame. Individual threads, or groups of threads, are then tied together with fibre and leaves. In some areas wax is then smeared on top to help in the resist process. The main colour is usually dyed first, secondary colours later.

With complex patterns (which are done from memory, plans are only required for new designs) and using natural dyes, it may take up to six months to produce a piece of cloth. Today, the pressures of the market place mean that it is more likely that cloth is produced using chemical dyes (which need only one short soaking, not multiple long ones – six hours or so – as with some natural dyes), and design motifs have generally become larger and less complex. Traditionally, warp *ikat* used cotton while weft *ikat* used silk. Silk in many areas has given way to cotton, and cotton sometimes to synthetic yarns.

along the stretch opposite the Asian Pavilion Hotel; there are also some gold shops further west towards the Chinese quarter.

Doris Jewelry, 2 shops in Lao Plaza Shopping Centre. Silverware, gems and antiques.

Saigon Bijoux, 367-69 Samsenthai Rd (opposite the big wine barrel), T021-214783. Wide range of jewellery including quality imported diamonds from Belgium. All settings are handmade on site.

Markets

Vientiane has several excellent markets. **Talaat Sao** (Morning Market), off Lane Xang Av, is currently undergoing major renovations that are expected to be finished sometime in 2007 but it's still the biggest and the best. It's busiest in the mornings (from around 1000), but operates all day. There are money

exchanges here (quite a good rate), and a good selection of food stalls selling Western food, soft drinks and ice cream sundaes. It sells imported Thai goods, electrical appliances, watches, DVDs and CDs, stationery, cosmetics, a selection of handicrafts (see above), an enormous choice of Lao fabrics, and upstairs there is a large clothing section, silverware, some gems and gold and a few handicraft stalls. **Talaat Kudin**, on the other side of the bus stop, has an interesting produce section, in addition to many of the same handicrafts and silks as the Morning Market. It is a lot cheaper than Talaat Sao and can be even more so, if you're prepared to bargain hard.

Talaat Thong Khoun Khum, on the corner of Khoun Khum and Dong Miang roads, is the largest produce market. It is sometimes known as the evening market but it's busiest in the mornings.

Other markets include **Talaat That Luang**, south of the parade ground, **Talaat Dong Palane**, Dong Palane Rd (there's a sign near the temple pointing down a lane as the bulk of the market has been moved just away from the main road), and **Talaat Chin**, which is good for electrical goods, CDs and DVDs, kids' toys, kitsch decorations, clothes, furniture and cheap imported tat.

Photo processing
Konica Plaza, 110/5 Samsenthai Rd, is the best film developer in Vientiane and also offers cheap CD-burning and photocopying services. Next door are **Kodak Express** and **Venus Colorlab** (also on Heng Boun Rd). Many more dotted around the town and in the **Morning Market**.

Tailors
There are many Vietnamese tailors along Samsenthai and Pang Kham roads (north of Nam Phou fountain). **Queen's Beauty Tailor**, by the fountain, is quite good for women's clothes, but allow at least a week. Also try **Adam Tailleurs**, 72 Pang Kham Rd, and **TV Chuong**, 395 Samsenthai Rd. There are also a few tailors in the **Morning Market**.

Textiles
Every hue and design is available in the **Morning Market**. For cheaper (but still very good-quality) fabric just pop across the road to **Talaat Kudin**; the fabric section is at the back of the market, in the covered area. A *sinh*, the traditional Lao skirt, can be made within the day for a US$1-2 extra; just pick the length of fabric and the patterned band for the bottom of the skirt.
Kanchana, 102 Samsenthai Rd, That Dam Square or Ban Nongtha Tai, handwoven silks and cottons.
Lao Cotton, Luang Prabang Rd, out towards Wattay Airport, approximately ¼ mile on right from Novotel Hotel, T021-215840. Good range of material, shirts, handbags and housecoats, ask to see the looms. Another branch on Samsenthai.
Lao Textiles by Carol Cassidy, Nokeo Koummane Rd, T021-212123, F021-216205, 0800-1200 and 1400-1700 Mon-Fri, 0800-1200 Sat. Exquisite silk fabrics, including *ikat* and traditional Lao designs, made by an American in a beautifully

renovated colonial property. Dyeing, spinning, designing and weaving all done on site (and can be viewed). It's pricey, but many of the weavings are real works of art; custom-made pieces available on request.

Videos
Cheap DVDs and VCDs can be bought from the **Morning Market**. **Walkman Village**, Fa Ngum Rd, T021-213609, also stocks a selection of good-quality DVDs and CDs, along with goods geared towards foreigners, from handbags through to binoculars.

▲ Activities and tours

Vientiane *p64, maps p68, p72 and p80*
Aerobics
Open-air aerobics sessions are held at the amphitheatre on the riverfront (Fa Ngum) every evening 1700-1730. Locals love it when foreigners join in. Less public aerobics at **Sengdara Gym** (see below).

Cooking
Thongbay Guesthouse (see Sleeping), T021-242292. Cooking classes, covering all aspects of meal preparation, from purchasing the ingredients to eating the meal. Must be arranged in advance.

Cycling
Bicycles are available for hire from several places in town, see Transport, page 93. A good outing is to cycle downstream along the banks of the Mekong. Cycle south on Tha Deua Rd until Km 5 and then turn right down one of the tracks (there are a number) towards the river bank. A path, suitable for bicycles, follows the river beginning at about Km 4.5. There are monasteries and drink sellers en route to maintain interest and energy.

Go-karting
ITECC Go Karts, in the car park underneath ITECC, 1200-2200 daily. Only 4 karts but they are very good quality on a smooth track. Helmets and racing gloves provided. You can try to solve logic puzzles to win extra laps – not as easy as it sounds. 45,000 kip for 5 mins, 70,000 kip for 10 mins or pay by the lap.

Golf

Santisuk Lane Xang Golf Club, Km 14, Tha Deua Rd, T021-812022, 0700-1800 daily. 9-hole course, open to the public, with modest green fees and caddies available. To get there, catch Bus No 14 from the Morning Market.

Vientiane Golf Club, Km 6, Route 13 South, T021-515820, 0630-sunset daily. Short 9-hole course that's a favourite for its friendly atmosphere and swimming pool. Cheap green fees include the caddy; clubs available for rent. It's customary to tip your caddy about US$1 per 9 holes. To get there, turn right at the Peugeot showroom (6 km south of town), left after bridge, right at the fork and right at the top of the hill.

Language courses

Vientiane College, That Luang Rd, T021-414873. The best Lao courses. Ask for Seng.

Massage, saunas and spas

The best massage in town is given by the blind masseuses in a little street off Samsenthai Rd, 2 blocks down from Simuang Minimart (across from Wat Simuang). There are 2 blind masseuse businesses side-by-side and either one is fantastic: **Traditional Clinic**, T020-5659177 and **Porm Clinic**, T020-627633 (no English spoken). They are marked by blue signs off both Khou Vieng and Samsenthai roads. Recommended.

LV Spa, Samsenthai Rd, T030-5256699, 0900-2000 daily. Opened in early 2005, this is the first large-scale spa in town and has certainly raised the bar in terms of service. Featuring all the usual forms of treatment at a fraction of the prices you'd expect to pay in the West.

Mixay Massage, Fa Ngum, 1700-2100 daily. Lao massage (US$5 per hr), facials, manicure, pedicure and sauna.

Oasis Massage and Beauty, 7 Mixay Rd, T021-243579. Very good, strong massages (*keng* – means strong in Lao).

Papaya Spa, opposite Wat Xieng Veh, T021-216550, 0900-2000 daily. A favourite among locals looking to spoil themselves. Surrounded by beautiful gardens, you feel more relaxed from the minute you walk through the gates. Massage, sauna, facials. Lovely environs. Recommended.

Wat Sok Paluang, Sok Paluang. Peaceful leafy setting in the compound of Wat Sok Paluang. Herbal sauna, followed by herb tea (2,000 kip) and massage by 2 young male masseurs (4,000 kip); very relaxing but ladies should watch out for groping. Vipassana meditation is held every Sat 1600-1730, free, T021-216214. To get there, walk through the small stupas to the left of the Wat; the sauna is a rickety building on stilts on the right-hand side, recognizable by the blackened store underneath.

Soccer

Soccer is very popular in Laos, with regular national league matches being played at the **National Stadium** in Vientiane. In fact, this is probably one of the few places in the world where you can see World Cup qualifying matches for under US$1.

Sports clubs and fitness centres

Several hotels in town permit non-residents to use their fitness facilities for a small fee, including the **Tai Pan** (rather basic), **Lao Plaza**, **Lane Xang**, **Don Chan** and **Novotel** (for all, see Sleeping, above).

Australia Club Recreation Centre, Km 3, Tha Deua Rd, T021-314921. A beautiful setting, with one of the nicest pools in Vientiane. It's a lovely place for a swim followed by a glass of wine as the sun sets. Also a small restaurant and a squash court. Short-term membership for US$10 per day or US$20 for a family. It is cheaper if you get a member to sign you in; loiter around some of the expat drinking holes and you might find someone willing. A tuk-tuk from the centre costs 20,000-30,000 kip.

Sengdara, 5/77 Phonthan Rd, T021-414061, sengdara_fitness@yahoo.com, 0500-2200 daily. Modern, well-equipped fitness centre with gym, pool and sauna. US$5 for use of all the facilities for a day, massage extra.

Swimming

Australia Club, (see Sports clubs, above).
Lane Xang Hotel (see Sleeping). Visiting the pool is a massive nostalgia trip. Swimmers are required to wear caps and the pool features a very old springboard. US$3.
Lao Plaza Hotel (see Sleeping). A very clean pool on the 3rd floor, with a great view of the city, open to non-guests for US$5.

Settha Palace Hotel, 6 Pang Kham Rd (see Sleeping). Lovely pool in landscaped gardens. US$6.

Sokpaluang Swimming Pool, Sok Paluang Rd, south of centre, 0800-2000 daily, 9,000 kip for the day. Good-sized pool for serious swimmers, paddling pool for children, costumes for hire, restaurant and bar.

Tai-Pan Hotel (see Sleeping). Open to non-guests for US$5.

Tennis

Vientiane Parkview, Luang Prabang Rd, T021-250888. Expensive at US$5 an hour but easily the best tennis court in town. Book in advance.

Vientiane Tennis Club, National Stadium. 3,000 kip per hr, equipment for hire. Floodlit courts stay open until 2100, bar.

Ten-pin bowling

Bowling is very popular, particularly as the bars in the bowling centres are often the only ones open after curfew. The **Lao Bowling Centre**, behind the Lao Plaza Hotel is good value at US$1 per person, shoe hire is included but bring your own socks. An alternative is on the way out to the airport (Luang Prabang Rd) where you'll find **Marina Bowling** which is aimed at a younger clientele, with retro lighting, and fluorescent balls and pins. Not a great selection of larger shoe sizes for hire, though, so if your feet are over a size 9 you'll be bowling barefoot.

Tour operators

The best bet for organizing any kind of ecotour is to visit the **National Tourism Authority**, as they have been working hard on a number of ecotourism projects. Most agents will use 'eco' somewhere in their title but this doesn't necessarily mean anything.

Diethelm Travel, Nam Phou Circle, Setthathirat Rd, T021-213833, F021-216294, www.diethelm-travel.com.

Exotissimo, 6/44 Pang Kham Rd, T021-241861, F021-262001, www.exotissimo.com. Various tours and travel services. Excellent service.

Green Discovery Laos, Setthathirat Rd, next to Xayoh Café, T021-251564/511203, F021-223022, www.greendiscoverylaos.com. Specializes in ecotours and adventure travel. Recommended.

Lao Travel-Eco Tourism Co, 248 Khou Vieng Rd, T021-263063, F021-263064, www.laoecotour.com. Quite upmarket tour company providing an interesting variety of travel experiences.

Wildside Asia, T/F021-223321, www.wildside-asia.com. Travel and ecotourism specialists.

Weaving and dyeing courses

Houey Hong Vocational Training Centre, Ban Houey Hong, 20 mins north of Vientiane, T021-560006, hhwt@laotel.com. This small NGO runs training courses for underprivileged ethnic minorities. Tourists are welcome to join in the course for US$15 per day. To get there ask the *songthaew* to drop you off at Talaat Houey Hong, and follow the track 200m west. It is easier if you call the centre in advance.

⦿ Transport

Vientiane *p64, maps p68, p72 and p80*
See also Ins and outs, page 64.

Air

Prices and schedules are constantly changing, so always check in advance.

China Yunnan Airlines, Luang Prabang Rd, in the same building as Thai Airways, T021-212300. **Lao Airlines**, 2 Pang Kham Rd (near Fa Ngum), T021-212054, F021-212065, www.laoairlines.com, also at Wattay Airport; call T021-212057 for international flights (0800-1700 daily); call T021-512000 for domestic flights (0800-1200 and 1300-1600 Mon-Fri, 0800-1200 Sat); flights to **Bangkok** (Thailand, 80 mins), **Luang Prabang** (40 mins), **Pakse** (70 mins) and **Siem Reap**. **Thai Airways**, Head Office, Luang Prabang Rd, past the Novotel towards the airport, T021-222527/9, www.thaiairways.com, 0830-1200 and 1300-1500 Mon-Fri, 0830-1200 Sat; also on Pang Kham Rd, next to the bookshop, and at Wattay Airport, 1st floor, Rm 106, T021-512024, 0700-1200 and 1300-1600 daily; flights to **Bangkok** (70 mins). **Vietnam Airlines** Head office, Lao Plaza Hotel, T021-252618/217562, www.vietnamairlines.com, 0800-1200 and 1330-1630 Mon-Fri, 0800-1200 Sat; flights to **Hanoi** (Vietnam, 60 mins), to **Saigon** (Vietnam, 3 hrs).

Lao Air, Wattay Airport, T/F021-512027, runs charter flights and helicopter services. Lao Westcoast Helicopters, Hangar 703, Wattay Airport, T021-512023, F021-512055.

Bicycle and motorbike

For those energetic enough in the hot season, **bikes** are the best way to get around town. Many hotels and guesthouses have bikes available for their guests, including Lani I, Syri, Day Inn, Lao-Paris and Douang Deuane (see Sleeping). Expect to pay about 5,000-10,000 kip per day depending on the state of the machine. There are also many bike hire shops around town, sometimes attached to restaurants, sometimes to shops specializing in other things. Markets, post offices and government offices usually have 'bike parks' where it is advisable to leave your bike. A small minding fee is charged.

Motorbikes are available for hire from many guesthouses and shops within the city centre. Expect to pay around US$5 per day and leave your passport as security. Trail bikes can be hired for around US$20 per day, although the price goes down to around US$15 per day if you hire the bike for a longer period. Insurance is seldom available anywhere in Laos on motorbikes but most places will also hire out helmets, a necessity. Check your insurance policy before you venture out, as most have a clause saying they won't cover motor bike accidents.

PVO, Samsenthai Rd, corner of Nam Phou Circle, has the most reliable selection of bicycles, motorbikes and trail bikes.

Boat

Improved roads means the old boat transport system has disappeared, with people preferring to stay on terra firma. The only real pier offering transport out of Vientiane is at Tha Hua Kao Liaw, 8 km west of the Novotel in Ban Kao Liaw. Departures are intermittent and unreliable so you may need to charter your boat if you're determined to travel by river; this will need to be organized at least a day in advance. Every now and then speed boats make the trip to Pak Lai (115 km, US$20). If you have 5 or 6 people you can charter speed boats to Luang Prabang (8 hrs) for US$45 per person but it isn't the most comfortable journey.

Bus

There is no real city bus service but buses, trucks and pick-ups to destinations around Vientiane all leave from the station next to the Talaat Sao bus station, next to the Morning Market (see below). Many private tour operators also run buses to popular locations like Vang Vieng and will pickup/dropoff around Nam Phou or pick up passengers from their guesthouse.

Vientiane has 3 main public bus terminals: **Northern**, **Southern** and **Talaat Sao** (Morning Market). There is currently confusion surrounding services from these terminals as the government restructured the schedules and stations in late 2005, so always check before you set off. Many of the buses that traditionally departed from the Talaat Sao bus station have now been divided between the Southern and Northern terminals. Local taxis and tuk-tuks are still unfamiliar with the schedule changes, so leave enough time to get to another bus station, if necessary. Occasionally, buses heading out of the city into Vientiane Province will pass by the Talaat Sao bus station but this is to be phased out officially during 2006. The most comfortable buses are run by private companies, usually from the Southern terminal; check in advance. They only offer only a limited service but are best chance of a decent sleep, if travelling at night – watch out that they don't swap the normal VIP bus for a karaoke one! They provide snacks and have waitresses. Robberies have been reported on the night buses so keep your valuables somewhere secure. **KVT Buses**, T021-242101, and **Laody**, T021-242102, run daily services down south. This is probably the best bet for travel to Thakhek or Pakse, as it's quick and easy. To **Pakse**, 2030 daily, 110,000 kip with a/c, also stop in **Thakhek**, 80,000 kip; schedule says it also stops in Savannakhet but it doesn't, it dumps you in a town called **Xeno**, 30 km from Savannakhet very early in the morning (80,000 kip). A/c buses also depart for Pakse at 0515, 1800, 1900, 2000 (110,000 kip).

Southern bus station Route 13, 9 km south of the city centre. Public buses depart daily for destinations in southern Laos. To **Paksan**, 0500, 0600, 0700 daily, 143 km, 1 hr 30 mins, 20,000 kip, continuing to **Lak Sao**

(for the Vietnamese border), 334 km, 8 hrs, 50,000 kip. To **Thakhek**, 0400, 0500, 0600, 1200 daily, 332 km, 6 hrs, 40,000 kip. To **Savannakhet**, 0530, 0630, 0700, 0730, 0800, 0830, 0900 daily, 457 km, 8 hrs, 55,000 kip. To **Pakse**, 1000, 1230, 1300, 1330, 1400, 1430, 1500, 1530 daily, 659 km, 15 hrs, 85,000 kip; there are also a/c express buses to Pakse at 1800, 1830, 1900, 1930, 2000 daily, 11 hrs, 110,000 kip, and a VIP service at 2030 daily, which takes about the same time but has water, snacks etc, 130,000 kip. To **Salavan** and **Sekong**, 1630 daily, 774 km, 20 hrs, 100,000 kip. To **Attapeu**, 0930 and 1700 daily, 812 km, 23 hrs, 110,000 kip. To **Voen Kham** (Cambodian border, see page 284), 1100 daily, 818 km, 18 hrs, 110,000 kip. To **Don Talaat**, 1130 daily, 100,000 kip. To **Muang Khong** on Don Khong, 1030 daily, 788 km, 18 hrs, 110,000 kip.

SDT Transport, T021-740521, runs a bus to northern Vietnam at 1900 daily, with stops in **Vinh** (19 hrs, US$16); **Thanh Hoa** (20 hrs, US$18) and **Hanoi** (23 hrs, US$20). Another bus for southern Vietnam also departs at 1900 daily, with stops in **Hué** (21 hrs, US$20); **Danang** (23 hrs, US$20) and **Ho Chi Minh City** (48 hrs, US$45).

Northern bus station Route 2, towards the airport from the centre of town, T021-260255. Some southbound buses still depart from here (no logic to it but *bopenyang*): to **Thakhek**, 0400, 0500, 0600, 1200 daily, 40,000 kip; to **Savannakhet**, 0530, 0630, 0700, 0730, 0800, 0830, 0900 daily, 55,000 kip; to **Pakse**, 1000, 1200, 1300, 1400, 1500, 1600 daily, 85,000 kip; to **Don Khong**, 1030 daily, 100,000 kip); to **Voen Kham**, 1100 daily, 100,000 kip; to **Salavan**, 1630 daily, 100,000 kip.

Northbound buses are regular and have a/c. For the more popular routes, there are also VIP buses which will usually offer snacks and service. To **Luang Prabang** (384 km), standard buses at 0730, 1100, 1330, 1600, 1800 daily, 11 hrs, 70,000 kip; a/c buses at 0630, 0900, 1930 daily, 10-11 hrs, 80,000kip; VIP buses at 0800 daily, 9 hrs, 100,000 kip. To **Udomxai** (578 km), standard buses at 0645, 1400 daily, 14-15 hrs, 100,000 kip; a/c buses at 1630 daily, 110,000 kip. To **Luang Namtha**, 0830 daily, 676 km, 19 hrs, 120,000 kip. To **Phongsali**, 0715 daily, 811 km, 26 hrs, 135,000 kip. To **Houei Xai**, 1730 Mon, Wed and Fri,

869 km, 25-30 hrs, 170,000 kip. To **Sayaboury** (485 km), standard at 1750 daily, 12-15 hrs, 90,000 kip; a/c at 0700 daily, 100,000 kip. To **Xam Neua**, 0700, 1000, 1230 daily, 612 km, 14-23 hrs (depending on whether it goes via Phonsavanh), 130,000 kip. To **Phonsavanh** (374 km), standard at 0630, 0930, 1600 daily, 10 hrs, 75,000 kip; a/c at 0730 daily, 85,000 kip; VIP bus at 0800 daily, 95,000 kip. A bus departs every Thu and Sun for the Chinese border at **Boten**.

Talaat Sao bus station Across the road from Talaat Sao, in front of Talaat Kudin, on the eastern edge of the city centre. Destinations, distances and fares are listed on a board in English and Lao. Most departures are in the morning and can leave as early as 0400, so many travellers on a tight schedule have regretted not checking departure times the night before. There is a useful map at the station, and bus times and fares are listed clearly in Lao and English. However, it's more than likely you will need a bit of direction at this bus station: staff at the ticket office only speak a little English so a better option is to chat to the friendly chaps in the planning office, who love a visit, T021-216506. The times listed below vary depending on the weather and the number of stops en route.

To the **Southern Bus Station**, every 30 mins 0600-1800, 2,000 kip. To get to the **Northern Bus Station**, catch the Nongping bus (0630, 0810, 0940, 1110, 1230, 1430, 1600 and 1720 daily) and ask to get off at "*Thay Song*" (1,500 kip). To **Wattay Airport**, every 30 mins 0640-1800, 3,000 kip.

There are numerous buses criss-crossing the province; most aren't very useful for tourists. To **Barksarp** (via Som Sa Mai for the boat to **Ban Pako**), 0630, 0930, 0730, 1330, 1530, 1730 daily, 5,000 kip. To **Ban Keun** (via Ban Thabok for **Phou Khao Khouay**), 0630, 0745, 0900, 1000, 1130, 1245, 1400, 1515, 1730 daily, 7,000 kip. To **Xieng Khuan**, bus No 14 every 10-20 mins 0530-2030, 1 hr, 3,000 kip. To **Nam Ngum**, direct bus 0700 daily, 3 hrs, or catch a bus to **Ban Talaat**, every hr 0630-1630, 2½ hrs, 8,000 kip, and then get a *songthaew* to the lake. To **Kasi** (via **Vang Vieng**, 20,000 kip, but unless you're dead broke, there are much better ways of getting to Vang Vieng), 0830 and 1500 daily. To the **Friendship Bridge** (Lao side), every 30 mins 0650-1710, 3,000 kip. To **Nong Khai** (Thai side of the Friendship Bridge), 0730, 1030, 1530 and 1800 daily, about 1 hr including immigration, 8000 kip. To **Udon Thani** (Thailand), 0700, 0930, 1500, 1700 daily, allow 3 hrs (times vary depending on immigration procedures), 22,000 kip; this is a very cheap way to get to Udon Thani.

Other private bus services To **Vang Vieng**, Green Discovery, from their office on Setthathirat, 0100 and 1400 daily, 45,000 kip; also **Sabaidee Bus** for the same price and at the same time. Both services will pick you up from your guesthouse if you arrange in advance. Sabaidee Bus to **Luang Prabang**, Tue and Thu, 130,000 kip, with a stopover in Vang Vieng on the way.

Car
It is not essential to hire a driver but note that in the event of an accident a foreigner is likely to shoulder the responsibility and any costs. Car hire rates vary according to state and model of vehicle and also whether out-of-town trips are planned. Expect to pay about US$50-90 per day. Many hotels and guesthouses will have cars for hire.
Asia Vehicle Rental, 354-56 Samsenthai Rd, T021-217493/223867, www.avr.laopdr.com, 0800-1900 Mon-Fri, 0800-1200 Sat. Most competitive prices in town with the best range. Vientiane city US$55 per day with driver up to 130 km, US$15 per additional 100 km. Outside of Vientiane rates are about US$80 per day plus petrol. Discounts for longer periods of hire.

Taxi
These are mostly found at the Morning Market (Talaat Sao) or around the main hotels. Newer vehicles have meters but there are still some ageing jalopies. Flag fall is 8,000 kip. A taxi from the Morning Market to the **airport**, US$5; to **Tha Deua** (for the Friendship Bridge and Thailand), 30,000 kip or US$9, although you can usually get the trip much cheaper but the taxis are so decrepit that you may as well take a tuk-tuk, US$4-5 (see below). To hire a taxi for trips outside the city costs around US$20 per day. To **Nam Ngum**, US$40.

Lavi Taxi, T021-350000 is the only reliable call-up service in town but after 2000 in the evening it is a lottery whether someone will answer the telephone.

Tuk-tuks
Tuk-tuks usually congregate around tourist destinations: Nam Phou, Talaat Sao and Talaat Kudin. Tuk-tuks can be chartered for longer out-of-town trips (maximum 25 km, US$10-15) or for short journeys of 2-3 km within the city (5,000 kip per person). There are also shared tuk-tuks, which run on regular routes along the city's main streets. Tuk-tuks are available around the fountain area until 2330 but are quite difficult to hire after dark in other areas of town. To stop a vehicle, simply flag it down. A reliable driver is **Mr Souk**, T020-7712220, who speaks good English and goes beyond the call of duty. **Saamlors** are as rare as hen's teeth in Vientiane.

⊙ Directory

Vientiane *p64, maps p68, p72 and p80*
Banks
See Money, page 28, for details on changing money in Laos. At the time of writing the most reliable ATM in the city was at the **BCEL Bank** (see below) on the corner of Fa Ngum and Pang Kham roads), which takes all the usual credit cards. There are others in town but many of them have a maximum withdrawal limit and don't always work properly. **Banque Pour le Commerce Exterieur** (BCEL), 1 Pang Kham Rd, traditionally offers the lowest commission (1.5%) on changing US$ TCs into US$ cash; there is no commission on changing US$ into kip; also has an international ATM. **Joint Development Bank**, 33 Lane Xang Av (opposite market). **Vientiane Commercial Bank**, 33 Lane Xang Av (opposite Morning Market), T021-222700/5, cash advance on Visa at 3% commission.

With the loosening of banking regulations a number of Thai banks have set up in Vientiane; many are situated along Lane Xang Av. They all offer efficient and competitive exchange facilities: **Thai Military Bank**, 69 Khoun Boulom Rd; **Bangkok Bank**, 28/13-15 Hat Sady Rd, cash advance available on Mastercard for 3% commission.

Embassies and consulates
For details of visa regulations for neighbouring countries, see page 27. **Australia**, Nehru, Ban Phonxay Rd, T021-413602. **Britain**, no embassy; served by the

⦂ Border essentials: Friendship Bridge

The bridge is 25 km southeast of Vientiane; catch bus No 14 from the Talaat Sao terminal (1,000 kip) or hire a tuk-tuk, 20-40 minutes, US$5 (see page 95).

The border is open from 0600 to 2200 daily. Immigration and customs are on either sides of the bridge and shuttle minibuses take punters across the bridge every 20 minutes for 2500 kip or ฿20, stopping at the Thai and Lao immigration posts where an overtime fee is charged after 1630 and at weekends.

There are good facilities at the Lao border, including a telephone box, a couple of duty free shops, some drinks and snack stalls and a post office. Allow up to one hour 30 minutes to get to the bridge and through formalities on the Lao side. The paperwork is pretty swift, unless you are arriving in Laos and require a visa (15-day allowance) or are leaving the country and have over-stayed your visa. In the latter case you will be escorted into the immigration office to pay the US$10-per-day fine.

The Thai side is über-efficient but not nearly as friendly. Tuk-tuks wait to take punters to Nong Khai

(10 minutes), the nearest Thai town of any size to the Friendship Bridge. A number of tour companies here provide travellers to Laos with visas but since these are now available on arrival at the bridge this service has become redundant; ignore the random shady characters at the bus station in Nong Khai who will try to divert you to travel agencies, with whom they have a mutually beneficial agreement. If you get stuck in Nong Khai, **Mut Mee Guesthouse** is recommended.

Udon Thani is another hour beyond Nong Khai; taxis from the Thai side of the border charge about ฿500 to get you there; add another ฿300 from the Lao side. It is necessary to bargain particularly assiduously on the Thai side of the border, as sharks loom awaiting to relieve you of your crisp baht notes. From Udon Thani you can get to Bangkok easily by budget airline. Another option is to catch the overnight train from Nong Khai to Bangkok's Hualamphong Station (11 hrs, ฿800 for a sleeper). Buses also run from both Udon Thani and Nong Khai to Bangkok.

Australian Embassy. **Cambodia**, Tha Deua Rd, Km 2, T021-314952, F021-312584, visas 0730-1030 daily. **Canada**, no embassy; served by the Australian Embassy. **China**, Wat Nak, T021-315100/3, visas 0900-1200 daily. **Czechoslovakia**, Tha Deua Rd, T021-315291. **France**, Setthathirat Rd, T021-215253. **Germany**, 26 Sok Paluang Rd, T021-312110/1. **India**, That Luang Rd, T021-413802. **Indonesia**, Phon Kheng Rd, T021-413910. **Japan**, Sisavangvong Rd, T021-414400/13, F021-414403, 0900-1200 and 1330-1600, visas take up to 1 week and cost 300,000 kip. **Malaysia**, That Luang Rd, T021-414205/6, 0800-1200 and 1300-1700. **Myanmar (Burma)**, Sok Paluang Rd, T021-314910-1, 0800-1200 and 1300-1630 daily. **Russia**, T021-312219, 0730-1800 Mon,

Tue and Thu; Wed and Fri 0700-1200. **Sweden**, Sok Paluang Rd, T021-315018, F021-315001, 0800-1200 and 1300-1700 Mon-Thu, 0800-1300 Fri. **Thailand**, Phon Kheng Rd, T021-214581/2, F021-216998 (consular section on That Luang), 0830-1200 Mon-Fri. If crossing by land, 30-day visas are also issued at the Friendship Bridge, see above. **USA**, That Dam Rd (off Samsenthai Rd), T021-212580, F021-212584. **Vietnam**, That Luang Rd, T021- 413400, visas 0800-1045 and 1415-1615 daily.

Emergencies
Ambulance, T195 but note that you are taking a significant risk by placing your life in their hands; in cases of medical emergency see Dr Ben at the **Australian Clinic** (see

Medical services, below). **Police Tourist Office**, Lang Xang Av (next to the National Tourism Authority of Laos), T021-251128.

Internet

Internet cafés have opened up all over the city, many on Setthathirat Rd. Most offer drinks and newspapers and are generally open 0800-2200/2300 daily. Shop around for the best rates; you shouldn't have to pay more than 200 kip per min. Connection speeds are improving with the arrival of broadband but don't ask questions that are too technical or you'll be met with blank stares. Internet phones are now very popular, with most cafés providing this service for under US$1 per min. The following are the most reliable places in town: **PlaNet Computers**, 205 Setthathirat Rd, on the corner, planet@laonet.net, 0830-2300 Mon-Fri, 0900-2300 Sat and Sun, is the pick of the bunch. Another option is **Star-net**, Mixay Rd, T021-504550, whose owner, Somphane Sihavong, is helpful and speaks good English. **Fastest Net**, a block down from the Lao Plaza on Samsenthai Rd, is OK but doesn't deserve the name.

Laundry

Laundrettes can be found all over Samsenthai Rd and the streets around Nam Phou. Try **Delight House of Fruit Shakes** (see Cafés, cakeshops and juice bars, above).

Media

There are 2 English newspapers available in Vientiane. Most articles pertinent to foreigners appear in the English-language *Vientiane Times*, 3,000 kip, which runs Lao news, plus some quite interesting out-on-the-street interviews and quirky snippets that have been translated from the local newspapers. Up-to-date listings and events are at the back of the paper. There is also the French-language *Le Renovateur*, 3,000 kip, which takes a more serious approach and includes lots of news on events in France.

Medical services

There are 2 pretty good pharmacies close to the Talaat Sao Bus Station. Vientiane's hospitals do not come highly recommended. However, there are a few very good private clinics in town: **Australian Clinic**, Australian Embassy, Nehru Rd, T021-413603 (or T021-511462 after hours), 0800-1200 and 1400-1700 Mon, Tue, Thu, Fri, 0830-1200 Wed, by appointment only, for Commonwealth patients only (except in emergencies), US$50 to see the doctor. **International Clinic**, Mahosot Hospital, Setthathirat Rd, T021-214022, 24 hrs daily. Mahosot is said to be staffed by Cubans and is very under-equipped, so only advisable for minor conditions. **Clinique Setthathirat**, next to That Luang, T021-413720. **Phia-Watt Clinic**, Sakarindh Rd, T021-217041, small Lao clinic that can deal with diarrhoea and minor ailments, extremely cheap.

If you need a decent hospital, the closest is the **Wattana General Hospital**, in Nong Khai, Thailand. Even better is **AEK Udon Thani Hospital**, Udon Thani, Thailand. For both, see page 54. In cases of extreme emergency where a medical evacuation is required, contact **Lao Westcoast Helicopters**, Hangar 703, Wattay International Airport, T021-512023, F021-512055. A charter to Udon Thani costs US$1,500-US$2,000, subject to availability and government approval.

Post

Post Office, Khou Vieng Rd/Lane Xang Av (opposite market), T021-216425, offers poste restante, local and international telephone calls and fax services (see page 59 for more detailed information). Also a good packing service and a philately counter. To send packages, use **DHL**, Nong No Rd, near the airport, T021-214868, or **TNT Express**, in the Thai Airways Building, Luang Prabang Rd, T021-261918.

Telephone

Area code: 021 for landlines and 020 for mobile phones. Dial 170 for international operator. The international telephone office is on Setthathirat Rd, near Nam Phou Rd, 24 hrs daily, fax service 0730-2130 daily.

Useful contacts

Immigration office, Phai Narn Rd (near Morning Market), 0730-1200, 1400-1700, Mon-Fri. For visa information, see page 25. **Vientiane University**, Dong-Dok, Route 10, 10 km north of the city, buses run from Talaat Sao every 30 mins 0640-1700, 1,500 kip.

Around Vientiane

There are plenty of short trips from Vientiane, ranging from the popular backpacker hotspot of Vang Vieng, through to the stunning Phou Khao Khuoay National Park. Vang Vieng has become very popular with action sports enthusiasts, with kayaking, caving and rock climbing all on offer. For years the Nam Ngum dam has been a popular weekend escape for Vientiane residents and is starting to gain appeal with the tourist set. ▶ *For Sleeping, Eating and other listings, see pages 106-112.*

South of the city

Bus No 14 from the Talaat Sao bus station follows Route 2 southeast towards Tha Deua, the Friendship Bridge to Thailand and the Garden of the Buddhas. The observation area by the bridge makes a good picnic spot, or it would be possible to take lunch in Thailand for visitors with multi-entry visas. ▶ *For immigration formalities at the bridge, see Border essentials, page 97.*

Along Thanon Tha Deua (Route 2)

Although it isn't officially recognized as a tourist destination, the **Beer Lao factory** ⓘ *Km 12, Thanon Tha Deua (Route 2), T021-812000,* is surprisingly interesting and worth the trip. Numerous people have visited and been welcomed with open arms, given a mini tour and plied senseless with the award-winning ale. Beer Lao has inadvertently become something of a national symbol and the locals swell with pride

Around Vientiane

To Phonsavanh

Kasi · To Luang Prabang

SAYSOMBOUN SPECIAL ZONE

Phu Bia (2,819m)

Vang Vieng

Ban Houay (North Port)

North Town

Nam Ngum Dam · Santipat Island

Phou Khao Khouay

Ban Talaat · Nam Ngum Reservoir

Ban Phonhong

South Port

Ban Hat Khai

Ang Nam Leuk

Rt 13

Vangxang

Tulakhom · Tad Leuk

Thabok

Paksan

Vientiane Zoo

Ban Keun

Ban Na

Tha Pabat Phonsanh

Rt 10

Som Sa Mai · Nam Ngum · Ban Naxai

Rt 13

Mekong

Xieng Khuan

Rt 13

THAILAND

VIENTIANE

Tha Deua

Nong Khai

N

0 km   10
0 miles   10

Sleeping 🛏
Ban Pako Resort **2**
Nam Ngum Resort **1**

Bridging the Mekong

In April 1994, King Bhumibol of Thailand and the President of Laos, accompanied by prime ministers Chuan Leekpai of Thailand and Keating of Australia, opened the first bridge to span the lower reaches of the Mekong River, linking Nong Khai in northeast Thailand with Vientiane in Laos.

The bridge had taken a long time to materialize. It was first mooted in the 1950s but war in Indochina and hostility between Laos and Thailand scuppered plans until the late 1980s. Then, with the Cold War ending and growing rapprochement between the countries of Indochina and ASEAN, the bridge, as they say, became an idea whose time had come.

The 1,200-m-long Friendship Bridge, or Mittaphab, was financed with US$30 mn of aid from Australia. It is a key link in a planned road network that will eventually stretch from Singapore to Beijing. For land-locked Laos, it offers an easier route to Thailand and through Thailand to the sea. For Thailand, it offers an entrée into one of the least developed countries in the world, rich in natural resources and potential, while, for Australia, it demonstrated the country's Asian credentials.

The Thais would like to build two further bridges. One will probably link Savannakhet and Mukdahan; final agreement was reached at the end of 2001 and is due for completion in 2006/7. The Lao and Thai governments have also signed a memorandum of understanding to build a bridge between Thakhek and Nakhon Phanom, although Vientiane is decidedly cool about the prospect. The Lao government worries that the bridges will not only bolster trade with Thailand but may also bring consumerism, crime, prostitution and environmental degradation to their relatively unspoiled country.

if you share their enthusiasm for a tipple of their amber liquid. Two kilometres further on is **555 Park (Saam Haa Yai)**. These extensive but rather uninspiring gardens encompass Chinese pavilions, a lake and a small zoo. In the 1980s, a white elephant was captured in southern Laos. Revered in this part of the world for its religious significance, it had to be painted to ensure it was not stolen on the way to the capital. It was originally kept in the Saam Haa gardens but has since been moved to a 'secret' location, the zoo, where it is paraded in front of the crowds during the That Luang festival. White elephants are not really white, but pink.

Xieng Khuan

ⓘ *Route 2 (25 km east of Vientiane). Daily 0800-1700. Admission 5000 kip, plus 5000 kip for cameras. Food vendors sell drinks and snacks. Getting there: 1 hr by bus No 14, charter a tuk-tuk for approximately 100,000 kip, hire a private vehicle for up to US$15, or cycle because the road follows the river and is reasonably level the whole way.*

Otherwise known as the **Garden of the Buddhas** or **Buddha Park**, Xieng Khuan is a few kilometres beyond **Tha Deua** on Route 2, close to the frontier with Thailand. It has been described as a Laotian Tiger Balm Gardens with reinforced concrete Buddhist and Hindu sculptures of Vishnu, Buddha, Siva and various other assorted deities and near-deities. There's also a bulbous-style building with three levels containing smaller sculptures of the same gods.

The garden was built in the late 1950s by a priest-monk-guru-sage-artist called Luang Pu Bunleua Sulihat, who studied under a Hindu *rishi* in Vietnam and then combined the Buddhist and Hindu philosophies in his own very peculiar view of the world. He left Laos because his anti-Communist views were incompatible with the

ideology of the Pathet Lao (or perhaps because he was just too weird) and settled
across the Mekong near the Thai town of Nong Khai, where he proceeded to build an
equally revolting and bizarre concrete theme park for religious schizophrenics, called
Wat Khaek. With Luang Pu's forced departure from Laos his religious garden came
under state control and it is now a public park. Luang Pu died in 1996 at the age of 72
and remains very popular in Laos and northeastern Thailand.

East of the city 🖳 ▸▸ *pages 106-112.*

Kaysone Phomvihane Museum
ⓘ *Km 6, Route 13 South. Bus from the Morning Market or cycle.*
The Kaysone Phomvihane Museum commemorates the exploits and leadership of
the Lao PDR equivalent of Vietnam's Ho Chi Minh. Kaysone was certainly the critical
character in Laos' recent history: revolutionary fighter, inspired leader and statesman
(see page 294). This dedicated museum is mostly visited by Lao schoolchildren.

Ban Pako → *Colour map 2, B2*
Ban Pako lies 50 km northeast of Vientiane, on the banks of the Nam Ngum river (off
Route 13). There is a quiet and secluded 'nature lodge' here, established by an
Austrian couple a few years back. The owners have 50 ha of land, through which they
have cut paths and planted trees. It's a lovely place to retreat to, for swimming,
boating, trekking, rafting and walks to local Lao villages and, after all the physical
exertion, you can unwind in the herbal sauna. To reach Ban Pako, take the Paksan
bus from Vientiane's Morning Market and get off at Som Sa Mai (one hour). From Som
Sa Mai, take a local boat to Lao Pako (another 25 minutes). Alternatively, the route
makes a great trail bike ride; the last 20 km are on dirt and can get quite wild,
especially during the wet season.

Tha Pabat Phonsanh
About 80 km down the Paksan road, is Pabat Phonsanh, built on a plug of volcanic
rock in the middle of a coconut plantation. It is known for its footprint of the Buddha
and has a statue of a reclining Buddha (*mudra*) rarely seen in Laos.

Phou Khao Khouay National Park 🖳 ▸▸ *pages 106-112.*

Phou Khao Khouay (pronounced 'poo cow kway'), 40 km northeast of Vientiane, is one
of Laos' premier national parks. Established in 2003, it is one of the most accessible
protected areas in the country, with several Vientiane-based tour operators offering
trips to the park. The park extends across 2,000 sq km, incorporates an attractive
sandstone mountain range and is crossed by three large rivers, smaller tributaries and
two stunning waterfalls, which weave their way into the **Ang Nam Leuk reservoir**.

Ins and outs
Getting there The park is a two-hour drive from Vientiane, along Route 13 South; a
good vehicle is recommended as the roads are terrible. To get to Ban Na you need to
turn off at Tha Pabat Phonsanh, 80 km northeast of Vientiane (see above). For Ban Hat
Khai continue on Route 13 to Ban Thabok, where a *songthaew* can usually take you the
extra 7 km to the village. However, at the time of publication, vehicular access was
impossible here as a bridge was down en route (it could stay that way for a long time). If
this is still the case, you may need to book a boat in advance for the 40-minute journey
from Ban Thabok to Ban Hat Khai. Buses to Paksan from the Talaat Sao bus station and
That Luang evening market in Vientiane stop at Thabok.

Saysomboun Special Zone

The Saysomboun Special Zone, an area forged out of the northern parts of Vientiane Province and the southern parts of Luang Prabang and Xieng Khouang provinces in 1994, is pretty much a no-go zone for tourists. The government views this area as dangerous due to the presence of armed Hmong insurgents and doesn't wish to risk any foreign fatalities.

There are mixed reports about foreign access here; a number of tourists have been swiftly escorted by police from the area, after being heavily fined and having their motorbikes impounded. On the other hand, some tour operators run rafting and kayaking expeditions through some parts of the zone. It is believed that the authorities are trying to relax the restrictions on the area but, in 2005, it was pretty much off limits. However, as areas have been declared safe they are gradually breaking away from the special zone. In 2000 two districts were handed over to Vientiane Province.

This was once an important opium growing region but since the government's opium eradication policy, the crops have disappeared (or so they say!), which could be another reason why it's out of bounds for now. The area is believed to contain some fantastic sites of interest to visitors, including the country's highest mountain.

Tourist information Although treks can be organized in Ban Na (T020-2208286) and Ban Hat Khai (T020-2240303), advance notice is required so it's advisable to go with a tour operator from Vientiane instead. Visit www.trekkingcentrallaos.com and contact the **National Tourism Authority** in Vientiane, T021-212248, or **Green Discovery Tours** (see Activities and tours, page 93).

Tad Leuk

Accessed by dirt track (one hour) or boat from Ban Thabok (the waterfall sign is easily seen on the left), these are the most visited falls in the park and contain several large, undulating tiers. It is a good picnic spot, with swimming possible in the lake behind the waterfall although it is sometimes too rough. Tad Leuk has a visitor information centre which has toilets and washing facilities and also rents camping equipment. There's also a nice little snack stand on a platform, offering a view of the falls. Mr Khamsavay Kingmanolath, the supervisor at Tad Leuk, organizes cheap treks from Tad Leuk, about US$7-10 per group.

Tad Sae

These are the most stunning falls in the park but don't boast the facilities of Tad Leuk. The falls tumble down seven tiers, flowing for about 800 m before plummeting 40 m into a magnificent river gorge. There is a small, clear pool that's perfect for swimming. To get to the waterfall, take the road from Ban Thabok and turn right at the fork – it's signposted.

Ban Na

These days the principal draw-cards for Phou Khao Khouay are the organized treks and the elephant observation tower, both of which are based out of the small farming village of **Ban Na**. The village's sweet sugar cane plantations attract a herd of wild elephants, which has, in the past, destroyed the villagers' homes and even killed a resident. An elephant observation tower has now been built to keep a lookout for the big pachyderms, which tourists are more than welcome to visit. The village, in conjunction with the National Tourism Authority, has also started running trekking tours to see these massive creatures in their natural habitat. One- to three-day treks can be organized through the amazing national park, crossing waterfalls, pristine jungle and, hopefully, spotting the odd wild elephant. This is the only ecotour of its kind in Laos.

Ban Hat Khai

This village contains 90 families from the Lao Loum and Lao Soung ethnic groups and is another starting point for organized treks through amazing mountain landscapes, crossing the Nam Mang river and the Phay Xay cliffs. Tad Sae falls can be reached on a small boat trip from the village.

North of the city 🖿 ▸▸ *pages 106-112.*

▸▸ *pages 106-112.*

Route 13 North
Tad Kaukhanna ① *10,000 kip per car plus 2,000 kip per person*, is 11 km off the Phonhong road (Route 13), about 18 km north of Vientiane. It's a lesser known waterfall with a campsite and a restaurant. Tuk-tuks normally only head this way on public holidays, so a private car or taxi may be necessary to get here. A day trip in a *songthaew* should cost about US$15-20 return.

About 30 km from Vientiane, on the Luang Prabang road, is **Dane Soung**, an area where large fallen rocks have formed a cave. There are Buddhist sculptures inside and a footprint of the Buddha on the left of the entrance. This is a popular spot with locals at the weekend. Too steep for tuk-tuks, it tends to be only private cars and motorbikes that make it here. Turn left at the 22 km mark towards Ban Houa Khoua. Dane Soung is 6 km down the track and is only accessible in the dry season. About 10 km further along Route 13, turn left at the former **Lao-Australian Livestock Project Centre** and left again before the bridge along a precipitously narrow track to reach **Nam Soung** rapids and waterfall; they are only impressive during the rainy season. Alternatively, turn right before the bridge to reach an absurdly out-of-place, English-style picnic spot by the water.

Vientiane Zoo
① *Route 10, near Ban Keun, 50 km north of Vientiane. Daily 0800-1630, 5,000 kip.*
This zoo is really not much to get excited about: a small collection of animals and nothing of great zoological note. There's a café and picnic area. Take a public bus bound for Ban Keun and ask to be let off at the '*Suan Sat Wiang Chan*'.

Vangxang
Located 80 km north of Vientiane on Route 13, Vangxang, which means elephant drinking hole, is a lovely place to stop on the way to Vang Vieng. Worth a look are the amazing Buddha sculptures carved into a cliff face 2 km from the Vangxang Resort. The 10 Angkorian relief sculptures are believed to be over 500 years old, with two of them hovering at about 4 m. Aside from the Buddha carvings, walks through the jungle are the only diversion.

Nam Ngum dam and reservoir 🖿🍴 ▸▸ *pages 106-112.*

▸▸ *pages 106-112.*

The Nam Ngum dam, 90 km from Vientiane, is the pride of Laos and figures prominently in picture postcards. It provides electricity for much of the country and its energy exports to Thailand are the country's second biggest foreign exchange earner. The lake is very picturesque and is dotted with hundreds of small islands.

Many people believe that the dam was built with Soviet aid and assistance following the victory of the Communists in 1975. In fact construction began in the 1960s under the auspices of the Mekong Development Committee and was funded by the World Bank and Western nations. Indeed a large slice of the country's aid budget went into the construction of the dam, which was officially opened in the early 1970s. After the Communist victory, two of the lake's islands came in handy as open prisons for the most 'culturally polluted' of Vientiane's population. Two thousand drug addicts, prostitutes and other assorted hippies and 'low life' were rounded up and shipped out here. One island was allocated for men and the other for women. In addition to the islands, huge semi-submerged tree-trunks pose a navigational hazard, as no one had the foresight to log the area before it was flooded. The untapped underwater cache of timber has now been spotted by the Thais looking for alternative sources of timber; sub-aqua chainsaws are used to take out the 'treasure'.

Exploring the lake

Access to the Nam Ngum reservoir is via Phonhong on Route 13: turn right at the strategically placed concrete post in the middle of the road, then head left to the village of **Ban Talaat** on the southwest shores of the reservoir. The market here is worth a browse (the word '*talaat*' means market), as minority groups from the surrounding area come here to sell their produce. From Ban Talaat, turn right across the narrow bridge to reach the dam, about 4 km up the road. An alternative route to the dam is via Route 10 out of Vientiane, which passes through much prettier countryside and traverses the Nam Ngum by ferry. Turn right at the end of the road for the dam. One bus leaves the Morning Market in Vientiane daily for Nam Ngum, otherwise you will need to catch a bus to Ban Talaat and organize a *songthaew* from there. There are boats from the dam to **Ban Pao Mo** on the other side of the reservoir. The trip should take around two hours and cost about US$10 per hour but it is necessary to bargain hard with boatmen before crossing the lake. Boats can also be hired out; again, barter hard to get a good hourly rate. Vang Vieng is two hours' ride from the dam.

> ❣ *No photographs are allowed at the dam wall or at the power plant.*

Vang Vieng and around 🖥🛈🏠🛏⛰🚻🛈 ▸▸ *pages 106-112.*

The drive to Vang Vieng, on the much improved Route 13, follows the valley of the Nam Ngum north to Phonhong and then climbs steeply onto the plateau where Vang Vieng is located, 160 km north of Vientiane. The surrounding area is inhabited by the Hmong and Yao hill peoples and is particularly picturesque: craggy karst limestone scenery, riddled with caves, crystal-clear pools and waterfalls. In the early morning the views are reminiscent of a Chinese Sung Dynasty painting.

The town itself is also attractive, nestled in a valley on the bank of the Nam Xong river, amid a misty jungle. It enjoys cooler weather and offers breathtaking views of the imposing mountains of Pha Tang and Phatto Nokham. There are a number of 16th and 17th century **monasteries** in town of which the most notable are **Wat That** at the northern edge of the settlement and **Wat Kang**, 100 m or so to the south.

The town's laidback feel has made it a popular haunt for the backpacker crowd, while the surrounding landscape has helped to establish Vang Vieng as Laos' premier outdoor activity destination, especially for rock climbing, caving, and kayaking. (It is also a convenient stop-off point on the gruelling journey to Luang Prabang.) Its popularity in many ways has also become its downfall: Vegas-like neon lights, pancake stands, 'happy' this, 'happy' that and an oversupply of pirated *Friends* videos now pollute this former oasis. Nevertheless, the town and surrounding area is still full of wonderful things to do and see.

Getting there and around Vang Vieng is on Route 13 between Vientiane and Luang Prabang so a bus between Vientiane and anywhere up north (or vice versa) will pass Vang Vieng even if it is not on the itinerary. The journey to/from the capital takes about three to four hours and buses come and go from a inconspicuous spot on the side of the road along the old airstrip near the centre of town. You generally don't have to wait too long for a bus that's heading in your direction.

Safety Laos is a very safe country for tourists but a disproportionate number of accidents and crimes seem to happen in Vang Vieng. **Theft** is routinely reported, ranging from robberies by packs of kids targeting tubers on the river to the opportunist theft of items from guests' rooms. It is usually advisable to hand in any valuables to the management of your guesthouse or to padlock your bag and leave cash stashed in a very good hiding spot. Another major problem is the sale of illegal **drugs**. Police often go on sting operations and charge fines of up to US$600. There have even been unsubstantiated reports of the police planting drugs on tourists. Legal issues aside, numerous travellers have become seriously ill from indulging in the 'happy' supplements supplied by the restaurants. ▸▸ *For details of the significant safety risks involved in adventure activities, see Activities and tours, page 111.*

Tourist information The **Tourist Information Office** has a few maps on the walls but can't provide much useful information. The **Centre for the Protection of Foreigners**, next door, is also of little use; it was operating as a goat farm in 2005.

Caves

Vang Vieng is best known for its limestone caves, sheltered in the mountains flanking the town. Pretty much every guesthouse and tour operator offers tours to the caves (the best of these is **Green Discovery**) and, although some caves can be accessed independently, it is advisable to take a guide to a few as they are dark and difficult to navigate. Often children from surrounding villages will take tourists through the caves for a small fee. Don't forget to bring a torch, or even better a head-lamp, which can be picked up cheaply at the market both in Vang Vieng and Vientiane. Each cave has an entrance fee of 3,000 -10,000 kip and many have stalls where you can buy drinks and snacks. You can buy hand-drawn maps from the town but all the caves are clearly signposted in English from the main road so these are not really necessary. ▸▸ *For further details, see Activities and tours, page 111.*

Of Vang Vieng's myriad caves, **Tham Chang** ① *access via the Vang Vieng Resort (see Sleeping), 1,000 kip*, is the most renowned of all. Tham Chang penetrates right under a mountain and is fed by a natural spring perfect for an early morning dip. From the spring it is possible to swim into the cave for quite a distance (bring a waterproof torch, if possible). The cave is said to have been used as a refuge during the 19th century from marauding Chinese Haw bandits and this explains its name: *chang* meaning 'loyal' or 'steadfast'. To reach the cave, cross the rickety bamboo bridge in rainy season or wade across during the dry season. For your US$1 or 10,000 kip entrance fee you not only get into the caves but the lighting system will also be turned on. Although the cave is not the most magnificent, it serves as a superb lookout point.

Another popular cavern is **Tham Poukham** ① *7 km from Vang Vieng, 5,000 kip.* The cave is often referred to as the cave of the Golden Crab and is highly auspicious. It's believed that if you catch a golden crab you will have a lifetime of fortune. To get there you need to cross the foot-bridge near the **Nam Song Hotel**, and then follow the road for a further 6 km until you reach the village of Ban Nathong. From the village the cave is 1 km walk and a short climb up quite a steep hill. Mossy rocks lead the way into the main cavern area where a large bronze reclining Buddha is housed. Here there is an idyllic lagoon with glassy green-blue waters, perfect for a dip.

Tham None ⓘ *4 km north of Vang Vieng, 5,000 kip*, is known locally known as the 'Sleeping Cave' because 2000 villagers took refuge there during the war. The large cave is dotted with stalagmites and stalactites, including the 'magic stone of Vang Vieng', which reflects light. There are also lots of bats residing in the grotto. In the wet season it is possible to swim here. The cave is very popular with tour groups and rock climbers.

Tham Xang ⓘ *14 km north of Vang Vieng on the banks of the Nam Xong, 2,000 kip*, also known as the 'Elephant Cave', is named after the stalagmites and stalactites that have created an elephant formation (you may need to squint to see it). The cave also contains some Buddha images, including the Footprint of Buddha. From this cave there is a signposted path that leads to **Tham Hoi** ⓘ *15 km from town, 5,000 kip*, a long spindly cave that is believed to stretch for at least 7 km. It takes about two hours to explore the cavern and at the end of one of the off-shoots is a crystal-clear pool, perfect for a dip. The cave is guarded by a large Buddha figure and is home to loads of bats, which the locals capture by splashing water on them.

‼ *Do not visit Tham Hoi without a guide as there have been a couple of fatalities here.*

There are many more caves in the vicinity of town, most to the west and north. It is possible to hire a bicycle in Vang Vieng (around 10,000 kip per day), take it across the river and cycle to the caves and villages on the other side of the Nam Xong as all the sites are between 2 km and 15 km from Vang Vieng. Alternatively you can catch a Lao-style tractor on the far side of the river (5,000-8,000 kip depending on distance; bargain hard).

Kasi → *Colour map 2, A2*

This is one of those towns that seem to exist for no better reason than that people need to rest and have a bite to eat. It is a trucking stop on Route 13 and, as it is only 60 km north from the much more attractive town of Vang Vieng, it entices few people to tarry here for longer than necessary. According to some of the locals, the countryside around Kasi boasts what is reputedly the second largest cave in the world, Khoun Lang. To date, this has remained a well-kept secret; the cave hasn't popped up on the tourism radar yet and no official tours have been established. Delightfully, the introduction of tourists to the area looks set to be done in a traditional Lao style, with trips incorporating local food and living, including showers in the river and such like. There is plenty of interest to be had by walking around local ethnic villages. The children learn English at school and welcome the opportunity to talk to strangers.

The 45 km stretch of hilly road north of Kasi, up towards **Muang Phou Khoun**, is notorious for Hmong rebel attacks, although it has calmed down in the last few years. **Muang Phou Khoun** is an old colonial garrison at the junction of Route 13 and Route 7. Its strategic position was heavily fought over during the second Indochina war.

🛏 Sleeping

Ban Pako *p101, map p99*
C-E Ban Pako Resort, T021-451970, F021-451844. Accommodation is in a Lao-style longhouse or in single bungalows overlooking the river. You can also sleep under the stars on the verandah. Can be crowded at weekends. The restaurant (♈♈♈) serves excellent Lao and European food.

Phou Khao Khouay *p101*
The visitor centre at Tad Leuk rents out tents, mattresses, mosquito nets and sleeping bags. It costs 40,000 kip per night to rent a tent and 15,000 kip a night to hire a sleeping bag. Toilets and washing facilities on site. It is also possible to organize a homestay in one of the surrounding villages.

Vangxang *p103*
D Vangxang Resort, 13 Neau Rd, Ban Phonegnern, T021-211526. The resort has cute little cottage-style bungalows, with hot water. Great Lao restaurant and scenic manmade lake. US$6 a night.

Nam Ngum *p103, map p99*

A Nam Ngum Resort, southern end of Nam Ngum, T021-217592, www.dansavanh.com. Perplexingly advertized as an ecotourist option, this is a Malaysian and Lao government joint-venture hotel with 209 rooms, Chinese and Thai restaurant, health centre, video games and 1 of only 2 legal casinos in the country. Future plans include marine sports facilities, fun fair and golfing links. Rates include breakfast and a shuttle bus from Vientiane.

B Nam Lik Eco Resort, Ban Vang Mong, about 8 km from Ang Nam Ngum, turn off Route 13 at Km 75, T020-5508719. Lovely bungalow rooms, affording brilliant views. Myriad adventure sports, from kayaking through to rock-climbing.

Vang Vieng and around *p104, map p108*

This is one of the most popular destinations in the country for foreign travellers and numerous guesthouses and Western-style restaurants have sprung up to accommodate this influx. Unfortunately, the town's popularity has also ensured a uniformity among almost all the places catering to tourists: most restaurants feature the same menu (with the same typos) and there isn't much individuality in the guesthouses either. The accommodation in town is far from mind-blowing but the riverfront places, further from the centre, do promise stunning karsk limestone cliffs and water views right on your front doorstep. Most guesthouses are geared to the needs of travellers and offer a laundry service, guides, bicycles, inner tubes (for the river) and maps of the area. They are good sources of information regarding the caves and other sights in the vicinity of town. Below is by no means an exhaustive list of the accommodation available.

A-B Thavonsouk Resort, on the river, T021-511096, thavonsouk@hotmail.com. This lovely place was the choice of Kylie Minogue when she came to town and offers several different styles of accommodation. There is a traditional Lao house, decorated with Lao furnishings, suitable for a family or big group, plus suites (TV, fridge, bath, a/c) and standard accommodation. Fantastic restaurant. Keep your eye out for local home-grown pop star, Aluna, who runs the place. Highly recommended.

B Ban Sabai Bungalows, on the banks of the river, T021-511088, F021-511403. A stunning complex of bungalows in a spectacular location, with all the modern fittings. Hot water, a/c, breakfast included. A fire in 2005 burnt a few of the bungalows but the place is still in top form. Recommended.

B Nam Song Hotel, T021-213506, milestone at the gate. This hotel sits in a beautiful location overlooking the Nam Xong within its own spacious grounds, but has a bit of a Communist institution feel. However, the renovations underway at the time of publication looked pretty promising and, when the completed project is finally unveiled, expect large rooms with bath, television and a/c.

B Vang Vieng Resort, close to Tham Chang, T021-219380. A Chinese-owned resort, with bar and noodle restaurant. Some chalets have bathrooms but there's no a/c and the rooms smell musty.

C Vang Vieng Orchid, on the river road, T021-511172. Very new-looking building with rooms ranging from US$6 (fan) to US$15 (a/c). Hot water bathrooms, clean tiled floors, very comfortable. Friendly owners. The rooms with the private balconies are well worth the few extra dollars to have your own personal piece of the phenomenal view. Recommended.

D Malany Guesthouse, on the main road, T021-511083. Smack bang in the centre of town. Big concrete building, not the most forthcoming in friendliness. The rooms are very clean and surprisingly nice, with en suite bathrooms, hot water and fan. Hardish beds, though.

D Maylyn Guesthouse, T020-560 4095. Very atmospheric setting on the opposite side of the river to town. Basic rattan-style bungalows, with shared facilities. In summer a footbridge leads to the bungalows; in the wet season small boats make the short trip for around 2,000-5,000 kip.

D-E Dokkhoun, T021-511032. Two-storey villa with balcony area, clean rooms with hot water en suite bathrooms and hot water. A/c rooms for a few dollars extra.

D-E Erawan, T021-511093. This place is a hotbed of tourists and is a font of useful information on things to do in the area. Rooms are similar to all the others in town, but this place also boasts a TV, bar and restaurant and is always buzzing with people. Restaurant menu is disappointingly international, but food is good.

D-E **Saysong Guesthouse**, by the river behind the post office, T021-511130. The cheaper rooms (US$3) have en suite

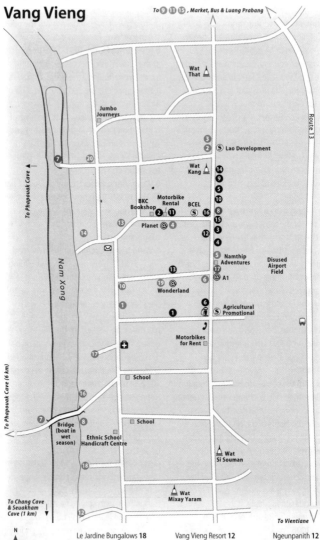

Vang Vieng

N

Not to scale

Sleeping
Amphone 1
Ben Sabai
  Bungalows 17
Bountang 2
Chanthala 3
Dokkhoun 4
Erawan 6

Le Jardine Bungalows 18
Malany Guesthouse 5
Maylyn Guesthouse 7
Morodok Guesthouse 9
Nam Song 8
Organic Mulberry
  Farm 11
Phou Bane 10
Saysong Guesthouse 14
Thavonsouk Resort 16
Thavisouk Guesthouse 19
Vang Vieng Eco-Lodge 15
Vang Vieng Orchid 20

Vang Vieng Resort 12
Viengvilay 13

Eating
Ahea 1
Fathima 2
Give Pizza a Chance 9
Keomani & Paddle
  Adventures 10
Luang Prabang
  Bakery 11
Nangbot 3
Nazim's 4

Ngeunpanith 12
Nisha 5
Organic Farm Café 6
Rising Sun 13
Sokphaserd 14
Vieng Champa 15
Xayoh Café & Green
  Discovery Tours 16

Bars & clubs
Island Bar 7
Jay Dees 17
Nam Lao 8

bathrooms and are a tad mouldy. The doubles are substantially better, cleaner and bigger. There's a small coffee shop downstairs and a fantastic communal balcony overlooking the river.

E Amphone, T021-511180. Nicer than many alternatives, although nothing particularly out of the ordinary. Spotless rooms with hot water in the en suite bathrooms and a friendly proprietor, who also just happens to be a dab hand at knocking up beautifully tailored trousers, shorts and skirts in his shop opposite. Recommended.

E Bountang, near Wat Kang. Large 3-storey white villa with weaving loom and handicrafts in the garden. Choice of cold and hot showers.

E Chanthala, next to Wat Kang. One of the older cheap guesthouses in Vang Vieng, with shared toilet facilities, clean.

E Phou Bane, close to the market and the bus station. One of the original guesthouses in Vang Vieng which may lend the place atmosphere, but the rooms are not as clean or well-equipped as others; shared shower and toilet downstairs. Good restaurant and nice garden to lounge in. A friendly place.

E Viengvilay, T021-511177. Bit of a mixed bag, this one: all rooms are reasonably clean and have en suite bathrooms, some on the 2nd floor offer spectacular views of the mountains.

E-F Le Jardine Bungalows, about 900 m from the centre of town along the river, T020-511 1340 (mob). There are 3 sets of bungalows here: the best are superb; the worst, falling down. It is far enough from town for the surrounding beauty to remain undisturbed but close enough for convenience (a tuk-tuk runs into town until 2000). The views are remarkable and the restaurant is quite good too. Recommended.

E-F Thavisouk Guesthouse, T5111340. Cheapish rooms in a central location. Hot water and a/c or fan. Bit damp but otherwise reasonably good value.

Out of town

The places out of town are great for those who wish to escape into a more natural landscape. The lack of facilities and transport in the area ensures tranquillity but also makes it quite difficult to get to town.

A-B Morodok Guesthouse, 2 km north off Vang Vieng off Route 13, T021-511488, morodok2003@yahoo.com. 13 rattan and brick bungalows set in a pleasant riverside valley. The gardens are a tad overgrown but nonetheless very pleasant. The rooms are comfortable with en suite bathroom, hot water and nice balconies. Thai restaurant.

A-B Vang Vieng Eco-Lodge, 7 km north of town, T020-5513785 (mob), tatluang @laotel.com. Although this isn't an ecolodge it is still an exceptionally beautiful place to stay. Set on the banks of the Nam Xong river, with stunning gardens and beautiful rock formations, this newly established 'resort' is a perfect place to get away from it all and not be disturbed. The 10 chalet-style bungalows have been nicely decorated, with beautiful balconies, comfortable furnishings and a big hot water bathtub. It is quite far out of town but management assures a tuk-tuk is just a phone call away. Good Lao restaurant. Also arranges kayaking, camping and trekking. Low season discount.

D-E Organic Mulberry Farm, 3 km north of town, T021-511220, www.laofarm.org. This mulberry farm is a very popular drop-off spot for tubers. The farm is engaged in community development (its latest project is the construction of a local library) and, originally, people volunteering at the farm would get free board but this is no longer the case. You don't have to be a volunteer to stay here, although a helping hand is more than welcome. Basic rooms with net US$5, dorm accommodation US$3, full board US$10. Cheaper rates in the low season. Hugely popular restaurant, serving great star-fruit wine (20,000 kip) and famous mulberry pancakes (10,000 kip).

Kasi *p106*

Rooms are available in Kasi at several guesthouses.

E Somchith, Route 13 Main Rd. The most popular place is this small guesthouse above a restaurant in the centre of town.

● Eating

Nam Ngum Dam *p103, map p99*

❦❦ **Lao Food Rafts**, there are several floating restaurants lining the shore.

There is a string of eating places on the main road through town, with the same menu duplicated in almost every establishment. Generally available are hamburgers, pasta, sandwiches, basic Asian dishes and the local 'Israeli Salad'. Most of the restaurants offer 'happy' upgrades – marijuana or mushrooms in your pizza, cake or lassi. Although many people choose the 'happy' offerings, some of these wind up very ill. The police have also been known to go on drug-busting sprees.

On the main road

Give Pizza a Chance. This little place offers a broad sample of Western fillers, including pesto spaghetti, salads, burgers and baked potatoes. Lao food is referred to as 'ethnic food' on the menu.

Keomani Restaurant, T021-511122. Sandwiches, pasta, some Lao and Thai dishes. Very friendly owners. Also serves as the headquarters for **Paddling Adventures**.

Nangbot, T021-511018. This proper sit-down restaurant is one of the oldest tourist diners in town and serves a few traditional dishes, such as bamboo shoot soup and *laap* with sticky rice, alongside the usual Western fare.

Nazim's, T021-511214. Largest and most popular Indian joint in town. Good range of South Indian and buriyani specialities, plus selection of vegetarian meals.

Ngeunpanith, attached to the guesthouse, T021-511150. May as well be called *Friends* Café, as this is what folk seem to come here for. The appeal? Who knows, maybe it's the 'happy' supplements.

Nisha Restaurant, T020-5685538. Pretty good-value Indian food and Lao dishes.

Organic Farm Cafe, further down the main road. Small café offering over 15 tropical fruit shakes and a fantastic variety of food. Mulberry shakes and pancakes are a must and the harvest curry stew is absolutely delicious. The sister branch is at the **Organic Mulberry Farm** (see Sleeping). You can while away the afternoon sipping star-fruit wine and watching the world go by on the river. Highly recommended.

Sokphaserd Restaurant, T020-5623360 (mob). Seating on an elevated platform offering steak, pizza, shakes (11 different types) and Israeli Salad. Lots of neon.

Thank-you Restaurant. Long narrow place with big breakfast menu, plus salad and burgers.

Vieng Champa Restaurant, T021-511037. Refreshingly, this family-run restaurant seems to have a greater selection of Lao food than most other places on the street. Most meals between 15,000 and 20,000 kip. The only drawback is the highly unflattering green fluorescent lighting.

Elsewhere in town

Ahea, T021-511141. Sweet little place, set away from the main strip and offering a good line in decent, cheap Lao food. The milkshakes are to die for and the breakfast comes highly recommended. A welcome break for anyone looking to escape the crowds.

Fathima, just up from the post office, T020-5111198 (mob). Indian and Malay cuisine, including good nasi goreng. Halal food.

Luang Prabang Bakery Restaurant, just off the main road, near BCEL. Excellent pastries, cakes and shakes and pretty delicious breakfasts. The rotund proprieter has cultivated the Italian Mama look down to a tee. Highly recommended.

Rising Sun, just off the main road. They've tried to cultivate a different atmosphere here to every other restaurant in town. The decor is brightly coloured and the menu features good comfort food, such as cottage pie.

❶ Bars and clubs

Vang Vieng and around *p104, map p108*
Island Bar, across the footbridge on the river. Crowds gather here in the dry season.
Jay Dees, main street. Very popular, if pokey. The punters jam pack the place, giving it a very cosy feel.
Nam Lao, main street. A small nightclub and restaurant, although food seemed quite scarce at the time of publication. Dim lighting, bar, dancefloor for hip-hop and dance music. Popular with younger locals.

❷ Shopping

Vang Vieng and around *p104, map p108*
BKC Bookshop, next door to Fathima restaurant, T021-511303. A reasonable but limited bookshop and exchange.

Ethnic School Handicraft Centre, near the hospital, by the river, has a small shop selling good-quality bags, purses and other handicrafts made by the Khmu, Yao and Hmong students at the school. The proceeds go towards the school.
New Market, 2 km north of town has the greatest selection of goods. .

▲ Activities and tours

Vang Vieng and around *p104, map p108*
Tour guides are available for hiking, rafting, visiting the caves and minority villages from most travel agents and guesthouses. Safety issues need to be considered when taking part in any adventure activity. There have been fatalities in Vang Vieng from boating, trekking and caving accidents. The Nam Xong river can flow very, quickly during the wet season (Jul, Aug) and tourists have drowned here. Make sure you wear a life-jacket during all water-borne activities and time your trip so you aren't travelling on the river after dark. A price war between tour operators has led to cost cutting, resulting in equipment that is not well maintained or does not exist at all. With all tour operators it is imperative that you are given safety gear and that canoes, ropes, torches and other equipment is in a good state of repair. The more expensive, reputable companies are often the best option (see also Vientiane Tour operators, page 93).
Green Discovery, attached to Xayoh Café. Probably the best operator in town. Caving, trekking, rafting and kayaking trips. Also rock climbing courses. Very professional and helpful. Highly recommended.
Namthip Adventures, near the centre . Rents out tubes for US$4 per day, including transport to drop-off site. Also offers a range of other tourist services, but for adventure tourism it's better to go with either **Paddling Adventures** or **Wild Side** (Vientiane).
Paddling Adventures, Keomani Restaurant, T020-5624783. Rafting and kayaking expeditions at reasonable rates.

Elephant trekking
Jumbo Journeys, close to the Vang Vieng Orchid Hotel, T020-5624923. This outfit offers great half day treks through and along the river. These trips are combined with visiting a cave. US$20. Recommended.

Kayaking and rafting
Kayaking is a very popular activity around Vang Vieng and competition between operators is fierce. There are a wide variety of trips available, ranging from day trips (with a visit to the caves and surrounding villages), to kayaking all the way to Vientiane (for experienced kayakers only), US$15-25, about 6 hrs, including a 30-min drive at the start and finish. All valuables are kept in a car which meets kayakers at the end of their paddle. A few companies also offer 2-day rafting trips down the Nam Ngum river, one of the only ways to see the off-limits Saysamboun Special Zone (see page 102). The trip includes several grade 4 and 5 rapids and usually an overnight camp on an island on Nam Ngum Lake. US$$100 per person or less for groups of more than 3. The trips can be tailormade to include other attractions.
Both **Green Discovery** and **Paddle Adventures** are recommended for kayaking and rafting trips. Be wary of intensive rafting or kayaking trips through risky areas during the wet season as it can be very dangerous.

Rock climbing
Vang Vieng is the only really established rock climbing area in the country, with over 50 sites in the locality, ranging from grade 5 to 8A+. By 2005 almost all of these climbs had been 'bolted'. **Green Discovery** runs climbing courses almost every day in high season (US$20-45 per day, including equipment rental). The best climbing sites include:
Sleeping Cave (see Caves, above).
A popular destination, accessed by dug-out canoe across the Nam Xong river. The cave offers 14 separate routes, after which you can jump into the water on one of the rope swings to cool off.
Sleeping Wall, near to Sleeping Cave.
A tough 20-m crag, which features 19 separate climbs, including a few ascents requiring some tricky manoeuvring and steep overhangs. Boatmen offer climbers a lift along the Nam Xong river (5,000 kip) to get to the wall. There are refreshment stalls at both Sleeping Wall and Sleeping Cave.
Tham Nam Them, 7 km from town.
Fantastic clambers around the entrance of the cave. There are 19 bolted tracks here, both inside and outside the cave.

Trekking

Almost all guesthouses and agents in town offer hiking trips, usually incorporating a visit to caves and minority villages and, possibly, some kayaking or tubing. Tour operators will provide an English-speaking guide, all transport and lunch for US$10-15 per day.

Tubing

No trip to Vang Vieng is complete without tubing down the Nam Xong. Floating slowly along the Nam Xong is an ideal way to take in the stunning surroundings of misty limestone karsks, jungle and rice paddies. The drop-off point is 3 km from town near the organic farm, where several bars and restaurants have been set up along the river. Start early in the day as it's dangerous to tube after dark and the temperature of the water drops sharply. Tour operators and guesthouses offer tube rental, life jackets and drop-off for US$3-4. It is essential that you wear a life jacket as people have drowned on the river, particularly in the wet season (Jul and Aug) when the river swells and flows very, very quickly.

❺ Transport

See also Vientiane Transport, page 93.

Vang Vieng and around *p104, map p108*
Bicycle and motorbike hire
There are many bicycles for rent along the road east up from the market (10,000 kip per day). There are also a few motorbike rental places (US$5 per day).

Bus

Buses leave from the make-shift bus terminal on the east side of the airstrip, T021-511341. There were plans to relocate all buses to the terminal at the New Market, 2 km north of town but this still hadn't happened by Aug 2005. Check before departing to either station. Public buses leave for **Vientiane** at 0530, 0600, 0630, 0700, 1230 and 1330 daily, 20,000 kip; *songthaew* depart every hour or so. Also to **Luang Prabang** at 0900, 7hrs, 40,000 kip, or else catch a Vientiane-Luang Prabang bus as it passes through town. The upgrading of the road from Vang Vieng to Luang Prabang was finally completed at the end of 1996. Although safe at the time of publication, check on conditions before

travelling as, in the past, buses on this leg of the route north have been periodically ambushed by bandits. Route 13 continues north 60 km to Kasi. *Songthaew* regularly ply along this route.

VIP buses, which aren't really VIP buses at all, more like cramped, stinking, mini-vans, make trips to **Vientiane**, 0900, 1000, 1330 daily, 40,000 kip. Also to **Luang Prabang**, 0900 and 1000, 7 hrs, 75,000 kip. Every guesthouse and travel agent can book the VIP/mini-vans and they will pick-up from your guesthouse. Seats get booked up really quickly and buses take at least half an hour to make all their pick-ups, so expect long delays.

Tour companies sell tickets from Vang Vieng to **Bangkok** for ฿825 but there are better, more efficient and cost-effective ways to get back to the Thai capital.

Tuk-tuk
A day trip to the caves should cost US$7-10 but there have been reports of some drivers offering trips to the caves for 10,000 kip per person and then demanding an outrageous fee for the return leg. Make sure all prices are set in stone before departing town.

Kasi *p106*
Bus/truck
There are connections south to **Vang Vieng** (2 hrs) and north to **Luang Prabang** (4 hrs).

❶ Directory

Vang Vieng and around *p104, map p108*
Banks Agricultural Promotion Bank and the Lao Development Bank, on the main road both exchange cash, 0830-1530 daily. BCEL, T021-511480, exchanges cash and TCs and will also do cash advances on Visa and Mastercard, 0830-1530 daily. **Internet** There are a number of internet cafés along the main drag, all 200 kip per min; most offer international net calls from 3,000 kip per min. The best are Wonderland Internet, just off the main road and A1net. **Medical services** Vang Vieng Hospital is located on the road that runs parallel to the river; it's terribly under-equipped. The hospital is proof positive of the need for travel insurance. In most cases it is better to go to Vientiane or even into Thailand. **Post office** next to the former old market, 0830-1600 daily.

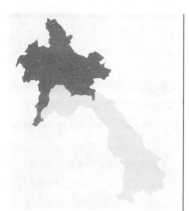

⁞ Footprint features

Introduction

Much of Laos's northern region is rugged and mountainous, a remote borderland with a significant minority population of hill peoples. Until recently, in some areas at least, the only way to travel was by boat, along one of the rivers – many fast-flowing – which have cut their way through this impressive landscape. Today road travel is much improved, although still not easy. The key centre of the north is the old royal capital of Luang Prabang, one of the world's most beautiful cities. To the east is the Plain of Jars and Vieng Xai, a former stronghold of the Pathet Lao, while to the north is a string of small towns that are becoming increasingly popular places to visit. Eco-resorts in peaceful forest settings, treks to upland villages, dips in icy mountain streams and rafting trips down innumerable rivers are among the highlights of this region. And, as tourist numbers rise, local people are learning to cater for the peculiar demands of foreigner visitors.

★ Don't miss...

1 **Luang Prabang** Saunter through the old royal capital, taking time to visit the incomparable Wat Xieng Thong and to climb Mount Phousi, see page 116.

2 **Pak Ou caves** Catch a boat upstream to cliff-side caves, stuffed with 4000 images of the Buddha, see page 135.

3 **Kwang Si falls** Take a dip in these cascades, south of Luang Prabang, page 136.

4 **Cruising on the Mekong** Take a slow boat along the river between Luang Prabang and Houei Xai on the border with Thailand, pages 147, 165 and 179.

5 **Trekking around Phongsali** Head north to this upland town for hiking amid stunning scenery, page 153.

6 **Muang Sing** Use the attractive hill town as a base for exploring the hill villages and minority peoples of the area, page 163.

7 **Boat Landing Guesthouse** Stay at the country's premier ecotourism resort on the river in Luang Namtha and enjoy great food, too, page 169.

8 **Plain of Jars** Construct your own hypothesis for the creation of Xieng Khouang's giant stone jars, page 185.

9 **Vieng Xai** Explore the caves that served as the stronghold of the Pathet Lao, page 198.

Northern Laos

Luang Prabang and around

→ *Phone code: 071. Colour map 2, A2.*

In terms of size, Luang Prabang hardly deserves the title 'city' – the capital district has a population of less than 20,000, and there are probably just 10,000 inhabitants in the town proper. But in terms of grandeur the appellation is more than deserved. Luang Prabang is the town that visitors often remember with the greatest affection. Its rich history, incomparable architecture, relaxed atmosphere, good food, friendly population and stunning position, surrounded by a crown of mountains, mark Luang Prabang out as exceptional.

At daybreak, scores of saffron-robed monks silently amble out of the monasteries bearing gold-topped alms boxes in which to collect offerings from the town's residents.

Anchored at the junction of the Mekong and Nam Khan rivers, the former royal capital is home to a spellbinding array of gilded temples, weathered French colonial shopfronts and art deco shophouses. Luang Prabang was founded on Mount Phousi – a small rocky hill with leafy slopes – and has been a mountain kingdom for over 1000 years. Despite a few welcome concessions to modern life, including great food, internet cafés, electricity and the occasional car, Luang Prabang still oozes the magic of bygone days. In the 18th century there were more than 65 wats in the city; many have been destroyed over the years but over 30 remain intact, including the former royal Wat Xieng Thong; Wat Visoun, built in 1513 (the oldest operational temple in Luang Prabang); That Pathum (Lotus Stupa), noted for its odd watermelon-like shape, and Wat Aham, formerly the seat of the Lao Supreme Patriarch. The continuing splendour and historical significance of the town led UNESCO to designate Luang Prabang a World Heritage Site at the end of 1995 and declare it the best preserved traditional city in Southeast Asia.

Yet for all its magnificent temples, this royal 'city' feels more like an easy-going provincial town: in the early evening children play in the streets, while women cook, old men lounge in wicker chairs and young boys play takro. The town's timelessness can be observed by simply walking the ancient cobbled paths. ➤➤ *For Sleeping, Eating and other listings, see pages 137-149.*

Ins and outs

Getting there Until quite recently visitors to Luang Prabang were advised by Vientiane's foreign consular staff to fly rather than risk the road journey. This was because vehicles on the stretch of Route 13 between Vientiane and Luang Prabang, particularly north of Kasi, were periodically attacked by Hmong bandits. Flying is still the easiest option, with daily connections from Vientiane, plus flights from Bangkok and Chiang Mai to **Luang Prabang International Airport** (LPQ) ① *4 km northeast of town, T071-212172/3.* Don't expect anything too jazzy but the airport does have a phone box, a couple of restaurants and handicraft shops. There is a standard US$5 charge for a tuk-tuk ride from the airport into the centre; on the way back you can probably negotiate a cheaper price.

Route 13 is now safe, with no recent attacks reported, and the road has been upgraded, shortening the journey from Vientiane to a relatively painless eight or nine hours. There are also overland connections with other destinations in northern Laos including Sayaboury, Nong Khiaw, Xieng Khouang (Phonsavanh), Xam Neua, Luang Namtha, Udom Xai, Muang Ngoi and Pak Mong. Luang Prabang has two main bus stations: **Kiew Lot Sai Nuan** (northern bus station), located on the northeast side of

---

● *Luang Prabang's famously laidback atmosphere even extends to crime and punishment.*
● *Prisoners at the Nam Pha 'free-range' jail were reportedly reluctant to be released.*

❝❞ Luang Prabang is a tiny Manhattan, but a Manhattan with holy men in yellow robes in its avenues, with pariah dogs, and garlanded pedicabs carrying somnolent Frenchmen nowhere, and doves in its sky.

Norman Lewis, A Dragon Apparent, *1950*

Sisavangvong Bridge, for traffic to and from the north; and **Naluang** (southern bus station) for traffic to and from the south. Occasionally buses will pass through the opposite station to what you would expect, so be sure to double-check. The standard tuk-tuk fare to/from either bus station is about 15,000 to 20,000 kip. If there are only a few passengers, it's late at night or you are travelling to/from an out-of-town hotel, expect to pay 20,000 to 30,000 kip. These prices tend to fluctuate with the international cost of petroleum. There is a third, smaller station, south of town, on the road to the falls, which operates as a terminal for buses to Sayaboury.

A third option is to travel by river: a firm favourite is the two-day trip between Houei Xai (close to the Thai border) and Luang Prabang, via Pak Beng. Less frequent are the boats between Luang Prabang and Vientiane, via Pak Lai, and to Muang Ngoi and Nong Khiaw, via Muang Khua. ►► *For further details, see Transport, page 147.*

Getting around Luang Prabang is a small town and the best way to explore the 'city' is either on foot or by bicycle. Bicycles can be hired from most guesthouses for US$1 per day and the ruling that banned foreigners from hiring bicycles has now been lifted (although there's no guarantee that it won't happen again). Strolling about this beautiful town is a real pleasure but there are also tuk-tuks and saamlors available for hire. Note, however, that road names are not widely used and there seems to be some confusion over precisely what some of the roads are called. Buses provide links with out-of-town destinations (although the service is limited and intermittent), and there are also boats and minibuses for charter.

When to visit Luang Prabang lies 300 m above sea-level on the upper Mekong, at its confluence with the Nam Khan. The most popular time to visit the town is during the comparatively cool months of November and December but the best time to visit is from December to February. After this the weather is warming up and the views are often shrouded in a haze, produced by shifting cultivators using fire to clear the forest for agriculture. This does not really clear until May or, sometimes, June. During the months of March and April, when visibility is at its worst, the smoke can cause soreness of the eyes, as well as preventing airplanes from landing.

Tourist information Luang Prabang Tourism Office is near Wat Vissunarat (Wat Visoun), on Visunnarat St, T071-212487. Aside from provincial information, it offers a couple of good ecotourism treks (which support local communities), including one to Tad Kwang Si and one in Chompet district. Ask for Vongdavone. Probably the best city map is the one compiled by the **Lao National Tourism Authority**, with support from the Asian Development Bank and GT Rider; the tourist office should have free copies. In 2000, a 3-D city map was released; it's not really practical for travellers, as it's large and cumbersome, but it makes a fairly attractive souvenir. Other maps are increasingly available, including a detailed map by Hobo maps.

History

According to legend, the site of Luang Prabang was chosen by two resident hermits. Buddha was believed to have glanced in Luang Prabang's direction, saying a great city would be built there. The discovery of large, stone container-like artefacts nearby Luang Prabang allude to an ancient history yet to be unravelled by archaeologists. Some believe the artefacts are linked with the Vietnamese Dong Son period (500 BC-AD 100), while others suggest a prehistoric connection to the Plain of Jars. Details are sketchy regarding the earliest inhabitants of Luang Prabang but historians imply the ethnic Khmu and Lao Theung groups were the initial settlers. They named Luang Prabang, 'Muang Sawa', which literally translates as Java, hinting at some kind of cross-border support. By the end of the 13th century, Muang Sawa had developed into a regional hub.

A major turning point in the city's history came about in 1353, when the mighty Fa Ngum barrelled down the Nam Ou river, backed by a feisty Khmer army, and captured Muang Sawa. Here, the warrior king founded Lane Xang Hom Khao, the Kingdom of a Million Elephants, White Parasol and established a new Lao royal lineage, which was to last another 600 years. The name of the city refers to the holy Pra Bang, Laos's most sacred image of the Buddha which was given to Fa Ngum by his father-in-law the King of Cambodia.

Fa Ngum imported Khmer traditions including Theravada Buddhism and great architecture, but his constituents and army, wary of his warmongering ways, exiled him in 1373, and his son, Oun Heuan, then assumed the throne. Oun Heuan was known as 'Samsenthai', a name that indicated the size of his army – a man-force of 300,000 – and, during his reign, the city was renamed Muang Xieng Thong, the City of Gold.

In 1478 the city was invaded by Vietnamese. After several years occupying and ransacking the place, they were finally driven out and the Kingdom embarked upon a massive reconstruction campaign. During this period some of Luang Prabang's finest monuments were built, including Wat Xieng Thong. The city had been significantly built up by the time King Visunarat came to power in 1512 and remained the capital until King Setthathirat, fearing a Burmese invasion, moved the capital to Vieng Chan (Vientiane) in 1563.

Luang Prabang was a religious as well as a trading centre. To begin with, it seems that Theravada Buddhism was creatively combined with ritualistic elements from the Hinduist and animist past. Mendez Pinto, in his account of 1578, describes Luang Prabang (or what historians take to be Luang Prabang) as having 24 religious sects and writes that there is "so great a variety and confusion of diabolical errors and precepts, principally in the blood sacrifices they employ, that it is frightful to hear them". The royal chronicles of the 16th century describe successive attempts to erase these sects from the kingdom.

Luang Prabang's importance diminished in the 18th century, following the death of King Souligna Vongsa and the break-up of Lane Xang, but it remained a royal centre until the Communist takeover in 1975. During the low point of Laos' fortunes in the mid-19th century, when virtually the whole country had become tributary to Bangkok (Siam), only Luang Prabang retained a semblance of independence. The tiny kingdom, shorn of most of its hinterland, paid tribute to Siam, Hué and Peking, hoping to play one off against the other. (The country's approach to foreign affairs since 1975 neatly mirrors this strategy.) What the king in Luang Prabang did not envisage, however, was the arrival of a power stronger than all three of these: the French.

The French and the British competed diligently for control of mainland Southeast Asia. France's piece of the cake became French Indochina and their attempt to wrest control of Laos from Siamese suzerainty was linked to the energy, perseverance and force of will of one man: Auguste Pavie. Contemporary accounts describe Pavie as

Mekong monsters, real and imagined

It is said that the *pla buk*, the giant catfish of the Mekong, was only described by Western science in 1930. That may be so, but the English explorer and surveyor, James McCarthy, goes into considerable detail about the fish in his book *Surveying and exploring in Siam*, which was first published in 1900 and draws upon his travels in Siam and Laos between 1881 and 1893.

He writes: "The month of June in Luang Prabang is a very busy one for fishermen. Nearly all the boats are employed on fishing, each paying a large fish for the privilege. Two kinds of large fish, *pla buk* and *pla rerm*, are principally sought after... A *pla buk* that I helped to take weighed 130 pounds; it was 7 ft long and 4 ft 2 ins round the body; the tail measured 1 ft 9 ins. The fish had neither scales nor teeth, and was sold for 10 rupees. The roe of this fish is considered a great delicacy. The fish is taken in... June, July and August, when on its upward journey. Returning in November, it keeps low in the river, and a few stray ones only are caught." McCarthy also recounts the story of a mythical river serpent of the Mekong: "It lives only at the rapids, and my informant said he had seen it. It is 53 ft long and 20 ins thick. When a man is drowned it snaps off the tuft of hair on the head [men wore their hair in this manner], extracts the teeth, and sucks the blood; and when a body is found thus disfigured, it is known that the man has fallen victim to the *nguak*, or river serpent, at Luang Prabang."

"thin and weak-looking" but this physical demeanour disguised a man of extraordinary abilities. He was appointed French vice-consul in Luang Prabang in May 1886, after accumulating 17 years' experience in Cambodia and Cochin China (south Vietnam). According to Martin Stuart-Fox in *A History of Laos* (1997), Pavie had not only acquired a comprehensive knowledge of the people, cultures and languages of the area, but also developed a deep dislike of the Siamese. His part in securing Laos for France was achieved when he rescued King Unkham from marauding Haw and Tai bandits in 1887. The protecting Siamese and their Lao soldiers had departed from Luang Prabang, leaving Pavie with the opportunity to save the day. He plucked the aged king from a burning palace, escaped downstream and was rewarded when the king requested France's protection. The events marked the dispossession of the Siamese by the French. The city had been ransacked and set ablaze by the bandits but the French helped to rebuild the city, using indentured labour from Vietnam and giving Luang Prabang much of the look it has today.

James McCarthy, an otherwise rather plodding recorder of events and sights, wrote of Luang Prabang at the end of the 19th century: "In a clear afternoon, Luang Prabang stood out distinctly. At evening the pagoda spires and the gilded mouldings of the wats, glancing in the light of the setting sun, added their effect to that of the natural features of the landscape – and caused in me a feeling of irresistible melancholy. Since my visit in February 1887, Luang Prabang had passed through much suffering. It had been ravaged by the Haw; its people had been pillaged and murdered or driven from their homes, and the old chief had only been rescued by his sons forcing him to a place of safety. The town seemed doomed to suffer, for within two months past it had again been burned, and, more recently still, about 500 of its inhabitants had died of an epidemic sickness." Yet, by 1926 American Harry Franck could find paradise in Luang Prabang, as recorded in his book, *East of Siam*: "It is not a city at all, in the crowded, noisy, Western sense, but a leisurely congregation of dwellings of simple lines, each ... with sufficient ground so that its opinions or doings need not interfere with its neighbours. In short, Luang Prabang town is in many ways what idealists picture the cities of Utopia to be".

Luang Prabang didn't suffer as greatly as other provincial capitals during the Indochina wars, narrowly escaping a Viet Minh capture in 1953. Rumour has it that as the Vietnamese troops approached Luang Prabang, the citizens remained calm because a blind monk had prophesized that the city wouldn't be taken. During the Second Indochina War, however, the Pathet Lao cut short the royal lineage, forcing King Sisavang Vatthana to abdicate and sending him to a re-education camp in northeastern Laos where he, his wife and his son died from starvation.

Despite the demise of the monarchy and years of revolutionary rhetoric on the city's tannoy system, Luang Prabang's dreamy streets have somehow retained the aura of old Lane Xang. In the early 1990s it was suggested that a highway be constructed through Luang Prabang, to the Chinese border. Fortunately, with UNESCO's designation of Luang Prabang as a World Heritage Site, the scope for redevelopment was substantially restricted. The old town – essentially the promontory – is fully protected while elsewhere only limited redevelopment and expansion is permitted (no building, for example, can be higher than three storeys). The road building went ahead but the local authorities constructed a bypass to ensure that the fragile town wasn't disrupted.

Luang Prabang

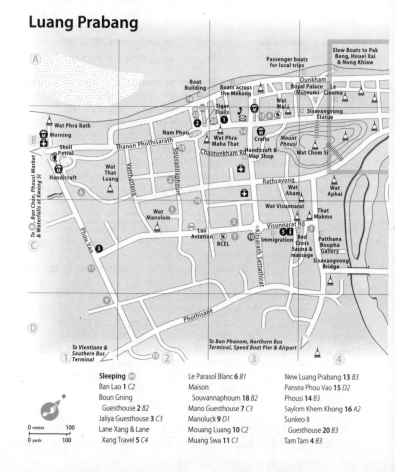

Sleeping

Ban Lao **1** *C2*
Boun Gning
    Guesthouse **2** *B2*
Jaliya Guesthouse **3** *C3*
Lane Xang & Lane
    Xang Travel **5** *C4*

Le Parasol Blanc **6** *B1*
Maison
    Souvannaphoum **18** *B2*
Mano Guesthouse **7** *C3*
Manoluck **9** *D1*
Mouang Luang **10** *C2*
Muang Swa **11** *C1*

New Luang Prabang **13** *B3*
Pansea Phou Vao **15** *D2*
Phousi **14** *B3*
Saylom Khem Khong **16** *A2*
Sunkeo II
    Guesthouse **20** *B3*
Tam Tam **4** *B3*

Sights

The sights are conveniently close together in Luang Prabang. Most are walkable – the important ones can be covered leisurely within two days – but a bike is the best way to get around. To begin with it may be worth climbing Phousi or taking a stroll along the Mekong and Nam Khan river roads to get a better idea of the layout of the town. Most of Luang Prabang's important wats are dotted along the main road, Phothisarath. When visiting the wats it is helpful to take a guide to obtain entry to all the buildings, which are often locked for security reasons. Without a guide, your best chance of finding them open is early in the morning. ▶▶ *For a walking tour of the town, see page 129.*

Royal Palace

ⓘ *Sisavangvong Rd. Daily 0800-1100 and 1330-1600. Admission 20,000 kip. Shorts, short-sleeved shirts and strappy dresses are prohibited; shoes should be removed and bags must be put in lockers. No photography.*

Also called the **National Museum**, the Royal Palace is right in the centre of the city on the main road, Sisavangvong, which runs along the promontory and allowed royal guests ready access from the Mekong. Unlike its former occupants, the palace survived the 1975 revolution and was converted into a museum the following year. It replaced a smaller wooden palace on the same site.

Construction of the palace started in 1904, during the reign of Sisavang Vong, and took 20 years. It was built by the French for the Lao king, in an attempt to bind him and his family more tightly to the colonial system of government. Although most of the construction was completed by 1909, the two front wings were extended in the 1920s and a new, more Lao-style, roof was added. These later changes were accompanied by the planting of the avenue of palms and the filling in of one of two fish ponds. Local residents regarded the ponds as the 'eyes' of the capital, so the blinding of one eye was taken as inviting bad fortune by leaving the city unprotected. The subsequent civil war seemed to vindicate these fears. The palace is Khmer in style, cruciform in plan and mounted on a small platform of four tiers. The only indication of French involvement can be seen in the two French lilies represented in stucco on the entrance, beneath the symbols of Lao royalty. There are a few Lao motifs but, in many respects, the palace is more foreign than Lao: it was designed by a French architect, with steps made from Italian marble; built by masons from Vietnam; embellished by carpenters from Bangkok, and funded by the largesse of the colonial authorities. The palace itself is modest; its contents, spectacular.

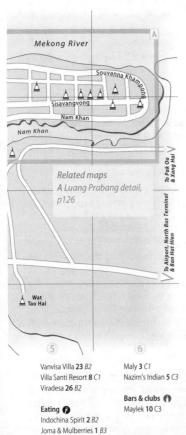

Related maps
A Luang Prabang detail, p126

Vanvisa Villa **23** *B2*
Villa Santi Resort **8** *C1*
Viradesa **26** *B2*

Maly **3** *C1*
Nazim's Indian **5** *C3*

Eating 🍴
Indochina Spirit **2** *B2*
Joma & Mulberries **1** *B3*

Bars & clubs 🍸
Maylek **10** *C3*

The museum now contains a collection of 15th- to 17th-century Buddha statues and artefacts from many of the wats in Luang Prabang such as the Khmer bronze drums from Wat Visoun. Notable pieces include an ancient Buddha head, an offering from Indian dignitaries; and a reclining Buddha with the unusual addition of mourners. The most important piece, however, is the Pra Bang, or **Golden Buddha**, from which the city derives its name. The Buddha is in the attitude of Abhayamudra or 'dispelling fear' (see page 334). Some believe that the original image is kept in a bank vault, although most dispel this as rumour. It is 90% solid gold, stands 83 cm high and weighs around 53 kg. Reputed to have originally come from Ceylon, and said to date from any time between the first and ninth centuries, the statue was brought to Cambodia in the 11th century, given to King Phaya Sirichanta, and was then taken to Lane Xang by King Fa Ngum, who had spent some time in the courts of Angkor and married into Khmer royalty. An alternative story has the Pra Bang following Fa Ngum to the city: it is said that he asked his father-in-law, the King of Angkor, to send a delegation of holy men to assist him in spreading the Theravada Buddhist faith in Lane Xang. The delegation arrived bringing with them the Pra Bang as a gift from the Cambodian King. The Pra Bang's arrival heralded the capital's change of name, from Xieng Thong to Nakhon Luang Prabang – 'The great city of the big Buddha'. In 1563 King Setthathirat took the statue to Lane Xang's new capital at Vientiane. Two centuries later in 1779 the Thais captured it but it was returned to Laos in 1839 and rediscovered in the palace chapel in 1975. The Pra Bang is revered in Laos as its arrival marked the beginnings of Buddhism in Lane Xang. The Pra Bang is currently kept in a small enclosure to the right of the entrance but is expected to be moved to the Wat Ho Prabang during 2006.

Entrance hall The main entrance hall of the palace was used for royal religious ceremonies, when the Supreme Patriarch of Lao Buddhism would oversee proceedings from his gold-painted lotus throne.

King's reception room The room to the immediate right of the entrance was the King's reception room, also called the **Ambassadors' Room**. It contains French-made busts of the last three Lao monarchs, a model of the royal hearse (which is kept in Wat Xieng Thong) and a mural by French artist Alex de Fontereau, depicting a day in the life of Luang Prabang in the 1930s.

Coronation Room (Throne Room) To the rear of the entrance hall, the Coronation Room was decorated between 1960 and 1970 for Sisavang Vatthana's coronation, an event which was interrupted because of the war. The walls are a brilliant red with Japanese glass mosaics embedded in a red lacquer base with gilded woodwork. They depict scenes from Lao festivals, such as boat racing. The carved throne has a gold three-headed elephant insignia; on one side is a tall pot to hold the crown. To the right of the throne, as you face it, are the ceremonial coronation swords and a glass case containing 15th- and 16th-century crystal and gold Buddhas, many from inside the 'melon stupa' of Wat Visoun. Because Luang Prabang was constantly raided, many of these religious artefacts were presented to the king for safekeeping long before the palace became a national museum. At the back of the room to the right of the entrance is the royal *howdah*, a portable throne that was used during battle. The throne is covered with shields to protect it.

Private apartments In comparison to the state rooms, the royal family's private apartments are modestly decorated. They have been left virtually untouched since Sisavang Vatthana and family left for exile in Xam Neua Province. The **King's library** backs onto the Coronation Room: Sisavang Vatthana was a well-read monarch, having studied at the École de Science Politique in Paris. Behind the library, built around a small inner courtyard are the Queen's modest bedroom, the King's bedchamber and the royal yellow bathroom, with its two regal porcelain thrones standing side by side. These rooms are cordoned off but you can still see them. The King's bed is a marvellous construction with a three-headed elephant insignia. The remaining rooms include a small portrait gallery, dining room and the former children's bedroom, which is decorated with musical instruments and headdresses for Ramayana actors. In the hallway linking the rooms is a miscellany of interesting objects, including a an intricately patterned *sinh*, worn by the queen, and a royal palanquin (the King's tuk-tuk), which would have been tied to an elephant. Domestic rooms, offices and library are located on the ground floor beneath the state apartments.

Other reception rooms To the left of the entrance hall is the reception room of the **King's Secretary**, and beyond it, the **Queen's reception room**, which together house an eccentric miscellany of state gifts from just about every country except the UK. Of particular note is the moon rock presented to Laos by the USA following the Apollo 11 and 17 lunar missions. Also in this room are portraits of the last King Sisavang Vatthana, Queen Kham Phouy and Crown Prince Vongsavang, painted by a Soviet artist in 1967.

King's chapel On the right wing of the palace, next to the King's reception room, is the King's private chapel, which housed the Pra Bang until 2005. It also contains four Khmer Buddhas, ivories mounted in gold, bronze drums used in religious ceremonies and about 30 smaller Buddha images from temples all over the city.

Wat Ho Prabang This small ornate pavilion is located in the northeast corner of the palace compound, to the right of the entrance to the Royal Palace. It was designed by the Royal Secretary of the time to house the Pra Bang and was paid for by small donations sent in from across the country. The Pra Bang should move in here in 2006.

Other buildings In the left-hand corner (south) of the compound, is the **Luang Prabang Conference Hall**, built for the official coronation of Savang Vatthana, which was terminally interrupted by the 1975 Revolution. The southwestern corner of the compound is now used as the **Royal Theatre**, where traditional performances are held.

Wat Mai

ⓘ *Sisavangvong Rd. Daily 0800-1700. Admission 5000kip.*

Next to the Royal Palace is Wat Mai. This royal temple, inaugurated in 1788, has a five-tiered roof and is one of the jewels of Luang Prabang. It took more than 70 years to complete. It was officially called Wat Souvanna Phommaram and was the home of the Buddhist leader in Laos, Phra Sangkharath until he moved to That Luang in Vientiane. Auguste Pavie and his crew took up residence here while trying to win Luang Prabang over from the Siamese who controlled the Lao court at the time. The Siamese thought that detaining Pavie in the compound would keep him out of their way but the Frenchman struck up a friendship with a local abbot, who acted as a runner between the King and Pavie. The temple housed the Pra Bang from 1894 until 1947 and, during Pi Mai (New Year), the Pra Bang is taken from the Royal Palace and installed at Wat Mai for its annual ritual cleansing, before being returned to the Palace on the third day.

Today, Wat Mai is probably the most popular temple after Wat Xieng Thong. The façade is particularly interesting: a large golden bas-relief tells the story of Phravet (one of the last reincarnations of the Gautama or historic Buddha), with several village scenes, including depictions of wild animals, women pounding rice and people at play. Inside, the interior is an exquisite amalgam of red and gold, with supporting pillars similar to those in Wat Xieng Thong and Wat Visoun. The temple is indicative of Luang Prabang architecture aside from the standout roofed verandah, whose gables face the sides rather than the front. The central beam at Wat Mai is carved with figures from the Hindu story of the birth of Ravanna and Hanuman. Behind the temple is an open construction where two classical racing boats are kept, ready to be brought out for Pi Mai (Lao New Year) and the August boat racing festival

▸▸ For details, see Festivals and events, page 144.

Mount Phousi

ⓘ *The western steps lead up from Sisavangvong Rd. Daily 0800-1800. Admission at western steps 10,000 kip. If you want to watch the sun go down, get there early and jostle for position – don't expect to be the only person there.*

Directly opposite the Royal Palace is the start of the steep climb up **Mount Phousi**, the spiritual and geographical heart of the city and a popular place to come to watch the sunset over the Mekong, illuminating the hills to the east. Luang Prabang was probably sited at this point on the Mekong, in part at least, because of the presence of Phousi. Many capitals in the region are founded near sacred hills or mountains, which could become local symbols of the Hindu Mount Mahameru or Mount Meru, the abode of the gods and also the abode of local tutelary spirits.

As you start the ascent, to the right is **Wat Pa Huak**, a disused wat suffering from years of neglect. It is usually locked but, occasionally, monks will open the building up for a small donation. It is worth the trouble because the monastery has some fine 19th-century murals, depicting classic scenes along the Mekong. There are a few Buddha images here that date from the same period and a fine carved wooden mosaic on the temple's exterior, depicting Buddha riding Airavata, the three-headed elephant from Hindu mythology.

From Wat Pa Huak, 328 steps wind up Phousi, a gigantic rock with sheer forested sides, surmounted by a 25-m-tall *chedi*, **That Chomsi**. The *chedi* was constructed in 1804, restored in 1914 and is the designated starting point for the colourful Pi Mai (New Year) celebrations in April (see Festivals and events, page 144). Its shimmering gold-spired stupa rests on a rectangular base, ornamented by small metal Boddhi trees. Next to the stupa is a little sanctuary, from which the candlelit procession descends at New Year, accompanied by effigies of Nang Sang Kham, the guardian of the New Year, and naga, protector of the city. The drum, kept in the small *hor kong* on the east side of the hill, is used only on ceremonial occasions. The summit of Phousi affords a splendid panoramic view of Luang Prabang and the surrounding mountains. The Mekong lies to the north and west, with the city laid out to the southeast.

A path next to the ack-ack cannon leads down to **Wat Tham Phousi**, which is more like a car port than a temple, but which is home to a rotund Buddha, Kaccayana (also called Phra Ka Tiay). At the top of the steps leading out of the wat are two tall cacti, planted defiantly in the empty shell casings of two large US bombs – the local monks' answer to decades of war.

Wat Siphouttabath (Wat Pha Phoutthabat)

Located down a path to the north of Wat Tham Phousi, just off the central road running along the promontory, is a compound containing three monasteries. Of them, **Wat Pa Khe** is most notable, predominantly for its carvings of 17th-century Dutch and Italian traders. Why these traders are depicted in a Buddhist temple in Luang Prabang remains a mystery, although many suspect it may have been influenced by trading merchants from the East India Company, who travelled through the area in the late 16th century. Behind the *sim* is a shrine housing a 3-m-long footprint of the Buddha. The shrine is normally only open during festive occasions, so you will need to ask someone on the premises for a key. Flanking the shrine is a small pavilion where Cambodia's former King Sihanouk entertained the press (in his usual publicity-centric fashion) during King Sisavang Vong's cremation ceremony.

A block back from Sisavangvong Road is the old monastery site of **Wat Xieng Muang**. The *sim* here was constructed in 1879, although initial construction is believed to have started decades earlier. The temple features a few impressive sculptures and an imposing fresco of *nagas* on the ceiling. UNESCO has funded an artistic training centre for monks here to ensure that adequate skills are available to continue restoration work in the future. The novices are being taught the crafts of wood-carving, painting and Buddha-making. Also in the same block is **Wat Pa Phai**, called the Bamboo Monastery, although there isn't an overwhelming amount of bamboo in evidence. The *sim*, however, is decorated with colourful serpents and peacocks.

Wat Sene (Wat Saen)

Further up the promontory, Wat Sene was built in 1718 and was the first *sim* in Luang Prabang to be constructed in Thai style, with a yellow and red roof. The exterior may lack subtlety, but the interior is delicate and rather refined, painted red, with gold patterning on every conceivable surface. Sen means 100,000 and the wat was built with a local donation of 100,000 kip from someone who discovered 'treasure' in the Nam Khan river. At the far end of the wat compound is a building containing a large, gold, albeit rather crudely modelled, image of the Buddha in the 'calling for rain' *mudra* (standing, arms held stiffly down). Note the torments of hell depicted on the façade of the building (top, left). The temple was restored in 1932, with further renovations in 1957. One of Laos's most sacrosanct abbots, Ajahn Khamjan, was ordained at the temple in 1940.

Wat Xieng Thong

ⓘ *Xiengthong Rd. Daily 0800-1700. Admission 10,000 kip.*

Wat Xieng Thong Ratsavoraviharn, usually known as just **Wat Xieng Thong**, is set back from the road, at the top of a flight of steps leading down to the Mekong. It is arguably the finest example of a Lao monastery, with graceful, low-sweeping eaves, beautiful stone mosaics and intricate carvings. The Wat has several striking chapels, including one that houses a rare bronze reclining Buddha and another sheltering a gilded wooden funeral chariot. The back of the temple is encrusted with a stunning glass mosaic depicting a boddhi tree, while inside, resplendent gold-stencilled pillars support a ceiling with *dharma* wheels. The temple's tranquillity is further enhanced by beautiful gardens of bougainvillea, frangipani and hibiscus, shaded by banyan and palm trees.

This monastery was a key element in Luang Prabang's successful submission to UNESCO for recognition as a World Heritage Site. The striking buildings in the tranquil compound are decorated in gold and post-box red, with imposing tiled roofs, intricate carvings, paintings and mosaics, making this the most important and finest royal wat in Luang Prabang. It was built by King Setthathirat in 1559, and is one of the few buildings to have survived the successive Chinese raids that marked the end of the 19th century. It retained its royal patronage until 1975 and has been embellished and well cared for over the years: even the crown princess of Thailand, Mahachakri Sirindhorn, has donated funds for its upkeep.

The sim The sim is a perfect example of the Luang Prabang style, with its low, sweeping roof in complex overlapping sections. The roof is one of the temple's most outstanding features and is best viewed at a distance. Locals believe that the roof has been styled to resemble a bird, with wings stretched out to protect her young. The eight central wooden pillars have stencilled motifs in gold and the façade is finely decorated. The beautiful gold-leaf inlay is predominantly floral in design but a few images illustrate Ramayana-type themes and the interior stencils depict *dharma* wheels and the enigmatic King Chantaphanit.

In an ancient form of the modern-day Mousetrap game, a serpent-like aqueduct sits above the right-hand side of the main entrance. During Lao New Year water is poured into the serpent's tail, causing it to gush along to its mouth and tip onto the Buddha image below. The water then filters down a drain, flowing under the floor and eventually spouting out of the mouth of the mirrored elephant on the exterior wall.

At the rear of the sim is a mosaic representation of the thong copper 'Tree of Life' in glass inlay. This traditional technique can also be seen on the 17th-century doors of That Ingheng, near Savannakhet in central Laos (see page 227).

Side chapels Behind the *sim* are two red *hor song phra* (side chapels): the one on the left is referred to as **La Chapelle Rouge** (the Red Chapel) and houses a rare Lao reclining Buddha in bronze, dating from the 16th century, which was shown at the 1931 Paris Exhibition. The image was kept in Vientiane and only returned to Luang Prabang in 1964. Several other Buddha images, of varying styles, dates, and materials, surround the altar. The exterior mosaics on the *hor song phra*, which relate local tales, were added in 1957 to honour the 2,500th anniversary of the Buddha's birth, death and enlightenment. Somewhat unusually, the fresco features a heroic character from local Lao folklore, Siaw Sawat. The other *hor song phra*, to the right of the sim, houses a standing image of the Buddha which is paraded through the streets of the city each New Year and doused in water. A small stone chapel with an ornate roof stands to the left of the sim.

Chapel of the Funeral Chariot The **hor latsalot** (chapel of the funeral chariot) is diagonally across from the *sim* and was built in 1962. The centrepiece is the grand 12-m-high gilded wooden hearse, with its seven-headed serpent, which was built for King Sisavang Vong, father of the last sovereign, and used to carry his urn to the stadium next to Wat That Luang (see below) where he was cremated in 1959. It was built on the chassis of a six-wheel truck by the sculptor Thid Tan. On top of the carriage sit several sandalwood urns, none of which contain royal ashes. Originally the urns would have held the bodies of the deceased in a foetal position until

Luang Prabang detail

Sleeping
Apsara 1
Bougnasouk Guesthouse 2
Bounthieng Guesthouse 3
Chautanome 4
Kongsarath 18
Le Calao Inn 5
Merry Lao Swiss 6
Pa Phai Guesthouse 8

Pack Luck 7
Sala Luang Prabang 9
Say Nam Khan Guesthouse 10
Sayo 11
Silichit Guesthouse 12
Sok Dee Guesthouse 13
Three Nagas 14
Tum Tum Cheng 15
Villa Santi 16

Villa Savanh 17

Eating
Café Ban Vat Sene 1
Café des Artes 2
Coleur Café 6
Dao Fa 3
Khemkhan Food Garden 5
Le Elephant 7

0 metres 50
0 yards 50

cremation. The mosaics inside the chapel were never finished but the exterior is decorated with some almost erotic scenes from the *Ramakien* (or local *Ramayana*), sculpted in enormous panels of teak wood and covered with gold leaf. Glass cabinets feature several puppets that were once used in royal performances.

Other structures The **tripitaka library**, near the boat shelter, was added in 1828. The **hor kong** at the back of the garden was constructed in the 1960s and near it is the site of the copper tree, from which Wat Xieng Thong took its name.

Wat Pak Khan

At the far northeast end of Phothisarath Road is **Wat Pak Khan**, which is not particularly noteworthy other than for its scenic location overlooking the confluence of the two rivers. It is sometimes called the Dutch Pagoda, as the sculptures on the south door are of figures dressed in 18th- and 19th-century Dutch costume.

> ‼ *The Pra Bang was housed here from 1507 to 1715 and again from 1867 to 1894.*

Wat Visunnarat (Wat Wisunarat)

ⓘ *Daily 0800-1700. Admission 10,000 kip.*

This is better known as Wat Visoun and is on the south side of Mount Phousi. It is a replica of the original wooden building, constructed in 1513, which had been the oldest building in Luang Prabang, until it was destroyed by marauding Chinese tribes. Louis Delaporte's sketches from the 1860s show the original temple as boat- or coffin-shaped. The wat was rebuilt in 1898 and, in keeping with the original style, renovators tried to ensure that the brick and stucco construction resembled the original medieval shapes of the lathed wood. The arch on the northwest side of the *sim* is original and the only remaining piece of the 16th-century building.

The *sim* is virtually a museum of religious art, with numerous 'Calling to the Rain' Buddha statues: most are more than 400 years old and have been donated by locals. One of the biggest philanthropists was Prince Phetsarat who donated them in order to redeem the temple after the Haw invasion. Wat Visoun also contains the largest Buddha in the city and old stelae engraved with Pali scriptures (called *hiu chaluk*).

The big stupa, commonly known as **That Makmo** ('melon stupa'), was built by Queen Visunarat in 1504. It is of Sinhalese influence with a smaller stupa at each corner, representing the four elements. The stupa originally contained hundreds of small Buddha images, many of which were pilfered by the Haw. The remaining images were relocated to the Royal Museum for safe-keeping.

Wat Aham

ⓘ *next door to Wat Visoun. Daily 0800-1700. Admission 10,000 kip.*

Wat Aham was built by a relative of the king in 1823 and, before Wat Mai took over, Wat Aham was the residence of the Supreme Patriarch of Lao Buddhism, Sangkharat. The interior has rather beautiful pillars and roof and overbearing modern murals of the torments of hell, as

Tourist port (boats to Pak Ou)

Wat Xieng Thong

World Heritage Office

Souvanna Khampong

Sakkaline

Wat Khi Li

Wat Pak Khan

L'Etranger **8**
Luang Prabang Bakery **9**
Luang Prabang Pizza **10**
Nazim's Indian **11**
Nisha's **12**
Pak Houay Mizay **13**
Samsara **14**

Tamnak Lao **15**
Tum Tum Cheng **16**
View Khaem Khong **4**
Yongkhoune **17**

Bars & clubs 🍸
Hive **18**
Khob Jai **19**
Lemongrass **20**

Northern Laos Luang Prabang & around

well as a panoramic view of Luang Prabang. The two huge Banyan trees outside are important spirit shrines.

Wat Phra Maha That

Close to the **Hotel Phousi** on Phothisarath Road, this is a typical Luang Prabang wat, built in the 1500s and restored at the beginning of this century. The ornamentation of the doors and windows of the *sim* merit attention, with their graceful, golden figures from the *Phra lak phra lam* (the *Ramayana*). The pillars, ornamented with massive *nagas*, are also in traditional Luang Prabang style and reminiscent of certain styles adopted in Thailand. The front of the *sim* was renovated in 1991. The monastery contains a stupa, holding the ashes of Prince Phetsarath and his younger brother Prince Souvanna Phouma.

Wat Phra Bath

Behind the market at the far northwest end of Phothisarath Road is **Wat Phra Bath** (or Phraphoutthabat Tha Phralak). The original wooden temple on this site dated back to the 17th century but most of the present structure was built in 1959 by the local Chinese and Vietnamese community. It certainly doesn't evoke the grandeur of other temples in town but is worth a visit for its picturesque position above the Mekong. It is renowned for its huge Buddha footprint – 'bath' is the Pali word for footprint.

Wat That Luang

Close by, behind the stadium, on Phou Vao Rd, is **Wat That Luang**. Rumour suggests that the original structure was built by Indian missionaries, although this is probably no more than hearsay as all evidence suggests that the royal wat was built in 1818 by King Manthaturat. Note the bars on the windows of the *sim* in wood and gold leaf, typical of Luang Prabang. The gold stupa, at one end of the compound, was built in 1910 and contains the ashes of King Sisavang Vong and his brother. King Sisavang Vong is remembered fondly in the city and many offerings are left here. The stone stupa contains relics of the Buddha and is the site of the Vien Thiene (candlelit) festival in May (see Festivals and events, page 144). There are also some traditional style *kuti*, or monks' quarters, with carved windows and low roofs.

When James McCarthy visited Wat Luang at the end of the 19th century, he was told of the ceremonies that were performed here on the accession of a new 'chief'. In his book *Surveying and exploring in Siam* (1900) he writes that the "Kamus assembled and took the oath of allegiance, swearing to die before their chief; shot arrows over the throne to show how they would fight any of its enemies, and holding a lighted candle, prayed that their bodies might be run through with hot iron and that the sky might fall and crush them if they proved unfaithful to their oaths".

Wat Manolom

South of Wat That Luang (between Phou Vao and Kisarath Settathirat), Wat Manolom was built by the nobles of Luang Prabang to entomb the ashes of King Samsenthai (1373-1416) and is notable for its large armless bronze Buddha statue, one of the oldest Lao images of the Buddha, which dates back to 1372 and weighs two tonnes. Locals maintain that the arm was removed during a skirmish between Siamese and French forces during the latter part of the 19th century. The Lao have unsuccessfully replaced the missing appendage with a concrete prosthetic. The monastery has an attractive weathered look and the usual carved doors and painted ceilings. While it is not artistically significant, the temple – or at least the site – is thought to be the oldest in the city, dating back, so it is said, to 1375 and the reign of Fa Ngum. Close by are the ruins of an even older temple, **Wat Xieng Kang**, which dates back to 1363.

ⓘ *3 km out of town to the northeast, near Ban Phanom. Daily 0800-1000 and 1300-1630. Donation expected.*

Outside town, Wat Pa Phon Phao is a forest meditation centre renowned for the teachings of its famous abbot, Ajahm Saisamut, one of the most popular monks in Lao history. More famous to

❧ *The small huts to the right of the entrance are meditation cells or 'kutis'.*

tourists, though, is **Wat Phra That Chedi**, known as the Peace Pagoda. It looks as though it is made of pure gold from a distance and it occupies a fantastic position. The wat's construction, funded by donations from Lao living abroad and from overseas Buddhist federations, was started in 1959 but was only completed in 1988; the names of donors are inscribed on pillars inside. It is modelled on the octagonal Shwedagon Pagoda in Yangon (Rangoon) and its inner walls are festooned with gaily painted frescoes of macabre allegories. The lurid illustrations depict the fate awaiting murderers, adulterers, thieves, drunks and liars who break the five golden rules of Buddhism. Less grotesque paintings, extending right up to the fifth floor, document the life of the Buddha. On the second level, it is possible to duck through a tiny opening to admire the Blue Indra statues and the view of Luang Prabang.

An architectural tour of Luang Prabang

→ *Numbers in the text are marked on the map below.*

In a town as small as Luang Prabang, it is easy enough just to set out and find your own route, however, we have provided a walking tour that takes in Luang Prabang's architectural highlights (secular as well as religious). It concentrates on the peninsula and the streets that form the original core of the city. The route and the most interesting buildings are shown on the map below. ▸▸ *For a guide to the secular architectural styles described in this tour, see page 130.*

Luang Prabang walking tour

Royal Palace **1**	Wat Xieng Muang **8**	Le Calao Inn **16**
Traditional Lao house **2**	Traditional Lao house **9**	Lao houses with French
Gendarmerie **3**	Compartment buildings **10**	colonial influence **17**
Lao Bank **4**	French colonial	School of Fine Arts **18**
Lao-French colonial	school **11**	French colonial
house **5**	Villa Santi **12**	hospital **19**
Lao-French colonial	Villa Savanh **13**	Lao-French colonial
house **6**	Wat Xieng Thong **14**	buildings **20**
Royal Taxes office **7**	Bamboo house **15**	Maison Souvannaphoum **21**

⦂ A guide to Luang Prabang's secular buildings

Traditional Lao The traditional Lao house is rectangular, supported on timber stilts, with a two-sided steep roof and built of bamboo, wood or daub. The stilts help to protect the occupants against wild animals at night and also help to keep the living area dry, especially during the rainy season. The underside also provides a shaded spot for working during the day, as well as area for storage. Living above ground is said to be a characteristic of the Lao and a 16th-century Lao text, the Nithan Khun Borom, records that the Lao and Vietnamese Kingdoms of Lane Xang and Dai Viet agreed to demarcate their respective zones of influence according to house style: people living in houses raised on stilts would owe allegiance to Lane Xang, those living on the ground, to Dai Viet.

The traditional Lao house is divided into three principal sections, recognizable from the exterior: the sleeping room, the verandah, and the kitchen. Under the main roof is the sleeping area and the very characteristic verandah is contiguous to it. The kitchen is linked to the main building by an open deck commonly used for bathing and washing. Roof, gables, rafters and balustrade are ornamented with lots of savoir-faire. The building process of traditional Lao houses was governed by strict rules: its orientation, the date when building could commence, the setting of the wooden piles, and so on, had to conform to spiritual guidelines.

French colonial The French introduced new technologies and materials into house construction, in particular the fired brick and the ceramic roof tile. Traditionally, these materials were reserved for wat construction – explaining why almost all buildings of pre-colonial vintage in Laos today are religious. The main characteristicsof French colonial architecture are: extensive roof area to protect against sun and rain; large window openings, paned and shuttered; verandahs; arcades; a monumental entrance; a fireplace and chimney breast; brick and wooden decorative details expressingdifferent construction systems (for instance, columns, capitals, rafters and lintels) and ceramic roof tiles.

The start of the tour is on Thanon Phothisarath in front of the **Royal Palace** (**1**; see page 121). Historically, the area to the west of the palace was considered the noble quarter of town, the east was inhabited by the middle classes, while the working class lived around the foot of Phousi. Walking from the Royal Palace along Phothisarath Road southwest towards the post office, look out for the **traditional Lao house** (**2**) in front of Wat Mai. This is a construction on stilts with a closed verandah. Continuing along Phothisarath Road, the former French colonial **Gendarmerie** (**3**) – now the information and culture department – is on your left, with gables on the façade. There's another example of a French colonial building, the **Lao Bank** (**4**), on your right.

Turn right onto Kittsarath Setthathirat Road and walk down towards the Mekong. Past the post office, on the right, is a Lao house showing French colonial influences (**5**). Take the first road on your right to see more examples of traditional Lao houses. In some cases the formerly open ground level area has been enclosed to increase the habitable space, using a variety of different materials: bricks, wood and bamboo, for example. (This is also very common in Thailand. Traditionally the under-house area was used for weaving and lounging during the hottest hours of the day. At night, animals were corralled under the house to keep them safe. Fires were also lit here at night at the coldest times of year.)

Lao-French colonial As French influence grew, so Lao builders began to incorporate some aspects of French design into their constructions. For example, some houses which in all other respects conform to the traditional Lao house style, have French openings and a grandiose doorway leading to a flight of impressive stairs.

French colonial-Lao In the same way as Lao builders adopted some French elements, so French architects and builders embraced Lao stylistic features. This is most evident in the use of temple-style ornamentation, on the roof for example.

International-modern Many houses are now built of concrete and the bungalow has become common. In many cases, traditional Lao architectural motifs and designs are merely made from concrete rather than the traditional wood. But concrete has also allowed some innovations in design: cantilevers, flat roofing, pre-fabricated elements and geometric ornamentation are all linked in part to the change in building medium from wood and bamboo, to concrete. 'International modern' includes both domestic buildings and compartments (shophouses).

Lao contemporary

Lao contemporary houses tend to fall into two categories. Either they are respectful of traditional Lao style; or they embrace modern design and construction materials wholesale. Houses in the first category can be seen to be part of an evolution of the traditional Lao house: the main entrance has shifted to the gable side, the verandah is smaller, while the open area between the piles below the main house is enclosed with brick or concrete walls and has physically become part of the house. Wood is still used for exterior facing for the first floor, but the walls of the ground level floor are made from stone and bricks. This is the most common form of house built today.

The second category of Lao contemporary house is built entirely of brick and concrete and most Lao consider it to be more luxurious.

At the very end of this street, just beside the Royal Palace, are two opulent Lao-French colonial-style houses (**6**). Turn left to reach the Mekong River road and then right to walk along the river bank. The **Royal Taxes office** (**7**), now operating as a tourism company, lies behind the Royal Palace. It is decorated with the classic three-headed elephant insignia. To see some truly beautiful examples of traditional architecture, enter **Wat Xieng Muang** (**8**; see page 125) and take the exit into the alley behind the temple. Opposite the wat is a **traditional Lao house** (**9**).

Continue up to Phothisarath Road, turn left and take a look at the **compartment buildings** (**10**) on both sides of the street. These skillfully combine commercial and residential functions under the same roof, much like the Chinese 'shophouse' found throughout Southeast Asia, in which the ground floor serves as a business, shop or workshop. The Lao traditionally never lived and worked in the same building; they always ran their businesses from some other location, even if it was a street-side stall just a few yards away from their home. It is therefore safe to assume that these 'compartments' were used by Chinese and Vietnamese immigrants. They are built in a variety of styles, mainly French colonial and Lao-French colonial.

Walking on towards the tip of the peninsula, there are several other notable buildings, including the **French colonial school** (**11**) and the **Villa Santi Hotel** (**12**), on the left-hand side of the road, and **Villa Savanh** (**13**), a traditional Lao compartment building on the right. At **Wat Xieng Thong** (**14**; see page 125) take the exit from the monastery on the east side to look at the modest **bamboo house** (**15**) down the alley.

At the tip of the peninsula, turn back along the Mekong River road. On the left is the **Calao Inn** (**16**), an example of a renovated colonial building and the only Portuguese building on the peninsula. Immediately after the inn, take the first road on your left and then turn right. Along this road, at the first intersection, are two very fine **Lao houses** showing **French colonial influences** (**17**). Past the intersection further along the same street, the **School of Fine Arts** (**18**) is one of few Lao traditional-style buildings in Luang Prabang, with two adjoining roofs. Return to the Mekong River road along which are a number of buildings showing various degrees of international influence.

Cross the peninsula to the Nam Khan river road and then follow the road south around Phousi. Along the road are a number of examples of Lao traditional and Lao-French colonial buildings. On Rathsavong Street is the **French colonial hospital** (**19**). Further along, turn right towards Nam Phou. This street has a number of **Lao-French colonial buildings** (**20**), showing French influences on Lao architecture. Follow the road until it reaches the **Maison Souvannaphoum** (**21**) on the left. Take a minute to have a look at the main building (not the new annexes), which was built in 1962 in a modern French-colonial style. The tour ends north of here at the post office.

The west bank of the Mekong

The monasteries and villages on the right bank of the Mekong are accessible by boat from Luang Prabang. For anyone who does not fancy spending three hours on a boat travelling to and from the Pak Ou caves, this makes for an enchanting alternative excursion. Also on the right bank are two hills, **Phou Thao** and **Phou Nang**, named after Luang Prabang's very own Romeo and Juliet. Thao Phouthasene and Nang Kang Hi were two lovers who died in tragic but romantic circumstances only to find themselves transformed into rock and incorporated in the local landscape. The hills are said to look like a man and woman sleeping next to each other.

Ins and outs

It is simpler to explore sights outside the city with a tour operator, as roads are unmarked and rural communities are less used to tourists. Many hotels organize trips. Boats run from the boat pier downstream from the Royal Palace to the other side of the river, near Wat Long Khoun or Ban Xiang Men, 35,000 kip return. If you can't find a boat here, try the pier behind the Royal Palace. Remember to fix a return time with the ferryman. Ferries also run irregularly across the river for 2,500 kip. ▸▸ *For further details, see Activities and tours, page 146, and Transport, page 147.*

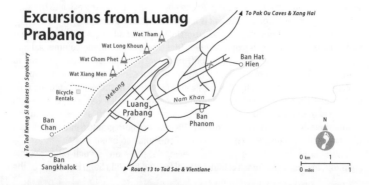

Excursions from Luang Prabang

To Pak Ou Caves & Xang Hai

Wat Tham

Wat Long Khoun

Wat Chom Phet

Wat Xiang Men

Ban Hat Hien

Bicycle Rentals

Mekong

Luang Prabang

Nam Khan

Ban Phanom

To Tad Kwang Si & Buses to Sayaboury

Ban Chan

Ban Sangkhalok

Route 13 to Tad Sae & Vientiane

N

0 km   1
0 miles   1

Wat Long Khoun

ⓘ *Daily 0800-1700. Admission 3,000 kip for foreigners.*

The first stop is usually Wat Long Khoun at the top of a flight of steps leading up from the river bank, almost opposite Wat Xieng Thong. This wat was built in two stages and was renovated by the École Française de l'Extrême-Orient in January 1994 at a cost of FF400,000. The oldest section is at the back and dates from the 18th century. The beautifully sculpted door was made in 1937. The *sim* on the river side of the compound is a delightful building, small, well-proportioned and intimate. It has some vibrant but fading Jataka murals. On the exterior, either side of the main doorway, are two bearded warriors, with swords slung over their backs, that seem to be representations of Chinese Haw soldiers. The kings of Lane Xang are said to have come on three-day retreats to this spot, to prepare for their coronation.

Wat Tham

ⓘ *100 m upstream from Wat Long Khoun. Daily 0800-1700. Admission 5,000 kip.*

A well-trodden path leads upstream to Wat Tham, literally 'cave monastery', nestled in Sakkarin Savannakuha cave, above a dilapidated sala. The wat is a limestone cave temple with stairs and balustrades cut out of the stone. The interior is very dark but is worth exploring, as it is stacked with ancient, rotting Buddha images. During Pi Mai celebrations the temple comes alive with pilgrims, candles and those coming to worship the images in the masses. A resident monk, with the aid of dim torches, will lead visitors down into the airless cavern pointing out rock formations and Buddha images. Fearful that the torches may not be powered by long life batteries, visitors may emerge into the light with a degree of relief. Not for the claustrophobic. If the cave is locked ask someone at Wat Long Khoun to let you in.

Wat Chom Phet and Wat Xiang Men

Leading from Wat Long Khoun downstream is another well-trodden track. Before reaching the small community of Ban Xiang Men, a stairway leads up to **Wat Chom Phet**, a hilltop *sim* offering fine views over the Mekong and Luang Prabang. The site has been apparently abandoned as a religious site, although the mouldering *sim*, kiltering *chedis* and profusion of apricot-coloured lilies give the place a rather attractive 'lost wat in the forest' feel. It also enjoys a perfect view at sunset.

Continuing downstream, the track passes through **Ban Xiang Men**, a peaceful village where households cultivate the exposed river banks during the dry season, taking advantage of the annual deposition of silt. **Wat Xiang Men** was originally built in 1592 by Chau Naw Kaewkumman, son of Setthathirat, and has undergone extensive renovations since. The doors date from the original construction, as do several artefacts within the wat. This temple is particularly sacred to local residents because the Pra Bang was located here for a week when it first returned to Luang Prabang from Vientiane in 1867. About 1 km downstream, in a clearing in the middle of the forest, is the **royal cemetery**. There are sculptures depicting those members of the royal family who could not be cremated for religious reasons, such as children who died as infants and victims of contagious diseases. It is hard to find a local guide willing to take you there as most are terrified of ghosts.

Ban Chan

Ban Chan is a few kilometres downstream from Luang Prabang (about 15 minutes by boat; US$6) or 4 km on the road beyond the evening market to Ban Sangkhalok and a short crossing by boat (villagers will paddle you across). The village is known for its local pottery industry and mostly produces thongs (large water storage jars) and salt pots. Boats regularly cross the river – although the fare varies depending on the number of passengers. You can charter a boat from the main pier on the Mekong for a couple of hours (about 70,000 kip). It is possible to cross over to Wat Long Khoun, walk downstream and catch another boat back to the Luang Prabang bank of the river either at Ban Xiang Men or Ban Chan. Or the circuit can be completed in the reverse direction. There are a couple of food stalls in Ban Xiang Men.

East of the city 🖂 ➤ *pages 137-149.*

➤ *pages 137-149.*

Ban Phanom and around

Ban Phanom, or Tit Cliff Village, is 6 km east of Luang Prabang. This is a 300-year-old weaving village, where shawls (*pha biang*) and sarongs (*pha sin*) are made from silk and cotton. Although best known for its weaving, the village's main economic activity is rice cultivation. The 100 or so families in Ban Phanom are members of the Lue minority, who originated from Yunnan in southern China. They were traditionally the king's weavers, soldiers and palace servants. King Sisavang Vong's dancers were traditionally hand-picked from this village at the age of six or seven and were required to undergo intensive training aimed at increasing their flexibility.

A few years ago cloth was sold from a street market in the middle of the village. However, some of the larger producers have turned their houses into small shops and it is now possible to buy lengths of cloth at any time. Tourists are more than welcome to wander around and look at the process of silk manufacture, from the silk worm's inception to finish, with the weavers clacking away at their looms. The village has turned into somewhat of a tourist trap and those looking for a bargain might be disappointed to find that the silk is almost the same price as in town.

> ❧ *A trip to this village can be combined with a visit to Phra That Kong Chedi and Henri Mouhot's tomb. A tuk-tuk to all three will cost US$8-9 return.*

The French explorer Henri Mouhot stumbled across Angkor Wat in 1860 but succumbed to a malarial attack in Luang Prabang on 10 November the following year: his last journal entry read, "Have pity on me, O my God". Resident foreign aid workers spent months searching for his grave before rediscovering it in 1990, 2 km beyond Ban Phanom, at the top of a bank looking down into the Nam Khan, a tributary of the Mekong. **Henri Mouhot's tomb** was constructed six years after his death, in 1867, and was designed by another French explorer, Doudart de Lagrée. The town of Mouhot's birth, Montbéliard, donated a plaque inscribed simply, 'Proud of Our Son', and the French government has granted an allowance for the tomb's upkeep. When going to the tomb by foot, bicycle or motorbike, follow the road along the river until you see the sign and turn left; follow this path for a further 300 m. It is also possible to get a boatman to take you the extra kilometres for a couple of dollars. If you are unsure ask villagers in Ban Phanom for directions; children will sometimes show visitors the way.

Ban Hat Hien

This village is on the airport road; fork right before the terminal and at the end of the road is Luang Prabang's knife-making village. Residents beat scrap metal over hot stoves to make blades and tools. The flames are fanned by bellows, originally made from teak tubes and operated with plungers; several craftsmen use old 155-mm Howitzer propellants and say their "little presents from the US come in very handy". One shed is stacked with hundreds of old car batteries from which the lead is extracted and poured into moulds for ball bearings and gunshot. The results of their labours can be seen in the markets in town. From the nearby Nam Khan, villagers harvest 'seaweed', which is dried, fried and eaten with sesame in a dish known as *khai pehn*; it is sold all over the country.

Pak Ou caves

The Pak Ou caves are perhaps the most popular excursion from Luang Prabang and are located 25 km upstream from the city, set in a limestone cliff opposite the mouth of the Nam Ou tributary (Pak Ou means 'Mouth of the Ou'). The two caves are studded with thousands of wood and gold Buddha images – 2,500 in the lower cave and 1,500 in the upper – and are one of the main venues for Pi Mai in April, when hundreds make the pilgrimage upriver from Luang Prabang. During the dry season the river shrinks, exposing huge sandbanks, which are improbable gold fields. Families camp out on the banks of the Mekong and pan for gold, most of which is sold to Thailand.

Ins and outs

Many restaurants, hotels, guesthouses and tour companies in Luang Prabang will arrange this trip and this is probably the best way to reach the caves. Otherwise, boats can be chartered from Tha Heua Me or from one of the stairways leading down to the river along Manthatourath, where boatmen wait for business. The going rate for the journey – about two hours upstream and one hour down with stops en route – is US$10-15. Boats vary in size but the larger ones can take up to eight people. Long-tailed boats also depart from the pier in Luang Prabang and charge US$25 for up to five people. Boats will often stop at Xang Hai (see below) and Ban Pak Ou, across the water from the caves, where enterprising villages have set up thatched stalls serving sticky rice, barbecued Mekong fish and *somtam*, plus cold drinks and snacks. Although rest houses, tables and a basic toilet have been built below the upper cave, there is no restaurant and no drinks stall at the caves themselves.

Background

The two sacred caves were supposedly discovered by King Setthathirat in the 16th century but it is likely that the caverns were associated with spirit (*phi*) worship before the arrival of Buddhism in Laos. For years the caves, which locals still believe to be the home of guardian spirits, were inhabited by monks. The king visited them every New Year, staying at Ban Pak Ou on the opposite bank of the Mekong, where there is a royal wat with beautiful old murals on the front gable. The famous French traveller, Francis Garnier, also visited the caves on his travels in the 1860s.

Some of the Buddha images in the caves are thought to be more than 300 years old, although most date from the 18th and 19th centuries. In the past, gold and silver images were in abundance but these have all been stolen; now the Buddha images are crafted from wood, copper or stone. Both the caves and the many Buddhas they contain were restored with Australian funds but since the Australian government completed its conservation project in 1998, theft has been a chronic problem, particularly between 2001 and 2002, when hundreds of statues were stolen and sold to Thai antique dealers and tourists in Luang Prabang.

Exploring the caves

ⓘ *Admission US$1, free for children.* Torches are available but candles make it possible to see reasonably well after your eyes have become accustomed to the dark. The lower cave, really a deep overhang, is named **Tham Thing**, while the upper, an enervating climb up 100 or so slippery steps, is called **Tham Phum**. A carved wooden frieze, supporting two massive wooden doors flanks the entrance. Aside from the numerous Buddha images, the cave features a statue of one of Buddha's disciples and a carved wooden water channel for the ceremonial washing of the sculptures. The cave is around 54-m-long and the sculptures range from 10 cm to 1.5 m in height. Many of the images are in the distinctive attitude of the Buddha calling for rain (with arms held by the side, palms turned inwards).

Xang Hai is 20 km upstream from Luang Prabang, on the way to Pak Ou caves and a popular stop-off. The name of this village translates as 'making wine pots'. In the rainy season the villages grow glutinous or 'sticky' rice and in the dry season they ferment it in water and yeast to brew *lao-lao*, a moonshine whisky, which is sold illegally in Luang Prabang. The village has now become rather touristy, with scores of stalls selling textiles, ceramics, souvenirs from Thailand, opium pipes and weights, ethnic clothes, and some *lao-lao* too. Villagers are delighted to give visitors a tasting session.

> ☙ Lao for 'cheers' is seung dium!

South of the city 🖼 ➜ *pages 137-149.*

Tad Sae

Seventeen kilometres (one hour) south of Luang Prabang are the beautiful multi-tiered, limestone cascades of Tad Sae, which make for a great half-day trip during the rainy season. (In the dry season, the waterfall is reduced to a mere trickle.) The falls sit at the confluence of the Huay Say and Nam Khan rivers and feature a multitude of crystal-clear swimming holes, similar to Kwang Si but on a smaller scale. They are not as touristy as Kwang Si and offer greater privacy. To get there, head south along Route 13 for 17 km and turn off for Ban En (signposted); follow this track for 2 km. From the village you can hire a boat for around US$1 to take you to the falls. Food stalls and facilities are also available. A tuk-tuk from Luang Prabang will cost about US$8-9.

Tad Kwang Si

ⓘ *30 km south Luang Prabang. Admission US$1.50, parking 2500 kip.*

These waterfalls are 30 km south of Luang Prabang on a tributary of the Mekong. The trip to the falls is almost as scenic as the cascades themselves, passing through small Hmong and Khmu villages and vivid green, terraced rice paddies. Travel agents run tours to the falls or you can charter a tuk-tuk for about US$15 return (make sure you agree how long you want to spend at the falls). Slow boats take one hour down and two hours back up river, via **Ban Muang Khai** (a pretty little village), where it is necessary to take a tuk-tuk the last 6 km or so to the falls. A third possibility is to take a speedboat from either Tha Leua Sing Kaeo (about 3 km downstream from Luang Prabang) or Ban Don, a few kilometres upstream.

The falls are stunning beautiful, misty cascades flowing over limestone formations, which eventually collect in several tiered, turquoise pools. In 2003 a large section of the limestone cliff collapsed, so the falls are a little shorter these days but just as scenic. Originally the waterfall's surroundings were inhabited by numerous animals, including the deer that give the falls their name, Kwang Si. However, the only wildlife you're likely to see today is Phet the tiger and some Asiatic black bears, rescued from poachers, in enclosures halfway between the entrance and the falls. The UNDP has cleared a path to the falls which winds right up to the top. The bottom level of the falls has been turned into a park and viewing area, with a small platform that affords good photo opportunities. The local village's economy seems increasingly to depend on the tourist business, so you'll find a large number of vendors selling snacks and drinks and some souvenirs. The site also has public toilets and changing rooms.

Although the waterfall is impressive year round, in the summer, the water cascades so gently over the various tiers of the falls that it's possible to scramble behind the curtains of water without getting wet. In the rainy season, the gallons of water roaring down the mountain catch at the imagination and could form the backdrop for any Indiana Jones or James Bond adventure. Best of all, and despite appearances, it's still possible to take the left-hand path halfway up the falls and strike out through the pouring torrents and dripping caves to the heart of the waterfall. Exhilarating and highly recommended. The pools above the falls are sheltered and comparatively private and make a wonderful spot for a swim; the second tier is best for a dip. If you follow the water either upstream or downstream there are plenty of other shady swimming spots. Note that swimming is only permitted in designated pools and, as the Lao swim fully clothed, you should wear modest swimwear and bring a sarong.

Hmong villages

There are numerous Hmong villages within a shortish distance of Luang Prabang and on the way to Kwang Si falls. Hmong children kids will usually come out on the road and stop your vehicle to sell you wristbands or embroidery. It is better to buy something from them than to give them cash or lollies. ▶▶ *For more information about the Hmong, see Background, page 324.*

Ban Longlan is east of town. To get there, take the main road upstream. At Ban Pak Xuang, just before the bridge over the river Xuang, turn right to follow this tributary of the Mekong. Just before reaching Ban Kokvan turn right onto a track to Ban Natan. From here an even smaller track leads off to the left. It follows the Houei Hia, a small stream, between two mountains and works its way upwards to the mountain village of Ban Longlan. Allow two hours to get there. Few tourists visit this village so dress modestly and be especially sensitive to local sensibilities. In the rainy season you will need a trail bike or four-wheel drive to get there.

Another Hmong village downstream from Luang Prabang is **Ban Long Lao** (one hour by tuk-tuk, US$15). Take the road southwest from town and after about 8 km turn left (after Ban Lekpet and before Ban Naxao). At the radio transmitter, continue straight ahead (rather than turning right to a waterfall). The road climbs steeply, passing a small dam and ends at the village of Long Lao. Again this is a village rarely visited by tourists. ▶▶ *For more details of how to get to the villages, see Transport, page 147.*

⊜ Sleeping

Luang Prabang *p116, maps p120 and p126*
The restored colonial villas on the peninsula and along Phou Vao tend to get booked up, particularly during national holidays, so, if you are thinking of plumping for an upper range hotel, it is advisable to arrange accommodation in advance. Around Lao New Year, hotels and guesthouses can almost charge what they like but in the wet season, prices tend to be a lot less, with most smaller establishments quoting approximately half the price given here and more expensive hotels generally knocking off about 20%. For the more upmarket hotels, check their websites, as internet rates are usually cheaper than rack rates. Also contact **Lao Airlines** as they usually have deals with some of the top-notch hotels.

There are plenty of hurriedly constructed budget guesthouses springing up all the

time, particularly in the narrow streets between the post office and the river and now also inland from Phothisarath Rd. However, many of them are distinctly mediocre and the older ones tend to get rundown pretty quickly. New establishments can be found on the tip of the peninsula heading towards Wat Xieng Thong and in the quiet streets around Phou Vao.

AL Le Calao Inn, river road (Souvanna Khampong section), T071-212100, http://calaoinn.laopdr.com. Enclosed by yellow walls, this recently renovated French colonial (1902) building boasts beautiful rooms in an incomparable position overlooking the Mekong. The balcony view is a real plus, so ensure you ask for a room with water views. Clean, relaxed and well run, with a/c and breakfast included.

AL Maison Souvannaphoum, Phothisarath Rd, T071-212200, www.coloursof angsana.com /souvannaphoum/ Formerly Prince Souvanna's residence, this place really is fit for royalty. Owned by Colours of Angsana (part of the Bayon Group Chain) and recently opened, after US$1 mn in renovations. There are 4 spacious suites and 18 rooms, with a/c, aromatherapy burners and special treats left in the rooms. The service is top-notch: rooms are cleaned twice daily and staff address customers by name. VISA and TCs accepted.

AL Pansea Phou Vao, Phou Vao Rd, T071-212194, F071-212534. Recently renovated and now under the management of the very upmarket **Pansea** group, this hotel is set on a hill slightly out of town. The 58 rooms are now beautifully decorated and there are good views from the bedroom balconies. Very comfortable accommodation, with a/c, restaurant and pool. Credit cards accepted.

AL Three Nagas Boutique Hotel, Sakkaline Rd (further down Sisavangvong Rd), T071-253888, www.3nagas.com. Housed in a beautifully restored building, with an annexe across the road, this boutique hotel is a running contender for best room in town. Attention to detail is what sets this hotel apart: from the 4-poster bed covered with local fabrics through to the large deep-set bathtub with natural handmade beauty products. There's a lovely sitting area in each room, plus traditional *torchis* walls and teak floors. Breakfast (included) is served in the fantastic café downstairs. Highly recommended.

AL Villa Santi Hotel, Sisavangvong Rd, T071-252158, www.villasantihotel.com. Almost an institution in Luang Prabang, this is a restored house from the early 20th century that served as the private residence of first King Sisavang's wife and then Princess Manilai. It's a charming place, full of character and efficiently run. There are 11 traditional rooms in the old building, each of a different size, and 14 newer rooms, with baths and showers, in a stylishly built annexe. The daughter of the official Royal Cook rustles up mouthwatering French cuisine in the Princess Restaurant (see Eating) and there are attractive seating areas in the garden, lobby or on the balcony.

Guests are also able to exploit the facilities of its sister establishment, the **Villa Santi Resort** (see below). **Lao Airlines** often offers a very cheap deal, so it is worth checking out before you book. Free pick-up from airport, if you call in advance.

AL-A The Apsara, Kingkitsarath Rd, T071-212420, www.theapsara.com. Ivan Scholte, wine connoisseur and antique collector has done a perfect job on this establishment. Stunningly beautiful rooms themed by colour, with 4-poster beds, changing screen, big bathtub and lovely balcony. Very, very romantic, with a modern twist and recommended by a gamut of notable publications. The foyer and lovely restaurant (see Eating) are decorated with Vietnamese lanterns, Burmese offering boxes and modern art pieces. Highly recommended.

A Le Parasol Blanc, Phou Vao Rd, T071-252194. A modern construction, with teak finish, houses 30 nicely decorated rooms, with mini-bar, surrounded by secluded, beautiful gardens.

A Manoluck (sometimes **Manoruck**), 14/3 Phou Vao Rd, T071-212250, F071-212508. Quasi-classical hotel. Rooms have good facilities (a/c, cable TV, mini-bar, polished wooden floors) but there's a surfeit of ostentatious furnishings in the lobby. Western/Asian restaurant. Credit cards accepted.

A Mouang Luang, Boun Khong Rd, T/F071-212790. Rather grandiose and lavish 2-storey reinterpretation of traditional Lao architecture in cement. There are 35 beautifully decorated a/c rooms, with polished wooden floors, marble bathrooms and enthusiastic staff endeavouring to make their mark on the Luang Prabang hotel scene. Lao and European food in the restaurant, small kidney-shaped pool. Credit cards accepted.

A Pack Luck, opposite Le Elephant Restaurant, T071-253373, packluck@ hotmail.com. This boutique hotel is a relative newcomer. The 5 rooms are on the smallish side but are tastefully decorated with beautiful fabrics and have brilliant bathrooms with deep slate bathtubs. Recommended.

A Phousi, Kittsarath Setthathirat Rd, T071-212192, www.phousihotel.laopdr.com.

Upgraded and expanded in the mid-1990s. Twin rooms with wooden floors, a/c, satellite TV and decent shower rooms, plus restaurant and extensive garden with seating. Very pleasant location alluding to another era. Credit cards accepted.

A Sala Luang Prabang, 102/6 Ounkham Rd, T071-252460, salabang@laotel.com. Very chic, renovated 100-year-old building overlooking the Mekong. Nice use of exposed beams and stone inlay in communal areas. Rooms have a minimalist, up-to-date edge with a/c and modern bathrooms, and doors either opening onto a small courtyard or river balcony (more expensive). Bus, car, bicycle hire available. Rates include breakfast and are substantially cheaper in the low season. Very, very nice. Highly recommended.

A Tum Tum Cheng, off Sisavangvong Rd, T071-253262, tumtumcheng@yahoo.com. Large white building with murals lining the walls. Big rooms have local artefacts, a/c and hot water. A very tranquil atmosphere but perhaps a tad too pricey at US$30 for a double.

A-B Merry Lao Swiss, Kingkitsarath Rd, T071-260211, samoraphouma@hotmail.com. Clean rooms with traditional-style furniture. Funky chequered floor. All have a/c, TV. Prices vary between US$20 and US$80 but always include breakfast.

A-B Say Nam Khan, overlooking the river, T071-212976, saynamkhan_lp@hotmail.com. Attractive renovated building with a homely feel created by its friendly owners. White paint and wooden furnishings, clean a/c rooms, although the inner ones are quite dark. Private bathrooms and hot water. Sitting on the terrace overlooking the Nam Kham emphasizes what a lovely setting it is. Very friendly and helpful. Often booked out.

A-B Sayo Guesthouse, Sotikoumman Rd, T071-252614, sayo@laotel.com. Seriously lovely. When Villa Santi's full, the staff often show their disappointed guests towards this old French colonial building. The front rooms are beautifully and tastefully decorated with local fabrics and woodwork, polished wooden floors and furniture, and they boast a fantastic view over Wat Xieng Muang – you can watch the monks carving and painting and woodworking. The back ones aren't as good value but still recommended.

B Muang Swa, Phou Vao Rd, T071-212192. A/c, restaurant, noisy disco. 17 reasonable rooms, with en suite bathrooms.

B New Luang Prabang Hotel, Sisavangvong Rd, T071-212264, F071-212804. Four floors and 15 rooms in a rather ugly building, decorated with the odd piece of local tapestry. Rooms are liveable but a tad pricey. Free pick-up to and from the airport.

B-C Ban Lao, Souvannaphoum Rd, T071-252078. An impressive white mansion with polished wooden floors. Large double rooms have en suite bathrooms and a/c; others have shared facilities. New annexe has reasonable, clean rooms with showers, hot water and satellite TV. Good value for money.

B-C Kongsavath Hotel, Ounkham Rd, T071-212994, khongsavath@hotmail.com. Nice clean guesthouse overlooking the Mekong, with comfy beds, a/c, hot water and lovely views from the window. Teak doors throughout this wonderful, restored building. Restaurant attached with good breakfast selection, stir-fry and drinks (US$2-3).

B-C Lane Xang, Visunnarat Rd, T071-212749. This attractive chalet-style hotel is run by **Lane Xang Travel Co**. Clean doubles with en suite bathroom and fridge. Good views of Wat Visunnarat.

B-C Silichit Guesthouse, just off Ounkham Rd, T071-212758. Fairly new, clean guesthouse. Comfortable rooms with fan, en suite bathroom and hot water. Very friendly owners can speak English and French, and often invite guests to sit down and have a family dinner with them. As with most budget places, it drops its prices dramatically in the low season. A guide runs popular tours to the Crystal Cave; he will probably show you the rave reviews he's received from past clients. Good value and highly recommended.

B-C Tam Tam, Sisavangvong Rd, T071-253300, chantavong@hotmail.com. You're paying for the great location here. The big rooms are ok, with bathroom, hot water and a/c. Pay US$25 for a TV and fridge. Large restaurant attached with outdoor seating, serving a wide selection of drinks, big breakfast menu (around US$2-3), burgers, salads, spaghetti and some Lao food.

C **Bougnasouk Guesthouse**, Ounkham Rd, T071-212749. This riverfront guesthouse has rather cramped, fan-cooled rooms, with en suite bathrooms with hot water. Lao restaurant serves exceptionally cheap Asian breakfast. A pungent odour of old pipe tobacco wafts through the place.

C **Bounthieng Guesthouse**, Khem Kong Rd, T071-252488, bounthiengsolo@yahoo.com. Riverside guesthouse with great communal balcony overlooking the river. Rooms are comfortable enough with fan and en suite bathrooms with hot water. Cheaper rooms have shared facilities. Pretty good value. Recommended.

C **Chantanome Guesthouse**, off Ounkham Rd, T020-770060. Neat rooms with fan and hot water. Very snazzy stone-inlay bathrooms.

C-D **Boun Gning Guesthouse**, 109/4 Ban That Luang, T071-212274. Attractive balcony, triples available, rooms are quite bare. Friendly and helpful English-speaking management.

D **Mano Guesthouse**, Phamahapasaman Rd, T071-253112. Clean, with a tiled ground floor and wooden upstairs, this place is a relaxed and charming, family-run option, offering some a/c. Ideal for chess enthusiasts, as a large chess set is carved into one of the stone tables outside. Owners speak good English and some French.

D **Sok Dee Guesthouse**, just off Ounkham Rd, T071-252555. Down a quiet, pleasant side street. Clean rooms with TV, fan and hot water baths. Small restaurant attached that offers a limited breakfast menu. Bicycle rental. Pretty good value. Recommended.

D-E **Kounsavan**, Chaotonkham Rd, T071-212297. This beautifully situated guesthouse is easy to miss because it's halfway down a sleepy looking street but it's definitely worth tumbling upon this oasis of tranquillity. Green grass, flowers, balconies, showers with hot water. Some rooms have en suites, others share facilities. This place is extremely friendly, and within easy striking distance of the town centre. Recommended.

D-E **Vanvisa Villa**, just off the river road, near Indochina Spirit (see Eating), T071-212925, vandara1@hotmail.com. Brightly coloured guesthouse down a quaint street. This is a little gem, with teak floors, large, characterful and immaculate rooms and friendly owners.

The downstairs has beautiful handicrafts and antiques. Recommended.

D-E **Viradesa**, off the river road, T071-252026. An old house with an extension. Good source of local knowledge for information-hungry travellers. Some rooms have their own good-sized hot water bathrooms (US$10) and others have shared facilities, all have portable fans. This previously sleepy street is becoming increasingly popular with tourists, and has even been (somewhat ambitiously!) referred to as the Khao San Road of Laos.

D-F **Jaliya**, Phamahapasaman Rd, near Mano Guesthouse, T071-252154. Comfortable bungalow-type rooms, with varied facilities ranging from shared bathrooms and fan through to a/c and TV. Relaxing garden area with a very friendly pet deer. Bicycle rental.

E **Sunkeo II**, just behind the post office, T071-252804. Basic rooms, shared hot water bathrooms. Friendly, clean.

E-F **Saylom Khem Khong**, T071-212304, wonmany2001@yahoo.com. Basic rooms on the river with fan and shared facilities. Bit cramped. Not much English spoken.

F **Pa Phai**, opposite Wat Pa Phai. This guesthouse is run by an elderly lady who speaks good English and French. It is a bit rundown but classic Laos: an attractive little wooden place with a shady garden and a verandah on the first floor. 10 clean rooms (separated only by rattan walls – which don't leave much to the imagination), very clean bathrooms, bikes for rent and same day laundry service. Recommended.

Other accommodation

Villa Savanh, Sisavangvong Rd, T071-212420, info@theapsara.com. A traditional wooden but fully restored, self-contained house, with 3 double bedrooms and bathrooms. Good use of Lao fabrics and furniture. Set in beautiful gardens. Steep stairs could pose a difficulty for some. Same management as the **Apsara** (see above). Short-term stays US$250 per night, discount for longer rental.

Out of town

AL-L **Grand Luang Prabang Hotel & Resort**, Ban Xiengkeo, 4 km from town, T071-253851/7, www.grandluang prabang.com. Very beautiful restored hotel in the former Prince Phetsarath's residence. Simple, classically decorated rooms set in lovely gardens. Try to get a room which offers the stunning Mekong River view. The 80 rooms have all the mod cons including IDD telephone, mini-bar, TV and marble bathroom. The drawback is that it is a bit of a hike from town.

East of the city p134

AL Lao Spirit Resort, 15 km east of Luang Prabang, T071-252655, www.tigertrail-laos.com. Eco-friendly accommodation, beautifully decorated glass-fronted bungalows with open-air bathrooms. The **Tiger Trail Elephant Camp** is located on the opposite side of the river and elephant treks can be organized. The bungalows are usually booked in conjunction with one of the Tiger Trail tours but can also be booked independently. Restaurant with Asian and European food. US$70 including breakfast and transfer. Discounts in low season. Gets rave reviews. Recommended.

B-C Thongbay Guesthouse, 10 mins from the airport and town centre on the Nam Khan, T071-253234, www.thongbay-guesthouses.com. Lovely small, family-run guesthouse perched on the bank of the Nam Khan. Very cosy bungalows with mosquito net, balcony and en suite bathroom. Relaxing atmosphere and fantastic restaurant serving Lao and Western food. Transport from town US$5. Highly recommended.

South of the city p136

AL Villa Santi Resort, Ban Na Dui, T071-252157/212267, F071-212158. This new 55-room resort, under the same management as Villa Santi Hotel, could hardly be more dreamy. It's set in 10 ha of beautiful countryside 6 km from town on the road to Kwang Si falls and backs onto a local village and fields of rice paddies. The foyer is decorated with beautiful art deco-style furniture and the rooms are very comfortable. There is a pool but it is often empty of water. If you can get on one of the Laos Airlines deals, this hotel is very good value. Shuttle buses into town are scheduled to leave every 30 mins throughout the day. Recommended.

Eating

Luang Prabang p116, maps p120 and p126

Luang Prabang produces a number of culinary specialities that make interesting souvenirs. The local market is a good starting point, although most restaurants have now clicked onto the popularity of the local delicacies. The most famous is *khai pehn*, dried river weed, mainly from the Nam Khan, which is mixed with sesame and eaten nationwide. It is particularly good fried as a sandwich between garlic and sesame. *Chao bong*, a mildly hot pimento purée, is also popular throughout the country. Other delicacies include: *phak nam,* a watercress that grows around waterfalls and is commonly used in soups and salads; *mak kham kuan* (tamarind jam) and *mak nat kuan* (pineapple jam).

Perhaps the best places to eat – at least in terms of ambience – are the cafés and restaurants along the Mekong, where the procession of boats and people make for fascinating viewing. The food can also be pretty good. Some enterprising souls have opened a row of French restaurants on Sisavangvong Rd. Although there is little to distinguish them, they are tastefully decorated with a combination of traditional Lao handicrafts and Western styles. Lantern-lit at night, they exude a good atmosphere and serve Lao fare, along with mainly French and some Italian dishes.

Note that, as Luang Prabang has a curfew, most places won't stay open past 2200.

Cafés and bakeries

There are so many bakeries in town, or so-called bakeries, that one starts to lose count.

Café Ban Vat Sene, opposite Wat Sene. A seriously nice option, with a breezy, colonial air. White walls and polished dark wooden floors, tables and chairs. Some locals suggest that this café double's as UNESCO's canteen. The food (French) is a treat. Good place for coffee or tea.

Joma, Sisavangvong Rd near Nam Phou fountain, T071-252292. Utterly delicious array of comfort foods: shakes, coffee, sandwiches, lasagne, quiche and more. Nice and cool a/c interior. **Mulberry Handicrafts** is upstairs.

L'Etranger, Kingkitsarath Rd, near Hive Bar, T020-5471736. Great little bookshop-cum-café. The upstairs is exceptionally comfortable with cushions and low tables. This is the perfect place to wind down, grab a book and have a cuppa. The café serves tacos, salads and sandwiches (US$2-3) as well as a great range of teas. A movie is shown daily at 1600 (and usually another later in the evening). Good music, good books, good food. Highly recommended.

Luang Prabang Bakery, Sisavangvong Rd, T071-252499. Croissants, lemon bars, raisin slices, brownies, muffins, coffee, rolls, all to eat on premises or to take away. Also sells muesli, making it a good place for breakfast. One of the best selections of chocolate cakes in the country.

At the time of publication, the Scandinavian Bakery had closed and was relocating further along Sisavangvong Rd. When it reopens it is expected to have the same wide range of Danish pastries, croissants, quiche, pies, cream cakes, filtered coffee and yoghurt.

Foodstalls

A tempting choice of early evening stalls is to be found on Kittsarath Setthathirat, towards the river, and on the sidestreet down towards the river near the night market on Sisavangvong Rd. Roast chicken and sticky rice, a Lao favourite, are among the foods on offer. Very cheap and usually pretty good food. Baguettes can be bought at many roadside stalls.

French and European

Le Elephant, Ban Vat Nong, T071-252482, contact@elephant-restau.com. About as fine as dining gets in Luang Prabang. Very upmarket and utterly delectable cuisine. Pan-fried fillet of snapper, with capers and basil-flavoured mash is delicious, as are the simmered scallops. Also a number of Lao dishes. Most are US$10-15 but there are 3 set menus too: Lao (US$12), vegetarian (US$12) and French (US$18). The extensive wine list has over 20 wines ranging from US$13 to US$120 per bottle. Open for dinner. Good place to treat yourself. Highly recommended.

Samsara, Sisavangvong Rd. French-Asian inspired fusion food for around US$7-8. Beef with blue cheese and pan-fried salmon with tea sauce are nice enough. Pleasant lamp lighting and beautiful seating upstairs but tends to lack the chutzpah required for these prices.

Café des Arts, Sisavangvong Rd, T071-252162. Pleasant and reasonably priced French restaurant with artwork for sale on the walls but a bit lacking in atmosphere. Good salads, disappointing pizzas, scrumptious crème caramel. Some of the steak dishes are a bit expensive, US$6-7 but the chicken dishes are delicious.

Coleur Café/Restaurant, Ban Vat Nong, opposite Silichit Guesthouse, T020-5621064. The French expats in town have nothing but praise for this place, with its reasonably priced French and Lao meals and ambient setting. The Lao casseroles are fantastic. At the time of publication a new menu was being created, set to include salads, pizzas, quiches, steaks and a few Lao dishes. Fri is ear-marked for a US$5 steak-and-wine special. Recommended.

Dao Fa, Sisavangvong Rd, T071-252656, www.daofa-bistro.com. Crêperie with good savoury and sweet crêpes, great selection of teas and coffees, fab ice creams and tasty homemade pasta. The latter is the real draw-card and is recommended. Brightly decorated space with pavement seating. Breakfast, lunch, dinner.

Luang Prabang Pizza, Sisavangvong Rd. No surprises for guessing that their signature dish is pizza. Pizzas and pasta are cheap and passable but the real highlight here is the fantastic Lao staff.

Indian

Nazim's Indian Restaurant, Sisavangvong Rd. Luang Prabang's first Indian restaurant appears to be a roaring success. The menu offers a huge selection of authentic Indian food from both north and south of the country, plus halal dishes. The management and the chefs are all Indian which ensures that the food is traditionally prepared. The servings are huge, and the service is efficient; the interior remains bare.

Nisha's, Sisavangvong Rd, Mt Phousi. Whoever goes into Nisha's emerges singing its praises. The varied dishes are delicious as well as reasonably priced.

Lao, Thai and Vietnamese

¥¥¥ Phou Vao, Phou Vao Rd. This restaurant is attached to the Phou Vao Pansea hotel and is set on a hill outside town with great views over the city. Good Lao and continental à la carte menu. Locals worship the buffet.

¥¥ Apsara, see Sleeping. Lao/Thai restaurant offering cuisine, such as braised pork belly and pumpkin, great fish cakes. Good value.

¥¥ Indochina Spirit, Phothisarath Rd. Colonial building with an attractive courtyard. Average Lao and Italian food from pizza to Luang Prabang dishes, including a vegetarian selection. Luang Prabang pizza is a mixture of Luang Prabang sausage, river-weed and a few other local specialities – nice concept but it doesn't really work. On the tour group itinerary but don't be put off, reasonable.

¥¥ Tamnak Lao, Sisavangvong Rd, opposite Villa Santi, T071-252525. Brilliant restaurant, serving modern Lao cuisine, with a strong Thai influence. The freshest ingredients are used: try fish and coconut wrapped in banana leaf or pork-stuffed celery soup. Atmospheric surroundings, particularly upstairs but often packed to the brim with tourists so service can be very slow at times.

¥¥ Tum Tum Cheng, Sakkaline Rd, T071-252019. Lao food prepared by a Hungarian returnee. Tasty fusion-style meals. Very comfy outdoor seating. Also classes in Lao cooking and classical Lao dancing.

¥¥ View Khaem Khong, Ounkham Rd, T071-212726. The most popular of the dining establishments along the river. Good for a beer at sunset. The locals call the manager the 'King' because he seems to survey his mini outdoor kingdom from a throne. Service is a bit swifter during the day. Tasty Luang Prabang sausage and *laap*. Recommended.

¥¥ Yongkhoune, Sisavangvong Rd. Open 0800-1000 daily. Quite popular with travellers, thanks to its large menu, with pretty good Asian interpretations, noodle soup and a selection of Western dishes. Indoor and pavement seating.

¥¥-¥ Khemkhan Food Garden, Nam Khan Rd, T071-212447. A reasonable line in spicy foods but it's better for a beer than a feed. Very pleasant terrace setting overlooking the Nam Khan.

¥¥-¥ Pak Houay Mixay, Sisavang Vatthana Rd, Ban Xing Mouang, T071-212260. Tucked away off the main Sisavangvong Rd, this is a firm favourite with Westerners and Lao alike. Lao food with a Western twist: delicious fish, anise-flavoured stew and *laap*. At times the chef can go a bit ballistic with the oil.

¥ Bougnasouk, attached to the riverside guesthouse of the same name (see Sleeping). Open 0700-1000 daily for the best value Asian breakfast in town: noodle soup, fruit salad, juice, coffee or tea and fruit salad for under US$2.

¥ Maly Restaurant, Phou Vao Rd, T071-252013. It's a bit off the beaten track but most tuk-tuks know it as it's the most famous Lao restaurant in town. The building is nothing to look at but the food is brilliant. The specialty is the *sindad*, or Lao barbecue, where a hole in the centre of the table filled with burning coals serves as a barbecue. Anything you get here will be good, including fantastic fried chicken and fish in coconut milk. Serves lunch and dinner. Packed at night.

✿ Bars and clubs

Luang Prabang *p116, maps p120 and p126*
It took a few years for Luang Prabang to catch up but now there's a drinking hole for almost every occasion and budget. There are several wooden platform restaurants built over the bank of the Mekong, which make incomparable places to have a beer at sunset. **Le Elephant** and **Apsara** also provide attractive settings for a drink. An occasional disco is held at the **Muang Swa Hotel**, although **Chao Fa Discotheque**, out towards the southern bus terminal, is more popular with the young Lao.

Hive Bar, Kingkitsarath Rd, next to L'Etranger. Luang Prabang's most happening bar-club is good for a dance. Cosy and dark with loud hip-hop and dance music. Serves tapas. At closing time patrons are herded out onto the streets in scenes all too reminiscent of UK watering holes. Happy hour 1700-2100.

Khob Jai, Kingkitsarath Rd (opposite Hive Bar). Dedicated gay bar. Slightly outrageous, and at times a bit too full-on, but loads of fun. Often *kittoys* (lady boys) will perform a show. Has the added benefit that the owner will often go past the curfew.

Lemongrass, Ounkham Rd. Very slick, upmarket wine bar, with green theme. Extensive wine list, tad pricey but pleasant. Also stocks accessories and beauty products.
Maylek, corner of Kitsarath Settathirat and Visunnarat rds. LP's first pub was designed by a French-Canadian architect with a definite eye for dim lighting and artfully arranged modern furniture. It's a surreal experience walking into a place such as this in Laos. Its steep prices, too, are more akin to London than Luang Prabang.
Mr Hong's Coffee Shop, Ban Thongchaleun. Although this is designed as a restaurant (with exceptionally cheap Lao food), Mr Hong has garnered more of a reputation for his famous cocktails. Popular with backpackers.

⏺ Entertainment

Luang Prabang *p116, maps p120 and p126*
Cinema
There isn't a cinema in Luang Prabang anymore but **Le Cinema**, close to the Royal Palace, T020-577 4724, has 5 film-viewing rooms for hire, with 34-inch screens and comfy cushions. 30,000 kip for 1st person, 10,000 kip for each extra person. **L'Etranger** (see Cafés, above) also shows arthouse and other well-reviewed movies every evening.

Theatre and dance
Traditional dance performances, influenced by the Ramayana, are held at the **Theatre Phalak Phalam** in the Royal Palace compound, T071-253705, Mon, Wed and Sat at 1700, US$15. The traditional dance of Luang Prabang, which is incorporated into most shows is over 600-years old.

✱ Festivals and events

Luang Prabang *p116, maps p120 and p126*
Apr
Pi Mai (Lao New Year; movable) is the time when the tutelary spirits of the old year are replaced by those of the new. It has special significance in Luang Prabang, with certain traditions celebrated in the city that are no longer observed in Vientiane. In the past the King and Queen would symbolically clean the principal Buddha images in the city's main wats, while masked dancers pranced

through the streets re-enacting the founding of the city by 2 mythical beasts. Today, people from all over the province, and even further afield, still descend on the city. The newly crowned Miss New Year (Nang Sang Khan) is paraded through town, riding on the back of the auspicious animal of the year.
Day 1 Bazaar is held in the streets around the post office; sprinkling of Buddha statues with water; release of small fish into Mekong from pier behind Royal Palace – a symbolic gesture, hoping for good luck in the New Year; construction of sand stupas on western bank of Mekong, next to Wat Xiang Men; fireworks in the evening.
Day 2 1st procession from Wat That to Wat Xieng Thong; dance of the masks of Pou Nheu Nha Nheu and Sing Kaeo Sing Kham; fireworks and festivities in the evening.
Day 3 2nd procession from Wat Xieng Thong to Wat That; procession of monks; *baci* celebrations; fireworks in evening.
Day 4 Pra Bang is moved from the Royal Palace to Wat Mai.
Day 5/6 All-day traditional washing of Pra Bang at Wat Mai.
Day 7 Pra Bang Buddha is returned to Royal Palace.
Days 9-11 Wat Xieng Thong Phraman image brought outside for ritual washing.

May
Vien Thiene (movable), the candlelit festival.

Aug
Boat races (movable) are celebrated in Luang Prabang in Aug unlike other parts of the country, where they take place in Sep. Boats are raced by the people living in the vicinity of each wat.

⭘ Shopping

Luang Prabang *p116, maps p120 and p126*
Antiques
Authentic antiques are almost impossible to find as the Thai dealers have whole-heartedly scavenged through the place. Real antiques are considered immensely valuable and will usually be priced accordingly.
Patthana Boupha Antique Gallery, Ban Visoun, T071-212262. This little gem can be found in a partitioned-off area in a fantastic colonial building. Antique silverware and

jewellery, Buddhas, old photos and fine textiles. Less common are furniture and household items. The owner is of aristocratic lineage. Reasonable prices. Often closed, so ring beforehand.

Art galleries

Quite a few little operations are popping up now, since the German owner of **Ban Khiily Café and Paper Gallery**, Sakkaline Rd, T071-212611, opened his place, trained up all his staff, and then had to watch as most of them went off with their newly learnt skills to set up on their own. This is a *sa* crafts centre (*sa* is a rough, leaf-effect paper). The 1st floor sells scrolls, temple stencils, paper lanterns and cards. On the2nd floor is a small art gallery and a comfortable balcony café that sells drinks and overlooks the string of wats on Sisavangvong Rd.

L'Etranger and **Mekong Art Gallery** have regular art exhibitions.

Baskets

The best collection can be found in several shops along Sisavangvong Rd, near to Villa Santi.

Books

A small selection of second-hand books is available at **Luang Prabang Bakery Restaurant**, Sisavangvong Rd (not to be confused with the Luang Prabang Bakery Restaurant that sells all the chocolate cakes, see Cafés). A wider selection of books can be purchased or rented from **L'Etranger** (see Cafés), the best bookshop in the country.

Handicrafts

There is a handicraft market, geared to tourists, close to the intersection of Phou Vao Rd and the river road. A row of shops lines Phothisarath Rd, upriver from the **Luang Prabang Handicraft Shop**, Ounkham Rd, which offers a good range of silks and cottons and handicrafts. The Lao owner gets his products from local villages. **Satri Lao Silk**, Sisavangvong Rd, T071-219295. Truly beautiful silks and handicrafts for sale. Overpriced, but definitely worth a look. **Mulberries**, above Joma Café (see Eating), sells a range of silk homewares and clothes, as well as local teas.

Jewellery

Naga Creations, Sisavangvong Rd, T071-212775. A large collection of jewellery and trinkets, combining Lao silver with quality semi-precious stones. Both contemporary and classic pieces, from traditional spirit boxes through to funky plastic Buddhist statues.

Markets

There is a small **ethnic minority market** near the post office on the stretch of Sisavangvong Rd that runs down to the Mekong. It sells fruit, wild honey, roots and tubers, fresh and dried fish, and knives and other ironmongery made by the smiths of Ban Hat Hien. In the evening, food stalls also set up shop here. This area bustles with activity; it seems to be an important trading and shipment area. Boats dock at Tha Heua Me pier to unload their goods. There's also a **night market** in the same area, sprawling down several blocks of Sisavangvong Rd. Hundreds of villagers flock to the market to sell their handicrafts, ranging from silk scarves through to embroidered quilt covers and paper albums. Open 0500-2230 daily, the market is a 'must see' and most visitors won't leave without a great souvenir or two. Note that the night market may move to Kingkitsarath Rd or to the former central market building (see below) during 2006.

The **central market**, on the corner of Rathsavong and Kittsarath rds, is currently closed, having been overshadowed by the newer **Phousi market**, 1.5 km from the centre of town. The latter is a fantastic place to pick up quality silk garments. Pre-made silk clothes are sold here for a fraction of the price of the shops in town. The clothes just need the odd button sewn on here or the hem taken in there. Make sure that you are very detailed with instructions though and ensure the same colour thread is used in any alterations. There is also a colourful outdoor fruit and vegetable section, which makes for stunning photographs.

Silver

One of Luang Prabang's traditional crafts is silversmithing. During the Communist era between 1975 and 1989 many silversmiths turned to other occupations, such was the lack of demand. However, with the rise in tourism and the economic reforms, demand has increased and many silversmiths have returned to their craft. Most tourists buy their silver – and other crafts – from the main market in Luang Prabang (see above). However, almost none of the pieces on sale here are from the Luang Prabang area – despite what the marketeers might say. Most are made in Vientiane and trucked to the royal capital. Expert silversmiths like Thithpeng Maniphone maintain that these Vientiane-made pieces are inferior, and certainly the engraving and silverwork does appear cruder.

The silversmith along the river, near the rear of the Royal Palace, produces good workmanship; his father made one of the King's crowns. There are also several other Lao silversmiths around the Nam Phou area (fountain), where you can watch the artisans ply their trade. **Thit Peng**, signposted almost opposite Wat That, is a workshop and small shop with jewellery and pots.

Weaving
OckPopTok, near Le Elephant restaurant, T071-253219. OckPopTok, which literally translates to 'east meets west', truly incorporates the best of both worlds in beautiful designs and fabrics. It specializes in naturally dyed silk, which is of a much better quality than synthetically dyed silk, as it doesn't run. Clothes, household items, hangings and custom-made orders. Recommended.

Woodcarving
Caruso Gallery, Sisavangvong Rd (towards the Three Nagas Hotel) has some lovely but very *peng lai* (expensive) pieces.

▲▲ Activities and tours

Luang Prabang *p116, maps p120 and p126*
Courses
Tum Tum Cheng, see Eating, T071-252019. Lao cooking courses for 1 day (5 hrs; US$25) or 2 days (US$45), starting at 0900 Mon-Sat. Learn how to shop for fresh produce and get tips on food preparation, herbs and spices. Finally get to eat the delicious meal you prepare. Book in advance. The restaurant also holds traditional ballet lessons by the star performer of the Royal Ballet, Hattarath

Dhamma Chaleun (US$24 for one-on-one tuition, US$10 per person for 3 or more). You need to sign up at least the day before at the restaurant.

Sauna and massage
There are numerous massage places along Sisavangvong Rd. For sheer indulgence, the **Maison Souvannaphoum** (see Sleeping) has a spa with a range of luxurious and expensive treatments.
Red Cross Sauna, opposite Wat Visunnarat, reservations T071-212303. Open daily 0900-2100 (1700-2100 for sauna). Massage 30,000 kip per hr, traditional Lao herbal sauna 10,000 kip. Bring your own towel/sarong.
Spa Garden, Ban Phonheauang, T071-212325, spagardenlpb@hotmail.com. More upmarket. Offers a wide selection of massage and beauty treatments. Aromatherapy massage US$12 per hr, skin detox US$25 per hr. Also a treatment described as "big plus breast up".
Steam Bath Massage, near Wat Xieng Thong on Souvanna Khampong Rd. Open 1600-2030 daily. A low-key affair where one entrepreneurial family have set up a sauna and massage in their home. Very friendly. Massage US$3 per hr, sauna US$1. Bring a towel and shower first.

Tour operators
Action Max, Ban Xieng Muan, T071-252417, www.actionmaxasia.com. Trekking and adventure-based tours. Good ecotourism based treks including a trek to Chompet district.
All Laos Service, Sisavangvong Rd. Large successful travel agency organizing ticketing and travel services.
Exotissimo, www.exotissimo.com.
Green Discovery, T071-212093, www.greendiscoverylaos.com. Kayaking trips on the Nam Ou and treks around Tad Kwang Si. Home stays, rafting, kayaking, plus the usual trips to Pak Ou caves etc.
Tiger Trail, Chau Fa Ngum, T071-252655, www.tigertrail-laos.com. Adventure specialists: elephant treks, trekking, mountain biking tours, rafting, rock climbing etc. Their resort gets rave reviews, see Sleeping.

Treasure Travel Laos, Sisavangvong Rd, T071-254403. Almost every travel service possible, from tours to Phonsavanh, through to ticketing and transport. Good local operator, recommended.

◯ Transport

Luang Prabang *p116, maps p120 and p126*
See also Ins and outs, page 116.

Air
Luang Prabang International Airport (LPQ) about 4km from town, T071-212172/3. Lao Airlines, Phamahapasaman Rd, T071-212172, has 2 daily connections with **Vientiane**, 40 mins, US$56 single/US$108 return, and a service to **Chiang Mai**, US$85 single; flights to/from **Phonsavanh** have been curtailed for the time being. **Bangkok Airways** runs daily flights between Luang Prabang and **Bangkok**, 1400 daily, US$107/US$205, check the schedule as timings tend to change. **Siem Reap Airways** runs flights to **Siem Reap**, US$170 single.

Early morning departures are often delayed during the rainy season, as dense cloud can sometimes make Luang Prabang airport inoperable until about 1100. Airline tickets are more often than not substantially cheaper from travel agents (see Tour operators, above) than from the actual airline. There is a standard 5,000 kip departure tax for all domestic flights, US$10 for international departures. Confirm bookings a day in advance and arrive at the airport early as flights have been known to depart as soon as they're full.

Bicycle hire
There is no doubt that the best way to explore Luang Prabang is by bicycle. Bikes can be rented for US$1 per day from most guesthouses, depending on the state of the machine.

Boat
Luang Prabang was established at the confluence of the Mekong and Nam Khan rivers because of the transport and communication opportunities that such a position affords in an otherwise mountainous and inaccessible area. However, with the development of overland links and the

upgrading of the Vientiane- Luang Prabang road, river transport has languished. Nonetheless, while few passengers take the boat option south to Vientiane via Pak Lai, the route upstream to Houei Xai via Pak Beng, on the border with Thailand, remains very popular. There are 3 departure areas, with most boats leaving from the 2 docks behind the Royal Palace. **Tha Heua Me Pier** is the most popular departure point and has a blackboard listing all the destinations and prices available (daily 0730-1130 and 1300-1600). Prices are largely dependent on the price of gasoline. A boat to the **Pak Ou caves** (2 hrs upstream, 1 hr down) should cost about US$10-15. The 3rd dock is at **Ban Don** (15 mins north of town by tuk-tuk, US$1-2).

To Houei Xai via Pak Beng
Speedboats depart from Ban Don to **Houei Xai** (on the Thai border) in around 6 hrs, with a short break in **Pak Beng**. Tickets, Houei Xai (US$30) or Pak Beng (US$20), are available from most travel agents. The boats are horribly noisy and dangerous (numerous fatalities have been reported from boats jack-knifing when hitting waves). Ear plugs are recommended and ensure boatmen provide a helmet and life jacket. A much more enjoyable alternative is to take the languid slow boat between Luang Prabang and Houei Xai, which is now one of the most popular ways of entering or leaving Laos. The daily slow boat leaves from the boat pier behind the Royal Palace in Luang Prabang. The journey takes 2 days, with a break in Pak Beng after 6-7 hrs on the 1st day. If you wish to visit Hongsa hop off at Tha Suang (before you hit Pak Beng). The boat is often packed to the brim so wear something comfortable and bring some padding to sit on. (If the boat to Pak Beng is full, you can charter your own for about US$200-300.) Most travel agents in Luang Prabang sell tickets to Pak Beng for US$9; tickets for the onward trip to Houei Xai can be purchased in Pak Beng.

The most comfortable option is to go on the **Luang Say Cruise**, T071-252553, www.mekongcruises.com, www.asian-oasis.com, a purpose-built, 34- m luxury river barge that stops over at the beautiful Luang Say Lodge at Pak Beng (see page 172). Departs Luang Prabang Tue, Wed and Sat in high season (low season subject to change);

departs Houei Xai Mon, Thu and Fri in high season and Fri in low season. The trip costs US$225-US$300, depending on how many days you are going for.

To Vientiane via Pak Lai The passenger service between Vientiane and Luang Prabang has ceased but you may be able to squeeze yourself on to one of the rare southbound cargo boats. This is difficult and unreliable. Larger boats only travel in the rainy season and you may have to hang around for several days, while the freight is loaded. It may be helpful to use a translator in order to negotiate the price. The stretch of river from Luang Prabang to Pak Lai is quite hazardous, with a fair number of rapids, so a more practical alternative may be to take the bus to **Sayaboury** (see Bus, below) and on to **Pak Lai**, where there is a basic guesthouse, then catch the boat to Vientiane from there. Slow boats depart Pak Lai for Vientiane at 0730 and take all day (US$10). Or you can hire a speed boat, 5-6 hrs, US$150 for up to 6 people. It is possible to see working elephants on the journey between Pak Lai and Sanakham (Xana Kham), the next significant settlement downstream. Sanakham has 3 wats, one with a ruined stupa and another wat with an unusual Buddha image. There is a river border crossing here to Chiang Khan in Thailand, but foreigners are not permitted to cross (although frequent boats ply the Mekong and it is said that no-one asks for your passport). Boats from Sanakham to Vientiane are intermittent, and take about 8 hrs, arriving at the northern jetty.

To Nong Khiaw and Muang Khua A few boats travel up the Nam Ou to Nong Khiaw and Muang Ngoi. However, these are infrequent, especially when the river is low. The journey usually takes 6 hrs to Nong Khiaw, 65,000 kip, and a further 1 hr to Muang Ngoi. The Nam Ou joins the Mekong near the Pak Ou caves, so it is possible to combine a journey with a visit to the caves en route. Most of the travel agents on Sisavangvong Rd organize small slow boats to make this journey and advertize individual seats depending on how many places they have booked, usually around US$10 per person. Alternatively, you can charter a slow boat for 1-6 people for US$100. Speedboats to Nong Khiaw leave from Ban Don (5 km

from Luang Prabang), expect to pay 150,000 kip. The speedboats are hazardous, uncomfortable and not environmentally friendly but make for exhilarating travelling. From Nong Khiaw some vessels continue upriver to Muang Khua (198,000 kip all the way from Luang Prabang to Muang Khua).

Bus/truck
Luang Prabang has two main bus stations: the northern for northbound traffic and the southern for traffic to/from the south. Always double-check which terminal your bus is using, as unscheduled changes are possible. There's a third, smaller station, south of town on the road to the falls, for buses to Sayaboury.

From the northern terminal To **Nam Bak**, 0800-0900 daily (the truck leaves when full), 3 hrs, 18,000 kip. To **Luang Namtha**, 1500 and 1730 daily, 8 hrs, usually via Udom Xai, 50,000 kip. The roads are reasonable and paved but quite hilly. The 1730 bus has usually come from Vientiane and is often full. An alternative is to break the journey by catching the bus to **Udom Xai**, 0800 and 1100 daily, 5 hrs, 30,000 kip, and then continuing on to Luang Namtha in the afternoon.

There are also daily departures (usually in the morning) to **Houei Xai** on the Thai/Lao border, US$7, a pretty uncomfortably, bumpy trip. Road upgrades in 2005 should make the road more bearable.

From the southern terminal There are up to 10 buses to **Vientiane** on any given day, although scheduled departures tend to decline in the low season. The ordinary service departs at 0730, 0830, 1030, 1230, 1530, 1630 and 1800 daily, 10-11 hrs, 60,000 kip; the 1530 service stops in **Vang Vieng**, 6 hrs, 45,000 kip. VIP buses to Vientiane depart 0630, 0830, 0900, 1930, 9 hrs, 80,000 kip; the 0900 service stops in Vang Vieng, 55,000 kip. There is also an additional so-called VIP service to Vang Vieng at 1000, 5 hrs, 65,000 kip.

To **Phonsavanh**, 1750 daily, 8-9 hrs, 70,000 kip. To **Xam Neua**, twice a week, 10-13 hrs depending on road conditions, 80,000 kip. To **Nong Khiaw** via Pak Mong, 1330, 1 hr, 20,000 kip; there are also several daily *songthaew*/trucks to Nong Khiaw, 4 hrs, 18,000 kip, and to **Vieng Kham**, 6 hrs, 25,000 kip, departing from the same place.

From the Sayaboury terminal

Songthaew for **Pak Khon**, on the Mekong, depart several times a day, when full, 3 hrs, 25,000 kip/US$1.50. From Pak Khon there is a Mekong ferry to **Tha Deua**, 3000 kip, from where buses continue to **Sayaboury**, 1 hr, 10,000 kip. This is the route you need to take if you want to catch a boat from Pak Lái to Vientiane (see above).

Minibus

Minibuses with driver are available from several hotels and the tour companies, US$50 per day around Luang Prabang, US$60 per day if travelling further afield. Check out the notice boards for services to **Vang Vieng**, 5 hrs, 85,000 kip, and **Vientiane**, 7 hrs, 180,000 kip; quicker than the bus, but more expensive. If you have a big group you can organize independent min-van rental.

Saamlor and tuk-tuk

Lots around town, which can be hired to see the sights or to go to nearby villages. Barter hard! A short stint across town should cost about 10,000 kip per person, but expect to pay 15,000 kip for anything more than 1 km. Most of the nearby excursions will cost US$5-10. Tuk-tuks leave the centre of town frequently for **Ban Phanom**, 30,000 kip. To **Ban Hat Hien**, 50,000 kip.

---

❶ Directory

Luang Prabang *p116, maps p120 and p126*
Banks Lao Development Bank, 65 Sisavangvong Rd, 0830-1200 and 1330-1530 Mon-Sat, will change US$/Thai ฿/TCs into US$ or kip, but doesn't accept Visa; there's another branch on Sisavangvong Rd, near Nisha Restaurant.

Banque pour le Commerce Exterieur Lao (BCEL), Mahapatsaman Rd, 0830-1200 and 1330-1530 Mon-Sat; all transactions in kip, will exchange Thai ฿, US$, AU$, UK£, € and TCs, also cash advances on Visa cards; another booth branch near Nazim's. Many of the jewellery stalls in the old market, plus restaurant and tourist shop owners, will change US$ and Thai baht.

Communications Area code: 071.
Post and telephone office, corner of Chau Fa Ngum and Setthathirat Sts, 0830-1730 Mon-Fri, 0830-1200 Sat, express mail service, fax and international telephone facilities, philately section. There are IDD call boxes around the post office and on Sisavangvong Rd. Hotels and some guesthouses also allow international calls from their reception phones (about US$5 a min). You are better off making international calls from one of the many internet cafés, which are dramatically cheaper.
Internet Plenty of internet cafés have cropped up around town, with a concentration on Sisavangvong Rd, including **Luang Prabang Internet**, **PN Computers**, **English IT Centre** and a plethora of others; most places charge 100 kip per min. Connection speeds leave a lot to be desired. **PlaNet**, Sisavangvong Rd, can be a bit grumpy at times. **Luang Prabang Internet**, opposite Silichit Guesthouse, is probably the best value deal in town, with the friendliest service.
Medical services Medical services in Luang Prabang are limited. The main hospital is on Settathirat, T071-252049. There is also the **Chinese Hospital**, Ban Phu Mok, T071-254026. Neither rank highly in terms of medical service. If you are caught seriously ill it is recommended to make for Bangkok. There are a few quite well-equipped pharmacies towards Villa Santi on Sisavangvong Rd.

North of Luang Prabang

In recent years the settlements of Nong Khiaw and Muang Ngoi Neua in the north of Luang Prabang Province have become firm favourites with the backpacker set. In fact, idyllic Muang Ngoi Neua is often heralded as the new Vang Vieng, surrounded by stunning scenery and the fantastic ebb of life on the river. It is far more pleasant to travel between Luang Prabang and Nong Khiaw/Ban Saphoun by long boat, than by bus. The Nam Ou passes mountains, teak plantations, dry rice fields and a movable water wheel mounted on a boat, which moves from village to village and is used for milling. But with the improvements that have been made to Route 13, road travel has now become the preferred option for many – partly because it is cheaper, and partly because it is quicker. Route 13 north runs parallel with the river for most of the journey to Nam Bak. ▸▸ *For Sleeping, Eating and other listings, see pages 154-159.*

Nam Bak → *Colour map 1, B3.*

The town of Nam Bak lies on the banks of the Nam Bak. It is a rather beautiful place and is worth an overnight stop. The market is interesting in the very early morning, when hill people including Blue Hmong converge to sell a miscellany of pickings from

> ❢ *The road west from Nam Bak to Udom Xai is beautiful, passing Blue Hmong villages.*

the forest. There is a small wat on the right, at the end of town as you come from Luang Prabang, called **Wat Tiom Tian**. From here there are good views of the surrounding countryside. There is a small children's graveyard behind the wat.

Nong Khiaw and Ban Saphoun → *Colour map 1, B4.*

 ▸▸ *pages 154-159.*

Nong Khiaw lies 22 km to the northeast of Nam Bak and is a delightful little village on the banks of the Nam Ou, surrounded by limestone peaks. There are, in fact, two settlements here; Ban Saphoun on the east bank of the Nam Ou and Nong Khiaw on the west. Confusingly, the combined village is sometimes called one name, sometimes the other and sometimes **Muang Ngoi**, which is actually another town to the north (see opposite) and also the name of the district.

One reason why Nong Khiaw/Ban Saphoun has become such a popular stopping place for travellers is because of its pivotal position on the Nam Ou. It is also on the more scenic route to Phonsavanh via Route 1 (see page 201). But, most importantly, it is a beautiful spot, the sort of place where time stands still, journals are written, books read and stress is a deeply foreign concept.

It is possible to swim in the river (women should wear sarongs) or walk

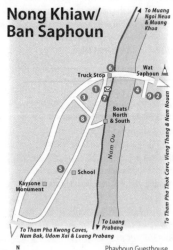

Nong Khiaw/ Ban Saphoun

To Muang Ngoi Neua & Muang Khua

Wat Saphoun

Truck Stop

Boats North & South

Nam Ou

School

Kaysone Monument

To Tham Pha Kwong Caves, Nam Bak, Udom Xai & Luang Prabang

To Luang Prabang

To Tham Pha Thok Cave, Vieng Thang & Nam Nouan

N

Not to scale

Sleeping
Manipoon Guesthouse 1
Mexay Guesthouse & Restaurant 2
Pha Noi Guesthouse 4

Phayboun Guesthouse & Restaurant 3
Phosoi Guesthouse 5
Sanhty Guesthouse & Restaurant 7
Sendoro Guesthouse 6
Somgnot Guesthouse & Restaurant 8
Sunset Guesthouse & Restaurant 9

Around Nong Khiaw

The most obvious attractions in the area are **Tham Pha Thok** (2 km away, 1,000 kip
per person in a tuk-tuk) and **Tham Pha Kwong** (3 km away, 1,000 kip per person), two
caves that were used by locals when the US bombed the area. It is possible to walk to
the caves; turn left out of the village heading towards Nam Bak
and the Tham Pha Kwong caves are about half an hour's walk, up
on the right. There is a shrine to the Buddha, various relics, and a
pile of old ammunition and bombshells inside. Take a strong
torch to explore the tunnel at the back. It's a 30-minute trek to
Tham Pha Thok: go over the bridge and follow the main road. The
caves are signposted.

> ❗ *Word on the ground
> is that the caves are
> connected via an
> underground tunnel but
> don't even try to explore,
> it's far too dangerous!*

Also in the area, close to Ban Sopkhong, is the **Than Mok** waterfall. To get there,
you can either walk for about 3 km or charter a boat (around 20,000 kip per person for
the return trip); remember to agree a return time. There's a 2,000 kip fee to see the
waterfall, and some cheeky little child will likely charge you a further 10,000 kip to
guide you there (40 minutes each way). It's difficult to find on your own. It's best to go
in the morning, so as not to have to rush the climb up to the falls or cut short your time
there before dark.

Muang Ngoi Neua → *Colour map 1, B4.*

🏠🍴🔺🚌🅘 → *pages 154-159.*

The town of Muang Ngoi Neua lies 40 km and one hour north of Nong Khiaw, along
the Nam Ou. This small town surrounded by ethnic villages has become very popular
with the backpacker set over the last few years, with many calling it the new Vang
Vieng. The town is a small slice of utopia, set on a peninsula at the foot of Mount
Phaboom, shaded by coconut trees, with the languid river breeze wafting through the
town's small paths. Most commonly known as **Muang Ngoi**, the settlement has had
to embellish its name to distinguish it from Nong Khiaw, which is also often referred
to as Muang Ngoi (see above). It's the perfect place to go for a trek to surrounding
villages, or bask the day away swinging in your hammock. A market is held every 10
days to which the villagers come to sell their produce and handicrafts.

Around Muang Ngoi Neua

Tham Kang cave, a large limestone cave, with a glassy river running through it, is a
pleasant 30-minute walk south of town. Follow the road out of town, turn left near
Kaikaew Restaurant and head through the school grounds and along a narrow path
through vegetation. Follow the path on the left to avoid wading through very deep and
very cold water. Just past the school, villagers will collect the entrance fee of 2,000
kip. The cave is over 30 m high and exceptionally dark inside, so bring a torch. There's
a swimming hole at ground level. **Tham Pa Kaew** is a further five minutes' walk along
the trail. Inside the cave is a small Buddha image and there's also a crystal-clear pool
that's great for a dip. On the other side of the path are sticky rice paddies, where you
can catch a glimpse of locals planting or harvesting the rice by hand. Another 30
minutes' walk along the same path leads to some friendly Khmu and Lao villages; the
people of **Ban Ha** are exceptionally friendly. Another 30 minutes' walk leads to **Ban
Huay Baw**, from where you can reach the **Than Mok** waterfall by boat (see page 151). It
is a 20-minute trip downstream to **Ban Sopkhong** (60,000 kip per boat), where you
disembark for a one-hour walk to the waterfall. Villagers are more than obliging to
assist in directions.

Muang Khua → *Phone code: 081. Colour map 1, B3.*

😊🍴🏠📱 ▸▸ *pages 154-159.*

Muang Khua is nestled into the banks of the Nam Ou, close to the mouth of the Nam Phak, in the south of Phongsali Province. Hardly a destination in itself, it's usually just a stopover between Nong Khiaw and Phongsali. This, in itself, makes Muang Khua a great place to kick back for a few days, if you want to take a break from the well-worn traveller's path.

Located at the junction of two rivers and on Route 4 to Vietnam, the town has long been a crossroads between Vietnam and Laos. A French garrison was based in Muang Khua until 1954, when it was ousted by Vietnamese troops in the aftermath of the battle at Dien Bien Phu. For a brief period from 1958, Polish and Canadian officials of the Comité International de Contrôle were quartered in the town to monitor the ceasefire between the Pathet Lao and the Royal Lao government. Nowadays, Muang Khua is home to a burgeoning market in Vietnamese goods, trucked in from Dien Bien Phu. There is speculation that the border with Vietnam will soon open to tourists, which will certainly change the character of the town, for better or worse.

Muang Khua is an attractive town to walk about, but be prepared for a group of children to join you on your saunter. There is a small new wat and a 30-m-long wood-and-iron pedestrian bridge across the Nam Phak to a small village on the other side. The bridge offers excellent views up and down the river but, as it tends to wobble, it is not for vertigo-sufferers. The morning market, which sometimes attracts Akha women, sells fresh vegetables and meat, while the goldsmith, just off the main square, is usually surrounded by a small group watching his very delicate work.

Around Muang Khua

The Akha, Khmu and Tai Dam are the main hill tribes in the area. The nearest villages are 20 km out of town and you will need a guide if you want to visit them. Trekking around Muang Khua is fantastic and still a very authentic experience, as this region remains largely unexplored by backpackers. The friendly villages are very welcoming to foreigners, as they don't see as many here as in somewhere like Muang Sing. For these very reasons, it is important to tread lightly and adopt the most culturally sensitive principles: don't hand out sweets and always ask before taking a photograph. Treks usually run for one to three days and involve a homestay at a villager's house (usually the Village Chief). ▸▸ *For further details, see Activities and tours, page 157.*

Towards Phongsali

You can travel from Muang Khua to Phongsali either by truck, bus or boat. Trucks, on their way from Udom Xai, depart from the nearby village of **Pak Nam Noi**; buy lunch from the market there before departure. The ride is a long one, made more difficult when the pick-up is full, however, the hill tribes you come across along the way are very interesting and the scenery toward the Phongsali end of the trip is utterly breathtaking. A great experience. Alternatively, catch a boat direct from Muang Khua. It's a beautiful trip, especially for birdwatching, with kingfishers everywhere. The river is quite shallow in places and there is a fair amount of white water, so take a blanket. Boats stop at **Hat Xa**, 20 km or so to the northeast of Phongsali, where you may find yourselves stuck, as there are no buses to Phongsali after mid-afternoon. Note there is no electricity in Hat Xa. ▸▸ *For further details, see Transport, page 158.*

Phongsali → *Phone code: 088. Colour map 1, A3.*

▸▸ *pages 154-159.*

High up in the mountains at an altitude of about 1628 m, this northern provincial capital provides beautiful views and an invigorating climate. It is especially beautiful from January to March, when wildflowers and opium poppies bloom in the surrounding hills. The town can be cold at any time of the year, so take some warm clothes. Mornings tend to be foggy and it can also be very wet.

Phongsali was one of the first areas to be liberated by the Pathet Lao in the late 1940s. The old post office (just in front of the new one) is the sole physical reminder of French rule. The town has a very different feel to the southern towns and its architecture is a strange mix of Chinese post-revolutionary concrete blocks, Lao wood and brick houses with tin roofs, and bamboo or mud huts with straw roofs. The Chinese influence is very prominent here, mainly dating from the year when the new road network linked the town with the border. New Chinese shophouses are under construction and the roofs are mainly galvanized iron.

The town itself is home to about 20,000 people, mostly Lao, Phou Noi and Chinese. The wider district is a potpourri of ethnicities, with around 28 minorities inhabiting the area, depending on how you define them. The principal groups are the Phou Noi, Akha, Lu, Yunnanese and Lao Soung. The so-called **Museum of Tribes** ⓘ *close to Lao Telecom, daily 0800-1100 and 1330-1630 , 2000 kip*, displays hill tribe costumes and photographs; opening hours are erratic, but if you go there during the week and ask around, someone will probably open up for you.

> ❢ *The Chinese border west of Phongsali is only open to Lao and Chinese nationals. Foreigners must use the crossing at Boten, see page 177.*

Around Phongsali

Many paths lead out of town over the hills; the walking is easy and the views are spectacular. It is not possible to hire bikes, tuk-tuks or even ponies here so walking is the only way to explore the fantastic landscapes of this region. Climb the 413 steps to the top of **Mount Phoufa** for humbling views of the surrounding hills. Some people trek north from Phongsali to **Muang Uthai**, staying in Akha villages en route. Muang Uthai is probably as remote and unspoilt as it gets. During the rainy season, it may be possible to take a boat back downriver from Uthai to Luang Prabang. ▸▸ *For further details, see Activities and tours, page 157.*

Northern Laos North of Luang Prabang

Phongsali

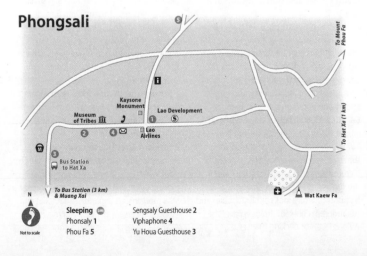

To Mount Phou Fa

To Hat Xa (1 km)

Kaysone Monument

Museum of Tribes 血

Lao Development

Lao Airlines

Bus Station to Hat Xa

To Bus Station (3 km) & Muang Xai

N
Not to scale

Wat Kaew Fa

Sleeping
Phonsaly **1**
Phou Fa **5**

Sengsaly Guesthouse **2**
Viphaphone **4**
Yu Houa Guesthouse **3**

The road from Phongsali to Udom Xai has been upgraded relatively recently and, although it remains only partially sealed, is in good condition. The surroundings and scenery are incredible. It is possible to break the journey at **Pak Nam Noi,** which lies at the intersection of the two roads going either to Muang Khua or Udom Xai. There's an elephant farm near Km 14 and elephants can sometimes be seen from the road.

Sleeping

Nam Bak *p150*

E-F **Bounthiem,** canary yellow building opposite the wat at the opposite end of town to the market, T071-253640. Five double or twin rooms, with clean, comfy mattresses, fans and mosquito nets. Balcony area, Western-style toilet downstairs and shower with hot water. Friendly. Recommended.

E-F **Viengthong Guesthouse,** 100 m past the bridge on the right. Nine very clean and comfortable rooms, singles, twins and doubles, with fan and mosquito nets. Separate Western-style toilet and scoop showers downstairs. Free bottle of water on check-in.

F **Khounvilay Guesthouse,** next door to Bounthiem, T071-253647. Basic doubles, triples and twins. Quite scruffy with a squat toilet and shower out the back. Mosquito nets, cold drinks available. The wonderfully friendly family owners are likely to invite you to share their evening meal – an extravaganza of spices that is liable to blow your mouth away! Mr Somchith is a good source of travel information.

Nong Khiaw and Ban Saphoun *p150, map p150*

D **Phayboun Guesthouse,** 1st guesthouse on the right as you enter Nong Khiaw from the west, T071-253928. Solid building with reasonable and clean doubles and twins. Balcony, toilet and en suite shower. Restaurant attached. Quiet location. Friendly owner.

E-F **Sunset Guesthouse,** down a lane about 100 m past the bridge, Ban Saphoun, T071-253933. Slap bang on the bank of the river – you couldn't ask for a more picturesque setting from which to watch the sunset. The charming, sprawling bamboo structure looks out onto tables and sun umbrellas liberally arranged over the various levels of decking that serve as a popular restaurant in the evenings (European food and curries). A good spot to read or write, whilst soaking up the sun during the day. Western toilet and hot water shower outside. Eight rooms with hard mattresses on the floor but definitely worth it. A great favourite with travellers. Trekking can be arranged here, too. Recommended.

F **Manipoon Guesthouse,** near the post office, Nong Khiaw, T071-253908. Slightly grander rooms than the other guesthouses, separated by wooden walls rather than just bamboo. Verandahs offer unspectacular views of nearby rooftops. Bathroom downstairs.

F **Mexay Guesthouse,** on the Ban Saphoun side of the bridge. Six dirt-cheap but clean and comfortable doubles and twins. Separate squat bathroom downstairs. The food is not as inviting as its more successful neighbour, **Sunset** (see above).

F **Pha Noi Guesthouse,** on the right as you cross the bridge, Ban Saphoun, T071-235919. Five simple double and twin bungalows nestled near the river's edge. Basic Western toilet and shower.

F **Phosoi Guesthouse,** south of the boat landing and opposite the school. A small, rickety 2-floored structure with 5 small doubles and twins. Balcony upstairs, café downstairs, with small Lao menu. Squat toilet and scoop shower in garden. Recently renovated. Friendly owners can speak a little English.

F **Sanhty Guesthouse,** a few doors down from the post office facing the river, Nong Khiaw. Six tiny twin and double rooms, squat toilet and shower out back.

F **Sendoro Guesthouse,** on the left just before crossing the bridge, Nong Khiaw. Five double and twin bungalows with balconies looking out across the river, and 5 more set a little more inland, separate squat toilet and scoop showers, with a washing machine. Also a large restaurant with a good selection.

F Somgnot Guesthouse, a few doors down from the Sanhty Guesthouse, close to where the boats leave, Nong Khiaw. Five 'spaces' – it's difficult to call them rooms – separated by bamboo screens, Oriental feel, with Indian paintings. Run by a friendly old man with a little English. Tasty cheap Lao food served downstairs.

Muang Ngoi Neua *p151*

The surge of tourists now visiting Muang Ngoi Neua has led to an increase in the number of guesthouses and bungalows, so that there are now over 18 places to stay. All the accommodation in town is dirt cheap and of the same standard: bungalows with extremely welcoming hammocks on their balconies. Most offer a laundry service for around 10,000 kip per kg and all have electricity 1800-2200 only. Rats are a problem here but, luckily, the mosquito nets tend to keep them at bay.

F Banana Café and Guesthouse, riverside in the centre of town. Five basic bungalows with balconies overlooking the Nam Ou. Western-style toilet and scoop shower. Also a restaurant on the roadside with the standard Laos menu. Trekking, hiking and fishing can be arranged here. Movies are shown in the evening on request (when the power is on). The owners are friendly.

F KaiKeo Bungalows, just beyond the south end of the main road, beside the Nam Ou (take the small track on the right-hand side). The very friendly proprietor, Nuan Chan, and her family have been in the business since 1998. Her son, Sy, guides treks and can organize fishing trips. A paddle boat is available for rent. Recommended.

F Ning Ning Guesthouse, beside the boat landing. Double and twin bungalows, overlooking the river, with separate Western toilet and shower. The food in the adjoining restaurant is great and the owner speaks good English. Popular spot.

F Phet Davanh Guesthouse, on the main road, near the boat landing. Newly opened concrete guesthouse, with 10 double and twin rooms. Comfy mattresses on the floor, Western toilet and shower, restaurant with Lao menu. Good for those who don't want to stay in a bungalow.

F Riverview Bungalows, centre of town. Double and twin bungalows on the river.

Separate scoop shower and squat toilet. Restaurant with a good Lao menu and a few foreign dishes too – claims to serve the best *lao-lao* in Laos. Trekking, fishing and river tubing trips.

F Sainamngoi Bungalows, at the south end of the main road (on the left-hand side). Five rundown bungalows with double beds overlooking the stream to Mount Phaboom. Squat toilet and shower outside. Very tranquil; you won't be disturbed.

F Tali Guesthouse, next to KaiKeo Bungalows. Set in a shady area amid trees. Basic rooms, separate Western toilet and scoop shower. Restaurant with a few Lao dishes.

F Vita Guesthouse, on the river down a path toward the north of the road. The customary bungalow set-up but the owner here goes out of her way to take care of you and cooks great food as well. Recommended.

Muang Khua *p152*

C Sernnali Hotel, in the middle of town, near the top of the hill, T081-212445. The newest and by far the most luxurious lodging in town. 18 rooms with large double and twin beds, hot water scoop showers and Western-style toilets, immaculately clean. Balconies overlook the Nam Ou.

E Keophila Guesthouse, almost at the top of the hill, T081-210907. A reasonably new building with 7 clean, completely tiled double and twin rooms, with hard beds, hot water showers and squat toilets, interesting decor in the bathrooms.

E Ketsana Guesthouse, down a lane at the bus station, T081-210821. Basic rooms with mosquito nets and fan, some have squat toilet and shower. A balcony out front for relaxation. The cheery family that own it don't speak any English.

E Nam Ou Guesthouse & Restaurant, follow the signs at the top of the hill, T081-210844. Looking out across the river where the boats land, this guesthouse is the pick of the budget bunch in Muang Khua. Singles, twins and doubles, some with hot water bathrooms en suite, and 3 new rooms with river views. Great food (see Eating, below). A popular spot with travellers.

E-F Singsavanh Guesthouse, on the top of the hill next to the market, T088-210812. Clean concrete structure. Basic twins and doubles, with mosquito net, some have toilet and shower attached. Very friendly staff. The budget rooms in the basement have an eclectic collection of buffalo and deer heads – an experience.

F **Sengali Guesthouse**, about halfway up the hill from the river, T088-210838. Three-storey building with miserable twin and double rooms, mosquito nets. Squat toilet and shower on the 2nd floor. Cheap.

Towards Phongsali p152

Hat Xa now has a guesthouse, run by the chief, 15,000 kip for a space in a bamboo shelter with a pillow and mattress. The Nam Ou serves as the toilet and shower! The chief also runs a very pricey and basic restaurant, and the only shop with a fridge. There is a small noodle shop on the hill towards Phongsali which serves much better and cheaper fare.

Phongsali p153, map p153

C **Phou Fa Hotel**, turn up the hill just past the Phongsaly Hotel and follow the signs. This hotel has good views over the town but feels a bit like an army barracks. Clean double rooms with en suite bathrooms and hot water. Large and gloomy restaurant, nightclub, and its best facility – a beer garden overlooking the town, an excellent spot for an afternoon beer. Friendly staff speak excellent English.

D **Viphahone Hotel**, next to the post office. Three-storey building with 24 very clean, large and airy twin and double rooms, with excellent hot water bathrooms, some with Western flush toilets, some with squats. There is a coffee table with chairs in most rooms as well as Laos tea. Good value. Restaurant on the ground floor.

E **Phongsaly Hotel**, opposite Kaysone Monument. This Chinese 4-storey monstrosity is the tallest building in town. There are 2 floors of large and airy triple rooms, some with hot water bathrooms. Excellent views from the roof and a good restaurant. The Chinese owner is rumoured to have come by his money by poaching elephants. Price negotiable for longer stays.

E **Sengsaly Guesthouse**, up the hill and around the bend from the market, T088-210165. Worn but comfortable rooms in a concrete building, with squat toilets and scoop showers. The friendly owners will bring you hot water in the evening for the Lao tea provided in your room, or if you prefer – to shower with.

E-F **Yu Houa Guesthouse**, across the road from the market, T088-210186. Six clean fresh twin and double rooms in a 3-storey building. The more expensive rooms have a bathroom with Western toilet. Shared shower on the 2nd floor with squat toilet for the other rooms. Sweeping views of the valley from the rooms at the back. Restaurant downstairs.

Towards Udom Xai p154

F **Sinsay Guesthouse**, Pak Nam Noi. Simple rooms for 20,000 kip.

🍴 Eating

Nam Bak p150

There are 2 or 3 noodle shops, the best is **Han Nang Nit**, opposite the market. No English but very friendly service – good place to wait for onward transport as the trucks stop outside.

Nong Khiaw and Ban Saphoun p150, map p150

Most of the guesthouses have cafés attached, although the food is generally quite bland. A better option are the noodle shops alongside Sendoro selling very tasty fried rice, sticky rice and vegetables – ask to see the English menu. Great Lao coffee.

Muang Ngoi Neua p151

Aside from the guesthouse restaurants, which serve quality Lao food, there are also a number of places to eat along the main road. Most have exactly the same food; in fact, many of them just copy their competitors' menus. The fruit shake stands in the centre of town are good value.

Sainamgoi Restaurant & Bar, in the centre of town, serves tasty Lao food in a pleasant atmosphere, with good background music. There are tables and chairs or cushions on the floor. The bar, the only one in town, is in the next room. Further along the main road, with a bomb casing out front, is **Sengdala Restaurant & Bakery**, which serves very good, cheap Lao food, terrific pancakes and freshly baked baguettes. Next to Banana

Guesthouse, **Nang Phone Keo Restaurant**, serves all the usual Lao food plus some extras: try the 'Falang Roll' for breakfast (a combination of peanut butter, sticky rice and vegetables). **Sky Restaurant** is ambient in the evening although the food is not great.

Muang Khua *p152*

This is a small town with very few eateries, although what it lacks in restaurants, it makes up for in pool tables; very small children show a frightening aptitude and you should be prepared to have an instant audience if you try your hand; there is usually a box in which you are expected to make a donation.

The **Nam Ou Guesthouse & Restaurant** (see Sleeping) is up the mud slope from the beach, an incomparable location for a morning coffee overlooking the river; it has an English menu and friendly staff. The restaurant opposite the **Singsavanh** has tasty fried noodles and rice dishes and an English menu. There is also a restaurant next door to **Keophila Guesthouse** that serves nice and cheap Vietnamese style feu. Noodles and baguettes are available in the market.

Phongsali *p153, map p153*

It is possible to buy apples, pears and even potatoes in Phongsali and the few restaurants along the only road sell chips; a welcome relief after days of *feu*. The rice here is steamed rather than sticky. A few doors down and across the road from the Phongsaly is a small Chinese restaurant. There are also *feu* stalls opposite the market.
₸₸ **Phongsaly Hotel** (see Sleeping). Good food and the best chips in town.
₸₸ **Yu Houa Guesthouse** (see Sleeping). A short Lao section on an English menu. Cheap and good.

▲ Activities and tours

Muang Ngoi Neua *p151*

Trekking, hiking, fishing, trips to the waterfalls and boat trips can be organized through most of the guesthouses.
Kongkeo, who lives in the centre of town, is a former English teacher, who has been running treks since 1998. He does an overnight trek to the top of Mount

Phaboom, US$15 per person per night for a group of 4, including food and accommodation in the villages. It is also possible to canoe to nearby villages. A lovely 1-day hike into the rainforest can be arranged.
Lao Youth Travel, www.laoyouthtravel.com, 0730-1800 daily. Half-day, day, overnight or 2-night treks, starting from US$10 per person. Also kayaking trips.

Muang Khua *p152*

Singsavanh Guesthouse can arrange tours to the surrounding hill villages for around US$30 per person for 2 days and 1 night, or about half that per day for trekking. The guides speak good English. **Mr Khammane**, khammaane@hotmail.com, is a former monk and chemistry teacher who guides treks to surrounding villages Jun-Aug and at weekends. **Mr Kak**, of the **Nam Ou Guesthouse**, guides 2- and 3-day treks for US$15 per person, including food and accommodation.

Phongsali *p153, map p153*
Trekking

A few independent local guides lead treks in the region. The **tourism office**, on the way to Phou Fa Hotel, T088-210098, Mon-Fri 0730-1130 and 1330-1630, can also arrange guided treks for up to 7 nights for around US$25 per day (1 person) or US$35 (2 people). **Chantha Sone**, T020-5688315, offers 1- or 2-day treks over the weekend for US$17 per person per day (1 person) or US$12 (2 people), including food and accommodation; he has a number of different routes, visiting some of the 35 ethnic villages in the area. **Mr Phonsai**, T020-5688357, is another local guide who comes recommended. Agencies in Luang Prabang and Luang Namtha also organize group treks around Phongsali.

⊖ Transport

Nam Bak *p150*

There are regular trucks/buses to **Luang Prabang**. To **Nong Khiaw**, 1 hr by truck on a good road. In theory, the trucks wait for the boats to arrive from Luang Prabang and Muang Khua. To **Muang Ngoi Neua**, 0700 and throughout the day as soon as they're full, 7,000 kip; be prepared to wait around for a few hours, tuk-tuks are more frequent for the same price. To **Udom Xai** (94 km), you need to take a *songthaew* to **Pak Mong**, 10 km west of Nam Bak, 8,000 kip, and change there for a bus to Udom Xai, 3 hrs, 15,000 kip. Don't be surprised if you have to wait in Pak Mong. To **Nam Nouan**, flag down one of the vehicles from Vientiane travelling east along Route 1, which usually pass the market at around 2000, 60,000 kip.

Nong Khiaw and Ban Saphoun *p150, map p150*

Boat

Boat services have become irregular following road improvements, although you may find a service to **Muang Ngoi Neua**, 1 hr, 13,000 kip, from the boat landing. Some vessels also head upriver to **Muang Khua**, 5 hrs, 60,000 kip.

Songthaew/truck

Regular connections to **Luang Prabang**, 3-4 hrs, 18,000 kip. Also several departures daily to **Nam Bak**, 30 mins, 7,000 kip and on to **Udom Xai**. Alternatively, take one of the more regular *songthaew* to **Pak Mong**, 1 hr, 10,000 kip, where there is a small noodle shop, and then catch a vehicle on to Udom Xai (see Nam Bak transport, above).

Travelling east on Route 1, there are buses to **Vieng Kham**, 2-3 hrs, 15,000 kip, and **Nam Nouan**, and from here south on Route 6 to **Phonsavanh** and the **Plain of Jars**, 75,000 kip, or north to **Xam Neua**, 6 hrs. The bus to Nam Nouan can be caught from the toll gate on the Ban Saphoun side of the river when it comes through from Vientiane at around 0730, 60,000 kip; it's usually quite crowded and you will probably have to stay overnight in Vieng Thong en route.

Muang Ngoi Neua *p151*

Boat

From the landing at the northern end of town, slow boats travel north along the Nam Ou to **Muang Khua**, 5 hrs, US$6, however, if there is no boat going, which is often the case, you will have to charter your own for US$50 per boat. Slow boats also go south to **Nong Khiaw**, 1 hr, 13,000 kip, and **Luang Prabang**, 8 hrs, US$100 per boat. Speedboats to Nong Khiaw take 30 mins

and cost 20,000 kip per person. Departure times vary; for more information and tickets, consult the booth at the landing.

Muang Khua *p152*

Boat

Road travel is now more popular but irregular boats still travel south on the Nam Ou to **Muang Ngoi Neua/Nong Khiaw**, 4-5 hrs, 60,000 kip, if there is enough demand. Also north to **Phongsali** via **Hat Xa**, 6 hrs, US$7 slow boat or 3 hrs, US$6 in a speedboat. Boats will only run when there is enough water, so check before travelling in the dry season (Mar-May). A jeep or truck transports travellers on from Hat Xa to Phongsali itself, 20 km, 2 hrs along a very bad road, $US25.

Songthaew/truck

To **Phongsali**, take a *songthaew* to nearby village **Pak Nam Noi**, 0800 daily, 1hr 10,000 kip, then take the truck that passes through from Udom Xai around 1030 daily, 7½ hrs, 40,000 kip.

To **Udom Xai**, pick-ups leave 0700-0800 daily from outside the Singsavanh Guesthouse and later in the day if you're prepared to wait around, about 4 hrs, 15,000 kip, and, again, a beautiful ride.

Phongsali *p153, map p153*

Air

Lao Airlines, next door to the Viphahone, T020-980180, runs flights to Vientiane, Thu and Sun, US$89 one-way, although flights can be cancelled at short notice due to the small number of prospective passengers.

Bus and boat

Buses to **Hat Xa** leave 0700-0730 daily, 5000 kip, from the bus station across the road from the market; if you miss the morning departures you may have to wait another day. From Hat Xa, boats leave for **Muang Khua**, 4-5 hrs, 60,000 kip; it can be cold and wet so wear waterproofs. Buses to **Udom Xai**, 237 km, 9-10 hrs, 50,000 kip, leave from the bus station 3 km south of town at 0730 daily; to get to this bus station catch a *songthaew* from opposite the market.

❶ Directory

Nam Bak *p150*
Bank There's an exchange by the market.
Post office 100 m west of the market.

Nong Khiaw and Ban Saphoun *p150, map p150*
Internet The only connection is at Sunset Guesthouse (600 kip per min. **Post office** at the bridge, on the Nong Khiaw side.

Muang Ngoi Neua *p151*
Bank Lattanavongsa Money Exchange is on the main road at the northern end of town. **Communications** There is no internet or telephone in this remote town.

Muang Khua *p152*
Bank Lao Development Bank, near the truck stop, 0800-1130 and 1300-1630 Mon-Fri, can change US$, Thai ฿, € and Chinese ¥ at quite bad rates. They won't change TCs or do cash advances on credit cards, so make sure you have plenty of cash before you come here. **Communications** Post office is opposite the wat; turn right at the top of the hill. International calls can be made from the Telecom office, a small unmarked hut with a huge satellite, halfway up the winding road, behind the bank, open 0700-1130 and 1300-1630 daily, domestic calls 1,000 kip per min; international calls vary by destination, 14,000-23,000 kip per min. **Electricity** 1900-2200 daily.

Phongsali *p153, map p153*
Banks There is a branch of the Lao Development Bank, 20 m along from Phonsaly Hotel. It will only change US$, Thai ฿ and Chinese ¥. **Communications** The post office is just down the road from the Viphahone. Calls can be made from Lao Telecom Office next door or there is an IDD call box on the opposite side of the road.

Northwest Laos

Northwestern Laos is comprised of dramatic, misty mountainous scenery, clad with thick forests and peppered with small villages. This area is home to a large variety of ethnic minority groups including the Akha, Hmong, Khmu and Yao and has become a firm favourite with trekkers. The mighty Mekong forges its way through picturesque towns, such as Pak Beng and Houei Xai, affording visitors a wonderful glimpse of riverine life. ▸▸ *For Sleeping, Eating and other listings, see pages 168-181.*

Udom Xai (Oudom Xai) and around

→ *Phone code: 081. Colour map 1, B3.* 🅑🄯🔺🄴❶ ▸▸ *pages 168-181.*

Udom Xai, the capital of Udom Xai Province, is a hot and dusty town. It was razed during the war and the inhabitants fled to live in the surrounding hills; what is here now has been built since 1975, which explains why it is such an ugly settlement. Since the early 1990s, the town has been experiencing an economic boom, as a result of its position at the intersection of roads linking China, Vietnam, Luang Prabang and Pak Beng, and commerce and construction are thriving. It also means that Udom Xai has a large population of Chinese and Vietnamese, a fact that appears to rile the locals.

The town's truck-stop atmosphere doesn't enamour it to tourists and, unfortunately, the other bad elements which come with major transport thoroughfares seem to be raising their heads here. However, the town does make a decent stop-off point at a convenient junction; it's one of the biggest settlements in northern Laos and has excellent facilities. The **Provincial Tourism Office** ① *near the river on the main road in the centre of town, T081-211797, Mon-Fri 0800-1630*, can offer helpful advice.

Udom Xai Province is populated by 23 different ethnic minority groups, with strong contingents of Hmong, Akha and Khmu. The village of **Ban Ting**, behind Udom Xai is interesting to wander through. Its wat, just the other side of the stream, has a ruined monastery and a bizarre life-size tree made of concrete, with tin leaves, concrete animals in the foliage and two reclining Buddhas on the topmost branches. The wat also includes a Buddhist high school for monks and offers a good view of the town and surrounding mountains.

Ban Mok Kho is a Hmong village 16 km along Route 1 to Nam Bak, where the inhabitants wear traditional dress and live in longhouses. To get there, catch a ride on a pick-up going to Nam Bak, or negotiate a price with a taxi or tuk-tuk.

The local tourism authorities have teamed up with **Udom Xai Travel** to offer treks in the **Houay Nam Kat Nature Reserve** and **Nam Kat** waterfall. A few tourists who have gone on the trip have reported only a trickle of water from the falls. ▸▸ *For further details, see Activities and tours, page 175.*

Muang La

Muang La is located 28 km north of Udom Xai, off Route 4 to Phongsali and makes a lovely stop en route. **Wat Ban Pakkla** is considered one of the most sacred temples in the area, due to the presence of a 400-year-old, gold-plated Buddha image, known as the Pra Xaek Kham. Steeped in superstition and highly auspicious, the temple is the place to go if you want to make your dreams come true.

Muang La has gained popularity with travellers for its **hot springs**. Set in beautiful surroundings, the springs are a favourite afternoon bathing spot for the locals who come for a dip in the very hot waters. If you bathe here, wear a sarong or something discreet. The springs haven't really been developed and, at the time of publication, were full of algae but the authorities are trying to improve the site, so it is worth enquiring in Udom Xai before you make the trip.

Muang Houn → *Colour map 1, B2.*

This is a new town (although it looks as old as any other), built in 1986 by the government to entice people down from the hills, in an attempt to stop them growing opium. There are quite a number of Blue Hmong in town.

Luang Namtha and around → *Phone code: 086. Colour map 1, B2.*
🌐🍴🛏️⛰️🚌🏤🅿️ ▸▸ *pages 168-181.*

The provincial capital was obliterated during the war and the concrete structures erected since 1975 have little charm. Like other towns in the north, the improvement in transport links with China and Thailand has led to burgeoning trade. The main attraction is the food market, where members of the many minorities who inhabit the area can be found selling exotic species. Despite this dubious trade, the area has firmly established itself as a major player in Laos' ecotourism industry, primarily due to the **Nam Ha National Protected Area** (see page 162) and the environmentally friendly **Boat Landing Guesthouse** (see page 169).

Sights

Apart from the town's market, the **Luang Namtha Museum** ① *near the Kaysone Monument, daily 0830-1530 (closed for lunch), 5000 kip*, is also worth a visit. The small museum houses a collection of old coins, traditional ethnic clothing, Khmu bronze drums and other interesting artefacts from the region, alongside the usual testaments to the war.

That Poum Pouk sits in a ruinous state on a hill, 3 km west of the airfield. Local sources suggest that the stupa was built as part of a competition between the Lanna Kingdom (in northern Thailand) and the Lane Xang Kingdom to prove who had the most merit. Severe damage due to bombing in 1964 led local villagers and monks to reconstruct the stupa but this proved a somewhat fruitless exercise as further bombing in 1966 dislodged the stupa, parts of which still remain on the ground. Incredibly, much of the original stucco and an incripted stelae survived. The trip to the stupa is most pleasant in the afternoon; tuk-tuks will do the return trip from the market for US$5.

Villages around Luang Namtha
Luang Namtha Province has witnessed the rise and decline of various Tai Kingdoms and now over 30 ethnic groups reside in the province, making it the most ethnically diverse in the country. Principal minorities include Tai Lu, Tai Dam, Lang Ten, Hmong and Khamu. There are a number of friendly villages around the area. As with all other minority areas, you should only visit the villages with a local guide or endorsed tourism organization.

Luang Namtha

To Muang Sing (58 km)

To Udom Xai

Nam Tha River

Sports Ground

Luang Namtha Museum

EU Project
Kaysone Monument
Lao Telecom
BCEL
Lao Development Bank
KNT
Green Discovery
Lao Airlines

To ⑫ Boat Landing, Airfield & Houei Xai

N

Not to scale

Sleeping
Boat Landing Guesthouse & Restaurant **12**
Bounthavong **11**
Bus Station Guesthouse **5**
Cha Rueh Sin Guesthouse **9**
Guesthouse Restaurant **13**
Hong Tha Xay Som Boun **8**
Lao Mai Guesthouse & Restaurant **3**

Luang Namtha Guesthouse & Restaurant **7**
Manychan Guesthouse & Restaurant **4**
Palanh Guesthouse **2**
Saikhonglongsack Guesthouse & Restaurant **1**
Sinsavanh Guesthouse **6**
Vila Guesthouse **10**

Eating
Bakery **1**
Lao Lao **5**
New Restaurant **3**
Panda **2**
Yamuna **4**

Ban Nam Chang is a Lang Ten village 3 km walk along a footpath outside Luang Namtha; ask your way. Lang Ten women are easily recognized: they wear their hair back and pluck their eyebrows from the age of 15. Their clothes are black, with coloured borders, and they wear a lot of delicate silver jewellery.

Ban Lak Khamay is quite a large Akha village 27 km from Luang Namtha on the road to Muang Sing. It was resettled from a nearby location higher in the hills in 1994 as part of a government policy to protect upland forests. The community now grows teak and rubber trees. The village chief speaks Lao. The settlement features a traditional Akha entrance; if you pass through this entrance you must visit a house in the village, or you are considered an enemy. Otherwise you can simply pass to one side of the gate but don't touch it. Other features of interest in Akha villages are the swing, located at the highest point in the village and used in the annual swing festival, and the meeting house, where unmarried couples go to court and where newly married couples live until they have their own house. There is another, smaller Akha village a few kilometres on towards Muang Sing. ▸▸ *For further information, see Visiting an Akha village, page 162.*

Ban Nam Dee is a small bamboo papermaking Lang Ten village about 6 km northeast of Luang Namtha. There's a beautiful waterfall close by: take a right turn down the stream after 500 m.

⁙ Visiting an Akha village

Many people have complained that visiting tribal villages is similar to visiting a human zoo. Here are some tips on how to avoid this experience:

· Always visit with an Akha or locally endorsed guide rather than on your own.
· Do not touch the spirit symbol, spirit gate, spirit house or swing and do not walk through the Akha entrance gate. Touching any of these things is believed to bring incredibly bad luck to the village.
· If you wish to give gifts, such as money, these should be offered only to the Village Chief.
· Accept food a drink if it is offered. The Akha may also offer you a massage; it's OK to accept.
· Rather than watching people go about their work, ask if you can help them.

The small Tai Lue village of **Ban Khone Kam** is also worth a visit. The settlement is based on the banks of the Nam Tha, halfway between Luang Namtha and Houei Xai, and is only accessible by boat or by foot. The friendly villagers offer **homestays** here (30,000 kip per night, includes meals), for one or two nights, providing an interesting cultural insight into the daily lives of the region's boatmen and rice farmers. For information, contact the **Luang Namtha Boat Station**, T086-211305; BAP Guesthouse in Houei Xai, T084-211083, or the **Boat Landing Guesthouse** in Luang Namtha.

Vieng Phouka and around

Before the roads were upgraded, Vieng Phouka was the place to stay overnight when travelling between Luang Namtha or Muang Sing and the Mekong. Located south of Luang Namtha (and 125 km north of Houei Xai), the town is surrounded by minority villages, Akha, Hmong, Lahu and Khmu, with the latter comprising about 90% of the population. The local tourism authority runs treks around the area. ⇥ *For further details, see Activities and tours, page 175.*

The 5-km-long **Nam Aeng cave**, 12 km north of Vieng Phouka, is famous locally for an annual ceremony on 13 January, when elders call up the large fish in the cave. The **Nom cave**, a four-hour walk from the town, was once home to a famous sacred Buddha, which has now been pilfered. During the revolution it served as a hideout. Around the area are a few scattered remains of the wall from the ancient city of Kuvieng, much of which has been dismantled by local villagers at the government's insistence.

Vieng Phouka is a great base from which to venture into the **Nam Ha National Protected Area** (NPA), one of a few remaining places on earth where the rare black-cheeked gibbon can be found. If you're lucky you can hear the wonderful singing of the gibbons in the morning.

Nam Ha National Protected Area

The Nam Ha Ecotourism Project was established by UNESCO and the Lao government in 1993 to help preserve Luang Namtha's cultural and environmental heritage. The 2224-sq-km National Protected Area encompasses over 30 ethnic groups and 37 threatened mammal species. The organization currently leads two- and three-day treks in the area for small groups of four to eight culturally sensitive travellers. The treks offer the chance to visit traditional villages, explore various forest habitats, take

● *The residents of Ban Boolahn Village, about 14 km north of Vieng Phouka, are renowned*
● *locally as bat hunters; the creatures are used for cooking.*

river trips and support local conservation efforts. A relatively new trek to **Phu Sam Yord**, Three Peak Mountain, has recently been unveiled. The trek is a fantastic way to witness a variety of cultures, partake in local village activities and see stunning landscapes. New, longer routes to other villages are also being explored. Treks leave three to four times a week; check with the **Luang Namtha Guide Service Unit** or **Green Discovery** for departure days; an information session about the trek is given at the Guide's Office. The price will cover the cost of food, water, transportation, guides, lodging and the trekking permit. All the treks utilize local guides who have been trained to help generate income for their villages. Income for conservation purposes is also garnered from the fees for trekking permits into the area. The Nam Ha project has won a UN development award for its outstanding achievements in the area. ►► *For further details, see Activities and tours, page 175.*

Nateui → *Colour map 1, B2.*

Nateui is a small roadside settlement northeast of Luang Namtha at the junction of Route 3 and Route 1. Route 3 runs southeast from here to Udom Xai, while Route 1 runs north 18 km to the border settlement of Boten and then into China. This stretch of road is currently being rebuilt as part of the Chinese highway through to Myanmar; as a result it's quite painful and dusty at the the moment but in the near future will be one of the more enjoyable bits of travelling in Laos. Nateui has become a stopover town for trucks driving from Luang Prabang, through Boten, to Mengla in China.

Boten → *Colour map 1, B2.*

Boten lies on the border with China and, until recently, was nothing more than a trucking stop for drivers, with a couple guesthouses here and a handful of noodle shops. However, the town is set for dramatic change, with the construction of the massive Chinese-funded 'Golden Boten City' project. The ten-year project aims to build warehouses, several marketplaces, 2000 hotel rooms and 500 guesthouses, entertainment venues and a golf course. The first foundation stone was laid in 2005 but whether these grandiose plans actually come to fruition remains to be seen. The city project is hoping to capitalize on the upgrading of Highway R3, which will eventually run from Kunming, China, through Luang Namtha and Bokeo provinces to Bangkok, Thailand.

Muang Sing → *Colour map 1, B2.* 😊🏍️🔺🏢🍴 ►► *pages 168-181.*

Many visitors consider this peaceful valley to be one of the highlights of the north. Lying at the terminus of the highway in the far northwest corner of Laos, it is a natural point to stop and spend a few days recovering from the rigours of the road, before either heading south or moving on to China. This area is a border region that has been contested by the Chinese, Lao and Thai at various points in the last few centuries. While it is now firmly Lao territory, there is a gnawing sense that the Chinese have again invaded by stealth; their economic presence is all too evident. There are also several NGOs, as well as bilateral and multilateral development operations, in the area. The only way to get to Muang Sing is by truck or pick-up from Luang Namtha. The road is asphalt but is sometimes broken and the terrain on this route is mountainous with dense forest.

> ‡ *A road leads from Muang Sing to the Chinese border but the crossing is not open to foreigners - at least officially. Boten is still the only point where foreign nationals can cross to or from China.*

● *Local folklore suggests that Muang Sing was founded hundreds of years ago, when two*
● *lions (sing) came down from the Himalayas and settled here.*

66 99 Muang Sing is a supremely picturesque village of golden rattan huts glowing among misty, blue-green peaks.

Sights

Muang Sing itself is little more than a supremely picturesque village, situated on an upland plateau, where golden rattan huts glow among misty, blue-green peaks. The town features some interesting old wooden and brick buildings and, unlike nearby Luang Namtha and several other towns in the north, it wasn't bombed close to oblivion during the struggle for Laos. The **old French fort**, built in the 1920s, is off limits to visitors, as it is occupied by the Lao army, but the **market** is certainly worth a look if you're up very early in the morning; it starts about 0545 and begins to wind down after 0730. Along with the usual array of plastic objects, clothes and pieces of hardware, local silk and cotton textiles can be purchased.

Numerous hill peoples come to the market trade, including Akha and Hmong tribespeople, along with Yunnanese, Tai Dam and Tai Lu.

The tourist office has loads of local information, from transport details through to local history.

The **Muang Sing Exhibition** ⓘ *in the centre of town, Mon-Fri 0900- 1200 and 1300-1600, 5000 kip*, is a beautiful building housing a range of traditional tools, ethnic clothes, jewellery, instruments, religious artefacts and household items, like the loom. The building was once the royal residence of the Jao Fa (Prince), Phanya Sekong. There is another, enigmatic museum, near the central market, although it is not officially open. If you knock on the building next door the occupants might be able to point you in the direction of the gate-keeper, who holds the key. Most Buddhist monasteries in the vicinity are Tai Lue in style. The most accessible is **Wat Sing Chai**, on the main road.

From Muang Sing, trek uphill past Phoutat Guesthouse for 7 km to reach **That Xieng Tung**, the most sacred site in

Muang Sing

To ① & Chinese Border ④
School

Bikes for hire
Nam Sing

To Morning Market

Muang Sing Exhibition ⑨ ❶

Wat Sing Jai
Tour Guide
Library ③ ⑫

⑤
❷ ⑬ ⑩
To Museum

ℹ ⑪

Lao Development ⓢ ❷

Kaysone Monument
⑦

⑥

To ⑧ , Xieng Kok, Luang Nam Tha & Burmese Border

N
Not to scale

Sleeping 🛌
Adima Guesthouse 1
Charmpy Thong Guesthouse 2
Daennuea Guesthouse 3
Inthanon Guesthouse (Lü Tribe) 4
Muang Sing Guesthouse 5
Phouiou 2 7
Phouiou Guesthouse 6
Phoutat Guesthouse 8

Sengdeuane Guesthouse & Restaurant 9
Sengkhatiyavang Guesthouse 10
Sing Xai Guesthouse 11
Taileu Guesthouse
Viengxai Guesthouse & Restaurant 13

Eating 🍴
Music Oasis Bar 1
Viengphone Guesthouse 2

Opium

Most ethnic groups in Muang Sing still live traditionally and practise slash-and-burn agriculture, growing rice, corn and even some cotton. Many of the local Akha villages were originally built on slopes as high as 600-1500 m but the government relocated villages down to 400-600 m in an attempt to eradicate opium farming in the hills. For a long time Muang Sing was highly reliant on the opium trade, with the drug used for medicinal purposes for over a hundred years. The government crackdown (in the face of international pressure) has impoverished many farmers but, despite the government's best efforts, opium is still readily for sale in the town. Needless to say, don't buy it under any circumstances.

One tourist who had taken too much opium ran naked into an ethnic minority village in the middle of the night, only to be beaten up by local villagers who thought an evil ghost (*pii*) had come to attack their village. There are two morals to this story: never take opium and always dress modestly in Laos.

Northern Laos Northwest Laos

the area. The stupa was built in 1256 and is believed to contain the Buddha's adam's apple. It attracts lots of pilgrims in November for the annual full moon festival. Originally a city was built around the stupa but everyone migrated down to lower lands. There is a small pond near the stupa, which is also believed to be very auspicious: if it dries up it is considered very bad luck for Muang Sing. It is said that the pond once dried up and the whole village had no rice and starved. Most tourism operators will run treks up to the stupa and will also stop at **Nam Keo** waterfall, a large cascade with a 10-m drop that trickles down into a little brook. It's a nice place for a picnic lunch. The local tourism authority runs treks to the falls for upwards of US$10. Bring good shoes.

Around Muang Sing

The area around Muang Sing is home to many minorities who have been resettled, either from refugee camps in Thailand or from highland areas of Laos. The town is predominantly Tai Lue but the district is 50% Akha, with a further 10% Tai Neua. The population of the district is said to have trebled between 1992 and 1996 and, as a result, it is one of the few places in northern Laos where hilltribe villages are readily accessible. The main activity for visitors is to hire bicycles and visit the villages that surround the town in all directions; several guesthouses have maps of the surrounding area and trekking is becoming increasingly popular. However, please do not undertake treks independently as it undermines the government's attempts to make tourism sustainable and minimize the impact on the culture of local villages.
▶▶ *For further details, see Activities and tours, page 175.*

Along the Mekong 🌐🚤🏔️🚌🎭 ▶▶ *pages 168-181.*

Houei Xai (Houay Xai) and around → *Phone code: 084. Colour map 1, B1*
This town is in the heart of the Golden Triangle and used to derive its wealth from the narcotics trade on the heroin route to Chiang Mai in Thailand. Today trade still brings the town considerable affluence, although it is rather less illicit: timber is ferried across the Mekong from Laos to the Thai town of Chiang Khong and, in exchange, consumer goods are shipped back. Sapphires are mined in the area and, doubtless, there is also still some undercover heroin smuggling.

Houei Xai is a popular crossing point for tourists travelling to and from Thailand and a considerable amount of money flows in from the numerous guesthouses and restaurants that have been built here. However, few people spend more than one night in the town. Most passengers arrive close to the centre at the passenger ferry pier. The vehicle ferry pier is 750 m further north (upstream), while the post office is about 500 m south, at the edge of town. Although the petite, picturesque town is growing rapidly as links with Thailand intensify, it is still small and easy enough to get around on foot.

Wat Chom Kha Out Manirath, in the centre of town, is worth a visit for its views. The monastery was built at the end of the 19th century but, because it is comparatively well endowed, there has been a fair amount of re-building and renovation since then. There is also a large former French fort here called **Fort Carnot** now used by the Lao army (and consequently out of bounds). The **Morning Market** can be entertaining, particularly for first-time visitors who have entered from Thailand, as this will be their first experience of a Lao market. There is little of note about the products on display but local tribespeople come from their villages to sell things here. To get there, take a tuk-tuk (3,000 kip). There is a **sapphire mine** south of the town, near the fast boat terminal. The miners pan in the morning and clean the stones in the afternoon, so the afternoon is the best time to visit.

❣ Houei Xai is a good place to shop for Lao weaving and gems, as it is cheaper than Vientiane.

Ban Nam Chan is a pleasant Chinese-speaking village, about 17 km from Houei Xai. The Lang Ten tribespeople who live here are famous for their textiles: the women wear black, kaftan-style dresses and shave their eyebrows and wear a headpiece once they are married; the men wear black shirts and blue trousers. Along the way, the road passes Hmong villages (15 km in). **Ban Nam Keun**, a small traditional village on the high plateau not far from the main town, is worth a visit for its natural beauty.

Pak Beng → *Colour map 1, C2.*

This long thin strip of a village is perched halfway up a hill, with fine views over the Mekong. Its importance lies in its location at the confluence of the Mekong and the Nam Beng. There is not much to do here but it's a good place to stop on the slow boat between Houei Xai and Luang Prabang (or vice versa). The village is worth a visit for its traditional atmosphere and the friendliness of the locals, including various minorities. Just downstream from the port is a good spot for swimming in the dry season, but be careful as the current is strong. There are also a couple of monasteries in town. The locals are now organizing guided treks to nearby villages; check with **Bounmy Guesthouse** (see Sleeping).

Hongsa and around

From Pak Beng you can take a boat downriver to the small town of **Tha Suang** and then catch a *songthaew*, through beautiful jungled hills, to the valley of Hongsa.

Hongsa district is renowned for its 70 working elephants, which are used as all-purpose heavy 'machinery' for the timber trade and other agricultural purposes. Hongsa town is usually just a jump-off point for excursions to nearby **Vieng Ghiaw**, whose men have a long tradition as *mahouts* (elephant handlers), training elephants specifically for use in the local timber trade. ➤➤ *For details of elephant treks, see Activities and tours, page 175.*

❣ Hongsa is under 50 km from the Thai border. At the time of publication the crossing at Muang Ngeun wasn't open to foreigners, though it is said to be opening up soon.

Vieng Ghiaw is surrounded by overgrown, ruined city walls, believed to be hundreds of years old, and an extensive moat system that spans several kilometres. The predominatly Tai Lue village features traditional stilt houses, made of solid Mai Du (an Asian rosewood) and designed to house both elephants and humans, with a large spacious area underneath so that the mahout can step straight off his verandah onto the elephant's back. Locals are actively involved in the preservation of these unique houses and are hoping, through sponsorship, to keep their village homes rather than replacing them with ugly, concrete equivalents. Displayed beneath the verandah are miscellaneous items, usually weaving looms or elephant saddles, which symbolize the family's social status. The Tai Lue use a variety of saddles, separate ones for training, hunting, weddings or religious celebrations. The village is also well known for its textiles, woven by the Tai Lue women.

Sayaboury (Xayaboury) → *Phone code: 074. Colour map 1, C2.*

⬛📁🗄🎧 ▸▸ *pages 168-181.*

Sayaboury is not on many visitors' agendas. This is partly because it is a difficult place to get to and partly because there doesn't seem any obvious reason to make the effort. There is no direct road between Vientiane and Sayaboury so the only way to get here from the capital is to take a boat upriver to Pak Lai and then to catch a bus – if the road isn't washed away. Rather easier is to catch a bus from Luang Prabang through Muang Nan, cross the Mekong by ferry, and then take a bus to Sayaboury – a comparatively painless four- to seven-hour journey. Having reached Sayaboury and sampled its limited enticements, it is then necessary to retrace your steps or set out for Pak Lai and hope for a downstream boat to Vientiane – wishful thinking for the most part.

These transport difficulties have given Sayaboury a rather charming forgotten atmosphere. It may be the capital of a province covering over 16,000 sq km – equivalent to the area of Hawaii or Northern Ireland – and with 300,000 inhabitants, but it doesn't feel like it. The town is located in an attractive setting on the Nam Houn – a tributary of the Mekong – and has a number of **monasteries**; those of note, according to local historians, are Wat Thin, Wat Pha Phoun, Wat Natonoy and Wat Sisavang Vong, named after the king who reigned during the de facto Japanese occupation of French Indochina. The province is mountainous with Phu Khao Mieng, Laos's ninth highest peak, just exceeding 2000 m.

Gluttons for punishment or very adventurous souls, depending on which way you look at it, may care to take the seven- to 10-hour *songthaew* trip from Sayaboury to Hongsa (see page 166). The trip covers some stunning territory and you may see some working elephants en route but it is a bone-jarringly bumpy trip on unsealed roads and, in the rainy season, they are often flooded.

Pak Lai → *Colour map 2, B1.*

Pak Lai is not very much more than a convenient place to stop on the long river journey between Vientiane and Luang Prabang and it grew up as a boating equivalent to a truck stop. There are a sprinkling of colonial shopfronts and old wooden Lao houses, a couple of guesthouses, a few restaurants and shops, and a desultory branch of the Lao Development Bank.

Pak Lai does, however, enjoy a footnote in Laos's colonial history which is worth recounting. In 1887 Luang Prabang was attacked by a band of Chinese Haw and northern Tai bandits. Auguste Pavie, the newly appointed French vice consul, rescued King Unkham from his burning palace and escaped downstream to Pak Lai. Here they remained while the old and frail King recovered from the journey and Pavie researched the early history of Lane Xang. This piece of quick-thinking indebted the

● *Sayaboury has more alternative spellings than most – and this in a country which is*
● *replete with imaginative transliterations: you'll come across Sainyabuli, Sayabouri,*
  Sayaboury, Sayaburi, Xaignabouli, Xaignabouri, Xayabury and others.

king to Pavie and therefore also to the French. Within five years of this heroic rescue Laos was French and the Siamese had lost control of the country.

⊜ Sleeping

Udom Xai *p159, map p168*

C Fu Shan, T081-312198. Two doors down from the Sing Tong and a step up in the friendliness stakes. Another Chinese establishment, offering bare doubles with en suite hot shower and Western toilet, TV and fan. Restaurant downstairs.

C Sing Tong, opposite the market on the main street, T081-312061, T071-212813, T/F021-412686. En suite baths and Western toilets, with hot water, towels and soap provided. Sometimes live pop music in the courtyard.

C-D Litthavixay Guesthouse, about 100 m before the turn onto the airport road, T081-212175. This place has the best rooms in town, large single, double and triple rooms, carpeted and all very clean. Rooms are furnished with desk, closet, TV, fridge and kettle, and drinking water is provided. Hot water shower attached. Car rental service and free pick-up from the airport. Breakfast (not included) is served in the lobby. Also best value internet in town.

D Saylomyen Guesthouse, about 200 m from the airport, T081-211377. Very clean, comfortable rooms, some with adjoining bathrooms and hot water. Also an 'open air' room for use in the warmer months.

D-F Sai Xi, opposite the post office. A basic Chinese establishment with very rude, blunt staff; also noisy at night with partying clientele. Cheapest beds are in a 5-bed dorm on the 4th floor with communal (very dirty) toilet and shower 1 floor down. Other rooms have en suite bathrooms, hot water, TV and fan. Good views of the town and hills beyond from the roof.

E Dokbouadeng, T081-312142. Rooms with en suite shower and Western toilet, small restaurant downstairs.

E Kongchi Guesthouse, T081-211141. Very clean furnished rooms with separate hot shower and squat toilet.

E Linda Guesthouse, downhill from the market and across the bridge, T081-312147. Reasonably new 3-storey white building, with gold frescoes and lobby with comfortable sofa. Clean, furnished rooms, some with bathroom en suite, Western toilet and hot water. Rooms have fan and balcony.

E Linda No2 Guesthouse, on the street behind the Kaysone Monument, next door to Mexai, T020-5681188. Clean rooms with hot water, bath and a TV. Although their English is not great, the staff here are friendly. Restaurant downstairs. Good value.

E Yang Lu Guesthouse, a few doors up from the Sai Xi, T081-312067. Large rooms with TV, en suite shower, hot water and toilet; a bit gloomy but friendly staff.

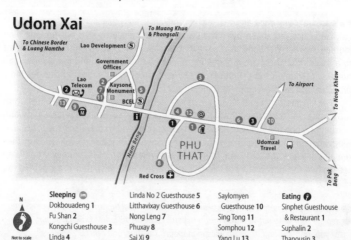

Udom Xai

N
Not to scale

Sleeping ⊜
Dokbouadeng **1**
Fu Shan **2**
Kongchi Guesthouse **3**
Linda **4**

Linda No 2 Guesthouse **5**
Litthavixay Guesthouse **6**
Nong Leng **7**
Phuxay **8**
Sai Xi **9**

Saylomyen
  Guesthouse **10**
Sing Tong **11**
Somphou **12**
Yang Lu **13**

Eating ⊘
Sinphet Guesthouse
  & Restaurant **1**
Suphalin **2**
Thanousin **3**

E-F Somphou Guesthouse, next to Linda Guesthouse. Not so clean doubles with en suite hot water baths and Western toilets. Comfy lounge with a TV. Also dorm beds for 10,000 kip each, with shared toilet and shower. Restaurant downstairs.

F Nong Leng, between the Sing Tong and Fu Shan hotels. Disinterested staff but clean rooms with en suite cold shower and toilet.

F Phuxay, T081-312140, downhill on the main street from the market and across the bridge, turn right after the petrol station (there is a sign at the petrol station), up the road from the police counter-narcotics unit. Newly revived, clean rooms with en suite hot shower and toilet, TV and mini-bar. The double beds are massive. Nice garden with sitting area.

Around Udom Xai p160

A Kamu Lodge, Ban Nyong Hay, Udom Xai Province, T071-241861. On the banks of the Mekong, 3 hrs upstream from Luang Prabang. Visitors usually stay here en route from Houei Xai, when booking an ecotour with Exotissimo but you can also stay here independently. Good if you're after a few days' isolation. Management plans to turn this into a major ecoresort but for now accommodation is in modern canvas tents, decorated with local furnishings. The Lao restaurant serves excellent fish. Also runs some treks and activities, such as gold panning. Can be booked through Exotissimo in Luang Prabang (see Tour operators, page 129), which will arrange transport (additional).

Muang La p160

If you wish to stay, the Hot Springs Resort is your only option, with US$3 accommodation in basic wood and bamboo constructions, with fan and river-water showers. The resort also has a very basic restaurant.

Muang Houn p160

E Bounnam Guesthouse, T081-212289. Basic no-frills guesthouse, with reasonable facilities for a short stay.

E Miss Manyvane. A 2-storey concrete house, with a little balcony upstairs. Basic facilities, 4 rather mouldy twin rooms, with tattered mosquito nets, shared toilet and scoop shower. The family lives downstairs.

There has been a sudden rush of guesthouses popping up here over the last few years yet, despite this, Luang Namtha has very little in the way of decent accommodation aside from the **Boat Landing**, the best ecotourism venture in the country and the stand-out choice in the area.

A-B Boat Landing Guesthouse & Restaurant, out of town towards the airport, T086-312398. Farther out of town than most other guesthouses, this place is located right on the river. It's an ecoresort that has got everything just right: pristine surroundings, environmentally friendly service and a brilliant restaurant serving traditional northern Lao cuisine. Live traditional Lao music is often performed. The rooms are very homely, combining modern design with traditional materials and decoration; they'll even give you a sample of the local fabric. Bill is a fantastic source of local information and speaks good English. An exceptional place that can't be recommended highly enough.

D Guesthouse Restaurant. Clean and bright twin and double rooms, with en suite squat bathrooms. The twin rooms have large, comfy beds. There's satellite TV in most rooms and a/c in the most expensive rooms. Restaurant offers many Chinese delicacies – not for vegetarians.

D Hong Tha Xay Som Boun, T086-312079, F086-312078. Chinese-owned hotel with nice garden area, restaurant, bar and disco (noisy after 2000). However, the rooms are nothing special for the hefty price, with stone floors, ceiling fan, toilet and cold shower en suite. Adequately clean. A/c in the more expensive rooms.

D Palanh Guesthouse, T086-312439. Relatively clean rooms, with fan. Big ones are airy and spacious with en suite bathrooms; smaller (and cheaper) rooms have no attached bathrooms, but rather delightfully, you walk along the verandah to get to the communal facilities. Rustic.

D Vila Guesthouse, further on from the Lao Mai on the right, T086-312425. A new 2-storey building with 11 of the cleanest rooms in town, lounge and sparkling en suite bathrooms, with hot water.

D-E Lao Mai Guesthouse and Restaurant, , T086-312232. Nice wooden building, lovely rooms with wooden floors, bamboo walls and hard but comfortable beds. Communal toilets are clean and well maintained. Double rooms downstairs have en suite bathroom. Beautiful verandah with some spectacular views, depending on which side of the building you're on. Internet and CD-burning facilities in the lobby, plus table football. Restaurant food is delicious, as is the homemade yoghurt and muesli. Trekking and rafting arranged. Recommended.

E Bounthavong Guesthouse, T086-312256, Very basic double and twin rooms with massive communal bathroom with hot water. A small Lao/Chinese restaurant downstairs.

E Cha Rueh Sin, T086-312393. Bare, basic, but not uncharming rooms, with en suite bathrooms in a monster of a building. Breezy verandahs overlook parts of the town.

E-F Bus Station Guesthouse, T086-211090. Sweet little rooms, clean and airy but with hard beds. Some have hot water. Friendly staff. Ideally sited for an early morning start.

E-F Luang Namtha Guesthouse, T086-312087/312407. Run by 2 friendly Hmong brothers, one of whom speaks English. The house is an impressive building for Luang Namtha, with a grand staircase. All rooms are beautifully clean and furnished, with en suite bathrooms, hot water and balconies. Satellite TV in the more pricey rooms. Free pick-up from the bus station if you telephone ahead. Great setting. Recommended.

E-F Sinsavanh Guesthouse, T086-211141. A wooden building with pleasant garden. The rooms inside are quite cramped but quaint, with wooden shutters and flowers. Toilets and hot showers are separate. The rooms on the top floor are a little grubby.

F Manychan Guesthouse, opposite the smaller bus station, T086-312209. One of the most popular places in town, probably due to the location and the restaurant, rather than the rooms, which are small and gloomy but reasonably clean, with shared bathroom and toilet. They were renovating in 2005; on completion prices will rise to US$5. Bikes can be hired next door for 15,000 kip per day. The staff are very friendly.

F Saikhonglongsack Guesthouse, next to the Kaysone Monument, T086-312257. Large rooms with en suite squat toilet and shower.

Friendly staff. The house has tiled floors and a breezy balcony overlooking the main street. Communal areas are a bit grubby. Cheap restaurant downstairs.

Vieng Phouka *p162*

There are a few very, very basic guesthouses in town, try the **Don Vieng**, T084-212394, US$2-3 or the **Bo Kung**.

Nateui *p163*

E Tali Guesthouse, on the main road. No traffic in the evening, so it is quiet. Reasonably good food served.

Boten *p163*

At present there is a small, unmarked guesthouse right on the border (**E**). Basic doubles, clean enough, geared to Chinese, Vietnamese and Lao truckers. Expect a few more to crop up soon as the major construction work begins. Boten also has a couple of *feu* stalls but little else.

Muang Sing *p163, map p164*

C Phouiou Guesthouse and **Phouiou 2**, at the southern end of town, T086-212348. Two guesthouses across the road from each other and owned by the same people. Phouiou has large, clean double rooms, with en suite bathrooms and hot water. From the balcony there is a superb view out over the town. Phouiou 2 has double bungalows of the same high quality and provides towels and bottled water. The lack of scenery here at the latter is its only downfall. Prices for both include breakfast, cheaper without. There is also a sauna here.

C-D Adima Guesthouse, near Ban Oudomsin, north of Muang Sing towards the Chinese border, T020-2249008. A little hard to get to, but in a fantastic location: peaceful bungalows constructed in traditional Yao and Akha style, plus a lovely open-air restaurant. There are only 10 rooms (more on the way) and they fill up quickly, so get there early. A calm and peaceful retreat surrounded by rice fields. Minority villages are literally on the doorstep. However, Footprint does not endorse DIY treks using the guesthouse map, which are having a negative effect on local villages. If you wish to trek please visit the local tourism office to organize a bonafide ecotrek.

To get there, take a tuk-tuk (no more than 20,000 kip) to Ban Oudomsin or hire a bike (some guesthouses or restaurants have basic maps). Alternatively, the owner runs in and out of town about 3 times a day (depending on bus arrival times) and will pick you up from the bus station for a small fee.

C-D Phoutat Guesthouse/Black Stupa, 6 km out of Muang Sing towards Luang Namtha. 10 wooden bungalows perched on the side of a hill, looking over the small town, mountains and rice paddies. Hot water, fan, Western toilet and fantastic balcony. Stunningly beautiful. There is also quite a good restaurant on site The guesthouse was for sale at the time of publication but should still be one of the best places to stay when someone buys it. Highly recommended.

D Sengdeuane Guesthouse, at the far end of town from the bus stop, T086-212376. A quiet spot. Rooms have iron doors which make the place resemble a dungeon, but there's an attractive view from the roof. Shared bathroom outside. The owners have

now built large clean rooms out the back, which boast adjoining bathrooms, hot water and enormous double beds.

D-E Inthanon Guesthouse, about 1 km north from the bus station. Run by the Lue tribe. Traditionally styled thatched huts, with en suite clean toilet and shower (**E**). Also 4 brand-spanking-new doubles (**D**), very clean, big rooms with hot shower. Friendly owners and a peaceful setting, away from the crowds of tourists in the village. Cows low at the window in the morning.

E Charmpy Thong Guesthouse, behind the clothes market. Four basic but clean double rooms with en suite bathroom. The staff here are quite friendly.

E Daenneua Guesthouse, T086-212369. Friendly staff, good restaurant, slightly better rooms than Taileu, now with hot water and laundry service.

E Singxai Guesthouse, just behind the market. Doubles and triples, en suite bathrooms, with squat toilet and shower, mosquito nets, slow service but the rooms and huts in the back garden are fairly clean. In a beautiful spot by paddy fields.

E-F Taileu Guesthouse, next door to Daenneua. Similar, but not quite as good.

F Additional guesthouses in the centre of town include **Muang Sing**, **Viengxai** (see Eating) and **Sengkhatiyavang**. There's nothing to really distinguish between them: basic, cramped double rooms, with shared squat toilets and shower and paper-thin walls, although the Viengxai now has some en suite bathrooms.

Houei Xai *p165, map p171*

There is a cluster of hotels on Sekhong Rd, which is the main street running through the town.

C Thaveesinh, Sekhong Rd, north of the immigration intersection, T084-312039. Previously the best hotel in town. Good rooms and location. Don't mix this one up with the other similar sounding guesthouse at the other end of town (see below).

C-D Arimid Guesthouse, at the northwest end of the town, T084-9804693. The owners M and Mme Chitaly speak excellent French and a little English. Comfortable individual rattan-style bungalows, bathroom attached, hot water, nice garden area and great balconies. Some with a/c. Mme Chitaly will

Houei Xai

To Nam Khong Hills

Vehicle
Ferry Pier

Red Cross

Mekong

Sekhong

Passenger
Ferry Pier,
Immigration
& Customs

Wat Chom Kha
Out Manirath

Bokeo
Travel Agency

Morning

To Tin That Pier (2km),
That Nevsouvanna (3km)
& Airport (9km)

N

Not to scale

Sleeping
Arimid Guesthouse 1
BAP Guesthouse 2
Houei Xai 3
Keo Champa 4
Sabaydee Guesthouse 5
Thanormsub Guesthouse 6
Thaveesinh Guesthouse 7

Eating
Khemkhong 1
Mouang Neua 2
Nutpop 3
Riverside 4
Sousada 5

cook tasty Luang Prabang food and serve it to you at your bungalow. Recommended.

E Houay Xai, in the centre of town. Rooms with en suite bathroom, including hot shower. Basic but clean hotel, with friendly staff.

E Sabaydee, T020-5483233. Big, tiled rooms, with en suite hot showers and Western toilets. Recommended.

E Thanormsub Guesthouse, Sekhong Rd. Double rooms, clean, hot water, fan and satin curtains to boot. Nice helpful staff.

E-F BAP Guesthouse, Sekhong Rd, north of immigration, T084-211083. Rooms have a dorm-room feel about them, even when they aren't. Reasonable value for the price, with fan, bathroom, but a bit damp.

E-F Keo Champa, Sekhong Rd, 200m south of the immigration intersection. Rooms are basic with attached bathroom, fan and 2 single beds for under US$2. Very clean and quite nice view of the river. Possibly the best value for money. Recommended.

F Thavesinh Guesthouse, on the main road, south of the immigration stand, T084-271155. Pretty stark rooms – concrete floor and outside bathroom. Very, very basic.

Pak Beng p166, map p172

A word of advice: during peak season, when the slow boat or 'backpacker ferry' arrives from Luang Prabang, about 60 people descend on the town at the same time. As Pak Beng doesn't have an endless supply of great guesthouses, it is advisable to get someone you trust to mind your bags, while you make a mad dash to get the best room in town. Note, too, that rats are a problem in some of the cheaper places.

A Luang Say Lodge, on the fork to the left, past Bounmy, T081-212296. A beautiful ecolodge primarily used by passengers aboard the **Luang Say Cruise**, a luxury, purpose-built river barge (see page 147). There are a number of large, beautifully styled bungalows, 19 rooms, fan, hot water. Lovely deck overlooking the river. Restaurant.

A Pakbeng Lodge. A wooden and concrete construction, built in Lao style, this stunning guesthouse sits perched on a hillside above the Mekong and includes 20 rooms with fan, toilet and hot water. Good restaurant and wonderful river views. Owned by the same people who own the **Elephant Lodge** in Hongsa (see page 173). Guided tours of the area are planned.

C-D Sarika, T081-212306. Completely rebuilt after a fire a few years back, this is an elegant structure on the steep cliff overlooking the river. It was once the best place to stay in town, but is now over-shadowed by new arrivals, such as the Luang Say and Pakbeng Lodges. Big, clean rooms with toilet and shower en suite, tiled floors. Prices vary: anything from US$5 to US$20. There is a great restaurant, serving reasonably priced meals (see Eating).

D-E Bounmy Guesthouse. Smallish bamboo rooms, with bed, fan, mosquito net and good, clean, bathrooms with hot water (some shared facilities). Although it occupies a quiet location, the walls are paper thin, which can be a bit annoying.

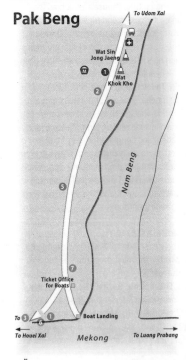

Pak Beng

To Udom Xai

Wat Sin Jong Jaeng

Wat Khok Kho

Nam Beng

Ticket Office for Boats

To Houei Xai

Boat Landing

Mekong

To Luang Prabang

N

Not to scale

Sleeping
Bounmy 1
Donevilisack Guesthouse 2
Luang Say Lodge 3

Monhamy Guesthouse 4
Monsavan Guesthouse 5
Pakbeng Lodge 6
Sarika Guesthouse & Restaurant 7

Eating
Khor Khor Bookstore & Café 1

D-E **Donevilisack Guesthouse**, T081-212315. Sprawling across 2 buildings, the popular Donevilisack offers a pretty reasonable choice of rooms. In the older building are basic budget rooms, with fan, mosquito net and shared hot showers. More expensive rooms are in the newer concrete building and have private cold water bathrooms. Recommended.

F **Monhamy**. Not so much a guesthouse as a Lao home trying to make a few bucks by renting out sub-standard rooms. Dark, cramped, no fan and you have to share a squat toilet. There are a number of other shack-like bamboo lodgings running up the hill.

F **Monsavan**. Comparatively clean, bamboo rooms, with fan and mosquito net. It is reportedly rat-free, which is a plus, but the shared toilets are a bit of a hike away, on the other side of the road! Guests say the owner prepares good sandwiches for the boat-trip to Luang Prabang.

Hongsa *p166*
A **Elephant Lodge**, T074-252841. An upmarket choice that must be booked in conjunction with a tour from **Lao Travel Ecotourism**, T021-213180. The tour is quite expensive. Restaurant.

D **Jumbo Hotel**. At US$8 per night this isn't really the best value in town. Five rooms, with cold water mundi shower only.

E **Sunflower Guesthouse**. Clean 2-storey guesthouse next to a beautiful lotus pond. The nearby **Lotus Café** is the best place for a quick bite to eat, with a surprising menu which includes a few Italian dishes and a Korean barbecue plus the usual Lao fare.

Sayaboury *p167*
In 1994 the National Tourism Authority recorded that the entire province had no hotels or guesthouses. Fortunately, things have changed.

E **Hongvilai Guesthouse**, south of the centre on the banks of the Nam Houn, T074-211068. This place has a good outlook but the rooms are a bit squalid– shared cold water bathrooms and not quite clean. Even so, it makes a nice spot to stay.

E **New Sayaboury Hotel**. Large, 3-storey hotel with clean, fair-sized rooms boasting fan, en suite bathroom and hot water. For a few extra dollars you can get even a/c. Recommended.

Pak Lai *p167*
E **Banna Guesthouse**, along the river road, east of the boat landing, T074-211995. Very clean, 3-storey guesthouse, 17 rooms with fan and shared facilities.

E **Lamdouan Guesthouse**, to the west of the boat landing, along the river road. Very friendly, family-run guesthouse, basic rooms with shared facilities.

There is a nice little restaurant beside the boat landing that serves *feu* and *pad gow*.

🍴 Eating

Udom Xai *p159, map p168*
Stalls in front of the market sell beer and snacks from nightfall.

🍴 **Suphalin**, up the hill in a small alley near the post office. One of the better options in town. A tad more expensive but worth it as the meals are larger. Great fruit shakes and spring rolls, although you will have to order the latter in advance. Locals rave about owner Suphalin, who can cheer up even the grumpiest souls. Recommended.

🍴 **Thanousin**, on the corner of the road to the airport. Friendly service, menu in English, good basic Lao food.

🍴 **Sinphet Guesthouse & Restaurant**, opposite Linda Guesthouse. One of the best options in town. English menu, delicious iced coffee with ovaltine, great Chinese and Lao food. Try the curry chicken, *kua-mii* or yellow noodles with chicken. Also stocks some French wines.

Somphou and **Dokbouadeng** guesthouses both have small cafés on the ground floor (see Sleeping). There are also a number of restaurants on the 1st left turn after the bridge; all do good Laos and Chinese food. A bakery with tasty cakes and buns is located across the road and noodle soup shops are scattered throughout town.

Muang Houn *p160*
There are two eating places facing each other next to the market. Both serve noodles, eggs and sticky rice, no menu. Fresh baguettes are available from the market in the morning.

Northern Laos Northwest Laos Listings

¶¶ Boat Landing Guesthouse & Restaurant, see Sleeping, T086-312398. Best place to eat in town, with a beautiful dining area and exceptionally innovative cuisine: a range of local northern Lao dishes made from ocal produce that supports local villages. Highly recommended.

¶¶ Guesthouse Restaurant, see Sleeping. A large dining area serving traditional Chinese food – everything from fried bamboo insects and turtles to dogs.

¶¶ Manychan, see Sleeping. A very popular restaurant with outdoor seating and a variety of toned-down Lao dishes plus a few Western interpretations.

¶¶ New Restaurant, on the main road, towards the internet shop, T020-5718026. This restaurant is gaining flavour with the locals and tourists for its good fruit shakes and Lao food. A few Western dishes, too.

¶¶ Yamuna Restaurant, on the main road, T020-5405698. A delicious Indian restaurant with veg and non-veg dishes and halal cuisine. Extensive, predominantly south Indian menu. Most dishes around US$2.50.

¶¶-¶ Lao Mai, attached to the guesthouse (see Sleeping). A large selection of Lao and Thai food, all of which is seriously good. The restaurant itself is tastefully decorated with tiled floors, brick walls, pebble stone pillars and rotating fans. There is an outside seating area, as well, with a mini waterfall to set the mood. Recommended.

¶ Lao Lao Restaurant, across the road from Sinsavanh. An excellent picture menu of Lao food. Chalet-like, with wide verandahs and a pleasant view, friendly owners.

¶ Ouann Villay Restaurant. The usual Lao-influenced dishes plus a few foreign dishes, such as French fries and macaroni.

¶ Panda Restaurant, T086-211304. A goodie – very clean and small, with coloured lanterns strung throughout. Cheap and tasty food. The curries are outstanding. Friendly owner with good English.

¶ Saikhonglongsack Guesthouse, see Sleeping, T086-312257. Clean restaurant with friendly staff and the usual selection of dishes. It seems to attract many Lao customers, which is a good sign, and is popular with tourists, too.

There is a bakery and cake shop next door to the Cha Rueh Sin, that sells mouthwatering treats; try the green tea cake. There are a few *feu* stalls by the main market and the morning market near the bus stop, useful when waiting for those ever-delayed *songthaew*. At night, food vendors gather along the main road, with little, pretty, candle-lit stalls, selling meat on a stick and waffles.

Muang Sing *p163, map p164*

It is highly recommended to try and eat some of the delicious ethnic food while you're in Muang Sing as there aren't many places elsewhere you will be able to sample these meals.

¶¶ Adima Guesthouse, see Sleeping. Western offerings, such as the usual backpacker pancakes, fried eggs, as well as some Lao inspired meals.

¶¶-¶ Taileu Guesthouse, see Sleeping. The most popular place to eat due to its indigenous Tai Lue menu. Well worth the trip with some unique and tasty meals including baked eggplant, with pork, soy mash and fish soup.

¶ Music Oasis Bar, just over the bridge. Sells the heavenly combination of ice cream and beer and, as the name suggests, plays the music of your choice.

¶ Sengdeuane Guesthouse, see Sleeping. A quieter option with an English menu, nice garden setting and a pair of green parakeets. Popular with the locals.

¶ Viengphone Guesthouse, next door to the Viengxai Guesthouse. This place has an English menu offering the usual fare, US$1-2 per dish. Excellent fried mushrooms.

¶ Viengxai Guesthouse, see Sleeping. Very good food, with some of the best chips in Laos, English menu, friendly service, reasonable prices.

These last 3 restaurants are all popular at night and can get crowded. They are also prime places for the minorities to come and sell their wares.

Houei Xai *p165, map p171*

¶¶-¶ Khemkhong Restaurant, opposite the immigration stand. Good option for those who want a drink after the cross-border journey. Selection of Lao and Thai food.

¶¶-¶ Riverside, just off Sekhong Rd, near the Houay Xai Guesthouse, T084-211064. Huge waterfront restaurant on large platform. Most dishes US$1-2. Mixture of Lao and

Thai-inspired food: basil chicken, tom yum, sweet and sour pork etc. The live music sounds suspiciously like karaoke. Recommended for dinner.

BAP Guesthouse, see Sleeping. Without doubt the best breakfast menu in town: wide range of dishes including pancakes, croissants and eggs.

Lao Chinese Restaurant, Sekhong Rd, down from Houay Xai Guesthouse. No prizes for guessing what cuisine this restaurant specializes in. Reasonably priced food.

Mouang Neua, Sekhong Rd, opposite Thaveensinh. Very good Lao and Thai food, cooked to perfection and ridiculously cheap. Also a good place to get information about trips to the Bokeo Nature Reserve. Recommended.

Nutpop, Sekhong Rd, down from Thanormsub Guesthouse, T084-211037. The fluoro lights and garish beer signs don't give a good impression. However, this is quite a pleasant little garden restaurant, set in an atmospheric little lamp-lit building. Good Lao food – fried mushrooms and nice curry.

Sousada, Sekhong Rd, just down from Keo Champa Guesthouse. Loads of dishes – pork, duck, fish, chicken – in a variety of Lao and Thai styles. Good fruit shakes made from local pasteurized milk. Good chicken curry (8000 kip).

Pak Beng *p166, map p172*
Restaurants serve breakfast (baguettes, pancakes and coffee) really early. The two ecolodges have pretty upscale restaurants.

Khok Khor Bookstore & Café. Stands out for its great coffee. Run by a friendly Australian called Wendy.

Sarika, see Sleeping. An atmospheric restaurant downstairs has wonderful river views, fresh flowers on the table, amazing variety on the menu, including cheese omelette, but interminably slow service.

There are several restaurants lining the main road towards the river; all seem to have the same English menu, basic Lao dishes, eggs and freshly made sandwiches. The local market has an array of dishes from *feu* through to frogs!

Sayaboury *p167*
There are a number of restaurants, along with the usual noodle shops and stalls, near the market and on the streets leading off the market. None is particularly noteworthy. Simple Chinese and Lao dishes.

O Shopping

Luang Namtha *p160, map p161*
KNT internet Shop sells textiles woven by the women of Luang Namtha: silk skirts, curtains, cushions etc. There is also a handicrafts store around the corner from Saikhonglongsack.

▲▲ Activities and tours

Udom Xai *p159, map p168*
Traditional Lao herbal sauna and massage is offered by the **Red Cross Centre**, behind the main stupa past the Phuxay Hotel, 1500-1900 daily, 40,000 kip per hour. Look out for the signs on the main road.
Udomxai Travel, near the bus station, T081-212020, travel_kenchan@yahoo.com, offers ecotours and travel services.

Luang Namtha *p160, map p161*
Massage and sauna
There's a herbal sauna not far from Sengchanh film processing, open daily 1630-1730, 15,000 kip for a sauna; 25,000 kip for a massage, 50 mins. The towels they provide are utterly disgusting, so bring your own.

Tour operators
Green Discovery, near Manychan Guesthouse, T086-211484. Offers 1- to 7-day kayaking/rafting and trekking excursions into the Nam Ha NPA.
Luang Namtha Guide Service Unit, T086-211534. Information on treks into the Nam Ha NPA; ask to speak to Mr Bountha or Ms La Ong Kham.

Vieng Phouka *p162*
The local tourism authority runs treks around the local villages, the Nam Ha national park and caves with food and accommodation and camping with a host family. The guides are usually Khmu and Akha locals from the surrounding villages and have excellent local knowledge. Contact the **Vieng Phouka Guide Service Unit**, T084-212400, or speak to the **National Tourism Authority** in Vientiane.

Trekking

Trekking has become a delicate issue around Muang Sing as uncontrolled tourism was beginning to have a detrimental effect on some of the surrounding minority villages. Luckily some sensible procedures and protocols have been put in place to ensure low impact tourism which still benefits the villages concerned.

Exotissimo (www.exotissimo.com) in cohoots with GTZ, a German aid agency, launched some very good treks in late 2005. Details were not available as this guide went to press but the treks will include tasty meals prepared by local Akha people, using banana flowers, pumpkin leaves, sesame paste, bamboo soup or whatever ingredients can be found in the jungle on the day.

The **tourist office**, in the centre of town, can also organize pretty good treks for 1, 2 or 3 days, US$13 per day, including accommodation and food. The guides are supposedly from local villages and can speak the native tongue, Akha or Tai Lue.

Houei Xai *p165, map p171*

Gibbon Experience, next to Mouang Neua Restaurant, T084-212021, www.ecotourism laos.com. Loads of tourists have been raving about this unique ecotourism operation, which provides the rare opportunity to see or hear the soprano-singing, black-cheeked crested gibbons (once thought to be extinct) from a network of canopy huts and zip-lines. Sightings are seasonal. Accommodation is in a tree house, affording sensational views of the surrounding Bokeo Forest Reserve. At the time of publication the operation had not yet officially been 'opened', so phone for details of trial tours.

Phoudoi Travel and Tours, in the centre of town, T084-211676. Arranges tours to the mines and hill tribe villages and offers an international phone service, helpful people.

Pak Beng *p166, map p172*

There is a small massage and sauna on the riverbank, massage 40,000 kip per hr.

Hongsa *p166*

Elephant treks are organized through **Jumbo Guesthouse** (see Sleeping) or as part of a tour through Vientiane-based **Lao**

Travel-Ecotourism, T021-213180, www.laoecotourism.com. Elephant treks can also be organized independently for US$18 for 2 hrs for 2 people.

◉ Transport

Udom Xai *p159, map p168*

Air

There are flights to **Vientiane**, Tue, Thu and Sat, US$72. **Lao Airlines** has an office at the airport, T081-312156.

Bus/truck/songthaew

One of the nicest ways to get to Udom Xai from either Luang Prabang or Houei Xai is to catch the boat to Pakbeng (see pages 147 and 179) and then take a bus from there.

Udom Xai's bus station is 1 km east of the town centre. To get to **Muang La** either hop on a bus bound for Phongsali or grab a *songthaew*, which leave every few hours. To charter a *songthaew* should cost around US$15-20 return, they depart from the street near the Kaysone Monument.

There are 5 buses daily (last around 2000) south to **Muang Houn**, 3 hrs, 17,000 kip, and **Pak Beng**, 5 hrs, 30,000 kip; it's an attractive journey on a bad road through a valley with paddy fields and many villages. From here, there are boat connections on to Houei Xai west or Luang Prabang east (8 hrs).

Departures east to **Nam Bak** and **Nong Khiaw**, 3 hrs, are fairly frequent. To **Luang Prabang**, direct, 0800, 1130 and 1400 daily, 5 hrs, 38,000 kip. There is also a direct bus to **Vientiane**, 1530 and 1800 daily, 15 hrs, 100,000 kip. Pick-ups and buses run west to **Boten** (for the Chinese border, see page 177), 0800 and 1130 daily, 4 hrs, 23,000 kip. Also to **Luang Namtha**, 0800, 1130 and 1530 daily, 4 hrs, 26,000 kip. There are services north on Route 4 to **Muang Khua**, 0800, 1130 and 1400 daily, 4 hrs, 20,000 kip, and **Phongsali**, 0800 daily, 9 hrs, 50,000 kip; this trip is long so bring something soft to sit on and try to get a seat with a view.

Muang Houn *p160*

Regular buses south to **Pak Beng**, 2 hrs, 15,000 kip, and north to **Udom Xai**, 4-5 hrs, 25,000 kip.

• Border essentials: Boten-Mohan

The border between Boten (Laos) and Mohan (China) is open to international traffic 0800-1600 daily, but no Chinese visas can be obtained here. (The nearest Chinese embassy is in Vientiane.) Travelling from Luang Namtha or Udom Xai to China, the earliest you can arrive in Boten is 1100. This means that when you cross into China you have to stay in Mengla (2 hours away). Mengla is a nasty introduction to China, reverberating with the tiresome sounds of karaoke and prostitutes until the early hours. It is better to stay in Boten overnight and then make an early start to reach the much nicer town of Jinghong (5-6 hours from Mengla).

Coming into Laos, you can pick up a 15-day Lao visa for US$30 at the border or a 30-day visa in advance from the Lao consulate in Kunming, which is inside the Camelia Hotel (T0871-3176624); the latter takes three working days to process or 24 hours on payment of a surcharge.

You can change remaining yuan into Lao kip at the border. The bus station is a walk down the hill. There is limited accommodation in Boten so if you want to make it to the bigger settlement of Luang Namtha, you should aim to cross in the morning when transportation is ubiquitous, rather than in the afternoon when you could find yourself stranded. If there isn't a direct bus, take the bus to Udom Xai and change at Natuei. If you want to go to Vientiane and there isn't a direct bus, your best bet is to catch a bus to Udom Xai and transfer there to Vientiane/Luang Prabang.

Luang Namtha *p160, map p161*
Air
The airport is 7 km south of town – 15,000 kip by tuk-tuk. Small planes fly to **Vientiane** 4 times per week, 55 mins, US$55 single, US$140 return. **Lao Airlines**, T086-312180, has an office at the airport and another south of town on the main road. Book flights at least 1 day in advance.

Bicycle hire
Bicycles for hire from next door to the Manychan Guesthouse for 15,000 kip a day.

Boat
Officially, fast boats are not allowed on the Nam Tha. Slow boats are the best and most scenic travel option but their reliability will depend on the tide and, in the dry season (Mar–May) they often won't run at all as the water level is too low. There isn't really a regular boat service from Luang Namtha, so you will have to either charter a whole boat and split the cost amongst the passengers or hitch a ride on a boat making the trip already. If you manage to organize a boat it should cost around US$30-40 to **Na Lae**; US$80-90 to **Pak Tha** and US$100 to **Houei Xai**; these prices are highly variable, and need to be established in advance of the trip. Note that boats travelling upriver (eg Pak Tha to Na Lae) will usually be more expensive. If you wish to go to Luang Prabang you should change boats at Pak Tha. The **Boat Landing Guesthouse** is a good source of information about boats; if arrangements are made for you, a courtesy tip is appreciated.

Bus, truck, songthaew
The bus station and its ticket office are located about 100 m north of the Morning Market, T086-312164/211977, open 0700-1600 daily. If you want to get somewhere quickly and there's no bus, speak to the women in the nearby restaurants, who might be able to arrange transport, although it will come at a price. Otherwise hop on a bus to Udom Xai for more frequent connections.

To **Boten** on the Chinese border (see page 177) via Nateui, by pick-up, 0800, 0930 and 1100 daily, 2 hrs, 15,000 kip. Chinese visa required to cross into China (Meng La).

❧ Border essentials: Houei Xai-Chiang Khong

Small boats ferry passengers across the Mekong between Houei Xai and Chiang Khong every 10-20 minutes, ฿20. Thai immigration is open 0800-1800 daily; two-week visas are given at the border. Buses and taxis travel from Chiang Kong to Chiang Rai Airport.

Crossing into Laos, immigration is open 0800-1800 daily, but expect to pay a ฿15 over-time fee at the weekend or after 1600. A two-week tourist visa is available at the border for US$30 or you can get a 30-day visa from travel agents in Chiang Khong (it will take a couple of days). The Lao border has to be one of the nicest in the world, with the gaggle of lovely officials, offering a snack to tourists and giving out tourist information. There is a bank at the Lao border (open 0830-1600).

To **Muang Sing**, 0800, 0930 and 1100 daily, 2 hrs, 15,000 kip, additional pick-ups may depart throughout the rest of the day, depending on demand. To **Udom Xai**, 0830, 1200 and 1430 daily, 100 km, 4-6 hrs, 26,000 kip, additional services will leave in the early afternoon if there is demand. To **Houei Xai**, 0800-0830 daily, 9-10 hrs by pick-up in the dry season and almost impossible during rainy season, 60,000 kip; the road is largely unpaved and potholed but at the time of publication was receiving an overhaul. *Songthaew* will also usually depart once a day for **Na Lae** (on the Nam Tha), 3 hrs, 35,000 kip.

To **Luang Prabang**, 0830 daily, 10 hrs, 55,000 kip, continuing to **Vientiane**, 20 hrs, 120,000 kip. To **Pakmong**, 35,000 kip, for connections to **Nam Bak**, 3,000 kip, and **Nong Khiaw**, another 7,000 kip.

Vieng Phouka *p162*

Buses and *songthaew* depart for **Houei Xai**, a few times daily from the market, usually in the morning, 5 hrs, US$5. It is also possible to get buses to **Luang Namtha** and **Udom Xai**.

Nateui *p163*

There are infrequent *songthaew* connections with **Luang Namtha**, 34,000 kip, and **Udom Xai**, 80 km, 15,000 kip, and rather more frequent departures for the border at **Boten**, 18 km.

Boten *p163*

Pick-ups to **Luang Namtha**, 0830, 1100 and 1300 daily, 15,000 kip. To **Udom Xai**, 0930, 1200 and 1400 daily, 23,000 kip. For international connections with China, see Border essentials, page 177.

Muang Sing *p163, map p164*
Bicycles

Available for rent from some of the guesthouses. There are also some bicycle hire shops on the main street. The going rate is 10,000 kip per day.

Bus, truck, songthaew

To **Luang Namtha**, by bus or pick-up, 0800, 0900, 1100, 1300 and 1500 daily, 2 hrs, 15,000 kip. To charter a *songthaew* or tuk-tuk to Luang Namtha costs upwards of 150,000 kip.

There are also trucks to **Muang Long**, 1100 and 1430 daily, 48 km, 2 hrs, 13,000 kip, and to **Xieng Kok** (located on the Mekong at the Myanmar/Burma border), several times a week, 75 km, 2½ hrs, 25,000 kip. Foreigners are not officially permitted to cross into Myanmar (Burma) here, but there have been reports of travellers being granted a visa and entering. It is sometimes possible to charter boats from Xieng Kok downstream on the Mekong to **Houei Xai**, 3-4 hrs. This is expensive – around US$150; contact Mr Chom. If you can't find a boat to Houei Xai, aim for Muang Mom, which will be cheaper and is a more common route for the speedboats.

Houei Xai *p165, map p171*
Lao National Tourism State Bokeo, near immigration, T084-211555, organizes the sale of boat, bus, pick-up and other tickets and will deliver tickets to most hotels.

Air

The airport is located 5 km south of town and has flights to **Vientiane**, US$80; book in advance as it is a small plane and tends to fill up quickly.

Boat

The BAP Guesthouse is a good place to find out about boat services. For services across the Mekong to Thailand, see Border essentials, page 178.

The slow boat to **Pak Beng** is raved about by many travellers. It leaves from a jetty 1½ km north of town, 0930-1000 daily, 6-7 hrs, 75,000 kip to Pak Beng or 160,000 kip for the whole journey to **Luang Prabang**; it's a charming trip through lovely scenery, worth getting a seat on the roof. Speedboats are a noisy, unrelaxing alternative; they leave from the Tin That pier south of town, to Pak Beng, 3 hrs, 130,000 kip and to Luang Prabang, 270,000 kip. There have been reports of unscrupulous boatmen claiming there are no slow boats in the dry season to encourage travellers to take their fast boats. This is usually untrue. The most luxurious option is the Luang Say Cruise to Luang Prabang (see page 147).

It is also possible to take a speedboat north along the Mekong to **Xieng Kok**, 200,000 kip, on the Burmese border (no legal crossing for foreigners). The boats depart 20 km upstream from Houei Xai (a tuk-tuk to the embarkation point costs 30,000 kip). The trip is an upstream battle, so slow boats tend not to make it. Chartering a boat is possible, but quite an investment at anything from US$100 up to US$300. A row of new bungalows to the left of the boat drop in Xieng Kok provide accommodation at 40,000 kip per night in good rooms with verandahs, bathrooms, mozzie nets and electricity 1800-2200 daily. From Xieng Kok, it's possible to get to **Muang Sing** by bus (25,000 kip). It is reported that Xieng Kok was the centre of a major drug-smuggling racket but whether this holds true now that Laos is reportedly opium-free is yet to be seen.

There are also boat services from Pak Tha (30 km downstream from Houei Xai) north on the Nam Tha to **Na Lae**, US$60, despite what most boatmen may say. However, you're unlikely to get all the way to Luang Namtha from here.

Bus, truck, songthaew

The bus station is located at the Morning Market, 2 km out of town; a tuk-tuk to the centre costs 5000-10,000 kip. To **Nam Chan** by taxi, 1 hr, 80,000 kip for the whole vehicle.

Trucks, buses and mini-vans run to **Vieng Phouka**, 0930-1030 daily, 5 hrs, 45,000 kip; to **Luang Namtha**, 0930-1130 daily, 170 km, 8 hrs, 60,000 kip; to **Udom Xai**, 0900 daily, 95,000 kip; to **Luang Prabang**, 0930 daily, 6 hrs, 120,000 kip; to **Vientiane**, 0900 daily, 20 hrs, 160,000 kip.

Pak Beng *p166, map p172*
Boat

The times and prices for boats are always changing so it's best to check beforehand. The slow boat to **Houei Xai** leaves at around 0800 from the port and takes all day. The slow boat to **Luang Prabang** leaves around the same time. Speedboats to Luang Prabang (2-3 hrs) and Houei Xai leave throughout the day, when full, until early afternoon. You can also take a boat downriver to **Tha Suang**, 1 hr, US$5, and then catch a *songthaew* from here to **Hongsa**, US$3.

Bus, songthaew

Buses leave from the jetty in the morning for the route north to **Muang Houn**, 2 hrs, 20,000 kip, and **Udom Xai**, 6-7 hrs, 30,000 kip. Direct *songthaew* to Udom Xai are few, so an alternative is to take one to Muang Houn and catch a rather more frequent service from there. The road to Udom Xai is through spectacular scenery and is currently being renovated. There is no road between Pak Beng and **Houei Xai**.

Sayaboury *p167*
Air

Flights to **Vientiane**, Sat and Wed, 45 mins, US$51/US$97. On each occasion the plane makes a round trip. Tickets can be purchased at the airport, about 1 km south of town.

Bus

There are 2 bus terminals, the South Bus Station, 2 km southeast of town, and the North Bus Station, 2 km north of town.

There are no direct road links with Vientiane. The road south from Sayaboury only goes as far as Muang Ken Thao, close to the border with Thailand. This road passes through Pak Lai, on the Mekong, where it is possible to catch a boat downstream to **Vientiane**. There are buses to **Pak Lai** at 0730- 1000 daily, 4 hrs, US$2.50. Note that the road is in poor condition – although it is gradually being upgraded – and transport during the wet season (Jun/Jul-Oct/Nov) is difficult and sometimes impossible.

You can catch a *songthaew* north to **Tha Deua** on the Mekong, 23 km, 1 hr, from where a ferry crosses to **Pak Khon**, 3000 kip. There are regular buses from Pak Khon to **Luang Prabang**, 4 hrs, US$1.50. Speedboats also run from Tha Deua direct to Luang Prabang, 1 hr, US$20 but you may have to rent the whole boat, which is costly.

Pak Lai *p167*
Boat
There are connections by slow boat (downriver) to **Vientiane**, 0730 daily, 8 hrs, US$7. However, due to the upgrading of Route 13 between Vientiane and Luang Prabang, there are no longer any scheduled boats upriver to Luang Prabang; instead you need to head to Sayaboury then Tha Deua (see above).

Songthaew
Songthaew services terminate 3 km out of town; share a tuk-tuk into the centre. *Songthaew* run north to **Sayaboury**, 4 hrs, US$3, twice daily.

❶ Directory

Udom Xai *p159, map p168*
Banks Lao Development Bank, just off the road on the way to Phongsali, changes US$, Chinese ¥ and Thai ฿, cash and TCs. The BCEL Bank, on the main road near the Kaysone Monument, T081-211260, is much more convenient and offers the same services. No credit card advances. **Communications** Post office and Lao Telecom, opposite the Sai Xi Hotel, uphill from the Chinese market; international calls available. Telephone code: 081. **Internet** is available on the main street opposite the petrol station for around 500-600 kip per min; also internet calls overseas, with pretty bad connection but at a cheaper rate than the Lao Telecom office. The most reliable

internet is at **Litthavixay Guesthouse**, see Sleeping, which is leagues ahead of the competition. **Useful information** Electricity available 24 hrs.

Luang Namtha *p160, map p161*
Banks Lao Development Bank, in the centre of town, changes US$, Chinese ¥ and Thai ฿ to kip, also exchanges TCs but charges a sizeable commission. The BCEL opposite the Telecom Office, changes US$, Chinese ¥ and Thai ฿ and does cash advances on Visa. **Communications** Telephone code: 086. KNT Computers, on the main road, south of Manychan Guesthouse, have a fully set-up internet café, 500 kip per min. You can make international calls from **Lao Telecom**, near Saikhonglongsack Guesthouse. **Useful information** Electricity available 24 hrs.

Muang Sing *p163, map p164*
Banks There is a small branch of the **Lao Development Bank** opposite the market which will exchange Thai ฿, Chinese ¥ and US$.

Houei Xai *p165, map p171*
Banks Lao Development Bank, right next to the immigration office, changes TCs, US$ cash and Thai ฿, open 0830-1600 daily. **Communications** Post office with telephone facilities about 500 m south (downstream) from the centre of town. Area code: 084. **Immigration** At the boat terminal and the airport, open 0800-1800 daily, ฿15 service fee is charged Sat and Sun (see also Border essentials, page 178).

Pak Beng *p166, map p172*
Banks There is no bank in town, but most of the guesthouses and restaurants will exchange Thai ฿ and US$ cash at a hefty commission. **Communications** The post office is up over the hill on the main road. **Useful information** Electricity is sporadic and sometimes only available 1800-2200 daily.

Sayaboury *p167*
Banks There is only one bank in town, the Lao Development Bank. just down from the Kaysone Monument, 0830-1600 Mon-Fri. It does not accept TCs but will change US$ and Thai ฿. The rate of exchange is poor.

Communications Telephone code: 074. The post office, 0800-1100 and 1300-1700 Mon-Fri, and Lao Telecom Office are in the centre of town, on the other side of the road from the market. International call cards are available.

Pak Lai *p167*

Banks The Lao Development Bank, a block north of the boat landing, will change Thai ฿ and US$. **Communications** There is a small telephone office and post office a block west of the bank.

Xieng Khouang Province

Apart from the historic Plain of Jars, Xieng Khouang Province is best known for the pounding it took during the war. Many of the sights are battered monuments to the plateau's violent recent history. Given the cost of the return trip and the fact that the jars themselves aren't that spectacular, some consider the destination oversold. However, for those interested in modern history, it's the most fascinating area of Laos and helps one to gain an insight into the resilient nature of the Lao people. The countryside, particularly towards the Vietnam frontier, is beautiful – among the country's best – and the jars, too, are interesting by dint of their very oddness: as if a band of carousing giants had been suddenly interrupted, casting the jars across the plain in their hurry to leave. ▸▸ *For Sleeping, Eating and other listings, see pages 191-195.*

Background

Xieng Khouang Province has had a murky, blood-tinted, war-ravaged history. The town of Phonsavanh has long been an important transit point between China to the north, Vietnam to the east and Thailand to the south and this status historically made the town a target for neighbouring countries. What's more, the plateau of the Plain of Jars is one of the flattest areas in northern Laos, rendering it a natural battleground for the numerous conflicts that ensued from the 19th century to 1975.

The earliest known settlers in this area were believed to be of the ethnic Tai origin and a Phuan kingdom was established in the region in the 14th century. The kingdom suffered numerous sackings by the Vietnamese over hundreds of years, until, in 1832, they invaded Phonsavanh, executing the Phuan king and turning the area into an Annan vassal state. The region was incorporated into the kingdom of Lane Xang by King Fa Ngum briefly in the 16th century but was more often than not ruled by the Vietnamese (who called it Tran Ninh) because of its proximity to the border. The Chinese Haw also ravaged Phonsavanh in the 19th century, an event that, along with the sacking of Luang Prabang, became a catalyst for the government's acceptance of French protection.

Under the French, Xieng Khouang supported tea plantations and many colonial settlers took to the temperate climate. Like the Boloven Plateau to the south, the French colonial administration had visions of populating the Plain of Jars with thousands of hard-working French families. Only in this way, it was reasoned, could Laos be made to pay for itself.

Once the French departed, massive conflicts were waged in 1945-1946 between the Free Lao Movement and the Viet Minh. The Pathet Lao and Viet Minh joined forces and, by 1964, had a number of bases dotted around the Plain of Jars. From then on, chaos ensued, as Xieng Khouang got caught in the middle of the war between the Royalist-American and Pathet Lao-Vietnamese (see also page 182).

● *Both the Vietnamese and the US signed a 1962 Geneva Accord, prohibiting military involvement in Laos, yet more bombs were dropped on Laos during the 1960s and 1970s than on both Germany and Japan combined in World War II.*

⁑ Secret War on the Plain of Jars

The Plain occupies an important niche in modern Lao history as it became one of the most strategic battlegrounds of the war. For General Vang Pao's Hmong, it was the hearthstone of their mountain kingdom; for the royalist government and the Americans it was a critical piece in the Indochinese jigsaw; for Hanoi it was their back garden, which had to be secured to protect their rear flank. From the mid-1960s, neutralist forces were encamped on the Plain (dubbed 'the PDJ' during the war). They were supported by Hmong, based at the secret city of Long Tien, to the southwest. US-backed and North Vietnamese-backed forces fought a bitter war of attrition on the PDJ; each time royalist and Hmong forces were defeated on the ground, US air power was called in to pummel from above. In mid-February 1970, American Strategic Air Command, on presidential orders, directed that B-52 Stratofortress bombers should be used over the PDJ for the first time. Capable of silently dumping more than one hundred 500-lb bombs from 40,000 ft, they had a devastating effect on the towns and villages of the Plain but a minimal effect on Communist morale. Even if the B-52s had managed to wipe out North Vietnamese and Pathet Lao forces, the US-backed troops were unable to reach, let alone hold, the territory. Hanoi had garrisons of reinforcements waiting in the wings.

On the Plain, the B-52 proved as inappropriate and ineffective a weapon as it would later on the Ho Chi Minh Trail. As US bomber command increasingly turned its attention to the Trail, the Pathet Lao quickly seized the upper hand and retook the PDJ. The Communists were beaten back onto the surrounding hills and ridges by Vang Pao's forces and American bombers but they kept swarming back and, by March 1972, the North Vietnamese Army had seven divisions in Laos supporting the Pathet Lao. The so-called 'Mountain of Courage' – the hill behind the new airport to the northwest) – was the scene of some particularly hard fighting. It was here that the royalists, encamped on Phu Kheng, were trapped on two fronts by the Communists. When the Pathet Lao retook Xieng Khouang for the last time in 1973, they consolidated their position and bided their time.

During the 'Secret War' (1964-1974) against the North Vietnamese Army and the Pathet Lao, tens of thousands of cluster bomb units (CBUs) were dumped on Xieng Khouang Province, as testified by the (former) scrap metal trade in CBU casings. Each unit was armed with 150 anti-personnel plastic 'pineapple' bomblets, which still regularly kill children and cripple adults. The Plain of Jars was also hit by B-52s returning from abortive bombing runs to Hanoi, who jettisoned their bomb loads before heading back to the US air base at Udon Thani in northeast Thailand. One bombing raid destroyed 1600 buildings in Xieng Khouang town alone. Suffice it to say that, with over 580,944 sorties flown (one-and-a-half times the number flown in Vietnam), whole towns were obliterated and the area's geography was permanently altered. Today, as the **Lao Airlines** Y-12 turbo-prop begins its descent towards the plateau, the meaning of the term 'carpet bombing' becomes clear. On the final approach to the town of Phonsavanh, the plane banks low over the cratered paddy fields, affording a T-28 fighter-bomber pilot's view of his target, which in places has been pummelled into little more than a moonscape. Some of the craters are 15 m across and 7 m deep.

The so-called 'collateral damage' is also staggering. There is no official figure on the number of dead but, since over 80% of the population is believed to have inhabited the northern and southern provinces targeted by US bombing, some sources estimate 300,000 Lao were killed – between a ninth and a tenth of the country's total population at the time. Others suggest the figure may be closer to 800,000 or up to a quarter of the population. One survivor from just outside Phonsavanh recalled his experiences of the bombing campaigns: "I was just a boy, coming home and saw a bomb hit my house. It exploded and split my home right in two! My parents and my brother were killed; my sister, killed; the family, killed; my dog was killed, the buffaloes, killed. Everything gone." He remembers how "the kids would run out to the streets and pick up these things that had fallen from the sky, like parachutes, thinking they were chocolate bars or something, and their arms would catch fire and no matter how hard you tried you couldn't put it out, these screaming children on fire. It was horrific, truly horrific."

Today, hundreds of thousands of bomblets – and equally lethal impact mines, which the Lao call *bombis* – remain buried in Xieng Khouang's grassy meadows. Because the war was 'secret', there are few records of what was dropped and where and, even when the mines have been uncovered, their workings are often a mystery – the Americans used Laos as a testing ground for new ordnance so blueprints are unavailable. One aid worker relates how in the mid-1980s, a specially designed, armour-plated tractor was terminally disabled by *bombis*, while attempting to clear them from the fields. The UK-based **Mines Advisory Group** (MAG) is currently engaged in clearing the land of Unexploded Ordnance (UXO). The process began in schools and hospitals and has now moved on to those clear areas where fatalities are greatest. Villagers can also put requests in to have their back gardens cleared of ordnance. The fact that MAG found a 500 lb bomb close to their own HQ in Phonsavanh a few years ago illustrates the scale of the problem. Note that MAG's work should not be viewed as a tourist 'attraction'.

Uncle Sam has, however, bequeathed to local people an almost unlimited supply of twisted metal. Bombshells and flare casings can frequently be seen in Xieng Khouang's villages where they are used for everything from cattle troughs and fences, to stilts for houses and water-carriers. In Phonsavanh steel runway sheets make handy walls, while plants are potted out in shell casings.

Xieng Khouang remains one of the poorest provinces in an already wretchedly poor country. The whole province has a population of only around 250,000, a mix of different ethnic groups, predominantly Hmong, Lao and a handful of Khmu. Government attempts to curtail shifting cultivation and encourage the Hmong to settle have not been very successful, largely because there are no alternative livelihoods available. Travelling through the province there is a sense not just that the American air war caused enormous suffering and destruction, but that the following decades have not provided much in the way of economic opportunities.

Ins and outs

Getting there Phonsavanh Airport (aka Xieng Khouang airport) is 4 km west of Phonsavanh. **Lao Airlines** flies to and from Vientiane; check www.laoairlines.com for up to date information. A tuk-tuk to town costs 10,000 kip per person.

The most direct route by road from Luang Prabang to Xieng Khouang Province is to take Route 13 south to Muang Phou Khoun and then Route 7 east; note that this road is periodically attacked by anti-government bandits, so check the security situation before travelling. Take motion sickness tablets as it's quite a bumpy trip. An alternative, albeit rather longer, route to Xieng Khouang is via Nong Khiaw (see page 150), from where there are pick-ups to Pak Xeng and on to

❖ Note that travel agents and airlines tend to refer to the provincial capital, Phonsavanh, as 'Xieng Khouang', while the old town of Xieng Khouang is now usually known as 'Muang Khoune'.

Phonsavanh via Vieng Thong on Route 1. This is a very convoluted way to do the trip but is quite scenic. Some visitors have said that this loop is impassable during the wet season due to the state of the road at Vieng Thong but this should have improved by late 2005; check before you depart.

The new bus station is 3 km west of Phonsavanh on Route 7; a tuk-tuk to/from the centre costs 5000 kip. Many services still use the terminal in the centre of town but eventually all services will use the new station.

> ❆ It is cold here Nov-Mar. Several jumpers and a thick jacket are required.

Getting around Public transport is limited and sporadic. Word on the ground is that soon a miscellany of transport options will become available, from bicycles through to tuk-tuks but, at the time of publication, it was illegal to rent your own vehicle. Until the regulations change and tourists are allowed more freedom, the only real way to get to outlying sites is by rented car, with driver. ▸▸ *For further details, see Transport, page 194.*

▸▸ For further details, see Transport, page 194.

Phonsavanh → *Phone code: 061. Colour map 1, C4.*

🄿🄵🄾🄾🄰🄴🄲 ▸▸ *pages 191-195.*

Phonsavanh is the main town of the province today – old Xieng Khouang having been flattened – and its small airstrip is a crucial transport link in this mountainous region. Surrounding the town are huge mountains, among them Phu Bia, one of the country's highest. The town itself is notable mainly for its ugliness. It was established in the mid-1970s and sprawls out from a heartless centre with no sense of plan or direction. While Phonsavanh will win no beauty contests, it does have a rather attractive 'Wild West' atmosphere. As journalist Malcolm Macalister Hall wrote in 1998: "I liked this ugly, rough-hewn town: for its unlikely invitations, its mad breakfasts, and the beautiful landscapes that surrounded it". What's more, it's the only base from which to explore the Plain of Jars, so it has a fair number of hotels and guesthouses. The daily market is busy but rather undistinguished, with the usual assortment of cheap Chinese bric-a-brac. The food market, behind the post office, is more lively and worth a look.

Phonsavanh

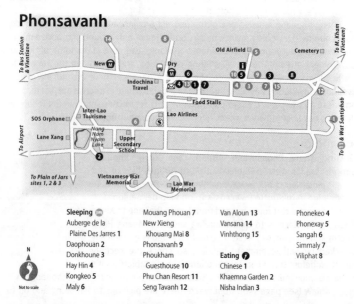

Sleeping 🛏	Mouang Phouan 7	Van Aloun 13	Phonekeo 4
Auberge de la	New Xieng	Vansana 14	Phonexay 5
Plaine Des Jarres 1	Khouang Mai 8	Vinhthong 15	Sangah 6
Daophouan 2	Phonsavanh 9		Simmaly 7
Donkhoune 3	Phoukham	**Eating 🍴**	Viliphat 8
Hay Hin 4	Guesthouse 10	Chinese 1	
Kongkeo 5	Phu Chan Resort 11	Khaemna Garden 2	
Maly 6	Seng Tavanh 12	Nisha Indian 3	

N ⟡ Not to scale

South of Phonsavanh, on two small hills, a pair of white and gold monuments can be seen. It is worth the short hike up, if only for the views they afford of the surrounding countryside. The **Vietnamese war memorial** ① *daily from dawn till dusk, 1,000 kip*, on the west side, was built to commemorate the death of over one million Vietnamese troops in the war against the anti-Communists. It contains the bones of Vietnamese soldiers and is inscribed 'Lao Vietnamese Solidarity Forever'. The newer **Lao war memorial** ① *daily from dawn till dusk, 1000 kip*, to the east, is more rounded in the Lao style and was built later in memory of 4500 Pathet Lao soldiers who died, including Hmong and Khmu fighters (often only remembered as fighting for the US).

Plain of Jars → *Colour map 1, C5.* 🍴🏨🍽 ⇢ *pages 191-195.*

The undulating plateau of the Plain of Jars (also known as Plaine de Jarres, or Thong Hai Hin), stretches for about 50 km east to west, covering an area of 1,000 sq km at an altitude of 1,000 m. In total there are 136 archaeological sites in this area, containing thousands of jars, discs and deliberately placed stones. Of these only three are open to tourists. Note that the plateau can be cold from December to March.

Background
Most of the jars are generally between 1 m and 2½ m high, around 1 m in diameter and weigh about the same as three small cars. The largest are about 3 m tall. The jars have long presented an archaeological conundrum, leaving generations of theorists non-plussed by how they got there and what they were used for. Local legend relates that King Khoon Chuong and his troops from Southern China threw a stupendous party after their victory over the wicked Chao Angka and had the jars made to brew outrageous quantities of *lao-lao*. However attractive this alcoholic thesis, it is more likely that the jars are in fact 2000-year-old stone funeral urns. The larger jars are believed to have been for the local aristocracy and the smaller jars for their minions.

Some archaeologists speculate that the cave below the main site was hewn from the rock at about the same time as the jars themselves and that the hole in the roof possibly indicates that the cave was used for cremation or that the jars were made and fired in the cave. But this is all speculation and the jars' true origins and function remain a mystery. In fact, the stone from which the jars at Site one are made doesn't seem to come from that area. Instead, using the evidence of some half-hewn jars made of the same stone found near Sites two and three, archaeologists have postulated that the jars were carved here and then transported to Site one.

Tools, bronze ornaments, ceramics and other objects have been found in the jars, indicating that a civilized society was responsible for them but no-one has a clue which one, as the artefacts bear no relation to those left behind by other ancient Indochinese civilizations. Some of the jars were once covered with round lids and there is one jar, in the group facing the entrance to the cave, that is decorated with a rough carving of a dancing figure.

Over the years, a few jars have been stolen and a number have been transported by helicopter down to Vientiane's Wat Phra Kaeo and the back yard of the National Museum (see pages 71 and 74). Local guides will claim that despite four or five B-52 bombing raids on the plain every day for five years during the Secret War (see page 182), the jars remained mysteriously unscathed. However, several bomb craters and damaged jars at the main site show this to be a fanciful myth. During heavy fighting on the Plain in the early 1970s, the Pathet Lao set up a command centre in the cave next to the jars and then posed among the jars for photographs (which can be seen in the Revolutionary Museum in Vientiane). Around the entrance to the cave are numerous bomb craters, as the US targeted the sanctuary in a futile attempt to dislodge the Communists.

A vast aviation fuel depot was built next to the jars, early in the 1990s, to supply the huge new airbase just to the west. The base, designed by Soviet technicians, is the new headquarters for the Lao Air Force, although why the government needs a large airbase here remains a mystery and something of a political minefield. On the grasslands around the jars are stumpy little flowers, known as '*baa*' by the Hmong and '*dok waan*' by the Lao; the stems are boiled to make a soup, while the red buds are fried. Once the flower has bloomed (turning yellow), they are no longer tasty. Along with the bomb craters that scar the landscape there are also patches of bare earth that have nothing to do with the Indochina conflict. These are sparrow free-fire zones: after the first rains, local people clear the land of grass over an area of about 10 sq m and build a small hide; they then put sticky rice down and wait for the poor creatures to alight for a leisurely lunch before being blasted.

❧ *The road to the Plain passes through a Hmong resettlement village. Their distinctive homes are not built on stilts and there is no separate kitchen area on the side.*

Ins and outs

Getting there and around At the time of publication the sites were only accessible by vehicles from Phonsavanh and tuk-tuks were barred indefinitely from ferrying customers around the area. A 4WD with driver is your best chance of making it successfully over the somewhat hairy roads. It should be possible to drive to the Plain of Jars, see Site one and return to town in two hours. Expect to pay in the region of US$25 for an English-speaking guide and vehicle for four people, or US$60 for seven people and a mini-van. Alternatively, hotels, guesthouses and tour companies in Phonsavanh run tours to the Plain of Jars, Muang Khoune (Xieng Khouang) and to Hmong villages to the northeast of Phonsavanh. If you arrive by air, the chances are you'll be inundated with official and unofficial would-be guides as soon as you step off the plane. Note that it is not possible to walk from the airport to Site one, as there is a military base in

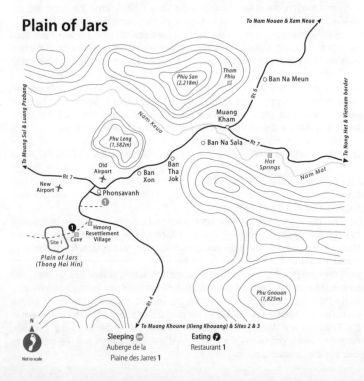

Plain of Jars

Sleeping
Auberge de la
Plaine des Jarres 1

Eating
Restaurant 1

Not to scale

❝❞ The site looks as if a band of carousing giants had been suddenly interrupted, casting the jars across the plain in their hurry to leave.

between. It is recommended that you hire a guide, for at least a day, to get an insight into the history of the area. The cost of admission to each site is 7000 kip. ▸▸ *For further information, see Activities and tours, page 194, and Transport, page 194.*

Site one
More than 300 jars survive, mainly scattered on one slope at so-called 'Site one' or **Thong Hai Hin**, 10 km southwest of Phonsavanh. This site is closest to Phonsavanh and has the largest jar – along with a small restaurant. A small path, cleared by MAG, winds through the site, with a warning not to walk away from delineated areas as UXO are still around. There are 250 jars at the site, each of which weighs about a tonne, although the biggest, called **Hai Cheaum**, is over 2 m tall and weighs over 6 tonnes. Folklore suggests that the jar is named after a Thai-Lao liberator, who overthrew Chao Angka. Further downhill is another smattering of jars, some of which feature carvings. The smallish cave in the hill to the left was used by the Pathet Lao as a hideout during the war and may have been the ancient kiln in which the jars were fired (see Background, above).

Sites two and three
True jar lovers should visit Site two, known as **Hai Hin Phu Salatao** (literally 'Salato Hill Stone Jar Site'), and Site three, called **Hai Hin Laat Khai**. Site two is 25 km south of Phonsavanh and features 90 jars spread across two hills. The jars are set in a rather beautiful location, affording scenic views. A further 10 km south of Site two, Site three is the most atmospheric of all the sites, set in verdant green rolling hills, swiss-cheesed with bomb craters. To get there you have to walk through some rice paddies and cross the small bamboo bridge. There are more than 130 jars at this site, which are generally smaller and more damaged than at the other sites. There's also a very small, basic restaurant here, serving *feu*. Nearby is **Ban Xieng Dai**, a friendly village, home to a monastery featuring some Buddha images, which were badly damaged during the war. Villagers will lead treks to the nearby Lang waterfall for 10,000 kip.

Muang Khoune (old Xieng Khouang) → *Colour map 1, C4.*

The old town of Xieng Khouang – now rebuilt and renamed Muang Khoune – was destroyed during the war, between 1964 and 1969, and now the population is reduced to a mere 14,000. Prior to the bombing, the town was extremely picturesque, similar to Luang Prabang, with over 400 old colonial buildings and 30 wats and pagodas but today it holds nothing in the way of aesthetic charm and a sense of impermanence pervades; it consists of a row of wooden Lao houses and a market area. However, while Muang Khoune itself is spectacularly unimpressive, its position, surrounded by mountains, is noteworthy.

Xieng Khouang was founded by Chao Noi Muang and was a stronghold for the Xieng Khouang royal family. In 1832 the Hmong mountain state was annexed by Vietnam and renamed Tran Ninh; the king was marched off to Vietnam and publicly executed in Hué, while the population of Xieng Khouang was forced to wear Vietnamese dress.

Many important temples were built here in the distinctive Xieng Khouang style but these were completely obliterated by the American bombing. The religious architecture of the province was one of Laos's three main architectural styles (Luang Prabang and Vientiane styles being the other two). The town was also the main centre for the French in this area during the colonial period and remnants of French colonial architecture are still in evidence.

Xieng Khouang was most heavily bombed during 1969 and 1970, when US air power was called in to reverse the success of the Communists' dry season offensive on the Plain of Jars. In his book *The Ravens*, Christopher Robins interviews several former US pilots who describe the annihilation of the town in which 1,500 buildings were razed, together with another 2,000 across the plain. Three towns, he says, "were wiped from the map. By the end of the year (1970) there would not be a building left standing". During this time most villagers left their homes and lived in caves or in the forest, subsisting on rice from China and Vietnam. So incessant was the bombing and strafing that peasants took to planting their rice fields at night. One brave woman recalled, "I would have to get the rice at two or three in the morning so as not to be seen. I would carry it on my back, sometimes 100 kg, it was so heavy that I was doubled over, my head almost touching the ground."

The town, which is in fact little more than a village, was rebuilt after 1975 and renamed Muang Khoune.

Sights

Those excited about the prospect of visiting a unique collection of 500-year-old wats must, for the most part, be content with piles of bricks. There is virtually nothing left of the 16th-century **Wat Phia Wat** (at the far end of town on the right-hand side by the road), except the basement and several shrapnel-pocked Buddha statues, including a large, seated Buddha which is believed to be over 600 years old. The once-picturesque wat underwent a series of renovations in 1930 only to be bombed into oblivion by the Americans. The half-hearted attempt at further renovation is barely noticeable. Walking up the hill, the remains of the French colonial Governor's house, built in the 1930s, can be seen, with some old tile floors still in place and a hospital, patched together Lao-style.

Two stupas perch on a pair of hills above the town. **That Chompet** is a stump of its former self and is relatively overgrown. A better alternative is the 16th-century **That Foun**, which is quite sizeable and similar to That Dam in Vientiane. The *that* is said to contain relics of the Indian emperor Asoka but this legend should be taken with a large pinch of *nam pa*. It may, however, explain why the heart of the stupa has been hollowed out, as thieves have searched, apparently in vain, for buried treasure, in particular old Buddha images.

Wat Si Phoum (opposite the market below the main road) was also destroyed by the war and now a new inelegant wat has been built next to the ruined *that*. There is a small monastery attached.

The market in Muang Khoune holds little interest for the tourist, with nothing on sale but the bare essentials. Head to the Black Tai village, about 500 m northwest of town, to buy local handicrafts and scarves.

West of Phonsavanh

Muang Sui

Muang Sui lies 45 km west of Phonsavanh on Route 7. The town was formerly known for its vast array of old Buddhist Temples and traditional Lao architecture but its fate was sealed once it became a primary landing site for US planes. The town was later razed by the North Vietnamese Army. It is part of a district called Phu Kut, an area known for Hmong insurgency, so don't be surprised if you see armed personnel around. The strip of road, in particular, has experienced ongoing difficulties with Hmong insurgents and, although things are settling down now, with a large group surrendering to the government in 2005, there is still a small risk of attack. There aren't many sights in the actual town and a day trip from Phonsavanh should be more than sufficient to take in the outlying caves and picturesque **Nong Tang Lake**, a short drive east of town. It's crowned by limestone karsk formations and believed to be very deep.

The caves around Muang Sui make the trip worthwhile; a US$1 entrance fee is paid at **Buddha Cave** (Tham Pha), a large honeycomb network of labyrinthine passages, grottoes and caverns that is said to house over 1000 Buddha images, many dating back 1,200 years. Another nearby cave, was used by the Vietnamese Army as a hospital and is still known as **Hospital Cave. Water Cave** is named after the water that falls though its roof but it isn't as interesting as the other caves. Nearby is the large **Stupa Cave** (Tham That), which contains the ruins of an old stupa believed to be several hundred years old. Within walking distance is **Coffin Cave**, nestled high up in a limestone cliff. It's a bit of a climb to the cave but worth it as it contains prehistoric coffins carved out of old tree trunks. The caves have been raided but there are a few human remains and remnants scattered around the floor.

When travelling between Phonsavanh and Muang Sui, stop off to look at the old Russian tank, about 20 km west of Phonsavanh.

East of Phonsavanh 🍴🛏🚌 » pages 191-195.

Route 7 heads east from Phonsavanh towards Muang Kham and the border with Vietnam (see page 190). The journey is characterized by attractive rolling hills and grassy meadows in the wet season but becomes very barren in the dry season, especially where the bomb craters have pock-marked the landscape. The drive is an abject lesson in the potentially destructive nature of some forms of shifting cultivation. Some authorities estimate that up to 100,000 ha of forest were being destroyed in this area by slash-and-burn agriculture before the government implemented a policy to minimize the practice. The difficulty is that minority shifting cultivators – especially the Hmong – often farm land that has already been logged by commercial timber firms (for the simple reason that it is easier to cultivate) and then find themselves blamed for the destruction.

About 12 km east of Phonsavanh is the village of **Ban Xon**, which lays claim to two famous daughters, Baoua Kham and Baoua Xi, who are reported to have shot down a US B-52 with small arms fire. War historians are very sceptical about this claim but a Lao popular song was nonetheless written about them. The ballad is said to extol the beauty and courage of the women of Xieng Khouang.

Hmong villages

Route 7 winds its way down off the plateau along the Nam Keua, a fertile area where Hmong villagers grow rice and maize. About 25 km east of Phonsavanh is the Hmong market, held on Sundays from 0400 to 1000. Hundreds of people come in from surrounding villages to the colourful market to sell local produce, animals and

⁞ Border essentials: Nam Khan

Nong Het is approximately 60 km east of Muang Kham. It is deep in Hmong country and is an important trading post with Vietnam, which is just a few kilometres down the road at **Nam Khan**. Not many tourists seem to use this border crossing, although trucks and *songthaew* ply between Phonsavanh and the border daily, 4-5 hrs, US$4-5. There are also buses via Nong Het from Phonsavanh's central bus station at 0630 Tue and Fri, US$10. Fifteen-day Lao visas are available on arrival; Vietnamese visas are required in advance.

handicrafts. Many of the older people wear traditional attire. Seven kilometres further east is the roadside Hmong village of **Ban Tha Jok**, where there are some old Hmong houses that use old bomb casings as stilts.

If you wish to visit a more traditional Hmong settlement, leave your vehicle at Ban Na Sala Mai on the main road and walk south for 5 km, up a very pleasant valley to **Ban Na Sala**. This is a very beautiful village, perched in the hills. During the war, the Pathet Lao occupied the hills surrounding this village, so the US army was not able to go anywhere near it. Ban Na Sala is one of the best places to see the creative architectural and household application of war debris, as here, too, the people have utilized bomb casings to construct their houses.

Muang Kham

This small trading town, 53 km east of Phonsavanh, is situated in the centre of a large open valley on the route to Vietnam. It was devastated during the war but now has a thriving economy dealing in Vietnamese and Chinese goods. The valley is an important fruit and rice growing area. There's a market early every morning in the centre of town and there are also a couple of groups of stone jars close by.

Tham Phiu

ⓘ *East of Muang Kham, off Route 7, just after the Km 183 post. A rough track leads down to an irrigation dam, built in 1981. To Tham Phiu, either go the easy way and hire a vehicle and driver US$30-40 from Phonsavanh. Or the hard way, public transport. For the latter, take the bus to Nong Het, and request to stop at the Tham Phiu turn-off. From here walk towards the towering limestone cliff and follow the small trails for the last km. It is best to do this with a guide as there are still UXOs littered in the area.*

Evidence of the dirty war can be seen in the area immediately surrounding Muang Kham. The intensity of the US bombing campaign under the command of the late General Curtis Le May was such that entire villages were forced to take refuge in caves. (Curtis Le May is infamously associated with bragging that he wanted to bomb the Communists "back into the Stone Age".) In **Tham Phiu**, a cave overlooking the valley, 365 villagers from nearby Ban Na Meun built a two-storey bomb shelter and concealed its entrance with a high stone wall. They lived there for a year, working in their rice fields at night and taking cover during the day from the relentless bombing raids. On the morning of 8 March 1968 two T-28 fighter bombers took off from Udon Thani air base in neighbouring Thailand and located the cave mouth which had been exposed on previous sorties. It is likely that the US forces suspected that the cave contained a Pathet Lao hospital complex. Indeed, experts are at odds whether this was a legitimate target or an example of collateral damage. The first rocket destroyed the wall; the second, which was fired as the planes swept across the valley, carried the full length of the chamber before exploding. There were no survivors and 11 families were completely wiped out; in total 437 people died, many reportedly women and children. Local rescuers claim they were unable to enter the cave for three days, but eventually the dead were buried in a bomb crater on the hillside next to the cave mouth. Today there is no official memorial, just the eerily black walls. The interior of the cave was completely dug up by rescue parties and relatives and today there is nothing but rubble inside. It makes for a poignant lesson in military history and locally it is considered a war memorial. Further up the cliff is another cave, **Tham Phiu Song**, which fortunately didn't suffer the same fate. Visitors are welcome to explore but you will need a torch.

Bor Yai and Bor Noi
ⓘ *Hot Springs Resort, off Route 7. Daily 0900-1900. 5000 kip. Taxi from Muang Kham 50,000 kip or tour from Phonsavanh.*

Not far from Muang Kham, off the Vietnam road, are two hot springs (*bor nam lawn*) on the Nam Mat, imaginatively named Bor Yai (Big Spring) and Bor Noi (Little Spring). They are locally known for their curative properties and are said to have enormous potential for geothermal power but this is hard to believe as they do not appear to be particularly active. The murky water is distinctly uninviting but it is piped to showers and wooden tubs, where a therapeutic soak can be quite pleasant. The springs are owned and operated by the government, so to bathe you have to go to the resort, which has a number of private bathrooms that tourists can use for the day. The resort was purportedly built by Kaysone Phomvihane's wife for visiting dignitaries.

● Sleeping

Phonsavanh *p184, map p184*
None of the streets in Phonsavanh are named – or at least the names aren't used. Consult the map on page 184 to check the exact locations of hotels, guesthouses and restaurants.

A Auberge de la Plaine des Jarres (aka Phu Pha Daeng Hotel), 1 km from the centre of Phonsavanh, T/F061-312044. In a spectacular position on a hill overlooking town are 16 attractive stone and wood chalets, with living room, fireplace and shower-room, (occasional hot water). Clean and comfortable, lovely views, roses, geraniums and petunias planted around the chalets. Restaurant serves good food. More expensive Oct-May. The friendly owner speaks French.

A Phu Chan Resort, on a hill on the outskirts of town, T061-312264. Cosy spacious wooden bungalows with all the modern fittings. Nice view of town and the cemetery.

A Vansana, on a hill about 1 km out of town, T061-213170. One of the newest in town, opened in Nov 2004. Big, modern rooms with telephone, TV, mini-bar, polished floor-boards and tea/coffee-making facilities. Phenomenal views of the countryside. Opt for the rooms upstairs, with free-form bathtub and picturesque balcony views.

Restaurant offers Lao and foreign cuisine. Airport pick-up (look for Vong) and tour services available. Highly recommended.

B-C Maly Hotel, down the road from local government offices, T061-312031, F061-312003. All rooms have hot water and are beautifully furnished with lovely local artefacts, including a small (defused!) cluster bomb on the table. More expensive rooms on the upper floors have satellite TV, sitting area and other luxuries. Fireplace in the lobby. Restaurant. Transport services available. The owner, Mr Sousath Phetrasy, runs exceptional tours in this area and to the north around Xam Neua (see Activities and tours, page 194).

B-C New Xieng Khouang Mai, behind the dry market, T061-312049. This hotel has been recently renovated and offers huge triples, with en suite showers and hot water. More expensive rooms have baths and TV. Rates include breakfast.

C-D Daophouan Hotel, opposite the food market, T061-312092. Clean doubles, with en suite bathrooms and hot water, breakfast included, but still overpriced. Rundown and lacks atmosphere.

D Phoukham Guesthouse, on the main road through town. A Hmong-owned hotel. Large rooms with bathroom and hot water but beds are a bit like sleeping on a rockface. The tour services, which use local Hmong guides, are recommended.

D-E Donkhoune Guesthouse, on the main road through town. 36 rooms. The ones in the new annexe out the back are better: clean and comfy with en suite bathroom, hot water and fan.

E Mouang Phouan, T061-312046. 12 rooms in motel style with well-kept garden at the front. A bungalow-style annexe, with partitioned rooms and sitting area, is situated down a quiet side street, also looking onto a little garden. Shared squat loos and wash area for annexe rooms, private toilets and washbasin in main hotel. Looks as though the place has chopped down a forest to decorate its foyer – a huge, single, 6-m tree-top table is the showpiece. Price includes breakfast, hot water in thermos flasks and blankets in cold season. Recommended.

E Seng Tavanh, T061-211131. Smallish rooms either with bathrooms and hot water or with shared squat toilet. Nice, helpful owners who can help manage tours and logistics around the area. Russian jeep for rent, with driver, US$35-40 per day. Restaurant attached. Some gems from the menu include: baked eel; swallow; frogs; hedgehog; intestine or beef placenta salad.

E Van Aloun, T061-312070. An ugly Chinese concrete house. Some rooms have their own bathrooms. Clean enough and friendly, although rooms are a bit shabby.

F Hay Hin, T061-312252. Basic, warren-like guesthouse, with rooms partitioned by hardboard. Upstairs is a balcony and a communal sitting area and slightly better rooms. Tea provided. The manager does not speak English but is extremely enthusiastic.

F Kongkeo. Nice new house with large, clean rooms, some with en suites, some with shared bathrooms. Also several wooden huts out the back. The attached restaurant serves extremely cheap and spicy food.

F Phonsavanh Hotel, T061-312206, T020-5561193. Mammoth building houses huge dark rooms with en suite bathrooms or shared facilities – the water supply is erratic. Also operates as a part-time brothel. Unhelpful staff.

F Vinhthong, T061-312047. Very basic guesthouse. Mosquito net, bed, toilet, hot

shower. The US$3 rooms are cell-like but others are clean and serviceable and some have enormous bathrooms. Friendly Vietnamese owner. The lobby is like a taxidermy centre cum war museum with a display of shell casings, weapons and ammunition and interesting pictures, circa 1953, prior to the bombing of Old Xieng Khouang town. Tours of the Plain of Jars organized. Excellent value.

Plain of Jars p185
There are no hotels or guesthouses in the town of Muang Khoune.

Bor Yai and Bor Noi p191
C Hot Springs Guesthouse, Bor Yai. Two lovely wooden bungalows, each with 4 rooms and 1 bathroom. Recommended.
C Senebot, around the corner from Hot Springs Guesthouse. Rooms are a tad on the small side.

🍴 Eating

Phonsavanh p184, map p184
♥♥♥ Auberge de la Plaine de Jarres, see Sleeping. Reasonable menu of Lao dishes and some French food, somewhat overpriced given the competition.
♥♥♥-♥♥ Maly Hotel, see Sleeping. A great little restaurant serving fantastic food from a very extensive menu: everything from duck curry through to beef steak. Most dishes are around US$2. The best deal in town. Highly recommended.
♥♥ Chinese restaurant, near Van Aloun. Hot Sichuan dishes on the menu, a bit pricey, and be prepared to wait a long time.
♥♥ Phonekeo, main road through town. Limited menu with some dishes to raise the eyebrows, including placenta salad. "Chewy rubber" was the opinion of the only patron we found – and he was talking about the chicken.
♥♥-♥ Khaemna Garden Restaurant, 3 km from town centre. A fabulous setting by a lake overlooking a long stretch of rice paddies (don't forget your mozzie repellant!). This place is great: super food (from the usual menu) and friendly service. Best restaurant in town. Recommended.
♥♥-♥ Meuangphone, close to Hay Hin guesthouse. A large restaurant that appears

⁞ Parasol renaissance

Aside from the war paraphernalia, Phonsavanh is also the best place in Laos to pick up a traditional paper parasol. The art of making paper and wood umbrellas, also known as *khan nyu*, has undergone a renaissance in the last decade. The tradition is a centuries-old practice, originally bequeathed to the domain of monkhood. Novices and monks would make the parasols to give as gifts to the villages they were visiting. After 1975, the paper umbrellas were quickly usurped by plastic and metal ones from China. The frame of the umbrella is formed from bamboo and the paper made from a pulp of mulberry trees and usually dyed with colour from fruits, such as apple. The paper is stuck to the frame with glue made from persimmon resin and the outside spokes are painted with a charcoal compound. The umbrellas sell from US$5 upwards and can be found in the market and at guesthouses, such as Seng Tavanh.

impersonal but the service is friendly and quick. Lao and Western dishes.

🍴-🍴 **Sangah**, next to the market, opposite the Van Aloun Hotel, T061-312318. Formerly the best restaurant in town. Thai, Lao and Vietnamese (good noodle soup) dishes all available, as well as some Western fare including steak and chips. Enormous portions.

🍴 **Nisha Indian**, on the main road. Wins the prize for most unexpected find in Phonsavanh. North and south Indian food – very welcome if you need a reprieve from the same Asian dishes found throughout the north of Laos. The owner, endeavouring to exhibit some marketing prowess, has handwritten his name and phone number on every single water bottle. Open 0600-2230.

🍴 **Phonexay**, on the main road, towards the Tourism Office. Excellent fruit shakes and good Asian dishes – fried noodles, sweet and sour (all dishes 10,000-15,000 kip). Exceptionally friendly service.

🍴 **Simmaly**, 30 m from the market, T061-211013. Very popular restaurant offering Asian interpretations 0700-2200 daily. Specialist Western dishes can also be made to order. The staff are overwhelmingly helpful but, if the place is jam-packed, service can be a bit slow. Recommended.

🍴 **Viliphat**, on the main road, T061-211422. Small hole-in-the-wall style Vietnamese restaurant, serving great *feu* and coffee.

Plain of Jars *p185*

There are many good restaurants in Muang Khoune. **Manivanh**, for example, has good soup and fried rice/noodles dishes. There's also good *pho* opposite the market.

O Shopping

Phonsavanh *p184, map p184*

There are a multitude of shops at the town's market. The dry market is beside the town bus station and sells local handicrafts including the famous Phonsavanh parasols, textiles and silver. Most products from shoes to biscuits can be purchased here. Another Chinese market is being built and will probably offer the same kind of products (if the dry market isn't completely superceded altogether). Behind the post office is a fresh produce market with a gamut of fruit and vegetables on offer. There is a surprisingly well-equipped camera shop on the corner, adjacent to the town's bus station. Many of the guesthouses sell local handicrafts and war paraphernalia.

❀ Festivals and events

Phonsavanh *p184, map p184*

Dec National Day on the 2nd is celebrated with horse-drawn drag-cart racing. Also in Dec is **Hmong New Year** (movable), which is celebrated in a big way in this area. Festivities centre around the killing of a pig and offering the head to the spirits. Boys give cloth balls, known as *makoi*, to girls they've taken a fancy to.

▲ Activities and tours

Phonsavanh *p184, map p184*
Tour operators
There are no shortage of tour operators in Phonsavanh and most guesthouses can now arrange tours and transport. A full day tour for 4 people, travelling about 30 km into the countryside, should cost up to US$50-60, although you may have to bargain for it. The tourist office, just off the main road, is also quite helpful and runs tours to the hot springs near Muang Kham.

Indochina Travel, based at **Phoukham Guesthouse** (see Sleeping). Tour services.

Inter-Lao Tourisme, slightly out of town, opposite the government office. Ask for Phet, a long-time guide, who has had rave reviews and knows the history of the area inside out.

Lane Xang, T/F061-312171. Tours to Plain of Jars, trekking, caves, hot springs and more. Ask for Vong (the only English speaker), who comes highly recommended and will chatter away about local legends and history.

The most knowledgeable tour guide, however, is the owner of the Maly Hotel (see Sleeping). **Sousath Phetrasy** spent his teenage years in a cave at Xam Neua during the war and has helped foreign researchers with projects in the region. He also claims to be able to access some of the sites other guides can't reach, such as Long Tien. He is probably the best guide you can get, in terms of local and historical knowledge, and speaks fluent English and German. His tours are slightly more expensive thatn others at US$50-80 per day but well worth it.

◎ Transport

Phonsavanh *p184, map p184*
Air
Lao Airlines runs flights to **Vientiane**; check www.laoairlines.com for current schedules.

Bus
Buses currently depart from both the central bus station, next to the dry goods market, and the new bus station, 4 km west of town, but, in the future, buses will only use the latter terminal; check before travelling. Bus prices have a tendency to fluctuate. If taking one of the hilly routes, to Xam Neua, for example, take motion sickness pills.

To **Muang Sui** in Phu Kut district, 50,000 kip. To **Luang Prabang**, 0830 daily, 265 km on a sealed road, 7-8 hrs, 60,000 kip. To **Vientiane**, 0700, 0900, 1500 daily, 9-10 hrs, 75,000 kip, also a VIP bus (with a/c and TV) at 0730 daily, 85,000 kip. To **Vang Vieng**, 0715 daily, 65,000 kip, and a VIP bus at 0730, 70,000 kip. To **Muang Kham**, 3 hrs, 20,000 kip. Also north to **Nam Nouan**, 4-5 hrs, 30,000 kip (change here for transport west to **Nong Khiaw**), and to **Xam Neua**, 0800 daily, 60,000 kip, a 10-hr haul through some of the country's most beautiful scenery. To **Nong Het** for the Vietnam border, 0630 Tue and Fri, US$10.

Car with driver
This is the easiest way of touring the area. A full car to the **Plain of Jars** will cost US$20 (US$5 each) to Site one, or US$30-40 to all 3 sites. The tour could be combined with a trip to the hot springs, west of Muang Kham, for an extra US$20-30. To **Muang Sui**, US$60-80 return. Jeeps are available from Seng Tavanh (see Sleeping) for US$35-40 per day.

Tuk-tuk and taxi
Taxis and tuk-tuks wait at both bus terminals. It is illegal to hire them to the **Plain of Jars** but they can be used to reach **Muang Kham**, 3 hrs, 30,000 kip. Alternatively hire a jeep or taxi for the whole day and visit the minority villages and other sights around Muang Kham, US$35-40. Shared taxis to **Muang Khoune** (32 km) depart when there are enough passengers to warrant the trip, 20,000 kip per person (depending on the number of passengers), with up to 9 people jam-packed in the car.

Plain of Jars *p185*
Route 1D is surfaced between Muang Khoune and Phonsavanh (32 km). Buses to **Phonsavanh** depart daily from the Morning Market, 45 min, 15,000 kip.

Muang Kham *p189*
The only way to visit the minority villages en route to Muang Kham is by hiring a taxi. A taxi from Muang Kham to the hot springs costs 50,000 kip

❶ Directory

Phonsavanh *p184, map p184*
Banks Lao Development Bank, near Lao Airlines Office, 2 blocks back from the dry market, changes cash and Tcs, open 0800-1200 and 1330-1600 Mon-Fri.
Communications Area code: 061. The post office is opposite dry market and has IDD telephone boxes outside. At the time of

writing, there were only 2 internet cafés in town, at the photo shop and next door, 500 kip per min. **Medical facilities** There is a small clinic near the Daophouan Hotel and the Lao-Mongolian Hospital on the road to the airport; neither are recommended for any complicated procedures or treatment. Pharmacies are ubiquitous in town, particularly around the market.

Hua Phan Province

Hua Phan Province has a total population of 270,000 and is one of the most isolated areas of the country. Over 20 ethnic groups, mostly mountain-dwellers, inhabit the province, whose character has been shaped over the centuries by a variety of shifting rulers: it was part of the Tai Neua Kingdom, then integrated into the Annamese state of Ai Lao and also experienced stints as a Siamese protectorate and French colonial outpost. Until recently, Hua Phan remained relatively sheltered from the free market ethos that has spilled into towns along the Thai and Chinese borders, and memories of the period when it was the base for the revolutionary struggle are still close to the surface. Traders from China and Vietnam are more common these days but Hua Phan is still known in Laos as the 'revolutionary province'.

Hua Phan is spectacularly beautiful but largely overlooked by tourists, with the government only recording 700 visitors in 2004. This is a shame, as it is one of the most scenic parts of the country. It is also one of the country's poorest provinces, with over 75% of the population living below the poverty line. Local authorities hope that the area's large tourism potential will help to alleviate the plight and they have teamed up with the NGO SNV to develop infrastructure. There are plans for new guesthouses, a new runway, a visa facility at the Vietnam border and, generally, more open access, which at the time of publication was still quite limited. ▸▸ *For Sleeping, Eating and other listings, see pages 202-204.*

Background

Together with Phongsali Province, Hua Phan was the base for left-wing insurgency from the late 1940s until the final victory of the Pathet Lao over the royalist forces in 1975. Members of the Lao Issara, who had fled to Vietnam after French forces smashed the movement in 1946, infiltrated areas of northeast Laos in 1947-49 under the sponsorship of the Viet Minh. The movement coalesced when Prince Souphanouvong, who had fled to Thailand, arrived in Hanoi and organized a conference in August 1950 at which the Free Lao Front and the Lao Resistance Government were formed. Thereafter, the Pathet Lao adopted strategies developed by the Viet Minh in Vietnam, who in turn drew on the strategies of Mao Zedong and the Chinese Communists: establishment of bases in remote mountain areas; use of guerrilla tactics; exploitation of the dissatisfaction of tribal minorities, and mobilization of the entire population of liberated areas in support of the revolutionary struggle. By the time of the Geneva Agreement of 1954, following the French defeat at Dien Bien Phu, Communist forces effectively controlled Hua Phan and Phongsali provinces, a fact acknowledged in the terms of the settlement, which called for their regroupment inside these provinces pending a political settlement. The Pathet Lao used the breathing space and the succession of coalition

⁝ Border essentials: Na Maew-Nam Xoi

Route 6A heads east from Xam Neua to the Vietnamese border at **Na Maew**. The crossing to Nam Xoi in Than Hoa Province, Vietnam, was opened to tourists in April 2004. 15-day Lao visas are usually issued at the border but Vietnamese visas must be obtained in advance from a Vietnamese embassy or consulate.

A truck/*songthaew* leaves Xam Neua for the border at around 0600 daily, 20,000 kip; you can also go via Vieng Xai by tuk-tuk, a reasonably quick trip.

governments in the late 1950s and early 1960s to reorganize their operations. The Lao People's Revolutionary Party was formed at Xam Neua in 1955 and the Neo Lao Hak Sat, or National Front, was established in 1956.

While Party President Prince Souphanouvong spent a good deal of time in Vientiane, participating in successive coalition governments between 1958 and 1964, Secretary-General Kaysone Phomvihane remained in Hua Phan overseeing the political and military organization of the liberated zone. The beginning of the American bombing campaign in 1964 forced the Pathet Lao leadership to find a safe haven from which to direct the war. Vieng Xai was chosen because its numerous limestone karsts contained many natural caves which could be used for quarters, while their proximity to each other inhibited attack from the air. American planes tried to dislodge the Communists from their mountain hideout but, protected in their caves, they survived the onslaught. Nevertheless, phosphorous rockets and napalm caused many casualties in the less fortified caves. After the war, senior members of the Royal Lao Government were sent to re-education camps in the province.

Ins and outs

Getting there Tourists are often put off visiting Hua Phan by the long bus haul to get there but, considering the road passes through gorgeous mountain scenery, the trip is well worth the endeavour. There are three main sealed roads to Xam Neua: Route 6 from the south, linking Xam Neua with Phonsavanh; Route 1 from Vieng Thong and the west, and Road 6A from the Vietnamese border. Due to the upgrading of Route 6, it is now possible to make the journey between Phonsavanh and Xam Neua in a day without an overnight stop in Nam Nouan en route – if you start out early enough. Already, however, a few rainy seasons have taken their toll, so always check on road conditions before setting off. There is an airport at Xam Neua, 3 km from the centre of town on the road to Vieng Xai and Vietnam. However, at the time of publication, all flights were suspended. ▸▸ *For further details, see Transport, page 204.*

Getting around Tourists should exercise caution when travelling independently throughout the province, as some of the authorities harbour a residual suspicion of Westerners and there are very few guides that can speak English. The provincial tourism office is probably the best first port of call, and can organize a car with driver/guide to Vieng Xai caves or Hintang Archaeological Park.

When to visit Summer is pleasant in Xam Neua but temperatures at night reach freezing in winter and you should bring a pullover, even in summer. The area is at its most picturesque in October, when the rice is almost ripe. Mosquitoes are monstrous here, so precautions against malaria are advised (see Health, page 56).

# Xam Neua (Sam Neua) → *Phone code: 064. Colour map 1, B5a.*

🛏🍴🚌🌐 ⤻ *pages 202-204.*

The small capital of Hua Phan Province, Xam Neua is set against a picture-perfect mountain backdrop, amid forested hills and rice fields. The town itself was obliterated during the war and rebuilt after 1973, so it offers little in the way of sights. However, it has a bustling atmosphere, thanks to the many villagers who descend from mountain tops to sell their wares here, and provides visitors with the increasingly rare chance to experience a culturally intact, unspoilt town. It is also a staging post for visiting the caves at Vieng Xai.

Sights

The **market** is a good place to see the province's mixture of cultures and peoples – Hmong, Yao, Tai Dam (Black Tai), Tai Khao (White Tai), Tai Neua (Northern Thai) and other ethnic groups – who can all be found buying and selling various commodities. In the adjoining dry market, examples of the distinctive weaving of Xam Neua and Xam Tai can be found at reasonable prices, along with goods trucked in from China and Vietnam. Loudspeakers in the market area often blast music and propaganda from 0600 in the morning and there is a strong military presence. Archways throughout the town – many of them painted for the 20th anniversary celebrations in 1995 – commemorate the final victory of the Pathet Lao in 1975. The province is known for its **weaving** and many houses in Xam

❖ Walk 1 or 2 km back along Route 6 towards Muang Kham for excellent views of the town and an adjoining valley.

Neua have looms on their verandahs. There are also several workshops with four or five looms each; some of these still use traditional vegetable dyes rather than the aniline (chemical) dyes that are the norm in most other areas.

p# South of Xam Neua

South of Xam Neua are the **Houiyad** falls, located amid undulating hills in a stunning river valley, and surrounded by fields, rice paddies and ethnic minority villages. The falls themselves don't rank highly in the Lao waterfall stakes but make a nice half-day picnic trip from Xam Neua. Nearby **Ban Houaiyad** is renowned for making belts from aluminium gathered from crashed aircrafts, although these days recycled cans are used instead. A few kilometres away are the **Nameuang hot springs** ① *17 km south of Xam Neua, off Route 6; at the junction follow the unpaved road for 3 km, 5,000 kip*, which feature a small bathing pool and six washrooms, three of which have bathtubs. The site is currently managed by local villagers.

Continuing south on Route 6 towards Nam Nouan, the waterfall of **Nam Tok Dat Salari** is visible on the left, 3 km after the village of Ban Doan. The falls are difficult to miss as there are numerous empty houses and stalls by the road, used once a year by the people of Xam Neua for Pi Mai celebrations. A track on the right leads up through the jungle to the top of the falls, a very good swimming and picnic spot.

Sao Hintang

① *Off Route 6, 74 km south of Xam Neua and 36 km north of the junction with Route 1 at Phou Lao. For further information contact the tourist office in Xam Neua. Tours can also be organized from Phonsavanh through Mr Sousath Phetrasy of Maly Hotel (see Sleeping, page 191).*

The beguiling Hintang Archeological Park is located just off Route 6 south of Xam Neua. At the billboard-sized sign in Ban Liang Sat, turn up the dirt road heading east. This road is quite rough in places so you'll need a 4WD car or all-terrain motorbike in order to reach

rfvriantrp

the site in one piece. Three kilometres up the road is a sign for the Kechintang Trail, a 90-minute walking trail that takes you to some of the sites. The first is visible from the road after a further 3 km, with Site two located another 3 km after that.

The park features hundreds of ancient upright stone pillars, menhirs and discs, gathered in Stonehenge-type patterns over a 10-km area, surrounded by jungle. The megoliths have been cut into narrow blades, up to 2 m tall, and stand one behind the other, with the tallest usually in the middle. According to local sources they are at least 1500 years old. Interspersed between the stone sites are burial chambers dug deep into the bedrock. These were originally covered with large stone discs, up to 7 m wide, and could only be accessed via a narrow vertical chimney.

The enigmatic stones are as mysterious as the Plain of Jars: no-one is quite sure who, or even which ethnic group, is responsible for erecting them and they have become steeped in legend. It is believed that the two sites are somehow linked, as they are fashioned from the same stone and share some archaeological similarities. In 1931, the sites were surveyed and partially excavated by an archaeological team, led by Madeleine Colani, although, by this time, the contents of the chambers had already been raided or simply washed away. The exploration uncovered a number of objects – funerary urns, ceremonial stones, bronze bracelets and ceramic pendants – that give credence to the theory that the stone park was an ancient burial site.

While travelling along Route 6 to the park keep your eyes peeled for the numerous roadside **fox-holes**. These small bolt-holes were used as air-raid shelters during the US bombardment of the area. A large number actually expand into large bunkers capable of accommodating 10 or 12 people.

East of Xam Neua

Xam Tai
Hua Phan is supposed to be a 'cradle' of traditional Lao weaving. The province's remoteness means that the diversity of designs produced here is second to none and techniques that have become rare elsewhere are still practised here. The premier centre for weaving is **Xam Tai** (local pronunciation, Xam Teua), 100 km southeast of Xam Neua, close to the Vietnamese border. You can try to charter a pick-up to Xam Tai from the market, or hire a car at the **Lao Houng** hotel, but note that the road is bad and there is no guesthouse at Xam Tai.

Sop Hao
This town, 60 km east of Xam Neua on the Vietnam border, features a trade fair each Saturday but is pretty much a no-go zone for foreigners due to the presence of one of the country's last re-education centres. The border crossing here is only open to Lao and Vietnamese.

Vieng Xai (Viengsay) → Colour map 1, B6. 🅟🅔🅒 ›› pages 202-204.

The village of **Vieng Xai** lies 31 km east of Xam Neua on a road that branches off Route 6 at Km 20. The trip from Xam Neua is possibly one of the country's most picturesque journeys, passing terraces of rice, pagodas, copper- and charcoal-coloured karsk formations, dense jungle with misty peaks and friendly villages dotted among the mountains' curves. Vieng Xai itself is in a stunning setting, very similar to Vang Vieng, with its rocky outcrops and caves, but without the river, 'herb' pizza or usual backpacker hoopla. The area is characterized by lush tropical gardens, a couple of smallish lakes and spectacular limestone karsts, riddled with natural caves that proved crucial in the success of the left-wing insurgency in the 1960s and 1970s.

Although it only takes one day to see the caves, five of which are open to the public, it is worth spending some more time exploring the area. The valley contains many other poignant reminders of the struggle, although there is less obvious war debris here than in Xieng Khouang.

Background

From 1964 onwards, Pathet Lao operations were directed from cave systems at Vieng Xai, which proved an effective refuge from furious bombing attacks. The first bombing raid on the area took place in 1965 and the caves were enlarged and reinforced with concrete during 1965, 1966 and 1967 to create living quarters, offices, garages, supply depots, hospitals, schools and ammunition dumps. At the height of the war, thousands of soldiers, government officials and their families occupied the valley at Vieng Xai and more operated from the surrounding region. Previously, the valley had been home only to two small villages, Ban Bac and Nakay. The Pathet Lao leadership renamed the area Vieng Xai, meaning 'City of Victory' and it became the administrative and military hub of the revolutionary struggle. In the run-up to the fall of Vientiane, there was even talk among the Pathet Lao leadership of making Vieng Xai an alternative capital but this idea was dropped after 1975.

A conservation survey of the area in 1982 identified over 95 caves of historical significance alone. Included in these was a former hospital complex approximately 15 km from Vieng Xai and a school for children of government officials at Ban Bac. A separate cave complex at Hang Long, 25 km from Xam Neua, housed the provincial government during the war years but is now completely abandoned. Other caves, called 'Embassy Caves', were intended for VIPs from other countries, with individual caves set aside for Russia, Vietnam, Cuba and China. Locals make unsubstantiated suggestions that King Sihanouk from Cambodia also spent a long time hiding out in Vieng Xai during the war.

Vieng Xai village

Built in 1973, when the bombing finally stopped and the short-lived Provisional Government of National Union was negotiated, the former capital of the liberated zone is an unlikely sight: surrounded by rice fields at the dead end of a potholed road, it features street lighting, power lines, sealed and kerbed streets and substantial public buildings – all in varying stages of decay.

Just before the market and truck stop, a wonderful socialist-realist statue in gold-painted concrete pays tribute to those three pillars of the revolution: the farmer, the soldier and the worker; the worker has one boot firmly planted on a bomb inscribed 'USA'. Behind this statue is a **small museum**, which contains some interesting old photographs, many of them unlabelled. Few of the guides seem to know about the museum, so make a point of asking to visit it.

The main street divides as it reaches the top of the village to form a town 'square' which is in fact a triangle. At the apex is a war monument topped by a red star, while at the southern end is a yellow two-storey building housing government offices; the cave tourist office is next door. Follow the road past this building to the caves of Kaysone and Nouhak; go right to reach Khamtai's cave and what was once a recreation area; the road along the northern edge of the 'square' leads to the caves of Souphanouvong and Phoumi. All the caves are within walking distance of the village. Visitors have to buy tickets, 10,000 kip, from the **Kaysone Memorial Cave Tour Office** ⓘ *on the left-hand side of the government building, T020-765194, 0900-1630 daily*; contact Mr Siphon. Officials may insist you take an attendant with you, which isn't a bad idea as the history of the caves is just as interesting as the sites themselves. Expect to pay around US$5 for a guide (depending on the number of people). On public holidays you can buy tickets at the entrance to the caves. The caves have been fitted with electric bulbs but you may find a torch useful.

There is a fairly spectacular **waterfall**, 8 km before Vieng Xai. About 3 km after the turn-off from Route 6, a swift stream passes under a steel and concrete bridge. A path just before the bridge leads off to the left, following the river downstream. It takes just a few minutes to reach the top of the waterfall, but the path leads all the way to the bottom, about 20 minutes' walk. Swimming is not advised.

Vieng Xai caves

The caves of Vieng Xai, like the Cu Chi tunnels in Vietnam, show the ingenuity of the Pathet Lao in outsmarting relentless US bombing raids. At present the site is rundown, having had virtually no maintenance since 1976, but moves have been underway to restore it since Kaysone's death in 1992 and some preliminary work has been done under the auspices of the Kaysone Memorial Fund. Five **caves**, formerly occupied by senior Pathet Lao leaders (Prince Souphanouvong, Kaysone Phomvihane, Nouhak Phounsavanh, Khamtai Siphandon and Phoumi Vongvichit) are officially open to tourists but further work, scheduled for 2006, should result in another two or three caves being opened to the public.

The setting is a delight, with crags jutting vertically from fields of snooker-table green. The caves themselves have a magic, secretive, Garden of Eden feel about them, with fruit trees, sweet smelling frangipani and colourful gardens decorating the exteriors.

Each cave burrows deep into the mountainside and all of them feature 60-cm-thick concrete walls, encompassing living quarters, meeting rooms, offices, dining and storage areas. All but Khamtai's cave have an outside kitchen and at least two exits. Each cave also contains a centrally located 'emergency room', installed in case of a gas attack or similar eventuality. This consists of a fully sealed concrete bunker with room for 10 to 20 people, in the corner of which can be found the remains of a hand-cranked oxygen pump of Soviet manufacture. Below and outside the entrance to each cave, buildings house additional accommodation and meeting rooms. The occupants of the caves actually slept in these buildings, as raids rarely took place at night. Until recently the original furniture and other items, including books, maps and papers, remained in the caves but since restoration work began, most of the furniture has been removed, leaving the caves relatively bare.

There are also many abandoned caves around Vieng Xai which were obviously used during the war and at least one, on the left past Phoumi's cave, is quite extensive. However, the attitude of local authorities and the risk of unexploded bombs means you should not be tempted to fossick about in them.

Tham Than Souphanouvong

A mossy path flanked by large grapefruit trees leads to the cave home of Prince Souphanouvong, the 'Red Prince' and son of the Queen of Luang Prabang. To the right of the path, stands a pink stupa, the tomb of the prince's son, who was captured and beaten to death by infiltrators a few kilometres away in 1967 at the age of 28. Watch your head at the far entrance of the cave, as rocks have been known to fall from time to time. Below the cave is an attendant's room, with an ancient black and white photograph of Souphanouvong and Khruschev stuck to the wall. The next building contains a makeshift memorial to the prince decorated with a few dusty souvenirs from the USSR. Souphanouvong and Phoumi's caves both feature a 'garage cave' at the base of the karst, a cavity in the limestone large enough to accommodate a car.

Tham Tham Kaysone

Kaysone Phomvihane's cave is reached by mossy steps cut into the cliff face and extends over 100 m. The cavern is surrounded by blossoming bushes and large frangipani trees.

The cave's construction started sometime prior to 1963 but Kaysone and his followers didn't move in until 1964. About 10 people lived in the cave: Kaysone, his children, a doctor, intelligence officer, cook and bodyguards, but Kaysone's wife relocated to Yunnan, China, at the start of the war, where she was head of a school; these days she lives in Vientiane. Kaysone rarely left the cave and only allowed the most important of visitors inside, mostly other Communist leaders. The Americans knew of Kaysone's whereabouts but were unable directly to attack the cave or infiltrate it, due to its position and to the large number of Pathet Lao soldiers mounted on the summit. The cave remained Kaysone's official residence until 1973, when he relocated to the building in front of the cave. In 1975 he moved to Vientiane.

Like the other caves, this one has a suite of rooms, including a bedroom, meeting room and library. A few of Kaysone's books are on display, including, not surprisingly works by Marx, Engels, Ho Chi Minh and an economic text from Vietnam. There are also a few gifts from foreign dignitaries, such as a framed picture of Che Guevara courtesy of Fidel Castro, a lacquer-ware vase from Vietnam and a bust of Lenin. An interesting feature of the cave is a long, narrow passage, which connects the living quarters to a large meeting area and emergency accommodation for dozens of guests. In true Lao style a large bomb crater at the front of the cave was ingeniously filled with cement and turned into a lavish swimming pool (now empty).

Tham Than Khamtai

Khamtai's cave is slightly different to the others. The first thing the visitor notices is a set of three bomb craters within metres of the entrance. The craters, now overgrown, are so close together they almost touch. Possibly inspired by their arrival, the entrance is shielded by an enormous, tapering slab of concrete, 4½ m high and nearly 2 m wide at the base. Inside, the cave is darker and more claustrophobic than the others, with no outside areas. Deep inside the cave, at the bottom of some stairs, the attendant may lead you through a thick steel door, which gives access to a steeply descending staircase, ending in a sheer drop of several metres to the floor of a small underground theatre. A long-ish tunnel, featuring a number of stalactites and lit by daylight, runs from here to the far larger theatre cave of Tham Xang Lot.

Tham Xang Lot

A small distance from Khamtai's cave is the large and obvious entrance to **Tham Xang Lot**, or the 'cave that an elephant can walk through'. Formerly used as an enclosure to keep animals such as elephants and monkeys, this natural cavern was converted into a theatre during the war, complete with stage, arch, orchestra pit and a concrete floor with space for an audience of several hundred. It is hard to imagine now, but this damp, dark area once entertained numerous dancers, symphonies, circuses and foreign dignitaries from Romania, Bulgaria, Vietnam and China who would pop in for a boogie. As one local recalls: "I snuck in for a look and an orchestra was playing. I got so excited but was trying to contain myself because I was worried that the grenade in my pocket would go off." At times up to 2,000 soldiers were hidden in the two caves.

West on Route 1 🚌🚌 ▸▸ *pages 202-204.*

Nam Nouan

The junction of Routes 1 and 6 is known as **Phou Lao**; just to the south is the larger settlement of Nam Nouan. Now that Route 6 between Xam Neua and Nam Nouan has been upgraded, it is no longer necessary to stay in Nam Nouan en route to or from Phonsavanh. However, if you're heading to or from Muang Ngoi, you will probably have to spend a night either here or in Vieng Thong, three hours to the west. As of 2005, Route 1 between Nam Nouan and Vieng Thong was being upgraded.

Vieng Thong, also known as Muang Hiam, lies 158 km west of Xam Neua on Route 1 and is a reasonable stopover for those journeying to or from Nong Khiaw. The town itself has little to offer but the surrounding area is nothing short of spectacular and improved access in the near future should enable tourists to sample its attractions. The Nam Khan flows through the town, straight from Luang Prabang, so it's rather annoying that no tour operators have yet capitalized on what could be an amazing journey between the two areas.

✦ Surrounding Vieng Thong are numerous ethnic minority villages, mostly Hmong.

Close to town are the Vieng Thong **hot springs** ① *cross the bridge, turn right and walk for 1 km, ask locals along the way, 5000 kip*, which offer great respite from what can be quite a tiring journey. There's a decent bathing area and washrooms are available.

Nam Et/Phou Loei NPA

Just 10 km beyond Vieng Thong is Laos's largest protected area, the Nam Et/Phou Loei National Protected Area. Camera trap studies conducted in recent years by the Wildlife Conservation Society have discovered a vast array of large mammals here, including tiger, guar, bear, leopard, macaque, wild pig and deer. The NPA also contains a couple of impressive caves that have piqued archaeologists' interests. The cavern of **Tham Han** is 20 km north of Vieng Thong, towards the Vietnamese border. A swift 20-minute stroll, following the road along the Nam Neun, will bring you to this river cave, which stretches a considerable distance into the hillside and leads to a village on the far side. It can also reportedly be accessed by boat (if there are any around).

✦ Don't try to venture into the caves without a guide who has good local knowledge.

Ban Secock, a small village 40 km west of Vieng Thong, is the place to go if you want to trek to the stunning Phou Loei waterfall, which should take around two hours. In the future it is hoped that there will be organized treks to Phou Loei, the second highest peak in Laos.

For the time being this area remains undeveloped, particularly from a tourism perspective. There aren't any major ecotourism operators running tours through the NPA yet although there are concerted efforts to get something up and running in the near future. In 2005 roads were being upgraded to improve access to the sites within the protected area.

● Sleeping

Xam Neua *p197, map p203*

D **Boun Home**, in the lane around the corner from Shuliyo, T064-312223. Newish guesthouse, with very clean rooms, private bathrooms and hot showers. One of the best deals going. Highly recommended.

D **Kheam Xam Guesthouse**, on the corner by the river, T064-312111. Large twin rooms across 3 floors, excellent views from top balcony, shared hot shower and toilet, tiled floors, good restaurant downstairs. Drawback? Management can be very rude so best avoided.

D **Outhaithany Guesthouse**, T064-312121, F064-312414, opposite the airport, a few km out of town. Reasonably sized, rustic

bungalows, popular with tour groups. Great restaurant with fantastic views.

D **Shuliyo**, about 100 m from the bus station. A new addition with very lovely owners. Clean rooms, exceptionally comfortable beds, sparsely but nicely decorated, en suite bathroom with squat toilet. Recommended.

D-E **Lao Houng**, next to the bridge over the Nam Xam facing the market, T064-312018. There are 28 fairly grotty rooms, some with en suite bathrooms, with Western toilet and hot shower. The communal bathrooms are dirty, with squat toilets and scoop baths. There is a pleasant view of the town and hills from upstairs, the staff are friendly and one of the girls speaks good English but there are much better deals around.

E-F Phanhsam Guesthouse, on the main road near the bus and truck stop, T064-312255. Vietnamese establishment offering small, cell-like concrete rooms. Grungy bedding, shared bath, squat toilet, hot shower.

F Phatpuosay, just round the corner from the bus station, T064-312942. Rundown guesthouse, with smallish rooms and shared bathroom. Bit grubby.

Vieng Xai *p198*
Most visitors to Vieng Xai and the caves stay in Xam Neua and make a day trip out here. But there is accommodation if required.

E-F Swampside Guesthouse, on the lake behind the statue. Basic and not very clean. Dorm rooms and outside toilet.

F Naxay Guesthouse, near the caves, T064-314336. Wooden blue guesthouse set in quite a pretty garden. Basic accommodation, with mosquito nets and shared facilities. The most popular option.

F Viengsay Guesthouse, follow the road that leads to Khamtai's cave but turn left at the football field; the hotel is the first building on the left, T020-5881305. The hotel is the mouldering remnant of what were once comfortable quarters for visiting

dignitaries. The big Communist edifice is extremely rundown but still offers a few threadbare comforts, such as silk bedspreads and tea-sets in some rooms, evoking past splendour. Doubles and triples available, ask for an upstairs room, shared bathroom. Basic restaurant attached, with food, beer and cigarettes available. Electricity 24 hrs. The ramshackle building has a disturbing history as a re-education centre but its setting is superb, amid eucalyptus and Norfolk Island pines, with views of surrounding karsts.

Nam Nouan *p201*
This isn't the nicest place to stay but if you find yourself stuck here overnight, **Nam Nouan Guesthouse**, signposted with a small blue sign just near the row of restaurants, would suffice.

Vieng Thong *p202*
Vieng Thong has 3 below-average guesthouses, all with shared facilities, in the 20,000-30,000 kip range. **Souksavan** is probably the pick of the bunch. There are a few local restaurants and *feu* stalls.

🍴 Eating

Xam Neua *p197, map p203*
Two pieces of advice when it comes to eating in Xam Neua: first, all the restaurants in Xam Neua display their menus in Lao script on white boards but they usually have an English menu tucked away somewhere, so ask to see it; second, beware of power cuts as you will not find any place to cook food for love nor money.

🍴 **Dan Xam Muang**, a block back from the river. Reasonably clean restaurant offering mostly Asian interpretations and a few quasi Western dishes. Very attentive, friendly service but 9 times out of 10 your order will be mixed up, so make sure you're very clear.

🍴 **Joy's Place**. This is the best of many noodle shops in the market area along the street adjacent to the river.

🍴 **Mitsamphan**, opposite Boun Home Guesthouse, T064-312151. This place seems pretty accustomed to tourists and has an English menu. Staff can understand English. Quick service, good food, recommended.

🍴 **Sam Neua May**. Delicious fried noodles but very rarely has any food.

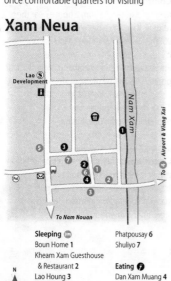

Xam Neua

Sleeping 🛏

Boun Home **1**

Kheam Xam Guesthouse
 & Restaurant **2**

Lao Houng **3**

Outhaithany
 Guesthouse **4**

Phanhsam Guesthouse **5**

Phatpousay **6**

Shuliyo **7**

Eating 🍴

Dan Xam Muang **4**

Joy's Place **1**

Mitsamphan **2**

Sam Neua May **3**

N

Not to scale

There is also a good *feu*/coffee shop on the corner opposite the bus station.

Vieng Xai *p198*
There are a few noodle shops on the main street opposite the post office and in the market. **Nang Sang Jan Restaurant**, near the lake/swamp as you enter town, serves tasty *feu* and coffee. No English spoken but very helpful and friendly.

◎ Transport

Xam Neua *p197, map p203*
Bus/truck
Buses and trucks currently leave from the market area, although the bus station is likely to move out of town in 2006. There are regular services during the morning and early afternoon to **Vieng Xai**, 60-90 mins, 10,000 kip; there are virtually no services after 1500. *Songthaew* to **Nam Nouan**, 0600 daily, 3-4 hrs on an excellent road; from Nam Nouan there are daily connections to Phonsavanh, 6 hrs, and, less regularly, to Muang Ngoi. *Songthaew* depart at 0700 for **Vieng Thong**, 6-7 hrs, 30,000 kip or catch the bus to Vientiane at 0730. To **Phonsavanh**, 0900 and 1200 daily, up to 10 hrs, 60,000 kip. An additional service to Phonsavanh at 0730 is scheduled to continue on to **Vientiane**, about 100,000 kip, but this is unreliable. To **Luang Prabang**, usually around 0800 daily, 60,000 kip.

Motorbike hire
You can charter motorbikes from the market for US$15 per day. *Songthaew* will make the trip to **Vieng Xai** for US$15-20. It is obvious that most *songthaew* riders aren't used to tourists as they will initially try to charge a small fortune for the trip and aren't very open to negotiation.

Tuk-tuk
A tuk-tuk to **Nameuang hot springs** should cost US$15 return; to **Vieng Xai**, 31 km, 50 min, 15,000-20,000 kip per person.

Vieng Xai *p198*
Pick-ups and passenger trucks run from in front of the market in Vieng Xai to **Xam Neua** regularly until 1500, 60-90 mins, around 10,000 kip. It will cost around 200,000 kip to charter a pick-up if you miss the last truck back to Xam Neua. It's a better option to charter a vehicle in Xam Neua for a whole day trip to Vieng Xai.

Vieng Thong *p202*
The so-called public transport system is a bit hit and miss. The intersection near the market is the best place to catch a bus or truck east to **Xam Neua**, 158 km, 5-6 hrs, 30,000 kip, or west to **Nong Khiaw**, 175 km , 3-4 hrs, 20,000 kip, and **Luang Prabang**, 30,000 kip. Route 1 west from Vieng Thong is rough but was being upgraded in 2005. Some tourists have reported that this trip is impossible during the rainy season but this should change once the road has been completed.

◑ Directory

Xam Neua *p197, map p203*
Banks The Lao Development Bank will change Thai ฿, US$ and Chinese ¥ into kip but will only accept TCs in US$.
Communications Internet at 500 kip per min is available from a house near the temple. Xam Neua has a **post office**, open 0800-1100 and 1300-1600 Mon-Fri, but it's best to wait until you are in either Phonsavanh or Luang Prabang. International phone calls can be made from **Lao Telecom**, behind the post office, 0800-1100 and 1300-1600 daily; prices vary widely depending on the destination.

Vieng Xai *p198*
Communications There's a **post office** in town by the market but don't bother sending any mail from here. The police station is behind the disused department store on the town square.

Central Provinces

⁝ Footprint features

Introduction

Laos's central provinces, sandwiched between the Mekong (and Thailand) to the west and the Annamite mountains (and Vietnam) to the east, are the least visited in the country. Travellers entering Laos from Vietnam cross the border via Lak Xao or Xepon but few choose to linger for long. This is a shame because the scenery here is stunning, with dramatic limestone karsts, enormous caves, beautiful rivers and forests. In particular, the upland areas to the east, off Route 8 and Route 12, are a veritable treasure trove of attractions, mottled with scores of caves, lagoons, rivers and rock formations. Tourists will require some determination in these parts, as the infrastructure around here is still being developed, although a lot of new roads are planned to coincide with the construction of the Nam Theun II Dam. The Mekong towns of Thakhek and Savannakhet are also elegant and relaxed.

★ Don't miss...

1 **Travelling overland to Vietnam** Catch a bus across the Annamite Mountains on Route 8 via Lak Xao or Route 9 via Lao Bao, pages 209 and 230.
2 **Boat trip to Tham Kong Lor** Travel along the Nam Hinboun river through awe-inspiring Kong Lor cave, page 209.
3 **That Sikhot** Take a tuk-tuk to one of Laos's holiest sites, where Chao Sikhot is said to have come to a grisly end, page 215.
4 **The caves off Route 12** Head east from Thakhek to explore underground caverns in the limestone landscape, page 216.

Central Provinces

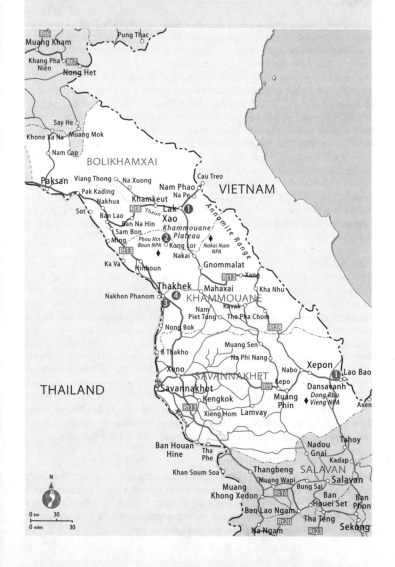

Paksan to Lak Xao → *Phone code: 054.*

East of Paksan the adventurous visitor can encounter some of county's most stunning landscapes. This little known region contains a maze of limestone karst peaks, studded with thousands of caves, a beautiful river and pristine jungle. Kong Lor cave, the principal tourist attraction in this area, smacks of Lord of the Rings, with the river cave running straight through the centre of a mountain. ➨ *For Sleeping, Eating and other listings, see pages 212-214.*

Paksan (Paxsan) and around → *Colour map 2, B4.*
🖥🔌❄🚌 ➨ *pages 212-214.*

In the mid-1990s people used to stop in Paksan to break the journey south (or north) but, now that road upgrading has shortened the journey between Vientiane and Thakhek to a bearable five to six hours, the town's one purpose in life, for most tourists, has been rendered obsolete. However, you might just find yourself stranded here on your way to Vientiane from the Vietnamese border at Lak Xao. It is possible that Paksan will regain its significance when – and if – proposed Route 22 is upgraded, making it possible to reach Xieng Khouang, Phonsavanh and the Plain of Jars. However, this has been on the planner's desk for over a decade now and seems no closer to realization. There are other potential visitor draws, however, in the shape of **Wat Prah Bat**, an important pilgrimage site for Lowland Lao. Built in 1933, the stupa boasts a footprint of the Buddha as well as one of the largest drums in Laos. Overlooking the Mekong is the more modern **Phonsane Temple**, which isn't anything spectacular in itself but has become famous for its annual Naga Fireball Festival (see Festivals and events, page 213). And for those travellers who feel all 'templed out', there are also several opportunities to explore the province's natural heritage by boat, canoe or kayak 50 km east of Paksan, where the **Nam Kading** river flows into the Mekong.

Pak Kading
Pak Kading is a small whistle-stop of a town at the mouth of the Nam Kading. Many commentators slate it as the next major ecotourism centre but it's not quite ready for the hordes yet: there aren't really any tours set up and it's very difficult to arrange transport; the best option is to charter your own boat. The picturesque Nam Kading is known as a local fishery goldmine and is one of the most pristine rivers in the country. A worthwhile boat trip travels upstream through the Nam Kading NPA to **Nam Tok Taat Wang Fong**, a pretty, undulating set of small rapids spectacularly set in a small valley flanked by primary jungle and steep hills. The trip takes three hours there and back and boatmen wait at the boat landing at the south end of town, US$20, bargaining required.

Alternatively you can pick up a boat 15 km east of town to **Ban Phonsi**, where there are signposts advertising the boat trips. There are a few good restaurants on the main road through Ban Phonsi, as it has developed into a bit of a truck stop.

Ban Lao (Vieng Kham/Tham Beng)
Sitting at the junction of Route 13 and 8 is the small settlement of Ban Lao. The town's folk aren't quite sure of the official name, which creates a lot of confusion, but it seems Ban Lao is the safest bet (try Vieng Kham or Tham Beng if Ban Lao pulls a blank). The settlement is pretty nondescript and only noteworthy for its position at the western end of Route 8 to Kong Lor cave and Lak Xao.

East on Route 8 🚌🚐 ▸▸ *pages 212-214.*

After leaving the north-south Route 13, take Route 8 east towards Lak Xao. This road leads into the hills, with tremendous views over a karst landscape of pinnacles, cones and a patchwork of forest. Big charcoal grey, jagged rocks cut through the surrounding jungle, conjuring a somewhat daunting, gothic fairytale images. Two-thirds of the way to Ban Na Hin on the right-hand side look out for **Phu Phu Man Limestone Forest**, a cluster of sharp limestone pillars, saw-toothing across the country-side. There is a a small look out where you can stop; most *songthaew* passengers won't mind if you stop for a minute to take a picture.

Ban Na Hin (Khoun Kham)
Ban Na Hin is a real end-of-the-earth town, low on the charm front and redeemed only by the phenomenal landscapes surrounding it. Its two main *raisons d'etre* are as a centre for the Nam Theun dam operations and as a transit point for Kong Lor cave to the south; the settlement is also known as Khoun Kham – the 'Gateway to Kong Lor'. Ban Na Hin has quite a big market where you can pick up fresh fruit and vegetables, bread and other supplies; if you haven't got a torch, it's a good idea to pick one up here. There are also a few cheap *feu* shops dotted around the market's periphery.

There isn't a whole lot here but just outside of town is **Namsanam waterfall**. Take the signposted path on the left-hand side of Route 8, beside a colourful monastery. The trek to the falls is roughly 3 km through quite pleasant surroundings. The two-tiered, 70-m-tall falls are stunning and flow year round. There are reputed to be wild elephants in the area but the likelihood of seeing one is next to nil. Apparently local guides do exist but you will probably find the waterfall before you find a guide.

Towards Tham Kong Lor
The first stage of the journey is by *songthaew* or tractor from Ban Na Hin to **Ban Napur**. (For details of this route by motorbike, see page 218.) From Ban Napur catch a boat along the Nam Hinboun to either **Ban Phonyang**, where ecolodge **Sala Hinboun** is located (see Sleeping, page 212), or to **Ban Kong Lor**, the closest village to the caves, where you can find a homestay for 50,000 kip, including food. The boat trip from Ban Napur to Ban Phonyang is fascinating, with excellent views of impressive limestone cliffs along the way and classic riverside scenes with people fishing and bathing. Take some padding for your bum as the wooden seats, even if they are cushioned, can be a bit uncomfortable. There are also reputed to be homestays at Ban Natan on the other side of Kong Lor.

> ⁘ *It is almost impossible to do the 9- to 10-hour return trip from Ban Na Hin to Kong Lor in a day, as boat drivers won't travel in the dark.*

Some people have reportedly trekked from Ban Na Hin to Ban Kong Lor (47 km) but there isn't much shade and you will need to bring loads of water, as there isn't anywhere to stock up until you reach Ban Phonyang. Some have suggested hitching a ride with a local tractor for the first 20 km as it is quite boring. The river trip is still undoubtedly the most scenic route. ▸▸ *For further details, see Transport, page 213.*

Tham Kong Lor (Kong Lor cave) → *Do not miss this!*
ⓘ *Boat trip from Ban Phonyang 2-3 hrs return, including a brief stop at Ban Natan on the other side of the mountain. Boat costs US$10-20 for up to 3 passengers; this usually includes the entrance fee, 3000 kip.*

Kong Lor cave is one hour upstream from Ban Phonyang and the boat trip is gorgeous, with small fish skipping out of the water, languid buffalo bathing, kids taking a dip and ducks floating by – all surrounding by breathtaking cliffs and rocky outcrops. The rocks look like a Picasso painting: odd bits and pieces jig-sawed together to create the most surreal of landscapes.

The Mlabri – spirits of the yellow leaves

The elusive Mlabri 'tribe', which occupies the forests around Lak Xao as well as parts of Thailand, represents one of the few remaining groups of hunter gatherers in Southeast Asia. They are also known as the Phi Tong Luang or 'Spirits of the Yellow Leaves'; when their shelters of rattan and banana leaves turn yellow they take this as a sign from the spirits that it is time to move on. Traditionally the Mlabri hunted using spears. If they were stalking larger game, they would brace the weapon against the ground, rather than throwing it, and allow the charging animal to impale itself on the point. In this way, the Mlabri were able to kill the great saladang wild buffalo (Bos gaurus), as well as bears and tigers. Smaller game was more common, however, and this was supplemented with tubers, nuts, honey and other forest products to provide a balanced diet.

Many of the Mlabri's traditions are already on the verge of extinction. The destruction of the forest means that the Mlabri have been forced to lead more sedentary lives, turning to settled agriculture in place of hunting and gathering, while inter-marriage with other tribes is reducing their number. Perhaps this is no bad thing: as recently as the 1980s, a Mlabri was displayed in a cage in a Bangkok department store. Today, many of the few Mlabri that remain have been forced to become cheap labourers for groups such as the Hmong.

The cave itself can only be described as sensational and, at 6 km in length, it is so large that no-one should suffer from claustrophobia. It is named after the drum makers who, once upon a time, were believed to make their instruments here. (It's hard to imagine with the current waterway surging through the grotto.) Another more believable theory is that the cave is named after the constant drum beat of bombs falling. The Nam Hinboun river has tunnelled through the mountain, creating a giant rocky cave, 90 m wide and 100 m high, which opens out into the blinding bright light at Ban Natan on the other side, an amazing river valley flanked by large limestone cliffs. Fisherman will often come into the cave to try their luck as it is believed that 20-kg fish lurk below the surface.

Tham Natan is another enormous cave set in this remote countryside, requiring a 4x4 and a good guide to find it.

At the start of the cave, you will have to scramble over some boulders while the boatmen carry the canoe over the rapids, so wear comfortable shoes with a good grip. A torch or, better, a head-lamp (2000 kip at Thakhek market), is also recommended. It is eerie travelling through the dark, cool cave, with water splashing and bats circulating. There are a few miniscule rapids inside and the cave's surface is bumped with nooks and crannies, crevices and holes. About two-thirds of the way through the cave is an impressive collection of stalagmites and stalactites.

It is possible to continue downstream into the awesome Hinboun gorge. This is roughly 14 km long and, for much of the distance, vertical cliffs over 300 m high rise directly from the water on both sides. The discovery of some valuable religious documents indicates the historical significance of the gorge both during the Vietnamese War and much earlier. There is no white water but the river frequently flows quite fast. More impressive scenery then follows until the village of **Paktuk**, close to Route 13 where any journey can be continued.

West of Kong Lor, in the beautiful **Pathene valley**, a visit to the rickety **Phontiou tin mine** is fascinating, but not encouraged by the Korean manager. A few kilometres past the mine, open panning is done by the local people, mainly of Vietnamese origin.

⁞ Border essentials: Nam Phao-Cau Treo

The border is 20 km east of Lak Xao at **Nam Phao** and has been a legal crossing point since September 1997. The Vietnamese border town is **Cau Treo** (30 km, one hour from Lak Xao). There are buses to the border from Vientiane (via Paksan, see page 213) as well as regular transport from Lak Xao (see page 213). The border is open 0800 to 1700 and the official exit fee is 3,000 kip, although the Lao border officials are quite lacksadaisical. Be prepared for slow service around lunchtime and an overtime fee at weekends. You need to organize Vietnamese visas in advance (ideally in Vientiane) as they aren't issued at the border. Crossing into Vietnam can induce culture shock as you will be descended upon by a gang of 'sharks', trying to extort ridiculous amounts for mini-van/bus services to Vinh (reports of up to US$30!). Take your time to bargain for the right price (US$6-7 is reasonable), rather than rushing your travel arrangements. Arriving from Vietnam, 15-day Lao visas are issued at the border (US$30).

They are allowed to sell their tin to the Phontiou mine and receive about 5000 kip per kg. At the head of the valley a great limestone amphitheatre houses more caves.

Lak Xao (Lac Sao) → *Colour map 2, B5.*  ⟩⟩ *pages 212-214.*

Lak Xao is a new town. It was established by the army's Bolisat Phathana Khet Phoudoi (BPKP or Mountainous Area Development Company) back in 1968 in a remote and sparsely populated area close to the border with Vietnam, and still retains a frontier atmosphere. It is sometimes called Muang Kham Keut, which is confusing because there is another Kham Keut, 30 km to the west of town. (This was the original settlement and is worth a visit as it is over 500 years old.) The surrounding countryside is beautiful but Lak Xao itself has little to recommend it, except that it provides a necessary break on the journey overland to Vietnam.

This part of Laos was once one of the richest in terms of wildlife. Unfortunately, you only have to look around the town to see that it's also a major logging centre, with big bulky timber trucks rumbling through to Vietnam. It is believed that Lak Xao was once a mini fiefdom controlled by an old, Lao general, who logged the town into oblivion. Another threat to the forests and fauna is the area's great hydropower potential. Many fear that the controversial **Nam Theun II** dam project will open up the region to yet more loggers and settlers. Construction of the dam has been monitored by a hawk-eyed bunch of consultants and it was rumoured that, if even one fish species were to become extinct as a result of the dam-building efforts, then the World Bank and other financiers would pull the funds. The **Lak Xao Wildlife Centre** used to operate in the town, trying to protect animals displaced by the logging and dam construction. Unfortunately the centre has now closed and an assortment of wildlife is now to be found for sale at the market stalls: monkeys, reptiles, frogs and basically anything else the locals can get their hands on.

⁞ *In the distance looms a line of cliffs, the last of which is known locally as Pa Pi Hai – the 'Ghost that Cries'.*

The local army of tuk-tuk drivers is also worth mentioning as a breed apart. The town's wild west atmosphere seems to have gone to their heads, so it's a question of holding on to your hats and your wallets, too, as they will probably do their level best to fleece you.

Paksan *p208*

Accommodation seems insufficient, given the number of backpackers passing through the town.

D-E **B&K Guesthouse**, across the river, on the 1st road on the right, T054-212638. The friendly owners of this establishment speak very good English, and with clean rooms and en suite bathrooms, it's worth a try. Has a very good restaurant attached.

F **Paksan Phattana Hotel** (better known as the **Phou Doi**), 1 km south of the bus station, Route 13. Simple rooms with shared bathrooms and a/c. Clean but some of the rooms have leaky roofs and lots of peep-holes.

Ban Lao *p208*

If you get stuck en route there are 2 guesthouses on Route 13, just past the Route 8 intersection, which, by and large, are better than those found at Ban Na Hin.

D-E **Bunthieng Guesthouse**, on the righthand side of Route 13. Reasonable accommodation, with basic furnishings.

F **Vieng Thong**, on the left-hand side of the road. Quite big rooms with fan.

Ban Na Hin *p209*

You may need to stay either here or in Ban Lao for 1 night if you are trying to make your way back quickly from Kong Lor cave. Accommodation is of a 'rustic' nature – to put it very, very nicely.

E **SP Guesthouse**. A wooden house, smack-bang in the centre of town. It's a little lacklustre, but the big verandahs are quite nice, US$4.

E **Xok Sai**, Route 8 before the village, T054-233629. The better of the 2 guesthouses, nicely isolated from the town. Simple rooms, with shared facilities.

Towards Tham Kong Lor *p209*

B-C **Sala Hinboun**, Ban Phonyang, T051-214315, 8 km from Kong Lor cave. A scenic location, set on the river banks amongst karst rock formations. 10 rooms in 2 bungalows – well equipped and very pleasant. The river view bungalows are more expensive, US$23. Mr Kham, the manager, is very helpful and will arrange a boat to pick you from Napua US$25, with advance notice. A tour to Kong Lor for 2-3 people is US$30 with picnic lunch. Discounts in the low season.

E **Bounhome Homestay**, Ban Kong Lor. Three rooms with shared facilities, rates include food.

E **Sala Kong Lor Lodge**, 1.5 km from Kong Lor cave, T051-214315. Four small huts with twin bed (US$4) and a couple of rooms in a building. There is also a campsite for US$2 per night.

Lak Xao *p211*

There are now several relatively pleasant places to stay in Lak Xao.

D **Phoutthavong Guesthouse** , T054-341074. Spotless rooms with a/c or fans, tiled floor, polished wooden furniture and wonderfully white paintwork that is at odds with the dusty atmosphere of the town. Recommended.

D **Souriya Hotel** , T054-341111. Another pleasant alternative with 20 spotlessly clean, simple rooms (some a/c) with TV and some baths (hot water). Friendly owner speaks quite good English.

D **Vongsouda Guesthouse**, T054-341035. Quite a nice guesthouse with a/c and en suite bathrooms with Western loos and hot water. Not the most comfortable mattresses in the world but rooms are clean and serviceable. Clean and airy lobby but the real selling point is the large verandah outside the main entrance where you can sit and relax with a drink. Motorbike hire (US$15).

D-E **Phoudoi Hotel**, Route 8B, 4 km out of the main town. A range of rooms for varying budgets in 3 buildings. A stone's throw from the bus station, so there's no need to deliver yourself into the unscrupulous hands of the tuk-tuk drivers.

● **Eating**

Paksan *p208*

There are many small restaurants along the main drag. Few have English menus and most are of poor quality and not particularly cheap. One alternative is **Tavendang Saysane Restaurant**, on the waterfront, which serves good Lao and Thai food.

⁞ Border essentials: Paksan-Beung Kan

The Thai border is 2 km from Paksan on the Mekong, where there's a small port and immigration office, open 0800-1200 and 1330-1630 daily. Fifteen-day Lao visas are available here, US$30. Boats to

Beung Kan on the Thai side leave when they are full, ฿25, usually every half an hour.

From Beung Kan there are regular onward buses to both Udon Thani and Bangkok.

Ban Lao *p208*
There is a small market at the intersection, with several *feu* restaurants.

Lak Xao *p211*
🍴 **Only One Restaurant**, 200 m from Phoutthayong Guesthouse, on the same side of the road. Plenty of tables in a pleasant, if unextraordinary, setting. Reasonable Vietnamese and Lao food, open 0600-2200 daily.

❊ Festivals and events

Paksan *p208*
Every year, usually in **Jul**, Wat Prah Bat hosts a full moon festival. More famous is the Naga Fireball Festival (**Bang Fai Phayanuk**) at Phonsane Temple in **mid Oct** (movable), when small, colourful fireballs shoot out of the river.

⊖ Transport

Paksan *p208*
Bus
The bus stop is next to the Morning Market. To **Vientiane**, 0600, 0700, 0800, 0900, 1030, 1100 and 1330 daily, 1-2 hrs, 15,000 kip. In the other direction, most buses from Vientiane to southern destinations ply through the town every couple of hours, so it's just a matter of waiting at the bus stop/market to pick up a lift: to **Thakhek**, 190 km, 4-5 hrs, 15,000 kip; to **Savannakhet**, 25,000 kip. To reach the Vietnam border at **Nam Phao** (see Border essentials, page 209), catch one of the border-bound buses that starts from the southern terminal in Vientiane (see page 94) or travel by pick-up to Lak Xao, 5-6 hrs, 30,000 kip, for onward transport (see below).

Ban Lao *p208*
There is a small transport terminus at the intersection. If a bus/*songthaew* happens to dump you here, hop on one of the northbound buses to Vientiane or a southbound bus to Thakhek, Savannakhet and Pakse. Songthaews generally scurry through here from early in the morning to well into the afternoon, to **Ban Na Hin** (for Kong Lor cave, 15,000 kip), and **Lak Xao**, 25,000 kip.

Towards Tham Kong Lor *p209*
Generally, a pick-up waits in Ban Na Hin to take passengers all the way to **Ban Kong Lor**, 3 hrs, where you can pick up a cheap boat trip into the cave for US$10-15. Alternatively, pick up a *songthaew*, tuk-tuk or tractor from the centre of **Ban Na Hin** (opposite the market) for the 10-km journey to **Ban Napur**, 30 mins, and then catch a boat to **Ban Phonyang**, 2-3 hrs, and onto the cave, a further 1 hr, US$20. (If you are staying at **Sala Hinboun**, see Sleeping, they will send you a boat to Ban Napur to collect you, US$25).

Lak Xao *p211*
Songthaew depart for **Paksan**, every hour from 0700 daily, 5-6 hrs, 40,000 kip, and **Thakhek**, every hour 0730-noon daily, 40,000 kip. If you wish to leave after midday, go to Ban Lao and pick up a lift from there.

The road up into the mountains is excellent, partly because there is a hydropower dam here – the Nam Hinboun – and also because of the need to establish and maintain good infrastructural links with neighbouring countries. A road also snakes its way northwest through the mountains to Xieng Khouang and the Plain of Jars, but it is in a terrible state and is currently closed to all but the most intrepid.

Central Provinces Paksan to Lak Xao Listings

Pick-ups depart from the Lak Xao market throughout the day to the Vietnam border at **Nam Phao**, 1 hr, 10,000 kip each if you can fill a whole tuk-tuk but be prepared to barter hard. Often tour buses to Vietnam leave from the **Phou Doi Hotel**, so it is worth checking as it is an infinitely more comfortable mode of transport. There is also a mini-van service from Lak Xao market to **Chung Thom**, near Vinh, 1100 daily. Otherwise, it's sometimes cheaper to catch a ride in the mornings, as there's a better chance the drivers will be able to pick up passengers, but the chances deteriorate exponentially as the day goes on.

ⓘ Directory

Lak Xao p211,
Banks BCEL and Lao Development Bank, open 0800-1500 daily, with an hour lunch break, quite a competitive exchange rate on major currencies. **Communications** The post office is open 0800-1200 and 1300-1600 daily.

Thakhek and around

→ *Phone code: 052. Colour map 2, B5.*

Thakhek is sometimes translated as Indian (Khek or Khaek) Port (Tha), although it probably means Guest (Khaek) Port after the large number of people who settled here from the north. During the royalist period (through to the mid-1970s) it was a popular weekend destination for Thais who came here in droves to gamble. After the Communist victory, when Laos effectively shut up shop, everything went very quiet. But the recent recovery of commercial traffic has brought some life back to this small settlement, although Thakhek remains a quiet town, set in beautiful countryside.

The origins of Thakhek can be traced back to the Cambodia-based kingdoms of Chenla and Funan, which reached their heyday in the seventh century AD. But modern Thakhek was founded in 1911-12, under the French, clearly evident in the architecture. Apart from Luang Prabang, this is probably the most outwardly French-looking town, particularly with the fading pastel hues of the villas around the town's fountain area.

As in Savannakhet and Pakse, the locals are hoping that their town will be blessed by a bridge over the Mekong, linking it with the Thai city of Nakhon Phanom. In June 1996 Vientiane and Bangkok signed a memorandum of understanding but the bridge is yet to be built and the Lao are noticeably less enthusiastic about the project than the Thai. Instead, the two countries are concentrating on a larger project – Nam Theun II Dam (see page 220). The impressive karst landscape of the Mahaxai area is visible to the northeast of town and has now become a popular route for those doing 'the Loop' (see page 218). ▸▸ *For Sleeping, Eating and other listings, see pages 222-224.*

Ins and outs

Getting there and around Flights between Vientiane and Thakhek have been discontinued, as the improving quality of the road north to the capital makes flying unnecessary. The bus terminal is 4 km from town and runs services to and from Savannakhet, Pakse, Vientiane and Paksan. Boats no longer run between Thakhek and Vientiane. Across the Mekong is the Thai town of Nakhon Phanom; this is one of the points where it is possible for foreigners to cross between Thailand and Laos. Tuk-tuks ferry people in from bus terminals and are available to hire for out-of-town trips. Thakhek itself is small enough to negotiate on foot or by bicycle. ▸▸ *For further details, see Transport, page 223.*

Tourist information The tourism office is on Vientiane Road, T052-212512. The staff are particularly helpful and are champing at the bit to take tourists on their new ecotours to Buddha Cave and Phou Hin Protected Area. The tours give proceeds to poor, local communities. Money well spent; recommended.

Sights

There are few officially designated sights in Thakhek but many visitors consider it to be a gem of a settlement. Quiet and elegant, with some remaining Franco-Chinese architecture, including a simple fountain square, it has a fine collection of colonial-era shophouses, a breezy riverside position and a relaxed ambience. What locals regard as the central business district at the river end of Kouvoravong Road is wonderful for its peeling buildings. Other visitors, in contrast, look more critically at the dusty streets, seeing pockets of squalor, dilapidated buildings and an uncharacteristic atmosphere of disinterest amongst the locals. ▶▶ *For details of the town's three markets, see Shopping, page 223.*

> ‡ *Thakhek is also known as Muang Khammouan, after Khammouane Province, of which the town is the capital.*

That Sikhot

ⓘ *6 km south of Thakhek. Daily 0800-1800 (the gate is always open). Admission 2000 kip. Private tuk-tuk 100,000 kip return or public tuk-tuk from the intersection of Ounkham and Kouvoravong rds.*

That Sikhot or **Sikhotaboun** is one of Laos's holiest sites. It overlooks the Mekong and the journey downstream from Thakhek, along a quiet country road, reveals bucolic Laos at its best. The *that* was restored in 1956 but is thought to have been built by Chao Anou at the beginning of the 15th century, around the same time as That Ingheng in Savannakhet Province (see page 227). The *that* houses the relics of Chao Sikhot, a local hero, who founded the old town of Thakhek. According to local legend, Sikhot was an ordinary man who cooked some rice which he stirred with dirty – but as it turned out magic – sticks. When the local people refused to eat the dirt-ridden rice he did so instead and, as a result, was bestowed with Herculean strength. He conquered most of the surrounding area as well as Vientiane, whereupon he married the King of Vientiane's daughter. (The legend does not mention Chao Anou's name, but who wants to spoil a good story?) The king asked his daughter to discover whether Sikhot had any weakness. Her husband foolishly revealed to her that he could only be killed through his anus, so the King of Vientiane placed an archer at the bottom of Sikhot's pit latrine (a messy business that does not bear contemplating) and when the unfortunate Oriental Hercules came to relieve himself, he was killed by an arrow.

> ‡ *That Sikhot is yet another place that is said to contain some of the Buddha's bones.*

That Sikhot consists of a large gold stupa raised 29 m on a plinth, with a viharn upstream built in 1970 by the last King of Laos. The *that* is partly surrounded by a high wall. The tip of the stupa is said to be fashioned after a banana flower and there are reliefs of the Buddha in various *mudras* along the base. Stalls selling drinks and some food are to be found under the trees to the left. A major annual festival is held here in July and during February.

Kong Leng lake

Fed by a natural spring, this small lake is almost 30 km north of Thakhek and is

Thakhek

Sleeping
Khammuan
  International **1**
Khammouan Saykhong **2**
Mouthong Guesthouse **3**
Sooksomboon
  Guesthouse **4**
Southida Guesthouse **5**
Thakhek Travel Lodge **6**

Eating
Kaysone **1**
Lao-named Restaurant **2**
Noodle Stall **3**
Vanthiu **4**
Zukiyaki **5**

spectacularly beautiful. The water is a very light blue colour, resulting from the dissolved calcium from the surrounding limestone crops. You need to ask permission of the Village Chief in Ban Nar Kur to swim in the lake; fishing is not permitted.

The lake is only accessible in the dry season and even then you will need a good bike or 4WD vehicle. Take Route 13 north for 25 km; turn right and follow the road for 2 km before getting to the next major junction, where you turn right again. Continue for 16 km to **Ban Nar Kur**; the lake is 1 km further on. Alternatively, if you are taking public transport, take a northbound bus (towards Vientiane) and ask to hop off at Houei Aek; from here ask a tractor to take you Ban Nar Kur. The easiest option is to go on a tour with the provincial tourism office, who conduct treks around the area in the dry season, very cheap and easy.

Excursions off Route 12 🚌🏍🚲 ▸▸ *pages 222-224.*

Tham Xang (Tham Pha Ban Tham)

This is the closest cave to Thakhek, around 9 km northeast of town. The cave is considered an important Buddhist shrine and contains a number of Buddhist artefacts, including some statues and a box containing religious scripts. The Buddhist component, however, pales into insignificance compared to what locals herald as a 'miracle': a formation of stalagmites that looks something like an elephant's head. Visitors will need a flashlight to find the formation along a small passage at the right-hand corner of the cave, behind the golden Buddha. To get there follow Route 12 for about 7 km until you pass the bridge, then turn right. Difficulties can arise reaching the cave in the wet season due to flooding. Of lesser interest but in the same general direction are a few **railway bridges**, part of a project, designed by the French in the early 1900s, to connect Laos and Vietnam, but abandoned in 1920. The best remnant is the bridge crossing the Nam Don river. To get there, turn north off Route 12 at Km 8 and follow the road for 1 km until you hit the old railway bed. Then turn right and continue along the dirt track for another 1 km until you cross the bridge.

Tham Pha Pa (Buddha Cave)

ⓘ *Ban Na Khangxang, off Route 12, 22 km from Thakhek. 2000 kip for motorbike and 2000 kip for entry.*

A farmer hunting for bats accidently stumbled across Buddha Cave in April 2004. On climbing up to the cave's mouth, he found 229 bronze Buddha statues, believed to be over 450 years old, and ancient palm leaf scripts. Since its discovery, the cave has become widely celebrated, attracting pilgrims from as far away as Thailand, particularly around Pi Mai (Lao New Year). A new wooden ladder has now been built to access the cave but it is quite difficult to get to, as the road from Thakhek is in poor condition. It is recommended that you organize a guide through the Thakhek Tourism Office to escort you. In the wet season, it is necessary to catch a boat.

Tha Falang (Wang Santiphap)

This lovely emerald billabong is surrounded by pristine wilderness and breathtaking cliffs. The swimming pool, created by the Nam Don river, was a favourite French picnic spot during the colonial period and it's a nice place to spend the afternoon or break your journey if you're doing 'the Loop' (see page 218). The water can become a bit stagnant in the dry season. To get there, follow Route 12 for 13 km and then turn north for 2 km. In the wet season it may be necessary to catch a pirogue or canoe from the Xieng Liab Bridge.

Tham Xiang Liab

Turn off Route 12 at Km 14 (1 km past the turn-off for Tham Xang) and follow the track south to reach Tham Xiang Liab, the first cave in the province to be officially opened to tourists. The cave is reasonably large and sits at the foot of a 300-m-high limestone cliff, with a small river running through it. Local lore states that a former monk smitten with a local girl searched the cave to find her (the name translates as 'former monk sneaking '). There are limestone formations on the roof and experts have suggested that there may be some historical drawings hidden among the shadows. The 200-m-long cave has a small swimming hole (in the dry season) at the far end.

It is not easy to access the interior of the cavern on your own and, in the wet season, it can only be navigated by boat, as it usually floods (US$10).

Tham Sa Pha In

This little-visited cave contains a small lake, reputed to be 75 m long, and a couple of interesting Buddhist shrines. Swimming in the lake is strictly prohibited as the auspicious waters are believed to have magical powers. To reach the cave, follow Route 12 to Km 17; beyond the narrow pass turn to the left (north) and follow the path for 400 m.

Tham Nan Aen

ⓘ *To reach the cave, follow Route 12 until you see a sign on the right (south) at Km 18, which reads '700 metres'; follow this path to the entrance. Admission 5000 kip.*

The giant of the local caverns is said to be 1.5 km long and stands over 100 m tall. It is worth a visit, if only to catch the cool breeze, which rushes from within the rock and emanates from the cave entrance. Outside the cave is a shady, wooded picnicking area and a rather motley collection of animals, a disgrace considering this is supposed to be a protected area. The large cave is accessed by a wooden platform, purpose-built in 1987, for the visiting Princess of Thailand. The breezy cave is like a labyrinth, with multiple chambers and entrances, and also contains a small underground freshwater pool. The cave has bizarre looking stairs and fluorescent lighting.

Nam Don Resurgence

Close to Ban Na, off Route 12 at Km 14, 25 km northeast of Thakhek, is a beautiful lagoon, located within a cave and shaded by a sheer 300-m-tall cliff. The lagoon offers about 20 m of swimming then filters off into an underground waterway network, believed to extend for 3 km. In 1998 French surveyors found a rare species of blind cave fish 23 m below the surface. If you follow the cave wall around, there is another entrance which offers a good vista of the turquoise pool below. A trip to Nam Don Resurgence can be done in conjunction with 'the Loop' but requires a few hours. It is a bit tricky to find on your own so you might need to ask the locals or recruit a local tour guide. During the wet season, access is often only by boat. The Provincial Tourism Office runs some pretty good tours including this sight.

Mahaxai

Visible from Thakhek is the karst landscape of the **Mahaxai** area to the north and east. Mahaxai itself is a beautiful small town 50 km east of Thakhek on Route 12. The sunset here is quite extraordinary but even more beautiful is the surrounding scenery of exquisite valleys and imposing limestone bluffs. A visit to Mahaxai should be combined with a visit to one or more of the spectacular caves along Route 12 and some river excursions to see the Xe Bang Fai gorges or run the rapids further downstream.

The Loop

A motorbike tour loops around Mahaxai, Lak Xao, the caves and other beautiful scenery along the way, and has become increasingly popular with the backpacker set. However, by doing the entire 'circuit' by motorbike you will miss some of the most beautiful landscapes in the country, much of which can only be accessed by boat, in particular the trip to Kong Lor cave (see page 209). The circuit should take approximately three days but count on four – particularly if you want to sidetrack to Kong Lor – to allow for the normal punctures and muddy shenanigans that are par for the course in this part of the world. It is a wild ride in parts, so pack lightly: you will need a torch for darker cavernous areas, helmet and a sarong for bathing; a Lao phrase book is imperative as even the best navigators will probably require some assistance from the locals.

A word of warning: the Nam Theun II dam is one of the biggest things to happen in Laos in the last decade (see page 220), so this whole region is very susceptible to change over the next few years, particularly between Mahaxai and Lak Xao. This area will probably be flooded in parts and new roads will undoubtedly be built, so it is imperative that you check for up-to-date information.

Thakhek to Mahaxai From Thakhek take Route 12 east. The 45 km trip to Mahaxai should take two to three hours, without stops. It can be a little bumpy, pot holed and particularly muddy during the rainy season. Most travellers will want to stop off at some of the caves, swimming holes or the railway line en route (see above). Close to Mahaxai there is a small village, with a large, blue-coloured factory, and a good *feu* soup restaurant. After this, turn right at the T-junction to Mahaxai, where there are a few cheap guesthouses (see Sleeping, page 222).

Around Thakhek: The Loop

Mahaxai to Nakai/Ban Tha Long Alternatively you can continue on to Nakai (an additional one and a half to two hours), where there are also basic guesthouses and fuel. There is a 5 km hilly section en route to Nakai, where the sandy roads can be difficult to navigate (although nothing compared to the hike into Kong Lor). There is a guesthouse in Nakai (40,000 kip, clean but with quite a few bugs) but this isn't the nicest of towns in which to stay so you might want to continue a further 20 km to Ban Tha Long, which has a lovely riverfront guesthouse, serving pretty good omelettes (40,000 kip).

Nakai to Lak Xao Lak Xao is 70 km and four to five hours from Nakai or 50 km and three to four hours from Tha Long. The road is relatively smooth due to the kindly efforts of the Nam Theun dam crew. From Nakai you can either take the left or right fork: the left fork is the shortest option, with a detour via the Nam Theun site; the most common route, though, is to take the right fork along the forested, paved road to Lak Xao. Lak Xao offers extraordinary scenery but doesn't emanate the kind of vibe which makes you want to stay for long.

Lak Xao to Kong Lor To get to Kong Lor from Lak Xao follow the road to **Ban Na Hin** (also known as Khoun Kham), the last town before Kong Lor. It has a couple of small guesthouses (see page 212). Follow the main road through town and turn south after the hydroelectric project. Follow the hydroelectric waterway along the dusty road and after a few kilometres turn right at the intersection marked by red painted barrels. (You'll know you have the correct turning when you can see a settlement on the other side of the waterway.) Keep following the road along until you hit a rusty bridge at Namsanam. Here you have two options, left or right. If you want it easy, turn right after the bridge and follow the mammoth power lines until you reach the crossroads, turn left and head for **Ban Napur** (also known as Naphouk Village). Here, there is a small enclosure where you can leave your bike or motorbike for a day or two, while you continue your journey to Kong Lor by boat. The boat trip is recommended over the final motorbike leg, as it takes in some absolutely stunning scenery (see page 209). Eight kilometres from Kong Lor is **Sala Hin Boun**, which can make a pleasant stopover (see page 212). Alternatively, turn left at the bridge in Namsanam for a more adventurous ride, although this route can be impassable in the wet season, when you may have to carry your bike – not much fun. You'll drive through challenging but beautiful terrain for two hours – the first hour forest and the second hour farmland.

Ban Na Hin to Thakhek Once you get back to Ban Na Hin, check out **Namsanam waterfall** (see page 209), 3 km off the main road, then continue on Route 8 towards the intersection with Route 13. You will hit a little uphill stretch followed by a big downhill run; don't miss out on the stunning lookout point, well worth a break. At the intersection is the small village of Ban Lao (see page 208), from where it is 100 km back to Thakhek; this last stretch should take two hours and passes through some pretty boring scenery.

Nakai Nam Theun NPA

The **Nakai Plateau** was once a royal hunting ground, but today it is part of a National Protected Area (NPA). Over 3700 sq km of stunning landscape have been designated for protection, making it the largest area of its type in Laos and some of the most pristine wilderness remaining in Southeast Asia. Gradually rising from the Nakai Plateau, the heavy jungle looms up into the Annamite Mountain range, bordering Vietnam. Although numbers are dwindling, there is a great wealth of rare and endangered flora and fauna in this region, including elephants, tigers, the giant

☃ Nam Theun II: the arguments for ...

The Nam Theun II hydroelectric project has been identified by the World Bank as a key project for economic and social development in Laos. Its design and preparation has been ongoing for more than 10 years and in 2005 the project had reached construction stage. Nam Theun II has a capacity of 1,070 MW and will sell 95% of its electricity to Thailand. It has a reservoir size of 450 km² that will inundate 40% of the Nakai Plateau, through which the Nam Theun river flows. The Nakai Plateau is currently composed of agricultural land, heavily degraded forest, and both permanent and seasonal wetlands. The inundation will require the resettlement of 1,000 families or approximately 6,000 people onto the shores of the new reservoir. The developers are convinced that, because the level of poverty on the Nakai Plateau is currently very high, such resettlement will represent a considerable improvement to the livelihoods of these people.

Since turbined water will be released downstream into the Xe Bang Fai river, which flows through an adjacent Mekong plain, a development programme has also been established properly to manage any possible effects on the livelihoods of the approximately 50,000 people who live along relevant lower sections of the river and nearby tributaries. The Lao PDR Government and its development partners aim to enhance

... and against

Despite the World Bank's endorsement in March 2005 of the Nam Theun II project, many independent analysts have serious concerns relating to the project's social and environmental impacts. The US$1.45 billion hydropower project will displace more than 6,200 indigenous people and impact on more than 100,000 villagers who depend on the Xe Bang Fai and Nam Theun rivers for fish, agriculture and other aspects of their livelihood.

There will also be a large environmental impact, including the dramatic effects on the two river basins involved. Even the developer, Nam Theun II Power Company (NTPC), admits that many of these effects cannot be mitigated and instead will permanently alter river ecology and river-based livelihood systems. NTPC predicts "a collapse in the aquatic food chain," along the Xe Bang Fai. Fish catches are predicted to drop by 40-60% due to poor water quality and altered hydrology. Aquatic plants, snails, mussels and shrimp, traditionally collected for food or sale at local markets, would disappear. Riverside land, used for high-value crops in the dry season, would be permanently flooded by the dam's discharges.

Critics of the project also state that, while the project will generate revenues for watershed management and needed foreign exchange for the central Lao government, the government's capacity to manage protected areas and utilize project revenues for the benefit of Laos's poorest people is questionable. This is a critical issue given that the World

muntjac, Asiatic black bears, Malayan sun bears, clouded leopards and the very rare saola (or spindlehorn).

During 2005 tourist access to the area was limited, almost certainly due to the **Nam Theun II Dam** project (see page 220). Nam Theun NPA was thrown into the international spotlight over the controversial dam, which will supply electricity to nearby Thailand the benefits of bringing extra water to this area.

Furthermore, the government is committed to protecting and conserving 4,000 km^2 of forest and wildlife habitats situated in the nearby project watershed, otherwise known as the Nakai Nam Theun National Protected Area (NPA), thanks to an annual funding of US$1 million by the Nam Theun II project company.

The project sponsors and the government are convinced that Nam Theun II represents an important and unique opportunity for both Laos and Thailand to obtain significant economic and social benefits. On a macro-economical standpoint, Nam Theun II is of crucial importance for Laos as it will be the largest single contributor to the government's public finance and will be used to alleviate poverty and promote environmental protection throughout the country, whilst providing an opportunity to gradually reduce the country's dependence on international aid. Nam Theun II is at the forefront of the Lao National Poverty Eradication Programme (NPEP), the national development plan for the next decade.

The dam's commercial operation should begin in late 2009. For further information about the Nam Theun II Project, visit www.namtheun2.com.

Stuart Gillon, Nam Theun II

Bank is supporting the project largely on the basis of poverty reduction. While there have been numerous consultations to share project plans with villagers and elicit feedback, genuine consultations on development options have not occurred. Truly independent NGOs are not permitted to operate within Lao PDR, which means there has been no independent monitoring of consultations. According to the US State Department's 2003 Country Report for Laos, the human rights record "remained poor" and the government "prohibited most criticism that it deemed harmful to its reputation". Furthermore, the right to organize and join associations is "restricted in practice" and the government "prohibited associations that criticized the government". This environment makes it extremely difficult for Lao citizens to question the government and to seek redress when agreements or commitments are not met. The only country not to endorse the project in the World Bank Board of Directors was the USA.

Nam Theun II is an extremely large and complex project. Critical documents and studies have never been released to the public and, after more than a decade of project development, unanswered questions remain. A compelling case has not been presented to demonstrate that the benefits justify the economic, environmental and social risks of Nam Theun II.

An anonymous Vientiane-based source

and will eventually be a major source of income for the Laos government. Many conservationists believe the project is an environmental minefield. The dam is expected to be flooded by 2008, with effects undoubtedly reverberating throughout the whole area. Visitors to the region should ask advice before travelling, as certain areas will be flooded, villages will be moved and new roads will replace the old ones.

◯ Sleeping

Thakhek *p214, map p215*

C **Mekong Hotel**, Setthathirat Rd (or Mekong Rd), T052-250777, F052-250778. Prime location – hideous building. The putrid baby blue colour stands out like a psychedelic wart on what would otherwise be a pretty classic riverfront scene. Exterior aside, the large 1950s hotel has 60 or so a/c rooms overlooking the Mekong. No windows facing the river but the wide balconies are perfect for the sunset vista. Large, plain but clean, with TV, telephone, fridge and bathtub. Since you're not exposed to the exterior from your room, the US$10 asking price is one of the best deals in town. The Vietnamese management are friendly enough but don't speak much English. Brilliant restaurant attached.

C **Mouthong Guesthouse**, Nongbuakham Rd, T052-212387. Charmless concrete rooms, on the smallish side. Some have baths.

C-D **Sooksomboon Guesthouse** (formerly the Sikhot Hotel), Setthathirat Rd, T052-212225. An immensely attractive building that was once the provincial police station. It faces the Mekong and has the most character in Thakhek. The interior has been decorated with art deco-inspired charm. The a/c rooms in the main house are best, with en suite bathrooms, fluffy chairs, some padded walls, fridge and TV. Also cheaper rooms in the motel-esque annexe. Restaurant. Helpful staff.

C **Southida Guesthouse**, Chao Anou Rd (1 block back from the river), T052-212568. Pleasant family-run guesthouse. Clean rooms with TV, balcony and fridge. Overshadowed by some of the mammoth constructions towering over it, this quaint little place offers a very welcoming atmosphere and a homely feel. There is a small restaurant below.

D **Thakhek Travel Lodge**, 2 km from the centre of town, T020-5754009. Popular guesthouse set in a beautifully restored and decorated house. Fantastic outdoor seating area and the furniture and embellishments are outstanding. However, the rooms are pretty average for the price (US$5 standard room, US$2 dorm room and US$10 if you want an en suite toilet) and the service is a bit on the *bopenyang* side – so much so that you actually feel guilty if you ask the staff for anything. Hotel restaurant is only passable but does have an espresso machine. On the up side, the Danish owners can provide travel advice, when they're around, and there's an excellent log-book for those intending to travel independently around 'the Loop'. Motorcycle hire, US$15 per day. Recommended for those planning adventure travel around the area.

E **Khammuan International** (formerly the Chaleunxay Hotel), Kouvoravong Rd, T052-212171. Oldish villa with potential but rooms are small without windows and haven't seen a lick of paint in years. Some have a/c. The en suite bathrooms are good with hot showers. Cheaper single rooms with super-powerful ceiling fans are also available. The hotel has a large courtyard with a/c restaurant attached.

Mahaxai *p217*

E-F **Mahaxai Guesthouse**. 10 large clean airy rooms, with en suite showers, upstairs rooms are brighter. There is an attractive balcony overlooking the river, ideal for sitting and watching the world go by. Around 40,000 kip.

◯ Eating

Thakhek *p214, map p215*

Thakhek is not a place to come to for its cuisine. There is the usual array of noodle stalls – try the one in the town 'square' with good fruit shakes. Warmed baguettes are also sold at the square in the morning. The best place to eat is definitely at one of the riverside restaurants on either side of fountain square, where you can soak up the languid atmosphere, while knocking back a Beer Lao and tasty BBQ foods, and watching the spectacular river sunset morph through its various pinky tones. Otherwise, most restaurants are attached to hotels:

†† Lao-named restaurant, on the corner of Ounkham Rd and the east-west street leading to Wat Nabo. English menu with Lao and some Western dishes, mainly centred around seafood. Popular with local expats.

†† Kaysone, T052-212563. This is not the revolutionary place its name would suggest but, nonetheless, quite a nice spot to eat

Lao, Chinese and of course, Vietnamese dishes. If you're hankering for some ice cream, it is delicious here.

¶¶ **Mekong Hotel**, see Sleeping. The best of the hotel restaurants is very tastefully designed with proper tablecloths and what can almost be described as silver service. Menu has *Sukiyaki* plus a large array of Vietnamese-inspired dishes. Recommended. The **Southida Guesthouse** restaurant is also quite good value and does a reasonable Western breakfast.

¶¶ **Vanthiu Restaurant**. Walk through a wine shop to get to the Vietnamese restaurant out back . Friendly establishment, no English menu but some English dishes.

¶¶ **Zukiyaki Restaurant**, Vientiane Rd, T052-212334. Reasonably good Korean food, particularly BBQ, plus a few other generic Asian dishes.

Mahaxai *p217*
Food is generally of a high quality in the local noodle shops and food stalls.

○ Shopping

Thakhek *p214, map p215*
A few duty-free shops at the pier stock Chinese 'champagne', French wines, spirits, perfume and cigarettes.

Markets
There are 3 markets in Thakhek, although the goods on sale are not geared to the weird predilections of visiting *falang*. The largest, **Talaat Souk Somboun** (Talaat Lak Saam), is at the bus terminal, 4 km east of town. It is a good place to pick up odds and ends, with tuk-tuks constantly ferrying market-goers to and fro (5,000 kip). **Talaat Lak Song** is at the eastern end of Kouvoravong Rd, about 1½-2 km from the town centre. It is a mixed, largely dry goods market, although functional basketry and hand-crafted buffalo bells are also available. Finally, north on Chaoanou Rd is the **Talaat Nabo**.

○ Transport

Thakhek *p214, map p215*
There are no longer regular air or boat services to Vientiane. For boats to Thailand, see Border essentials, page 224.

Bus/truck
Thakhek's bus station is 4 km northeast of town. Daily connections northbound to **Vientiane**, 0400, 0530, 0700, 0830, 0900 and then hourly until 2300 daily, 346 km, 6-7 hrs, 40,000 kip; the VIP bus also dashes through town at 1300 daily, 60,000 kip. Scheduled buses to **Paksan**, 1100, 1200, 1500, and then every hr until late daily, 190 km, 4-5 hrs, but it is also possible to pick up a bus to Paksan en route to Vientiane, barrelling in from the southern provinces, usually on an ad hoc basis. Get off at **Ban Lao**, 15,000 kip, for connections along Route 12.

Southbound buses to **Savannakhet**, every hr, 1100-2200 daily, 139 km, 2½ hrs, 20,000 kip; to **Pakse**, every hr until 2400 daily, 6-7 hrs; also to **Sekong**, 1030, 1530 and 2300 daily, 60,000 kip; to **Attapeu**, 1530 and 2200 daily, 65,000 kip; to **Don Khong**, 1600 daily, 60,000 kip.

To **Dong Ha** (Vietnam), 0800 Sat, 80,000 kip; to **Thien Hué**, 2000 Mon, Tue and Thu, 80,000 kip.

Because of the irregular bus hours there is a small so-called 'guesthouse' at the bus station, where you can rent a bed for 25,000 kip.

To get to **Mahaxai**, take a *songthaew* from the bus terminal, 20,000 kip, or charter a tuk-tuk, which makes it easier to reach the caves en route.

Motorbike hire
Bikes can be rented from **Thakhek Travel Lodge**, US$15 per day; the **Chansathid Hotel**, T052-212208, US$10 per day, and from the no-name rental shop, on the left-hand side, near the traffic lights, US$8 per day (ask for Mr Na).

Mahaxai *p217*
Songthaew leave from the market in the morning. The last bus back to Thakhek leaves Mahaxai at 1500.

○ Directory

Thakhek *p214, map p215*
Banks Banque Pour le Commerce Extérieur, Vientiane Rd, just across from the post office, T052-212686, will change cash and TCs and does cash advances on Visa. **Lao Development Bank**, Kouvoravong Rd

⁞ Border essentials: Thakhek-Nakhon Phanom

Thakhek is across the Mekong from Nakhon Phanom in Thailand. There's a customs and immmigration office by the pier in Thakhek, open 0800-1730 daily, and boats cross between the two towns every half-hour or so (although this tends to slow down to an hourly service around lunchtime), 15,000 kip or ฿60, slightly cheaper in the other

direction. There are usually 'overtime service fees' at weekends, when boats become less frequent and will generally ask for more money. From Nakhon Phanom, scheduled buses depart for Udon Thani and Bangkok. Arriving from Thailand, 30-day Lao visas are available from agents in Nakhon Phanom; or get the standard 15-day visa at the border, US$30.

(eastern end), T052-212089, exchanges cash but doesn't do cash advances. There is also a second exchange counter at the immigration pier.

Communications Area code: 052.
Post office Kouvoravong Rd (at crossroads with Nongbuakham Rd). **Telephone** International calls can be made from the post office.

Savannakhet Province → Phone code: 041.

Savannakhet Province consists of 15 districts, with 780,000 inhabitants dispersed within its boundaries. Like most other provinces in the country, Savannakhet is a kaleidoscope of ethnicities, including the Lao, Phouthai, Thaidam, Katang, Chali, Lava, Souai, Pako, Kaleng, Mangkong and Taoi. The cultural diversity is even more visible in Savannakhet city, which has large Chinese and Vietnamese populations. Vietnamese and Thai merchants sell their products throughout the city, while the ubiquitous colonial houses and fading shopfronts are an ever-present reminder of French influence. According to official figures, this province records some of the highest tourist numbers in the country, although much of this is probably just transit traffic. Because of its proximity to both Thailand and Vietnam, Savannakhet is considered an important economic corridor. Savannakhet Province has a multitude of natural attractions, although the majority are a fair hike from the provincial capital.
▸▸ *For Sleeping, Eating and other listings, see pages 230-234.*

Savannakhet → Colour map 2, C5. ▸▸ pages 230-234.

Situated on the banks of the Mekong and at the start of the Route 9 to Danang in Vietnam, Savannakhet – or Savan as it is usually known – is an important river port and the gateway to the south. It is also an important trading centre with Thailand. The population of the town proper is about 50,000, although the district as a whole supports well over 100,000 people.

Across the Mekong, high-rise Mukdahan in Thailand may be cocking a snook at its poorer neighbour to the east, but Savannakhet has got a lot to offer that Mukdahan has bulldozed away in the name of modernization. It feels as though the country never left Savan: goats and chickens graze and wander around the urban area and a large portion of the town's French colonial roots still stand, moulding gently in the tropical climate. With a good lick of paint, Savannakhet could scrub up well and, although it's not quite Luang Prabang, it certainly shares many of the same characteristics. Whether this will last long is questionable. Construction of a Japanese-sponsored bridge across the Mekong to Mukdahan, costing ¥4700 million, has been underway for years. Its progress has been fraught with difficulty, including the death of several people on site in 2005, when a construction crane toppled over, but the latest news is that it should be ready for use in 2006 (don't expect it before 2007).

Background

Savannakhet was established in 1642 by Prince Thao Keosimphali, the son of King Luang of Phonsim. The Prince relocated the majority of families from Ban Phonsim, 18 km east of Savannakhet, to the modern-day town, naming the new fiefdom Ban Thahae (Mineral Port Village). The name was later changed to Souvannaphoum and, in 1883, was adapted to Savannakhet by French colonizers. In 1989 US servicemen arrived in Savannakhet, searching for the remains of men missing in action (MIAs) and the whole town turned out to watch their arrival at the airport. Not realizing that the Lao bear absolutely no animosity towards Americans, the men kept their heads down and refused to disembark until the crowds dispersed. During the war against the Pathet Lao the Royal Lao Air Force operated out of Savannakhet and, towards the end of the conflict, even headquartered here.

Ins and outs

Getting there and around There are overland international connections from Savannakhet to both Thailand and Vietnam. But, although it is possible to cross the Mekong from Mukdahan in Thailand and enter Laos through Savannakhet, few foreign travellers choose to do so. Rather more popular is to enter Vietnam via Lao Bao (see Border essentials, page 232), east of Savannakhet, with bus connections direct from Savan to Vietnamese towns, including Danang, Dong Ha and Hué. Domestic links aren't so good. The daily air connections with Vientiane and Pakse were canned sometime ago and look unlikely to be reinstated and the boats that used to be so handy found most of their business evaporating as people abandoned the river in favour of the newly improved roads. There are now no scheduled ferry departures and if you want to travel by private boat, you should be prepared to pay a wad of dollars.

The government bus terminal is on the northern edge of town, near the market; a tuk-tuk to the centre should cost about 5,000 kip. There is an information desk (some English spoken) in the bus station office. A new private bus station currently offers connections with Pakse and Vientiane. Approximately 50 m west of the government bus station is the *songthaew* terminal, where vehicles depart to almost every provincial destination imaginable. Tuk-tuks of various shapes and sizes criss-cross town. They are locally known as '*Sakaylab*' (as in Skylab) because they are said to resemble that piece of space hardware. ▸▸ *For further details, see Transport, page 233.*

Tourist information The **Provincial Tourism Office** ① *just off the Mekong River, Savannakhet, T052-214203, savannakhetguides2@yahoo.com (ask for Mr Kaisee)*, is one of the best in the country and runs a number of excellent ecotours in the surrounding area, which should be organized in advance. The office can also arrange guides and drivers for other trips. ▸▸ *For further details, see Activities and tours, page 233.*

● *Savannakhet is one of the only towns in Laos where there is still a sizeable Chinese*
● *population, entrepreneurs who fled from the Communists during the Cultural Revolution.*

Like any town of this size, Savan has quite a number of wats but none is particularly notable, unless 'watting' is a new and novel experience for you. **Wat Sounantha** on Nalao Road has a three-dimensional raised relief on the front of the *sim*, showing the Buddha in the *mudra* of bestowing peace, separating two warring armies. **Wat Sayaphum** on the Mekong is rather more attractive and has several early 20th-century monastery buildings. It is both the largest and oldest monastery in town, although it was only built at the end of the 19th century. Two of the monks at **Wat Sayamungkhun** speak some English and are pleased to talk about their 50-year-old monastery. There

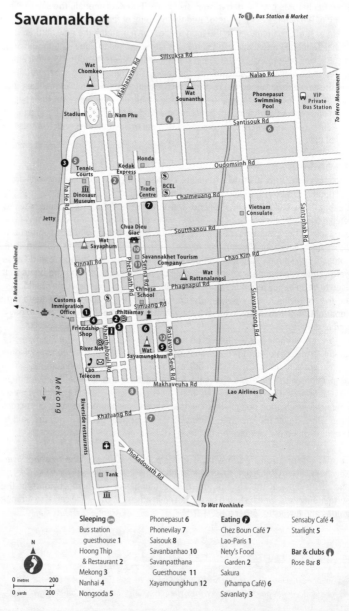

Savannakhet

N

| 0 metres | 200 |
| 0 yards | 200 |

is a large temple school here and, if you arrive during lessons, you may get roped into some impromptu English teaching.

Savan's **colonial heritage** can be seen throughout the central part of town. Perhaps the most attractive area is the square east of the Immigration office between Khanthabouli and Phetsalath roads. Simuang Road, near the Catholic church, is also rewarding in this regard. Evidence of Savan's diverse population is reflected in the **Chua Dieu Giac**, a Mahayana Buddhist pagoda at the intersection of Soutthanu and Phetsalath roads that serves the town's Vietnamese population. In deference to Theravada tradition, the *chua* has a *that* in the courtyard. There's also a Chinese school close to the Catholic church.

For those unable to get to the Ho Chi Minh Trail, there is some rusting war scrap in the grounds of the **Provincial Museum** ① *Khanthabouli Rd, Mon-Fri 0800-1130 and 1300-1600 (if it looks closed go across to the School of Medicine and knock on the curator's quarters, housed in the wooden building), 5000 kip*, and a tank just to the north. The museum has plenty of propaganda-style displays but little that is terribly enlightening, unless you are interested in the former revolutionary leader Kaysone Phomvihane.

Another attraction is the **Dinosaur Museum** ① *Khanthabouli Rd, south of the stadium, Mon-Fri 0800-1200 and 1400-1600, 5000 kip*, which houses a collection of four different dinosaur and early mammalian remains, and even some fragments of a meteorite that fell to earth over 100 million years ago. The first fossils in the region were unearthed in 1991 by a team of French and Lao scientists. All exhibits are accompanied by explanations in Lao and French; the staff speak good English and French and are happy to explain their work.

In the near future, the local tourism authority intends to open up a few more local sights to visitors, including Kaysone Phomvihane's former residence and the Thonglahasinh factory, where you can learn about the process of natural silk-dying (surprisingly interesting).

Around Savannakhet

That Inheng

This holy 16th-century *that* or stupa is 12 km northeast of Savannakhet. It was built during the reign of King Sikhottabong at the same time as That Luang in Vientiane, although local guides may try to convince you it was founded by the Indian emperor Asoka over 2,000 years ago. Needless to say, there is no historical evidence to substantiate this claim. The wat is the site of an annual festival in February or March akin to the one celebrated at Wat Phou, Champasak (see page 240). The regular tuk-tuks that ferry people between Savannakhet and Xeno will usually take you to That Inheng (60,000 kip return). If they will only drop you at the turning, it is a 3-km walk from the road. Alternatively hire a bicycle in town and cycle out here.

Salt works

Located northeast of the city, the salt works make for a good excursion. About 90% of Lao salt is produced here, either in large open saltpans or in an interesting Heath-Robinson contraption where the saline solution is pumped into small metal trays over wood fires in open sheds.

Kengkok

Kengkok is 35 km south of Savan along Route 13 and then a further 25 km inland. The main reason to come to this village is to see the beautiful surrounding countryside. The only way to get here is to hire a car or tuk-tuk (200,000 kip return); make sure you remember to agree a pick-up time.

Ho Chi Minh Trail

Throughout the Vietnam War, Hanoi denied the existence of the Ho Chi Minh Trail and, for most of it, Washington denied dropping 1.1 million tonnes of bombs on it – the biggest tonnage dropped per sq km in history. The North Vietnamese Army (NVA) used the Trail, really a 7000-km network of paths (trodden and cycled down by tens of thousands of men) and roads – some two-lane carriageways, capable of carrying tanks and truck convoys – to ferry food, fuel and ammunition to South Vietnam. Bunkers beneath the trail housed cavernous mechanical workshops and barracks. Washington tried everything in the book to stem the flow of supplies down the trail.

The Viet Minh had used it as far back as the 1950s in their war against the French. By 1966, 90,000 troops were pouring down the Trail each year, and four years later, 150,000 infiltrators were surging southwards using the jungle network. Between 1966 and 1971, the Trail was used by 630,000 communist troops; over the same period, it was also the conduit for 100,000 tonnes of provisions, 400,000 weapons and 50,000 tonnes of ordnance. At any given time, the Trail was guarded by 25,000 NVA troops and studded with artillery positions, anti-aircraft emplacements and SAM missiles.

The Trail wound its way through the Annamite mountains, entering Laos at the northeast end of the 'Panhandle', and heading southeast, with several access points into Cambodia and south Vietnam. Almost all roads running the north-south axis between southeastern and northeastern Laos were part of the Trail, and most towns sitting in these areas were obliterated by the US bombing campaign. The US airforce started bombing the Trail as early as 1964 in Operation Steel Tiger and B-52s first hit the Mu Gia pass on the Ho Chi Minh Trail in December 1965.

Carpet-bombing by B-52s was not admitted by Lao Prime Minister Prince Souvanna Phouma until 1969, by which time the US was dispatching 900 sorties a day to hit the Trail. It is estimated that it took 300 bombs for each NVA soldier killed on the Trail. The B-52 air strikes proved ineffective; they never succeeded in disrupting NVA supply lines for long.

In an effort to monitor NVA troop movements, the US wired the Trail with tiny electronic listening devices, infra-red scopes, heat- and smell-sensitive sensors, and locational

Champone District

An increasingly popular excursion, particularly for nature and wildlife enthusiasts, is a day trip to Champone District, location of Hai Suey Lake, the Monkey Forest and Don Deng Turtle Lake. A number of villages in the area provide an insight into the platitudes of local farming life. A tuk-tuk will do the round trip for US$40, divided amongst passengers. Otherwise contact the local tourist office, who should be able to hook you up with a guide/driver.

Take Route 13 south towards Pakse and turn left at Km 35; follow this road for approximately 20 km until you reach Ban Sokuan, a friendly village that's a great place to stop-off for a bite to eat to break the journey. **Hai Suey Lake**, the largest lake in Savannakhet Province, is located 4km further on. Boats will generally do short trips on the lake for about 5,000 kip. Another 7 km beyond Ban Sokuan is Ban Dong Meun, known as the **Monkey Forest**. The monkeys reign supreme from their forested habitat, not far from Champone River, and locals have attached many superstitions to their presence, such as imminent death if you hit a monkey. From Monkey Forest it is another 18 km north to Ban Dong Deng and **Turtle Lake**. There are fewer shelled beacons to guide fighter-bombers and B-52s to their target. The NVA carefully removed these devices to unused lengths of trail, urinated on them and retreated, while preparing to shoot down the bombers, which predictably arrived, on cue, from Clarke Field Air Base in the Philippines.

Creative US military technicians hatched countless schemes to disrupt life on the Trail: they bombed it with everything from Agent Orange (toxic defoliant) to Budweiser beer (an intoxicating inebriant) and washing up liquid (to make it into a frothing skid-track). In 1982 Washington finally admitted to dumping 200,000 gallons of chemical herbicides over the Trail between 1965 and 1966. The US also dropped chemical concoctions designed to turn soil into grease and plane-loads of Dragonseed – miniature bomblets which blew the feet off soldiers and the tyres off trucks. Nothing worked.

The US invasion of Cambodia in May 1970 forced Hanoi to further upgrade the Trail. This prompted the Pentagon to finally rubberstamp a ground assault on it, codenamed Lamson 719, in which south Vietnamese and US forces planned to capture the Trail-town of Tchepone, directly east of Savannakhet, inside Laos. The plans for the invasion were drawn up using maps without topographical features.

In February 1971, while traversing the Annamite range in heavy rain, the South Vietnamese forces were routed, despite massive air support. They retreated leaving the Trail intact, 5,000 dead and millions of dollars-worth of equipment behind. Abandoned vehicles, bomb casings and sometimes, gutted choppers and bombers can still be seen along the Trail. There is more war debris here than on the Plain of Jars as trucks cannot easily enter the area and pick up the scrap metal. For a map of the Ho Chi Minh Trail, see page 297.

Despite the herbicides, the mountainous region around the trail is still blanketed in dense tropical forest – much of it remarkably undisturbed – and, because of its inaccessibility, the forest has not been raided by the timber merchants. However, many of the rare birds and animals found in the markets at Salavan are caught in this area. Many of the tribal groups (mainly Lao Theung) that populated the area before the war were forced to move onto the Boloven Plateau because of the heavy bombing of the Ho Chi Minh Trail.

creatures here than monkeys at Dong Meun, but they are still reasonably visible. Locals revere these soft-shelled turtles (*paa faa*) and it is believed that certain residents can summon the creatures from the waters with a special call.

Ban Houan Hine

Ban Houan Hine, or Stone House, was built between the sixth and the end of the seventh centuries. It does not begin to compare with the better known Wat Phou outside Champasak but a visit here can be combined with a visit to **That Phone**, a hilly Buddhist *that* en route. It was previously possible to travel by boat down the Mekong to this lesser known Khmer site, 75 km south of Savannakhet, but, again, improvements in road conditions coupled with the usual tourist's disposition to press on elsewhere, has meant this is no longer an option. Instead, buses take Route 13 south, 60 km from Savan, and then turn right onto a track for a further 15 km (signposted 'Stone House Pillars').

East on Route 9 🍴🚲🚌 ⏵ *pages 230-234.*

Xepon (Sepon) and around → *Colour map 3, A3.*

It is possible to cross into Vietnam by taking Route 9 east over the Annamite chain of mountains to **Lao Bao** (just over the border) and from there to the Vietnamese town of Dong Ha and the cities of Hué and Danang (see Border essentials, page 232). The largest place on the Lao side of the frontier is Xepon. At first glance it might seem that there's not much to see and do in Xepon but as there is a government guesthouse here, travellers very occasionally use it as a stopping place en route to Vietnam.

The waterfall of **That Salen** is 25 km north of Xepon. The owner of Vieng Xai Guesthouse will be able to get you there and extremely fit visitors have been known to hire bicycles. The other waterfall, **Sakoy**, is about 4 km away by river, or 15 km by main road towards Vietnam. Wide without being high, it's nevertheless a great place for a picnic, and some travellers have even pitched camp here, situated as it is by the small village of Ban Sakoy, surrounded by coconut trees. There is a tourist office in the town office in Xepon, where they can organize a boat trip to a traditional Lao village, 2½ hours away.

Dong Phu Vieng National Protected Area

The provincial tourism office (see Ins and outs, page 225) runs excellent treks through the **Dong Phu Vieng National Protected Area**, south of Route 9, which is home to wildlife such as Siamese crocodiles, Asian elephants, the endangered Eld's deer, langurs and wild bison (most of which you would be incredibly lucky to see). Located within the NPA is a **Song Sa Kae** (Sacred Forest and Cemetery), revered by the local Katang ethnic group, who are known for their buffalo sacrifices. The well-trained local guides show how traditional natural produce is gathered for medicinal, fuel or other purposes. The tours are exceptionally good value. Most treks will only run during the dry season.

Ho Chi Minh Trail

This is an enticing prospect for some visitors but getting here is not easy from Savannakhet and should only be attempted in the dry season, November to March being the ideal time. It is necessary to hire a Soviet jeep or 4WD in order to cross the rivers because many of the bridges are broken so your best bet is to organize a tour from Savan (see Activities and tours, page 233), although you could also travel with a guide on public buses, staying overnight in Xepon (see Sleeping, page 231), the nearest town to the Trail. A guide will charge US$20-30 per day, including meals and accommodation, if required. The easiest access point to the trail is **Ban Tapung** .

> ‼ *Under no circumstances should you go anywhere near the Ho Chi Minh Trail without an experienced guide, as unexploded bombs abound.*

🛏 Sleeping

Savannakhet *p224, map p226*
Savannakhet has a good selection of places to stay for US$5 and upwards but real budget accommodation is scarce.
B **Hoong Thip**, Phetsalath Rd, T041-212262, F041-213230. A/c, satellite TV, dark rooms, big bathrooms en suite, breakfast included. Other services include sauna, and car hire with driver (US$25).

B **Nanhai**, Santisouk Rd, T041-212371, F041-212380. This 7-floor hotel is now considered one of the better places in town since the Auberge de Paris shut up shop. The 42 rooms, karaoke bars and dining hall are a prime example of a mainland Chinese hotel except that the staff here are quite polite. Mainly used by Chinese businessmen, there is little atmosphere for the tourist. Rooms have a/c, TV, fridge, IDD telephones and en suite bathrooms but they smell musty and the single rooms are minuscule. The pool has no water. The hotel boasts the only lift in town. For enquiries, write to 313 RM Lasavong Rd.

B Phonepasut, Santisouk Rd, 1 km from town centre in quiet street, T041-212158/212190, F041-212916. Motel-like place with 2 courtyards, restaurant and pool (US$1 for visitors). Rooms are clean, with hot water in the bathrooms, a/c and satellite TV. Friendly and well run with support services like fax and IDD telephones.

C-D Mekong, Tha He Rd, T041-212249. This place is housed in an attractive colonial villa on the Mekong, the rooms are large and generally clean, with good en suite bathrooms and some a/c. Mattresses vary hugely, so some spot-testing is a good idea. The hotel quite obviously operates as some kind of brothel and the Vietnamese management are diffident to the point of rudeness: if you can ignore these factors, then it's great.

C-E Savanbanhao, Senna Rd, T041-212202, F041-212944. Centrally located hotel composed of 4 colonial-styles houses set around a quiet courtyard, with a range of rooms. Most expensive have en suite showers and hot water. Beware the lethal Soviet water boiler. Some a/c. Large balcony. **Savanbanhao Tourism Co** is attached (see Activities and tours) and private buses (US$12 to Vietnam) depart from here. Motorbike hire US$10 per day. Good for those who want to be in and out of Savannakhet, quickly, with relative ease.

D Nongsoda, Tha He Rd, T041-212522. Oodles of white lace draped all over the house. Clean rooms with a/c and en suite bathrooms with wonderfully hot water. During the low season the hotel drops its room rates to US$8, which is exceptionally good value. Highly recommended.

D Saisouk, Makhavenha Rd, T041-212207. A real gem. This breezy new guesthouse has good-sized twin and double rooms, immaculately furnished and spotlessly clean, some a/c, communal bathrooms. Beautifully decorated with interesting *objets d'art* and what look like dinosaur bones. Plenty of chairs and tables on the large verandahs. Very friendly staff, reasonable English. Laundry service. Recommended.

D-E Phonevilay, 137 Phetsalath Rd, south of town centre, T041-212284. More expensive rooms with attached hot showers, cheaper rooms have musty bathrooms, hard mattresses and are like cells. Some a/c. Rude, uninterested staff.

D-E Savanpatthana Guesthouse, Senna Rd, next door to Savanbanhao, T041-213955. Ugly, grey building, bare and gloomy but with clean rooms. En suite bathrooms with squat toilet and rusty shower, no hot water. More expensive rooms upstairs are good value with a/c, although the 'VIP' rooms in the separate block are nothing to write home about, with tatty furniture and grubby albeit huge bathrooms. The predominantly male staff are helpful, when they are not too busy watching Thai boxing on TV.

E-F Xayamoungkhun (English sign just reads 'Guest House'), 85 Ratsavong Seuk Rd, T041-212426. An excellent little hotel with 16 rooms in an airy colonial-era villa. Centrally positioned with a largish compound. Range of very clean rooms available, more expensive have hot water, a/c and fridge. Very friendly owners. Second-hand books and magazines are available. Recommended.

F Bus station Guesthouse, at the bus station. Basic dorm rooms, useful for catching the daily Vietnam bus, which leaves at 0600.

Xepon *p230*
E Nangtoon Guesthouse, Route 9, 2 km from Xepon. Rooms with either fan or a/c and hot water in the bathrooms. Outstanding value. Recommended.
E Vieng Xai Guesthouse, T041-214895. A big house, wooden upstairs and concrete down, very clean, with shared bathroom. Friendly owners speak a little English.

🍴 Eating

Savannakhet *p224, map p226*
Several restaurants on the riverside serve good food and beer. The market also has stalls offering good, fresh food, including excellent Mekong River fish.
🍴 **Sakura**, T041-212882, near the church (signs read Khampa Café). This is a bit of a shock find – in a good way. A very atmospheric lantern-lit garden, with a

⁞ Border essentials: Dansavanh-Lao Bao

The Vietnam border is 236 km east of Savannakhet (45 km from Xepon). Getting through customs and dealing with potential obstacles on the other side means that it's impossible to state how long it may take to get into Vietnam itself.

The Lao border post is at **Dansavanh**, from where it is about 500 m to the Vietnamese immigration post and a further 3 km to **Lao Bao**, the first settlement across the border; motorbike taxis are available to carry weary travellers. We have received reports of long delays at this border crossing, as paperwork is scrutinized and bags are checked and double checked. Don't be surprised if formalities take 1 hour – and keep smiling! The problem seems to be at the Vietnamese end but those with a Vietnamese visa should be OK. The closest Vietnamese consulate is in Savannakhet; see page 234 for visa application details and opening hours. Lao immigration can issue 15-day tourist visas for US$30. Expect to pay 'overtime fees' on the Lao side if you come through on a Saturday or Sunday.

country and western meets Oriental sukiyaki feel. Acoustic guitarists often perform here. Good sukiyaki fondue and basic Asian fare, like fried rice, but it's the atmosphere that makes it special. Recommended.

† **Savanlaty**. Breezy setting overlooking 'landscaped' courtyard. Lots of pictures of snakes and elephants but they're too high up on the walls to see.

††-† **Chez Boun Cafe** opposite the big trade centre, T041-215190, ssingtao@yahoo.com. A tiny little café; you could easily walk straight past it as it isn't signposted. Great steak, pizza, espresso and cappuccino. Good for brunch. Recommended.

††-† **Nety's Food Garden**, east of the immigration office. A mini hawker centre. Awnings shield diners from the sun and a handful of stalls serve good and cheap single-dish Lao, Vietnamese and Thai food.

† **Lao-Paris**, formerly the Four Seasons Restaurant, between the derelict Santyphab Hotel and the customs/immigration office. A crumbling building with 4 tables on the grey verandah and a dingy interior. Tasty *falang* fare and Lao/Vietnamese dishes but there are better places around. A good cheap breakfast is served from 0800.

† **Sensaby Café**, next door to the derelict Santyphab Hotel. Cosy little café run by a young Chinese-Lao woman. Good atmosphere at night. Choice of Western food including salads, muesli and ice cream at very cheap prices, best milk shakes in town. Opening hours are erratic, best bet is in the evening, although they also offer breakfast. Good value. Recommended.

† **Starlight**, opposite Wat Sayamungkhun, on the corner. BBQ, deep fried dishes and spicy salads. Cheap and cheerful, and favoured by many Westerners. Don't expect any culinary masterpieces but the owners are a delight and speak good English.

Xepon *p230*

On the west side of the market there is a reasonable restaurant called **Bouphan**, which does good eggs, *feu* and coffee.

♦ Bars and clubs

Savannakhet *p224, map p226*
There are several large discos/beer gardens in town, most of which have live bands and are open 7 days a week. The reasonably surreal **Rose Bar** is popular, although it's not much of a bar, more a club-cum-beer garden, with lots of lights.

✿ Festivals and events

Savannakhet *p224, map p226*
Feb Than Ing Hang (movable) similar to the festival at Wat Phou, Champasak (see page 249).

○ Shopping

Savannakhet *p224, map p226*
Talaat Savan Sai Open 0700-1700 daily.
The central market has moved from its
former town location to a new site behind
the government bus station, north of town.
The brand spanking new building, built and
managed by a Singaporean company, comes
complete with parking spaces and one of the
few escalators in Laos (although it doesn't
work!). There is the usual selection of meat,
vegetables, fruit, dry goods, fabrics and
baskets, plus an abundance of gold and
silversmiths.

There is a branch of **Lao Cotton** on
Ratsavong Seuk Rd.

▲ Activities and tours

Savannakhet *p224, map p226*
**Savannakhet Provincial Tourism
Authority**, T041-214203, savannakhet
guides2@yahoo.com. In conjunction with
the NGO **SNV Netherlands**, the tourism
authority runs excellent ecotours in the area.
There are 14 keen-as-mustard English-
speaking guides to take tourists out to see
the local ethnic culture and sights. Highly
worthwhile 1- to 3-day treks have been
established, with proceeds filtering down to
local communities to help ease poverty and
encourage sustainable and culturally
sensitive tourism practices. (It is rumoured
that ethnic villagers are even given money
for each wild animal that the tourists see, to
ensure that rare and protected species aren't
hunted into extinction.) Recommended.
Savanbanhao Tourism Co, at the
Savanbanhao Hotel (see Sleeping, above),
open 0800-1200 and 1330-1630 Mon-Sat.
Tours and trips to most sights in the area,
including the Ho Chi Minh Trail, US$140 with
car and guide, or US$250-300 with an
overnight stay in a local village.

○ Transport

Savannakhet *p224, map p226*
Boat
Sadly boats no longer run to Vientiane, since
the road has been improved. The only river
services now are boats across the Mekong to

Mukdahan (Thailand) 0910, 1000, 1110, 1330,
1430 and 1630 Mon-Fri; 0930, 1130, 0230 and
0400 Sat; 1030 and 1500 Sun, ฿50. 30-day
visas for Laos are available from agents in
Mukdahan or you can get a 15-day visa at the
Lao customs and immigration in Savannakhet
(see Useful addresses, page 234).

Bus/truck
From the **government terminal**, northbound
buses depart daily to **Vientiane**, 0530, 0600,
0640, 0720, 0800, 0840, 0920, 1010, 1100,
1200 and then hourly until 2200 daily,
457 km on a good road, 8-9 hrs, 55,000 kip.
Most of the Vientiane-bound buses also stop
at **Thakhek**, 125 km, 2-3 hrs, 25,000 kip;
Paksan, 5-6 hrs, 55,000 kip, and **Pak Kading**
7-8 hrs, 55,000 kip. There are also specially
scheduled buses to **Thakhek** at 0730, 0915,
1015 and 1130 daily.

Southbound buses to **Pakse** depart at
0630, 0700, 0900, 1200 and 1430 daily,
6-7 hrs, 30,000 kip; buses in transit from
Vientiane to Pakse will also usually pick up
passengers here. To **Don Khone**, 0700 daily,
9-10 hrs, 50,000 kip; to **Salavan**, 1200 and
1700 daily, 8-10 hrs, 45,000 kip; to **Attapeu**,
0900 daily, 9-12 hrs, 65,000 kip. This road is
also in good condition.

Eastbound buses depart daily to **Xepon**
and **Lao Bao** (Vietnam border, see page
232), 0630, 0900 and 1200 daily, 4-5 hrs,
30,000 kip. A bus also departs at 2200 daily
for destinations within Vietnam, including
Hué, 13 hrs, 90,000 kip; **Danang**, 508 km,
15 hrs, 110,000 kip, and **Hanoi**, 22 hrs,
200,000 kip; there are additional services at
0700 and 1800 Sat and 0700 Sun. Luxury
Vietnam-bound buses can also be arranged
through the **Savanbanhao Hotel** (see
Sleeping), T041-212202, US$12.

Car, motorbike and bicycle hire
If you've time to shop around, it could be
worth it. Car and driver from the **Hoongthip
Hotel**, US$50 per day, and from
the **Savanbanhao Hotel**, prices vary. The
latter also has motorbikes, US$10 per day.
Sayamungkhun Hotel rents bicycles for
US$1 per day.

Songthaew/pick-up
The *songthaew* terminal, near the bus station
and market, serves countless destinations

within the province; most services depart at 0630-0700. To **Thakhek**, 0800, 0900, 1030, 1130, 1350, 1440, 1530 and 1620 daily, 3-5 hrs (depending on the number of stops), 20,000 kip. To **Ban Houan Hine**, 0700 daily when full, 20,000 kip. *Songthaew* to the **Vietnam border** depart with more frequency than the buses (see above) but are much slower.

Tuk-tuk

Most tuk-tuks charge around 5,000 kip per person for a local journey. Private charter to **Ban Houan Hine**, US$15. A tuk-tuk with good local knowledge and exemplary English is **Amphone**, T020-5440821.

Xepon *p230*

Buses depart from the market to **Savannakhet** at 0800 daily, 30,000 kip. There are numerous *songthaew* from the market to **Lao Bao**, 45 km, 1 hr, 20,000 kip but you'll need to get there by 0700 to ensure a space. It's also possible to jump on the various buses from Savannakhet to Vietnam, which pass through Xepon, the cheapest option being the service to Lao Bao (see above).

● Directory

Savannakhet *p224, map p226*

Banks Lao Development Bank, T041-212272, Oudomsinh Rd, open 0800-1200 and 1300-1530 Mon-Fri, will change most major currencies. **Banque pour le Commerce Exterieur Lao** (**BCEL**), Chalmeaung Rd, T041-212226, will exchange currency as well as do cash advances on Visa/Mastercard. There are exchange counters around the market, any currency accepted, and at the pier (bad rate). The goldsmiths in the market regularly change money; all currencies bought and sold.

Communications Area code: 041. Post office Khanthabouli Rd, T041-212205, 0800-2200 daily. Next door is **Lao Telecom Office**, for domestic and international calls. There are also plenty of IDD call boxes scattered around town (including 1 next to the immigration office at the river). Internet cafés here haven't really clicked onto net calls yet but it's only a matter of time. **Phitsamay**, Chalmeung Rd, is quite a decent internet café and shop in a convenient location. **Medical services** Savannakhet Hospital, Khanthabouli Rd, T041-212051. Dr Kongsy, T041-212711. **Police** A block back from the river, near the Tourist Office, T041-212069. **Useful addresses** Vietnam Consulate, Sisavangvong Rd, T041-212737, open 0730-1100 and 1400-1630 Mon-Fri, provides Vietnamese visas in 3 days on presentation of 2 photos and US$55. **Thai Consulate**, Kouvoravong Rd, open 0830-1200 for applications, 1400-1500 for visa collection, visas are issued on the same day if dropped off in the morning. **Lao customs and immigration**, Tha He Rd, at the passenger pier, for exit to Thailand and Lao visas, open 0830-1200 and 1300-1600 daily, overtime fees payable Sat and Sun.

Southern Laos

⁑ Footprint features

Introduction

Laos's southern provinces offer a varied array of enticements and a different character from the north of the country. Base yourself in the region's unofficial capital, Pakse, to explore the many attractions of Champasak Province, including the romantic, pre-Angkorian ruins of Wat Phou and Ban Khiet Ngong, with its elephants. Inland from Pakse is the Boloven Plateau, an area that was earmarked by the French for settlement and coffee production. The rivers running off the plateau have created a series of spectacular falls, including towering Tad Fan and stunning Tad Lo.

A highlight of any trip down south is Siphandon, where the Mekong divides into a myriad channels and 'Four Thousand Islands'. The idyllic, palm-fringed Don Khone, Don Deth and Don Khong provide perfect places to relax and absorb riverine life, as fisherman cast nets amongst lush green islets and children frolic on the sand bars.

★ Don't miss...

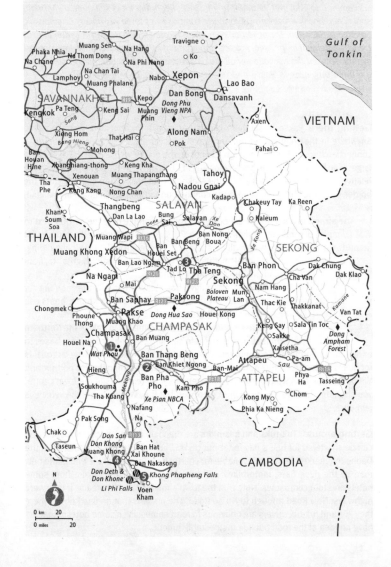

Pakse (Pakxe) and around

→ *Phone code: 031. Colour map 3, B2.*

Pakse is the largest town in the south and is strategically located at the junction of the Mekong and Xe Don rivers. Two bridges span the Xe Don here. The single lane bridge downstream was built by the French in 1925, while the upstream structure was erected by the Soviet Union and was not completed until about 1990. Pakse is a busy commercial town, built by the French early in the 20th century as an administrative centre for the south. The town has seen better days but the tatty colonial buildings lend an air of old-world charm. Pakse is a major staging post for destinations further afield, such as the old royal capital of Champasak, famed for its pre-Angkor, seventh-century Khmer ruins of Wat Phou (see page 240). The town's old colonial ebb is quickly succumbing to Thai and Vietnamese influence. Regardless it is still quite a charming spot. Champasak Province was formerly comprised of three provinces, Champasak, Sedon and Sitandon. The governor's office was located in Ban Muang in Sedon prior to French settlement in the area. Pakse's appointment as a French administrative outpost in 1905 spurred the relocation of all major government offices and businesses across the three provinces to Pakse and an amalgamation of provincial authorities. ►► *For Sleeping, Eating and other listings, see pages 245-253.*

Ins and outs

Getting there Pakse is Southern Laos's transport hub: from here you can get to anywhere in the southern region, and travel between local centres often requires a connection through Pakse. Although it is not on the **border** with Thailand, Pakse is the largest Lao town close to the border crossing at Chongmek. Traffic regularly crosses the relatively new Japanese Bridge over the Mekong, channelling passengers across the border. From the Thai side, *songthaew* continue on to Ubon Ratchathani in Thailand.
►► *For further details, see Border essentials, page 252.*

The **airport** is 2 km northwest of town; cross the bridge over the Xe Don next to Wat Luang and continue straight up No 13 Rd; tuk-tuks will make the journey for around 15,000 kip. There is a small café and BCEL exchange in the terminal building.

⁑ Two highways link Pakse with Danang in Vietnam via the Boloven Plateau. A crossing into Cambodia and Phnom Penh is under construction.

International flights, as well as domestic flights to/from Vientiane, run several times a week.

A public passenger **boat** leaves early in the morning for Champasak and Wat Phou, and also for Don Khong; boats can also be privately chartered.

There are three official bus terminals in Pakse: the **Northern terminal** (Km 7 on Route 13 north, T031-251508) is for buses to and from the north; the **Southern terminal** (Km 8 south on Route 13, T031-212981) is for buses to and from the south, and the **Central market terminal** is for northbound VIP buses. Tuk-tuks wait to transport passengers from terminals to the town centre; you shouldn't have to pay more than 5,000 kip but they will wait until the vehicle is jam-packed. ►► *For further details, see Transport, page 250.*

Getting around Tuk-tuks and **saamlors** are the main means of local transport and can be chartered for half a day for about US$5. The main tuk-tuk 'terminal' is at the Daoheung market. **Boats** are available for charter from the jetty at the end of the new road by the river. **Cars, motorbikes** and **bicycles** are available for hire from some hotels and tour companies. Note that the town's roads are numbered as if they were highways: No 1 Road through to No 46 Road. The result is that no-one knows where they live and tuk-tuk drivers are oblivious to road names. Even some hotel managers have no idea of the road outside their establishment.

Some patience is
required in dealing with officials here but, once you get past the initial bureaucratic
difficulties, you will find they have some fantastic ecotours on offer to unique
destinations (some are offered in conjunction with local travel agents, such as
Champa Mai, see Activities and tours, page 250). Mr Na, a guide at the office, speaks
very good English and is probably the best person to speak to.

Sights ●❷🛇▲🚉🛈 ↠ *pages 245-253.*

Pakse, by anyone's standards, is not a seething metropolis, which, of course, gives
it much of its charm. But this is starting to change now that the bridge has been built
and Pakse is firmly linked into the Thai economy; a strong Vietnamese influence is
also apparent. There's not that much to see in Pakse, so far as official sights are
concerned. Locals tend to mention the shopping centre-style market slap-bang in
the centre of town and the Daoheung (morning) market as the most interesting
places to visit; in fact, it may seem Pakse exists for little else (see page 249).
However, although it does not offer an overwhelming amount of tourist attractions,
it's a good place to base yourself to visit destinations further afield, including Tad
Lo, Tad Fan and Wat Phou.

Champasak Museum
① *No 13 Rd (the main highway) running east out of town, close to the stadium. Daily
0800-1130 and 1300-1600 except public holidays. Admission 5000 kip.*
This museum opened in 1995 and displays pieces recovered from Wat Phou,
handicrafts from the Lao Theung of the Boloven Plateau, weaponry, musical
instruments and a seemingly endless array of photographs of plenums, congresses
and assemblies and of prominent Lao dignitaries opening hydropower stations and
widget factories. Visitors are shown around by charming Lao guides who speak only
limited English, nor are the labels very informative. But it's still a treat for museum
aficionados. Opposite the museum is a *that*-like **Heroes Monument**.

Wat Luang
There are 40 wats in town but none figures particularly high in the wat hall of fame.
Wat Luang, in the centre of town, is the oldest. It was built in 1830, but was
reconstructed and redecorated in 1990 at a cost of 27 million kip. The *sim* now sports
a kitsch pink and yellow exterior complete with gaudy relief work. Lots of monks can
be found loitering around the premises, as this is one of the main centres where they
practise English. The hefty doors were carved locally. The compound was originally
much larger but, in the 1940s, the chief of Champasak Province requisitioned the land
to accommodate a new road. To the right of the main entrance stands a stupa
containing the remains of Khatai Loun Sasothith, a former Prime Minister who died in
1959. To the right of the *sim* is the monks' dormitory, which dates from the 1930s; the
wooden building behind the *sim* is the monastic school, the biggest in southern Laos,
and on the left of the entrance is the library, built in 1943. These earlier structures are,
needless to say, the finest – at least for Western sensibilities. The compound backs
onto the Xe Don.

● *According to ML Manich in his* History of Laos, *the French decided to make Pakse the local
administrative capital because they wanted to rule the country without interference from
the royal house of Champasak.*

Southern Laos Pakse & around

There are many more Lao monasteries in town. For those who desire a change there is also a Vietnamese/Chinese Mahayana Buddhist **Linh Bao Tu Pagoda** on No 46 Road, and a church on No 1 Road.

Boun Oum Palace
Situated on the road north towards Paksong, the Boun Oum Palace is now the **Champasak Palace Hotel** and by far the largest structure in town. Before Thai hotel interests bought the place, it was the half-finished palace of the late Prince Boun Oum of Champasak, the colourful overlord of southern Laos and a great collector of *objets d'art*. He began constructing the house of his dreams in 1968, with the intention of creating a monument with more than 1000 rooms. However, the Prince was exiled to France before his dream was realized. Looking at the hotel it is hard not to conclude that his exile was wholly for the best, at least architecturally.

Muang Khao
Muang Khao lies on the opposite bank of the Mekong to Pakse and, as the name suggests (it means 'Old Town'), was established before its larger sibling across the water. Once the French concentrated their attentions on Pakse, Muang Khao was neglected and, consequently, has a quaintness largely absent from Pakse. Most people come here en route to the Lao-Thai border at Chongmek but it does have some attractive buildings. A tuk-tuk to Muang Khao would cost around US$1.

Ban Saphay
ⓘ *5 km off Route 13, 15 km northwest of Pakse. Public tuk-tuks (US$5) travel from the 'terminal' near Daoheung market, especially in the morning.* This specialist silk-weaving village is 15 km north of town on the banks of the Mekong. Here about 200 women weave traditional Lao textiles on hand looms. The designs, like the classic *lao mut mee*, show clear similarities with those of northeastern Thailand, where the population is also Lao. However, there are also some unique designs. Prices vary according to quality and intricacy but a sarong length (1½ m) costs about 50,000-70,000 kip. There is also an unusual statue of Indra, Ganesh and Parvati at the local wat.

Wat Phou ☸ ↦ *pages 245-253.*

Wat Phou lies at the foot of the Phou Pasak, 8 km southwest of Champasak and is the most significant Khmer archaeological site in Laos. With its teetering, weathered masonry, it conforms exactly to the Western ideal of the lost city. The mountain behind Wat Phou is called **Linga Parvata**, as the Hindu Khmers thought it resembled a lingam – albeit a strangely proportioned one. Although construction of the original Hindu temple complex was begun in the fifth and sixth centuries, much of what remains today is believed to have been built in the 10th to 11th centuries.

Ins and outs
Getting there The nearest town to Wat Phou is Champasak (see page 243), which also lies on the west (or right) bank of the Mekong River; the main road is on the east bank. Most *songthaew* run from Pakse's Southern bus terminal on Route 13 to **Ban Lak Sarm Sip** (which translates as 'village 30 km'), where they take a right turn to **Ban Muang** (5 km). Here, people sell tickets for the ferry to **Ban Phaphin**, 2 km north of Champasak, 5000 kip. From the dock, you can catch a tuk-tuk to Champasak or the archaeological site for around 10,000 kip.

Public boats from Pakse make the journey to Champasak in 1½ hours, docking at the landing near Ban Lak Sarm Sip, from where you can catch a *songthaew* to Ban Muang. You can also charter a boat from Pakse to Wat Phou, which makes sense for a larger group and could be combined with a visit to Um Muang and Don Daeng (see page 244); expect to pay about US$50-60 for boat hire for 15-20 people. The boat will probably dock at **Ban Wat Muang Kao**, 4 km downstream from Champasak; take a bus or tuk-tuk from there. ▸▸ *For further details, see Transport, page 252.*

Wat Phou

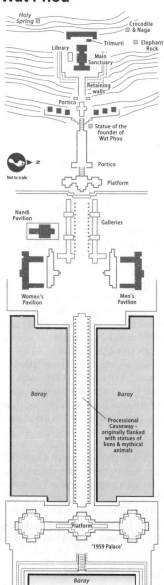

Tourist information The site is officially open 0800-1630 daily but the staff are happy to let you in if you get there for sunrise, even as early as 0530, and you won't get thrown out until 1800. Admission to the temple complex is 30,000 kip and goes towards restoration. There are foodstalls at the gate. The UNDP and UNESCO have agreed to finance and assist the renovation of Wat Phou and to establish a museum to hold some of its more vulnerable artefacts. A team of archaeologists is based at the site.

Background

Linga Parvata provides an imposing backdrop to the crumbling temple ruins, many of which date from the fifth and sixth centuries, making them at least 200 years older than Angkor Wat. At that time, the Champasak area was the centre of power on the lower Mekong. The Hindu temple only became a Buddhist shrine in later centuries. The French explorer, Francis Garnier, discovered Wat Phou in 1866 and local villagers told him the temple had been built by 'another race'. Unfortunately, not much is known about Wat Phou's history. Ruins of a palace have been found next to the Mekong at Cesthapoura (halfway between Wat Phou and Champasak – now an army camp) and it is thought the sixth-century Chenla capital was based there.

Archaeologists and historians believe most of the building at Wat Phou was the work of the Khmer king, Suryavarman II (1131-1150), who was also responsible for starting work on Angkor Wat, Cambodia. The temple remained important for Khmer kings even after they had moved their capital to Angkor. They continued to appoint priests to serve at Wat Phou and sent money to maintain the temple until the last days of the Angkor Empire.

1959 Palace and processional causeway The king and dignitaries would originally have sat on the platform above the 'tanks' or *baray* and presided over official ceremonies or watched aquatic games. In 1959 a palace was built on the platform so the king had somewhere to stay during the annual **Wat Phou Festival** (see page 249). The smaller house was for the king's entourage. A long avenue leads from the platform to the pavilions. The **processional causeway** was probably built by Khmer King Jayavarman VI (1080-1107), and may have been the inspiration for a similar causeway at Angkor Wat. The grand approach would originally have been flanked by statues of lions and mythical animals, but few traces remain.

Pavilions The sandstone pavilions, on either side of the processional causeway, were added after the main temple and are thought to date from the 12th century (most likely from the reign of Suryavarman II). Although crumbling, with great slabs of laterite and collapsed lintels lying aesthetically around, both pavilions are remarkably intact and, as such, are the most photographed part of the temple complex. The pavilions were probably used for segregated worship by pilgrims, one for women (left) and the other for men (right). The porticoes of the two huge buildings face each other. The roofs were thought originally to have been poorly constructed with thin stone slabs on a wooden beam-frame and later replaced by Khmer tiles.

Only the outer walls now remain but there is enough still standing to fire the imagination: the detailed carving around the window frames and porticoes is well-preserved. The laterite used to build the complex was brought from **Um Muang**, another smaller Khmer temple complex a few kilometres downriver (see page 244), but the carving is in sandstone. The interiors were without permanent partitions, although it is thought that rush matting was used instead, and furniture was limited – reliefs only depict low stools and couches. At the rear of the women's pavilion are the remains of a brick construction, believed to have been the queen's quarters. Brick buildings were very costly at that time.

Nandi Pavilion and temple remains Above the pavilions is a small temple, the Nandi Pavilion, with entrances on two sides. It is dedicated to Nandi, the bull (Siva's vehicle), and is a common feature in Hindu temple complexes. There are three chambers, each of which would originally have contained statues – these have been stolen. As the hill begins to rise above the Nandi temple, the remains of six brick temples follow the contours, with three on each side of the pathway. All six are completely ruined and their function is unclear. Archaeologists and Khmer historians speculate that they may have been Trimurti temples. At the bottom of the steps is a portico and statue of the founder of Wat Phou, Pranga Khommatha. Many of the laterite paving stones and blocks used to build the steps have holes notched down each side; these would have been used to help transport the slabs to the site and drag them into position.

Main sanctuary The main sanctuary, 90 m up the hillside and orientated east-west, was originally dedicated to Siva. The rear section (behind the Buddha statue) is part of the original sixth-century brick building. Sacred spring water was channelled through the hole in the back wall of this section and used to wash the sacred linga. The water was then thrown out, down a shute in the right wall, where it was collected in a receptacle. Pilgrims would then wash in the holy water. The front of the temple was constructed later, probably in the eighth to ninth century, and has some fantastic

Local legend has it that the Emerald Buddha – now in Bangkok – is a fake and the authentic one is hidden in Wat Phou; archaeologists, however, are highly sceptical.

carvings: apsaras, dancing Vishnu, Indra on a three-headed elephant (the former emblem of the kingdom of Lane Xang) and, above the portico of the left entrance, a carving of Siva, the destroyer, tearing a woman in two.

The Hindu temple was converted into a Buddhist shrine, either in the 13th century during the reign of the Khmer king Jayavarman VII or when the Lao conquered the area in the 14th century. A large Buddha statue now presides over its interior. There is also a modern Buddhist monastery complex on the site.

Around the sanctuary To the left of the sanctuary is what is thought to be the remains of a small library. To the right and to the rear of the main sanctuary is the **Trimurti**, the Hindu statues of Vishnu (right), Siva (central) and Brahma (left). Behind the Trimurti is the holy spring, believed by the Khmers to have possessed purificatory powers. Some of the rocks beyond the monks' quarters (to the right of the temple) have been carved with the figures of an elephant, a crocodile and a *naga*. They are likely to have been associated with human sacrifices carried out at the Wat Phou Festival; it is said the sacrifice took place on the crocodile and the blood was given to the *naga*. Present-day visitors to the festival in February (see page 249) should note that this practice has now stopped!

Around Wat Phou

For archeological enthusiasts who haven't had their fix from Wat Phou, there are several other ancient sites in close proximity, most in a state of disrepair. **Ho Nang Sida**, 1 km south of Wat Phou, is an understated ruined temple, overgrown with jungle and piles of rubble and rocks. The temple, called Lady Sida Hall, is believed to have sat on an ancient highway that linked Angkor Wat to Wat Phou; it was probably used as a hospital. One kilometre south of Ho Nang Sida is **Hong Nan Tao**, another set of ancient ruins, built under King Jayavarman VII and used as a shrine. Another 3 km along are three ancient stupas.

Champasak and around 🏠🍴❄️🚌 ›› pages 245-253.

The agricultural town of **Champasak**, stretches along the right bank of the Mekong for 4 km. It has a relaxed village ambience and, now that it has enough comfortable accommodation, is a good base from which to explore Wat Phou and the surrounding area. In 1970 Chao Boun Oum began work on yet another rambling palace on the outskirts of Champasak, but it was never finished as he was exiled to France in 1975. It

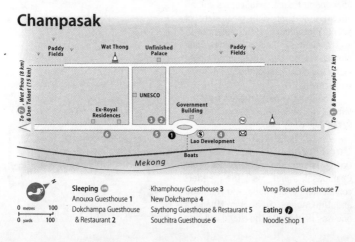

Champasak

Paddy Fields
Wat Thong
Unfinished Palace
Paddy Fields

To Wat Phou (8 km) & Don Talaat (15 km)

UNESCO

Ex-Royal Residences

Government Building

To & Ban Phapin (2 km)

Lao Development

Boats

Mekong

N

0 metres 100
0 yards 100

Sleeping 💤
Anouxa Guesthouse 1
Dokchampa Guesthouse & Restaurant 2

Khamphouy Guesthouse 3
New Dokchampa 4
Saythong Guesthouse & Restaurant 5
Souchitra Guesthouse 6

Vong Pasued Guesthouse 7

Eating 🍴
Noodle Shop 1

is now the official residence of Champasak's squatter community. The town's layout is quite compact with a number of colonial houses intermingled with traditional Lao wooden houses. The Prince's brothers owned the two French-style houses along the main road running south. These days the town doesn't really reflect the grandeur of bygone days. About 15 km southwest of Champasak is **Don Talaat**, which is worth a visit for its weekly market (Saturday and Sunday). It's renowned for the number of snakes on show.

Um Muang

ⓘ *Daily 0600-1630. Admission 10,000 kip (but it is unclear who you are supposed to give this to), some of the local children may act as guides (7000kip). A boat from Pakse (from the jetty at the end of No 11 Rd) costs US$45 return (split between the group). It is also possible to hire a car or tuk-tuk to make the journey. If you go by bus, you need to get off at Ban Huaytomo.*

Also known as Muang Tomo and Oup Moung, Um Muang is a lesser known temple complex built at about the same time as Wat Phou on the opposite (left) bank of the Mekong. It lies 40 km from Pakse and is accessible by boat from town or via the main road south from Pakse to Ban Thang Beng, Km 30, from where a track (vehicle access possible) leads 4 km to Ban Noi. From the village it is a 1-km walk to the temple.

In colonial days, Um Muang was a stopping point for ships travelling upriver from Cambodia. Its main treasure is a ninth-century Khmer-era temple complex built at roughly the same time as Wat Phou. The temple is thought to have been built by Yasarvoman I and is dedicated to Shiva's companion, Rudani. The site is an assortment of ruins, surrounded by jungle. A seven-headed sandstone *naga* greets you on arrival from the Mekong.

❣ *A chartered boat trip to Um Muang can easily be combined with visits to Wat Phou and Champasak for about US$50-60 for up to 6 people.*

Like Wat Phou, the main temple is built of laterite and its carvings are in similar style to those of the bigger complex upriver. It is thought, in fact, that the laterite blocks used in the construction of Wat Phou were taken from Um Muang. There are also the ruins of a second building, more dilapidated and moss-covered, making it difficult to speculate about its function, and, hidden in the jungle, are the remains of two *baray*. Um Muang is not on the same scale and nowhere near as impressive as Wat Phou but stumbling across a sixth-century Khmer temple in the middle of the jungle is nonetheless a worthwhile experience. Despite the presence of seemingly abandoned tourist facilities, it's still an atmospheric spot. With great slabs of laterite protruding from the undergrowth and ancient sandstone carvings lying around the bushes, there is no doubt that a great deal about the site remains undiscovered.

Some of the best artefacts from the temple can be found in the museum in Pakse (see page 239).

Don Daeng

Daeng Island sits right across from Champasak and is the perfect complement to any journey to Wat Phou and Um Muang. From Ban Muang a one-way boat trip to the island will cost

Around Wat Phou

Ban Saphay

To Thailand

Rt 10

Pakse

Muang Khao

To Paksong

Mekong River

Mount Kao (1,416m)

Ban Phaphin

Ban Lak Sarm Sip

Ban Muang

Champasak

Don Daeng

Um Muang (Muang Tomo)

To Attapeu

Wat Phou

Ban Wat Muang Kao

Don Talaat

Wat Muang Kang

Ban Noi

Ban Thang Beng

Don Khao Island

N

Rt 13

0 km   10

0 miles   10

To Ban Hat Xai Khoune

Southern Laos Pakse & around

around US$1. The island stretches across the Mekong, 8 km by 4 km, but its area increases and decreases in line with water levels on the river. Among the island's features is a crumbling brick stupa, built in the same century as Wat Phou. There are also a few ancient ruins in Sisak village. **Pouylao village** is known for the knife-making prowess of its inhabitants, who are more than happy to show tourists how they ply their trade. There is a lovely sand beach on the Champasak side, perfect for a dip. The best way to visit is on a pre-arranged ecotour, which may include treks and explorations of the local villages.

Hao Pa Kho island

One hour downriver from Pakse is this island, where Chao Boun Oum had his weekend house. It has lain abandoned since his exile to France.

Ban Khiet Ngong and Ban Pha Pho

⊟ 🍴 ▲ ↠ *pages 245-253.*

From Pakse follow Route 13 south and turn left at Km 38, onto Route 18b. Continue for another 13 km and you will reach **Ban Khiet Ngong**. This village has a community-based project which offers trekking and homestay accommodation on the edge of the **Se [Xe] Pian Wetlands**, which are rich in bird life and one of the most threatened land types in Laos. The provincial authorities are trying to promote ecotourism in this area, so please take this into consideration if you visit.

From Khiet Ngong, elephant treks can be organized either through the **Se Pian National Protected Area** or to the amazing fortress of **Phu Asa**. Located 2 km from Ban Khiet Ngong at the summit of a small jungle-clad hill, this ancient ruined fortress is an enigmatic Hindu-Khmer site. It was named after the local monk who apparently helped save the area from the Siamese in the 19th century but experts are unsure as to what purpose it originally served. Unlike Wat Phou, it isn't really intact but it does have over 20 interesting 2-m-high stone columns arranged in a semi-circle – they look a bit like a scaled-down Stonehenge.

Beyond Ban Khiet Ngong, about 27 km east of Ban Thang Beng on the road to Attapeu is **Ban Pha Pho**, a Suay village known for its working elephants. The Suay are a tribal group renowned across Thailand and Laos for their elephant-training abilities. There are more than 80 animals in the area, which are used to move hardwoods and to transport rice. These days it is quite difficult to organize an elephant trek by just turning up in Ban Pha Pho; a better bet is to make arrangements in **Ban Khiet Ngong**.

There are several two- to three-day trekking and home-stay ecotours offered in the area, contact the Provincial Tourism Information Office in Pakse and ask for Mr Sulichan. These tours are designed to ensure that local communities reap the rewards of tourism in a sustainable fashion and are highly recommended. Other tourism operators in Pakse can also organize tours to the area. ↠ *For further details, see Activities and tours, page 249.*

⊜ Sleeping

Pakse *p238, map p246*

AL-B Champasak Palace, No 13 Rd, T031-212263, F031-212781, champasak_palace_hotel@yahoo.com. This is a massive chocolate box of a hotel with 55 rooms. It was conceived as a palace for a minor prince (see Boun Oum Palace, page 240, for further details) and is now operated by a Thai firm.

Large rooms, ranging from economy (US$15-30) to the Presidential Suite. 40 more modern, less elaborate rooms were added in 2000. Never-ending construction seems on the agenda here. Despite the gaudy plaster additions of recent years and general lack of maintenance, some classic touches remain: wooden shutters, some art deco furniture and lovely tiles. The restaurant is the most atmospheric place to eat in town, set on a big verandah overlooking lovely frangipani trees and manicured gardens. Friendly staff, a good terrace and the best facilities in town, including a massage centre and a great position above the Xe Don. Family rooms are a good deal.

B Champa Residence (Residence du Champa), No 13 Rd, east of town near the stadium and museum, T031-212120, F031-212765, champare@laotel.com. Modern-style rooms, with a/c, mini-bar, hot water and satellite TV. Very clean and with some character. Attractive terrace and lush garden, visa accepted and tours arranged. Includes breakfast.

B-C Pakse Hotel, No 5 Rd (facing the new market), T031-212131. Recent renovations have rendered this one of the nicest places to stay in town with 65 rooms ranging from US$10 to US$27. The French owner, Mr Jerome, has integrated local handicraft decorations and tasteful furnishings into this slick hotel. Good restaurant attached, with the best pizza in town. Wonderful views of Pakse from the roof. Recommended.

B-C Seng Aroun, next door to Mengky Noodle Shop, T031-252111. The most modern hotel in town is so clean you can see your reflection on the floor tiles. At the time of publication, a long-running ₭500 promotion was still in place; at this price the hotel is really good value, but this is unlikely to last. 58 rooms with cable TV and a/c. More expensive rooms have a bathtub. Car rental, with driver, ₭1200 across the border.

C Lao Chaleun Hotel, opposite Salachampa, T031-251333, F031-251138. Opened in July 2001 on the corner of Rds 6 and 4, this place boasts 43 simply decorated a/c and fan rooms with TV and mini-bar. The name of the hotel means 'Modern Lao' but the façade of newness is starting to fade and the place is in need of some maintenance. A bit of an architectural eyebrow raiser: different areas of the hotel are separated by partitions under which you can duck to get to other

Pakse

Sleeping
Champasak Palace 1
Champa Residence 2
Lankham 3
Lao Chaleun 4
Pakse 5
Phonsavanh 6
Sabaidy II Guesthouse 7
Salachampa 8
Seng Aroun 9

Eating
Delta Coffee 1
Dorn Sok Dee 2
Jasmine 3
Ket Many 4

corridors. The outer rooms have a communal veranda. Motorbike rental and other tour services offered.

C **Salachampa**, No 10 Rd, T031-212273, F031-212646. The most characterful place in town. Choose a room in the main 1920s building: huge with wooden floors, large, en suite bathrooms with warm showers; the upstairs rooms with balconies are best. There are also some additional, quaintly rustic rooms in a 'new' extension and a nice garden area between the two. Recommended for those looking for a touch of colonial elegance and friendly service. Tours organized from here.

D **Lankham Hotel**, No 13 Rd, T031-213314. Void of character with a slightly haphazard, casual atmosphere downstairs. The rooms themselves are very clean and boast very comfortable beds. The downstairs restaurant is a hive of activity for breakfast. There is also an internet café attached to the premises.

D-E **Phonsavanh Hotel**, No 13 Rd, T031-212842. This has nothing else going for it except its central location and the fact that the popular Indian franchise, Nazim's, has moved downstairs. Rooms are grubby and basic with partitions which don't reach to the ceiling. Some have shared facilities, with cold water. Dismal feel.

D-F **Sabaidy 2 Guesthouse**, No 24 Rd, T031-212992. A wide range of rooms on offer, from US$2 dorm rooms through to US$5 rooms with private bathroom and hot water. The rooms are quite basic but the service here is exceptional. The proprietor, lively Mr Vong is a regular 'Mr Fixit' and offers tours, information and visa extensions. Mr Vong's grandfather, Liam Douang Vongsaa, was the first governor of Pakse and this building was the governor's residence, where Mr Vong was born in 1944. Highly recommended.

Champasak p243, map p243

C-D **Souchitra Guesthouse**, opposite former royal residences. A selection of rooms ranging from cheap cold-water rooms through to tastefully decorated clean rooms with fan, fridge and hot water. Good restaurant downstairs.

C-E **Anouxa Guesthouse**, 1 km north of the roundabout, T020-2275412. A wide range of good-value accommodation from wooden bungalows through to concrete rooms with either a/c or fan. The concrete villas are the best, with a serene river vista from the balconies. The only draw back is that it is a little out of town. Recommended.

E **Vong Pasued Guesthouse**, 450 m south of the roundabout. A firm favourite with the backpacker set, this small family-run guesthouse offers pretty reasonable but basic rooms (mosquito net, thin walls and cold water) in an old longhouse. Good restaurant, perfect for a natter with fellow travellers.

E-F **Dokchampa Guesthouse**, on the main road southwest of the roundabout, T020-2206248. Basic bamboo rooms with shared bathrooms and cold water. The newer establishment on the other side of the roundabout is of the same ilk. Just passable. Good-value restaurant.

Koveau Barbecue **5**
May Kham **6**
Mengky Noodle
  Shop **7**
Nazim's **3**

No 9 **9**
Seng Dao **10**
Sinouk **11**
Xuan Mai **12**

E-F **Khamphouy Guesthouse**, southwest of Dokchampa. Delightful family-run place. Fine bright rooms in the main house with shared facilities and 1 cottage (in the garden) with 2 rooms and en suite shower. Clean, comfortable, friendly, relaxed. Bikes for hire. Recommended.

E-F Saythong Guesthouse and Restaurant, opposite Dokchampa, T020-2209215. Riverside location. 5 basic rooms upstairs with shared toilet; 6 more rooms with private showers (3 with a/c) out the back. The rooms are reasonable but the restaurant is better: good food and ample portions.

Don Daeng p244

The island has only recently opened up for tourism. There is a very basic guesthouse, with single sex rooms, which can be booked through **Mr Ta**, Don Daeng Island Village or **Champa May Travel** in Pakse. Prices include meals and tours.

Ban Khiet Ngong and Ban Pha Pho p245

F **Boun Home Guesthouse**, Ban Khiet Ngong, very basic guesthouse with wooden rooms and shared facilities.

There are also a few basic wooden bungalows geared towards foreigners, US$4, and an ecolodge is due to open in 2006, www.kingfisherecolodge.com. Homestays can be arranged through the **National Tourism Authority** in Pakse (see page 239).

❶ Eating

Pakse p238, map p246

The town has numerous international eateries. Most close at around 2100-2200; Indian restaurants stay open latest.

Bakeries

Crusty baguettes are available across town; great for breakfast with wild honey and fresh Boloven coffee.

European/fusion

ᵀᵀ **Champasak Palace Hotel**, see Sleeping. Reasonable French interpretations in sublime surroundings.

ᵀᵀ **Delta Coffee**, Rd 13, opposite the Champasak Palace Hotel, T020-5345895. This place is a real find for those craving some Western comfort food. The extensive menu is tremendously varied and offers everything from pizza and lasagne to Thai noodles. Their coffee is brilliant and staff exceptionally friendly. They have an unusual ordering system in place where you write down orders by number.

ᵀᵀ **Sinouk**, opposite Lao Airlines on No 11 Rd, T031-212552. This is without a doubt the most tastefully decorated place in town, with tables adorned with glass-top coffee bean arrangements. There is a very reasonable breakfast and exceptionally good coffee. A creative menu is offered, which includes tomatoes stuffed with pork, ribs and a few other fusion-inspired meals, but coffee is their real forte.

Indian

ᵀᵀ-ᵀ **Jasmine Restaurant**, No 13 Rd, T031-251002. This small place has outdoor seating and is a firm favorite with travellers. Offering the standard Indian fare and a few Malaysian dishes, it's reasonable value. The town's conglomerate of tuk-tuk drivers gather here and very subtly tout for business.

ᵀᵀ-ᵀ **Nazim's Restaurant**, nearly next door to the Jasmine, T020-5832792. Serving a very similar menu but the setting and food is marginally better than their neighbour's.

Lao, Vietnamese, Thai and Chinese

ᵀ **Ket Many Restaurant**, 227 No 13 Rd, T031-212615. Chinese and Lao food from a limited menu in a/c restaurant. Deep-fried frog and Mekong River fish have both been recommended, or why not sample the spicy sour virgin pork uterus? Also serves European food (spaghetti etc).

ᵀ **Lankham Hotel**, see Sleeping. A reasonable choice, with good *feu* soup. Very popular for breakfast and lunch.

ᵀ **May Kham**, No 13 Rd, close to the bridge across the Don River, about 100 m from Wat Luang. Many local expats maintain this serves the best Vietnamese and Lao food in town, a/c restaurant but no pretensions, superb steamed duck with black mushroom and sweet and sour fish and morning glory stir fry.

ᵀ **Mengky Noodle Shop**, No 13 Rd. Serves bowls of tasty duck and beef noodle soup.

ᵀ **No 9**, No 13 Rd. Most Lao argue that this place has the best Lao food in town. The local *falang*, however, are not so impressed, particularly by the house speciality, dog.

⦿ Seng Dao Restaurant, No 13 Rd, T031-212507. A wide range of cakes, breads and pastries. There is also a buffet-style Lao food section, which by all accounts tastes great but does stand outside for a good part of the day, so be careful of salmonella.

⦿ Xuan Mai, near **Pakse Hotel**, T031-213245. Open-air restaurant serving Vietnamese, particularly good *feu*, and Lao dishes, excellent value and very good.

Korean

⦿⦿ Korean Barbecue, No 46 Rd (near corner with No 24 Rd), T031-212388. Classic Korean cook-it-yourself restaurant.

⦿ Dorn Sok Dee Restaurant, near the new market. Justifiably popular for its Korean grilled meat dishes.

Champasak *p243, map p243*

Most restaurants are in the guesthouses; all are cheap (⦿). **Anouxa Guesthouse** has a small menu but their offerings are delectable, opt for a fish dish. **Saythong Guesthouse** is also pretty good and its menu has some memorable typos such as "chicken can wish" and "fried morning yolky"; it's probably the best bet in town in terms of variety. There is also a pretty reasonably noodle *feu* shop near the roundabout.

Ban Khiet Ngong and Ban Pha Pho *p245*

Eating in the village is very basic and you will have to rely on the local food. *Feu* and noodle soup can be made on the spot; most other meals, such as *laap*, will need to be ordered in advance.

✪ Festivals

Wat Phou *p240, map p241*

Wat Phou Festival lasts for 3 days around the full moon of the 3rd lunar month (usually Feb). Pilgrims come from far and wide to leave offerings at the temple. In the evening there are competitions – football, boat racing, bullfighting and cockfighting, Thai boxing, singing contests and the like. There is also some pretty extravagant imbibing of alcohol.

◯ Shopping

Pakse *p238, map p246*
Film

There are a few shops on and around No 7 Rd and No 10 Rd where film can be developed, and a big Kodak shop on No 13 Rd.

Markets

Central market. The closest thing to a shopping centre in town remains half-filled with vendors mostly selling clothes. The initial plans were for it to be a pan-Asian centre, stocking Thai, Japanese, Vietnamese and Lao goods but this is yet to happen.

Daoheung market, opposite Champasak Museum. Even for Southeast Asia this is a major agglomeration of stalls and traders. It is best to get here between 0730 and 0800 when the place is in full swing; although it continues to function throughout the day, it does so in a rather semi-detached fashion. It's good for loads of unnecessary plastic and metal objects. Most people come here just to look but there are some fun things to buy: tin cans, clay pots, textiles and sarongs.

Textiles

Traditional handwoven silk cloth is available in the Daoheung Market (see above). There is a good handicraft shop opposite the small park near Wat Luang, which sells lovely woven baskets, wooden carvings and good-quality embroidery. Many people, however, prefer to visit **Ban Saphay** where the embroidery is actually produced and buy lengths there (see p240). The *mut mee ikat* designs are similar to those produced across the border in the northeastern or Isan region of Thailand. However, here in Laos it is more likely that the cloth will be produced from home-produced silk (in Thailand, silk yarn is often interwoven with imported thread) and coloured using natural rather than aniline dyes.

▲ Activities and tours

Pakse *p238, map p246*
Massage and sauna

Keo Ou Don Physiotherapy, Ban Ta Ou Dome, T031-251895. Although this place is just out of the main town area, it is well worth the short trip. A wide range of massage options are offered, from oil through to foot massage, as well as the Lao favourite: the 'reduced fat massage' (be warned, this is like burning fat off). All treatments and the sauna cost under US$3.

There is also a small sauna and massage centre at the **Champasak Palace Hotel**, and a brilliant new massage place across the road from the **Pakse Hotel**.

Swimming
There is a public pool on the way to the Southern bus station, 5,000 kip.

Tour operators
Most of the hotels in town arrange day tours to Wat Phou, Tad Lo and the Khong Phapheng Falls; of these the best is the **Pakse Hotel**. There are also a number of tour agencies in town, all of which will arrange tours to local sites like Wat Phou, Phu Asa, Khong Island and Champasak. They are also the best sources of information, although it is obviously in their interest to convince visitors that taking a tour is the best, possibly even the only, option.
Champa May, No 13 Rd, T031-212930, sonethida02 @yahoo.com, has teamed up with the NTA to offer a diverse range of unique ecotours for the benefit of local communities. Although you can approach the NTA directly, it is probably best to go with Champa May. Costs vary considerably according to numbers.
Lane Xang Travel, opposite **Jasmine Restaurant**, T020-2255176. Offers a variety of tours and useful tour services (including a mini-van service to Siphandon, 55,000 kip). Alex at Lane Xang is exceptionally helpful.
Sabaidy 2, see Sleeping, T031-212992. Mr Vong and crew offer a wide range of tours around a variety of top-notch provincial sites, very good value and recommended for visitors who are only around for a day or two (US$15 per person, 4 people min).
Sodetour, No 13 Rd, near No 24 Rd, T031-213431. Arranges adventurous tours to the Boloven Plateau, and other destinations.

Ban Khiet Ngong and Ban Pha Pho
p245
Elephant treks
There are several 2- to 3-day trekking/ homestay trips offered in the area; contact the **Provincial Tourism Information Office** in Pakse, T031-212021, and ask for Mr Sulichan. These tours are designed to ensure that local communities reap the rewards of tourism in a sustainable fashion and are highly recommended. Other tourism operators in Pakse can also organize tours to the area.

Elephant treks to the **Phu Asa** take about 3-4 hrs, US$13; the elephant baskets can carry 2 people. If you wish to travel independently to this area, you need to allow enough time for the elephants to be organized by the *mahouts* (elephant keepers) once you arrive. Contact **Mr Peua**, T020-5731207 (no English spoken) in advance. Otherwise, when you turn up in Ban Khiet Ngong, ask for **Mr Bounsome**, who runs the only bona fide guesthouse in the area (see Sleeping, above). Although only minimal English is spoken in the village, most of the locals will understand the purpose of your visit.

⊖ Transport

Pakse *p238, map p246*
For out-of-town journeys, hotels, such as the **Souksamlam** and **Champasak Palace**, and tour companies, such as **Lane Xang**, **Champa May** and **Sodetour**, charter cars and minibuses (with driver).

Air
The flight schedule changes frequently so it is best to check with a travel agent prior to making arrangements. There are currently flights to **Vientiane** on Tue, Wed, Fri and Sun, US$88; check with **Lao Airlines** for latest information; they have offices at the airport and by the river in town, T031-212252, open Mon-Fri. There is also a flight to **Siem Reap**, Wed, Fri and Sun, 50 mins, US$70. A flight between **Bangkok** and Pakse is being planned.

Boat
A public passenger boat leaves at 0800 daily for **Champasak** and **Wat Phou**, 1½-2 hrs, 40,000 kip per person, depending on numbers; boats can also be chartered for around US$50-60. In the dry season the public service continues to Ban Hua Khong on **Don Khong**, 8 hrs total, US$8/100,000 kip. Be warned, though, that the turnaround time is speedy, and by the time this boat

leaves Champasak, it's usually full to bursting and not apt to wait for any stragglers. In Ban Hua Khong you can catch a tuk-tuk to Muang Khong on the main part of the island. During the wet season, it is almost impossible to find a scheduled boat, in which case you can charter boats to Don Khong for around US$130 one way from the jetty at the end of No 11 Rd. Note that, even if you're chartering a boat, the boatmen will not make the journey in the dark, so embark before 0900 if you want to get to Don Khong in 1 trip.

Mr Bounmy, T020-5631008, will charter his speedy 30-seat, long-boat to Champasak and Don Khong for slightly cheaper rates.

For those that want to do the trip more comfortably, **Indocruise**, near BCEL bank, T031-215958, has an old slow boat, set up with a dining area, that cruises from Pakse to Wat Phou and Siphandon. Prices tend to vary depending on the season but are usually around US$330.

Bus/songthaew

Buses/trucks travelling north (to Savannakhet, Thakhek and Vientiane) leave from the Northern bus station, Km 7 on Route 13, across the Xe Don. The southern terminal is at Km 8 also on Route 13, heading south out of town. Lists of bus departures can be found in many of the hotels and guesthouses. There are regular morning departures to most destinations until 1600 and journey times are decreasing as the roads improve.

Songthaew for **Paksong**, 50 km, depart from another small bus terminal at Km 2 on the other side of the bridge, every 15 mins from 0800, US$1. Make sure you stipulate where you are hopping off.

From the Northern terminal Hourly departures 0600-1500 daily to **Savannakhet**, 250 km, 4-5 hrs, 30,000 kip; to **Tha khek**, 6-7 hrs, 60,000 kip; to **Lak Sao**, 8-9 hrs, 75,000 kip; to **Paksan**, 10 hrs, 80,000 kip; to **Vientiane**, 13-14 hrs, 85,000 kip.

From the Southern terminal There are regular bus connections with **Champasak** at the Southern bus station; stay on the bus if you are travelling to Wat Phou (see p240). Ask for Ban Lak Sarm Sip (translates as 'village 30 km'), here there is a signpost and you turn right and travel 4 km

towards Ban Muang (5 km). In the village there are people selling tickets for the ferry 7,000 kip. Also *songthaew* to **Champasak**, 1000 and 1300, 38 km, 1½ hrs, US$1.50.

Occasional buses to the **Siphandon** area but these can't be relied on; a cartel of *songthaew* drivers have some kind of scam that ensures buses won't operate while they are around. Buses are supposed to run down to the **Mekong Islands** but sit dormant for the most part. However, if you are travelling with a group you could probably hire a whole bus with little difficulty. Note, too, that buses are twice as likely to depart in the high season, usually at 1000 and 1200. Consider yourself lucky if you catch a bus but, if you do end up on a *songthaew*, aim for a seat on the inside, in case of rain, and try to find some padding for the seat as it can be a painful trip. To **Don Khong/Muang Khong**, 0800, 1000, 1200, 1400 and 1600 daily, 140 km, 4 hrs, US$3; to **Voen Kham** (Cambodian border), 0700 and 1100 daily, 3-4 hrs; to **Tad Lo**, 0700, 0900, 1000 and 1200 daily, 85 km, 2 hrs, US$2 (ensure that the bus is taking Route 20 and not the alternative Route 23 via Paksong); to **Tad Fan**, 0800, 0900, 1000 and 1200 daily, 50 km, 1 hr, US$1.50; to **Tha Theng**, 0900, 1100 and 1200 daily, 15,000 kip; to **Ban Khiet Ngong** (for elephant treks around Phu Asa, see page 245 and page 250) 1000 and 1200 daily, 56 km, 2 hrs, US$1; to **Ban Pha Pho**, 1000 and 1200 daily, 70 km, 2 hrs, 12,000 kip; to **Don Deth/Don Khone** (via **Ban Nakasong**), hourly 0800-1300 daily, 144 km, 4 hrs, from 25,000 kip. A more comfortable alternative, in the high season, is to take the mini-van service to **Don Deth/Don Khone** offered by Lane Xang Travel, 55,000 kip.

Local buses coming through from Vientiane provide the main means of transport to other destinations down south, so can be slightly off kilter. Buses depart for **Salavan**, 0700, 0900, 1000 and 1200 daily, 110 km, 2-3 hrs, US$2. This is a good alternative for those wishing to head to **Tad Lo** (20,000 kip), just make sure that the bus is taking Route 20 (not Route 23) and that the driver understands you want to get off at the junction. To **Sekong**, 0700, 0900 and 1300 daily, 144 km, 3-4 hrs, 25,000 kip; to **Attapeu**, 0600, 0800, 1000 and 1500 daily, 190 km, 3-4 hrs, 35,000 kip.

‡ Border essentials: Vang Tao-Chongmek (Thailand)

This route is an important exit point for Lao timber; timber trucks rumble their way towards the sizeable timber yard at Chongmek.

Songthaew for the border at Vang Tao depart from the Daoeuang market in Pakse, hourly, 0800-1600 daily, 45 km, 1 hr, US$1. The border is open 0500-2000 daily but allow yourself additional time to get there as the *songthaew* can be painfully slow. A faster alternative is one of the older taxis, 45 min, ฿300.

Once you've been dropped off at Vang Tao, walk 250 m to reach the official building where you will receive an exit stamp; you may need to pay 'overtime fees' if you cross the border at the weekend. Walk another 50 m or so to the Thai border, where you will automatically be issued with a 30-day visa. There is a post office and duty free shop at the border. Customs formalities are very relaxed.

From the Thai side, *songthaew* run to Phibun Mangsahan, 1 hr, ฿30, where you can pick up another *songthaew* (฿30) or a taxi-minibus (฿600 divided between all the passengers) to the city and airport of Ubon Ratchathani. Both airlines (Air Asia and Thai) and buses operate from Ubon Ratchathani direct to Bangkok (see page 31).

From the Central market These buses are a much quicker northbound alternative. **KVT Buses**, T031-212228, depart at 2030 daily for **Vientiane**, 10 hrs non-stop, US$16. **Laolee VIP** buses depart at 2000 daily for **Vientiane**, US$11, via **Savannakhet**, 5 hrs, US$6, and at 0700 daily for **Thakhek**, 7 hrs, US$8. **Sengjadut VIP** buses depart for **Vientiane** at 0800 daily, 10 hrs, US$11 (US$13 with toilet), via **Thakhek**, 7 hrs, US$8. Apparently the government does not favour the VIP buses so keep your fingers crossed that they won't be abolished.

Motorbike and bicycle hire
Sabaidy 2, see Sleeping, rents motorbikes with insurance for US$8 the 1st day and US$7 for subsequent days. The **Lankham Hotel** rents out bicycles (US$1 per day) and larger dirtbikes.

Tuk-tuk/saamlor
These are the main forms of local transport. A tuk-tuk to the northern bus station should cost 5,000-7,000 kip. Shared tuk-tuks to local villages leave from the Daoheung market and from the stop on No 11 Rd near the jetty. Tuk-tuks can also be chartered by the hour. For services to the Thai border, see Border essentials, above.

Champasak *p243, map p243*
Boat
It is almost as quick and far more entertaining to travel around this area by boat. A day tour of the local sites, with an early start, stopping off at Don Daeng, Wat Muang Kao and Um Muang, will cost US$15.

Boats coming upstream from Don Khong arrive at Champasak at about 1400 and continue on to **Pakse** but always check in advance that the boats are running. There's also a morning connection downstream to **Don Khong**, leaving 0830-1000 daily, 8,000 kip (see Pakse Transport, above). Be warned, though, that the turnaround time is speedy, and by the time this boat pushes off again, it's usually full to bursting and not apt to wait for any stragglers.

Tuk-tuk
A tuk-tuk to **Ban Thong Kop**, the village opposite Wat Phou costs around 10,000 kip; direct to **Wat Phou** is US$5 return.

❶ Directory

Pakse *p238, map p246*
Banks BCEL Bank, No 11 Rd (beside the river), changes US$ and most currencies (cash) and offers a better commission rate on cash exchange than other banks, also Visa/Mastercard cash advances at 3%

commission, Mon-Fri 0830-1530 (with 1 hr lunch break); **Lao Development Bank**, No 13 Rd, T031-212168, cash and TCs exchanged; there is a branch of the **Lao Viet Bank** on the main road but it only changes TCs and cash, open Mon-Fri 0830-1530. **Embassies and consulates** Vietnam, No 24 Rd, Mon-Fri 0800-1300, 1400-1630, visas for Vietnam cost US$50 and take 3 days to process, so you are better off organizing your Vietnamese visa in Vientiane. **Internet** Expect to pay around 200 kip per min but discounts kick in usually after an hour: **D@M's Internet & Email Service**, No 13 Rd; **Lankham Hotel** has about 5 computers; the **Canon** photocopy shop is another option; the best internet shop is **Vandersar Internet** run by a lovely Lao couple who are very helpful and offer good fruit shakes to boot.

Medical services There is a huge hospital between No 1 Rd and No 46 Rd, T031-212018, but neither their English skills nor medical service will suffice for complex cases; in case of emergencies you are better off going across to Ubon in Thailand; there is a pretty good pharmacy at the hospital which stocks most medications. **Police** T031-212145. **Post office** No 8 Rd, overseas telephone calls can also be made from here; express mail service available; note the ashtrays made from defused (one hopes) unexploded shells. **Telephone** Telecommunications office for fax and overseas calls on No 1 Rd, near No 13 Rd; all of the internet cafés have internet-call facilities which are by far the cheapest option.

Boloven Plateau

The French identified the Boloven Plateau, in the northeast of Champasak Province, as a prime location for settlement by hardy French farming stock. The soils are rich and the upland position affords some relief from the summer heat of the lowlands. Fortunately, their grand plans came to nought and, although some French families came to live here, they were few in number and all left between the 1950s and 1970s as conditions deteriorated. The area also suffered another setback during the war years, when the major surrounding towns were completely destroyed by US bombing campaigns. Even so, the area was developed as a coffee-, rubber-, tea- and cardamom-growing area. The cool breeze of the plateau, with an average altitude of 600 m, offers much respite from the stifling heat of surrounding lower lands, particularly in April and May. Today it is inhabited by a colourful mix of ethnic groups, such as the Laven, Alak, Tahoy and Suay, many of whom were displaced during the war and (to a lesser extent) by recent dam-building efforts. There are numerous villages dotted between the small settlement of Tha Teng and Salavan. The premier attraction in the area is the number of roaring falls plunging off the plateau. Today, Tad Lo and Tad Fan are particularly popular tourist destinations. A trip to a coffee or tea plantation also provides an interesting insight into the region. ›› *For Sleeping, Eating and other listings, see pages 264-270.*

Ins and outs

As tourism expands in Laos, so areas like the Boloven are sure to become more accessible. For the moment though the tourist infrastructure is limited. Tour companies, especially in Pakse, 30 km away (see page 249), can organize trips. Alternatively, the best base is Tad Lo (see page 255). Other places near or on the Boloven are Salavan (see page 258), Sekong (see page 260) and Attapeu (see page 261); guesthouses in these towns can also offer assistance and information. Note that it is not always possible to drive across the Boloven Plateau from Salavan to Attapeu, as bad weather rapidly deteriorates the roads. In the wet season, parts of the new road recently constructed from Paksong can be washed away.

The fertile farmland of the Boloven Plateau has given Salavan Province a strong agricultural base, supporting coffee, tea and cardamom plantations. The road from Paksong to Pakse is known as the Coffee Road. Coffee was introduced to the area by French settlers in the 1920s and 1930s, who then made a quick exit as the bombing escalated in the 1960s. It is mainly exported via Pakse to Thailand, Singapore and, formerly, the USSR. Fair Trade has also catapulted the coffee into the UK and US markets. Tea grown in this area, however, is for local use. The Boloven also has the perfect climate for durians; villages (particularly on the road from Paksong to Pakse) are liberally dotted with durian trees. The fruit is exceptionally rich and creamy and in the peak season, between May and July, can be bought from roadside stalls for just 1,000 kip or so. Thanks to its fertility, the plateau is now rapidly repopulating and new farms are springing up. One can see evidence of the government's relocation policy everywhere on the plateau, where villages have been moved from higher lands to the lower lands, with the end goal of minimizing slash-and-burn agriculture and providing people better access to infrastructure, markets and other facilities. As a result, many new farming practices and produce have been steadily introduced. Towards Salavan, lots of banana plantations are cropping up and, between Paksong and Tha Teng, many small-time village operations are producing cabbage and corn crops, often sold roadside.

During the bombing of the Ho Chi Minh Trail (see page 228), to the east, many hilltribes and other ethnic minority groups also migrated to the Boloven, which consequently has become an ethnographic goldmine with more than 12 obscure minority groups living in the area, including the Katu, Alak, Tahoy, Suay, Ya Houne, Ngai and Suk. Most of the tribes are of Indonesian (or Proto-Malay) stock and have very different facial characteristics to the Lao; they are mainly animist (see page 322).

Paksong (Pakxong) and around → *Phone code: 031.*

Colour map 3, B3. 🖼️🍴🛏️📞 » *pages 264-270.*

The main town on the Boloven Plateau is Paksong, a small market town 50 km east of Pakse. It was originally a French agricultural centre, popular during the colonial era for its cooler temperatures. Paksong was yet another casualty of the war and was virtually destroyed. The area is famous for its fruit and vegetables; even strawberries and raspberries can be cultivated here.

The town occupies a very scenic spot, however, the harsh weather in the rainy season changes rapidly, making it difficult to plan trips around the area. The town consists of little more than a couple of blocks of old shops and a big market, which acts as a trading centre for many of the outlying villages of the plateau.

Waterfalls around Paksong

Just 17 km from Paksong are the stunning twin falls of **Tad Mone** and **Tad Meelook**. Once a popular picnic spot for locals, the area is now almost deserted and the swimming holes at the base of the falls are an idyllic place for a dip. To reach the falls take Route 23 northeast of Paksong towards Tha Teng and Salavan, until you reach a signposted turning; follow the road for about 3½ km to reach the falls.

Not far from Paksong, 1 km off the road to Pakse, is **Tad Fan**, a dramatic 120-m-high waterfall, which is believed to be one of the tallest cascades in the country. The fall splits into two powerful streams roaring over the edge of the cliff and plummeting into the pool below, with mist and vapour shrouding views from above. The fall's name derives from the species of barking deer which formerly surrounded the area and local legends talk of large numbers of the species falling to their death down the mammoth falls. One of the best viewing spots for the falls is the **Tad Fan Resort**'s restaurant (see Sleeping, page 264), which offers an unobscured view of the magnificent site. Beware of the vendors aggressively hawking coffee, tea, orchids and other products on the entrance road. Further upriver, near Ban Lak, is **Tad Yeung**, an impressive set of falls, surrounded by coffee and tea plants, with good swimming and a few small food stalls. It's popular with local tourists. Take the trail from near the toilets at Tad Yeung to hike to the top of Tad Fan in about 40 minutes.

The falls sit on the edge of the **Dong Hua Sao National Protected Area** and access via the falls is one of the only ways to explore the area. Previously, it was inhabited by a number of rare species now dwindling in number. It is believed that a local population of tigers still resides in the protected area but the chances of spotting one are minimal. Trekking is offered around the waterfall but is quite difficult in the wet season due to slipperiness and leaches, so it's best to hire one of the guides at the **Tad Fan** resort. Take a track to the left off the main road at Ban Lak, Km 38; at the end of the track, a path leads down to a good viewpoint halfway down the horseshoe-shaped gorge. The magnificent falls offer stunning views but if you wish to swim you should trek further along to Tad Gniang, 2 km east of Tad Fan. **Tad Gniang**, named after the wild stags that populate the area, is only recommended for a dip during the dry season (October to the end of March). There is a charge of 2000 kip per person, plus an additional 3000 kip per motorbike. Tours to Tad Fan and Tad Gniang can be organized through most travel agents in Pakse, including the **Pakse Hotel**, **Sabaidy 2**, **Champa May Travel** and **Lane Xang Travel** (see page 250).

Tad Jampapa, another stunning waterfall can be found 42 km from Paksong on the way to Pakse; turn off at the sign on the north side of the road.

Tha Teng and around ⊞⊟ ›› pages 264-270.

On the Boloven Plateau, at the junction of Routes 23 and 16 between Salavan (45 km), Sekong (48 km) and Paksong (37 km), is **Tha Teng**, a village that was levelled during the war. Before that, it was the home of Jean Dauplay, the Frenchman who introduced coffee to Laos from Vietnam in 1920. Today the UNDP, in a joint venture with a private sector businessman, has set up a small wild honey-processing factory. Villagers are paid for the combs they collect from jungled hills around Tha Teng. The carefully labelled 'Wild honey from Laos' is exported to European health food shops. There are several ethnic minority villages in the area.

There isn't much to see in the town itself – essentially it's just a big roundabout, affording stunning views. There is, however, an excellent ethnic minority market starting at about 0600 daily, to which villagers come to sell produce from their plots. A convoy of tractors, horses and basket-carrying women puffing on pipes can be seen at day-break approaching the market.

Tad Lo and around → Phone code: 031. Colour map 3, B3
⊞⊘✲▲⊟ ›› pages 264-270.

Tad Lo is a popular 'resort' on the edge of the Boloven Plateau, 30 km from Salavan. There are now numerous places to stay in this idyllic retreat, good hiking, an exhilarating river to frolic in (especially in the wet season) and elephant trekking. In the vicinity of Tad Lo there are also hill tribe villages, which can be visited in the company of a local villager. The area has become particularly popular with the backpacker set, many of whom prefer to stay here rather than in Pakse.

The **Xe Xet** (or Houei Set) flows past Tad Lo, crashing over two sets of cascades nearby: **Tad Hang**, the lower series, is overlooked by the **Tad Lo Lodge** and **Saise Guesthouse** (see Sleeping, page 264), while **Tad Lo**, the upper, is a short hike away.

The fall of Tha Teng: a personal view

In 1968, I read about the fall of Tha Teng to the Pathet Lao. The small article was buried in a back page of the newspaper. Not many Americans really cared about this loss or even knew where Laos was, let alone Tha Teng. In 1969 I was flying over Tha Teng in my Bird Dog – a Cessna 170 – which was used in my work as a Forward Air Controller (Code name, Raven 58) for the United States Air Force. All that was left of this town was about 20 homes lining a road on the northern edge of the Boloven Plateau. The homes were gradually being overrun by heavy vegetation.

What was so important about this town that its loss would be reported in the United States? Tha Teng is strategically located on the northern edge of the Boloven Plateau. As a military outpost, it could be used to obtain intelligence about enemy activity. So, by occupying Tha Teng, the 'friendlies' – the Royal Lao Government – could, to a certain extent, control the gateway to the Boloven. With its loss, the Pathet Lao and North Vietnamese could move more easily in their efforts to control the plateau. The significance of the location of Tha Teng was well known to the Pathet Lao. It was rumoured that there was a cave northeast of Tha Teng which could hold a battalion of troops and whose entrance was large enough to walk an elephant through. Elephants were used to haul heavy equipment, ammunition and supplies into the cave. But, from the air, the terrain looked flat. Even the military topological maps did not indicate the possibility of a cave. However, on Thanksgiving Day 1969, I confirmed in fact the existence of that cave by

'clearing' away the 200-ft trees which protected its entrance. Further, it exposed a large permanent bivouac area in front of the cave entrance which provided facilities for at least a battalion-size unit. This staging area proved successful as the Pathet Lao captured the Boloven during their campaign of 1970.

The 'war-that-wasn't' in Laos was odd in more than just the sense that it wasn't a war. In Vientiane it was a common sight to see Pathet Lao soldiers coming down out of the mountains in full combat gear, including weapons, to obtain their daily rations. They could shop without concern of being captured and would then return to the mountains to join their combat units. These were the same soldiers that the Royal Lao army, who were also at the market, might be fighting later that same day. Three days each year, the war would stop in southern Laos. Officials from Salavan would get in a truck and head south toward the plateau. At the edge of the Bolovens they would stop to let armed Pathet Lao (PL) get on their truck so they could continue to each village on the plateau. These PL guards would make certain that the officials only went to the villages. As the officials visited each village, they would record the births, deaths and weddings which had taken place during the previous year. War or no war, official government records had to be maintained. Following the three-day yearly truce, the war would resume.

Source: Ken Thompson, Raven 58, who flew as a FAC over Laos and Vietnam from 1968 to 1970.

The Xe Xet is yet another river being dammed in the area to produce hydropower for export to Thailand.

Getting there The turning for Tad Lo is at to Ban Houei Set on Route 20 between Pakse and Salavan. Catch a bus or *songthaew* from either town; most drivers know Tad Lo and will stop at Ban Houia Set (2½ hours from Pakse and under an hour from Salavan). There is a blue sign here indicating the way to Tad Lo – a 1½-km walk along a dirt track and through the village of Ban Saen Wang. Usually you can get a tuk-tuk to Tad Lo for around 5,000 kip. ➤ For further details, see Transport, page 269.

Tourist information Each one of the guesthouses in Tad Lo can arrange guided treks to Ban Khian and Tad Soung. Before you set off, pop into **Tim's Restaurant** (see page 264) for a quick chat to Soulideth (Tim's English- speaking husband). A great source of free and friendly information, he is the foremost authority on all there is to do in the area and is unbelievably helpful. He can arrange tours and excursions – and anything else imaginable – with less hassle and more local involvement than anyone else. He'll also give you a map which you can copy. For more information, consult his website (www.tadlo.laopdr.com).

> ⚡ *You are advised to hire a local guide on all treks to tribal villages as there have been reports of trouble arising between independent visitors and the Nay Ban (Village Chief).*

Around Tad Lo

There are two Alak villages, **Ban Khian** and **Tad Soung**, close to Tad Lo. The Alak are an Austro-Indonesian ethno-linguistic group. Their grass-thatched huts, with rounded roofs, are not at all Lao in style and are distinct from those in neighbouring Lao Theung villages. Most fascinating is the Alak's seeming obsession with death. The head of each household carves coffins out of logs for himself and his whole family (even babies), then stacks them, ready for use, under their rice storage huts. This tradition serves as a reminder that life expectancy in these remote rural areas is around 40 (the national average is a little over 50) and infant mortality upwards of 120 per 1,000 live births; the number one killer is malaria.

Katou villages such as **Ban Houei Houne** (on the Salavan-Pakse road) are famous for their weaving of a bright cloth used locally as a *pha sinh* (sarong). This village also has an original contraption to pound rice: on the river below the village are several water-wheels which power the rice pounders. The idea originally came from Xam Neua and was brought to this village by a man who had fought with the Pathet Lao. Tours to the village are run by **Saise Guesthouse**: at 150,000 kip per tour; it's best to set off in a group. **Tim's Restaurant** can also make arrangements for you, negotiating directly with the tuk-tuk driver to keep the price down.

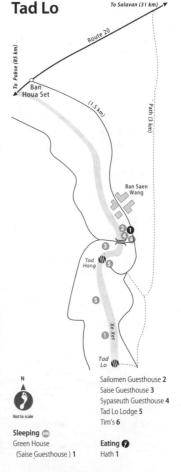

Tad Lo

To Salavan (31 km)
Route 20
To Pakse (85 km)
Ban Houa Set
(1.5 km)
Path (3 km)
Ban Saen Wang
Tad Hang
Xe Xet
Tad Lo

N
Not to scale

Sleeping
Green House
(Saise Guesthouse) 1

Sailomen Guesthouse 2
Saise Guesthouse 3
Sypaseuth Guesthouse 4
Tad Lo Lodge 5
Tim's 6

Eating
Hath 1

Salavan (Saravan) and around → *Phone code: 034. Colour map 3, B3.*

⊞⊘⊘⊡⊟⊙ ‣ *pages 264-270.*

The capital of one of the most beautiful provinces in Laos, the old French town of Salavan (also Saravan and Saravane) lies at the northern edge of the Boloven Plateau and acts as a transport hub and trading centre for the agricultural commodities produced on the plateau. The Xe Don, which enters the Mekong at Pakse, flows along the edge of town. Salavan is a charming town with no pretensions. Pigs and buffalo wander along the roads, children play in the streets and shops sell such practical goods as anvils, bicycle tyres, lengths of wire, transmission parts and brightly coloured functional plastic objects. There are few handicrafts or postcards in sight. In the cool of the evening, when people are at rest, talking, cooking and playing, the town seems – despite the legacy of the war – to epitomize a more innocent past. If you happen to be walking past the market at 1700 or thereabouts, you may even find yourself invited to join the locals in a game of petang.

Ins and outs

Getting there Most buses from Pakse turn off Route 23 and travel to Salavan via Route 20, a new and comparatively fast road that goes past the turning to Tad Lo (see page 255). They often also stop for a while at the small market town of Ban Lao Ngam on the Houei Tapoung (46 km from Salavan, 79 km from Pakse). Some buses, though, take the longer and rougher route via Paksong (Route 23). ‣ *For further details, see Transport, page 269.*

History

This area was an important Champasak kingdom outpost called Muang Mam and populated by mostly Mon-Khmer ethnic groups. In 1828 the Siamese renamed the area Salawan, which has evolved into the current name.

Salavan changed hands several times during the American war in Indochina, as the Pathet Lao and forces of the Royal Lao Government fought for control of this critical town located on a strategic flank of the Ho Chi Minh Trail. The two sides, with the RLG supported by American air power, bombed and shelled the town in turn as they tried to dislodge one another and Salavan was all but obliterated. (There is a

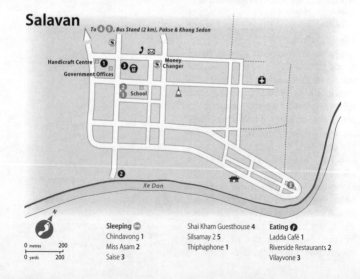

Salavan

Sleeping 😴
Chindavong 1
Miss Asam 2
Saise 3
Shai Kham Guesthouse 4
Silsamay 2 5
Thiphaphone 1

Eating 🍴
Ladda Café 1
Riverside Restaurants 2
Vilayvone 3

crude painting of the battle in the **Champasak Museum** in Pakse; see page 239.) Until a few years ago, there were still piles of war scrap, including unexploded bombs, shells and mortars in the streets. Now cleared away, reminders of the war are largely confined to the memories of older residents (most are under 30) and the pages of books. The consequences of the shelling and bombing today is that Salavan is a provincial capital with scarcely an ounce of physical beauty and almost no evidence of its French-era origins, except for the post office.

When US airforce pilots mounted bombing runs in Vietnam, their rules of engagement prohibited airstrikes within 500 m of a temple; in Cambodia, the margins were increased to 1 km. It has been said that in Laos such rules did not apply, but one retired US officer who was based there has written to us saying that "a complex web of rules [was] administered by levels of supervision stretching from the embassy in Vientiane, to Saigon, to Honolulu to the Pentagon, and included consultation with, and on the appropriate occasions approval by, the Lao government." Like Xieng Khouang, another critical town to the north, Salavan had one of the most beautiful temples in the country, **Wat Chom Keoh**, which was destroyed in an air raid in 1968. (The wat was commemorated on a postage stamp in the 1950s.)

Sights

Today all that remains of **Wat Chom Keoh** are two forlorn and shell-pocked corner-posts, one ruined chedi and a dilapidated wat building decaying still further in the grounds of the Salavan general hospital. The daily market in the centre of town is worth a visit, mainly, admittedly, because there is little else to see apart from the handicraft centre. In past years the market was an environmentalist's nightmare: all manner of wild creatures, some listed as endangered, would end up here, either for the cooking pot or for the trade in live wild animals (see Background, page 343). Today the frisson of such sights is, fortunately, no longer on offer. There's the usual array of frogs and fish, and perhaps a wild bird, squirrel or lizard, but not much else.

Look carefully and you can still see evidence of the war: many of the awnings and umbrellas in the market are made from parachute silk.

Ban Nong Boua

Ban Nong Boua, a beautiful lake near the source of the Xe Don, lies 18 km east of Salavan town. It is famed for its crocodiles (although apparently now only two remain), which move into the river in the dry season but usually stay out of sight. The locals have a number of cultural beliefs surrounding the crocodiles, so a donation – perhaps in order to offer a pig to the crocs, which the residents will actually consume themselves – is likely to be expected before they will escort you to the lake. The road to Ban Nong Boua is too rough to be negotiated by tuk-tuk, which means it is necessary to charter a jeep or other sturdy vehicle. There are two river crossings along the way, so any vehicle that won't fit in a small boat or brave the waters won't make it there. In the wet season it is advisable to travel by boat.

Ban Nong Boua is also rumoured to be a starting point for climbing **Phou Katae**, the 1588-m-high mountain that looms over Salavan from the south. However, *falangs* aren't welcome to climb it, either because of the American airstrip from the war that is supposedly up there, or because of the logging operations on the other side, which are not entirely legal nor public. Access to both Ban Nong Boua and Phou Katae is very difficult and is only recommended for the tougher independent traveller. There is nowhere to sleep near the mountain but it may be possible to sleep at the nearby temple if you have a mosquito net.

Salavan Province has a large hydroelectric power-generating capacity. The Xe Xet barrage, which emanates from the Nam Xe Xet, supplies power to Pakse; some electricity is also exported to Thailand.

Tahoy, northeast of Salavan along Route 15, is a major centre of the Tahoy minority ethnic group. There are 25,000 Tahoy spread across the two adjoining provinces but the largest population lives here. Aside from being an interesting cultural insight into the Tahoy culture, the town is also renowned for war junk, as the Ho Chi Minh Trail dissected the area. Locals believe that there is a large tiger population in the area and tales are rife of this person or that person being eaten by a tiger. However, it would seem that the tigers aren't very forthcoming, as even tiger specialists have difficulty tracking the creatures.

‼ *Ban Khan Nam Xiep on the Coffee Road is another Tahoy village.*

Toum Lan is a Katong village 46 km north of Salavan, notable for its longhouse and traditional weaving techniques (ask Mr Bousasone at **Saise Guesthouse** for details). They also celebrate the Lapup festival, where buffaloes are usually sacrificed around the full moon in March. During the rainy season it is difficult to access the site. A bus leaves for Toum Lan at 1430 (15,000 kip) and returns at 0700. Accommodation may be possible in the village (10,000 kip).

The **Phasuam** waterfall lies 81 km from Salavan on Route 20. It is a beautiful spot but is dominated by the resort that sits on the site. The proprietor has relocated a small ethnic village from their homes to the resort premises in order to make a distinctly dubious 'ethnic museum', where the villagers show tourists their 'traditional way of life'. As tourists approach, the villagers change out of their jeans and into traditional attire before running around, beating drums and playing traditional music.

Coffee Road

Heading south from Salavan, Route 20 reaches Ban Beng after 26 km (4 km from Tad Lo). Turn south (right if coming from Tad Lo or Pakse) on to Route 23 – the 'Coffee Road'. From here the road climbs up to the lower slopes of the Boloven Plateau. From Ban Beng, the road is poor as far as Tha Teng, although there are indications that upgrading is in the pipeline. From Tha Teng to Sekong, however, the road is paved and very scenic. The area is still largely forested with a sparse population concentrated along the road and mainly cultivating coffee. Buses and trucks usually stop at the local market centre of Ban Tha Teng.

Towards Sekong the land is more intensively cultivated; there is even some irrigated rice. This is also an area of resettlement with a number of new villages carving out a small area of civilized space in the forest. The large logging yard and saw mill at Ban Phon, about 12 km north of Sekong, demonstrates the local economy's dependence on timber.

Sekong (Xekong, Muang Lamam) and around

→ *Phone code: 031. Colour map 3, B4.* 🖃📞🖳🖂🌑 ➼ *pages 264-270.*

Sekong (or Xekong) is a new town and capital of the province of the same name. It is located on the Kong River at the eastern edge of the Boloven Plateau, about 100 km south of Salavan and a similar distance north of Attapeu, and was created comparatively recently from areas formerly part of Attapeu and Salavan. Much of Sekong's population voluntarily moved from Dakchung, close to the Vietnamese border, in the early 1980s, when the government created the new province and established better facilities.

For the moment, anyone travelling between Salavan and Attapeu (but probably not vice versa) must stay overnight here as the first bus from Salavan does not arrive until the last Pakse-bound bus for Attapeu has already departed (see Transport, page 268). As roads improve and journey times drop, however, it may become possible to make this trip without overnighting in Sekong.

Those hoping to chance upon an unknown gem of a town will be disappointed. In theory Sekong ought to be a good base to explore the people and scenery of the Boloven Plateau but there is simply no tourist infrastructure to make that possible. The only reason to come here, other than out of sheer perversity, is to take a boat down the Xe Kong to the much more attractive town of Attapeu (see Transport, below). The market, centered on the bus terminal, has some rather pathetic wild animals, such as giant flying squirrels, for sale – more, in fact, than Salavan which has an infamous reputation in this regard. There is a wat behind the market. A reminder of the war is the number of UXO that litter the area. The UXO office, near the Ministry of Finance, has set up a little exhibition and welcomes tourists.

Health warning Malaria is quite a serious problem in this area, particularly in the wet season, and precautions should be taken to avoid being bitten. If heading off the beaten track and away from immediate medical help for a few days, then it is recommended that an antidote is carried in the event of contracting malaria. The area is also littered with UXO, so stick to the well-worn path.

Towards Attapeu

The biggest draw-card in the area is the boat trip between Sekong and Attapeu down the stunning Xe Kong river. The four- to seven-hour journey through pristine wilderness, past riverside villages and the towering Boloven Plateau gives access to territory everyday tourists wouldn't get the opportunity to see. The trip should cost around US$30-40; opt for a boatman who provides lifejackets. Although the trip can get hot, try to avoid taking a dip as a nasty piranha-like blow-fish called the pa pao lives in the waters and apparently has a voracious appetite for the human penis.

Travelling by road to Attapeu, about 25 km south of Sekong near the Alak village of Ban Mun Hua Mung, the Xe Nam Noi crashes over a series of waterfalls: 100 m east of the bridge is **Tad Houakone**, while signposted 4 km downstream is **Tad Phek**; in between are a number of smaller falls. Those tempted to swim in the falls, should dip in the higher pool as the Pa Pao (see above) is rumoured to live in the lower pools. A track leads from one to the other; during the dry season you can walk downriver between the two. A tuk-tuk can be hired for a day to see these sights (US$10-15), but you may be better off trying to hire a motorbike from one of the locals.

The road between Sekong and Attapeu, along the eastern edge of the imposing Boloven Plateau, has finally been completed, aside from a few tiny sections, despite being put on hold for many years while the bridge contractor was in jail. The spectacular 120-m-high **Tad Sekatamtok** tumbles from the Xe Nam Noi about 16 km from the junction (Km 52) with the new road towards Paksong and Pakse. Local sources call this the highest waterfall in the country, although it seems that every province will claim their waterfall is Laos's highest. Unlike its closest counterpart, Tad Fan, this fall is comprised of one giant surge burgeoning over the cliff-top, certainly securing its ranking as one of the country's most spectacular. Along the road to Attapeu are clearings where new villages have been created for the 'upland' Lao. In a bid to resettle these people, the government provided land, aid and resources for building and a space by the banks of the Xe Kong to grow vegetables and other crops to sell.

Attapeu Province → Phone code: 031. Colour map 3, C4.

🚌🚉▲🏠🛈 » pp264-270.

Attapeu has an altogether different character from the Boloven Plateau, as the province is predominantly Lao Loum rather than comprised of ethnic minority groups. Attapeu Province was formerly administered under the Lane Xang Kingdom, King Saysetthathirath moved operations in 1571, later dying in the small town. Attapeu suffered greatly between 1964 and 1975, and evidence of this destruction is clear, particularly in the eastern corner along the Ho Chi Minh Trail, where the land is so cratered that some expats refer to it as 'moon-land'.

There are two National Protected Areas in Attapeu the **Dong Ampham Forest** and the eastern portion of the **Se Pian** (see page 245), covering almost 250,000 hectares in total. The NPAs (National Protected Areas) are home to numerous animal and plant species. You'll see giant logging trucks growling along the southern highway, transporting enormous trees, but visitor access to the sites is very difficult and tourism infrastructure is incredibly poor, rendering them almost impossible for a quick visit.

Ins and outs

Tourist information For information on the province, visit the **tourist office** in Attapeu town in the provincial hall, northwest of the town centre. It has large-scale relief maps of the area, good for hiking on or around the Boloven Plateau, and informative brochures on all there is to do in Attapeu. The office is run by Mr Phousavanh who is helpful and informative and will also offer his services as a guide. If intending to explore the countryside hereabouts, it is best to ask around for a guide. Other useful sources of information are Mr Bounkong who runs the **Pakong Restaurant** and Mr Boun Som at the **Sompasong Restaurant**.

Health warning Malaria is quite a serious problem in this area and precautions should be taken to avoid being bitten. If heading off the beaten track and away from immediate medical help for a few days, then it is recommended that an antidote is carried in the event of contracting malaria.

Attapeu town

Attapeu is an attractive, leafy town positioned on a bend in the Xe Kong, at the confluence of the Xe Kaman. Once referred to as the Golden Land for its gold deposits, Attapeu prides itself on the old provincial saying that "Attapeu people traded gold for chickens, while Salavan sold their own elephants to buy fire". According to ML Manich in his *History of Laos*, Attapeu should really be called Itkapü, which translates as 'buffalo dung', due to a misunderstanding between the original population and incoming Lao Loum people. The French, in their turn, transliterated Itkapü as Attapeu. For a pile of dung the town, however, is remarkably picturesque.

Apart from an unremarkable monastery, **Wat Luang**, dating from the 1930s, Attapeu is not over-endowed with obvious sights of interest. However, it is a pleasant place to walk around, with traditional wooden Lao houses with verandas and some French buildings. The people are friendly and traffic is limited. Vegetables are grown on the banks of the Xe Kong. Attapeu was fought over by the Pathet Lao and RLG, so it is a surprise that the town remains as attractive as it is. It was the only capital that was never taken by the RLG and is consequently far more attached to the early years of the Lao PDR than the rest of the country; the local tourism authorities seem more intent on providing patriotic propaganda than real tourist information. Due to the ongoing construction of a bridge over the Xe Kong, carrying a highway to Vietnam, the Vietnamese influence is obvious and growing rapidly and Attapeu, despite being one of the poorest provinces in Laos, is developing fast. The road is expected to be completed in 2006.

Outside Attapeu town to the northwest is a clearing on the hilltop which marks the spot of the new hydropower scheme – the **Houei Ho**. Built by the Korean firm, Daewoo, the scheme employed labour from South Africa to undertake the stupendous mining task: to dig a 740-m vertical shaft 4 m in diameter. Water is diverted down this shaft from a reservoir on the Boloven Plateau to produce electricity for sale to Thailand, as well as power for surrounding towns, including Pakse.

Nongfa Lake

The real treasure of Attapeu is Nongfa Lake, which was 'discovered' in 1930. The crystal-clear blue lake shares many of its attributes with the beautiful volcanic lake of Yaek Loam in Cambodia. The shores are surrounded by pristine wilderness and mountains and the lake is considered an auspicious site by the local population. Although no conservationists have officially surveyed the lake, the government has done its own survey. Official tourist brochures proclaim, proudly, that the lake is so large that "a shot of an AK47 rifle from one edge of the lake never reaches the other". Most locals can't pinpoint exactly how to get to the enigmatic lake, so it's best to organize a tour with the tourism authorities.

East of Attapeu

The sleepy town of **Xaisetha** (Saisettha), which stretches along the north bank of the Xe Kaman, lies 12 km east of Attapeu along Route 18. There is regular transport from the east bank of the Xe Kong across from Attapeu. A further 18 km along Route 18, 30 km in all from Attapeu, is the Alak village of **Pa-am**, which sits directly on the Ho Chi Minh Trail. War memorabilia freaks might be interested in the Soviet surface-to-air missile launcher (still apparently live), abandoned there by the Vietnamese. It will cost you 5,000 kip for a peek through the fence surrounding it.

West of Attapeu

The Lao Loum village of **Ban Mai** lies 50 km southwest of Attapeu. From Ban Mai it's 6 km to Ban Hinlat and, a further 6 km on, is the **Xe Pha** waterfall, which lies on the Se Pian. The falls are around 23 m high and 120 m wide. And another 9 km on from here, on the same river, are the **Xe Pang Lai** falls, the most stunning in the area.

From Ban Mai it is also possible to access 20-m-wide **Tad Samongphak** on a one-hour boat ride up the Se Pian. You may need a guide between the falls; ask locally, the tourism office is the best starting point. It should be possible to arrange accommodation in either village.

Southern Laos Boloven Plateau

Attapeu

Sleeping	Amphone	Soksomphone	Eating
Aloon Sot Sai	Guesthouse (2) 2	Guesthouse 4	Darawan 1
Guesthouse 1	ATP Palace 3		Thi Thi 2

0 metres 200
0 yards 200

Paksong and around *p254*

B **Tad Fan Resort**, T020-5531400, T020-5531400, Bangkok sales office +66 (0)2 9686832, www.tadfane.com. Perched on the opposite side of the ravine from the falls is a series of wooden bungalows with nicely decorated rooms and en suite bathrooms, with hot showers. The 2nd floor of the excellent open-air restaurant offers the best view of the falls and serves a wide variety of Lao, Thai and Western food. Great service. Treks to the top of falls and the Dan-Sin-Xay Plain cost from around US$5 per person and need to be organized in advance. Recommended.

E **Borlaven Guesthouse**, Route 23 about 2 km north of the market, beyond Paksong town. The new brick and wood building has a cabin feel and is surrounded by coffee trees, corn fields and a flower garden. The simple rooms are bright (pink floral sheets) and clean with en suite bathrooms but no hot water. 50,000 kip. Very friendly owner speaks English.

Apparently a casino/resort is due to be built in Paksong but details were sketchy as this guide went to press.

Tha Teng *p255*

D **Viphavahn Guesthouse**, T034-211970, about 1 km east on Route 16 towards Sekong. This is by far the best option in the village. Decent, clean, simply decorated rooms with hot water, fan and Western toilet.

E **Tatavin Guesthouse**, 2 km from the centre of town on Route 23 north to Salavan. This small place appears to be rarely occupied and is in a state of decay. The small rooms need a serious clean and consist of a simple bed and squat toilet.

Tad Lo *p255, map p257*

B **Tad Lo Lodge**, T031-211889; also through Sodetour in Pakse, T031-212122. Reception on the east side of the falls and chalet-style accommodation (13 rooms) built right on top of the waterfalls on the opposite side (doubles US$25, singles US$20, including breakfast and hot water). It is an attractive location (during the wet season) and the accommodation is comfortable – cane rocking chairs on the balconies overlook the

cascades on the left bank. Good restaurant serving plenty of Lao and Thai food. Elephant rides are available (US$10 per elephant for a 2-hour trek; each elephant can carry 2 people). Recommended.

C-D **Saise Guesthouse** (aka Sayse Guesthouse), T031-211886. The guesthouse comprises 2 sections: the lower part sits near the restaurant at the foot of Tad Hang and consists of rooms (US$12) and bungalows (US$6 or US$15 right next to the falls), all with hot water and fans. The more attractive and peaceful option is the so-called **Green House** (the roof's a giveaway) above the falls. This is a wooden chalet with 6 huge rooms, 4 with en suite shower and toilet, and 2 of those with balconies overlooking the river. Originally owned by the government, the guesthouse has been taken over by a private company which is currently looking into opening more guesthouses and resorts in Tad Lo and the surrounding area. The beautiful garden restaurant offers Lao and Thai food (US$1-4), service is less than attentive and the menu features illegal wildlife.

There are now a number of small bungalow guesthouses near the bridge on the east side of the river, including:

D-E **Sypaseuth Guesthouse & Restaurant**, right next to the bridge. Wooden bungalows right on the riverbank are slightly rundown but have fans and en suite bathrooms for only US$4. Also have 4 dingy concrete rooms set back from the river for US$6, and a couple of hovel-like triple rooms without a bathroom for US$2-3. Also a restaurant serving decent Lao food for US$1-2.

E **Sailomen Guesthouse**, next along the riverbank. Small but clean thatch bungalows with en suite bathrooms for US$2.50. The nicest of the cheap bungalows available.

E **Tim's Guesthouse & Restaurant**, just down the bridge road from the Sypaseuth, T031-214176, soulideth@laopdr.com. Twin and double bungalows for 30,000 kip with hot water, fans and lock boxes. Also internet access, international calls, room service, laundry, book exchange, a substantial music collection and CD burning, bike rentals (8,000 kip per hour or 30,000 kip per day) and just about anything else you could ask for. The place is backpacker heaven, but the very ragged stuffed cat in the restaurant is rather disturbing.

Salavan *p258, map p258*

D **Shai Kham Guesthouse**, on the road towards Pakse, T034-211186. Rooms are rarely occupied but are reasonably clean, with fan (70,000 kip with a/c). The en suite bathrooms only have squat toilets and cold water and the mattresses are pretty poor. Also a beer garden-style restaurant serving numerous Lao dishes, but no menu and little English spoken.

D **Silsamay 2 Guesthouse**, just down the road from **Shai Kham**, T020-5548054. Bright, clean, well-furnished rooms for 80,000 kip with a/c or 40,000 kip with just a fan. Bathrooms have hot water and Western toilets. Recommended.

D-E **Chindavong**, T034-211065. There are 2 types of room on offer here. For 25,000 kip you get a basic room, with fan but no en suite bathroom, whereas 70,000 kip will stretch to a beautifully decorated, bamboo-clad, homely twin or double, with a/c, en suite bathroom, writing table, television, and 'chill out' area. Restaurant attached (no menu!). Recommended.

D-E **Thiphaphone**, T034-211063. Next to the **Chindavong** on the market side. Clean (but musty) basic rooms with wooden walls and decent mattresses. Some have a/c, TV and hot water (70,000 kip), others only have fans (40,000 kip). Spotless bathrooms, some en suite, some communal.

E **Miss Asam**, next to the **Thiphaphone**, T034-211062. This is a tiny little place, with very basic rooms. Not in the least bit customer focused.

E-F **Saise Hotel**, 2½ km from the bus station on the other side of town near the river (get there by tuk-tuk), T034-211054/213775. Attractive guesthouse in large garden compound. The newer building has bright a/c rooms of a good standard with hot water; the older building has huge dank rooms with fans and large 'bathrooms' (tank of water and dipper, squat toilet). The management speak English and French – a useful source of information.

There are a couple of other establishments on the road to Pakse, about 1 km from the bus station.

B **Utayan Bajiang Champasak**, T031-251294. This resort, beside the lovely Phasuam waterfall, consists of ethnic-styled bungalows, a tree house and various other types of accommodation. There's also a restaurant by the water's edge. The resort caters predominantly to Thai package tourists and as a result there isn't much transport to get there. You will need to either travel independently or organize through a Pakse tour operator such as **Sabaidy 2**. There's a 5,000 kip fee to enter the compound.

Sekong *p260, map p267*

D **Koky Guesthouse**, just off the main road towards the post office, T031-211401. A little house with rooms for rent. Service is very friendly but no English is spoken. Rooms have a/c and TV.

D **Sackda**, between the market and the water tower, T031-211086. Clean and very blue: blue sheets, blue walls, blue curtains, resulting in an overall blue glow. Basic rooms for 75,000 kip with a/c or 45,000 kip with a fan. Attached bathrooms have a shower and squat toilet.

D **Sekong Souksamlane Hotel** (aka Sekong Hotel), a block back from the post office, T031-211030, pholsena@laotel.com. Old, but apparently popular with the few local *falangs*, partly due to the attached restaurant, which will cook whatever you want, as long as the food is available at the local market (or just order from the English menu). 16 rooms, with a/c (from 72,000 kip) or fan (from 45,000 kip), some with en suite bathrooms, cold shower, very functional and rather worn and dusty but OK for an overnight stop. Also 1 dorm room with 4 beds (E-F). The best rooms are upstairs; they have a balcony and get the mountain breeze. One of the rooms is reputedly haunted by some Malaysian UN officials who were drowned taking a boat downriver to Attapeu; they left their bags in their room and come back every so often to retrieve them.

D **Somchany Guesthouse**, near the water tower, T031-211316. A relatively new and quiet spot, with fan rooms for 40,000 kip and a/c for 60,000 kip. The colourful rooms, with children cartoon sheets, are a bit grimy and the bathrooms (Western toilet and *mundi*) have a bit of a pungent odour to them.

E **Woman Fever Kosment Center Guesthouse**, the block behind the post office, T031-211046. Looks like a Lao government office or a large school with cement foundations and a wooden 2nd storey. The very spacious, very basic rooms go for 30,000 kip with a fan, and the shared bathroom has a *mundi* and squat toilet.

A new and relatively luxurious hotel compound is under construction along the riverbank in the southeast corner of town, but no-one knows when it will be completed.

Attapeu *p261, map p263*

B-C **ATP Palace** (formerly the **Hotel Yingchokchay**), T031-212204, www.offroad.laotel.com. Renamed by the new owners who took over in 2005, and a favourite with government officials and businessmen, this enormous and slightly decaying building offers rooms from US$6 (with fan) to US$25 (suites). The lovely rooms are plain, large and simple, with sweet dream-enducing mattresses and great en suite bathrooms. Breakfast is included. Internet access is available (when it's working) for 1,000 kip per min.

E **Aloon Sot Sai Guesthouse**, 2 doors down from the **Sooksomphone**, T031-211250. Small somewhat dingy rooms with fan, TV and en suite bathrooms for US$3-5.

E **Amphone Guesthouse 2**, halfway between the bus station and the town centre. A peaceful location not far from the river. 7 good rooms (fan 50,000 kip, a/c 70,000 kip), most with en suite bathrooms. Also cheaper 4-bed dorm with shared facilities outside (literally). Quiet, but the service is not very good. The large restaurant boasts "Meat exposed to the sun fried" and other Lao specialities.

E **Soksomphone Guesthouse**, T031-211046. 16 small but well-furnished and airy rooms, some with en suites, some with TVs, others with enormous beds and clean shared bathrooms (*mundi* and squat toilet). Owners are slack but speak some English and French. Tours can be arranged to the surrounding area (but shop around first). Bicycles for hire (20,000 kip).

🍴 Eating

Paksong and around *p254*

🍴 **Borravan Plateau**, Rte 23 about 1 km from the market towards Tha Teng. The owner is very friendly. Standard selection of Lao dishes in an indoor setting, safe from the weather. Unfortunately there is no menu and no English spoken – so opt for something easy like *feu* or *laap*.

🍴 **Khihtavan Restaurant**, on the road between the bank and market, across from the Kaysone Monument, T020-5769874. Quiet place with very friendly service. Britney Spears poster turned menu board is written only in Lao. Also peddles jewellery and pirated VCDs. Standard Lao food and good coffee. Open 0800-2100.

There are a small string of barbecue restaurants, past the market away from Rte 23. The market also has a large restaurant section and there's a row of Vietnamese restaurants along Rte 23 near the bank.

Tad Lo *p255, map p257*

🍴 **Hath Restaurant**, behind the **Sailomen**, has a wide selection of Western and Lao food, including sandwiches, fish and chips, and vegetarian dishes for US$1-2; also international call services.

There are also a number of small Lao joints along the main road.

Salavan *p258, map p258*

Most restaurants in Salavan serve much the same range of dishes. Along the road to Pakse near the handicraft centre are a number of barbecue joints offering whatever parts of a pig can be found, including just the fat. Between the handicraft centre and the market is the **Ladda Café**, a small shop set beneath a few large trees serving ice cream, etc. By the market towards the road to Pakse are a number of restaurants offering Korean grilled meat, the Lao buffet, *khao piak* and *feu*, among other things. The road into town makes a 90° turn to the left; just beyond is a small road on the right heading towards the Xe Don and Sekong. There are a few decent little restaurants here. The 2nd of the 3 is the best, and will make whatever you ask for, if they can understand your Lao.

🍴 **Vilayvone**, on the airstrip side of the market. The only place in town with a written menu – and it's even in English. Offers MSG-laden Lao standards; the French fries are Salavan's sole attempt at Western food.

Sekong *p260, map p267*

All of the restaurants close relatively early, so last orders are no later than 2100. There are noodle shops in and around the market.

♥ **Khamting Restaurant**, next to Phathip. Popular with the locals, but no *falang* options and no English menu.

♥ **Phathip Restaurant**, opposite the Sekong Hotel. Owned by Nang Tu, a Vietnamese woman with considerable culinary expertise. The huge platters are a treat, especially the Vietnamese options. An amazing range of dishes on offer considering the location. The same *falangs* who have obviously helped with the menu must have also taught the chef a few things. The front of the menu boasts all sorts of information about the area, including dire warnings about both the contamination of Sekong Province with the residue from the Vietnam War, and 'the odd grumpy *falangs* that for one reason or the other seem to be more or less resident in this forgotten corner of South-east Asia'.

♥ **Saruya Restaurant**, between the bank and the post office, T031-211037. Standard Lao joint.

♥ **Somview Restaurant**, on the other side of the Phathip. Typical Lao food.

♥ **Souksamlane Restaurant**, attached to Sekong Hotel. Traditional Lao dishes and some European food. Tribal artefacts adorn the walls and are for sale.

Attapeu *p261, map p263*

Attapeu is a small town and looking for an open restaurant after 2100 could prove quite difficult. Most establishments serve the local breakfast speciality *feu* 0700-0800. Just up from Souksomphone Guesthouse towards the wat and almost opposite each other are a few places selling ready-made Lao food in pots, cheap and good. There are also a number of noodle shops in the same area and near the boat jetty on the south side of town.

♥ **Darawan Restaurant**, a block up from the post office, T031-211178. Serves not only typical Lao dishes, but an array of sweeter things, including *nam wan*, ice cream and milkshakes.

♥ **Sekong River Restaurant**, superb location down by the river. The speciality is goat, not fish as you might expect, prepared any way you can think of. Fish and other dishes are also available. It's also a good spot for a drink.

♥ **Thi Thi Restaurant**, between Wat Luang Muang Mai and the bridge, T031-211054. Vietnamese food, with lots of seafood, including eel and tortoise, cooked in a variety of imaginative ways; sometimes it's best not to ask!

☺ Entertainment

Salavan *p258, map p258*

Salavan lacks any sort of discos or bars but most restaurants serve Beer Lao. The closest thing to night-time entertainment is the beer garden on the road to Pakse across from the Shai Kham and Silsamay Guesthouses. It's popular with locals from about 1600 onwards, but beware that your drink order might be doubled and come complete with someone to drink it for you.

Southern Laos Boloven Plateau Listings

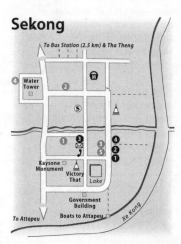

Sekong

To Bus Station (2.5 km) & Tha Theng

Water Tower

Kaysone Monument

Victory That

Lake

Government Building

To Attapeu

Boats to Attapeu

Xe Kong

N

Not to scale

Sleeping 😴
Koky Guesthouse **1**
Sackda **2**
Sekong Souksamlane **3**
Somchany Guesthouse **4**
Woman Fever Kosment Center Guesthouse **5**

Eating 🍴
Khamting **1**
Phathip **2**
Saruya **3**
Somview **4**

! Tahoy festival

The Tahoy village of Ban Paleng, not far from Tha Teng, is a fascinating place to visit, especially in March (in accordance with the full-moon), when the animist Tahoy celebrate their annual three-day sacrificial festival. The village is built in a circle around the *kuan* (the house of sacrifice). A water buffalo is donated by each family in the village. The buffalo has its throat cut and the blood is collected and drunk. The raw meat is divided among the families and surrounding villages are invited to come and feast on it. The head of each family throws a slab of meat into the *lak khai* – a basket hanging from a pole in front of the *kuan* – so that the spirits can partake too. The sacrifice is performed by the village shaman, then dancers throw spears at the buffalo until it dies. The villagers moved from the Vietnam border area to escape the war, but Ban Paleng was bombed repeatedly: the village is still littered with shells and unexploded bombs.

❃ Festivals and events

Tad Lo *p255, map p257*
Buffalo ceremony This traditional Tahoy ceremony (page 268) takes place in a nearby village on the first full moon in **Mar** and is dedicated to the warrior spirit, whom the local tribesmen ask for protection. Villagers are happy for tourists to come and watch (5,000 kip per person). The spectacle kicks off at about 2000, with dancing; the buffalo is sacrificed the next morning at 0500. Throughout the day, the entire village shares the meat of the sacrificed animal, as well as leaving some choice pieces for the spirits of the dead warriors in the Ceremony House. **Tim's Guesthouse** (see Sleeping) is the best place to go for the low-down on this event.

○ Shopping

Salavan *p258, map p258*
The **handicraft centre** near the market has a decent selection of locally made textiles, baskets and other locally made products. The shop selling electrical goods also has some allegedly tribal artefacts (probably overpriced and being passed off as antiques). Basketry items and traditional cloth pieces can be found in and around the **market**; a craft shop on the market square offers similar objects.

Sekong *p260, map p267*
Sekong Textile Handicraft Shop, Sekong Hotel, T031-211039, sells woven basket

'backpacks' and other local products. A few baskets and textiles are also for sale in the market and there is a small craft shop selling weaving, textiles and other items.

⛰ Activities and tours

Tad Lo *p255, map p257*
Elephant trekking
This is an excellent way to see the area as there are few roads on the plateau and elephants can go where jeeps cannot. It is also a thrill being on the back of an elephant. Contact any of the guesthouses (50,000 kip per person; 2 people per elephant).

Attapeu *p261, map p263*
Attapeu Tours & Travel Co Ltd, ATP Palace Hotel, T031-211204, will offer trekking, ticketing, and car rental service, once the highway to Vietnam is opened in 2006. Aimed at the Viet/Thai tourist crowds.

⊖ Transport

Paksong and around *p254*
Regular connections to **Pakse**, 0630-1200 daily, 1½ hrs, 10,000 kip; also buses to **Attapeu**, 0830 and 1200 daily, 3½-4½ hrs.

Tha Teng *p255*
Bus/songthaew
All transport departs from the market. To **Salavan**, 0730 and 0830 daily, 1½ hrs, 10,000 kip; to **Sekong**, 0730, 1 hr, 10,000 kip;

to **Pakse**, 0530, 0630, 0730 and 0830 daily, at least 2 hrs (87 km), 20,000 kip. Due to its location many unscheduled buses pass through Tha Teng between Pakse, Salavan and Sekong, or Salavan, Paksong and Attapeu. *Songthaew* leave intermittently (most in the morning) for nearby destinations.

Tad Lo p255, map p257
There are buses from Ban Houei Set (1½ km north of Tad Lo) to **Pakse**, 0830, 1000, 1100, 1300 and 1400 daily, 17,000 kip; also to **Salavan** (from either Pakse or Lao Ngam), every hr 0730-1600 daily, 40 mins, 7,000 kip. You may also be able to catch the daily service to **Vientiane** on its way north, 0930 and 1430 daily, 85,000 kip but don't expect it to be on time.

Salavan p258, map p258
Bus/truck
The bus terminal is 2 km west of the town centre; a tuk-tuk either way costs about 5,000 kip. Salavan is by no means a tourist hub, which means the reliability of buses is dicey at best; scheduled connection times are as follows: to **Pakse**, 0630, 0730, 0830, 1000, 1215 and 1330 daily, 116 km, 3 hrs, 20,000 kip; to **Sekong**, 0730 and 1300 daily, 98 km, 4 hrs, 18,000 kip; to **Khong Xedon**, 1030 daily, 76 km, 3½ hrs, 17,000 kip, but most Savannakhet-bound buses will pass through as well; to **Lao Ngam** (via **Tad Lo**), 0600, 0815, 0945 and 1200 daily, 1 hr, 10,000 kip; to **Ta Oy**, 1100 daily but departure time varies wildly depending on the season, 84 km, 6 hrs, 28,000 kip; to **Savannakhet**, 0630 daily, 40,000 kip; to **Tha Teng**, 1000 daily, 10,000 kip; to **Vientiane**, 0830 daily, 85,000 kip. There are no buses further north than **Toum Lan**, 1430 daily, 15,000 kip.

Trickier destinations to get to from Salavan include **Attapeu** (you have to go by bus to Sekong, then find a bus to Attapeu) and **Lao Bao** (the best way is via Savannakhet and then along Route 9).

Sekong p260, map p267
Boat
To **Attapeu** down the Xe Kong, a beautiful and worthwhile trip, 5-7 hrs, 250,000-400,000 kip for a boat, depending on the

price of gasoline. Boats take about 4 people and need to be chartered privately. The **Sekong Hotel** and **Phathip** restaurant can help make the arrangements. This trip comes highly recommended.

Bus/truck
The morning buses that are reputed to leave from outside the **Sekong Hotel** were not in evidence on our last trip, but are worth using if they're running. Otherwise, the bus station lies 2½ km out of town (tuk-tuk 2,000 kip); some also stop on the highway near the hospital. To **Salavan**, 0600 and 1330 daily, 98 km, 3 hrs, 10,000 kip; to **Pakse** (via **Paksong**), 0530 and 0600 daily, 5-7 hrs, 15,000 kip. The lone bus to **Attapeu** leaves at 0700 daily, 2-3 hrs, 10,000 kip.

Attapeu p261, map p263
Bicycle
Bikes can be hired from the **Souksomphone Guesthouse** for 20,000 kip.

Boat
An alternative way to get to **Ban Mai** is to charter a boat to Xe Nam Sai and pick up a connection from there.

It is possible to travel upriver from Attapeu to **Sekong**, but it would take much longer than downriver and be quite expensive.

Bus/truck
Efficiency around the bus station is simply not on the agenda, and although there are daily connections with the main tourist hubs, departure times are a source of great argument and debate. Prices are more definite. A rough departure schedule follows, but you should check all onward connections on your arrival. To **Pa-am**, 30 km, 5,000 kip (or charter a tuk-tuk, from 60,000 kip return); to **Pakse**, from the market, 0645, 0730 and 1000 daily, 4 hrs, 35,000 kip; to **Sekong**, 1430 daily, 2-3 hrs, 15,000 kip; to **Vientiane**, 0815 and 1100 daily, 20-24 hrs, 95,000 kip; to **Savannakhet**, 0600 daily, 10-12 hrs, 60,000 kip. To get to **Salavan** you will have to take the bus to Sekong and transfer. There are buses to **Ban Mai**, 0800, 1200 and 1400 daily, 1 hr (returning at 1600) but it is probably better to rent a tuk-tuk for around US$15 per day.

ⓘ Directory

Paksong and around *p254*
Bank Lao Development Bank, east side of
Route 23, opposite the Kaysone Monument,
open 0830-1530 daily, exchanges Thai ฿
and US$.

Salavan *p258, map p258*
Banks Lao Development Bank, near the
market, will exchange cash (US$ and Thai ฿)
and TCs, open Mon-Fri. The shop selling
electrical goods will also change money .
Communications The post office is in a
modern yellow building opposite the
market; local calls only from telephone
exchange in same building. For international
calls, go to the Telecoms centre, Mon-Sat.

Sekong *p260, map p267*
Banks Lao Development Bank will
exchange US$ and Thai ฿ only.
Communications Post office is in a
yellow building not far from victory *that*; the
telecommunications centre is next door,
international calls possible.

Attapeu *p261, map p263*
Banks Lao Development Bank, Mon-Fri
0830-1630, reputed to change US$ and Thai
฿ only, despite what it says. Money changers
can be found around the market area;
try the gold/jewellery shops.
Communications Post office, in town
centre, Mon-Fri 0800-1200 and 1300-1600.
The telephone office is next door, Mon-Sat
0700-1700, international calls.

Islands of the south

→ *Phone code: 031. Colour map 3, C2/3.*
This area is locally known as Siphandon, 'The 4,000 Islands'. Don Khong, Don Khone and Don Deth are just three of the many islands littered across the Mekong right at the southern tip of Laos near the border with Cambodia. Half of the islands are submerged when the Mekong is in flood. Just before the river enters Cambodia it divides into countless channels. The distance between the most westerly and easterly streams is 14 km – the greatest width of the river in its whole 4200-km course. The river's volume is swelled by the Kong, San Srepok and Krieng tributaries, which join just upstream from here. Pakha, or freshwater dolphins, can sometimes be spotted in this area between December and May, when they come upsteam to give birth to their young but they are increasingly endangered. ⟩⟩ *For Sleeping, Eating and other listings, see pages 277-284.*

Route 13 to Ban Hat Xai Khoune
The bus journey south from Pakse to Ban Hat Xai Khoune on Route 13 is 120 km and, until recently, progress was excruciatingly slow. But now the whole road, including the bridges, has been surfaced. The trip is worthwhile for the contrast it offers to conditions in northeastern Thailand, just 20 km or so west. Much of the area is still forested (large quantities of Lao timber are trucked to Thailand via Chongmek, west of Pakse; see page 238) and villages are intermittent even on this road, the national artery for north-south communications. Paddy fields sometimes appear to be fighting a losing battle against the encroaching forest and most houses are roofed in thatch rather than zinc. At **Ban Hat Xai Khoune**, a car ferry and boats wait to transport passengers across the Mekong to Don Khong and Muang Khong (see below).

Don Khong ⊕🅿❀⊟ⓘ ⟩⟩ *pages 277-284.*

Don Khong is the largest of the Mekong islands at 16 km long and 8 km wide. It's a tremendous place to relax or explore by bicycle. Visitors might be surprised by the smooth asphalt roads, electricity and general standard of amenities that exist on the island but two words explain it all – Khamtai Siphandone – Laos's president, who has a residence on the island. The island was electrified about five years before the surrounding mainland areas and it is not unusual to see heavily armed personnel cruising around the place. The president spends much of his time on the island, in his modest quarters near Ban Houa Khong, and ferries back and forth between Vientiane and the island in his own helicopter.

Ins and outs

Getting there In the high season *songthaew* depart Pakse's Southern bus terminal hourly between 0800 and 1200. The occasional bus will also ply through but *songthaew* are the most common transport option. The journey to Ban Hat Xai Khoune should take between four and five hours and cost US$3; in most cases the bus/truck will board the **car ferry** (3,000 kip) at Ban Hat (1 km south of Ban Hat Xai Khoune) and take you right across to Ban Naa on Don Khong (1 km south of Muang Khong). The ferries, which spend

> ✆ Make sure the bus or songthaew *driver knows that you wish to go to Don Khong and not Don Khone.*

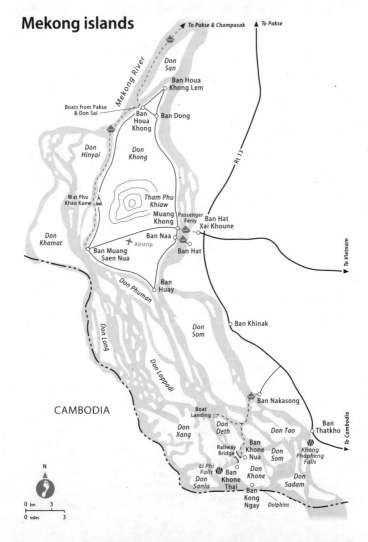

Mekong islands

most of their time transporting ancient Russian Zil trucks loaded with Cambodian rosewood across the Mekong, are made from two old US pontoon boats on either side of an ageing diesel river boat with a pallet lying crossways on top. There are also **motorboats** from Ban Hat Xai Khoune to Muang Khong (5,000 kip, dependent on the number of passengers). If there is not a bus directly to Don Khong, catch a bus bound for Ban Nakasong and jump off at Ban Hat Xai Khoune. If by chance you get dumped at Ban Nakasong, you can arrange a boat to Don Khong from there; although this is a very pretty route it is time-consuming and not the most efficient way to get to the island.

If you travel all the way from Pakse or Champasak by **boat**, alight at Ban Houa Khong on the northern tip of the island and arrange transport from there to Muang Khong (buses and tuk-tuks wait here). The boats often continue to Ban Muang Saen Nua, although they may arrive here considerably later, as they tend to visit neighbouring islands first. ▸▸ *For further details, see Transport, page 283.*

Getting around All of the guesthouses can arrange bicycle hire for 8000-10,000 kip per day. There are a few tuk-tuks in town but they are hardly required around tiny Muang Khong. It is, however, possible to charter a tuk-tuk, loaded with a bicycle or two, for the trip to the far side of the island and then cycle back.

Muang Khong

Don Khong's 'capital' is **Muang Khong**, a small former French settlement. 'Muang' means city but, although Muang Khong is the district's main settlement, it feels more like a village than a town, with only a few thousand inhabitants. Pigs and chickens scrabble for food under the houses and just 50 m inland the houses give way to paddy fields.

There are two wats in the town. **Wat Kan Khong**, also known as Wat Phuang Kaew, is visible from the jetty: a large gold Buddha in the *mudra* of subduing Mara garishly overlooks the Mekong. Much more attractive is **Wat Chom Thong** at the upstream extremity of the village, which may date from the early 19th century but which was much extended during the colonial period. The unusual Khmer-influenced *sim* may be gently decaying but it is doing so with style. The wat compound, with its carefully tended plants and elegant buildings, is very peaceful. The *naga* heads on the roof of the main *sim* are craftily designed to channel water, which issues from their mouths. The old *sim* to the left of the main entrance is also notable, although it is usually kept locked because of its poor condition.

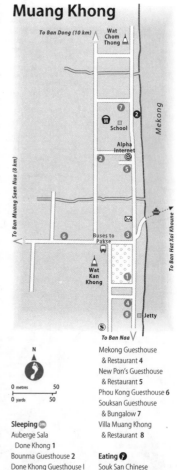

Muang Khong

To Ban Dong (10 km)
Wat Chom Thong
To Muang Saen Nua (8 km)
Mekong
School
Alpha internet
Buses to Pakse
Wat Kan Khong
Jetty
To Ban Hat Xai Khoune
To Ban Naa

N

0 metres 50
0 yards 50

The Mekong: mother river of Southeast Asia

The Mekong River is the heart and soul of mainland Southeast Asia, a sinuous thread that binds Vietnam, Cambodia and Laos geographically, historically, culturally and economically.

The Mekong's source in eastern Tibet has only been pin-pointed in the last 15 years. From here the giant river plies 4500 km through six countries, cutting through almost the entire length of Laos, dissecting Cambodia, and plunging into Vietnam's Mekong Delta before emptying into the South China Sea. The river is the 12th longest river in the world and is the 10th largest by volume of water dispersed into the ocean, at 475 km^3.

French explorer Francis Garnier commented that: "without doubt, no other river, over such a length, has a more singular or remarkable character". The Mekong has indeed woven itself into the cultural fabric of the region and shaped its history, from the ancient Funan settlement in the Mekong Delta, through to the Khmer Empire, which established its capital at Angkor and relied on the river for transport and agriculture. After several European expeditions, the French took an interest in the river and the region in the mid 19th century, developing grandiose plans to transform the Mekong into a river highway from China. (The plans were thwarted upon discovering that the Mekong could not be traversed.) The river later played an integral role in the Vietnam War for the running of Viet Cong supplies.

The river has been a major purveyor of culture, ushering in various religions, arts and customs and folklore, including enormous, colourful, boat races and annual water festivals, which celebrate the Mekong and its importance to agriculture. Nor is the river free from superstition or strange phenomena. In Laos thousands of people gather each year to witness naga fireballs rising from the river's surface.

Today, the Mekong is instrumental in the region's future prosperity, with more than 60 million people in Southeast Asia dependent on the river and its tributaries for their survival. Agricultural production, particularly the farming of rice, relies on the river's annual flood-drought cycle. During the monsoon, the river swells to 30 times its original size, depositing rich fertilizing sediments along the floodplains and riverbanks.

Fish are an important part of the Lao diet constituting 80% of many people's protein requirement. The river is home to between 770 and 1300 species of freshwater fish, including the world's largest, a giant 300 kg catfish (the size of a grizzly bear). It also shelters the endangered Irrawaddy dolphin (numbered at around 80).

However, it is unclear how much longer the Mekong can be relied on to support millions of Vietnamese, Cambodian and Lao people. In the last decade, more than 100 large dam proposals have been tabled for the Mekong basin, while China, the source of up to 45% of the lower Mekong's water, has embarked on a massive programme for the construction of eight new dams. Two of these have been completed so far and are already having a detrimental effect upon the Mekong, altering the river's natural ebb and flow. Chainarong Setthachua, director of South East Asia Rivers Network has said that: "Not only is the water the lowest in its history, it is also fluctuating; sometimes up, sometimes down. This comes from dam operations in China." The Mekong River Commission (MRC) agrees, pointing out that, in places, the river has reached rock-bottom levels.

For early risers the **morning market** in Muang Khong is also worthwhile – if only to see the fish before they are sold to the restaurants here and consigned to the cooking pot. Note that the market only really operates between 0530 and 0730. If you are getting up for the market, it is worth setting the alarm clock even earlier to get onto the banks of the Mekong before 0600, when the sun rises over the hills to the east, picking out the silhouettes of fishermen in their canoes.

Exploring the island

Most people come to Muang Khong as a base for visiting the **Li Phi** and **Khong Phapheng Falls** (see pages 276 and 277) in the far south of Laos. (Dolphin-watching trips are much easier to arrange from Don Deth or Don Khone.) However, the island itself is worth exploring by bicycle and deserves more time than most visitors give it. It is flat – except in the interior – the roads are quiet, so there is less risk of being mown down by a timber truck, and the villages and countryside offer a glimpse of traditional Laos. Most people take the southern 'loop' around the island, via **Ban Muang Saen Nua**, a distance of about 25 km (two to three hours by bike). The villages south of Ban Muang Saen Nua are wonderfully picturesque.

Tham Phou Khiaw is tucked away among the forests of the **Green Mountain** in the centre of the island. It's a small cave, containing earthenware pots. Buddha images and other relics and offerings litter the site. Every Lao New Year (April) townsfolk climb up to the cave to bathe the images. Although it's only 15 minutes' walk from the road, finding the cave is not particularly straightforward except during Lao New Year when it is possible to follow the crowds. Head 1½ km north from Muang Khong on the road until you come to a banana plantation, with a couple of wooden houses. Take the pathway just before the houses through the banana plantation and at the top, just to the left, is a small gateway through the fence and a fairly well-defined path. Head up and along this path and, after 300 m or so, there is a rocky clearing. The path continues from the top right corner of the clearing for a further 200 m to a rocky mound that rolls up and to the left. Walk across the mound for about 20 m, until it levels out, and then head back to the forest. Keeping the rock immediately to your right, continue round and after 40 m there are two upturned tree trunks marking the entrance to the cave.

About 6 km north of Ban Muang Saen Nua is a hilltop wat which is arguably Don Khong's main claim to national fame. **Wat Phou Khao Kaew** (Glass Hill Monastery) is built on the spot where an entrance leads down to the underground lair of the *nagas*, known as **Muang Nak**. This underground town lies beneath the waters of the Mekong, with several tunnels leading to the surface – another is at That Luang in Vientiane. Lao legend has it that the *nagas* will come to the surface to protect the Lao whenever the country is in danger. (This means, to most Lao, whenever the Thais decide to attack.) Some people believe that the Thais tricked the Lao to build *thats* over the holes to prevent the *nagas* coming to their rescue – the hole at Wat Phou Khao Kaew is covered.

Don Deth, Don Khone and around

⬤⬤⬤⬤⬤⬤ ⟫ *pages 277-284.*

The islands of Don Khone and Don Deth are the pot of gold at the end of the rainbow for most travellers who head to the southern tip of Laos, and it's not hard to see why. After the relative fever and bustle of Pakse, the transport headaches around the Boloven Plateau and the architectural wonder of Wat Phou, the bamboo huts that stretch along the banks of these two staggeringly beautiful islands are filled with contented travellers in no rush to move on. Travelling by boat in this area is very picturesque: the islands are covered in coconut palms, flame trees, stands of it demands a skilled helmsman to negotiate them. In the distance, a few kilometres to the south, are the Khong Hai Mountains, which dominate the skyline and delineate the frontier between Laos and Cambodia.

Background

For those who have travelled on the slow, lazy upper reaches of the Mekong, huge roaring waterfalls might seem rather out of character. But here, near the Cambodian border, the underlying geology changes and the river is punctuated by rapids and the Khone Falls. The name Khone is used loosely and there are in fact two impressive cascades in the area: the Li Phi (or Somphamit) Falls and Khong Phapheng Falls – the latter are the largest in Southeast Asia and reputedly the widest in the world. Francis Garnier was suitably impressed when he ascended the Khone cataract in 1860, his boatmen hauling their vessels "through a labyrinth of rocks, submerged trees, and prostrate trunks still clinging to earth by their many roots".

The French envisaged Don Deth and Don Khone as strategic transit points in their grandiose masterplan to create a major Mekong highway from China. In the late 19th century, ports were built at the southern end of Don Khone and at the northern end of Don Deth and a narrow-gauge railway line was constructed across Don Khone in 1897 as an important bypass around the rapids for French cargo boats sailing upriver from Phnom Penh. In 1920, the French built a bridge across to Don Deth and extended the railway line to Don Deth port. This 5-km stretch of railway has the unique distinction of being the only line the French ever built in Laos. Although the lucrative Chinese supply line was never properly realized, the route remained operational until 1940.

A colonial-style customs house still stands in the shadow of the impressive railway bridge on Don Khone. On the southern side of the island lie the rusted corpses of the old locomotive and boiler car. Before pulling into Ban Khone Nua, the main settlement on Don Khone, Don Deth's original 'port' is on the right, with what remains of its steel rail jetty.

Ins and outs

Getting there A number of companies run tours to this area, especially from Pakse (see Activities and tours, page 249). To get to Don Deth or Don Khone independently from Pakse the bus/*songthaew* will need to drop you off at Ban Nakasong. Note that some *songthaew* wait at Pakse airport to take travellers direct to Siphandon; price depends on numbers but a group of five can expect to pay US$5 per person. The *songthaew* trip from Pakse can be mildy uncomfortable, particularly if it's raining; aim for a seat away from the sides of the vehicle. There is a toothless, charmless policeman who sits in Ban Nakasong bullying tourists off the bus and forcing them to walk to the boat dock. It's not a long haul – perhaps 500 m – but can be uncomfortable if you're laden with luggage. The 'ticket office' is located in a little restaurant to the right-hand side of the dock. But you can literally ask anyone that's jumping across to the islands for a lift, at a dramatically reduced rate. The boats take about 15 to 20 minutes to make the easy trip to the islands and cost around US$2 to US$3 per person. Prices will be higher (US$5-6) if you are traveling solo.

❧ Make sure the bus or songthaew driver knows that you wish to go to Don Khone (via Nakasong) rather than Don Khong.

Getting around A boat between Don Deth and Don Khone costs 20,000 kip; alternatively you can walk between the two islands, paying the 9,000 kip charge to cross the bridge (also used as ticket to see Li Phi Falls). Both islands can easily be navigated by foot or bicycles can be rented from guesthouses for US$1 per day. There are also motorbikes for hire on Don Khone for US$6-8 per day. ▸▸ *For further details, see Transport, page 283.*

It seems that this small town's sole *raison d'etre* is as the jumping-off point for Don Khone and Don Deth. Ban Nakasong is not the most pleasant of Lao towns and several travellers have complained about being ripped off here. However, it has a thriving market, where most of the islanders stock up on their goods, so it's worthwhile having a look around before you head off to the islands, particularly if you need to pick up necessities like torches, batteries and film.

Don Deth

This island has really woken up to tourism in the last couple of years and the riverbank is peppered with cheap-as-chips bamboo huts and restaurants geared to accommodate the growing wave of backpacker travellers that floods south to stop and recoup in this idyllic setting. A good book, hammock and icy beverage are the orders of the day here, but those with a bit more energy should explore the truly stunning surroundings. It's a great location for watching the sunrises and sunsets, for walking through shady palms and frangipani trees and for swimming off the beaches, which attract the hordes in the dry season. Away from the picturesque waterfront, the centre of the island comprises rice paddies and farms; you should take care not to harm crops when exploring the island.

The national tourism authorities have been coordinating with locals to ensure that the beautiful island doesn't become 'Vang Vieng-ified', so you'll find no *Friends* videos or 'Happy' shakes here. The island has no electricity (except for a generator supply 1800-2200), no cars (except for the odd truck) and no other modern conveniences. Internet has amazingly made its way to the island, however, and it's still possible to get mobile phone coverage. Talk of electrification has been on the cards for many years but, so far, has not materialized.

Don Khone and Li Phi Falls

From the railway bridge, follow the southwest path through **Ban Khone Thai** and then wind through the paddy fields for 1.7 km (20 minutes' walk) to **Li Phi Falls** ① *aka Somphamit or Khone Yai falls, 9000 kip entry fee, paid at the bridge.* These are a succession of raging rapids, crashing through a narrow rocky gorge. In the wet season, when the rice is green, the area is beautiful; in the dry season, it is scorching.

From the main vantage point on a jagged, rocky outcrop, the falls aren't that impressive, as a large stretch of them are obscured. 'Phi' means ghost, a reference, it is believed, to the bodies that floated down the river from the north during the war.

≛ Do not be tempted to swim in the pools near Li Phi Falls. Several people have drowned here.

It's best to visit Li Phi around June or July, when all the fishermen are putting out their bamboo fish traps. Every year Cambodia's Tonlé Sap lake reverses its flow sending millions of fish up the Mekong into Laos. During this time, each fish trap can catch 1000-2000 kg of fish in a day. In theory, enough fish are caught in these two short months to feed half the population of Laos, although most of the catch is exported to Thailand.

Dolphin spotting

The Mekong, south of Don Khone, is one of the few places in the world where it is possible to see freshwater dolphins. They can be spotted in the late afternoon from December to May, from the French pier at the end of the island, not far from the village of **Ban Hang Khon**. The walk across Don Khone from the railway bridge is some 4 km and bicycles can be hired by asking around. It is easier, however, to catch a glimpse of the dolphins in a boat from **Ban Kong Ngay** or Ban Hang Khon, as they reside in deep water pools. In 1996 there were thought to be 30 dolphins, after which the numbers seemed to decline and, according to local data, there were fears that only

≛ Try to organize your trip for the late afternoon, so you can enjoy sunset on the return trip.

four or five were left, although a new calf has recently been spotted. The problem is that the Lao-Cambodian border transects the dolphin pool and the dolphins actually belong to Cambodia. Cambodian fishermen seem hooked on dynamite and hand grenade fishing technology – the piscine equivalent of the scorched earth approach. Lao boatmen have to pay US$1 to the Cambodian authorities in order to access the waters in which the dolphins reside. Cambodia gets a bit tetchy about these 'border incursions' and may, on the odd occasion, deny access.

Khong Phapheng Falls

ⓘ *Ban Thatko, US$1 entry fee for foreigners; there are a number of food and drinks stalls. Guesthouses on Don Deth and Don Khone organize trips to the falls for around 60,000 kip per person (min 5 passengers) and will usually be booked in conjunction with a trip to see the dolphins. A guesthouse at Khong Phapheng should be completed during 2006.*

About 36 km south of Ban Hat Xai Khoune at Ban Thatko, a road branches off Route 13 towards Khong Phapheng Falls, which roar around the eastern shore of the Mekong for 13 km. One fork of the road leads to a vantage point, where a large wooden structure, built up on stilts, overlooks the cascades for a fantastic head-on view of the falls. When you see the huge volume of white water boiling and surging over the jagged rocks below, it is hard to imagine that there is another 10 km width of river running through the other channels. A perilous path leads down from the viewpoint to the edge of the water. Unsurprisingly, the river is impassable at this juncture, as an 1860s French expedition led by adventurers Doudart de Lagrée and Francis Garnier discovered. Another road leads down to the bank of the Mekong, 200 m away, just above the lip of the falls; at this deceptively tranquil spot, the river is gathering momentum before it plunges over the edge. It was said that a tongue of rock once extended from the lip of the falls, and the noise of Khong Phapheng – literally 'the voice of the Mekong' – crashing over this outcrop could be heard many miles away. The rock apparently broke off during a flood surge but the cascades still make enough noise to justify their name.

● Sleeping

Don Khong (Muang Khong)
p272, map p272

A-B **Auberge Sala Done Khong**, T031-212077, www.salalao.com. This traditional wooden house, the former holiday home of the previous regime's foreign minister, was once the best place to stay on Don Khong but, although the exterior is still stunning, the rooms just aren't worth the price. There are 12 tastefully decorated, large rooms with a/c, hot water and en suite bathrooms; the best are in the main building on the 1st floor where there is an attractive balcony overlooking the Mekong with comfortable deck chairs. Clean and professionally run, tours arranged, bicycles for hire, good food – very relaxing. The best of the upper price-range places. Slightly cheaper rate in the low season.

A-B **Villa Muang Khong**, T020-5515993, also in Vientiane on T021-261870,

xbtrvlmk@laotel.com. A bungalow complex with 32 tidy a/c rooms and en suite Western bathrooms (hot water). Garden and pleasant restaurant serving Lao and European food. Bicycle, boat and mini-van hire plus other tour services. Again, this place is a bit on the expensive side for what is on offer and service is a little on the slack side.

B-D **Souksan Hotel and Bungalow**, northern end of town near Wat Chom Thong, T031-212071. A range of rooms, from well-designed a/c rooms with en suite bathrooms to simple rooms with fans and shared facilities, all set around an attractive garden. The rooms in a separate building, with bizarre river landscape paintings, are nicely decorated and comfortably set up with desk, cane chairs, tiled floor-boards and hot water (US$30 including breakfast). Much better value are the bungalows, with wooden floor-boards and hot showers for

US$5. Like most places, discounts are offered in the low season. The manageress, Mrs Khamsone, will arrange boats to visit the falls or see the freshwater dolphins, also motorbike hire (US$10 per day). She also runs one of the most popular and best-value guesthouses on Don Deth (see page 278). Recommended.

D Done Khong Guesthouse, beside the park, T031-214010. Big concrete edifice with reasonable fan or a/c rooms with cold showers. This is increasingly one of the more popular guesthouses on the island and has made the owners a bit complacent; some rooms flood when it rains and there seems to be a general laxity towards service. However, the rooms are still comparable to those found in the upper price bracket, so it's reasonably good value for money. The attached restaurant offers a bland but reliable selection of foods; a highlight is the 18,000 kip breakfast with juice, eggs, bread and coffee.

D Mekong Guesthouse, T031-213668. Beautifully simple and spotless rooms with fans, some overlooking the Mekong and all with comfortable mattresses. Some rooms have a/c and hot showers (US$20). There are also cheaper rooms with shared facilities (equally clean) in a wooden building.

E Bounma Guesthouse, just off the main river road. Set in an old wooden building are a number of pungent but homely rustic rooms, decorated with interesting artefacts, and en suite cold water bathrooms. There is a lovely communal area upstairs which looks over the grassy village area.

E New Pon's Guesthouse and Restaurant, T031-214037. This establishment has been renamed to reflect the massive renovations undertaken in recent months. The US$5 fan rooms are very good value, with hot showers, mozzie nets and comfortable beds. For an extra US$10 you get a/c. Mr Pon, who speaks French and English, is perhaps the most helpful of all accommodation proprietors on the island and can offer an endless supply of tourist information. Motorbike rental US$8 and bicycles US$1. He also runs a mini-van service to Pakse for US$6 per person (minimum 10 people).

E Phou Kong Guesthouse, just near the bridge, T031-213673. Very cheap rooms with tiny bathroom cubicles (cold water). If you can draw the owners away from the television for a second, they will organize tuk-tuks to Cambodian border and boats to Don Deth and Don Khone. Restaurant serves the standard quasi-Asian fare.

Ban Nakasong *p276*

Why anyone would want to stay in this town when the islands are 15 mins away is beyond comprehension but in case some kind of catastrophe strikes you can stay at the **Nakasong Guesthouse**, on the main road towards the river, a wooden house with very basic rooms and shared facilities (**E**).

Don Deth *p276, map p280*

Many people tend to make their choice of accommodation on the basis of word-of-mouth recommendations from other travellers; this is as good a way to choose as any, as the accommodation is all cheap and usually much of a muchness. It normally consists of spartan, thread-bare bungalows with bed, mosquito net and hammock, and shared squat toilets (unless otherwise stated). Always opt for a bungalow with a window, as the huts can get very hot. The wooden bungalows don't provide as much ventilation as the rattan equivalents but tend to attract fewer insects. Always check that the bungalow has a mosquito net. Other things to consider is the distance from the toilet to the bungalow, the state of the hammock, whether there is a restaurant attached and whether generator power is provided. Note that there may be a small price-hike in accommodation in the near future to ensure that tourism benefits all of the island's inhabitants, including the farmers. Costs are likely to double once the island gets electricity.

The accommodation runs across the two sides of the island, known as the **Sunset Side** and **Sunrise Side**. There is a large conglomeration of accommodation towards the northern tip, which is a good option for those wishing to socialize and hop between the various establishments' restaurants/bars; this is also the most common drop-off point. As a general rule, if you want peace and quiet, head for the bungalows towards the centre of each coast; ask the boat drivers to drop you off directly at the bungalows as it can be a difficult hike with baggage.

Sunset Side

C-D Souksan Guesthouse and Restaurant, T031-212071, Houa Deth at the northern tip of the island, at the pinnacle of the Sunset and Sunrise sides. Convenient and very close to the dock, this place justifiably claims to offer the best view of the sunset. Mrs Khamsone cleared the area which now houses 20 or so twin and double rooms built from wood and bamboo with shared shower and toilets, not to mention a legendary Chinese restaurant. There are also a couple of concrete bungalows that are slightly more expensive. The beautiful garden is home to hundreds of butterflies, with little paths linking up to the restaurant. It's a cracking place to chill out as you sip one of the many cocktails on offer. Water volleyball is a popular option in the dry season. Electricity 1800-2200; internet 1,200 kip per min (10 mins minimum). This is the hands-down winner on the island – no competition – and more than worth the extra few bucks. Highly recommended.

F Miss Noy's. Very close to the island tip and a small hike from the main drop-off dock, this place offers an excellent view of the sunset. Clean but very basic bungalows overlooking the river. Restaurant in a prime position.

F Mr B's, follow a small trail past Miss Noy's to reach Mr B's (signposted). The owner and staff here are tremendously friendly and the restaurant offers a semi-diverse range of options (it's all relative here!). It's famous for the pumpkin burger, which is OK but doesn't actually seem to have any pumpkin in it. The bungalows and grounds themselves are a bit lacklustre and the enormous pigs swilling around the backyard don't make for the most pleasing surroundings. However, the river views and the helpful staff make this an outstanding option. Recommended.

F Tena's Bungalows, also known as Sunset Bungalows, located further along the same path. Nine rattan bungalows with mozzie nets. The restaurant is more of an attraction and is a very popular meeting spot.

F Thon Don Family Guesthouse and Restaurant, further along Sunset Boulevard from Mr B's and right down a little lane. US$2 bungalows with outside toilet. Rickety restaurant that's a very popular night-time chill-out joint. The owners are exceptionally

friendly. Good for hanging around and swinging in a hammock. Recommended.

Sunrise Side

F Bouasone Bungalows, riverside midway along the Sunrise Side, T020-5833001. Secluded bungalows with shared facilities. Restaurant with guitar for those that want a jam session, which may be difficult above the loud Lao music blaring from the premises. Six threadbare bungalows with hammocks. It's difficult to get to from the main jetty, so ask the boat driver to drop you off right in front of the establishment.

F Bounhome, close to Bouasone towards the centre of the island. Five bungalows in either rattan or wood. Small badminton court. The pigs tied to the huts don't improve the atmosphere.

F Deng Bungalows, next to Mr Oudomsouk's. Three wooden bungalows on stilts. Very popular with those who want to hang on a hammock overlooking the water. Scenic position. Recommended.

F King Kong Guesthouse and Restaurant, riverside, midway along the Sunrise Side. Three spartan rattan bungalows and a smallish restaurant. Bike hire US$1. Tours and travel services.

F Mama and Papa, on the northern peninsula just up from **Paradise Bungalows**. Typical thatched bamboo bungalows with mozzie nets and shared facilities. Nice shady position. The restaurant has battery-powered lights for the night-time blackout and serves a pretty exceptional lentil curry.

F Mama Leuah, on the south side of the former French concrete port towards the centre of the island. Several bungalows that seem a bit newer and jazzier than most. Shared squat toilet facilities. Not bad value.

F Mama Tan Orn Rasta Café. This place has had numerous names but the atmosphere remains unchanged. There is a beautiful view from the communal balcony and the effervescent Mama is good value with her jovial demeanour and back-slapping, cheeky quips. The place is somewhat down-trodden, with rattan huts and communal facilities but is popular for hanging out in the hammocks.

F Mr Oudomsouk, north of the old concrete French port. Four Spartan huts, with a couple of newish wooden bungalows. Small restaurant with a few board games and dominoes. Seems to be where the local monks like to chill out.

F **Mr Phao's**, riverfront. Brand spanking new wooden bungalows with lovely carved wooden furniture.

F **Mr Tho's**, at the junction of the paths across and around Don Det. Eight bamboo bungalows set right on the water's edge with mid-sized verandas and hammocks. Mr Tho speaks good English and isn't above using it to try and rip you off. The bookswap

Don Deth & Don Khone

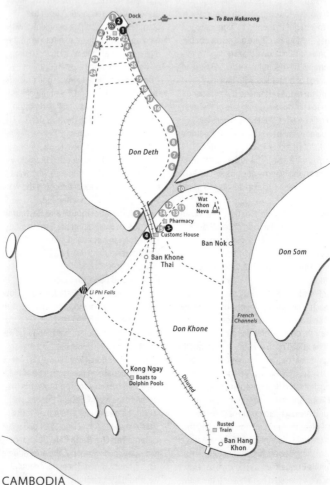

is the major draw here, with a better selection than anywhere else on the island.

F **Paradise Bungalows**, north of the centre, next door to **Deng Guesthouse**. Wooden stilted bungalows in a very enchanting location. Note that the shared facilities are a long way from the bunglows, which makes for an annoying midnight dash to the loo.

F **Phonepasack Restaurant and Guesthouse**, northern end of the island, 650 m from the dock. Five rooms in a wooden waterfront shack. Popular, perhaps due to the lively proprietor rather than the standard of accommodation. Cheap restaurant with meals at around US$0.50. Lovely fishing from hammocks hanging over the water.

F **Poonit Bungalows**, close to the dock. The big plus here is the sheer convenience of being close to the boats. However, the accommodation is very basic. Runs a generator so has a well-lit restaurant. Bike hire.

F **Santiphab Guesthouse**, far end of the island. Seven basic rattan bungalows right beside the bridge, most have the quintessential hammock. Idyllic setting, flanked by the Mekong on one side and rice paddies on the other – a friendly, timeless place. US$5 for bungalow with toilet attached. Good for those who want to be secluded. Very cheap restaurant serves tasty fare along with buckets of atmosphere.

Don Khone p276

Although Don Deth attracts the vast majority of tourists, Don Khone holds its own by offering some very pleasant accommodation alternatives and close proximity to most of the attractions.

B **Salaphae**, along from **Auberge Sala Don Khone**, T031-217526, F031-217108, www.salalao.com. This is the true stand-out accommodation in the whole of the Siphandon area. 3 rafts are managed by ex-lawyer Leusak and hold 2 bungalows per raft. The rooms have been decorated perfectly, with all the minor touches that can make accommodation outstanding. A wonderful deck, with seating overlooking the stunning river scenery. Fantastic restaurant. Solar power heating. Very romantic. Highly recommended

B-C **Auberge Sala Don Khone**, Ban Khone Nua, T020-5633718, www.salalao.com. A former French hospital built in 1927, this is

one of the nicest places to stay on the island. Two traditional Luang Prabang-style houses have been built in the grounds, with 6 rooms, all with en suite hot shower and toilet, some with a/c. The restaurant, across from the guesthouse, is one of the best places to dine on any of the 3 islands, with an unobscured waterfront view from the comfy deck-chairs and a unique cuisine selection that offers great relief from the menus found in every other establishment. Generator 1800-2200. Reduced rate in low season. Organizes tours/boat trips.

E-F **Boun Guesthouse**, next door to **Auberge Sala Don Khone**. Mr Boun has built a couple of basic thatched bungalow with shared facilities and a few, newer wooden ones, with en suite bathrooms.

F **Mr Bounpath**, next door to **Sompamit**. Small thatched bungalows overlooking the river, very basic, shared facilities. Bike hire US$1 per day. Small restaurant attached.

F **Sompamit Guesthouse**, across from **Boun Guesthouse**, on the riverside, T020-5733145. Threadbare rattan thatched bungalows with mosquito nets and shared bathroom facilities. Also a couple of basic rooms with en suite bathrooms.

F **Xaymountry Residence**, towards the bridge, T020-5735755. This old wooden villa with polished floor-boards does not live up to the grandeur of its exterior. Tacky linoleum floor covering but clean en suite bathrooms. No river views but magnificent old building.

🍴 Eating

Don Khong (Muang Khong)
p272, map p272

The majority of restaurants only serve fish and chicken: killing a pig or cow requires a lot of hungry diners. In the low season most restaurants will only be able to fulfill about half of the menu options. Special dishes such as a roast or *hor mok* will also need to be ordered a day in advance to ensure the proprieters have the required produce in stock. Although many other towns and areas also make such a claim, Don Khong is renowned for the quality of its *la-lao* (rice liquor). Local fish with coconut milk cooked in banana leaves, *Mok Pa*, is truly divine and makes a trip to the islands worthwhile in itself.

Southern Laos Islands of the south Listings

Ψ-Ψ Souksan Chinese Restaurant. Attractive place with a stunning, unobscured view of the river. It serves mostly Chinese food, including good local fish and tasty honeyed chicken. In recent years they have added a number of Western specialities, including the US$5 roast (beef, chicken or pork with potatoes and gravy), which needs to be ordered a day in advance. Recommended.

Ψ Done Khong Guesthouse, see Sleeping. The restaurant produces good food – nothing flash, just simple single-dish meals. It does a good line in pancakes.

Ψ Mekong Restaurant, attached to the Mekong Guesthouse, see Sleeping. This restaurant is pleasantly positioned near the bank of the Mekong and provides legendary fare at seriously low prices. Good *feu*.

Ψ New Pon's Restaurant, see Sleeping, T031-214037. Good atmosphere, excellent food, try the fish soup. Recommended.

Ψ Villa Muang Khong Hotel Restaurant, see Sleeping. Lao and European food – a limited but good selection of dishes.

Ban Nakasong *p276*

Two small thatched beachside restaurants serve good chicken *feu*. In the rainy season they move further up the bank. There are also food and drinks stalls on the right as you get off the boat.

Don Deth *p276, map p280*

Most people choose to eat at their guesthouses; they all have pretty much the same menu. A couple of stand-outs are:

Ψ Souksan, see Sleeping. Excellent Chinese-inspired dishes in addition to well-cooked fish. The restaurant is in a prime location to take in the sunset. Will cook up a roast for US$5 with advanced notice.

Ψ-Ψ Mr B's, see Sleeping. Italian bruschetta, rice pudding and a famous selection of burgers including chicken and pumpkin. Service is faultless. Recommended.

There are also two cheap (Ψ) restaurants beside the dock: **Riverside Restaurant** and **Khonsavanh Restaurant**. They both offer outstanding river views but mediocre food and service. The Riverside marginally wins out, predominantly due to the range of visa and travel services it can offer. Great places to watch the sun go down with an icy beverage but eat elsewhere.

Don Khone *p276*

Don Khone has better eateries and accommodation than Don Deth but remember that, in low season, most restaurants won't be able to provide many of their dishes due to the lack of supplies.

ΨΨΨ-ΨΨ Salaphae, see Sleeping. The best choice on the island, with a selection of scrumptious and creative dishes.

ΨΨ Auberge Sala Don Khone, see Sleeping. There's a beautiful view from the restaurant and some fine options on the menu, such as tuna and orange salad or steak salad.

Ψ Channihoummas Restaurant, further along the track towards the bridge. Basic, limited options – fruit shakes, coffee, baguettes, open from 0700.

Ψ Sengaroune, near the bridge, T020-5735009. Huge restaurant with large deck. Local Lao and Vietnamese-inspired cuisine. Good spring rolls. Very popular with the locals.

☻ Festivals

Don Khong *p270*

Dec A 5-day **Boat Racing** festival takes place early in the month, on the river opposite Muang Khong. It coincides with National Day on 2 Dec and is accompanied by a great deal of celebration, eating and drinking.

O Shopping

Don Deth *p276, map p280*

There isn't much to buy here. A small grocery store across from the port has a few essential items and snacks but is not very well stocked. If you're in desperate need of any items, make a quick trip to Ban Nakasong and pick up things from the market there. Most guesthouses go to Ban Nakasong on an almost daily basis and will usually buy things for you if you pay them 5,000 kip or so.

▲ Activities and tours

Don Deth, Don Khone and around *p274, map p271*

For boat trips, see Transport, page 283. Almost every guesthouse on the islands can arrange tours, transport and tickets. The best way to book yourself onto a tour on Don Deth is through the new 'whiteboard' system. A couple of whiteboards have been placed around the island (the most popular one is at the northern end, near the port); simply write your name down next to the tour or trip you wish to take. From Don Khone, it is possible to hire a boat for the day, to visit the islands and go fishing.

Dolphin watching

On **Don Khone**, boats depart either from Kong Ngay, US$7, or from the railway , US$4. Boats from **Don Deth** depart when they have enough passengers and charge about US$6 per person; put your name on the noticeboard the day before. Rates are highly subject to change as they are based on petrol prices and the individual boatman's prerogative more than anything else. The best bet is to gather 4 or 5 people and then approach a boatman.

Swimming

There is a sandy beach on **Don Khone** where many travellers like to take a dip. In the wet season this can be particularly dangerous as there is a nasty undercurrent and tourists have drowned here, so be careful. The other thing to consider is the nasty parasite called schistomosis.

⊖ Transport

Don Khong p270
Boat

See also Ins and outs, p270. **New Pon's Restaurant** (reliable and recommended) and **Souksan Hotel** can arrange boats to **Don Deth** or **Don Khone**. There are also several boatmen on the riverfront who are more than happy to take people for the right price. Fares tend to fluctuate according to international fuel prices but the going rate at the time of publication was US$15-20 for up to 10 people, one way. Most leave around 0800. Day trips can be tailored to suit (for example, to visit both waterfalls, or the dolphins and one fall). It is also possible to alight at **Ban Nakasong**, from where you can charter a tuk-tuk (50,000 kip round trip) to the **Khong Phapheng Falls**. On the return trip, boats leave the falls around 1600-1700, although check with your boatman, and be aware that they do have a habit of setting off without conducting a head count. It's a great

time to come back as you get a tremendous sunset thrown in.

Public passenger services going upriver from Don Khong leave around 0700 and take over 8 hrs to reach **Pakse**. Chartering a boat to/from Pakse costs around US$100-140 (max 20 people).

Bus/truck

A bus to **Pakse** departs from the intersection near Wat Kan Khong at around 0800 daily but it's worth asking the guesthouse owners for the most recent transport information; for earlier departures to **Pakse**, cross to **Ban Hat Xai Khoune** and pick up a bus heading north from Ban Nakasong (from 0600 onwards). To reach **Ban Nakasong**, walk to Route 13 from Ban Hat Xai Khoune and try for transport south.

Ban Nakasong p276
Boat

To **Don Deth** and **Don Khone**, 15-20 mins, 30,000 kip per person. To **Don Khong**, 2 hrs, US$15 (divided between max 5 passengers).

Bus

Decent buses depart from Ban Nakasong's market at 0600, 0700, 0800, 0900 and 1000 northbound for **Pakse**, 30,000 kip; some continue onwards to **Vientiane**; get off at **Ban Hat Xai Khoune** for the crossing to **Don Khong**, US$1. A scam is in operation on the Pakse-bound bus: *songthaew* drivers, in collusion with bus staff, get on the bus at a halfway point and tell foreign passengers they have to continue by *songthaew* to the terminal; this is not true. There's also a pick-up to Pakse at 1030 daily, US$5 per person. Buses to **Voen Kham** (for the Cambodia border; see page 284) depart in the morning, 13 km, US$1; alternatively, you can charter a *songthaew* for US$3, or hire a motorbike.To **Khong Phapheng**, take a tuk-tuk or motorcycle taxi for around US$6-7 return.

Don Deth, Don Khone and around
p274, map p271
Boat

Guesthouses organize boat trips around the area every day; the following rates are susceptible to change: to **Ban Nakasong**, US$2, divided by the number of passengers; to **Khong Phapheng Falls**, 60,000 kip, min

⚡ Border essentials: Voen Kham-Stung Treng (Cambodia)

Cambodia is easily accessible from this part of Laos – on paper. **Voen Kham** on the Mekong is 35 km south of Hat Xai Khoune. *Songthaew* can usually be arranged for US$3 but if you are staying on Don Khong, it is much easier to organize a mini-van through **Pon's Travel** or one of the other guesthouses (US$5-15 depending on the number of passengers). On reaching Voen Kham you must pay a Laos exit fee of US$2. There have been countless reports of dodgy Lao border officials hiking the rate up at weekends to as much as US$10.

Travellers face the same problems on the Cambodian side. From Voen Kham it is a one-hour journey by boat to **Stung Treng**, Cambodia. A decent price is US$30-40 for a four-seater boat but you will have to negotiate with the Cambodian boatmen and some people have reported being charged US$60-70. Try to stay as good humoured as possible. The boat trip between Voen Kham and Stung Treng is absolutely stunning. Note that coming from Stung Treng to Laos, the boat only costs US$6-7!

A highly unreliable alternative is the unofficial **Don Kalao** border (8 km from Voen Kham). This crossing includes a 60-km drive from the border to Stung Treng and is notorious for scams directed at travellers trying to cross.

5 people; to **Pakse** by boat and bus, 0600, 0700, 0800, 0900 and 1000 daily, 40,000 kip; to **Voen Kham** (for the Cambodian border, see above), 0800 and 1300, 30,000 kip, min 3 people (for around US$3-4 they will stop off at the **Khong Phapheng Falls** on the way). Otherwise you can do the border trip yourself from Ban Nakasong (see above).

There are two ways to get to **Don Khong**, from Ban Nakasong, either by boat, 2 hrs, US$15, or by bus (see above); motorbike taxis also make the trip for US$3. Although it's slower and more expensive, the boat trip is one of the loveliest in Laos.

❶ Directory

Don Khong (Muang Khong)
p272, map p272
Banks There is a basic Lao Agriculture Promotion bank in town; hours are erratic and it accepts only US$ or Thai ฿; guesthouses will also exchange cash at rates slightly poorer than market rate; New Pon's Guesthouse will change most major currencies and TCs but a photocopy of your passport is required.
Communications The post office is opposite the jetty in the centre of town – unreliable and slow mail service; international dialling available here; Alpha Internet offers

internet and internet telephone at 1000 kip per min; they also burn CDs, hire canoes and do laundry.

Don Deth *p276, map p280*
Banks There are no banks on the island; a foreign exchange service near the port will change most major currencies; Mr B of Mr B's guesthouse will also organize the cashing of TCs, but the commission here is quite hefty, so you are better off organizing your cash from Pakse. **Internet** There is a small internet café across from the port junction, 1000 kip per min; calls can also be made, min 10 mins. Souksan also has internet at 1200 kip per min. **Telephone** The best way to make a call is via the net, although most guesthouses will let you make calls from their mobiles, which can be incredibly expensive, up to US$4 a min. **Visas** The Riverside Restaurant can organize Cambodian visas in 3 working days for US$55 or 5 working days for US$45.

Don Khone *p276*
Communications No post office and no telephones on the island; guesthouses may allow you to make international calls from their mobile phones, for up to US$4 per min.
Electricity No mains electricity but many places run generators 1800-2200 daily.

History

Scholars of Lao history, before they even begin, need to decide whether they are writing a history of Laos; a history of the Lao ethnic group; or histories of the various kingdoms and principalities that have, through time, been encompassed by the present boundaries of the Lao People's Democratic Republic. Historians have tended to confront this problem in different ways without, often, acknowledging on what basis their 'history' is built. It is common to see 1365, the date of the foundation of the kingdom of Lane Xang, as marking the beginning of Lao history. But, as Martin Stuart-Fox points out, prior to Lane Xang the principality of Muang Swa, occupying the same geographical space, was headed by a Lao. The following account provides a brief overview of the histories of those peoples who have occupied what is now the territory of the Lao PDR.

Archaeological and historical evidence indicates that most Lao originally migrated south from China. This was followed by an influx of ideas and culture from the Indian subcontinent via Myanmar (Burma), Thailand and Cambodia – something which is reflected in the state religion, Theravada Buddhism.

Being surrounded by large, powerful neighbours, Laos has been repeatedly invaded over the centuries by the Thais (or Siamese) and the Vietnamese – who both thought of Laos as their buffer zone and backyard. They too have both left their mark on Lao culture. In recent history, Laos has been influenced by the French during the colonial era, the Japanese during the Second World War, the Americans during the Indochinese wars and, between 1975 and the early 1990s, by Marxism-Leninism.

It is also worth noting, in introduction, that historians and regimes have axes to grind. The French were anxious to justify their annexation of Laos and so used dubious Vietnamese documents to provide a thin legal gloss to their actions. Western historians, lumbered with the baggage of Western historiography, ignored indigenous histories. And the Lao People's Revolutionary Party uses history for its own ends too. The official three volume *History of Laos* is currently being written by Party-approved history hacks. The third volume (chronologically speaking) was published in 1989 and, working back in time, the first and second thereafter. As Martin Stuart-Fox remarks in his *A History of Laos*, "the communist regime is as anxious as was the previous Royal Lao government [pre-1975] to establish that Laos has a long and glorious past and that a continuity exists between the past and the present Lao state" (1997: 6). In other words, Laos has not one history, but many. Take your pick.

First kingdom of Laos

Myth, archaeology and history all point to a number of early feudal Lao kingdoms in what is now South China and North Vietnam. External pressures from the Mongols under Kublai Khan and the Han Chinese forced the Tai tribes to migrate south into what had been part of the Khmer Empire. The mountains to the north and east served as a cultural barrier to Vietnam and China, leaving the Lao exposed to influences from India and the West. There are no documentary records of early Lao history (the first date in the Lao chronicles to which historians attach any real veracity is 1271), although it seems probable that parts of present-day Laos were annexed by Lannathai (Chiang Mai) in the 11th century and by the Khmer Empire during the 12th century. But neither of these states held sway over the entire area of Laos. Xieng Khouang, for example, was probably never under Khmer domination. This was followed by strong Siamese influence over the cities of Luang Prabang and Vientiane under the Siamese Sukhothai Dynasty. Laos (the country), in effect did not exist; although the Laos (the people) certainly did.

⁝ Kings of Lane Xang

Fa Ngum	1353-1373	Pothisarath	1520-1548
Samsenthai	1373-1416	Setthathirat	1548-1571
Lan Kamdaeng	1417-1428	Saensurin	1572-1574
Phommathat	1428-1429	Mahaupahat (under	
Mun Sai	1429-1430	Burmese control)	1574-1580
Fa Khai	1430-1433	Saensurin	1580-1582
Khong Kham	1433-1434	Nakhon Noi (under	
Yukhon	1434-1435	Burmese control)	1582-1583
Kham Keut	1435-1441	Interregnum	1583-1591
Chaiyachakkapat-		Nokeo Koumone	1591-1596
Phaenphaeo		Thammikarath	1596-1622
(aka Sao Tiakaphat)	1441-1478	Upanyuvarat	1622-1623
Suvarna Banlang		Pothisarat	1623-1627
(aka Theng Kham)	1478-1485	Mon Keo	1627
Lahsaenthai Puvanart	1485-1495	Unstable period	1627-1637
Sompou	1497-1500	Sulinya Vongsa	1637-1694
Visunarat	1500-1520		

The downfall of the kingdom of Sukhothai in 1345 and its submission to the new Siamese Dynasty at Ayutthaya (founded in 1349) was the catalyst for the foundation of what is commonly regarded as the first truly independent Lao Kingdom – although there were smaller semi-independent Lao *muang* (city states, sometimes transliterated as *meuang*) existing prior to that date.

Fa Ngum and Lane Xang

The kingdom of Lane Xang (Lan Chang) emerged in 1353 under Fa Ngum, a Lao prince who had grown up in the Khmer court of Angkor. Fa Ngum is clearly an important man – that is, if the amount of space devoted to his exploits in the Lao chronicles is anything to go by. There is more written about him than there is about the following two centuries of Lao history. It is also safe to say that his life is more fiction than fact. Fa Ngum was reputedly born with 33 teeth and was banished to Angkor after his father, Prince Yakfah, was convicted of having an incestuous affair with a wife of King Suvarna Kamphong. In 1353 Fa Ngum led an army to Luang Prabang and confronted his grandfather, King Suvarna Kamphong. Unable to defeat his grandson on the battlefield, the aged king is said to have hanged himself and Fa Ngum was invited to take the throne. Three years later, in 1356, Fa Ngum marched on Vientiane which he took with ease and then on Vienkam which proved more of a challenge (see box, page). He is credited with piecing together Lang Xang – the Land of a Million Elephants (or, if not accented, the Valley of Elephants) – the golden age to which all histories of Laos refer to justify the existence (and greatness) of Laos.

In some accounts Lang Xang is portrayed as stretching from China to Cambodia and from the Khorat Plateau in present-day Northeast Thailand to the Annamite mountains in the east. But it would be entirely wrong to envisage the kingdom controlling all these regions. Lane Xang probably only had total control over a comparatively small area of present-day Laos and parts of Northeast Thailand; the bulk of this grand empire would have been contested with other surrounding kingdoms. In addition, the smaller *muang* and principalities would themselves have played competing powers off, one against another, in an attempt to maximize their own autonomy. It is this 'messiness' which led scholars of Southeast Asian history to suggest that territories as such did not exist, but rather zones of variable control. The historian OW Wolters coined the term '*mandala*' for "a particular and often unstable political situation in a vaguely defined geographical area without fixed boundaries and where smaller centres tended to look in all directions for security. *Mandalas* would expand and contract in concertina-like fashion. Each one contained several tributary rulers, some of whom would repudiate their vassal status when the opportunity arose and try to build up their own network of vassals."

Legend relates that Fa Ngum was a descendant of Khoum Borom, "a king who came out of the sky from South China". He is said to have succeeded to the throne of Nanchao in 729, aged 31, and died 20 years later, although this historical record is, as they say, exceedingly thin. Khoum Borom is credited with giving birth to the Lao people by slicing open a gourd in Muong Taeng (Dien Bien Phu, Vietnam) and his seven sons established the great Tai kingdoms. He returned to his country with a detachment of Khmer soldiers and united several scattered Lao fiefdoms. In those days, conquered lands were usually razed and the people taken as slaves to build up the population of the conquering group. (This largely explains why, today, there are far more Lao in northeastern Thailand than in Laos – they were forcibly settled there after King Anou was defeated by King Rama III of Siam in 1827 – see page 290.) The kings of Lane Xang were less philistine, demanding only subordination and allegiance as one part of a larger *mandala*.

Luang Prabang became the capital of the kingdom of Lane Xang. The unruly highland tribes of the northeast did not come under the kingdom's control at that time. Fa Ngum made Theravada Buddhism the official religion. He married the Cambodian king's daughter, Princess Keo Kaengkanya, and was given the Pra Bang (a golden statue, the most revered religious symbol of Laos), by the Khmer court.

It is common to read of Lane Xang as the first kingdom of Laos; as encompassing the territory of present-day Laos; and as marking the introduction of Theravada Buddhism to the country. On all counts this portrait is, if not false, then deeply flawed. As noted above, there were Lao states that predated Lane Xang; Lane Xang never controlled Laos as it currently exists; and Buddhism had made an impact on the Lao people before 1365. Fa Ngum did not create a kingdom; rather he brought together various pre-existing *muang* (city states) into a powerful *mandala*. As Martin Stuart-Fox writes, "From this derives his [Fa Ngum's] historical claim to hero status as the founder of the Lao Kingdom." But, as Stuart-Fox goes on to explain, there was no central authority and rulers of individual *muang* were permitted considerable autonomy. As a result the "potential for disintegration was always present ..."

After Fa Ngum's wife died in 1368, he became so debauched, it is said, that he was deposed in favour of his son, Samsenthai (1373-1416), who was barely 18 when he acceded the throne. He was named after the 1376 census, which concluded that he ruled over 300,000 Tais living in Laos: *samsen* means, literally, 300,000. He set up a new administrative system based on the existing *muang*, nominating governors to each that lasted until it was abolished by the Communist government in 1975. Samsenthai's death was followed by a period of unrest. Under King Chaiyachakkapat-Phaenphaeo (1441-78), the kingdom came under increasing threat from the Vietnamese. How the Vietnamese came to be peeved with the Lao is another story which smacks of fable more than fact. King Chaiyachakkapat's eldest son, the Prince of Chienglaw, secured a holy white elephant. The emperor of Vietnam, learning of this momentous discovery, asked to be sent some of the beast's hairs. Disliking the Vietnamese, the Prince dispatched a box of its excrement instead, whereupon the Emperor formed an army of an improbably large 550,000 men. The Prince's army numbered 200,000 and 2000 elephants. (Considering that the population of Lane Xang under Samsenthai was said to be 300,000 this beggars statistical belief. Still, it is a good story.) The massive Vietnamese army finally prevailed – two Lao generals were so tired they fell off their elephants and were hacked to pieces – and entered and sacked Luang Prabang. But shortly thereafter they were driven out by

Chaiyachakkapat-Phaenphaeo's son, King Suvarna Banlang (1478-85). Peace was only fully restored under King Visunarat (1500-1520), who built Wat Visoun in Luang Prabang (see page).

Increasing prominence and Burmese incursions Under King Pothisarath (1520-48) Vientiane became prominent as a trading and religious centre. He married a Lanna (Chiang Mai) princess, Queen Yotkamtip, and when the Siamese King Ketklao was put to death in 1545, Pothisarath's son claimed the throne at Lanna. He returned to Lane Xang when his father died in 1548. Once again an elephant figured as a prime mover in the event: Pothisarath was demonstrating his prowess in the manly art of elephant lassoing when he was flung from his mount and fatally crushed. Asserting his right as successor to the throne, he was crowned Setthathirat in 1548 and ruled until 1571 – the last of the great kings of Lane Xang.

At the same time, the Burmese were expanding East and in 1556 Lanna fell into their hands. Setthathirat gave up his claim to that throne, to a Siamese prince, who ruled under Burmese authority. (He also took the Phra Kaeo – Thailand's famous 'Emerald' Buddha and its most sacred and revered image – with him to Luang Prabang and then to Vientiane. The residents of Chiang Mai are reputed to have pleaded that he leave it in the city, but these cries fell on deaf ears. The Phra Kaeo stayed in Vientiane until 1778 when the Thai general Phya Chakri 'repatriated' it to Thailand.) In 1563 Setthathirat pronounced Vieng Chan (Vientiane) the principal capital of Lane Xang. Seven years later, the Burmese King Bayinnaung launched an unsuccessful attack on Vieng Chan itself.

Setthathirat is revered as one of the great Lao kings, having protected the country from foreign domination. He built Wat Phra Kaeo (see page 71) in Vientiane, in which he placed the famous Emerald Buddha brought from Lanna. Setthathirat mysteriously disappeared during a campaign in the southern province of Attapeu in 1574, which threw the kingdom into crisis (see page 261). Vientiane fell to invading Burmese the following year and remained under Burmese control for seven years. Finally the anarchic kingdoms of Luang Prabang and Vientiane were reunified under Nokeo Koumane (1591-96) and Thammikarath (1596-1622).

Disputed territory

From the time of the formation of the kingdom of Lane Xang to the arrival of the French, the history of Laos was dominated by the struggle to retain the lands it had conquered. Following King Setthathirat's death, a series of kings came to the throne in quick succession. King Souligna Vongsa, crowned in 1633, brought long awaited peace to Laos. The 61 years he was on the throne are regarded as Lane Xang's golden age. Under him, the kingdom's influence spread to Yunnan in South China, the Burmese Shan States, Issan in Northeast Thailand and areas of Vietnam and Cambodia.

Souligna Vongsa was even on friendly terms with the Vietnamese: he married Emperor Le Thanh Ton's daughter and he and the Emperor agreed the borders between the two countries. The frontier was settled in a deterministic – but nonetheless amicable – fashion: those living in houses built on stilts with verandas were considered Lao subjects and those living in houses without piles and verandas owed allegiance to Vietnam.

During his reign, foreigners first visited the country – the Dutch merchant Gerrit van Wuysthoff arrived in 1641 to assess trading prospects – and Jesuit missionaries too. But other than a handful of adventurers, Laos remained on the outer periphery of European concerns and influence in the region.

The three kingdoms After Souligna Vongsa died in 1694, leaving no heir, dynastic quarrels and feudal rivalries once again erupted, undermining the kingdom's cohesion. In 1700 Lane Xang split into three: Luang Prabang under Souligna's grandson, Vientiane under Souligna's nephew and the new kingdom of Champasak was founded in the south 'panhandle'. This weakened the country and allowed the Siamese and Vietnamese to encroach on Lao lands. *Muang*, which previously owed clear allegiance to Lane Xang, began to look towards Vietnam or Siam. Isan muang in present-day Northeast Thailand, for example, paid tribute to Bangkok; while Xieng Khouang did the same to Hanoi and, later, to Hué. The three main kingdoms that emerged with the disintegration of Lane Xang leant in different directions: Luang Prabang had close links with China, Vientiane with Vietnam's Hanoi/Hué and Champassak with Siam.

By the mid-1760s Burmese influence once again held sway in Vientiane and Luang Prabang and before the turn of the decade, they sacked Ayutthaya, the capital of Siam. Somehow the Siamese managed to pull themselves together and only two years later in 1778 successfully rampaged through Vientiane. The two sacred Buddha's, the Phra Bang and the Phra Kaeo (Emerald Buddha) were taken as booty back to Bangkok. The Emerald Buddha was never returned and now sits in Bangkok's Wat Phra Kaeo (see page 71).

King Anou (an abbreviation of Anurutha), was placed on the Vientiane throne by the Siamese. With the death of King Rama II of Siam, King Anou saw his chance of rebellion, asked Vietnam for assistance, formed an army and marched on Bangkok in 1827. In mounting this brave – some would say foolhardy – assault, Anou was apparently trying to emulate the great Fa Ngum. Unfortunately, he got no further than the Northeast Thai town of Korat where his forces suffered a defeat and were driven back. Nonetheless, Anou's rebellion is considered one of the most daring and ruthless rebellions in Siamese history and he was lauded as a war hero back home.

King Anou's brief stab at regional power was to result in catastrophe for Laos – and tragedy for King Anou. The first US arms shipment to Siam allowed the Siamese to sack Vientiane, a task to which they had grown accustomed over the years. (This marks America's first intervention in Southeast Asia.) Lao artisans were frog-marched to Bangkok and many of the inhabitants were resettled in Northeast Siam. Rama III had Chao Anou locked in a cage where he was taunted and abused by the population of Bangkok. He died soon afterwards, at the age of 62. The cause of his death has been variously linked to poison and shame. One of his supporters is said to have taken pity on the king and brought him poison. Other explanations simply say that he wished himself dead. Still others say that he choked to death. Whatever the cause, the disconsolate Anou, before he died, put a curse on Siam's monarchy, promising that the next time a Thai king set foot on Lao soil, he would die. To this day no Thai king has crossed the Mekong River. When the agreement for the supply of hydro-electric power was signed with Thailand in the 1970s, the Thai king was invited officially to open the Nam Ngum Dam, a feat he managed from a sandbank in the middle of the Mekong.

Disintegration of the kingdom Over the next 50 years, Anou's Kingdom was destroyed. By the time the French arrived in the late 19th century, the virtually unoccupied city was subsumed into the Siamese sphere of influence. Luang Prabang also became a Siamese vassal state, while Xieng Khouang province was invaded by Chinese rebels – to the chagrin of the Vietnamese, who had always considered the Hmong mountain kingdom (they called it Tran Ninh), to be their exclusive source of slaves. The Chinese had designs on Luang Prabang too and in order to quash their expansionist instincts, Bangkok dispatched an army there in 1885 to pacify the region and ensure the north remained firmly within the Siamese sphere of influence. This period was clearly one of confusion and rapidly shifting allegiances. In James McCarthy's book of his travels in Siam and Laos, *Surveying and Exploring in Siam* (1900), he states that an old chief of Luang Prabang remarked to him that the city had never been a tributary state of Annam (North Vietnam) but had formerly paid tribute to China. He writes:

"The tribute had consisted of four elephants, 41 mules, 533 lbs of nok (metal composed of gold and copper), 25 lbs of rhinoceros' horns, 100 lbs of ivory, 250 pieces of home-spun cloth, one horn, 150 bundles of areca-palm nuts [for betel 'nut' chewing], 150 cocoanuts [sic] and 33 bags of roe of the fish pla buk [the giant Mekong cat fish, see page 344]."

The history of Laos during this period becomes, essentially, the history of only a small part of the current territory of the country: namely, the history of Luang Prabang. And because Luang Prabang was a suzerain state of Bangkok, the history of that kingdom is, in turn, sometimes relegated to a mere footnote in the history of Siam.

The French and independence

Following King Anou's death, Laos became the centre of Southeast Asian rivalry between Britain, expanding east from Burma and France, pushing west through Vietnam. In 1868, following the French annexation of South Vietnam and the formation of a protectorate in Cambodia, an expedition set out to explore the Mekong trade route to China. Once central and north Vietnam had come under the influence of the Quai d'Orsay in Paris, the French became increasingly curious about Vietnamese claims to chunks of Laos. Unlike the Siamese, the French – like the British – were concerned with demarcating borders and establishing explicit areas of sovereignty. This seemed extraordinary to most Southeast Asians at the time who could not see the point of spending so much time and effort mapping space when land was so abundant. However, it did not take long for the Siamese king to realize the importance of maintaining his claim to Siamese territories if the French in the east and the British in the south (Malaya) and west (Burma) were not to squeeze Siam to nothing.

However, King Chulalongkorn was not in a position to confront the French militarily and instead he had to play a clever diplomatic game if his Kingdom was to survive. The French, for their part, were anxious to continue to press westwards from Vietnam into the Lao lands over which Siam held suzerainty. Martin Stuart-Fox argues that there were four main reasons underlying France's desire to expand West: the lingering hope that the Mekong might still offer a 'backdoor' into China; the consolidation of Vietnam against attack; the 'rounding out' of their Indochina possessions; and a means of further pressuring Bangkok. In 1886, the French received reluctant Siamese permission to post a vice consul to Luang Prabang and a year later he persuaded the Thais to leave. However, even greater humiliation was to come in 1893 when the French, through crude gunboat diplomacy – the so-called Paknam incident – forced King Chulalongkorn to give up all claim to Laos on the flimsiest of historical pretexts. Despite attempts by Prince Devawongse to manufacture a compromise, the French forced Siam to cede Laos to France and, what's more, to pay compensation. It is said that after this humiliation, King Chulalongkorn retired from public life, broken in spirit and health. So the French colonial era in Laos began.

What is notable about this spat between France and Siam is that Laos – the country over which they were fighting – scarcely figures. As was to happen again in Laos' history, the country was caught between two competing powers who used Laos as a stage on which to fight a wider and to them, more important, conflict.

Union of Indochina In 1893 France occupied the left bank of the Mekong and forced Thailand to recognize the river as the boundary. The French Union of Indochina denied Laos the area which is now Isan, northeast Thailand, and this was the start of 50 years of colonial rule. Laos became a protectorate with a *résident-superieur* in Vientiane and a vice-consul in Luang Prabang. However, as Martin Stuart-Fox points out, Laos could hardly be construed as a 'country' during the colonial period. "Laos existed again", he writes, "but not yet as a political entity in its own right, for no independent centre of Lao political power existed. Laos was but a territorial entity within French Indochina." The French were not interested in establishing an identifiable Lao state; they saw Laos as a part and a subservient part at that, of Vietnam, serving as a resource-rich appendage to Vietnam. Though they had grand plans for the development of Laos, these were only expressed airily and none of them came to anything. "The French were never sure what to do with Laos", Stuart-Fox writes, "either the parts or the whole." Unlike Cambodia to the south, the French did not perceive Laos to have any historical unity or coherence and therefore it could be hacked about and developed or otherwise, according to their whim, as if it were a piece of brie.

In 1904 the Franco-British convention delimited respective zones of influence. Only a few hundred French civil servants were ever in Vientiane at any one time and their attitude to colonial administration – described as 'benign neglect' – was as relaxed as the people they governed. To the displeasure of the Lao, France brought in Vietnamese to run the civil service (in the way the British used Indian bureaucrats in Burma). But for the most part, the French colonial period was a 50-year siesta for Laos. The king was allowed to stay in Luang Prabang, but had little say in administration. Trade and commerce was left to the omnipresent Chinese and the Vietnamese. A small, French-educated Lao élite did grow up and by the 1940s they had become the core of a typically laid-back Lao nationalist movement.

Japanese coup Towards the end of the Second World War, Japan ousted the French administration in Laos in a coup in March 1945. The eventual surrender of the Japanese in August that year gave impetus to the Lao independence movement. Prince Phetsarath, hereditary viceroy and premier of the Luang Prabang Kingdom, took over the leadership of the Lao Issara, the Free Laos Movement (originally a resistance movement against the Japanese). They prevented the French from seizing power again and declared Lao independence on 1 September 1945. Two weeks later, the north and south provinces were reunified and in October, Phetsarath formed a Lao Issara government headed by Prince Phaya Khammao, the governor of Vientiane. France refused to recognize the new state and crushed the Lao resistance. King Sisavang Vong, unimpressed by Prince Phetsarath's move, sided with the French, who had their colony handed back by British forces. He was crowned the constitutional monarch of the new protectorate in 1946. The rebel government took refuge in Bangkok. Historians believe the Issara movement was aided in their resistance to the French by the Viet Minh – Hanoi's Communists.

Independence In response to nationalist pressures, France was obliged to grant Laos ever greater self government and, eventually, formal independence within the framework of the newly reconstructed French Union in July 1949. Meanwhile, in Bangkok, the Issara movement had formed a government-in-exile, headed by Phetsarath and his half-brothers: Prince Souvanna Phouma and Prince Souphanouvong. Both were refined, French-educated men, with a taste for good wine and cigars. The Issara's military wing was led by Souphanouvong who, even at that stage, was known for his Communist sympathies. Within just a few months the so-called Red Prince had been ousted by his half-brothers and joined the Viet Minh where he is said to have been the moving force behind the declaration of the Democratic Republic of Laos by the newly-formed Lao National Assembly. The Lao People's Democratic Republic emerged – albeit in name only – somewhere inside Vietnam, in August 1949. Soon afterwards, the Pathet Lao – literally, 'the Lao nation' was born. The Issara movement quickly folded and Souvanna Phouma went back to Vientiane and joined the newly-formed Royal Lao Government.

By 1953, Prince Souphanouvong had managed to move his Pathet Lao headquarters inside Laos and with the French losing their grip on the north provinces, the weary colonizers granted the country full independence. Retreating honourably, France signed a treaty of friendship and association with the new royalist government and made the country a French protectorate.

Prince Souvanna Phouma: architect of independence and helmsman of catastrophe

Prince Souvanna Phouma was Laos' greatest statesman. He was Prime Minister on no less than eight occasions for a total of 20 years between 1951 and 1975. He dominated mainstream politics from independence until the victory of the Pathet Lao in 1975. But he was never able to preserve the integrity of Laos in the face of much stronger external forces. "Souvanna stands as a tragic figure in modern Lao history," Martin Stuart-Fox writes, a "stubborn symbol of an alternative, neutral, 'middle way'."

He was born in 1901 into a branch of the Luang Prabang royal family. Like many of the Lao élite he was educated abroad, in Hanoi, Paris and Grenoble, and when he returned to Laos he married a woman of mixed French-Lao blood. He was urbane, educated and, by all accounts, arrogant. He enjoyed fine wines and cigars, spoke French better than he spoke Lao, and was a Francophile – as well as a nationalist – to the end.

In 1950 Souvanna became a co-founder of the Progressive Party and in the elections of 1951 he headed his first government which negotiated and secured full independence from France.

Souvanna made two key errors of judgement during these early years. First, he ignored the need for 'nation building' in Laos. And, second, he underestimated the threat that the Communists posed to the country. With regard to the first of these misjudgements, he seemed to believe – and it is perhaps no accident that he trained as an engineer and architect – that Laos just needed to be administered efficiently to become a modern state. He appeared either to reject, or to ignore the idea that the government first had to try and inculcate a sense of Lao nationhood.

The second misjudgement was his long-held belief that the Pathet Lao was a nationalist and not a Communist organization. He let the Pathet Lao grow in strength and this, in turn, brought the US into Lao affairs.

By the time the US began to intervene in Lao affairs in the late 1950s, the country already seemed to be heading for catastrophe. But in his struggle to maintain some semblance of independence for his tiny country, he ignored the degree to which Laos was being sucked into the quagmire of Indochina. As Martin Stuart-Fox writes: "He [Souvanna] knew he was being used, and that he had no power to protect his country from the war that increasingly engulfed it. But he was too proud meekly to submit to US demands – even as Laos was subjected to the heaviest bombing in the history of warfare. At least a form of independence had to be maintained...".

When the Pathet Lao entered Vientiane in victory in 1975, Souvanna did not flee into exile. He remained to help in the transfer of power. The Pathet Lao, of course, gave him a title and then largely ignored him as they pursued their Communist manifesto. Again, Martin Stuart-Fox writes: "Souvanna ended his days beside the Mekong. He was to the end a Lao patriot, refusing to go into exile in France. The leaders of the new regime did consult him on occasions. Friends came to play bridge. Journalists continued to seek him out, although he said little and interviews were taped in the presence of Pathet Lao minions. When he died in January 1984, he was accorded a state funeral."

From Martin Stuart-Fox's *Buddhist Kingdom, Marxist State: the Making of Modern Laos* (White Lotus, 1996).

French defeat While all this was going on, King Sisavang Vong sat tight in Luang Prabang instead of moving to Vientiane. But within a few months of independence, the ancient royal capital was under threat from the Communist Viet Minh and Pathet Lao. Honouring the terms of the new treaty, French commander General Henri Navarre determined in late 1953 to take the pressure off Luang Prabang by confronting the Viet Minh who controlled the strategic approach to the city at Dien Bien Phu. The French suffered a stunning defeat which presaged their withdrawal from Indochina. The subsequent occupation of two north Lao provinces by the Vietnam-backed Pathet Lao forces, meant the kingdom's days as a western buffer state were numbered.

With the Geneva Accord in July 1954, following the fall of Dien Bien Phu in May, Ho Chi Minh's government gained control of all territory north of the 17th parallel in neighbouring Vietnam. The Accord guaranteed Laos' freedom and neutrality, but with the Communists on the threshold, the US was not prepared to be a passive spectator: the demise of the French sparked an increasing US involvement. In an operation that was to mirror the much more famous war with Vietnam to the East, Washington soon found itself supplying and paying the salaries of 50,000 royalist troops and their corrupt officers. Clandestine military assistance grew, undercover special forces were mobilized and the CIA began meddling in Lao politics. In 1960 a consignment of weapons was dispatched by the CIA to a Major in the Royal Lao Army called Vang Pao – or VP, as he became known – who was destined to become the leader of the Hmong.

US involvement: the domino effect Laos had become the dreaded 'first domino', which, using the scheme of US President Dwight D Eisenhower's famous analogy, would trigger the rapid spread of Communism if ever it fell. The time-trapped little kingdom rapidly became the focus of superpower brinkmanship. At a press conference in March 1961, President Kennedy is said to have been too abashed to announce to the American people that US forces might soon become embroiled in conflict in a far-away flashpoint that went by the inglorious name of 'Louse'. For three decades Americans have unwittingly mis-pronounced the country's name as Kennedy decided, euphemistically, to label it 'Lay-os' throughout his national television broadcast.

Coalitions, coups and counter-coups The US-backed Royal Lao Government of independent Laos – even though it was headed by the neutralist, Prince Souvanna Phouma – ruled over a divided country from 1951 to 1954. The US played havoc with Laos' domestic politics, running anti-communist campaigns, backing the royalist army and lending support to political figures on the right (even if they lacked experience or political qualifications). The Communist Pathet Lao, headed by Prince Souphanouvong and overseen and sponsored by North Vietnam's Lao Dong party since 1949, emerged as the only strong opposition. By the mid-1950s, Kaysone Phomvihane, later Prime Minister of the Lao PDR, began to make a name for himself in the Indochinese Communist Party. Indeed the close association between Laos and Vietnam went deeper than just ideology. Kaysone's father was Vietnamese, while Prince Souphanouvong and Nouhak Phounsavanh both married Vietnamese women.

Government of National Union Elections were held in Vientiane in July 1955 but were boycotted by the Pathet Lao. Souvanna Phouma became Prime Minister in March 1956. He aimed to try to negotiate the integration of his half-brother's Pathet Lao provinces into a unified administration and coax the Communists into a coalition government. In 1957 the disputed provinces were returned to royal government control and in May 1958 elections were held. This time the Communists' Lao Patriotic Front (Neo Lao Hak Xat) clinched nine of the 21 seats in the Government of National Union. The Red Prince, Souphanouvong and one of his aides were included in the cabinet and former Pathet Lao members were elected deputies of the National Assembly.

Almost immediately problems which had been beneath the surface emerged to plague the government. The rightists and their US supporters were shaken by the result and the much-vaunted coalition lasted just two months. The National Union fell apart in July 1958. Pathet Lao leaders were jailed and the right-wing Phoui Sananikone came to power. With anti-Communists in control, Pathet Lao forces withdrew to the Plain of Jars in Xieng Khouang province. A three-way civil war ensued, between the rightists, the Communists and the neutralists.

Civil war CIA-backed strongman General Phoumi Nosavan thought Phoui's politics rather tame and with a nod from Washington he stepped into the breech in January 1959, eventually overthrowing Phoui in a coup in December and placing Prince Boun Oum in power. Pathet Lao leaders were imprisoned without trial. Confusion over Phoumas, Phouis and Phoumis led one American official to comment that it all "could have been a significant event or a typographical error".

Within a year, the rightist regime was overthrown by a neutralist *coup d'état* led by General Kong Lae and Prince Souvanna Phouma was recalled from exile in Cambodia to become Prime Minister of the first National Union. Souvanna Phouma incurred American wrath by inviting a Soviet ambassador to Vientiane in October. With US support, Nosavan staged yet another armed rebellion in December and sparked a new civil war. In the 1960 general elections, provincial authorities were threatened with military action if they did not support the right-wing groups. Kong Lae backed down, Souvanna Phouma shuffled back to Phnom Penh and a new right-wing government was set up under Boun Oum.

Zurich talks and the Geneva Accord The new Prime Minister, the old one and his Marxist half-brother finally sat down to talks in Zurich in June 1961, but any hope of an agreement was overshadowed by escalating tensions between the superpowers. In 1962, an international agreement on Laos was hammered out in Geneva by 14 participating nations and accords were signed, once again guaranteeing Lao neutrality.

By implication, the accords denied the Viet Minh access to the Ho Chi Minh Trail. But aware of the reality of constant North Vietnamese infiltration through Laos into South Vietnam, the head of the American mission concluded that the agreement was "a good bad deal".

Another coalition government of National Union was formed under the determined neutralist Prince Souvanna Phouma (as Prime Minister), with Prince Souphanouvong for the Pathet Lao and Prince Boun Oum representing the right. It was no surprise when it collapsed within a few months and fighting resumed. This time the international community just shrugged and watched Laos sink back into the vortex of civil war. Unbeknown to the outside world, the conflict was rapidly degenerating into a war between the CIA and North Vietnamese jungle guerrillas.

Secret War

The war that wasn't With the Viet Minh denying the existence of the Ho Chi Minh Trail, while at the same time enlarging it, Kennedy dispatched an undercover force of CIA-men, Green Berets and US-trained Thai mercenaries to command 9000 Lao soldiers. Historian, Roger Warner believes that by 1965 "word spread among a select circle of congressmen and senators about this exotic program run by Lone Star rednecks and Asian hillbillies that was better and cheaper than anything the Pentagon was doing in South Vietnam." To the north, the US also supplied Vang Pao's force of Hmong guerrillas, dubbed 'Mobile Strike Forces'. With the co-operation of Prince Souvanna Phouma, the CIA's commercial airline, Air America, ferried men and equipment into Laos from Thailand (and opium out, it is believed). Owing to the clandestine nature of the military intervention in Laos, the rest of the world – believing that the Geneva settlement had solved the foreign interventionist problem

– was oblivious as to what was happening on the ground. Right up until 1970, Washington never admitted to any activity in Laos beyond 'armed reconnaissance' flights over northern provinces. Richard Nixon, for example, claimed that "there are no American ground combat troops in Laos", which was stretching the truth to breaking point. Souvanna Phouma appropriately referred to it as 'the forgotten war' and it is often termed now the 'non-attributable war'. The willingness on the part of the Americans to dump millions of tonnes of ordnance on a country which was

Vietnam War

ostensibly neutral may have been made easier by the fact that some people in the administration did not believe Laos to be a country at all. Bernard Fall wrote that Laos at the time was "neither a geographical nor an ethnic or social entity, but merely a political convenience", while a Rand Corporation report written in 1970 described Laos as "hardly a country except in the legal sense". More colourfully, Secretary of State Dean Rusk described it as a "wart on the hog of Vietnam". Perhaps those in Washington could feel a touch better about bombing the hell out of a country which, in their view, occupied a sort of political never-never land – or which they could liken to an unfortunate skin complaint.

Not everyone agrees with this view that Laos never existed until the French wished it into existence. Scholar of Laos Arthur Dommen, for example, traces a true and coherent Lao identity back to Fa Ngum and his creation of the kingdom of Lane Xang in 1353, writing that it was "a state in the true sense of the term, delineated by borders clearly defined and consecrated by treaty" for 3½ centuries. He goes on:

"Lao historians see a positive proof of the existence of a distinct Lao race (*sua sat Lao*), a Lao nation (*sat Lao*), a Lao country (*muong Lao*) and a Lao state (*pathet Lao*). In view of these facts, we may safely reject the notion, fashionable among apologists for a colonial enterprise of a later day, that Laos was a creation of French colonial policy and administration" (Dommen 1985:19).

American bombing of the North Vietnamese Army's supply lines through Laos to South Vietnam along the Ho Chi Minh Trail in East Laos (see page 228) started in 1964 and fuelled the conflict between the Royalist Vientiane government and the Pathet Lao. The neutralists had been forced into alliance with the Royalists to avoid defeat in Xieng Kouang province. US bombers crossed Laos on bombing runs to Hanoi from air bases in Thailand and gradually the war in Laos escalated. In his book *The Ravens* (1987), Christopher Robbins sets the scene:

"Apparently, there was another war even nastier than the one in Vietnam and so secret that the location of the country in which it was being fought was classified. The cognoscenti simply referred to it as 'the Other Theater'. The men who chose to fight in it were hand-picked volunteers and anyone accepted for a tour seemed to disappear as if from the face of the earth."

The secret war was conducted from a one-room shack at the US base in Udon Thani, 'across the fence' in Thailand. This was the CIA's Air America operations room and in the same compound was stationed the 4802 Joint Liaison Detachment – or the CIA logistics office. In Vientiane, US pilots supporting Hmong General Vang Pao's rag-tag army, were given a new identity as rangers for the US Agency for International Development; they reported directly to the air attaché at the US embassy (see Raven 58 crossing the fence, page 298). Robbins writes that they "were military men, but flew into battle in civilian clothes – denim cutoffs, T-shirts, cowboy hats and dark glasses ... Their job was to fly as the winged artillery of some fearsome warlord, who led an army of stone-age mercenaries in the pay of the CIA and they operated out of a secret city hidden in the mountains of a jungle kingdom ..." He adds that CIA station chiefs and field agents "behaved like warlords in their own private fiefdoms."

The most notorious of the CIA's unsavoury operatives was Anthony Posepny – known as Tony Poe, on whom the character of Kurtz, the crazy colonel played by Marlon Brando in the film *Apocalypse Now*, was based. Originally, Poe had worked as Vang Pao's case officer; he then moved to North Laos and operated for years, on his own, in Burmese and Chinese border territories, offering his tribal recruits one US dollar for each set of Communist ears they brought back. Many of the spies and pilots of this secret war have re-emerged in recent years in covert and illegal arms-smuggling rackets to Libya, Iran and the Nicaraguan Contras.

By contrast, the Royalist forces were reluctant warriors: despite the fact that civil war was a deeply ingrained tradition in Laos, the Lao themselves would go to great lengths to avoid fighting each other. One foreign journalist, reporting from Luang

⁑ "Raven 58, crossing the fence"

'Raven' was the call sign used by Forward Air Controllers (FACs) in Laos. It came to designate, however, a special breed of FAC – someone who was highly motivated, aggressive, decisive, daring and exceptionally skilled and professional in his work. The mystique was heightened by the secrecy of the assignment. Pilots would leave Vietnam and seemingly disappear.

To understand the importance of a Raven's mission, it is first necessary to understand the mission of an FAC. Essentially, a FAC had three responsibilities: (1) to conduct air reconnaissance to obtain first-hand information concerning enemy locations, activity and threats; (2) to control and direct Air Force or Navy aircraft bombers or Army artillery on enemy targets; and (3) to control, direct and coordinate air strikes with ground troops for close air support.

As a Raven Forward Air Controller (Raven FAC), I had the privilege of belonging to an elite group of pilots who flew covert operations in Laos in support of the Royal Laotian Army or the CIA Special Guerrilla Units (SGUs).

SGUs were trained by CIA Country Team members. They were an elite fighting force designed to interdict movement of the North Vietnamese along the Ho Chi Minh Trail in the south or in areas around the Plain of Jars in the north. When they operated along the trail or in other forward locations, their supplies would be flown in by a Porter aircraft, piloted by Continental Air Service or Air America pilots. The advantage of this aircraft was that it could land and take off on a very short 'runway' - about 100 feet in length.

Normally, I would support the SGUs from the air, providing reconnaissance or fighter aircraft support. However, on one day they returned the favour. My airplane crashed in a rice paddy south of Attapeu. Nine North Vietnamese were across the paddy as I made a judicious move toward the opposite side. I knew that the SGUs were in the area near Attapeu, as I headed in that direction. As I came upon them, I recognized that they were friendly and shortly thereafter I was picked up by an Air America helicopter and flown to a nearby Lima Site (PS-38) for the night.

During the time of the Ravens, 1966 to 1975, there were only a total of 191 pilots. Very few Americans actually ever went into Laos – except along the Ho Chi Minh Trail. My time in Laos was quite enjoyable. Officially, I was a 'forest ranger' working for the Lao Government. In fact, I worked for the American Ambassador and was assigned to provide visual reconnaissance and direct air support for the Royal Laotian Army and the CIA SGUs.

And, there was much to discourage volunteers. The casualty rate was said to be 50%. The conditions were more harsh. And, then there were the drug dealers and gold dealers. (At that time it was illegal to trade in gold in the United States. One could only buy 'jewellery'. For that reason, contracted CIA pilots from Air America and Continental Air Service would be seen wearing heavy gold bracelets which were not much more than gold bars formed into a bracelet.)

But, I had volunteered to join the Air Force for the specific purpose of going to Vietnam and Laos. I had been a student at Ohio State University and was exempt from the draft. I was 26

Prabang in the latter stages of the war, related how Royalist and Pathet Lao troops, encamped on opposite banks of the Nam Ou, agreed an informal ceasefire over Pi Mai (Lao New Year), to jointly celebrate the king's annual visit to the sacred Pak Ou Caves (see page 135). Correspondents who covered the war noted that without the constant years old when I joined the Air Force – just under the 26.5 age limit required of Air Force pilots. Having never flown before in my life I became a '90-day Wonder' as I received my commission as a second Lieutenant at Lackland Air Force Base in San Antonio, Texas. From Lackland I went to Laredo, Texas for Undergraduate Pilot Training. I completed my training in 1968, followed by 0-1 (Bird Dog) Special Operations Training, POW training and then on to the Philippines for Jungle Survival Training.

In Vietnam I was stationed at the Tuy Hoa MACV (Military Assistance Command Vietnam) compound where I flew in support of the Vietnamese Army. I volunteered for the Steve Canyon Program soon after arriving at Tuy Hoa. The Steve Canyon Program was named after 'Steve Canyon' – the flamboyant adventurist comic strip character. As I departed Bien Hoa Air Force Base near Saigon for Laos, I learned why it was called 'Steve Canyon'. The colonel who drove m e to the airplane which would take me to my first stop in Thailand said: "Well, now all you have to look forward to is ... glory, money and medals!"

Ravens were a breed apart. They would wear what they wanted when flying - shorts and T-shirts, homemade flying suits or cowboy outfits. They would disregard the Air Force standards for flying time and clock as much as 150 to 200 hours a month.

The monetary rewards were appealing. While not the income a true 'mercenary' might receive – for example, US$50,000 or US$100,000 for flying certain cargo in Southeast Asia or the Middle East - the extra per diem income, free in addition to being paid for board and room, maids and cooks, and combat pay, was welcome. It could amount to an extra US$1000 per month.

Arriving at Udon Air Force Base in Northeast Thailand, I was directed to a remote area of the base called 'Det-1'. The commander didn't know much about what I would be doing, but he had to maintain my Air Force records, since when I went into Laos, I would be a 'civilian'. Flying into Laos was quite different from flying into other countries. To protect my destination, when I crossed the border I would radio: "Raven 58, crossing the fence." 'Laos' would never be mentioned.

Along with the AOC (Air Operations Center) commander, a radio operator, two airplane mechanics and a medic, I lived in the town of Pakse, in a large colonial villa. The living conditions were excellent. After flying out into the war zone each day and returning, I would go down town to a movie or to the Mekong Bar for dancing and music, or to an inviting sidewalk café for dinner.

I believed that the Lao knew who I was. But, I found out that many did not. While trying to make a call to Vietnam to speak with my future Vietnamese wife, Kim Chi, a new Air Force Lieutenant received the call and became inquisitive as to why I referred to myself as "Mister Thompson" rather than "Captain". Even military personnel in Vietnam, including Air Force Forward Air Controllers, did not know about the clandestine operations of the Ravens.

Adapted from text written by Ken Thompson, or Raven 58, who flew as a FAC in Vietnam and Laos for over 26 months between 1968 and 1970. He was awarded two Distinguished Flying Crosses and a Bronze Star for valour.

goading of their respective US and North Vietnamese masters, many Lao soldiers would have happily gone home. Prior to the war, one military strategist described the Lao forces as one of the worst armies ever seen, adding that they made the [poorly regarded] "South Vietnamese Army look like Storm Troopers". "The troops lack the basic will to fight. They do not take initiative. A typical characteristic of the Laotian Army is to leave an escape route. US technicians attached to the various training institutions have not been able to overcome Lao apathy". (Ratnam, P, *Laos and the Superpowers*, 1980).

Air Force planes were often used to carry passengers for money – or to smuggle opium out of the Golden Triangle. In the field, soldiers of the Royal Lao Army regularly fled when faced with a frontal assault by the Vietnam People's Army (NVA). The officer corps was uncommitted, lazy and corrupt; many ran opium-smuggling rackets and saw the war as a ticket to get rich quick. In the south, the Americans considered Royal Lao Air Force pilots unreliable because they were loath to bomb their own people and cultural heritage.

The air war The clandestine bombing of the Ho Chi Minh Trail (see page 228) caused many civilian casualties – so-called collateral damage – and displaced much of the population in Laos' eastern provinces. A whole gamut of military devices and defoliants were used to destroy Lao territory and, although there are not really any official casualty figures in circulation, it is estimated that between a sixth and a tenth of the population were killed. By 1973, when the bombing stopped, the US had dropped 2,093,100 tonnes of bombs on Laos – equivalent to 700 kg of explosives for every man, woman and child in the country. It is reported that up to 70% of all B-52 strikes in Indochina were targeted at Laos. To pulverize the country to this degree 580,994 bombing sorties were flown. The bombing intensified during the Nixon administration: up to 1969 less than 500,000 tonnes of bombs had been dropped on Laos; from then on nearly that amount was dropped each year. In the 1960s and early 1970s, more bombs rained on Laos than were dropped during the Second World War – the equivalent of a plane load of bombs every eight minutes around the clock for nine years. This campaign cost American taxpayers more than US$2 mn a day but the cost to Laos was incalculable. The activist Fred Branfman, quoted by Roger Warner in *Shooting at the Moon*, wrote: "Nine years of bombing, two million tons of bombs, whole rural societies wiped off the map, hundreds of thousands of peasants treated like herds of animals in a Clockwork Orange fantasy of an aerial African Hunting safari."

The war was not restricted to bombing missions – once potential Pathet Lao strongholds had been identified, fighters, using rockets, were sent to attempt to destroy them. Such was the intensity of the bombing campaign that villagers in Pathet Lao-controlled areas are said to have turned to planting and harvesting their rice at night. Few of those living in Xieng Khouang province, the Boloven Plateau or along the Ho Chi Minh Trail had any idea of who was bombing them or why. The consequences were often tragic, as in the case of Tam Phiu Cave (see page 190).

In *The Ravens*, Robbins tells of how a fighter pilot's inauspicious dream would lead the commander to cancel a mission; bomber pilots hated dropping bombs and when they did, aluminium canisters were carefully brought back and sold as scrap. After the war, the collection and sale of war debris turned into a valuable scrap-metal industry for tribes' people in Xieng Khouang province and along the Ho Chi Minh Trail. Bomb casings, aircraft fuel tanks and other bits and pieces that were not sold to Thailand have been put to every conceivable use in rural Laos. They are used as cattle troughs, fence posts, flower pots, stilts for houses, water carriers, temple bells, knives and ploughs.

But the bombing campaign has also left a more deadly legacy – of unexploded bombs and anti-personnel mines. Today, over 30 years after the air war ended, over 500,000 tonnes of deadly unexploded ordnance (UXO) is believed to still be scattered throughout nine of Laos' 13 provinces. Frighteningly UXO casualties are increasing not decreasing, with nearly 200 casualties in 2004. Most casualties are caused by cluster bombs, or 'bombis' as they have become known. Cluster bombs are carried in large canisters called Cluster Bomb Units (CBUs), which open in mid-air, releasing around 670 tennis ball-sized bomblets. Upon detonation, the bombie propells around 200,000 pieces of shrapnel over an area the size of several football fields. This UXO contamination inhibits long-term development, especially in Xieng Khouang Province (see page 182), turning Laos' fertile fields, which are critical for agricultural production, into killing zones. The greatest irony of all, perhaps, is that most of Xieng Khouang was not even a military target – pilots would simply dump their ordnance so that they would not have to risk landing with their bomb bays packed with high explosive. Making farming in this part a Laos a highly dangerous occupation was simply one of those 'accidents' of war.

The land war Within Laos, the war largely focused on the strategic Plain of Jars in Xieng Khouang province (see page 182) and was co-ordinated from the town of Long Tien (the secret city), tucked into the limestone hills to the southwest of the plain. Known as the most secret spot on earth, it was not marked on maps and was populated by the CIA, the Ravens (the air controllers who flew spotter planes and called in air strikes) and the Hmong.

The Pathet Lao were headquartered in caves in Xam Neua province, to the north of the plain. Their base was equipped with a hotel cave (for visiting dignitaries), a hospital cave, embassy caves and even a theatre cave (see page 200).

The Plain of Jars (colloquially known as the PDJ, after the French Plaine de Jarres), was the scene of some of the heaviest fighting and changed hands countless times, the Royalist and Hmong forces occupying it during the wet season, the Pathet Lao in the dry. During this period in the conflict the town of Long Tien, known as one of the country's 'alternate' bases to keep nosy journalists away (the word 'alternate' was meant to indicate that it was unimportant), grew to such an extent that it became Laos' second city. James Parker in his book *Codename Mule* claims that the air base was so busy that at its peak it was handling more daily flights than Chicago's O'Hare airport. Others claim that it was the busiest airport in the world. There was also fighting around Luang Prabang and the Boloven Plateau to the south.

The end of the war Although the origins of the war in Laos were distinct from those which fuelled the conflict in Vietnam, the two wars had effectively merged by the early 1970s and it became inevitable that the fate of the Americans to the east would determine the outcome of the secret war on the other side of the Annamite Range. By 1970 it was no longer possible for the US administration to shroud the war in secrecy: a flood of Hmong refugees had arrived in Vientiane in an effort to escape the conflict.

During the dying days of the US-backed regime in Vientiane, CIA agents and Ravens lived in quarters south of the capital, known as KM-6 – because it was 6 km from town. Another compound in downtown Vientiane was known as 'Silver City' and reputedly also sometimes housed CIA agents. On the departure of the Americans and the arrival of the new regime in 1975, the Communists' secret police made Silver City their new home. Today, Lao people still call military intelligence officers 'Silvers' – and from time to time during the early 1990s, as Laos was opening up to international tourism, Silvers were even assigned as tour guides.

A ceasefire was agreed in February 1973, a month after Washington and Hanoi struck a similar deal in Paris. Power was transferred in April 1974 to yet another coalition government set up in Vientiane under the premiership of the ever-ready Souvanna Phouma. The neutralist prince once again had a Communist deputy and foreign affairs minister. The Red Prince, Souphanouvong, headed the Joint National Political Council. Foreign troops were given two months to leave the country. The North Vietnamese were allowed to remain along the Ho Chi Minh Trail, for although US forces had withdrawn from South Vietnam, the war there was not over.

The communists' final victories over Saigon (and Phnom Penh) in April 1975 were a catalyst for the Pathet Lao who advanced on the capital. Grant Evans in a *Short History of Laos* says that the most intriguing element of the communist take-over of Laos was the slow pace in which it was executed. Due to the country's mixed loyalties the Pathet Lao government undertook a gradual process of eroding away existing loyalties to the Royalist government. As the end drew near and the Pathet Lao began to advance out of the mountains and towards the more populated areas of the Mekong valley – the heartland of the Royalist government – province after province fell with scarcely a shot being fired. The mere arrival of a small contingent of Pathet Lao soldiers was sufficient to secure victory – even though these soldiers arrived at Wattay Airport on Chinese transport planes to be greeted by representatives of the Royal Lao government. It is even possible that they were not even armed. Nonetheless, rightist ministers, ranking civil servants, doctors, much of the intelligentsia and around 30,000 Hmong crossed the Mekong and escaped into Thailand, fearing that they would face persecution from the Pathet Lao. Many lived for years in squalid refugee camps, although the better connected and those with skills to sell secured US, Australian and French passports. For Laos, a large proportion of its human capital drained westwards, creating a vacuum of skilled personnel that would hamper – and still does – efforts at reconstruction and development. But while many people fled across the Mekong, a significant number who had aligned themselves with the Royalists decided to stay and help build a new Laos. They saw themselves as Lao patriots and their patriotic duty was to stay.

Administration of Vientiane by the People's Revolutionary Committee was secured on 18 August. The atmosphere was very different from that which accompanied the Communist's occupation of Saigon in Vietnam the same year. In Vientiane peaceful crowds of several hundred thousand turned out to hear speeches by Pathet Lao cadres. The King remained unharmed in his palace and while a coffin representing 'dead American imperialism' was ceremonially burned this was done in a 'carnival' atmosphere. Vientiane was declared 'officially liberated' on 23 August 1975. The coalition government was dismissed and Souvanna Phouma resigned for the last time. All communications with the outside world were cut.

While August 1975 represents a watershed in the history of Laos, scholars are left with something of a problem: explaining why the Pathet Lao prevailed. According to Martin Stuart-Fox, the Lao revolutionary movement "had not mobilized an exploited peasantry with promises of land reform, for most of the country was under-populated and peasant families generally owned sufficient land for their subsistence needs. The appeal of the Pathet Lao to their lowland Lao compatriots was in terms of nationalism and independence and the preservation of Lao culture from the corrosive American influence; but no urban uprising occurred until the very last minute when effective government had virtually ceased to exist... The small Lao intelligentsia, though critical of the Royal Lao government, did not desert it entirely and their recruitment to the Pathet Lao was minimal. Neither the monarchy, still less Buddhism, lost legitimacy." (Stuart-Fox 1997: 164). Stuart-Fox concludes that it was external factors, and in particular the intervention of outside powers, which led to the victory of the Pathet Lao. Without the Vietnamese and Americans, the Pathet Lao would not have won. For the great mass of Laos' population before 1975, Communism meant nothing. This was not a mass uprising but a victory secured by a small ideologically committed élite and forged in the furnace of the war in Indochina.

Laos under communism

The People's Democratic Republic of Laos was proclaimed in December 1975 with Prince Souphanouvong as President and Kaysone Phomvihane as Secretary-General of the Lao People's Revolutionary Party (a post he had held since its formation in 1955). The king's abdication was accepted and the ancient Lao monarchy was abolished, together with King Samsenthai's 600-year-old system of village autonomy. But instead of executing their vanquished foes, the LPRP installed Souvanna and the ex-king, Savang Vatthana, as 'special advisers' to the politburo. On Souvanna's death in 1984, he was accorded a full state funeral. The king did not fare so well: he later died ignominiously while in detention after his alleged involvement in a counter-revolutionary plot (see below).

Surprisingly, the first actions of the new revolutionary government was not to build a new revolutionary economy and society, but to stamp out unsavoury behaviour. Dress and hairstyles, dancing and singing, even the food that was served at family celebrations, was all subject to rigorous official scrutiny by so-called 'Investigation Cadres'. If the person(s) concerned were found not to match up to the Party's scrupulous standards of good taste they were bundled off to re-education camps.

Relations with Thailand, which in the immediate wake of the revolution remained cordial, deteriorated in late 1976. A military coup in Bangkok led to rumours that the Thai military, backed by the CIA, was supporting Hmong and other right-wing Lao rebels. The regime feared that Thailand would be used as a spring-board for a royalist coup attempt by exiled reactionaries. This prompted the arrest of King Savang Vatthana, together with his family and Crown Prince Vongsavang, who were all dispatched to a Seminar re-education camp in Sam Neua province. They were never heard of again. In December 1989 Kaysone Phomvihane admitted in Paris, for the first time, that the king had died of malaria in 1984 and that the queen had also died "of natural causes" – no mention was made of Vongsavang. The Lao people have still to be officially informed of his demise. (Some commentators – like Christopher Kremmer in his book *Stalking the Elephant Kings* published in 1997 – have used the incarceration of the King to mount a stinging critique of the current regime in Vientiane. However he does not adequately acknowledge the issue of the king's implication in a right-wing, counter-revolutionary plot.)

Re-education camps Between 30,000 and 40,000 reactionaries who had been unable to flee the country were interned in remote, disease-ridden camps for 're-education'. The reluctant scholars were forced into slave labour in squalid jungle conditions and subjected to incessant political propaganda for anything from a few months up to 15 years. Historian Grant Evans suggests that many internees were duped into believing that the government wanted complete reconciliation and so went away for re-education willingly. Evans says the purpose of the camps was to "break the will of members of the old regime and instill in them fear of the new regime." Old men, released back into society after more than 15 years of 're-education' were cowed and subdued, although some were prepared to talk in paranoid whispers about their grim experiences in Xam Neua.

By 1978, the reeducation policy starting to wind down, although, in 1986, Amnesty International released a report on the forgotten inhabitants of the re-education camps, claiming that 6000-7000 were still being held. By that time incarceration behind barbed wire had ended and instead the internees were 'arbitrarily restricted' rather than imprisoned. They were assigned to road construction teams and other public works projects. Nonetheless, conditions for these victims of the war in Indochina suffered from malnutrition, disease and many died prematurely in captivity. It is unclear how many died, but at least 15,000 have been freed. Officials of the old regime, ex-government ministers and former Royalist air force and army officers, together with thousands of others unlucky enough to have been on the wrong side, were released from the camps, largely during the mid to late 1980s. Most of the surviving political prisoners have now been reintegrated into society. Some work in the tourism industry and one, a former colonel in the Royal Lao Army, jointly owns the **Asian Pavilion Hotel** (formerly the **Vieng Vilai**) on Samsenthai Road in downtown Vientiane. After years of being force-fed Communist propaganda he now enjoys full government support as an ardent capitalist entrepreneur. The Lao, as scores of books like this one keep reminding their readers, are a gentle people and it is hard not to leave the country without that view being reinforced. Even the Lao People's Revolutionary Party seems quaintly inept and it is hard to equate it with its more brutal and sinister sister parties in Vietnam, Cambodia, China or the former Soviet Union. Yet five students who meekly called for greater political freedom in 1999 were whisked off by the police and have not been heard of since. So much for soggy ineptness.

Reflecting on 10 years of 'reconstruction' Laos' recent political and economic history is covered in more detail under Modern Laos (see page 304). But, it is worth ending this short account of the country's history by noting the brevity of Laos' experiment with full-blown Communism. Just 10 years after the Pathet Lao took control of Vientiane, the leadership were on the brink of far-reaching economic reforms. By the mid-1980s it was widely acknowledged that Marxism-Leninism had failed the country and its people. The population were still dreadfully poor; the ideology of Communism had failed to entice more than a handful into serious and enthusiastic support for the party and its ways; and graft and nepotism were on the rise.

The refugee camps By the late 1980s, a total of 340,000 people – 10% of the population and mostly middle class – had fled the country. At least half of the refugees were Hmong, the US's key allies during the war, who feared reprisals and persecution. From 1988, refugees who had made it across the border began to head back across the Mekong from camps in Thailand and to asylum in the US and France. More than 2000 refugees were also repatriated from Yunnan Province in China. For those prepared to return from exile overseas, the government offered to give them back confiscated property so long as they stayed for at least six months and become Lao citizens once again.

Modern Laos

Politics

Laos underwent the political equivalent of an earth tremor in March 1991 at the Fifth Congress of the Lao People's Revolutionary Party (LPRP). Pro-market reforms were embraced and the politburo and central committee got a much-needed transfusion of new blood. At the same time, the hammer and sickle motif was quietly removed from the state emblem and enlightened sub-editors set to work on the national credo, which is emblazoned on all official documents.

This shift in economic policy and ideology can be traced back to the Party Congress of 1986, making Laos one of the very first countries to embrace 'perestroika'. As late General Secretary Kaysone Phomvihane stated at the Fourth Party Congress in 1986:

"In all economic activities, we must know how to apply objective laws and take into account socio-economic efficiency. At the present time, our country is still at the first stage of the transition period. Hence the system of economic laws now being applied to our country is very complicated. It includes not only the specific laws of socialism but also the laws of commodity production. Reality indicates that if we only apply the specific economic laws of socialism alone and defy the general laws pertaining to commodity production, or vice versa, we will make serious mistakes in our economic undertaking during this transition period" (General Secretary Kaysone Phomvihane, Fourth Party Congress 1986; quoted in Lao PDR 1989:9).

Under the horrified gaze of Marx and Lenin – their portraits still dominate the plenary hall – it was announced that the state motto had changed from "Peace, Independence, Unity and Socialism" to "Peace, Independence, Democracy, Unity and Prosperity". The last part is largely wishful thinking for the poorest country in Southeast Asia, but it reflected the realization that unless Laos turned off the socialist road fast, it would have had great difficulty digging itself out of the economic quagmire that 15 years' adherence to Marxism had created. In August 1991, at the opening of the People's Supreme Assembly, Kaysone Phomvihane, the late President, said: "Socialism is still our objective, but it is a distant one. Very distant." With that statement, Kaysone embraced – somewhat reluctantly, it must be said – the country's market-orientated policy known as *Chin Thanakan Mai* or 'New Thinking'.

President Kaysone Phomvihane died in November 1992, aged 71. (His right hand man, Prince Souphanouvong – the so-called Red Prince – died just over two years later on 9 January 1995.) As one obituary put it, Kaysone was older than he seemed, both historically and ideologically. He had been chairman of the LPRP since the mid-1950s and had been a protégé and comrade of Ho Chi Minh, who led the Vietnamese struggle for independence from the French. After leading the Lao Resistance Government – or Pathet Lao – from caves in Xam Neua province in the north, Kaysone assumed the premiership on the abolition of the monarchy in 1975. But under his leadership – and following the example of his mentors in Hanoi – Kaysone became the driving force behind the market-orientated reforms. The year before he died, he gave up the post of Prime Minister for that of President.

His death didn't change things much, as other members of the old guard stepped into the breach. Nouhak Phounsavanh – a sprightly 78-year-old former truck driver and hardline Communist – succeeded him as President. Nouhak didn't last terribly long in the position and in February 1998 he was replaced by 75 year-old General Khamtai Siphandon – the outgoing Prime Minister and head of the LPRP. Khamtai represents the last of the revolutionary Pathet Lao leaders who fought the Royalists and the Americans.

With the introduction of the New Economic Mechanism in 1986 so there were hopes, in some quarters at least, that economic liberalization would be matched by political *glasnost*. So far, however, the monolithic Party shows few signs of equating capitalism with democracy. While the Lao brand of Communism has always been seen as relatively tame, it remains a far cry from political pluralism. Laos' first constitution since the Communists came to power in 1975, was approved in 1991. The country's political system is referred to as a 'popular democracy', yet it has rejected any significant moves towards multi-party reforms.

Take the elections to the 108-seat National Assembly on 24 February 2002. All of the candidates standing for election had been approved by the LPRP's mass organization, the Lao Front for National Construction. While it is not necessary for a candidate to be a member of the LPRP to stand, they are closely vetted and have to demonstrate that they have a 'sufficient level of knowledge of party policy'. As with the previous elections to the National Assembly at the end of 1997, only one of the 108 deputies elected was not a member of the Lao People's Revolutionary Party. Who was this sole, brave symbol of political pluralism? The minister of justice. When President Khamtai Siphandone turned up to cast his ballot (voting is compulsory), one journalist asked him what the election would change. His answer: "There won't be any change."

On the dreamy streets of Vientiane, the chances of a Tiananmen-style uprising are remote. But the events of the late 1980s and early 1990s in Eastern Europe and Moscow did alarm hardliners – just as they did in Beijing and Hanoi. They can be reasonably confident, however, that in their impoverished nation, most people are more worried about where their next meal is going to come from than they are about the allure of multi-party democracy. Day-to-day politics aren't on most Lao citizen's radar and many would find it hard to name the President and Prime Minister.

Nonetheless when students or others are tempted to suggest that there might be another way they are swiftly rounded-up and disappear.

The greatest concern for the Lao leadership (and in this sense the country mirrors developments in many other countries of Asia) is what effect 'westernization' is having upon the population. The economic reforms, or so the authorities would seem to believe, have brought not only foreign investment and new consumer goods, but also greed, corruption, consumerism and various social ills from drugs to prostitution. This was starkly illustrated at the March 1996 party congress. Observers were expecting to find the congress reaffirm the policy of economic reform and rubber stamp it 'business as usual'. Instead one of the architects of the reform programme, Deputy Prime Minister Khamphoui Keoboualapha, was unceremoniously dumped. The reason? It was thought that he had become too close to Thailand and in particular to influential Thai investors. He was blamed more than most for the emergence of the various social ills that the leadership have been so desperate to stem. Khamphoui was rehabilitated in a leadership reshuffle in February 1998 but this was probably because the leadership reasoned that they needed people with some knowledge of economic policy to see the country through the Asian crisis. It would be surprising if the process of economic reform was reversed – although it will probably slow down from time to time reflecting domestic developments and concerns – largely because there is simply no alternative.

In 2004, academic Martin Stuart-Fox painted a dismal picture of the progress of economic reform and development in Laos. The politburo still largely controls the country and, for now, sweeping changes are unlikely. Most of the country's leaders are well into their 60s and were educated in communist countries like Russia and Vietnam. However, the younger Lao people (particularly those that have studied abroad in Japan, Australia, the UK or the US) are starting to embrace new political and economic ideas. The government takes inspiration from Vietnam's success and is more likely to follow the lead of its neighbour rather than adopting any western model of government.

Foreign relations

Laos is rapidly becoming a 'keystone' in mainland Southeast Asia (see Economy below) and sees its future in linking in with its more powerful and richer neighbours. To this end Laos joined the Association of Southeast Asian Nations (ASEAN) on 23 July 1997, becoming the group's second Communist member (Vietnam joined in July 1995). By joining, Vientiane hoped to be in a better position to trade off the interests of the various powers in the region, thereby giving it greater room for manoeuvre. It was also hoped that tiny Laos would be able to develop on the economic coat tails of Southeast Asia's fast-growing economic 'tigers' – a hope rudely dashed by the region's economic crisis which began with the collapse of the Thai baht on 3 July 1997.

One of Laos' strategies for further integration into the Asian economy is to establish itself as a regional transit point, with new highways dissecting the country at 100 km intervals. Construction of one major highway was already underway in 2005, connecting Thailand's northernmost province of Chiang Rai to Kunming in China via the Lao provinces of Bokeo and Luang Namtha. The 700-km-long highway (of which 228 km will be in Laos) is expected to open in 2007 and could generate more income for the land-locked country. However, it also poses a major threat in terms of increased transmission of HIV from transient workers and truckers. To add insult to injury, China is opportunistically building a huge truck-stop near Boten in northwest Laos (see page 163), which is likely to wipe out a large proportion of the income Laos might have earned from transit vehicles.

Laos is the only landlocked country in Southeast Asia and Vientiane is keen to pursue a cooperative 'equilibrium policy' with its neighbours. There is a widely held view that Laos – a small, poor, weak and land-locked country – is best served by having

multiple friends in international circles. It has often been referred to as a 'buffer' state,
which exists to ensure that none of the surrounding countries have to border each other. The leadership in Vientiane is in the tricky situation of having to play off China's military might, Thailand's commercial aggressiveness and Vietnam's population pressures, while keeping everyone happy. The answer, in many people's minds, is to promote a policy of interdependence in mainland Southeast Asia. In 1993 a Western diplomat quoted by the French newspaper *Le Monde* said: "This country's only hope is to become, within the next 10 or 20 years, a bridge between its powerful neighbours, while at the same time managing to avoid being engulfed by either of them".

Relations with Thailand From the 1980s the government took steps to improve its foreign relations – and Thailand has been the main beneficiary. Historically, Thailand has always been the main route for international access to landlocked Laos. Survival instincts told the Vientiane regime that reopening its front door was of paramount importance. The 1990s began with an unprecedented visit by a member of the Thai royal family, Crown Princess Sirindhorn, and in 1994 the Friendship Bridge officially opened (see page 100) linking Laos and Thailand. The border disputes with Thailand have now been settled and the bloody clashes of 1987/88, when thousands on both sides lost their lives, are history. Thailand is Laos' largest investor and the success of the market reforms depend more on Thailand than any other country (but see below on the economic crisis). Economic pragmatism, then, has forced the leadership in Vientiane to cosy up to Bangkok. This does not mean that relations are warm. Indeed, Vientiane is irredeemably suspicious of Thai intentions, a suspicion born of a history of conflict.

The sleeping giant awakens: relations with China In 1988 China and Laos normalized relations and this was followed by a defence co-operation agreement signed in 1993. Recently, Beijing has taken a particular interest in developing Laos' infrastructure, more out of self-interest than altruism. As China continues to develop at a break-neck speed, its interest in Laos' natural resources is expected to escalate substantially, particularly in the areas of timber, iron ore, copper, gold, and gemstones. China is now Laos' third largest trading partner and foreign investor. The Asian Development Bank (ADB) reported that Lao-China trade grew from $33.1 million in 1990 to $118.3 million in 2003, for the most part, in China's favour. Over the last few years the economic giant has secured a deal to build numerous roads in Laos pro bono (see above), in exchange for logging the areas around the roads. In 2005, it seemed China had logged well beyond the limits that were initially agreed upon.

Laos' ever-tightening relationship with China could jeopardize ties with the country's closest ally, Vietnam, which shares a 1300 km-long border with Laos and historically has had poor relations with China.

Relations with Vietnam The Lao government has a special relationship with Vietnam, as it was Hanoi that helped the LPRP achieve power. Vietnam is also Laos' biggest trading partner. However, as Laos has turned to the West, Japan and Thailand for economic help, the government has become more critical of its closest Communist ally, Vietnam. Following Vietnam's invasion of Cambodia in December 1978, thousands of Vietnamese moved into northern Laos as permanent colonizers and by 1978 there were an estimated 40,000 Vietnamese regulars in Laos but, in 1987, 50,000 Vietnamese troops withdrew. In 1990 a Vientiane census found 15,000 Vietnamese living illegally in the capital, most of whom were promptly deported. With the death of President Kaysone Phomvihane in November 1992, another historical link with Vietnam was cut. He was half-Vietnamese and most of his cabinet owed their education and their posts to Hanoi's succour during the war years. As the old men of the Lao Communist Party, who owed so much to the Vietnamese, die off, so their replacements are looking elsewhere for investment and political support. They do not have such deep fraternal links with their brothers in Hanoi and are keen to diversify their international relations.

Relations with the USA Laos is the only country in Indochina to have maintained relations with the US since 1975, despite the fact that, thirty years since the illegal bombing campaign of Laos subsided, the US has neither offered a substantial sum of money for reparations nor helped to clear the tonnes of unexploded ordnance littering the eastern side of the country. Washington even expected the Lao government to allocate funds to help locate the bodies of US pilots shot down in the war. At a meeting between the Foreign Affairs Minister, General Phoune Sipaseuth, and the US Secretary of State, James Baker, in October 1990, Vientiane pledged to co-operate with the US over the narcotics trade (see Opium eradication, page 312) and to step up the search for the 530 American MIAs still listed as missing in the Lao jungle. In mid-1993, tri-lateral talks between Laos, Vietnam and the US allowed for greater cooperation in the search for MIAs, many of whom are thought to have been airmen, shot down over the Ho Chi Minh Trail. The MIA charity, based in Vientiane, has since assumed quite a high profile. In October 1992, America's diplomatic presence in Laos was upgraded to ambassadorial status from chargé d'affaires and, at the end of 1997, a high-level US mission to Laos promised greater support in the country's bomb-defusing work. However, until 2004, Laos remained one of the few countries to be denied Normal Trade Relations with USA, the others being North Korea, Cuba and Myanmar (Burma).

Furthermore, under duress from the US (a dangling carrot perhaps?) Laos has all but eradicated opium, at huge cost to the country socially and economically as it involved relocating lots of people, with minimal assistance from the US. Since 1989, the US government has handed over US$38 million for drug control to the Lao government but this money hasn't stretched far enough to ensure that former opium producers aren't left starving.

Relations with other countries Fortunately Laos is unwilling to put all its eggs in one basket. Japan is now Laos' biggest aid donor and Vientiane has also courted other Western countries, particularly Sweden (a long time friend), France, Germany and Australia, who have donated significant sums of aid. These days Washington and Tokyo offer more in the way of hope for the embattled regime than Moscow: in 1991, 100 Soviet economic and technical advisers were pulled out of the dilapidated flats they occupied on the outskirts of Vientiane; their withdrawal from the country signalled the end of the era of Soviet aid. While Russia gave Vientiane some leeway before it had to pay back its rouble debt, the country's former lifeline with Moscow has become of scant importance to Laos' economic future.

Economy

Until just a few years ago, if the world's financial markets crashed and international trade and commerce collapsed overnight, Laos would have been blissfully immune from the catastrophe. It would be 'farming as usual' the next morning. Since the mid-1980s, though, the government has gradually begun cautiously to tread the free-market path, veering off the old command system. Farms have been privatized and the state has to compete for produce with market traders at market prices. Many of the unprofitable state-owned businesses and factories have been leased or sold-off.

The logic for economic reform (about which, more below) and the integration of Laos into the regional – and world – economies was pretty compelling. During the decade of command planning from 1975 through to 1985 the economy grew at just

2.9% per year, barely sufficient to meet the needs of a growing population and not enough to fuel the desire for a better standard of living. The government's fear was that, like other communist countries, the failure to bring the Lao people a better standard of living might challenge the supremacy of the Lao People's Revolutionary Party. The decision to opt for reform seemed to be borne out as the economy picked up steam. During the early years of reform, between 1986 and 1990, the economy grew at 4.8% per year and from 1991-1995 increased again to 6.5% per year. However economic liberalization also has its risks. The collapse of the Thai baht at the beginning of July 1997 also dragged down the Lao kip while Thailand's fall from economic grace caused Thai investment in Laos to evaporate (Thailand is Laos' largest foreign investor). 1998 saw zero growth and inflation escalated to nearly 100% as the government rather ineptly tried to control events. Since then the economy has stabilized. GDP growth for 2004-2005 was estimated to be around 6%, with the industry and service sectors now accounting for almost half of GDP growth. In 2004 Laos had trade relations with over 50 countries (including bilateral agreements with 16 countries), accounting for US$454 million worth of exports, and a growth of 15% between 2000 and 2004. Primary trade areas include electricity production, handicrafts, foodstuffs, chemical production, mining and tourism. By the end of 2004, tourism was one of Laos's biggest sources of foreign exchange, with more than 800,000 visitors in the year. Inflation was around 10.6% for 2004 due to a widening fiscal deficit, excessive capital spending and declining revenue. In 2004-2005 Lao was still amending policy and legislation in order to prepare for accession to the World Trade Organization. Laos' stated aim is to graduated from LDC (least developed country) status by 2020.

The country's greatest economic potential lies in its natural resources – timber, gold, precious stones, coal and iron – and hydropower. It has been estimated that only 1% of the country's hydro-power potential of some 18,000 MW has so far been exploited and myriad schemes are being discussed (see below). By far the largest of these is Nam Theun 2, a US$1.2 billion hydroelectric dam project that is currently underway in Khammouane Province on the Nakai Plateau (see page 220). The huge 1070 MW dam is expected to generate up to US$150 million revenue a year for Laos or approximately US$2 billion over a 25 year period. The hydropower project will involve exporting 95% of the electricity to Thailand; the rest will be used domestically.

Malaysian, Taiwanese, Chinese and Thai firms have been awarded timber concessions in the country, many of them working in collaboration with the Lao army which has become an important economic player. (Strict reafforestation commitments were written into the contracts although there are grave doubts about how far the agreements are honoured.)

But though Laos has embarked on a path of economic reform (notwithstanding current debates) and has, since the mid-1980s, attracted large sums (for it) of foreign investment, there is no getting away from the fact that Laos is still – in economic terms – an extraordinarily poor place. In 1995 the government published its first ever survey of consumption and expenditure, undertaken with the help of the UNDP. It showed what most people already knew: that people don't have much surplus income. On average, the survey showed, 62% of household income is spent on food. The survey also showed that Laos does not have the deep disparities that are so painfully visible in neighbouring countries like Thailand (but see Emerging inequalities below).

A second expenditure and consumption survey (the so-called LECS II) was undertaken in 1997-98 and, in 2001, a participatory poverty assessment was published. These studies showed a number of worrying trends. First, a widening in spatial inequalities as some regions surge ahead and others get left in the economic doldrums. And second, a widening of inter-personal inequality as some individuals and households do very well out of the economic reforms, and others lag behind. The government is concerned that as the country 'embraces the market' it should not create a population of haves and have nots. The last lines of a World Bank analysis of the LECS II data concludes that a "key challenge facing policymakers developing a poverty reduction strategy for Laos will be to design policies that promote economic growth while keeping inequality in check." (World Bank 2001: 26).

Economic reform

Laos made the jump from a sleepy agrarian economy hidden behind a façade of socialism to a reforming economy like China and Vietnam's in the 1980s. In English this change is rather blandly named the New Economic Mechanism (NEM). Locally, the more evocative terms *chin thanakan mai* ('new thinking') and *kanpatihup setthakit* (the 'reform economy') are used. The origins of the NEM can be traced back to 1982 when the possibility of fundamental reform of the economy was first entertained by a small group within the leadership. For the next three or four years the debate continued within this small circle and it was not until 1985 that the NEM was actually pilot-tested in the Vientiane area. The success of the reforms there led to the NEM being presented at – and adopted by – the critical Fourth Party Congress of 1986. The NEM encompasses a range of reformist policies, much like those adopted in other countries from Russia to Vietnam: a move to a market determination of prices and resource allocation; a shift away from central planning to 'guidance' planning; a decentralization of control to industries and lower levels of government and the encouragement of the private sector; the encouragement of foreign investment and the promulgation of a new investment law allowing more relaxed foreign ownership and 'tax holidays'; a lifting of barriers to internal and external trade.

Former President Kaysone Phomvihane shouldered much of the blame for the miserable state of the economy, admitting that the Party had made mistakes. At the Congress in 1991 he set the new national agenda: Laos had to step up its exports, encourage more foreign investment, promote tourism and rural development, entice its shifting cultivators into proper jobs and revamp the financial system. In doing so he prioritized the problems but offered no solutions bar the loosening of state control and the promotion of private enterprise.

The first task for the government was to stabilize the value of the local currency, the kip and introduce market 'discipline' so as to eliminate a booming currency black market. So from 1986, when economic reforms were first introduced, Laos eliminated six of its seven official exchange rates to create a unified market-related rate. By the early 1990s the kip had stabilized at around 700 to the US$. The once-booming black market all but disappeared. Although still a non-convertible currency, the kip was as much in demand in Laos as the US dollar and Thai baht. This helped put Laos on a more commercially competitive footing. Unfortunately for supporters of economic reform, the collapse of the Thai baht and the consequent fall in the value of the kip encouraged the Lao government to reintroduce currency controls (see Reform in a period of economic crisis, page 316).

What Laos was able to achieve by introducing the NEM was a very rapid reorientation of its economy. But the question to be asked is: 'what exactly was being reformed?' The assumption is that Laos, as a so-called transitional economy, was making – is making – the transition from communism to capitalism, from state to market. This, though, misses the point that in 1986 there was remarkably little in Laos to reform. The great majority of the population were poor farmers (and they still are, around 85%) and the country's industrial base was almost non-existent. There were almost no communes to break up; and there was no large state industrial sector to dismember. It all meant that the task of the Lao leadership has been comparatively easy when compared with, say, Vietnam. In a sense, Laos was never socialist except in name and so the shift to a market economy involved not a move from socialism to capitalism, but from subsistence to capitalism.

Landmarks of economic reform

1975 **Dec**: full and final victory of the communist Pathet Lao.

1982 Reforms first touted.

1985 Pilot studies of financial autonomy in selected state-run industries.

1986 Decentralization of decision-making to the provinces including provincial tax administration. Freeing-up the market in rice and other staples.
Nov: NEM endorsed by the Party Congress.

1987 Restrictions on the cross-provincial movement of agricultural produce abolished; barriers to external trade reduced.
Jun: prices of most essentials market-determined.

1988 Forced procurement of strategic goods at below market price abolished; reduction in public sector employment; tax reforms introduced; private sector involvement in sectors previously reversed as state monopolies permitted; introduction of new investment law.
Mar: prices of fuel, cement, machinery and vehicles freed; tax reforms enacted; state and commercial banking sectors separated; state enterprises made self-reliant and autonomous; explicit recognition of the rights of households and the private sector to use land and private property.
Jun: nationwide elections held for 2410 positions at the district level.
Jul: multiple exchange rates abolished; liberal foreign investment code introduced; payment of wages in kind abolished.

1989 **Jun**: second tax reform enacted.
Oct: first joint venture bank with a foreign bank begins operation, the Joint Development Bank.

1990 **Mar**: privatization ('disengagement') law introduced.
Jun: key economic laws covering contracts, property, banking and inheritance discussed by National Assembly.
Jul: State Bank (Central Bank) of the Lao PDR established and fiscal management of the economy formally handed over to the new bank.

1992 Thai Military Bank begins operating a full branch in Vientiane.
Jan: Commercial Bank and Financial Institutions Act introduced.

1993 Accelerated privatization programme announced.
Dec: removal of last quantitative restrictions and licensing for imports.

1994 **Mar**: new investment and labour laws passed in March by the National Assembly, to be enforced within 60 days. As an incentive to foreign investors, the investment law lowers some import taxes and the tax on net profit, streamlines the approval process, and ends the foreign investment period limit of 15 years.

1997 Government tries to control currency transactions in the wake of Thailand's economic collapse
Apr: new land law introduced authorising transfer of land titles to relatives and use as collateral in obtaining bank loans.
July: Laos joins the Association of Southeast Asian Nations

2000 Direct foreign investment approvals decline from a peak of US$2.6 bn in 1995 to just US$20 mn in 2000.
Sources: Rigg, Jonathan (1997) Southeast Asia: the human landscape of modernization and development, London: Routledge, and other sources.

Background Modern Laos

⁝ Opium eradication

The Golden Triangle – the meeting point of Laos, Thailand and Myanmar (Burma) – is synonymous with the cultivation of the opium poppy (*Papaver somnifera*) and for many years provided at least 60% of the world's heroin supply, with Laos once the third largest producer after Burma and Afghanistan. The opium trade was legal in Laos until US pressure forced the government to outlaw it in 1971. The French quietly bought and sold the Hmong opium crop to finance their war efforts against Vietnam's Communists and the Americans turned a blind eye to the trade and allegedly fostered it too. During the 1960s, the drugs trade was run by a handful of high-ranking Royalist officers who became very rich. In Laos's northern provinces, the opium addiction rate of 50% in some villages was more than twice the literacy rate, and until recently small *parakeets* (sachets) of opium were an unofficial currency.

However, in October 1990, following accusations from the US State Department that the Lao government and military were actively involved in the narcotics trade, attempts have been made to combat the production and trafficking of illicit drugs. In exchange for aid, Laos agreed to co-operate with the US in narcotics control and to substitute opium poppies in the Houa Phanh province for cash crops, such as sesame, coffee and mulberry trees. Nevertheless, the Lao government remained reasonably understanding of the social and economic importance of the drug for minority villages, tabling a report in 1999 ('A Balanced Approach to Opium Elimination in Laos'), which stated that poppy cultivation could not be eradicated until alternative crops and economic development were firmly in place. Washington and international agencies responded with additional pressure. The US waved a carrot of $US80 million in aid if the drug was wiped out and the Lao government, desperate for the cash, drastically stepped up its campaign against opium. Seizures of raw opium and

This doesn't mean that reform has been a doddle, because although Laos may not have had to undo years of socialist reconstruction and development, there was also little that the leadership could build on to promote modernization. There are few skilled workers, there is a great dearth of engineers and graduates, the stock of roads is woefully thin, large slices of the country are almost impossible to reach, there is little domestic demand to fuel industrialization, there are few entrepreneurs and there are even fewer people with the money to invest in new ventures. In other words, Laos is short of most of the elements that constitute a modern economy.

Agriculture

Agriculture remains the mainstay of the Lao economy, accounting for more than 50% of GDP in 2004. Around 85% of Lao citizens are employed in some kind of subsistence agriculture, which they depend on for their survival. Rice is the staple food crop, cultivated by the majority of the population, and nearly three-quarters of Laos' farmers grow enough to sell or barter some of their crop. Output has more than doubled since 1980 and the country now produces 2.2 million tonnes of rice a year from 690,000 ha of paddy land. Moreover, the Fifth Five-Year Development Plan (2001-2005) states that rice production remains 'the most fundamental issue' for the country. However, although enough rice is produced to feed the Lao population, much of it is sold to Thailand. This was particularly problematic in 2003-2004, when the rice harvest was bad.

heroin increased and opium confiscated from traffickers was ceremonially burned. Traffickers were convicted in the Lao courts.

By mid-2005, Laos had almost totally eradicated opium and international anti-narcotic agencies were heralding a massive success. However, elimination of the crop before the proper safety nets were in place has come at a price. Historically, Laos' opium was grown in mountain areas and harvested by some of the poorest ethnic minority groups in the country. In order to eradicate it, the government had to relocate 65,000 people in northern Laos, many of whom are having terrible trouble adjusting to their new life: they face new diseases, such as malaria and gastro-intestinal troubles, and are finding it difficult to get food, particularly rice. The *Vientiane Times* may run stories about how happy the villagers are growing asparagus instead of opium but it just doesn't ring true. Another concern is the lack of care for opium addicts once the drug is withdrawn, with many addicts experiencing painful side-effects and even death. Furthermore, the drug was traditionally used by these poor groups for pain relief and for cultural purposes. In its absence, many people are turning to heroin and *yaa baa* (an amphetamine from Thailand), whose increased use has brought with it an increased risk of HIV transmission.

With hindsight, many international representatives are now saying that the eradication programme in Laos was too sudden. (Ironically, the US is one of the biggest critics of Laos' relocation programme in its annual human rights report.) Critics are also asking whether opium needs to be eradicated from developing countries at all, when it could easily be harnessed for commercial pharmaceutical exports. The International Narcotics Board provide licenses for countries, including India and Australia, legally to grow and trade opium. Critics argue that it is hypocritical for poor, developing countries to be denied the potential economic benefits of their biggest cash crop.

Background Modern Laos

While Laos may be land rich, this does not mean that everyone necessarily has enough to eat, and the achievement of food security is one of the government's priority objectives. Nationally the Lao PDR has achieved food self-sufficiency but at the regional, and more important village and intra-village levels, national self-sufficiency does not equate with local food security. Food deficits are common, resulting in many households experiencing both chronic and acute malnutrition. What's more, there is intra-regional variation. For example, Sekong, in the south, is traditionally a rice deficit province, as is Xieng Khouang in the centre. As we move down the scale levels from national to regional, provincial, district and village there are likely to be important variations in terms of food security. Even households that are in production surplus may face a consumption deficit due to their having to sell a portion of production to meet demands for cash or to pay off debts.

The main agricultural areas are on the Mekong's floodplains, especially around Vientiane and Savannakhet. The government has been successful in expanding the area capable of producing two rice crops a year by upgrading and developing the country's irrigation infrastructure. Cotton, coffee, maize and tobacco are the other main crops and the production of these and other 'industrial' crops such as soya and mung beans has increased in recent years. On the Boloven Plateau in the south, rice, coffee and cardamom – 500 tonnes of the latter is produced a year – are grown. Fisheries and livestock resources are being developed – the cattle population has risen from 446,900 head in 1990 to 986,600 a decade later.

While shifting cultivators continue to pose a 'problem' to the government, their numbers have dropped substantially since 1985 as the land allocation programme has been enthusiastically implemented. This is reflected by the fact that they are now said to cut down 100,000 ha of forest a year now, compared with 300,000 in the early 1980s. The situation has improved dramatically since the mid-1970s when Hmong General Vang Pao complained to a *National Geographic* reporter that "In one year a single family will chop down and burn trees worth US$6000 and grow a rice crop worth US$240."

Centuries of war and 15 years of Communism had little impact on the self-reliant villages of rural Laos. The government's attempts at cooperativization proved unpopular and unworkable. Just before the cooperativization programme was abruptly suspended in mid-1979 there were 2800 cooperatives accounting for perhaps 25% of farming families. But even these figures overestimate the role of cooperatives at that time, for many were scarcely functioning. The little work that has been undertaken on agriculture during this period has shown that even when cooperatives were functioning, their members were reluctant participants and there was a good amount of foot-dragging and petty obstructionism. The reasons why cooperatives were such a failure are numerous. To begin with and unlike China and Vietnam, there were almost no large landlords, there was little tenancy and there was abundant land. The inequalities that were so obvious in neighbouring countries simply did not exist in Laos. Second, most farmers were subsistence cultivators; capitalism had barely made inroads into the Lao countryside and the forces of commercialization were largely absent. Further and third, the LPRP provided little support either of a technical or financial kind. As a result, farmers – largely uneducated and bound to their traditional methods of production – saw little incentive to change. In some areas it was not so much a lack of interest in cooperatives, but a positive dislike of them. There were reports of farmers slaughtering their cattle, burning their fields and eating their poultry, rather than handing their livestock or crops over to the Party. By mid-1979, when the policy was suspended, the leadership in Vientiane had concluded that their attempts at cooperativization had been a disaster.

Since the suspension of the policy, the government has effectively returned to a free enterprise system in the countryside. Farmers now, effectively, own their land and, since a new land law was approved by the National Assembly in April 1997, they can pass it on to their children and use it as collateral to get a bank loan. They can produce whatever crops they like and can sell these on what has become virtually a 'free market'. Lao farmers, though they may be poor and though technology may be antiquated, are in essence no different in terms of the ways they work than their kinsfolk over the Mekong in Thailand.

Building up the economy

Laos, as books constantly reiterate, is poor. While it is tempting to mouth those favourite words 'poor but happy', there can be little doubt that the major challenge facing the country is how to promote development. There are few people – whether government ministers or shifting cultivators, businessmen or hawkers – who do not fervently hope that their children will be better off than they. And 'better off' means richer. Laos is playing a game of catch-up. As Houmpheng Souralay of the Foreign Investment Management Committe said to Singapore's *Sunday Times*, "We want to catch up with our neighbours like Thailand, Cambodia and Vietnam." But, he significantly added, only if those "investments are wholesome and do not erode our cultural identity".

Major development constraints are the shortage of skilled workers and capital, an undeveloped communication system poor educational and health resources, rugged terrain and low population density. Add to this a patchwork of cultures and different languages and it is easy to see why the country is difficult to manage. Even with large amounts of public expenditure going into infrastructure, the challenge of linking people to the market and the state remains supremely important. Without roads and transport farmers cannot obtain inputs for agriculture, cannot market any surplus production and cannot increase their incomes.

Traditionally, one of Laos' most important sources of foreign exchange was receipts from over-flight rights, as the Boloven Plateau lies on the flight path from Bangkok to Hong Kong and Tokyo. Nearly 100 international flights traverse Lao airspace every day and in the mid-1990s the government was receiving payment for each one. But, today, one of the country's biggest foreign-exchange earners is hydro-power, which generates not only electricity but more than US$20 mn a year in exports to Thailand. Plans are underway to further exploit the potential of the Mekong and its tributaries, with over 60 projects slated for development over the next decade. Laos has been dubbed the 'battery' or 'Kuwait' of Southeast Asia and the government has signed various deals with Thailand and Vietnam to sell electricity.

A few years ago these grand hydo-power plans all seemed eminently sensible: energy-hungry Thailand's economy was rapidly growing and Laos was well placed to meet its needs. But there were two issues that the Lao government and its international advisers failed to take sufficiently into account. The international environmental lobby and an economic slow-down. The US$1.5 bn Nam Theun 2 Dam (see page 220), for example, was delayed by the discoveries of rare bats and birds, with financial backing from multi-lateral agencies like the World Bank and the Asian Development Bank was held up for years. The World Bank, now all too conscious that its environmental credentials have been tarnished by dam developments in India and elsewhere, has gone out of its way to ensure that all the required environmental and other studies are undertaken. And the collapse of the Thai economy in mid-1997 also brought into question the economic rationale for the project.

But the Nam Theun 2 Dam is not quite the open-and-shut case it might appear, with the international environmental lobby on the side of local people and cuddly animals and the dastardly World Bank supporting shadowy businessmen and the interests of international capital. When local people were asked their views of the dam, many apparently welcomed it. An official explained that they did not want to stay "sitting on the porch in torn clothes, playing the *kaen* [a type of bamboo pan pipe] and having our picture taken by tourists" (*The Economist*, 30.8.1997). Even some environmentalists argued that having the dam might be preferable to having the forests logged. For without the money that can be earned from selling electricity to Thailand one of the few alternatives is selling wood.

Most of Laos' new enterprise has been in the service sector – there is little evidence that the reforms have prompted a significant increase in manufacturing activity. Most industry in Laos is small scale – rubber shoes, matches, tobacco processing, brewing and soft drinks and ice manufacturing. Saw-milling and timber processing account for the majority of factories. To give an idea of how limited Laos' industrial base is, the government's compendium of 'basic' statistics notes that in 2000 the country produced 250,000 boxes of chalk and 400,000 blocks of soap. Altogether, industry employs only a few thousand people and accounts for a tiny fraction of the gross domestic product. However, this is gradually changing, albeit from an extremely low base: textile manufacturers have set up shop in the country and garments are now one of Laos' most valuable exports as is the tourism industry (see below).

With the odds stacked against it, the government cannot afford to be choosy when it comes to investment. Several hundred foreign investment contracts have been approved since the government adopted a more liberal investment code in 1988, many of them textile factories and enterprises in the tourism sector. Unlike most of its Southeast Asian neighbours, Laos' embryonic garment industry is not subject to quotas from markets in the US and the European Community. The supposed 'flood' of foreign investment in this sector has been nothing more than blue jeans and T-shirt manufacturers from Thailand, Hong Kong, Macao and France, relocating to avoid export restrictions. Even with the cheap labour in Laos, it is impossible for them to compete with China.

In an effort to make the business climate more attractive, the state bank now supplies credit to all sectors of the economy. Provincial banks have been told to operate as autonomous commercial banks. State enterprises have been warned that if their bottom line does not show a profit, they are out of business. Provinces are free to conclude their own trading agreements with private companies and neighbouring countries – which generally means Thailand

Tens of thousands of people work for the government in a top-heavy and sometimes corrupt bureaucracy. Working for the Laos government is considered a job for life. Civil servants are paid the equivalent of US$20-40 per month while domestic servants working for expatriate families receive double this figure, or more. No wonder official corruption and profiteering are on the increase. The main financial incentive available to civil servants are the perks offered by NGOs – such as use of a car, per diems for trips away and scholarships to foreign universities. Admirably, most people who work for the civil service in Laos do so for prestige and personal pride, as there is little other incentive.

Reform in a period of economic crisis

While Laos might be poor it was not insulated from the effects of Asia's economic crisis. Indeed, it is the reforms of the years since 1986 which has made the country vulnerable to developments beyond its borders. The Lao kip was dragged down by the depreciation of the Thai baht and lost value from US$1 = 978 kip in December 1996 to US$1 = 1780 kip in November 1997. By March 1999 it had sunk still further to US$1 = 4200 kip and in November 1999 the unofficial rate of exchange was US$1 = 7600 kip. At the end of 2005 there were around 10,000 kip to the US$. In fact there is no currency in Southeast Asia, with the exception of the Burmese kyat, which has lost more value.

As the currency lost value the government lost its nerve and slapped on currency controls and rounded up the private money changers who have been operating for years in Vientiane. The governor of the Lao central bank blamed "speculative attempts by opportunists" for the Kip's collapse. The trade deficit widened and eight state-owned banks became effectively insolvent. Inflation during 1997 rose from 11% in January to 27% in September and in 1998 continued to escalate to reach 100% by the end of the year. There was also a sharp downturn in investment (remember, Thailand is Laos' largest foreign investor). From a peak of US$2.6 bn in approved projects in 1995, investment dropped to just US$150 mn in 1997 and shrunk still further to US$20 mn in 2000.

The leadership held very different views on how to deal with the crisis. The so-styled 'conservatives' in the politburo wanted the Lao government take a step back from the market and emphasize domestic resources. Reformists wanted further liberalization – à la the IMF – and to extricate the country from the economic mess by integrating still more rapidly into the regional and world economies. The outcome of this debate, in typically Lao style, was a bit of both. The leadership took their foot off the pedal of economic reform but did not substantially reverse what was already in place. It also seems that they may have realized the futility of trying to rein back trade with neighbouring Thailand and China given their lack of economic control in many areas.

What was perhaps most surprising about Laos' economic malaise was the absence of any public disturbances. With the economy contracting, inflation running at more than 100%, banks broke, foreign investment evaporating and the government apparently clueless and helpless as to what to do, one might have expected just a little more public debate and criticism. After all, Thailand and South Korea both saw a change of government, Malaysia the trial and imprisonment of its deputy prime minister Anwar Ibrahim and Indonesia the violent dumping of Suharto, president of more than three decades. Laos may be renowned for the relaxed and forgiving ways of its people, but it is hard not to wonder, 'for how much longer?'

Fears of dependency on Thailand

Thailand is Vientiane's lifeline to the outside world. Just two years after their last bloody border dispute in 1987-88, the old enemies patched up their differences. The Thai Crown Princess Sirindhorn visited Laos in early 1990 – the first visit by a member of the Thai royal family for 15 years – and Thailand lifted a ban on the export of 200 'strategic goods' to Laos, which had been in place since 1975 and which covered everything from military equipment to food and bicycles. The two old foes agreed to build the Mittaphab – or Friendship – bridge across the Mekong linking Vientiane with Nong Khai in Northeast Thailand. The bridge was built with Australian assistance and opened in 1994 (see page 100). However, fears of Laos becoming a Thai commercial colony has led the government to extend an extremely cautious welcome to Thai proposals to build another bridge at Savannakhet in the southern 'panhandle', which would provide a link west with the northeastern Thai town of Mukdahan and from there with southern Vietnam. Following prodding from the ADB and the Thai government this bridge appeared to get the final go-ahead in November 2001 and it is expected to be completed by 2006. There is also talk of a bridge linking Chiang Khong in Thailand's north with Houei Xai, allowing Thailand easier access to the rich market of Yunnan in southern China.

Historically, Thais have emerged as one of the biggest foreign investors in Laos. A number of Thai commercial banks have set up in Laos, along with businessmen, consultants and loggers. Young Lao who previously attended universities in the Soviet bloc are now being dispatched to Thai universities. The warming of relations between Bangkok and Vientiane has raised some eyebrows: sceptics say Laos' wealth of unexploited natural resources is a tempting reward for patching things up. Laos has about two million ha of forest – 400,000 ha of which is teak and other high quality timber – and it is disappearing fast, courtesy of its neighbours, Vietnam and China included. Thailand is also the most important player in the Nam Theun 2 hydropower project (see page 220). But to its credit, Thailand has prioritized aid to Laos and has signed joint ventures in almost every sector – from science and technology to trade, banking and agriculture. Thai businessmen have partially taken over the state beer and brewery and the Thai conglomerate Shinawatra (owned by the current Thai prime minister) has been given telecommunications concessions. Nonetheless, Thai diplomats are only too aware of the poor reputation that their businessmen have in Vientiane. They are regarded as over-bearing and superior in their attitude to the Lao and rapacious, predatory and mercenary in their business dealings. The Thai government has even run courses to try and improve business behaviour. But Thai perceptions of their neighbours are deeply entrenched. As one Thai critic once remarked: "Thai cultural diplomacy starts with the assumption that Thai culture is superior."

To understand Laos' fears of Thailand it is necessary to look back in history. Until the French absorbed Laos into Indochina, Laos came under Thai suzerainty and indeed the Siamese saw Laos as a junior, rather primitive, colony of theirs. When the foolhardy King Anou of Vientiane tried to recreate the great 14th-century Lao kingdom of Fa Ngum and invaded Siam he was soundly thrashed in a battle at Korat, in northeast Thailand, and then saw his capital Vientiane plundered, sacked and razed by Siamese forces – a fact which explains why today this ancient city is so devoid of architecture pre-dating the French period. Anou was captured and later died in captivity. Needless to say, Thai

When the Indian Ocean tsunami hit Thailand in December 2004, the Lao government collected money from every citizen to donate to the Thai government.

and Lao history is at odds on this period of history: Thai accounts paint Anou as a rebel; those written by Lao historians characterize him as a national hero. (This partly explains the emotional response of the Lao to a Thai producer's decision to make a film of these historical events – see the box History matters, above.)

It is only with this background in mind that Lao fears of Thai commercial hegemony can be fully appreciated. When, in 1988, former Thai Prime Minister Chatichai Choonhaven expressed a desire to turn Indochina "from a battlefield into a market place", this was viewed by many Lao – and some more thoughtful Thais – as tantamount to a threat of commercial invasion. (The theme was returned to in 1995 when a senior Thai diplomat, Suridhya Simaskul, remarked to the journalist Michael Vatikiotis, "We have passed the stage of turning battlefields into markets; now the market itself has become the battlefield.") Thailand, its own natural resources denuded through years of thoughtless exploitation, was hoping to pillage Laos' resource-rich larder. In July 1989, state run Radio Vientiane broadcast a commentary, presumably officially sanctioned, stating: "Having failed to destroy our country through their military might [referring to the Ban Rom Klao border conflict of 1987-88], the enemy has now employed a new strategy in attacking us through the so-called attempt to turn the Indochinese battlefield into a marketplace..." It is this fear of Thailand and of over-dependence on Thailand, which has prompted the Lao government to do its utmost to try and diversify its commercial links. In a rather novel departure from the usual state of affairs, the Lao are also more scared of Thai cultural pollution, than Western cultural pollution. The similarities between the two countries and the fact that many Lao households watch Thai television, make Thailand seem more of a risk. In 1993, former president and Pathet Lao veteran Phoumi Vongvichit warned against the dangers of prostitution, 'depraved' dancing and gambling. The source of these threats to pristine Lao culture was Thailand. Newspaper reports even dubbed the Mittapheap Bridge the AIDS Bridge, because it was expected that the bridge would bring prostitution and AIDS to the country.

Dependency on aid and development aims

Laos depends heavily on imports – everything from agricultural machinery and cars to petrol products, textiles and pharmaceuticals – 75% of which are financed by foreign aid. Western bilateral donors are enthusiastically filling the aid gap left by the Socialist bloc. Countries and private donors are falling over each other to fund projects, particularly anything that involves government reform; NGOs are homing in and multi-lateral development banks are offering soft loans and structural adjustment programmes. As Laos' foreign debt is mostly on highly concessional terms, it is not crippled by repayment schedules, though there is a reasonably hefty bill awaiting them. But with development banks accelerating their project-funding, fears are mounting that Laos is teetering on the edge of a debt trap.

The share of foreign assistance to GDP has nearly tripled since the mid-1980s. In 2005, Lao Foreign Minister Somsavat Lengsavat said that Laos had received an estimated US$3.465 billion in aid from foreign donors between 1975 and 1990, and more than $2.4 billion from foreign donors between 1991 and 2005. This figure accounts for roughly 70-80% of Laos' annual budget.

The country and its foreign strategists are looking to four distinct areas for future income. The first concentrates on mining and energy. Laos already has three HEP dams that generate power for export to Thailand and others are planned. The latest, built by South Korea's Daewoo group in southern Laos, began exporting electricity to Thailand in April 1998 (see page). Mining rights to some of Laos' huge lignite reserves have been sold to Thai investors. Other untapped mineral resources include reserves of gold, gemstones and iron ore, while foreign companies have undertaken preliminary searches for oil. The second area of interest is agriculture and forestry. Investors are looking at growing feed grains like soya beans and maize for export to

Thailand. Raw timber exports are being replaced by processed wood industries. More enlightened analysts also see Laos as a potential large exporter of organic agricultural products – after all, agriculture in the country has never had to rely on biochemical inputs or genetically engineered seeds. The third potential area for development is tourism but the government is wary of Laos going the same way as Thailand. The fourth and final strategy – and the most ambitious – is for Laos to become the 'service centre' between China, Vietnam, Cambodia and Thailand (see Laos as the 'keystone' of mainland Southeast Asia, below).

Poverty and human development

As in neighbouring Vietnam, the economic reforms are beginning to widen inequalities in society. Most of those who are doing well live in towns or at least close to one of the country's main roads. This means that off-road communities, and especially those in higher areas, are finding that – at least in relative terms – they are becoming poorer. In addition, because it is mostly minority Lao Soung and Lao Theung who live in these marginal areas, the economic reforms are widening inequalities between ethnic groups. One foreign aid worker was quoted in the *Far Eastern Economic Review* at the beginning of 1996 saying: "When they come down to Vientiane, where the lowland Lao [the Lao Loum] live, it's like Hong Kong to them. Here's money, here's development. In their own villages, there's nothing." As in Vietnam, the need to ensure that the economic reforms bring benefits to all and not just a few, is a key political question. The leadership are acutely aware that widening inequalities could fuel political discontent and this is perhaps one reason why the government seems so intent on increasing the number of members of the National Assembly from ethnic minorities.

The data that are available indicate that inequalities are widening. The first living standards survey was released in 1995 and showed what most people already knew: that Laos was a poor but relatively egalitarian place. The latest living standards survey, undertaken in 1997/98, shows that this equality is being eroded as the economic reforms progress. In Vientiane 'only' 14% of the population are officially designated 'poor'. But in the northern provinces of Hua Phanh and Udom Xai it is 70% and 65% respectively. Laos was ranked 135 out of 177 countries in the 2004 Human Development report and is the most underdeveloped countries in the Mekong region, ranking lower than Cambodia and Vietnam.

The government claims its "programme for the basic elimination of illiteracy among the masses", launched in 1984, was "an outstanding success". In 2004 UNDP reported that 79% of students aged between 15-24 are literate. Adult education has been expanded, schools upgraded, 62 classrooms built "for 1600 tribal youths" and a new university was set up in Vientiane. But while the government has been busy building schools, the quality of education has slipped further, as they cannot afford to pay teachers or buy textbooks. In 2004, only 62% of students who started grade one were still in school by grade 5.

Health care has suffered for the same reasons. Laos ranks 24 out of 28 countries in the region for deaths of children under five. One in ten children dies before the age of five, usually from communicable and preventable diseases such as acute respiratory infections, diarrhoea, malaria, measles, dengue fever and meningitis. Maternal mortality is also dangerously high, with around 530 maternal deaths per 100,000 births probably due to the fact that only 17% of pregnant women have their baby delivered by a trained doctor.

Laos as the 'keystone' of mainland Southeast Asia

In what sceptics might view as an ultimately futile effort, the leadership in Vientiane have chanced upon an economic future for their country: as the 'keystone' or 'crossroads' of Southeast Asia. Nor is it just Lao leaders who are drumming up enthusiasm for this notion. The Asian Development Bank (the Asian arm of the World

Bank) is at the forefront of developing – and funding – what has become known as the Greater Mekong Sub-region or GMS. This will link southwest China, Thailand, Myanmar, Cambodia, Vietnam and Laos. And within this scenario, Laos is the crucial pivotal country through which most road and rail links will have to go. There is talk of a 'Golden Quadrangle' (as opposed to the infamous Golden Triangle) – even of a Golden Land. This reference draws on ancient Indian texts which talked of 'Suvarnaphum' – a Golden Land – which encompassed modern-day Thailand, Laos, Myanmar and probably Peninsular Malaysia and parts of Indonesia too. Like most grand ideas, it looks great on paper but putting it into practice is something else. Indeed, Laos' current economic problems are in no small part due to its cosying-up to Thailand and integration into the regional economy of mainland Southeast Asia.

Culture

People

Laos has a population of 5,609,997, of which 2,813,589 are women, or 50.2 percent, while 2,796,408 are men. Savannakhet has the biggest population among provinces, with around 824,662 people. Vientiane city is second with around 695,473 people, while Champasak province is in third place, with 603,880 people. More than three-quarters of the population are subsistence farmers and only a tenth of its villages are anywhere near a road. Nearly one child in ten dies before its fifth birthday, and cars seem to have a longer life expectancy than people. More than one third of the population aged over 15 cannot read or write, the diet is inadequate, sanitation poor and only a quarter of the population have access to safe drinking water. Debilitating and fatal diseases, from malaria to bilharzia, are endemic in rural Laos while the health and education systems are limited. In northern provinces, a few years ago, the opium addiction rate was double the literacy rate, though this is starting to change now.

Ethnic groups

Laos is less a nation state than a collection of different tribes and languages. The country's enormous ethnic diversity has long been an impediment to national integration. In total there are more than 60 minority tribes which are often described as living in isolated, self-sufficient communities. Although communication and intercourse may have been difficult – and remains so – there has always been communication, trade and inter-marriage between the different Lao 'worlds' and today, with even greater interaction, the walls between them are becoming more permeable still.

Laos' ethnically diverse population is usually – and rather simplistically – divided by ecological zone into three groups: the wet rice cultivating, Buddhist Lao Loum of the lowlands, who are politically and numerically dominant, constituting over half of the total population; the Lao Theung who occupy the mountain slopes and make up about a quarter of the population; and the Lao Soung, or upland Lao, who live in the high mountains and practise shifting cultivation and who represent less than a fifth of Laos' total population. The terms were brought into general usage by the Pathet Lao who wished to emphasize that all of Laos' inhabitants were 'Lao' and to avoid the more derogatory terms that had been used in the past – such as the Thai word *kha*, meaning 'slave', to describe the Mon-Khmer Lao Theung like the Khmu and Lamet. Stereotypical representations of each category are depicted on the 1000 kip note.

⚬ Population by ethnic group

Group	Official category	% of total population
Tai	Lao Loum	55
Mon-Khmer	Lao Theung	35
Tibeto-Burman	Lao Soung	10

The French viewed the Lao (not to put too fine a point on it) as if they were an exasperating child. But, as Virginia Thompson put it in the late 1930s, "For the rare Frenchman who sees in the Laotians a silly, lazy and naïve people, there are hundreds who are charmed by their gentle affability ...". It was this affability which Henri Mouhout noted in the 1860s and which led some Frenchmen to express their concern as to what might happen to the Lao if the uncontrolled immigration and settlement of Siamese, Vietnamese and Chinese was permitted. (Norman Lewis in *A Dragon Apparent* said much the same about Frenchmen who had gone native: "Laos-ized Frenchmen are like the results of successful lobotomy operations – untroubled and mildly libidinous.") By the Second World War towns like Vientiane and Thakhek already had larger populations of Vietnamese than they did of Lao and had the Japanese occupation and independence not nipped French plans in the bud, Laos might well have become a country where the Lao were in a minority.

Although the words have a geographical connotation, they should be viewed more as contrasting pairs of terms: *loum* and *theung* mean 'below' and 'above' (rather than hillsides and lowland), while *soung* is paired with *tam*, meaning 'high' and 'low'. These two pairs of oppositions were then brought together by the Pathet Lao into one three-fold division. Thus, the Lao Theung in one area may, in practice, occupy a higher location than Lao Soung in another area. In addition, economic change, greater interaction between the groups and the settlement of lowland peoples in hill areas, means that it is possible to find Lao Loum villages in upland areas, where the inhabitants practise swidden, not wet rice, agriculture. So, although it is broadly possible to characterize the mountain slopes as inhabited by shifting cultivating Lao Theung of Mon-Khmer descent, in practice the neat delimitation of people into discrete spatial units breaks down and as the years go by is becoming increasingly untenable.

Lao Loum

It has been noted that the Lao who have reaped the rewards of reform are the Lao Loum of T'ai stock – not the Lao Theung who are of Mon-Khmer descent or the Lao Soung who are 'tribal' peoples, especially Hmong but also Akha and Lahu. Ing-Britt Trankell, in her book *On the Road in Laos: an Anthropological Study of Road Construction and Rural Communities* (1993), writes that the Lao Loum's "sense of [cultural and moral] superiority is often manifested in both a patronizing and contemptuous attitude toward the Lao Theung and Lao Sung, who are thought of as backward and less susceptible to socio-economic development because they are still governed by their archaic cultural traditions".

During the sixth and seventh centuries the Lao Loum arrived from the southern provinces of China. They occupied the valleys along the Mekong and its tributaries and drove the Lao Theung to more mountainous areas. The Lao Loum, who are ethnically almost indistinguishable from the Thais of the Isan region (the Northeast of Thailand), came under the influence of the Khmer and Indonesian cultures and sometime before the emergence of Lane Xang in the 14th century embraced Theravada Buddhism. The majority of Lao are Buddhist but retain many of their animist beliefs. Remote Lao Loum communities still usually have a *mor du* (a doctor

Background Culture

who 'sees') or medium. The medium's job description is demanding: he must concoct love potions, heal the sick, devise and design protective charms and read the future.

Today, the Lao Loum are the principal ethnic group, accounting for nearly half the population, and Lao is their mother tongue. As the lowland Lao, they occupy the ricelands of the Mekong and its main tributary valleys. Their houses are made of wood and are built on stilts with thatched roofs – although tin is far more popular these days. The extended family is usually spread throughout several houses in one compound.

There are also several tribal sub-groups of this main Thai-Lao group; they are conveniently colour-coded and readily identifiable by their sartorial traits. There are, for example, the Red Tai, the White Tai and the Black Tai – who live in the upland valley areas in Xieng Khouang and Hua Phan provinces. That they live in the hills suggests they are Lao Theung, but ethnically and culturally they are closer to the Lao Loum.

Lao Theung

The Lao Theung, consisting of 45 different sub-groups, are the descendants of the oldest inhabitants of the country and are of Mon-Khmer descent. They are sometimes called *Kha*, meaning 'slave', as they were used as labourers by the Thai and Lao kings and are generally still poorer than the Lao Loum. Traditionally, the Lao Theung were semi-nomadic and they still live mainly on the mountain slopes of the interior – along the whole length of the Annamite Chain from South China. There are concentrations of Akha, Alak and Ta-Oy on the Boloven Plateau in the south (see page 254) and Khmu in the north.

Most Lao Theung still practise slash-and-burn, or shifting, agriculture and grow dry rice, coffee and tobacco. They would burn a small area of forest, cultivate it for a few years and then, when the soil was exhausted, abandon the land until the vegetation had regenerated to replenish the soil. Some groups merely shifted fields in a 10-15 year rotation; others not only shifted fields but also their villages, relocating in a fresh area of forest when the land had become depleted of nutrients. To obtain salt, metal implements and other goods which could not be made or found in the hills, the tribal peoples would trade forest products such as resins and animal skins with the settled lowland Lao. Some groups, mainly those living closer to towns, have converted to Buddhism but many are still animist.

The social and religious beliefs of the Lao Theung and their general outlook on health and happiness, are governed by their belief in spirits. The shaman is a key personality in any village. The Alak, from the Boloven Plateau (see page) test the prospects of a marriage by killing a chicken: the manner in which it bleeds will determine whether the marriage will be propitious. Buffalo sacrifices are also common in Lao Theung villages and it is not unusual for a community to slaughter all its livestock to appease the spirits.

Viet Minh guerrillas and American B-52s made life difficult for many of the Lao Theung tribes living in East Laos, who were forced to move away from the Ho Chi Minh Trail. By leaving their birth places the Lao Theung left their protecting spirits, forcing them to find new and unfamiliar ones.

Lao Soung

The Lao Soung began migrating to Laos from South China, Tibet and Burma, in the early 18th century, settling high in the mountains (some up to 2500 m). The Hmong (formerly known as the Meo) and Yao (also called the Mien) are the principal Lao Soung groups.

Yao (or Mien)

The Yao mainly live around Nam Tha – deep inside the Golden Triangle, near the borders with Thailand, Burma and China. They are best-known as craftsmen – the men make knives, crossbows, rifles and high-quality, elaborately designed silver

The Mien or Yao are unique among the hilltribes in that they have a tradition of writing based on Chinese characters. Mien legend has it that they came from 'across the sea' during the 14th century, although it is generally thought that their roots are in South China where they originated about 2000 years ago.

The Mien village is not enclosed and is usually found on sloping ground. The houses are large, wooden affairs, as they need to accommodate an extended family of sometimes 20 or more members. They are built on the ground, not on stilts and have one large living area and four or more bedrooms. As with other tribes, the construction of the house must be undertaken carefully. The house needs to be orientated appropriately, so that the spirits are not disturbed and the ancestral altar installed on an auspicious day.

The Mien combine two religious beliefs: on the one hand they recognize and pay their dues to spirits and ancestors (informing them of family developments); and on the other, they follow Taoism as it was practised in China in the 13th and 14th centuries. The Taoist rituals are expensive and the Mien appear to spend a great deal of their lives struggling to save enough money to afford the various life cycle ceremonies, such as weddings and death ceremonies. The Mien economy is based upon the shifting cultivation of dry rice, maize and small quantities of opium poppy.

Material culture The Mien women dress distinctively, with black turbans and red-ruffed tunics, making them easy to distinguish from the other hilltribes. All their clothes are made of black or indigo-dyed homespun cotton, which is then embroidered using distinctive cross-stitching. Their trousers are the most elaborate garments. Unusually, they sew from the back of the cloth and cannot see the pattern they are making. The children wear embroidered caps with red pompoms on the top and by the ears. The men's dress is a simple indigo-dyed jacket and trousers, with little embroidery. They have been dubbed "the most elegantly dressed but worst-housed people in the world".

Akha (or Kaw)
The Akha, also called as the Ikho, Kho or Kha, have their origins in Yunnan, southern China, and from there spread into Burma (where there are nearly 200,000) and Laos and rather later into Thailand. There are three different Akha groups in northern Laos: the Akha Pouli, the Akha Pen and the Akha Jijaw. Around Muang Sing (see page 163) they constitute 22% of the population. They traditionally speak a Tibeto-Burmese language, which is believed to be represented in nine different written forms.

The Akha are shifting cultivators, growing primarily dry rice on mountainsides but also a wide variety of vegetables. The cultivation of rice is bound up with myths and rituals: the rice plant is regarded as a sentient being and the selection of the swidden, its clearance, the planting of the rice seed, the care of the growing plants and finally the harvest of the rice, must all be done according to the Akha Way. Any offence to the rice soul must be rectified by ceremonies. The Akha have no word for religion but believe in the 'Akha Way'. They are able to recite the names of all their male ancestors (60 names or more) and they keep an ancestral altar in their homes, at which food is offered up at important festivals and after the rice harvest. The two most important Akha festivals are the four-day Swinging Ceremony, celebrated during August, and New Year, when festivities also extend over four days. When someone dies they are wrapped in cloth, poor people in a white cloth, and rich people in a black cloth. They are kept in a wooden coffin, with a lid similar to a xylophone, for up to a month. A usual ritual baci will follow.

Akha villages are identified by their gates, a village swing and high-roofed houses on posts. At the upper and lower ends of the village are gates which are

Background Culture

renewed every year. Visitors should walk through them in order to rid themselves of the spirit of the jungle. The gates are sacred and must not be defiled. Visitors must not touch the gates and should avoid going through them if they do not intend to enter a house in the village. A pair of wooden male and female carved figures are placed inside the entrance to signify that this is the realm of human beings. The female and male parts of the house are divided and two doorways enter the house, one which is entered through and the other which serves as the exit. ▶▶ *For information on how to behave in an Akha village, see Visiting an Akha village, page 162.*

The Akha are relatively sexually liberal. Each village usually has a small courting house, where young men and women can rendezvous privately. Women will generally have a number of partners before settling into marriage and pregnancy prior to marriage is not deemed as being shameful but rather as a sign of fecundity. Sexual abstinence is often used as punishment for those who commit offences. Marriage is monogamous, however the rich and powerful are entitled to additional wives if their first wives can't conceive. Women adopt the husband's lineage upon marriage and usually move into or close to her partner's family home. Divorce exists but is not common, due to the financial pressures of raising children. A mid-wife generally delivers babies and men are not allowed in the house when the woman is in labour. Historically, twins born in villages were regarded as a very bad omen and were killed but this practice has now been outlawed and the children are put up for adoption.

Today the Akha are finding it increasingly difficult to follow the 'Akha Way'. Their complex rituals set them apart from both the lowland Lao and from the other hilltribes. The conflicts and pressures which the Akha currently face and their inability to reconcile the old with the new, is claimed by some to explain why the incidence of opium addiction among the Akha is so high.

Material culture Akha clothing is made of homespun blue-black cloth (dyed from indigo), which is appliquéd for decoration. The basic clothing of an Akha woman is a head-dress, a jacket, a short skirt worn on the hips, with a sash and leggings worn from the ankle to below the knee, though many are starting to wear more mainstream clothing, as they are self-conscious of their traditional dress. They wear their jewellery as an integral part of their clothing, mostly sewn to their head-dresses. This is the most characteristic item of Akha clothing and is adorned with jewellery and coins. The coins are made of pure silver and are used as currency (the small coins are worth about 15,000 kip and the large are worth about 50,000kip). Girls wear similar clothing to the women, except that they sport caps rather than the elaborate head-dress of the mature women. The change from girl's clothes to women's clothes occurs through four stages during adolescence. Unmarried girls can be identified by the small gourds tied to their waist and head-dress. Men's clothing is much less elaborate. They wear loose-fitting Chinese-style black pants and a black jacket which may be embroidered. Both men and women use cloth shoulder bags.

Hmong

Origins The Hmong are probably the best-known tribe in Laos. In the 19th century, Chinese opium farmers drove many thousands of Hmong off their poppy fields and forced them south into the mountains of Laos. The Hmong did not have a written language before contact with Europeans and Americans and their heritage is mainly preserved through oral tradition. Hmong mythology relates how they flew in from South China on magic carpets. Village story-tellers also like to propagate the notion that the Hmong are in fact werewolves, who happily devour the livers of their victims. This warrior tribe now mainly inhabits the mountain areas of Luang Prabang, Xieng Khouang and Xam Neua provinces where they practise shifting cultivation.

knew the Hmong as the Meo. Unbeknown to anyone except the Hmong, 'Meo' was a Chinese insult meaning 'barbarian' – conferred on them several millennia ago by Chinese who developed an intense disliking for the tribe. Returning from university in France in the mid-1970s, the Hmong's first highly qualified academic decided it was time to educate the world. Due to his prompting, the tribe was rechristened Hmong, their word for 'mankind'. This change in nomenclature has not stopped the Hmong from continuing to refer to the Chinese as 'sons of dogs'. Nor has it stopped the Lao Loum from regarding the Hmong as their cultural inferiors. But, again, the feelings are reciprocated: the Hmong have an inherent mistrust of the lowland Lao – exacerbated by years of war – and Lao Loum guides reluctantly enter Hmong villages.

The Hmong value their independence and tend to live at high altitudes, away from other tribes. This independence in addition to their former association with poppy cultivation and their siding with the US during the war has meant that of all the hilltribes, it is the Hmong who have been most severely persecuted. They are perceived to be a threat to the security of the state; a tribe that needs to be controlled and carefully watched.

Hmong villages tend not to be fenced, while their houses are built of wood or bamboo at ground level. Each house has a main living area and two or three sleeping rooms. The extended family is headed by the oldest male; he settles family disputes and has supreme authority over family affairs. Like the Karen, the Hmong too are spirit worshippers and believe in household spirits. Every house has an altar, where protection for the household is sought.

As animists, the Hmong believe everything from mountains and opium poppies to cluster bombs, has a spirit – or *phi* – some bad, some good. Shamans – or witchdoctors – play a central role in village life and decision making. The *phi* need to be placated incessantly to ward off sickness and catastrophe. It is the shaman's job to exorcise the bad *phi* from his patients. Until modern medicine arrived in Laos along with the Americans, opium was the Hmong's only palliative drug. Due to their lack of resistance to pharmaceuticals, the Hmong responded miraculously to the smallest doses of penicillin. Even Bandaids were revered as they were thought to contain magical powers which drew out bad *phi*.

Material culture   The Hmong are the only tribe in Laos who make batik; indigo-dyed batik makes up the main panel of their skirts, with appliqué and embroidery added to it. The women also wear black leggings from their knees to their ankles, black jackets (with embroidery) and a black panel or 'apron', held in place with a cummerbund. Even the youngest children wear clothes of intricate design with exquisite needlework. Traditionally the cloth would have been woven by hand on a foot-treddle/back-strap loom; today it is increasingly purchased from markets.

The White Hmong tend to wear less elaborate clothing from day to day, saving it for special occasions only. Hmong men wear loose-fitting black trousers, black jackets (sometimes embroidered) and coloured or embroidered sashes.

The Hmong particularly value silver jewellery; it signifies wealth and a good life. Men, women and children wear silver – tiers of neck rings, heavy silver chains with lock-shaped pendants, ear-rings and pointed rings on every finger. All the family jewellery is brought out at New Year and is an impressive sight, symbolizing the wealth of the family.

Hmong fighters in the 20th century   In the dying days of the French colonial administration, thousands of Hmong were recruited to help fight the Vietnamese Communists. Vang Pao – known as VP – who would later command 30,000 Hmong mercenaries in the US-backed war against the Pathet Lao, was first picked out by a French colonel in charge of these '*maquisards*' or 'native movements'. Later, the

Background Culture

Lao, Laos and Laotians

Most Lao are not Laotians. And not all Laotians are Lao. 'Lao' tends to be used to describe people of Lao stock. There are, in fact, several times more Lao in neighbouring northeastern Thailand (Issan) – roughly 20 million – than there are in Laos with a total population of some 5 million of whom perhaps a little over a half are ethnic Lao. At the same time not all Laotians – people who are nationals of Laos – are ethnic Lao. There are also significant minority populations including Chinese, Vietnamese, the Mon-Khmer Lao Theung and the many tribal groups that comprise the Lao Soung. After a few too many *lau-lao* it is easy to get confused.

Background Culture

Hmong were recruited and paid by the CIA to fight the Pathet Lao. Under General VP, remote mountain villagers with no education were trained to fly T-28 fighter-bombers. It is said that when these US aircraft first started landing in remote villages, locals would carefully examine the undercarriage to see what sex they were.

At its peak, VP's army consisted of 250,000 fighters, the majority of whom were Hmong. Around 30,000 Hmong lost their life in the war, over a tenth of the Hmong population at the time. Even after the Pathet Lao's 'liberation' of Vientiane in 1975, Hmong refugees, encamped in hills to the south of the Plain of Jars, were attacked and flushed out by Vietnamese troops. The Hmong claimed that chemical weapons were being used against them, most notably 'yellow rain' (the biological agent, trichothecane mycotoxins), although biologists at Yale University suggested the substance was, in fact, faeces from swarms of over-flying bees.

When the war ended in 1975 there was a mass exodus of Hmong from Laos. Hmong refugees poured into Thailand, the exodus reaching a peak in 1979 when 3000 a month were fleeing across the Mekong. Many ended up in Thai refugee camps, where they lived in terrible conditions, for many years, sometimes decades. A temporary refugee camp called Ban Vinai was established by the Thai government in June 1975 solely to accommodate the Hmong. These camps are now part of history but one of the best accounts of this period can be read in Lynellyn D Long's *Ban Vinai: the Refugee Camp*. As a Jesuit priest who worked at the camp explained to the author: "Before, they [the refugees] had a life revolving around the seasons... Here they cannot really work... Here people make only dreams."

Thousands of Hmong also ended up in the US and France, fresh from the mountains of Laos: unsurprisingly they did not adapt easily. Various stress disorders were thought to have triggered heart attacks in many healthy young Hmong – a condition referred to as Sudden Unexplained Nocturnal Death Syndrome. In *The Ravens*, Robbins comments that "in a simpler age, it would have been said that the Hmong are dying of a broken heart". Today more than 100,000 Hmong live in the US – mostly on the west coast and in Minnesota – where they regularly lobby politicians. They are a very powerful pressure group, with a habit for distributing sensationalized news, but they are increasingly out of touch with the situation in Laos. Where the US-based Hmong remain important, however, is in the money they remit to their relatives in Laos.

Hmong insurgency A small group of Hmong, led by Vang Pao, remained in Laos and continued to fight the Lao government through the 1980s and 1990s. There are probably still a small number of disaffected Hmong who cling to the cause but they have lost what credibility they may have had and, for the most part rely on left-over ammunition and guerilla tactics. The rebels' biggest public relations disaster came in

1989 when they shot dead several Buddhist monks while attacking a government convoy on the road to Luang Prabang.

Hmong insurgents have been staging reasonably regular attacks for years. A spate of bombings in Vientiane in 2000 was probably linked to the Hmong resistance and in 2004-2005 at least 15 civilians were killed by Hmong insurgents in the north of the country. The Hmong claim to be fighting for democracy and freedom but most are living in terrible conditions and starving, so robbery seems a more likely motivation behind their attacks.

The Lao government tends publicly to side-step the issue, saying there is no official policy towards the Hmong. However, the eradication of opium and related resettlement programme (see Opium eradication, page 312) has had a negative impact on the Hmong and there is undisputable evidence of human rights violations against the Hmong by the Lao government. In 2004, video footage was smuggled out of Laos showing the carnage of a military attack on a Hmong rebel group that had taken place in May 2004; the victims were children. Amnesty International also reported in 2004 that the Lao military was surrounding at least 20 known rebel groups and their families, preventing them from foraging for food. On the other hand, the Lao government recently appointed Hmong as governors of Phonsavanh, Xam Neua and Sayaboury provinces.

The donor community and international organizations continue keenly to watch the Lao government's response to the Hmong. Unfortunately, international pressure can destabilize important domestic policies. In 2005 it was reported that the government had requested groups involved in poverty alleviation in some provinces to prioritize the Hmong above all other ethnic groups when provincial budgets are allocated, regardless of their relative need.

Other communities

The largest non-Lao groups in Laos are the Chinese and Vietnamese communities in the main cities. Many of the Vietnamese were brought in by the French to run the country and stayed. In more recent years, Vietnam also tried to colonize parts of Laos. The Chinese have been migrating to Laos for centuries and are usually traders, restaurateurs and shop-owners. With the relaxation in Communist policies in recent years, there has been a large influx of Thais; most are involved in business. In Vientiane there is also a small community of Indians running restaurants, jewellery and tailors' shops. The majority of the Europeans in Laos are embassy or mining company staff or are involved with aid projects.

Architecture

The architecture of Laos reflects its turbulent history and has strong Siamese/Thai, Burmese and Khmer influences. Philip Rawson, in his book *The Art of Southeast Asia* (Thames and Hudson), goes so far as to state that "The art of Laos is a provincial version of the art of Siam." This is unjustified in so far as art and architecture in Laos, though it may show many links with that of Siam/Thailand (unsurprisingly as over the centuries the two countries have, at various times, held sway over parts of each other's territory), also has elements and styles which are unique to it. Unfortunately, little has survived because many of the older structures were built of wood and were repeatedly ransacked by the Siamese/Thais, Chinese and Vietnamese and then bombed by the Americans. Religious buildings best exhibit the originality of Lao art and architecture.

Like Thailand and Myanmar (Burma), the stupa is the most dominant architectural form in Laos. In its classic Indian form, it is a voluptuous half round – a hemisphere – very like the upturned begging bowl that it is supposed to symbolize.

The Lao wat

There is no English equivalent of the Lao word *wat* or *vat*. It is usually translated as either monastery or temple, although neither is correct. It is easiest to get around this problem by calling them wats. They were, and remain to some extent, the focus of the village or town; they serve as places of worship, education, meeting and healing. Without a wat, a village cannot be viewed as a 'complete' community. The wat is a relatively new innovation. Originally, there were no wats, as monks were wandering ascetics. It seems that although the word 'wat' was in use in the 14th century, these were probably just shrines, and were not monasteries. By the late 18th century, the wat had certainly metamorphosed into a monastery, so sometime in the intervening four centuries, shrine and monastery had united into a whole. Although wats vary a great deal in size and complexity, there is a traditional layout to which most of them conform.

Wats are usually separated from the secular world by two walls. Between these outer and inner walls are found the monks' quarters or dormitories (*kutis*), perhaps a drum or bell tower (*hor kong*) that is used to toll the hours and to warn of danger and, in larger complexes, schools and other administrative buildings. Traditionally the *kutis* were placed on the south side of the wat. It was believed that if the monks slept directly in front of the principal Buddha image they would die young; if they slept to the left they would become ill; and if they slept behind it there would be discord in the community of monks.

Generalized plan of a wat

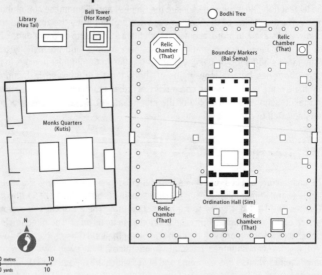

This is surmounted by a shaft representing the Buddha's staff and a stepped pediment symbolizing his folded cloak. In Thailand the stupa has become elongated while in Laos it is also more angular, with four distinct sides. They are referred to as *that* (rather than *chedi*, as in Thailand).

The inner wall, which in bigger wats often takes the form of a gallery or cloister (*phra rabieng*) lined with Buddha images, represents the division between the worldly and the holy, the sacred and the profane. It is used as a quiet place for meditation. Within the inner courtyard, the holiest building is the ordination hall or *sim*, reserved for monks only. This is built on consecrated ground, and has a ring of eight stone tablets or boundary markers (*bai sema*), sometimes contained in mini-pavilions, arranged around it at the cardinal and subcardinal points and shaped like stylized leaves of the bodhi tree, often carved with representations of Vishnu, Siva, Brahma or Indra, or of nagas. Buried in the ground beneath the *bai sema* are stone spheres – and sometimes gold and jewellery. The *bai sema* mark the limit of earthly power. The ordination hall is characteristically a large, rectangular building with high walls and multiple sloping roofs (always odd in number) covered in glazed clay tiles (or wood tiles, in the north). At each end of the apex of the roof are *dok sofa*, or 'bunches of flowers', which represent garuda grasping two nagas (serpents) in its talons. *Chao faa*, flame-like protrusions are attached to the extreme edge of the downward slope of the roofs. Inside, often through elaborately carved and inlaid doors, is the main Buddha image. There may also be numerous subsidiary images. The inside walls of the *sim* may be decorated with murals depicting the Jataka tales or scenes from Buddhist and Hindu cosmology. Like the Buddha, these murals are meant to serve as meditation aids. It is customary for pilgrims to remove their shoes on entering any Buddhist building (or private house

for that matter). Many complexes have secondary chapels, or *hor song phra* attached to the main sim.

Also found in the inner courtyard may be a number of other structures. Among the more common are that (*chedis*), tower-like relic chambers which in Laos and parts of north-eastern Thailand (which is also Lao in terms of culture) take the distinctive lotus bud form. These can be built on a massive scale (such as That Luang in Vientiane, see page 67), and contain holy relics of the Buddha himself. More often, thats are smaller affairs containing the ashes of royalty, monks or pious lay people.

Another rarer feature is the library or scripture repository (*hau tai*), usually a small, tall-sided building where the Buddhist scriptures can be stored safely, high off the ground. *Salas* are open-sided rest pavilions which can be found anywhere in the wat compound; the *sala long tham* or study hall is the largest and most impressive of these and is almost like a *sim* or *viharn* without walls. Here the monks say their prayers at noon.

Sometimes wats have a boat house to shelter the local boat used in the annual boat race.

In rural villages wats often consist only of a sala, or meeting hall.

It seems that wats are often short-lived. Even great wats, if they lose their patronage, are deserted by their monks and fall into ruin. Unlike Christian churches, they depend on constant support from the laity; the wat owns no land or wealth, and must depend on gifts of food to feed the monks and money to repair and expand the fabric of its buildings.

In addition to the *that*, a Lao monastery or *wat* (*vat*) will also have a number of other buildings of which the most important is the *sim* or ordination hall (in Thai, *bot* or *ubosoth*). See the box, above, for a short rundown on the main structures found in an orthodox Lao wat.

Architectural styles

Lao wats are generally less ornate and grand than those in Thailand, although the temples of Luang Prabang are stunning, with their layered roofs that sweep elegantly towards the ground. There are three main styles of temple architecture in Laos: Luang Prabang, Vientiane and Xieng Khouang. The last of these was almost lost forever because of the destruction wrought on the city of Xieng Khouang during the war (see page 188). Fortunately one or two examples exist in Luang Prabang.

The Vientiane style is influenced by the central Thai-style, with its high, pointed and layered roofs. Most of the main sanctuaries are rectangular and some, such as Wat Phra Kaeo in Vientiane, have a veranda around the entire building – a stylistic feature imported from Bangkok. Most of the larger *sim* have a veranda at the back as well as at the front. Vientiane's wats have higher roofs than those in Luang Prabang, the buildings are taller and the entrances more prominent. The steps leading up to the main entrance are often guarded by *nagas* or *nyaks*, while the doorways themselves are usually flanked by pillars and topped with intricately carved porticoes. That Luang, in Vientiane, historically provided a template for most Lao stupas and its unique shape is found only in Laos and some areas of North and Northeast Thailand. As in other Buddhist countries, many of the stupas contain sacred relics – bones or hairs of the Buddha, or the ashes of kings.

The Luang Prabang architectural style has been influenced by North Thai temples. The roofs of the main sanctuaries are very low, almost touching the ground – best exemplified by the magnificent Wat Xieng Thong in Luang Prabang. The pillars tend to narrow towards the top, as tree trunks were originally used for columns and this form was copied when they started to be constructed of stuccoed brick. The wats often has a veranda at the back and the front. The most famous wats in Luang Prabang and Vientiane were built with royal patronage. But most wats in Laos were and are, constructed piece-meal with donations from the local community. Royal wats can be identified by the number of *dok sofa*: more than 10 'flowers' signifies that the wat was built by a king.

The Xieng Khouang style appears to be an amalgam of Vientiane and Luang Prabang influences. The *sim* is raised on a multi-level pediment, as with Vientiane-style *sim*, while the low, sweeping roofs are similar to *sim* in Luang Prabang.

Arts and crafts

Lao art is well known for its wealth of ornamentation. As in other neighbouring Buddhist countries, the focus has been primarily religious in nature. Temple murals and bas-reliefs usually tell the story of the Buddha's life – the jataka tales. There has never been the range of art in Laos that there is in Thailand, as the country has been constantly dominated and influenced by foreign powers. Much of it has been destroyed over the centuries, as plundering neighbours ransacked towns and cities. The *Ramayana*, the Indian epic, has become part of the Lao cultural heritage and is known as the *Phra Lak Phra Lam* (see page 338). Many of the doors and windows of temples are engraved with scenes from this story, depicting the struggle between good and evil. Prime examples are the huge teak shutters at Wat Xieng Thong in Luang Prabang.

Sculpture

Sculpture in Laos is more distinctive in style; the best pieces originate from the 16th to 18th centuries. Characteristic of Lao Buddha images is a nose like an eagle's beak, flat, extended earlobes and tightly curled hair. The best examples are in Wat Phra Kaeo and Wat Sisaket in Vientiane.

¡ Weaving fundamentals

Colours/dyes:	red, orange, indigo and yellow
Motifs, animal:	naga/nyak (river serpent), hong (mythological goose-like bird), naak (dragon), to mom (deer), siharath (elephant lion), singh (lion)
Motifs, geometric:	zig-zag, triangles, spirals
Motifs, natural:	trees, flowers
Motifs, other:	palace buildings, that (stupas)
Primary pieces:	sinh/phaa sin (wrap around sarong worn by women usually finished with a separate hand woven border), pha baeng (shoulder cloth or shawl), pha tai luuk (shawl worn by mothers to carry their infants), pha mon (head scarf) wedding corsage, funeral outfits.

The above is very generalized; different weaving traditions of the country use different motifs, colours, techniques and designs.

The 'Calling for Rain' mudra (the Buddha standing with hands pointing towards the ground, arms slightly away from the torso) is distinctively Lao (see page 75). The 'Contemplating the Tree of Enlightenment' mudra is also uniquely Lao – it depicts a standing Buddha with hands crossed in front of the body. There are many examples in the Pak Ou Caves, on the Mekong, 25 km upstream from Luang Prabang (see page).

Textiles

Of all Laos' artistic traditions, perhaps none is more varied and more vital than its handwoven textiles. These inevitably show some stylistic links with Thailand, but in many respects Laos' tradition is richer and certainly the cloth being produced in Laos today is far finer, more complex and more technically accomplished than any currently being woven in Thailand (although there are those in Thailand who would dispute this, assuming – wrongly – that Thailand is more advanced than Laos in every regard).

Weaving is a craft almost entirely performed by women and it has always been a mark of womanhood. Traditionally, a girl was not considered fit for marriage until she had mastered the art of weaving and the Lao Loum women were expected to weave a corsage for their wedding day. Today these traditions are inevitably less strictly adhered to and there are also a handful of fine male weavers. (Indeed, it has been suggested that these few male weavers produce better – or at least more adventurous – work than their female counterparts because they are less constrained by tradition and more willing to experiment with new designs.) Even so, a skilled weaver is held in high regard and enjoys a position of respect. Cloth is woven from silk, cotton, hemp and a variety of synthetic materials (mostly polyester) – or in some combination of these.

The finest weaving comes from the north. Around Xam Neua (and especially near Xam Tai), the Lao Neua produce some outstanding pieces. These were handed down through a family as heirlooms, stored in lidded stone jars to protect them from insects, moisture and sunlight and only worn on special occasions. But the recent history of this area forced people to sell their treasured textiles and few remain in situ. Indeed it was feared that the art of traditional weaving had been lost entirely in the area. Only the work of some NGOs and committed supporters has resuscitated high quality weaving in the area (and in Vientiane where some of the finest weavers now live and work). Lao Neua textiles are usually woven with a cotton warp and a silk weft and pieces include *pha sinh* (sarong), *pha baeng* (shawl) and blankets. Various methods are employed including *ikat* (see the box on page) – where cotton is used as the Lao Neua consider that indigo dye does not take well on silk – and supplementary weft techniques. Pieces show bold bands of design and colour and the *pha sinh* is usually finished with a separate handwoven border. Among the designs are swastika motifs, *hong* (geese), diamond shapes, *nyak* (snake) heads, lions and elephants.

The Lao Loum of the Luang Prabang area also have a fine weaving tradition, different from that of the far north and northeast. *Pha sinh* produced here tend to have narrow vertical stripes, often alternating between dark and light. Silk tends to be used throughout on the finer pieces, although the yarn may be imported rather than locally produced and it is coloured using chemical dyes. Motifs include zig-zags, flowers and some designs that are French in inspiration.

Around Pakse in the south and also in central Laos around Savannakhet and Thakhek, designs are influenced by the Khmer and closest to those produced in the Isan region of northeast Thailand. *Matmii* ikat-woven cotton cloth is most characteristic. Designs are invariably geometric and today it is unusual to find a piece which has not been dyed using chemicals. Designs are handed down by mothers to their daughters and encompass a broad range from simple *sai fon* ('falling rain') designs where random sections of weft are tied, to the more complex *mee gung* and *poom som*. The less common *pha kit* is a supplementary weft *ikat*, although designs are similar to those in *matmii*. *Pha fai* is a simple cotton cloth, in blue or white and sometimes simply decorated, for everyday use and also used as part of the burial ceremony, when a white length of *pha fai* is draped over the coffin.

Literature

Lao literature is similar to Thai and is likewise also influenced by the Indian epic the *Ramayana*, which in Laos is known as the *Phra Lak Phra Lam* (see box, page 338). Scenes from the Phra Lak Phram Lam can often be seen depicted in temple murals. The first 10 jataka tales, recounting the last 10 lives of the Gautama Buddha (the historic Buddha), have also been a major inspiration for Lao literature. The versions that are in use in Laos are thought to have been introduced from Lanna Thai (northern Thailand, Chiang Mai) in the 16th century, or perhaps from the Mon area of present day Myanmar and Thailand. In these 10 tales, known as the *Vesantara Jataka*, the Buddha renounces all his earthly possessions, even his wife and children. Although the jataka tales in Laos are clearly linked, in religious terms, with Buddhism and therefore with India, the stories have little in common with the Indian originals. They draw heavily on local legends and folklore and have merely been incorporated within a religious literary milieu. They are essentially animist tales provided with a Buddhist gloss.

Traditionally, as in other parts of Southeast Asia, texts were recorded on palm leaves. The letters were inscribed with a stylus and the grooves darkened with oil. A palm leaf manuscript kept under good conditions in a well-maintained *hau tai* or library can last 100 years or more.

With the incorporation of Laos into French Indochina at the end of the 19th century, the Lao élite effectively renounced traditional Lao literature in favour of the French language and French artistic traditions. Many of the Lao élite were educated in France and those that were not still enjoyed a French-style education. The upshot was that Lao literature came to be looked down upon as primitive and simplistic and most scholars wrote instead in French.

As with traditional songs, much Lao poetry has been passed down the generations and remains popular. *Sin Xay* is one of the great Lao poems and has been written down (although many have not) and is found in many temples.

In 1778 the Thais plundered Laos and along with the two most sacred Buddha images – the Phra Bang and the Phra Kaeo (Emerald Buddha) – they pillaged a great deal of Lao religious literature and historical documents. Most Lao manuscripts – or *kampi* – are engraved on palm leaves and are 40-50 cm long, pierced with two holes and threaded together with cord. A bundle of 20 leaves forms a *phuk* and these are grouped together into *mat*, which are wrapped in a piece of cloth.

Language

The official language is Lao, the language of the ethnic majority. Lao is basically a monosyllabic, tonal language. It contains many polysyllabic words borrowed from Pali and Sanskrit (ancient Indian dialects) as well as words borrowed from Khmer. It has six tones, 33 consonants and 28 vowels. Lao is also spoken in Northeast Thailand and North Cambodia, which was originally part of the kingdom of Lane Xang. Lao and Thai, particularly the Northeast dialect, are mutually intelligible. Differences have mainly developed since French colonial days when Laos was insulated from developments of the Thai language. French is still spoken in towns – particularly by the older generation – and is often used in government but English is being increasingly used. Significant numbers of Lao have been to universities and colleges in the former Soviet Union and Eastern Europe, so Eastern European languages and Russian are also spoken, but not widely.

Many of the tribal groups have no system of writing and the Lao script is similar to Thai, to which it is closely related. One of the kings of the Sukhothai Dynasty, Ramkhamhaeng, devised the Thai alphabet in 1283 and introduced the Thai system of writing. Lao script is modelled on the early Thai script and is written from left to right with no spacing between the words.

Like many other newly independent countries, the leadership in the Lao PDR have attempted to make Lao the national language, in fact as well as in rhetoric. An oft-quoted phrase is 'Language reveals one's nationhood, manners reveals one's lineage'. Because Lao is so similar to Thai, there has also been a conscious attempt to maintain a sense of difference between the two countries' languages. Otherwise, some people believe, there exists the danger that Laos might simply become culturally absorbed within Greater Thailand. As scholars have pointed out, the cultural flows have essentially been one way: most people in Laos can understand Standard Thai, but few Thais (except in the Northeastern region) can understand Lao. Linguistically, Lao and Thai are both dialects of the same root language, but neither is the dialect of the other. (Many Thais view Lao as a linguistic off-shoot of Thai, and hence subordinate to Thai. Understandably, people in Laos take offence at this intimation.)

Because of this delicate intersection of nationality, identity and language, there has been a studied attempt to establish language principles for Lao that clearly separates it from Thai. To begin with it was necessary to establish an accepted, national version of spoken Lao (there are significant differences between areas). In other words, to produce Standard Lao which could be taught in schools, promoted in the media, and used in government. This effort at language engineering can be dated from the 1930s, and saw further refinements in the 1940s, 1950s, 1970s and 1990s. (Note that these attempts to develop Standard Lao bridge the colonial, royalist and communist periods.) While this has been successful to the extent that Lao remains noticeably and significantly different from Thai, the major influence on the Lao language today remains that of Thai. ▸ *See also Language, page 20; and Useful words and phrases, page 348.*

Background Culture

Mudras and the Buddha image

An artist producing an image of the Buddha does not try to create an original piece of art; he is trying to be faithful to a tradition which can be traced back over centuries. It is important to appreciate that the Buddha image is not merely a work of art but an object of and for, worship. Sanskrit poetry even sets down the characteristics of the Buddha – albeit in rather unlikely terms: legs like a deer, arms like an elephant's trunk, a chin like a mango stone and hair like the stings of scorpions. The Pali texts of Theravada Buddhism add the 108 auspicious signs, long toes and fingers of equal length, body like a banyan tree and eyelashes like a cow's. The Buddha can be represented either sitting, lying (indicating paranirvana), or standing, and (in Thailand) occasionally walking. He is often represented standing on an open lotus flower: the Buddha was born into an impure world, and likewise the lotus germinates in mud but rises above the filth to flower. Each image will be represented in a particular mudra or 'attitude', of which there are 40. The most common are:

Abhayamudra – dispelling fear or giving protection; right hand (sometimes both hands) raised, palm outwards, usually with the Buddha in a standing position.

Varamudra – giving blessing or charity; the right hand pointing downwards, the palm facing outwards, with the Buddha either seated or standing.

Vitarkamudra – preaching mudra; the ends of the thumb and index finger of the right hand touch to form a circle, symbolizing the Wheel of Law. The Buddha can either be seated or standing.

Dharmacakramudra – 'spinning the Wheel of Law'; a preaching mudra symbolizing the teaching of the first sermon. The hands are held in front of the chest, thumbs and index fingers of both joined, one facing inwards and one outwards.

Bhumisparcamudra – 'calling the earth goddess to witness' or 'touching the earth'; the right hand rests on the right knee with the tips of the fingers 'touching ground', thus calling the earth goddess Dharani/Thoranee to witness his enlightenment and victory over Mara, the king of demons. The Buddha is always seated.

Dhyanamudra – meditation; both hands resting open, palms upwards, in the lap, right over left.

Other points of note:
Vajrasana – yogic posture of meditation; cross-legged, both soles of the feet visible.

Virasana – yogic posture of meditation; cross-legged, but with the right leg on top of the left, covering the left foot (also known as paryankasana).

Buddha under Naga – the Buddha is shown in an attitude of meditation with a cobra rearing up over his head. This refers to an episode in the Buddha's life when he was meditating; a rain storm broke and Nagaraja, the king of the nagas (snakes), curled up under the Buddha (seven coils) and then used his seven-headed hood to protect the Holy One from the falling rain.

Buddha calling for rain – the Buddha is depicted standing, both arms held stiffly at the side of the body, fingers pointing downwards.

Bhumisparcamudra – calling the earth goddess to witness. Sukhothai period, 13th-14th century.

Dhyanamudra – meditation. Sukhothai period, 13th-14th century.

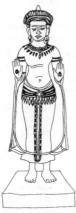

Abhayamudra – dispelling fear or giving protection. Lopburi Buddha, Khmer style 12th century.

Vitarkamudra – preaching, "spinning the Wheel of Law". Dvaravati Buddha, 7th-8th century, seated in the "European" manner.

Abhayamudra – dispelling fear or giving protection; subduing Mara position. Lopburi Buddha, Khmer style 13th century.

The Buddha 'Calling for rain'.

Background Culture

Dance, drama and music

Lao music, songs and dances have much in common with those of the Thai. Instruments include bamboo flutes, drums, gongs, cymbals and pinched or bowed string instruments shaped like banjos. The national instrument is the *kaen*, a hand-held pipe organ. It is made from bamboo and is similar in appearance to the South American pan pipes. Percussion is an important part of a Lao orchestra and two of the most commonly used instruments are the *nang nat*, a xylophone and the *knong vony*, a series of bronze cymbals suspended from a wooden frame. The *seb noi* orchestra – a consortium of all these instruments – is used to introduce or conclude vocal recitals. The *seb gnai* orchestra includes two big drums and a Lao-style clarinet as well; it was used in royal processions and still accompanies certain religious ceremonies.

Despite the lack of written notation, many epic poems and legends have survived to the present day as songs, passed, with the composition itself, from generation to generation. Early minstrels took their inspiration from folklore, enriched by Indian myths. Traditional Lao music can now only be heard during performances of the *Phra Lak Phra Lam*, the Lao version of the Indian epic the *Ramayana*. Many of the monasteries have experts on percussion who play every Buddhist sabbath. There is also a strong tradition of Lao folk music, which differs between tribal groups.

Secular songs, drawing largely on Lao literature for inspiration, are known as *mau lam* and can be heard at festival time not just in Laos but also in Northeast Thailand (where they are known as *mor lam*), which is also, culturally, 'Lao'. Indeed, there has been something of a Lao cultural revival in Northeast Thailand and some of the best performers are based there. It is also the best place to pick up cassette tapes of famous *mor lam/mau lam* singers.

In Vientiane and the provincial capitals, younger Lao tend to opt for Western-style pop. To the raucous strains of the likes of Joan Jett and the Blackhearts – with the lyrics roughly translated into Lao – local bands entertain Levi-clad dancers well into the early hours in Vientiane's discos and nightclubs. The Communist leadership have become increasingly concerned at this invasion of Western and Thai culture and there has been an attempt to limit the quantity of non-Lao music that is played in clubs and karaoke bars. The authorities have dictated that only a certain proportion of songs can be non-Lao and there are cultural police who occasionally check that these rules are being observed.

Classical Lao theatre and dance have Indian origins and were probably imported from the Cambodian royal courts in the 14th century. Thai influence has also crept in over the years.

Religion

Theravada Buddhism

Theravada Buddhism, from the Pali word *thera* ('elders'), means the 'way of the elders' and is distinct from the dominant Buddhism practised in India, Mahayana Buddhism or the 'Greater Vehicle'. The sacred language of Theravada Buddhism is Pali rather than Sanskrit, Bodhisattvas (future Buddhas) are not given much attention and emphasis is placed upon a precise and 'fundamental' interpretation of the Buddha's teachings, as they were originally recorded. By the 15th century, Theravada Buddhism was the dominant religion in Laos – as it was in neighbouring Siam (Thailand), Burma (Myanmar) and Cambodia. Buddhism shares the belief, in common with Hinduism, in rebirth. A person goes through countless lives and the experience of one life is conditioned by the acts in a previous one. This is the Law of Karma (act or deed, from Pali *kamma*), the law of cause and effect. But, it is not, as commonly thought in the West, equivalent to fate.

For most people, nirvana is a distant goal and they merely aim to accumulate merit by living good lives and performing good deeds such as giving alms to monks. In this way the layman embarks on the Path to Heaven. It is also common for a layman to become ordained, at some point in his life (usually as a young man), for a three month period during the Buddhist Rains Retreat.

Monks should endeavour to lead stringently ascetic lives. They must refrain from murder, theft, sexual intercourse, untruths, eating after noon, alcohol, entertainment, ornament, comfortable beds and wealth. They are allowed to own only a begging bowl, three pieces of clothing, a razor, needle, belt and water filter. They can only eat food that they have received through begging. Anyone who is male, over 20 and not a criminal can become a monk.

The 'Way of the Elders', is believed to be closest to Buddhist as it originally developed in India. It is often referred to by the term 'Hinayana' (Lesser Vehicle), a disparaging name foisted onto Theravadans by Mahayanists. This form of Buddhism is the dominant contemporary religion in the mainland Southeast Asian countries of Laos, Thailand, Cambodia and Myanmar (Burma).

In Theravadan Buddhism, the historic Buddha, Sakyamuni, is revered above all else and most images of the Buddha are of Sakyamuni. Importantly and unlike Mahayana Buddhism, the Buddha image is only meant to serve as a meditation aid; it does not embody supernatural powers and is not supposed to be worshipped. However, the popular need for objects of veneration has meant that most images are worshipped. Pilgrims bring flowers and incense and prostrate themselves in front of the image. This is a Mahayanist influence which has been embraced by Theravadans.

Buddhism in Laos

The Lao often maintain that the Vientiane area converted to Buddhism at the time of the Moghul emperor Asoka. This seems suspiciously early and is probably untrue. The original stupa at That Luang, so it is claimed, was built to encase a piece of the Buddha's breastbone provided by Asoka. Buddhism was undoubtedly practised before Fa Ngum united Lane Xang and created a Buddhist Kingdom in the mid-14th century. He was known as the Great Protector of the Faith and brought the Phra Bang, the famous golden statue – the symbol of Buddhism in Laos – from Angkor in Cambodia to Laos.

Buddhism was gradually accepted among the lowland Lao but many of the highland tribes remain animist. Even where Buddhism has been practised for centuries, it is usually interwoven with the superstitions and rituals of animist beliefs. Appeasing the spirits and gaining merit are both integral features of life. Most highlanders are animists and the worship of *phi* or spirits has remained central to village life throughout the revolutionary years, despite the fact that it was officially banned by the government. Similarly, the *baci* ceremony – when strings representing guardian spirits are tied around the wrists of guests – is still practised throughout Laos.

In the late 1500s, King Setthathirat promoted Buddhism and built many monasteries or wats. Buddhism was first taught in schools in the 17th century and prospered until the Thai and Ho invasions of the 18th and 19th centuries when many of the wats were destroyed. With the introduction of socialism in 1975 Buddhism was banned from primary schools and people prohibited from giving alms to monks. With the increasing religious tolerance of the regime it is now undergoing a revival and many of the wats are being rebuilt and redecorated. Males are expected to become monks for three months or so before marriage, usually during Buddhist Lent. All members of the priesthood are placed under the authority of a superior – the *Phra Sangharaja*– whose seat was traditionally in the capital of the kingdom.

⁞ The Lao Ramayana: the Phra Lak Phra Lam

The *Phra Lak Phra Lam* is an adaptation of the Indian Hindu classic, the *Ramayana*, which was written by the poet Valmiki about 2000 years ago. This 48,000 line epic odyssey – often likened to the works of Homer – was introduced into mainland Southeast Asia in the early centuries of the first millennium. The heroes were simply transposed into a mythical, ancient, Southeast Asian landscape.

In Laos, as in Thailand, the *Phra Lak Phra Lam* quickly became highly influential. In Thailand this is reflected in the name of the former capital of Siam, Ayutthaya, taken from the legendary hero's city of Ayodhia. Unfortunately, these early Thai translations of the *Ramayana*, which also filtered into Laos, were destroyed following the sacking of Ayutthaya by the Burmese in 1767. The earliest extant version was written by Thai King Taksin in about 1775.

The Lao, and Thai, versions of the *Ramayana*, closely follow that of the original Indian story. They tell of the life of Ram (Rama), the King of Ayodhia. In the first part of the story, Ram renounces his throne following a long and convoluted court intrigue and flees into exile. With his wife Seeda (Sita) and trusted companion Hanuman (the monkey god), they undertake a long and arduous journey. In the second part, his wife Seeda is abducted by the evil king Ravana, forcing Ram to wage battle against the demons of Langka Island (Sri Lanka). He defeats the demons with the help of Hanuman and his monkey army and recovers his wife. In the third and final part of the story – and here it diverges sharply from the Indian original – Seeda and Ram are reunited and reconciled with the help of the gods (in the Indian version there is no such reconciliation). Another difference from the Indian version is the significant role played by Hanuman – here an amorous adventurer who dominates much of the third part of the epic.

There are also numerous sub-plots which are original to the *Phra Lak Phra Lam*, many building upon local myth and folklore. In tone and issues of morality, the Lao and Thai versions are less puritanical than the Indian original. There are also, of course, differences in dress, ecology, location and custom.

In line with Buddhist tradition, materialism and the accumulation of personal wealth is generally frowned on in Laos. Poverty is admired as a form of spirituality. This belief proved rather convenient for the Communist regime, when it was taken to extremes. Today, in the new capitalist climate, the traditional attributes of spirituality sit uncomfortably with Laos' increasingly bourgeois aspirations.

Buddhism, as it is practised in Laos, is not the 'other-worldly' religion of Western conception. Ultimate salvation – enlightenment, or *nirvana* – is a distant goal for most people. Lao Buddhists pursue the Law of Karma, the reduction of suffering. Meritorious acts are undertaken and demeritorious ones avoided so that life and more particularly future life, might be improved. 'Karma' is often thought of in the West as 'fate'. It is not. It is true that previous karma determines a person's position in society, but there is still room for individual action – and a person is ultimately responsible for that action. It is the law of cause and effect.

It is important to draw a distinction between 'academic' Buddhism, as it tends to be understood in the West and 'popular' Buddhism, as it is practised in Laos. In Laos, Buddhism is a 'syncretic' religion: it incorporates elements of Brahmanism, animism and ancestor worship. Amulets are worn to protect against harm and are often sold in temple compounds. In the countryside, farmers have what they consider to be a healthy regard for the spirits (*phi*) and demons that inhabit the rivers, trees and forests. Astrologers are widely consulted by urban and rural dwellers alike. It is these aspects of Lao Buddhism which help to provide worldly assurance and they are perceived to be complementary, not in contradiction, with Buddhist teachings.

Most Lao villages will contain a 'temple', 'monastery' or wat (the word does not translate accurately). The wat represents the mental heart of each community and most young men at some point in their lives will become ordained as monks, usually during the Buddhist Rains Retreat, which stretches from July to October. Previously this period represented the only opportunity for a young man to gain an education and to learn how to read. An equally important reason for a man to become ordained is so that he can accumulate merit for his family, particularly for his mother, who as a woman cannot become ordained.

As in Thailand, Laos has adopted the Indian epic the *Ramayana* (see page 338), which has been the inspiration for much Lao art and sculpture. Complete manuscripts of the Lao *Ramayana* – known as the *Phra Lak Phra Lam*, used to be kept at Wat Phra Kaeo and Wat Sisaket.

Buddhism under Communism

Buddhism's relationship with Communism has been complex and usually ambivalent. As the Pathet Lao began their revolutionary mission they saw in the country's monks a useful means by which to spread their message. Many monks, though they may themselves have renounced material possessions and all desires, were conscious of the inequalities in society and the impoverished conditions in which many people lived their lives. Indeed most of them came from poor, rural backgrounds. In addition many monks saw themselves as the guardians of Lao culture and as the US became more closely involved in the country so they increasingly felt that it was their job to protect the people against the spread of an alien culture and mores. Therefore, right from the start, monks had a natural sympathy with the ideals of the Pathet Lao. Indeed, significant numbers renounced their vows and joined the revolution. Others stayed on in their monasteries, but used their positions and the teachings of the Buddha to further the revolutionary cause. The Pathet Lao, for their part, saw the monks as a legitimizing force which would assist in their revolutionary efforts. Monks were often the most respected individuals in society and if the Pathet Lao could somehow piggy-back on this respect then they too, it was reasoned, would gain in credibility and respect. The Rightist government also tried to do the same, but with notably less success.

With the victory of the Pathet Lao in 1975, their view of the *sangha* (monkhood) changed. No longer were monks a useful vehicle in building revolution; overnight they became a potential threat. Monks were forced to attend re-education seminars where they were instructed that they could no longer teach about merit or *karma*, two central pillars of Buddhism. Their sermons were taped by Pathet Lao cadres to be scrutinized for subversive propaganda and a stream of disillusioned monks began to flee to Thailand. So the *sangha* was emasculated as an independent force. Monks were forced to follow the directives of the Lao People's Revolutionary Party and the *sangha* came under strict Party control. Monasteries were expected to become mini-cooperatives so that they did not have to depend on the laity for alms and they were paid a small salary by the State for undertaking teaching and health work. In short, the LPDR seemed intent on undermining the *sangha* as an independent force in Lao society, making it dependent on the State for its survival and largely irrelevant to wider society. The success of the Pathet Lao's policy of marginalization can be seen in the number of monks in the country. In 1975 there were around 20,000 monks. By 1979 this had shrunk to just 1700.

● In Siddhartha's footsteps: a short history of Buddhism

Buddhism was founded by Siddhartha Gautama, a prince of the Sakya tribe of Nepal, who probably lived between 563 and 483 BC. He achieved enlightenment and the word buddha means 'fully enlightened one', or 'one who has woken up'. Siddhartha Gautama is known by a number of titles. In the West, he is usually referred to as The Buddha, that is the historic Buddha (but not just Buddha); more common in Southeast Asia is the title Sakyamuni, or Sage of the Sakyas (referring to his tribal origins).

Over the centuries, the life of the Buddha has become part legend, and the Jataka tales which recount his various lives are colourful and convoluted. But, central to any Buddhist's belief is that he was born under a sal tree, that he achieved enlightenment under a bodhi tree in the Bodh Gaya Gardens, that he preached the First Sermon at Sarnath and that he died at Kusinagara (all in India or Nepal).

The Buddda was born at Lumbini (in present-day Nepal), as Queen Maya was on her way to her parents' home. She had had a very auspicious dream before the child's birth of being impregnated by an elephant, whereupon a sage prophesied that Siddhartha would become either a great king or a great spiritual leader. His father, being keen that the first option of the prophesy be fulfilled, brought him up in all the princely skills – at which Siddhartha excelled – and ensured that he only saw beautiful things, not the harsher elements of life.

Despite his father's efforts Siddhartha saw four things while travelling between palaces – a helpless old man, a very sick man, a corpse being carried by lamenting relatives and an ascetic, calm and serene as he begged for food. The young prince renounced his princely origins and left home to study under a series of spiritual teachers. He finally discovered the path to enlightenment at the Bodh Gaya Gardens in India. He then proclaimed his thoughts to a small group of disciples at Sarnath, near Benares, and continued to preach and

However before the *sangha* could sink into obscurity and irrelevance, the government eased its policy in 1979 and began to allow monks and the *sangha* greater latitude. In addition and perhaps more importantly, the leadership embraced certain aspects of Lao culture, one of which was Theravada Buddhism. The memorial to the revolutionary struggle in Vientiane, for example, was designed as a Buddhist that (stupa) and government ministers enthusiastically join in the celebration of Buddhist festivals.

Animism

While the majority of the population (about 60-65%) follow Theravada Buddhism, Animism is practised by about 30% of the population. The term Animism derives from the Latin word 'anima', meaning mind or soul. At a very basic level, Animism refers to a belief in spirits. Animism is particularly common among Lao Theung and Lao Soung groups minority groups but elements of Animism have also infiltrated or been grafted onto Buddhism and Lao culture at a broader level. Most people believe in *phi*, spirits, which are seen as fundamental to their relationship with nature and the community. The word *phi* has even been adopted into Lao language to mean ghost, while *phi-baa* means crazy. Many Lao people believe that spiritual forces need to be placated, usually through a *baci* ceremony (see page 49), as they can cause illness, disease or attract followers until he died at the age of 81 at Kusinagara.

In the First Sermon at the deer park in Sarnath, the Buddha preached the Four Truths, which are still considered the root of Buddhist belief and practical experience: suffering exists; there is a cause of suffering; suffering can be ended; and to end suffering it is necessary to follow the 'Noble Eightfold Path' – namely, right speech, livelihood, action, effort, mindfulness, concentration, opinion and intention.

Soon after the Buddha began preaching, a monastic order – the Sangha – was established. As the monkhood evolved in India, it also began to fragment into different sects. An important change was the belief that the Buddha was transcendent: he had never been born, nor had he died; he had always existed and his life on earth had been mere illusion. The emergence of these new concepts helped to turn what up until then was an ethical code of conduct, into a religion. It eventually led to the appearance of a new Buddhist movement, Mahayana Buddhism which split from the more traditional Theravada 'sect'.

Despite the division of Buddhism into two sects, the central tenets of the religion are common to both. Specifically, the principles pertaining to the Four Noble Truths, the Noble Eightfold Path, the Dependent Origination, the Law of Karma and nirvana. In addition, the principles of non-violence and tolerance are also embraced by both sects. In essence, the differences between the two are of emphasis and interpretation. Theravada Buddhism is strictly based on the original Pali Canon, while the Mahayana tradition stems from later Sanskrit texts. Mahayana Buddhism also allows a broader and more varied interpretation of the doctrine. Other important differences are that while the Thervada tradition is more 'intellectual' and self-obsessed, with an emphasis upon the attaining of wisdom and insight for oneself, Mahayana Buddhism stresses devotion and compassion towards others.

bad luck. Unexplicable events – including strange behaviour by foreign visitors – are often attributed to 'ghosts'. Buddhist monks are often called upon to exorcize bad spirits and most wats have a small spirit house built on the monastic grounds. Animists generally suffer little discrimination from the government, however some practises, are discouraged for health and security reasons.

Christianity in post-1975 Laos

The smallest religious group represented in Laos are Christians, including Roman Catholics, who account for around 2% of the population. There are around 30,000 to 40,000 Catholics in the country, many of whom are ethnic Vietnamese, concentrated in major urban centers along the Mekong River.

Following the revolution, many churches in provincial towns were turned into community centres and meeting halls. Vientiane's Evangelical Church has held a Sunday service ever since 1979 but it is only in recent years that Christians have felt free to worship openly and even this 'freedom' comes with qualifications. In 1989 the first consultation between the country's Christian leaders (Protestant and Roman Catholic) was authorized by the government; it was the first such meeting since 'liberation' and was also attended by government representatives and two Hmong leaders of the Buddhist Federation.

It's illegal for foreigners to proselytize in Laos; persons found guilty can be subject to arrest and deportation for 'creating social divisions'. Foreign missionaries were ejected from Laos in 1975 and, today, foreign NGOs affiliated with religious organizations are only allowed to work in the country on the condition that they don't try to spread their religion. Not many Buddhists have converted to Christianity but it seems to be growing among the animist hilltribes. The US Bible Society has recently published a modern translation of the Bible into Lao but tribal-language editions do not yet exist. The shortage of bibles and other literature has prompted Christian leaders to 'offer unsolicited gifts' to the department of religious affairs to ease restrictions on the import of hymn books and bibles from Thailand.

While there is more freedom to worship today than during the pre-reform period, there is still a sense in the leadership that Christians are a political threat. In 1998 the authorities arrested 44 Christians, among them three Americans, for conducting unauthorized church services in people's private homes. The Americans were expelled but the Laotians were thrown in prison. This sort of knee-jerk reaction usually ends up being counter-productive. The US Congress responded to what they saw as religious persecution by blocking an economic agreement that was likely to significantly boost textile exports to the US. The fact that the leadership in Laos is hyper-sensitive to such issues was reinforced in November 1999 when six Christian leaders were reportedly arrested and imprisoned for planning a pro-democracy rally along with around 100 other activists.

Land and environment

Geography

Laos stretches about 1000 km from north to south, while distances from east to west range from 140 to 500 km. The country covers 236,800 sq km – less than half the size of France and just a third of the size of Texas. Only 24% of the population lives in towns. The country has the lowest population density in Asia, with 22 people per sq km.

Rugged mountains cover more than three-quarters of the country and with few all-weather roads (there are just 4000 km of sealed roads in the entire country), rivers remain important communication routes. Historically, the Mekong River has been the country's economic artery. On its banks nestle Laos' most important cities: in the north the small, colourful former royal capital of Luang Prabang, further south the administrative and political capital of Vientiane and farther south still the regional centres of Thakhek, Savannakhet and Pakse.

Laos is dominated by the Mekong River and the Annamite chain of mountains which both run southeast towards the South China Sea. Flowing along the borders of Laos are 1865 km of the 4000 km-long Mekong River. The lowlands of the Mekong valley form the principal agricultural areas, especially around Vientiane and Savannakhet and these are home to the lowland Lao – sometimes argued to be the 'true' Lao. The Mekong has three main tributaries: the Nam Ou and Nam Tha from the north and the Nam Ngum, which flows into Vientiane province.

Much of the northern half of Laos is 1500 m or more above sea level and its karsk limestone outcrops are deeply dissected by steep-sided river valleys. Further south, the Annamite chain has an average height of 1200 m. Heavily forested, rugged mountains form a natural barrier between Laos and Vietnam. Most of the country is a mixture of mountains and high plateau. There are four main plateau: the Xieng Khouang plateau, better known as the Plain of Jars, in the north, the Nakai and the limestone Khammuoane plateau in the centre and the 10,000 sq km Boloven Plateau to the south. The highest peak is the 2800 m Bia Mountain, which rises above the Xieng Khouang plateau to the northeast.

Climate

The rainy season is from May through to September-October; the tropical lowlands receive an annual average rainfall of 1250 mm a year. Temperatures during these months are in the 30s°C. In mountainous Xieng Khoung Province, it is cooler and temperatures can drop to freezing point in December and January. The first half of the dry season, from November to April, is cool, with temperatures between 10° and 20°C. This gives way to a hot, dry season from March to June when temperatures soar and are often in excess of 35°C. Average rainfall in Vientiane is 1700 mm, although in North Laos and the highlands it is much wetter, with more than 3000 mm each year.

Vegetation

Much of Laos is forested. The vegetation is rich and diverse: a mix of tropical and subtropical species. Grassy savanna predominates on plateau areas such as the Plain of Jars. In the forests, some hardwoods tower to over 30 m, while tropical palms and mango are found in the lowlands and large stands of pine in the remote northern hills.

Rural people rely heavily on the Mekong River and its watershed for everything from transport to rice production and fishing. It is estimated that 80% of the country is located near the Mekong, its tributaries or in the watershed. Over half of all vital protein consumed in rural areas comes from fish, frogs and other river creatures. Agriculture is of utmost importance to Lao people, with about 80% of the population engaged in subsistence farming.

In the mid-20th century over 70% of the country was covered with forest. Today, this number has been reduced to around 40% and of this only 17% remains old growth tropical forest. The rattan, cardamom, mushrooms, orchids and wild meat gathered from these forests are essential to rural livelihoods and in many cases generate over half of the income of a rural family. The Lao Government has established 20 National Protected Areas or NPAs (formerly known as National Biodiversity Conservation Areas, NBCAs), plus two corridor areas, covering 14.3% of the country. Although this is a step forward, illegal hunting and logging is still rife in most areas.

Logging provides Laos with a large proportion of its export earnings. Officially, around 450,000 cu m of forest are felled each year for commercial purposes but this is probably an underestimate owing to the activities of illegal loggers, many of whom are Chinese, Vietnamese and Thai. A ban on the export of logs in 1988 caused official timber export earnings to slump 30% but environmentalists claim that the ban has had little impact on the number of logs being exported. Another ban was imposed in late 1991. In addition, shifting cultivators clear an estimated 100,000 ha of forest a year. The government sees shifting cultivators (most of whom are from one of Laos' ethnic minorities) as the primary cause of forest loss and the current five year development plan has reiterated the government's commitment to 'totally eradicating' shifting cultivation. But if the situation is similar to neighbouring countries like Thailand and Vietnam then this will do little to preserve the forest because the primary culprits are commercial logging concerns. Government reforestation programmes far from compensate for the destruction. In October 1989 the Council of Ministers issued a decree on the preservation of forests of which the people appear to be blissfully unaware. There was a half-hearted propaganda campaign to 'teach every Lao citizen to love nature and develop a sense of responsibility for the preservation of forests'.

Wildlife

Mammals include everything from wildcats, leopards and tigers to bears, wild cattle and small barking deer. Laos is also home to the large Asian elk, rhinoceros, elephants, monkeys, gibbons and ubiquitous rabbits and squirrels. Ornithological life encompasses pheasants, partridges, many songbirds, ducks and some hawks and eagles – although in rural areas many birds (and other animals) have been killed for food. There is an abundant reptilian population, including cobras, kraits, crocodiles and lizards. The lower reaches of the Mekong River, marking the border between Cambodia and Laos, is the last place in Indochina where the rare Irrawaddy dolphin is to be found. However dynamite fishing is decimating the population and today there are probably under 20 left. Another rare denizen of the Mekong, but one that stands a greater chance of survival, is the pa buk catfish (*Pangasianodon gigas*) which weighs up to 340 kg. This riverbed-dwelling fish was first described by Western science only in 1930, although Lao fishermen and their Thai counterparts had been catching it for many years – as James McCarthy notes in the account of his travels through Siam and Laos published in 1900. The fish is a delicacy and clearly has been for many years – its roe was paid as tribute to China in the late 19th century. Because of over-fishing, by the 1980s the numbers of pa buk had become severely depleted. However a breeding programme is having some success and young pa buk fingerlings are now being released into the Mekong.

There is an enormous problem of smuggling rare animals out of Laos, mainly to South Korea and China. In 1978, the gall bladder of a black bear from Laos was auctioned in Seoul for US$55,000. Teeth and bones of wild cats from Laos are in demand for Chinese medicine. The English-language daily, *Khao San Pathet Lao*, published a report estimating that in 1992 more than 10 tonnes of protected wild animals had been slaughtered for export in the northeastern province of Houa Phanh.

Laos' wildlife has taken a caning due to poachers peddling animals across the country's borders. In 2001 the authors of "Wildlife Trade in Laos: the End of the Game" suspected that wildlife trade was the largest source of income in Lao villages after fishing and was worth an estimated $US35 million-per-year (a conservative estimate).

In 2004, the Lao Government joined CITES, the world's foremost conservation treaty regulating the international trade in endangered species. Regardless, Laos is still home to a diverse range of wildlife will some 800 bird and 100 mammal species. New species are popping up on an almost annual basis.

The degree to which Laos' flora and fauna are under-researched was illustrated in August 1999 when it was announced that a previously unknown species of striped rabbit had been discovered quietly nibbling the grass in the mountains dividing Laos from Vietnam. This area of Indochina has proved a veritable cornucopia of unknown animals. During the 1990s scientists have discovered one antelope, several species of deer, an ox and even a remnant herd of Javan rhinoceros, a species which was previously thought to be confined to a small corner of West Java.

Books

Laos

Art and culture
Dakin, Brett (2003), *Another Quiet American*, Asia Books. Dakin's experiences of working in Laos, with some interesting cultural insights.
Evans, Grant (1999), *Laos: Culture and Society*, Chiang Mai, Thailand: Silkworm Books. Edited volume written by assorted scholars of Laos. Highly informed; for those who really want to know about the country.
Fay, Kim (2005), *To Asia with Love: A Connoisseurs Guide to Cambodia, Laos, Thailand Vietnam*, Global Directions Inc/ Things Asian Press. Great anthology of ideas,

inspirations and experiences of Southeast Asia from the people who live there.
Phia Sing (1995), *Traditional recipes of Laos*, Totnes, Devon, UK: Prospect Books. The best Lao cookbook available. The recipes were collected by the chief chef at the Royal Palace in Luang Prabang, Phia Sing, in the 1960s. They have been translated into English and made West-friendly by replacing some of the more esoteric ingredients.

Economics, politics and development
Dommen, Arthur J (1985), *Laos: Keystone of Indochina*, Boulder: Westview Press. Out of date but a reasonable overview.

Evans, Grant (1990), *Lao Peasants under Socialism*, New Haven: Yale University Press. The definitive account of farmers in modern Laos. A new edition published by Silkworm Books in Chiang Mai (Thailand) takes into account economic changes brought about by the New Economic Mechanism.

Stuart-Fox, Martin (1982), *Contemporary Laos*, St Lucia: Queensland University Press. A useful overview of Laos up to 1980.

Stuart-Fox, Martin (1986), *Laos – Politics, Economics and Society*, London: Francis Pinter. Out of date but a good single volume summary of the country providing historical and cultural background.

Stuart-Fox, Martin (1996), *Buddhist Kingdom, Marxist State: the Making of Modern Laos*, Bangkok: White Lotus. A collection of Stuart-Fox's various papers published over the years and brought up to date. Especially good on recent history. Available in Bangkok.

Zasloff, J J and Unger, L (1991) (eds), *Laos: Beyond the Revolution*, Macmillan, Basingstoke. Edited volume with a mixed collection of papers; economics/politics chapters are already rather dated.

History

Kremmer, Christopher, *Bamboo Palace*, HarperCollins Australia. Traces Kremmer's attempts to unravel the mystery surrounding the Lao royal family.

Stuart-Fox, Martin and Kooyman, Mary (1992), *Historical Dictionary of Laos*, New York: the Scarecrow Press. Takes a dictionary approach to Laos' history which is fine if you are looking up a fact or two, but doesn't really lend itself to telling a narrative.

Stuart-Fox, Martin (1997), *A History of Laos*, CUP: Cambridge. Most up-to-date history of the country. Concentrates on the modern period.

Language

Higbie, James, *Lao-English/English-Lao Dictionary and Phrasebook*, Hippocrene Books, Inc.

Marcus, Russell (1983) *Lao-English/ English-Lao Dictionary*, Charles E Tuttle Co, USA. Perhaps the best dictionary available; US$20 from www.worldlanguage.com

Phone Bouaravong, *Learning Lao for Everyone*. Locally produced, with tapes.

Werner, Klaus *Learning and Speaking Lao*. Useful and cheaper than Marcus.

Laos and the Indochina War

Castle, Timothy (1993), *A War in the Shadow of Vietnam: US Military Aid to the Royal Lao Government 1955-1975*, New York: Columbia University Press.

Evans,Grant & Rowley, Kelvin (1990), *Red Brotherhood at War, Vietnam Cambodia & Laos since 1975*, Verso.

Evans, Grant (1983), *Yellow Rainmakers: Are Chemical Weapons Being Used in Southeast Asia*, Verso.

McCoy, Alfred W (1991), *The Politics of Heroin: CIA Complicity in the Global Drugs Trade*, Lawrence Hill/Chicago Review Press. Originally published at the beginning of the 1970s, it is the classic study of the politics of drugs in mainland Southeast Asia.

Parker, James (1995), *Codename Mule: Fighting the Secret War in Laos for the CIA*, Annapolis, Maryland: Naval Institute Press. Personal story of an Americans fighting in Laos. Much of it deals with fighting on the Plain of Jars.

Pyle and Faas (2003), *Lost Over Laos*, De Capo Press. The story of four photographers who died in Laos in 1971 and the search, years later, to recover the crash site.

Ratnam, P (1980), *Laos and the Superpowers*, Tulsi Publishing, India.

Robbins, Christopher (1979), *Air America: the Story of the CIS's Secret Airlines*, New York: Putnam Books. The earlier of Robbins' two books on the secret war. Made into a film of the same name with Mel Gibson in the starring role.

Robbins, Christopher (1989), *The Ravens: Pilots of the Secret War of Laos*, New York: Bantam Press. The best known of all the books on America's secret war in Laos. The story it tells seems almost incredible.

Warner, Roger (1995), *Back Fire: the CIA's Secret War in Laos and its Link to the War in Vietnam*, New York: Simon and Schuster. The best of the more recent books recounting the experiences of US servicemen in Laos. Excellent, engaging read. Also published as *Shooting at the Moon*.

De Carne, Louis (1872), *Travels in Indochina and the Chinese Empire*, London: Chapman Hall. Recounts De Carne's experiences in Laos in 1872, some years before the country was colonized by the French.

Dooley, Tom (1958), *The Edge of Tomorrow*, Farrar, Strauss & Cudahy.

Du Pont De Bie, Natacha (2004), *Ant Egg Soup: The Adventures of a Food Tourist in Laos*, Sceptre. A wonderful portrait of Lao culture and food through the eyes of a food tourist.

Garstin, Crosbie (1928), *The Voyage from London to Indochina*, Heinemann. Hilarious, irreverent journey through Indochina.

Hoskins, John (1991), *The Mekong*, Bangkok: Post Publishing. A large format coffee table book with good photographs and a modest text. Widely available in Bangkok.

Lewis, Norman (1951), *A Dragon Apparent: Travels in Cambodia, Laos and Vietnam*. One of the finest travel books; reprinted by Eland Books but also available second-hand from many bookshops.

Maugham, Somerset (1930), *The Gentlemen in the Parlour: a Record of a Journey from Rangoon to Haiphong*, Heinemann: London. An account of Maugham's journey through Southeast Asia, in classic limpid prose.

McCarthy, James (1994), *Surveying and Exploring in Siam with Descriptions of Laos Dependencies and of Battles against the Chinese Haws*, White Lotus: Bangkok. First published in 1900. An interesting account by Englishman James McCarthy, who was employed by the government of Siam as a surveyor and adviser.

Mouhot, Henri (1986), *Travels in Indochina*, Bangkok: White Lotus. An account of Laos by France's most famous explorer of Southeast Asia. He tried to discover a 'back door' into China by travelling up the Mekong, but died of Malaria in Luang Prabang in 1860. The book has been republished by White Lotus and is easily available in Bangkok; there is also a more expensive reprint available from OUP (Kuala Lumpur).

Murphy, Dervla (1999), *One Foot in Laos*, John Murphy Publisher. An interesting, off-the-beaten-track travelogue of adventures and mishaps through Laos.

Stewart, Lucretia (1998), *Tiger Balm: Travels in Laos, Cambodia and Vietnam*, London: Chatto and Windus.

Southeast Asia

White Lotus, www.thailine.com/lotus, is a Bangkok-based publisher specializing in English-language books (many reprints of old books) on the region.

Dingwall, Alastair (1994) *Traveller's Literary Companion to South-east Asia,* In Print: Brighton. Extracts from books by Western and regional writers on Southeast Asia. A good overview of what is available.

Dumareay, Jacques (1991), *The Palaces of South-East Asia: Architecture and Customs*, OUP: Singapore. A broad summary of palace art and architecture in Southeast Asia.

Fraser-Lu, Sylvia (1988), *Handwoven Textiles of South-East Asia*, OUP: Singapore. Large Well-illustrated book with informative text.

Higham, Charles (1989), *The Archaeology of Mainland Southeast Asia from 10,000 BC to the Fall of Angkor*, CUP: Cambridge. Best summary of changing views of the archaeology of the mainland.

Reid, Anthony (1988), *Southeast Asia in the Age of Commerce 1450-1680: the Lands below the Winds*, Yale University Press: New Haven. Perhaps the best history of everyday life in Southeast Asia, looking at such themes as physical well-being, material culture and social organization. Also Volume 2 (1993), *Southeast Asia in the Age of Commerce 1450-1680: Expansion and Crisis*, Yale University Press: New Haven.

Rigg, Jonathan (1997), *Southeast Asia: the Human Landscape of Modernization and Development*, London: Routledge. Focuses on how people have responded to the challenges and tensions of modernization.

SarDesai, DR (1989), *Southeast Asia: Past and Present*, Macmillan: London. Skillful but at times frustratingly thin history of the region from the 1st century to the withdrawal of US forces from Vietnam.

Steinberg, DJ et al (1987), *In Search of Southeast Asia: a Modern History*, University of Hawaii Press: Honolulu. The best standard history of the region.

Tarling, Nicholas (1992) (edit), *Cambridge History of Southeast Asia*, CUP: Cambridge. Two-volume edited study by theme and region, with contributions from most of the leading historians of the region. The history is fairly conventional.

Footnotes

Useful words and phrases

Greetings

Yes/No	men/baw
Thank you/	kop jai/
no thank you	baw, kop jai
Hello/goodbye	suh-bye-dee/lah-gohn
What is your name?	Chow seu yang?
My name is...	koi seu....
Excuse me, sorry	ko toat
Can/do you speak	Koy pahk pah-sah
English?	Anhg-geet?
A little, a bit	noi, hoi
Where?	you-sigh?
How much is...?	Tow-dai?
It doesn't matter,	baw penh yang
never mind	
Pardon?	kow toat?
I don't understand	Kow baw cow-chi
How are you?	Chao suh-bye-dee-baw?
not very well	baw suh-bye

Getting around

Where is the	Sa ta ni lot
train/bus station?	phai/mee yu sai?
How much to go to...?	Khit la ka taw dai...?
That's expensive	pheng-lie
Will you go for...kip?	Chow ja pai...kip?
What time does	Lot mea oak jay mong...?
the bus/train leave for...?	
Is it far?	Kai baw?
Turn left/turn right	leo sai/leo qua
Go straight on	pai leuy
River	Xe/Se, Houei/Houai
Town	Muang/Mouang
Mountain	phou

Sleeping

What is the charge	Kit laka van nuang
each night?	taw dai?
Is the room	Hong me ai yen baw?
air conditioned?	
Can I see the room	Koi ko beunghong dea?
first please?	
Does the room	Hong me nam hawn baw?
have hot water?	
Does the room	Me hang ap nam baw?
have a bathroom?	
Can I have the bill	Koi ton han bai hap?
please?	

Eating

Can I see a menu?	Kho beung lay kan arhan?
Can I have...?	Khoy tong kan...?
I am hungry	Koy heo kao
I am thirsty	Koy heo nahm
I want to eat	Koh yahk kin kao
Where is	Lahn ah hai you-sigh?
a restaurant?	
Breakfast	arhan sao
Lunch	arhan athieng
It costs....kip	Lah-kah ahn-nee...kip

Time

in the morning	muh-sao
in the afternoon	thon-by
in the evening	muh-leng
today	muh-nee
tomorrow	muh-ouhn
yesterday	muh van-nee
Monday	Van Chanh
Tuesday	Van Ang Khan
Wednesday	Van Pud
Thursday	Van Pa Had
Friday	Van Sook
Saturday	Van Sao
Sunday	Van Arthid

Numbers

1	nung	20	sao
2	song	21	sao-et
3	sahm	22	sao-song
4	see	30	sahn-sip
5	hah	100	hoy
6	hoke	101	hoy-nung
7	chet	150	hoy-hah-sip
8	pet	200	song-hoy
9	cow	1000	phan
10	sip	10,000	sip-phan
11	sip-et	100,000	muun
12	sip-song	1,000,000	laan

Basic vocabulary

airport	deune yonh	hotel	hong
bank	had xay	island	koh (or) hath
bathroom	hong nam	market	ta lath
beach	heva	medicine	ya pua payad
beautiful	ngam	open	peud
bicycle	loht teep	petrol	nahm-mahn-eh-sahng
big	nyai	police	lam louad
boat	quoi loth bath	police station	poam lam louad
bus	loht-buht	post office	hong kana pai sa nee
bus station	hon kay ya	restaurant	han arhane
buy	sue	road	tha nonh
chemist	han kay ya	room	hong
clean	sa ard	shop	hanh
closed	arte	sick (ill)	bo sabay
cold	jenh	silk	mai
day	vanh (or) mua	small	noy
delicious	sehb	stop	yoot
dirty	soka pox	taxi	loht doy-sanh
doctor	than mah	that	nahn
eat	kinh	this	nee, ahn-nee
embassy	Satan Tood	ticket (air)	pee yonh
excellent	dee leuth	ticket (bus)	pee lot mea
expensive	pheng	toilet	hong nam
food	ah-han	town	nai mouang
fruit	mak-mai	very	lai-lai
hospital	hong moh	water	nam (or) nah
hot (temp)	hawn	what	men-nyung

Glossary

Amitabha the Buddha of the Past

Amulet protective medallion

Arhat one who has perfected himself

Avadana Buddhist narrative, telling of the deeds of saintly souls

Avalokitsvara also known as Amitabha and Lokeshvara, the name literally means 'World Lord'; he is the compassionate male Bodhisattva, the saviour of Mahayana Buddhism and represents the central force of creation in the universe

Bai sema boundary stones marking consecrated ground around a bot

Ban village; shortened from muban

Batik a form of resist dyeing

Bhikku Buddhist monk

Bodhi the tree under which the Buddha achieved enlightenment (Ficus religiosa)

Bodhisattva a future Buddha. In Mahayana Buddhism, someone who has attained enlightenment, but who postpones nirvana to help others reach it.

Boun Lao festival

Brahma the Creator, one of the gods of the Hindu trinity, usually represented with four faces, and often mounted on a hamsa

Brahmin a Hindu priest

Bun to make merit

Caryatid elephants, often used as buttressing decorations

Champa rival empire of the Khmers, of Hindu culture, based in present day Vietnam

Chao title for Lao kings

Charn animist priest who conducts the basi ceremony in Laos

Chat honorific umbrella or royal parasol

Chedi religious monument (often bell-shaped) containing relics of the Buddha or other holy remains

Chenla Chinese name for Cambodia before the Khmer era

Deva a Hindu-derived male god

Devata a Hindu-derived goddess

Dharma the Buddhist law

Dok sofa frond-like construction surmounting temple roofs in Laos. Over 10 flowers means the wat was built by a king

Dtin sin decorative border on a skirt

Dvarapala guardian figure, usually placed at the entrance to a temple

Funan the oldest Indianised state of Indochina and precursor to Chenla

Ganesh elephant-headed son of Siva

Garuda mythical divine bird, with predatory beak and claws, and human body; the king of birds, enemy of naga and mount of Vishnu

Gautama the historic Buddha

Geomancy divination by lines and figures

Gopura crowned or covered gate, entrance to a religious area

Hamsa sacred goose, Brahma's mount; in Buddhism it represents the flight of doctrine

Hinayana 'Lesser Vehicle', major Buddhist sect in Southeast Asia, usually termed Theravada Buddhism

Hor kong a pavilion built on stilts where the temple drum is kept

Hor latsalot temple chapel of the funeral cart

Hor song phra secondary chapel

Hor takang bell tower

Hor tray/trai library where manuscripts are stored in a Lao or Thai temple

Hor vay offering temple

Ikat tie-dye method of patterning cloth

Indra the Vedic god of the heavens, weather and war

Jataka(s) the birth stories of the Buddha; they normally number 547; the last 10 are the most important

Kala (makara) a demon ordered to consume itself; often sculpted with grinning face and bulging eyes over entranceways to act as a door guardian; also known as kirtamukha

Kathin/krathin a one-month period during the eighth lunar month when lay people present robes and gifts to monks

Ketumula flame-like motif above the Buddha head

Kinaree half-human, half-bird, usually depicted as a heavenly musician

Kirtamukha see kala

Koutdi see kuti

Krishna incarnation of Vishnu

Kuti living quarters of Buddhist monks in a temple complex

Laterite bright red tropical soil/stone commonly used in Khmer monuments

Linga phallic symbol and one of the forms of Siva. Embedded in a pedestal shaped to allow drainage of lustral water poured over it, the linga typically has a succession of cross sections: from square at the base through octagonal to round. These symbolise, in order, the trinity of Brahma, Vishnu and Siva

Lokeshvara see Avalokitsvara

Mahabharata a Hindu epic text

Mahayana 'Greater Vehicle', major Buddhist sect

Maitreya the future Buddha

Makara mythological aquatic reptile often found with the kala framing doorways

Mandala a focus for meditation; a representation of the cosmos

Mara personification of evil and tempter of the Buddha

Matmii Lao cotton ikat

Mat mi see matmii

Meru sacred or cosmic mountain at the centre of the world in Hindu-Buddhist cosmology; home of the gods

Mondop from the sanskrit, mandapa. A cube-shaped building, often topped with a cone-like structure, used to contain an object of worship like a footprint of the Buddha

Muang administrative unit

Muban village, usually shortened to ban

Mudra symbolic gesture of the hands of the Buddha

Nak Lao river dragon, a mythical guardian creature (see naga)

Naga benevolent mythical water serpent, enemy of Garuda

Naga makara fusion of naga and makara

Nalagiri the elephant let loose to attack the Buddha, who calmed him

Nandi/nandin bull, mount of Siva

Nirvana release from the cycle of suffering in Buddhist belief; 'enlightenment'

Nyak mythical water serpent (see naga)

Pa kama Lao men's all-purpose cloth

paddy/padi unhulled rice

Pali sacred language of Theravada Buddhism

Parvati consort of Siva

Pathet Lao Communist party based in the northeastern provinces of Laos until they came to power in 1975

Pha biang shawl worn by women in Laos

Pha sin piece of cloth, similar to sarong

Phi spirit

Phra sinh see pha sin

Pra Lam Lao version of the Ramayana

Pradaksina pilgrims' clockwise circumambulation of holy structure

Prah sacred

Prang form of stupa built in Khmer style, shaped like a corncob

Prasada stepped pyramid (see prasat)

Prasat residence of a king or of the gods (sanctuary tower), from the Indian prasada

Quan Am Chinese goddess of mercy

Rama incarnation of Vishnu, hero of the Indian epic, the Ramayana

Ramakien Lao version of the Ramayana

Ramayana Hindu romantic epic

Sakyamuni the historic Buddha

Sal the Indian sal tree (Shorea robusta), under which the historic Buddha was born

Sangha the Buddhist order of monks

Sim/sima main sanctuary and ordination hall in a Lao temple complex

Singha mythical guardian lion

Siva the Destroyer, one of the three gods of the Hindu trinity; the sacred linga was worshipped as a symbol of Siva

Sofa see dok sofa

Sravasti the miracle at Sravasti when the Buddha subdues the heretics

Stele inscribed stone panel

Stucco plaster, often heavily moulded

Stupa chedi

Tam bun see bun

Tavatimsa heaven of the 33 gods at the summit of Mount Meru

Thanon street

That shrine housing Buddhist relics, a spire or dome-like edifice commemorating the Buddha's life or a funerary temple for royalty

Theravada 'Way of the Elders'; major Buddhist sect also known as Hinayana Buddhism ('Lesser Vehicle')

Traiphum the three worlds of Buddhist cosmology – heaven, hell and earth

Trimurti the Hindu trinity of gods: Brahma, the Creator, Vishnu the Preserver and Siva the Destroyer

Tripitaka Theravada Buddhism's Pali canon Ubosoth see bot

Urna the dot or curl on the Buddha's forehead, one of the distinctive physical marks of the Enlightened One

Usnisa the Buddha's top knot or 'wisdom bump'

Vahana 'vehicle', a mythical beast, upon which a deva or god rides

Viharn assembly hall in a Buddhist monastery

Vishnu the Protector, one of the gods of the Hindu trinity

Index

Credits

Footprint credits

Text editor: Sophie Blacksell
Map editor: Sarah Sorensen
Picture editor: Kevin Feeney
Proofreader: Sarah Chatwin

Publisher: Patrick Dawson
Editorial: Alan Murphy, Sarah Thorowgood,
Claire Boobbyer, Felicity Laughton,
Nicola Jones
Cartography: Robert Lunn, Claire Benison,
Kevin Feeney
Series development: Rachel Fielding
Design: Mytton Williams and Rosemary
Dawson (brand)
Sales and marketing: Andy Riddle
Advertising: Debbie Wylde
Finance and administration:
Sharon Hughes, Elizabeth Taylor

Photography credits

Front cover: Impact (Xieng Khuan)
Back cover: Claire Boobbyer (tuk-tuk)
Inside colour section: Alamy, Claire
Boobbyer, Jamie Marshall, Jock O'Tailan,
Superstock

Print

Manufactured in India by Nutech
Photolithographers, Delhi. Pulp from
sustainable forests

Footprint feedback

We try as hard as we can to make each
Footprint guide as up to date as possible
but, of course, things always change. If you
want to let us know about your experiences
– good, bad or ugly – then don't delay, go
to www.footprintbooks.com and send in
your comments.

Publishing information

Footprint Laos
4th edition
© Footprint Handbooks Ltd
April 2006

ISBN 1 904 777 53 8
CIP DATA: A catalogue record for this book is
available from the British Library

® Footprint Handbooks and the Footprint
mark are a registered trademark of
Footprint Handbooks Ltd

Published by Footprint

6 Riverside Court
Lower Bristol Road
Bath BA2 3DZ, UK
T +44 (0)1225 469141
F +44 (0)1225 469461
discover@footprintbooks.com
www.footprintbooks.com

Distributed in the USA by

Publishers Group West

Every effort has been made to ensure that
the facts in this guidebook are accurate.
However, travellers should still obtain advice
from consulates, airlines etc about travel and
visa requirements before travelling. The
authors and publishers cannot accept
responsibility for any loss, injury or
inconvenience however caused.

Acknowledgements

The absolute, biggest thank you has to go to Justin Armstrong, who has done everything, plus some. Daryl 'Razzler' McMahon and Luke 'Morgan' Burch: cheers to you both for all your help. A 'Cop Jai Deu' goes to local Phonsavanh star Vongsavath Douangdara, whose enthusiasm and initiative goes well beyond the call of duty. Also big thanks to Mr Sousath Phetrasy from the Maly Hotel; Bill Tuffin from the Boat Landing; Renae Stenhouse from WCS; Mr Vong and Co. from Saibaidy 2 in Pakse; Stuart from Nam Theun 2; Peg and Sapeth from Exotissimo; Gus and Dan for being very helpful; Sophie from Stickies for being ultra supportive; and Kay and Ban Simuang deck noi for keeping me laughing. Mum and Dad thanks for the endless support. And, last but not least, at Footprint HQ, Sophie and Alan. Previous editions of this guide were written by Joshua Eliot, Jane Bickersteth and Zee Gilmore.

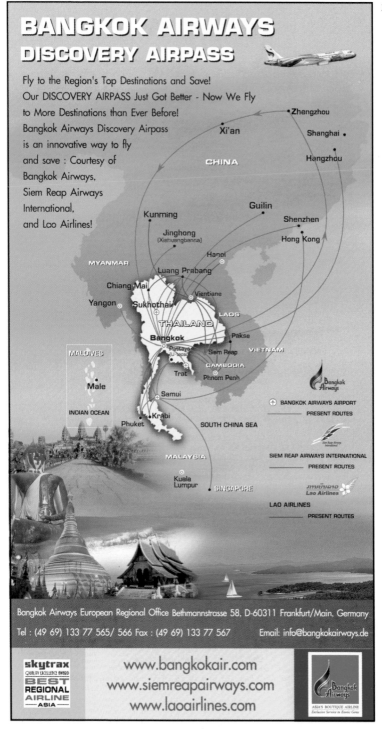

Laos

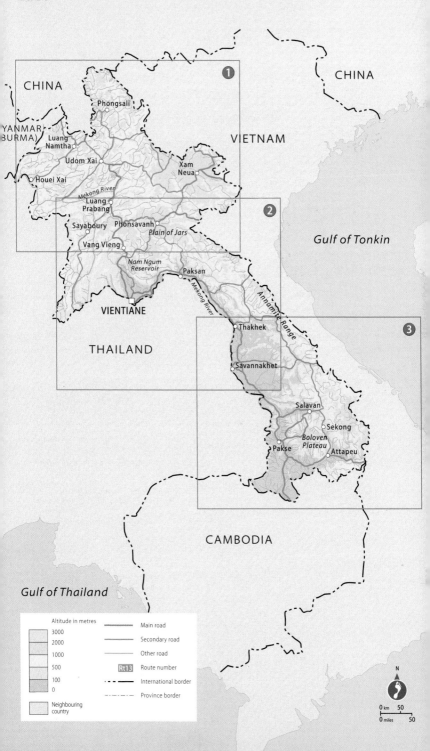

Map 1

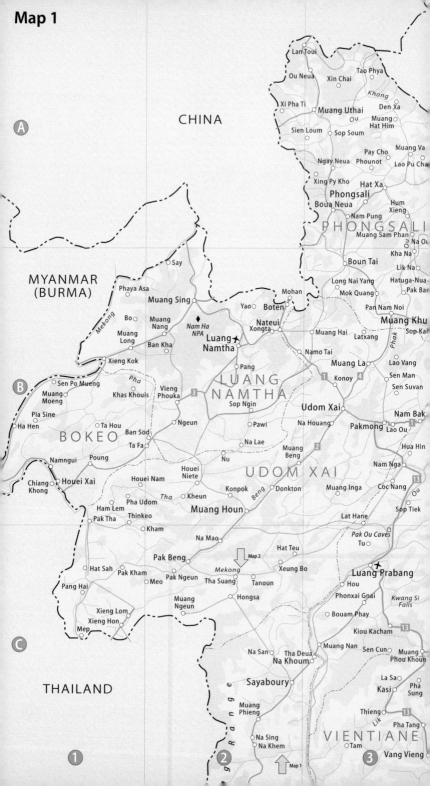

CHINA

Lan Toui

Ou Neua Xin Chai Tao Phya

Khang

Xi Pha Ti Muang Uthai Den Xa

Ou Muang
Sien Loum Sop Soum Hat Him

Pay Cho Muang Va
Ngay Neua Phounot Lao Pu Cha

Xing Py Kho Hat Xa

Phongsali

Boua Neua Hum
Xieng

Nam Pung

PHONGSALI

Muang Sam Phan Na Ou

Kha Na Lik Na

Boun Tai Hatuga-Nua

Pak Bar

**MYANMAR
(BURMA)**

Say

Phaya Asa

Muang Sing

Mohan

Phaya Asa Yao Boten

Bo Muang
Nang **Nam Ha
NPA** Nateui
Muang Xongta
Long Ban Kha **Luang
Namtha** Muang Hai Latxang Sop Kai

Long Nai Yang Mok Quang

Pan Nam Noi

Muang Khu

Mekong

Xieng Kok Pang Namo Tai **Muang La** Lao Vang

Sen Po Mueng *Pha* Vieng
Phouka **LUANG
NAMTHA** Konoy 4 Sen Man
Sen Suvan

Muang
Moeng Khas Khouis 3 Sop Ngin

Pia Sine Ta Hou Ngeun Pawi Na Houang **Udom Xai** **Nam Bak**
Ha Hen Ban Sod Lao Ou Hua Hin

BOKEO Ta Fa Na Lae Muang
Beng 2 Nam Nga

Namngui Poung Nu **UDOM XAI** Coc Nang 13

Chiang **Houei Xai** Houei Nam Konpok Donkton Muang Inga Sop Tiek
Khong Pha Udom *Tha* Kheun *Beng*
Ham Lem Thinkeo **Muang Houn** Lat Hane

Pak Tha Kham *Pak Ou Caves*
Na Mao Tu

Hat Teu

Hat Sah Pak Kham **Pak Beng** Map 2 Xeung Bo **Luang Prabang**
Pang Hai Meo Pak Ngeun *Mekong* Hou
Pak Kham Tha Suang Tanoun Phonxai Gnai *Kwang Si
Falls*
Muang Hongsa Bouam Phay
Xieng Lom Ngeun
Xieng Hon Kiou Kacham 13
Mep

C

THAILAND

Na San Tha Deua Muang Nan Sen Cun Muang
Na Khoum Phou Khoun

Sayaboury La Sa Pha
Kasi Sung

Muang Thieng Pha Tang
Phieng 13

Na Sing **VIENTIANE**
Na Khem Tam

Map 1 **3 Vang Vieng**

1 2 3

A

VIETNAM

N

0 km   20
0 miles   20

B

Na Lam
Phya
Sop Nhom
Sen Kattinia
Phya Lat
Muang Mai
Muang Khoa
Houei Tha
Pak Luong
Sop Kine
Muang
Ngoi Neua
Pha Nang
Muang Peu
Xieng Kho
Muang Et
B Na Men
Sop Bao
Senchitta
Na Veung
*Nam Et
NPA*
Sop Y
Sop Hao
Nong Khiaw &
Ban Saphoun
Muang Khao
Het
Sop Ka
Xam Neua
□ *Caves*
Vieng Kham
Muang Son
Vieng Xai
6A
Poun Song
Seng
Muang Ham
Muang Poun
Na Maew
*Phou Loei
NPA*
1
HUA
PHAN
Hoeui Sam
Me Kien
Houei Van
Muang Muoi
Muang Kout
Muang Vene
6
Muang Kan
LUANG
PRABANG
Vieng Thong
Hua Muong
Sam
Xam Tai
Tao
Nam Nouan
Nong Khai
Muang Na
Kha
Muang You
Khan
Pak Vang
Sam Thong
6
Neun
Pung Thac
Sa Mang
Song Hac
Muang Kham
Mat
Muang Sui
Xang
Khang Pha Nien
7
Nong Het
Nam Khan
Sen Kom
Xieng Dat
Khien
Phonsavanh
Muang
Khoune
Annamite Range
Plain of Jars
Phon
Na Vang
Sen Luang
Phouviang
Nam Ngum
XIENG
KHOUANG
Muang Ngat
Say He
Sop Tiong
Muang
Tiouen
Tam Kalong
4
Ta Viang
5
Khone Xa Na
Muang Mok
6
Muang Cha

C

Map 3

Map 3

THAILAND

KHAMMOUANE

SAVANNAKHET

SALAVAN

CHAMPASAK

Houai Aek
Gnommalath
Xang
Nakhon Phanom
Thakhek
Mahaxai
Kha Nhu
Kha Nhu
Nha Vet
Kham Phuang
Kavak
Napoung
Keng Khen
Nam Piet Tong
Tha Pha Chom
Boualapha
Xom
Yon
Na Phao
Nong Bok
Pha Ket
Travigne
Na Muong
Muang Sen
Na Hang
Ko
B Thakho
Phaka Nhia
Na Thom Dong
Xaibouli
Na Chane
Na Chan Tai
Na Phi Nang
Nabo
Xepon
Khone Kene
Lamphoy
Dansavanh
Xeno
Muang Phalane
Muang Phalane
Dan Bong
Lao Bao
Savannakhet
Pa Teng
Kepo
Muang Phin
Dong Phu Vieng NPA
Kengkok
Keng Sai
Xieng Hom
Sang
Lamvay
Along Nam
Bang Hieng
That Hai
Pok
Mohong
Ban Houan Hine
Xbanghiang-thong
Map 2
Keng Kha
Tahoy
Tha Phe
Xenouan
Muang Thapangthang
Nadou Gnai
Keng Kang
Nong Chan
Khan Soum Soa
Thangbeng
Done
Bung Sai
Salavan
Xe Don
Dan La Lao
Muang Wapi
Ban Nong Boua
Muang Khong Xedon
Ban Houei Set
Ban Beng
Ban Lao Ngam
Tad Lo
Tha Teng
Na Ngam
Mai
Boloven Plateau
Paksong
Ban Saphay
Chongmek
Pakse
Vang Tao
Dong Hua Sao
Houei Kong
Phoune Thong
Muang Khao
Champasak
Houei Na
Ban Muang
Wat Phou
Ban Thang Beng
Hieng
Ban Khiet Ngong
Ban-Ma
Soukhouma
Ban Pha Pho
Kam Pho
Mekong
Tha Kuang
Xe Pian NBCA
Nafang
Pak Song
Na
Chak
Don San
Taseun
Don Khong
Ban Hat Xai Khoune
Muang Khong
Ban Nakasong
Don Deth & Don Khone
Khong Phapheng Falls
Li Phi Falls
Voen Kham

Gulf of Tonkin

Axen

Pahai

Kadap

Chakeuy Tay   Ka Reen

Kaleum

SEKONG

Dak Chung

Ban Phon   Cha Van   Dak Klao

Sekong

Nam Hang   VIETNAM

un   Thakkanat

an   Thac Kie

Keng Say   Sala Tin Toc   Van Tat

Sakke   Dong
                 Ampham
Attapeu   Xaisetha   Forest

Pa-am

ATTAPEU   Phya Ha   18   Tasseing

Chom

Kong My

Phia Ka Nieng

CAMBODIA

Xe Kong

Kamone

Sau

4   5   6

Map symbols

Administration

- Capital city
- Other city/town
- International border
- Regional border
- Disputed border

Roads and travel

- Motorway
- Main road (National highway)
- Minor road
- Track
- Footpath
- Railway with station
- Airport
- Bus station
- Metro station
- Cable car
- Funicular
- Ferry

Water features

- River, canal
- Lake, ocean
- Seasonal marshland
- Beach, sandbank
- Waterfall

Topographical features

- Contours (approx)
- Mountain
- Volcano
- Mountain pass
- Escarpment
- Gorge
- Glacier
- Salt flat
- Rocks

Cities and towns

- Main through route
- Main street
- Minor street
- Pedestrianized street
- Tunnel
- One way-street
- Steps
- Bridge
- Fortified wall
- Park, garden, stadium
- Sleeping
- Eating
- Bars & clubs
- Building
- Sight
- Cathedral, church
- Chinese temple
- Hindu temple
- Meru
- Mosque
- Stupa
- Synagogue
- Tourist office
- Museum
- Post office
- Police
- Bank
- Internet
- Telephone
- Market
- Medical services
- Parking
- Petrol
- Golf
- Detail map
- Related map

Other symbols

- Archaeological site
- National park, wildlife reserve
- Viewing point
- Campsite
- Refuge, lodge
- Castle
- Diving
- Deciduous/coniferous/palm trees
- Hide
- Vineyard
- Distillery
- Shipwreck
- Historic battlefield